FROM

ALASKA

JOHN GOTTBERG

2ND EDITION

Published by Prentice Hall Trade Division
A Division of Simon & Schuster Inc.
15 Columbus Circle
New York, NY 10023

ISBN 0-13-218348-X
ISSN 1042-8283

Text Design: Levavi & Levavi, Inc.

Manufactured in the United States of America

*Although every effort was made to ensure the accuracy
of price information appearing in this book,
it should be kept in mind that prices
can and do fluctuate in the course of time.*

CONTENTS

MAPS

For Linda

ACKNOWLEDGMENTS

So many individuals and organizations assisted me in compiling the information in this book that I fear this list of acknowledgments may offend some while flattering others. Nevertheless, I offer my sincere thanks for the help of all businesses and organizations listed in this book. They opened their doors to me during my research.

In addition, I wish to give special thanks to the Alaska State Division of Tourism; the convention and visitors bureaus of Anchorage, Fairbanks, Juneau, Ketchikan, Kodiak, Matanuska-Susitna, Nome, Sitka, Skagway, and Valdez; the chambers of commerce of Cordova, Homer, Kenai, Seward, and Soldotna; the cities of Haines, Homer, Petersburg, and Wrangell; Denali, Glacier Bay, Kenai Fjords and Wrangell–St. Elias National Parks; Bradley/McAfee Public Relations; Brennan, & Brennan public relations; Alaska Airlines: MarkAir; Cruise Advisors, Inc.; Exploration Holidays; Gray Line of Alaska; Holland America Line/ Westours; and Princess Tours.

The following individuals went above and beyond the call of duty to show me things I might otherwise have missed, and/or to offer advice, guidance, or editing assistance: Connie Allison, Einar and Lilyan Anderson, Keith Anderson, Denise Belkoski, Cindy Bettine, Nancy Bird, Nathan Borson, Millie and Don Carlock, Dr. James A. Davis, Greg Edblom, Dr. Michael Farinha, Jim Gove, Mary Gross, Nancy Harrington, Amy Hayes, Kathy Herold, Laura Herrin, Karen Hofstad, Randy Kelsch, Steve Lay, Susan and Mark Lutz, Susan Lyon, Bill Marchese, George Mason, Terry Miller, Ernie Nygren, Jeff Osborne, Becky Paul, Joe Pentilla, Bill Quehrn, Jonathan Ramey, Thomas Scanlon, the Shady Ladies, Suzanne Sherwood, Veronica Slajer, Brad Snowden, John Stein, Bob Thomas, Sherry Thomas, Kim Tyner, Chip Waterbury, Caryn Wiegand, Aimee Youmans and Hank Adams, and especially Linda Carlock, Edie Jarolim, and Marilyn Wood.

I

INTRODUCING ALASKA

1. A CAPSULE HISTORY
2. THE ALASKANS
3. THE NATURAL ENVIRONMENT

The only way to speak of the state of Alaska is in superlatives. Larger than one-fifth of the continental United States, with more miles of coastline than the other 49 states combined, Alaska is bigger than all but 16 of the world's nations.

Visitors are awed by the sheer enormity of the landscape: everything seems to be on a grand scale, as if the physical features of the Lower 48 are mere miniatures. Not only is Mount McKinley, at 20,320 feet, the highest mountain in North America, but it rises directly from 2,000-foot lowlands to be joined by six other peaks over 14,500 feet. Not only does Alaska contain great glaciers like the Malaspina, itself larger than Rhode Island, but it has 100,000 glaciers covering over 28,000 square miles, more than 125 times the area covered by glaciers in the rest of the U.S. combined. Its bears are not just bears, they are the biggest bears. And so on.

Superimpose a map of Alaska over one of the contiguous U.S. and you'll begin to get an idea of its scale. If Ketchikan, the southeasternmost town, falls over Charleston, South Carolina, then Attu Island, the westernmost point of the Aleutians, will be near Yuma, Arizona, and Point Barrow, in the north, will fall somewhere near Bemidji, Minnesota. The state is 2,400 miles from east to west, 1,420 miles from north to south.

The name Alaska derives from the Aleut word *alaxsxaq,* a word that early Russian fur traders understandably found unpronounceable. So they called this territory Bolshaya Zemlya, "The Great Land." It fits. Some 590,000 square miles in size, but with a population of barely half a million, Alaska spans an awesome diversity of geographical zones and lifestyles. Commerical fishermen's homes cling to the slopes of densely forested southeastern fiords, while Eskimo walrus hunters live in Arctic villages where summers have no nights and winters no days. Solitary gold prospectors pan streams and chip rocks in the shadow of Mount McKinley as young executives in three-piece suits commute to offices in Anchorage high-rises. Descendants of Russian colonists worship their saints at onion-domed Russian Orthodox churches in Sitka, Kodiak, and other towns while U.S. military families in the stark, wind-swept Aleutians pray for a safe delivery home from their temporary exile.

Although construction of the Trans Alaska Pipeline in the mid-1970s opened up many parts of Alaska that had previously been inaccessible and drew many younger people from the Lower 48 to partake of the state's new wealth, the state

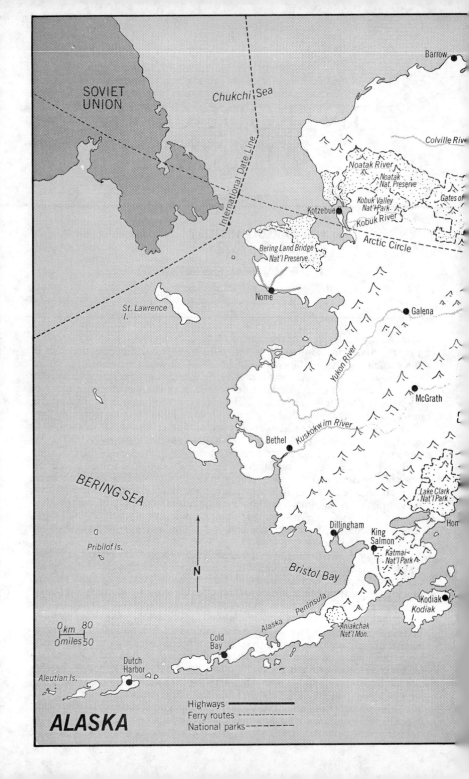

SOVIET
UNION

Chukchi Sea

International Date Line

Colville River

Noatak River
Noatak Nat'l Preserve
Kotzebue
Kobuk Valley Nat'l Park
Gates of
Kobuk River
Arctic Circle

Bering Land Bridge Nat'l Preserve

Barrow

St. Lawrence I.

Nome

Galena

Yukon River

McGrath

BERING SEA

Bethel

Kuskokwim River

Pribilof Is.

N

Lake Clark Nat'l Park

Hom

Dillingham

King Salmon
Katmai Nat'l Park

Bristol Bay

Kodiak
Kodiak

0 km 80
0 miles 50

Cold Bay

Alaska Peninsula

Aniakchak Nat'l Mon.

Dutch Harbor

Aleutian Is.

Highways ———
Ferry routes --------
National parks -------

ALASKA

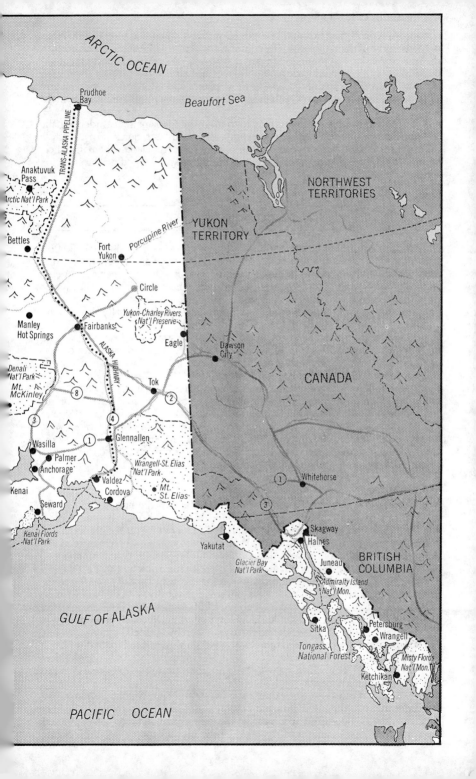

remains America's "last frontier." Despite its vastness, Alaska has only 16,000 miles of roads, most of them unpaved. (By contrast, the country of Austria, an eighteenth the size of Alaska, has some 25,000 miles of roads.) Most "bush" settlements—those inaccessible by road—depend on planes and air taxis to connect them with the outside world. Thus Alaska has far more planes and pilots per capita than any other state. Alaska also has more than 1,400 miles of ferry routes, or "marine highway."

Their traditional isolation has tended to make the Alaskans a very independent, self-sufficient people. They are also a friendly, gregarious sort, quick with a laugh at the expense of *cheechakos* (newcomers) but equally ready to welcome them into their homes. It's the unwritten law of the wilderness: they know you'd do the same for them.

1. A Capsule History

Human habitation began in Alaska sometime between 10,000 and 50,000 years ago, when nomadic Asiatics crossed the Bering land bridge in pursuit of game. They spread south and east—first the ancestors of today's Indians, then early Aleuts and Eskimos—gradually establishing homelands where they could eke a living from the alien land.

The first white man known to have visited Alaska was Vitus Bering, a Dane commissioned in 1725 by Russian Czar Peter the Great to explore the North Pacific. He sighted St. Lawrence Island and sailed through the strait now bearing his name in 1728; on a second voyage in 1741 he landed on Kayak Island, off south-central Alaska, while a second crew commanded by Alexei Chirikov weighed anchor off Prince of Wales Island in southeastern Alaska.

In the following three decades Russian visitors to Alaskan waters were almost exclusively fur traders. They hunted the playful sea otter almost to extinction, began an onslaught on the Steller fur seal, and made virtual slaves of the docile Aleuts. Other European powers made tentative voyages north from the American West Coast—Juan Perez of Spain in 1774, James Cook of England in 1776–1778, George Vancouver of England in 1791–1794—but it was left for the Russians to found a colony.

RUSSIAN AMERICA

Siberian fur merchant Grigori Shelekhov established the first Russian settlement in North America when he came to Three Saints Bay, Kodiak Island, in 1784 with 192 men and one woman (his wife, Natalie). In 1791 he turned management of the post over to Alexander Baranov, a colorful businessman who emerged as the dominant personality of Russian Alaska.

Many stories are told about Baranov's capacity for drink and of his taking a Kenai princess as his mistress. His most important action, historically, was founding Sitka as the capital of Russian America. Concerned about British activity in what he regarded as Russian territory, he took about 1,000 Aleuts and 100 Russians with him to build Redoubt Archangelsk Mikhailovsk (Fort St. Michael) in 1799. It was destroyed and its occupants massacred three years later by hostile Tlingit natives, but in 1804 Baranov—accompanied by a Russian warship—returned to the site, drove the natives from what today is Baranof Island, and built Novaya Archangelsk (New Archangel), now Sitka, which grew to become (for a time) the largest city on the west coast of North America.

In Russia, meanwhile, Shelekhov's son-in-law and heir, Nikolai Rezanov, had merged with rival fur merchants and obtained a royal charter granting the new Russian-American Company sole rights in the New World. Baranov was appointed the company's chief manager in America. Under his guidance it became a highly profitable venture. Baranov's interests did not extend far beyond business, although in 1808 he initiated the establishment of a Russian fort (now known as Fort Ross) on the California coast north of San Francisco, which remained in Russian hands until 1841. Baranov retired in 1817, and died of fever in the tropics while aboard a ship headed back to St. Petersburg.

Other Russian-American Company managers who succeeded Baranov were not as competent, nor did they demonstrate the capacity for self-sufficiency so necessary for survival in an isolated colony. Their most critical political action was an 1824 treaty setting the boundary (basically the one used today) between Russian America and British Canada, thus effectively ending Russian expansion in North America.

Less dramatic accomplishments had an equally lasting effect. As more Russian women moved to the colony, an ordered social life evolved, marked by the growth of schools, hospitals, and Orthodox churches. Native warfare and slavery became memories as Aleuts and some Eskimos and Indians were Christianized. Western and interior Alaska were explored and Russian settlements sprang up all over the territory. Coal was discovered on the Kenai Peninsula.

But by the middle of the 19th century the company was struggling financially and falling back on elaborate economic schemes like towing icebergs to San Francisco. The Crimean War and other pressing obligations in Europe convinced the Russian government to dispense with its North American possessions.

SEWARD'S FOLLY

Negotiations to sell Alaska to the United States began in 1859, when Baron Eduard de Stoeckel, Russian ambassador to the U.S., was granted the authority by Czar Alexander II to engineer a transaction. The American Civil War impeded progress on an agreement, but U.S. Secretary of State William H. Seward, acting for an ambivalent President Andrew Johnson, finally signed a treaty on March 30, 1867. Formal transfer took place on October 18 of that year at Sitka after ratification of the treaty by both governments.

The purchase price was $7.2 million, about 2¢ an acre. Seward was an ardent imperialist who envisioned Alaska as the first possession of a Pacific empire; many of his countrymen, believing that any available monies should be channeled into rebuilding the post–Civil War South, felt the price paid was exorbitant for what they imagined to be a frozen wasteland. Indeed, the purchase was labeled "Seward's Folly" by the nation's press.

For the next 30 years the territory languished as it hadn't done since the early years of Russian visitation. Population dropped sharply as the Russians headed home while only a small number of Americans moved in. The federal government created the Department of Alaska and put the army (and later the navy) in charge. There was some interest in the fur trade and salmon fishing, but with greater investment opportunities in the Lower 48, few Americans risked their capital this far north.

Gold was the element that shook Americans out of their Alaskan doldrums. Minor gold rushes hit Sitka and Wrangell in 1872, Juneau in 1880, and the Kenai Peninsula in 1895. The great Treadwell mine boomed outside Juneau, the first oil claims were staked in the Cook Inlet area, several corporate salmon canneries opened, and rough-and-ready frontier towns began to grow to serve the miners and fishermen. But these mini-booms were minor compared to what was to follow.

THE GREAT GOLD RUSHES

Ironically, the gold discovery that really established Alaska's name in the mind of the American public was one that didn't even occur on Alaskan soil. On August 17, 1896, a down-on-his-luck prospector named George Washington Carmack and two Indian companions, known to history as Tagish Charlie and Skookum Jim, found gold on Bonanza Creek—a tributary of the Klondike River near present-day

Dawson City in Canada's Yukon Territory. A few months later, when a supply ship laden with gold dust arrived in Seattle, the cry arose: "There's gold in the Klondike!" And by the following summer 30,000 fortune-hungry gold diggers were en route north.

A few of them did get wealthy. But for the most part, by the time these argonauts arrived in the Klondike they found the best claims long since staked by those prospectors already on the scene. And the people who got rich were the entrepreneurs and confidence men who provided services, scams, and entertainment in towns like Skagway, where most of the gold-seekers disembarked from steamers before heading inland.

Within a year of the start of the gold rush, Skagway, at the foot of the Chilkoot Trail to the Yukon, had become the largest city in Alaska, with a population near 20,000. (Fewer than 1,000 year-round residents live there today.) It was truly the great city of the north. Yet men can indeed be fickle when their minds are set on making a fortune. So when word came from far-off Nome that a new major gold strike had been made in September 1898, it was again "off to the races."

Few of the would-be miners imagined how hard life would be in Nome. Though much more accessible than the Klondike, this windswept Bering Sea port was devoid of trees for houses or fuel, and its harsh climate was alien to agriculture and animals alike. Most of the gold-seekers established temporary homes in tents on the frigid beach—a beach whose sands, it was soon discovered, were almost as rich in gold as the nearby hills being sluiced. With competition for riches so fierce, Nome developed a reputation for lawlessness that exceeded even Skagway's, John Wayne (remember *North to Alaska?*) notwithstanding.

Another big gold strike near modern Fairbanks in 1902 helped establish that city, the second largest in modern Alaska. But the main effects of the gold rushes were more far-reaching. Federal legislation extended the reach of several government agencies, most prominently justice and revenue, to the territory. Surveys and road construction got under way. Accorded a limited degree of self-government, Alaskans incorporated towns and elected their own officials. The territorial capital was moved from Sitka to Juneau in 1905, Alaskans were authorized a congressional delegate in 1906, and Congress granted the territory its own legislature in 1912.

By World War I, Alaska's population had stabilized at between 60,000 and 70,000, about half of the inhabitants Natives. More than 80% of the non-Natives were men. Copper surpassed gold as the chief economic base, then was itself supplanted by commercial fishing. Construction of the Alaska Railroad began in 1915 (it was completed in 1923) and resulted in the founding of Anchorage, now a thriving city of a quarter million people. The following year, 1916, the first bill for Alaska statehood was introduced in Congress by Delegate James Wickersham, one of the most famous names in 20th-century Alaskan history. But statehood was still many years away.

WORLD WAR II

The watershed years for Alaska's leap to modernity were those of World War II. Because of its proximity to Japan—Anchorage is almost equidistant between Washington and Tokyo, and the westernmost Aleutian island of Attu is a scant 650 miles from the Kuril Islands, then a Japanese possession—Alaska was regarded as a key link in the American military defense system.

Fort Richardson was established at Anchorage in 1940, and construction began on Elmendorf Air Base in the same year. As tensions grew on opposite sides of the Pacific, additional army and navy bases were built in Sitka, Kodiak, Fairbanks, and Dutch Harbor (Unalaska Island) at the eastern end of the Aleutian chain, while smaller garrisons were established in other locations. With the bombing of Pearl Harbor in December 1941, tens of thousands of troops rushed north. Government workers, meanwhile, required a mere eight months to construct the Alaska-Canada Highway in 1942.

The troop presence didn't stop the Japanese aggressors. In early June 1942 Dutch Harbor was attacked by a good-sized air and naval force intended to paralyze the American fleet while occupational forces landed on Adak, Kiska, and Attu islands farther to the west. Alerted to the Japanese invasion by a vigilant patrol plane, Dutch Harbor repelled the attack with antiaircraft guns and suffered but minor damage. In the following days the Japanese did succeed in overrunning the Aleut settlement on Attu and a temporary U.S. weather station on Kiska, but the Aleutian campaign was nevertheless a failure. Postwar studies reveal that its primary intention had been to divert American naval forces from the June 4, 1942, battle at Midway Island—a pivotal battle in the Pacific campaign that might have gone the Japanese way had the invaders succeeded in their shelling of Dutch Harbor.

Stung by the Japanese attack, the Americans moved quickly to drive them off Alaskan soil. The confrontation climaxed in May 1943 with 2½ weeks of bitter fighting on Attu, a stark, mountainous island 35 miles long and 15 miles wide. By the time it ended on May 29, of an initial force of 2,600 Japanese, only 28 survived. Most of those who had not died in the fighting had committed suicide rather than be captured. The Americans lost 549 men and suffered an additional 3,280 casualties. In proportion to the number of troops involved, it was the second-costliest battle (Iwo Jima was the first) of the Pacific campaign.

The retaking of Kiska was an anticlimax. For 2½ months, until mid-August, American planes and naval vessels bombarded the island almost mercilessly. When a landing force attacked on August 14, they found that the base and its complement of over 5,000 officers, enlisted men, and civilians had been completely evacuated under the cover of fog over two weeks previously.

With the Aleutians secured, America cut back sharply on its troops in Alaska. From a high of 152,000 in 1943 the numbers were reduced to 60,000 by 1945 and only 19,000 a year later. (Today about 22,000 active-duty military personnel are stationed in Alaska.)

The impact of World War II on Alaska, like the gold rush before it, far outpaced the actual events. Between 1941 and 1945 the federal government pumped over $1 billion into the state, much of that to develop transportation systems—the railroad, highways, airfields, docks, and breakwaters. Thousands of soldiers and construction workers who came north decided to remain when the war ended: the 1950 census indicated a territorial population of 112,000, a full 50% greater than in 1940. And while federal interest in Alaska waned slightly in the years immediately following the war, defense spending was quickly revived with the outbreak of the Cold War between the U.S. and Soviet Union in the late 1940s.

STATEHOOD

As the Pentagon bolstered the Alaskan economy, the residents of the territory were looking toward its rich natural resources to do the same for their personal bank accounts. They saw statehood as a panacea for developing their ailing and seasonal commercial fishing industry, a fledgling timber industry, and a mining industry that had long since outgrown its profitability.

In fact, Alaskan statehood had been discussed in seven separate hearings in Washington and three in Alaska between 1947 and 1956. But partisanship was a stumbling block. Alaska's ambitions were closely intertwined with those of Hawaii: Alaska was envisioned as a Democratic state, Hawaii as a Republican one, and neither political party was anxious to give the other an inch toward control of the House or Senate. The American public, on the other hand, was overwhelmingly in favor of admitting both to the Union.

Dreams finally became reality on June 30, 1958, when the U.S. Senate passed a bill approved by the House the previous August. Alaska became the 49th state of the United States on January 3, 1959, after President Dwight D. Eisenhower signed the proclamation. Democrat William A. Egan was elected Alaska's first state governor.

As part of its statehood Alaska received from the federal government a grant of

103,500,000 acres of public lands. But land alone would not solve the economic, social, and environmental problems that loomed in Alaska's future. Not only were the state's coffers dry, but the Native population was clamoring for compensation for lands taken from them by white settlers and a major confrontation was brewing between environmentalists who would protect natural resources and entrepreneurs who would exploit them for economic gains.

The brightest hopes for an economic boom were tourism, with its considerable potential, and the oil and gas industry. In 1957, in the Cook Inlet near Kenai, a modest oil strike was made and geologists indicated greater reserves might be found in Alaskan waters.

Nature appeared to be testing Alaska's mettle when, on March 27, 1964, one of the most powerful earthquakes in history struck the state's most populous region. Measuring 8.4 on the Richter scale, the Good Friday tremor wreaked almost unimaginable devastation on Anchorage, Prince William Sound, the Kenai Peninsula, Kodiak Island, and surrounding areas. When the last shock wave had ceased, 131 people had lost their lives and property damage was estimated at between $380 million and $500 million. The force of the quake was estimated at ten million times that of an atomic bomb. Alaskans' emotions and finances were taxed to the limit, but thanks to the support of industry and the federal government they rebounded with astonishing speed.

Then came the announcement in early 1968 that the Atlantic Richfield Oil Company (ARCO) had discovered a gigantic oilfield in the Arctic. Suddenly Alaskans were looking at the world through rose-colored glasses.

THE PIPELINE

The turn-of-the-century gold rushes in the Klondike and in Nome were mere footnotes to Alaskan history compared to the impact of the oil discovery at Prudhoe Bay. ARCO's find was verified at approximately 9.6 billion barrels of oil, making it one of the greatest oilfields on earth.

It can be argued that Alaska came of age on September 10, 1969. On that date, possibly the biggest auction in the history of mankind was held in Anchorage as oil companies and consortiums gathered for the sale of leases on some 450,000 acres of North Slope oil lands by the state of Alaska. ARCO, British Petroleum, Colorado Oil and Gas, Sinclair, and Union Oil sought to add to leases they already held, while North Slope newcomers wanted a foothold. In the decade since statehood Alaska had held 22 previous lease sales netting less than $100 million. On this day, after fewer than seven hours of bidding, the state collected a 20% down payment on more than $900 million in lease payments for less than .001% of its landmass.

Almost immediately, talk began of building an 800-mile-long pipeline to transport the oil from the North Slope, where Arctic Ocean ice prevented shipping for all but two months of the year, to the deep-water port of Valdez on the Gulf of Alaska. Eight oil companies set up the Alyeska Pipeline Service Company to construct and maintain the Trans Alaska Pipeline. But suits filed in 1970 by environmental groups, concerned with the potential negative ramifications of a pipeline on the natural environment, and Native villages, angered that there were no plans to compensate them for use of land through which the pipeline was to pass, prevented the start of construction pending 3½ years of legal and legislative actions. The original plan to build a conventional buried pipeline had to be shelved when it was demonstrated that oil moving at 160°F would have a disastrous effect on the Arctic permafrost. As finally built, more than half of the 48-inch-diameter pipeline is elevated above ground.

Pipeline legislation was signed on November 16, 1973, by President Richard Nixon. That winter, huge amounts of equipment and supplies were shuttled to temporary camps north of the Yukon River, and when spring arrived the construction effort got under way.

Over the next three years 21,600 workers operated out of 31 construction camps along the pipeline route. The working conditions were treacherous, but the men and women who tackled the pipeline were fed and paid like royalty—wages averaged $1,200 a week. They were followed to the north by fast-buck specialists: fly-by-night entrepreneurs, flimflam artists, and prostitutes. Fairbanks became their capital, more than doubling in size from about 15,000 to some 35,000 between 1973 and 1976.

Many pipeline workers made a sizable nest egg, returned to the Lower 48, and invested wisely. Others lost their money as quickly as they made it. All contributed to the boom that saw Alaska's gross product double to $5.8 billion between 1973 and 1975, and its population grow 32.4% between 1970 and 1980.

The Trans Alaska Pipeline was completed in 1977. Oil entered Pump Station No. 1 at Prudhoe Bay on June 20, reached the Marine Terminal at Valdez on July 28, and was headed for Puget Sound aboard a supertanker on August 1. The flow started at somewhat less than capacity, but increased so that today 1.9 million barrels of oil are pumped through the line daily.

Every resident of Alaska benefitted when, in 1980, the state legislature repealed the state income tax, refunded all 1979 taxes, and established a Permanent Fund wherein one-fourth of all royalty oil and mineral revenues were shared with the state's citizens in annual dividend checks constituting about 30% of the interest earnings. In 1982, with the state's oil revenues decreasing, the legislature called for a constitutional amendment limiting runaway state spending. In 1988 the rate of return to Alaska residents was just 5.3%, but that still resulted in dividend checks of $826.93 to every man, woman, and child.

An intense national search for oil and gas on the outer continental shelf of Alaska's North Slope was initiated in 1981 by Secretary of the Interior James Watt. Three separate competitive-bid lease sales on nearly one-third of the 23-million-acre National Petroleum Reserve were held in subsequent years. It is estimated that the original Prudhoe Bay oilfield was half depleted by 1986 and will be completely drained by the mid-1990s.

NATIVE LAND CLAIMS

A side issue of the pipeline boom, but one which has a long-reaching effect on Alaska, was the question of Native land claims. The state's Native peoples— Eskimos, Aleuts, Athabaskans, and Southeast Indians alike—sought assurance that they, too, would have an equal voice (and assume an equal share of the revenues) in Alaska's development. Through the long years of Alaska's exploitation by Russians and Americans alike, they had never received a kopeck or a penny of compensation.

After years of lobbying, Congress was shaken into action by a federal injunction forbidding the pipeline project to proceed until Native land claims were settled. The complex Alaska Native Claims Settlement Act was passed in 1971. In return for surrendering aboriginal claims to Alaska, the various Native groups were granted legal title to 40 million acres as well as $962.5 million, payable over a number of years. The settlement applied to all U.S. citizens with one-fourth or more Alaska Indian, Eskimo, or Aleut blood, except those for whom the Annette Island reservation had previously been established at Metlakatla.

Thirteen regional corporations were set up to administer the settlement, and each Native became the owner of 100 shares of stock in his or her particular corporation. With this new wealth, Native Alaskans quickly became influential in state politics and business. The corporations invested in hotels, real estate, natural resource development, commercial fishing, and transportation; some have done well, others have not.

WATCHDOGGING THE ENVIRONMENT

The early-1970s quarrels between environmentalists and developers over the potential impact of the pipeline on Alaskan wildlife and landforms were typical of the controversies that flare on many battlegrounds. The confrontation hit a peak in the late '70s when the state of Alaska filed suit in federal court to stop President Jimmy Carter from withdrawing millions of acres of Alaskan land from economic exploitation and making them federally protected lands. The feds won: the Alaska Lands Act of 1980 placed 53 million acres into the national wildlife refuge system, 43 million acres into national parks, 3.3 million acres into national forests, and parts of 25 rivers into the national wild and scenic rivers system.

Offshore waters were also a concern. A 200-mile fishing limit went into effect in 1978, restricting foreign vessels from entering Alaskan waters without permits. The Coast Guard is still kept busy enforcing the law against ambitious Japanese, Korean, Taiwanese, and Russian vessels. A widespread system of state hatcheries was set up to replenish the fishery.

No major controversies have arisen over the development of the Red Dog zinc mine northeast of Kotzebue, potentially a major revenue earner for the state as Alaska heads into the last decade of the 20th century.

Environmentalists have reacted with outrage to a 1987 Reagan Administration proposal that the entire 1.5-million-acre coastal plain of the Arctic National Wildlife Refuge be opened to oil development. Conservationists insist that the delicate ecological balance would suffer permanent damage. The U.S. Fish and Wildlife Service added fuel to their fire when it reported in 1988 that environmental damage in the Arctic plain was worse than projected before exploitation. The Fish and Wildlife Service cited significant air and water pollution, as well as loss of large tracts of wildlife habitat. Some 180,000 caribou make their homes in the 18-million-acre refuge.

If some view the Arctic National Wildlife Refuge issue as a disaster waiting to happen, they can point to the well-publicized events of March 1989 as the worst legacy of the oil era. The supertanker *Exxon Valdez* ran aground on a well-marked reef a mile outside the shipping lanes, spilling more than ten million gallons of crude oil into Prince William Sound. The resulting oil slick, when not immediately contained, spread across 3,000 square miles of coastal waters, sending its tar-like residue along once-pristine shorelines from the Kenai Fjords to Kodiak Island. The total monetary cost, not only for cleanup but in terms of lost income for fishermen and others, may not be known for years. The cost to wildlife may never be tallied. Many thousands of seabirds, fish, seals, and sea otters perished as a direct result of the spill.

Today Alaskans rank second lowest in average age but fifth in per capita income of any state in the Union. With oil revenues slumping, the population has leveled off at about half a million, but hopes are high that new oil or natural gas discoveries will establish a more stable economic growth pattern.

2. The Alaskans

The happenstance of history and climate has left Alaska only half a million independent souls spread over nearly 600,000 square miles. Half of them live in and around the only large city, Anchorage.

There are four major Native cultures: Tlingit and related Indian tribes in the southeast, Athabaskan Indians in the interior, Eskimos in the Arctic and the Bering Sea coast, and Aleuts in the southwest and Aleutian Islands. All told, they number about 64,000, or about 13% of Alaska's total population.

SOUTHEAST INDIANS

Because their homeland is in the more heavily settled Panhandle region, and because their culture is symbolized by the unmistakable totem pole, the Tlingit (pronounced "Klinkit") Indians are the Natives seen most often by Alaska visitors.

About 10,000 Tlingits live along the west coast and islands of the North American continent from Prince William Sound to and beyond Ketchikan. Distantly related to the Athabaskans of the interior, they probably followed the salmon down the rivers from the mountains to the coast many centuries ago. They have much in common with other (mainly Canadian) Northwest Coast Indians like the Haida, of whom about 800 live on southern Prince of Wales Island, and the Tsimshian, whose settlement of 1,000 at Metlakatla on Annette Island is the only Indian reservation on Alaskan soil.

Unlike other Native peoples of Alaska who had to survive in a harsh environment, the Tlingit were blessed with an abundance of food and natural resources. Excellent hunters and trappers, the men hunted deer, bear, ducks, and geese with bow and arrow, and harvested the wealth of the sea. They invented ingenious traps and hooks for snaring salmon, black cod, and herring; harpooned seals and sea lions; and stalked the sea otter for its warm fur, used for clothing. Children gathered berries from the forest undergrowth, dug clams, and gathered crabs from tidal flats. Their affluence enabled the Tlingit to conduct a steady upriver trade with the Athabaskans of the interior.

Thus economically established, the Tlingit developed a complex and sophisticated society. They recognized that their lives were inextricably interwoven with those of the natural world around them, and so evolved a religion based in kinship and communication with all living things. Differences between animate beings were seen as superficial. The clans were named for legendary creatures—Raven, Eagle, and Bear, for example—who, it was said, could appear in human form as teachers, perhaps, or heroes. Totemic symbols identified these real or imaginary animals.

Because Tlingit society was matrilineal, these legends and values were passed from male to male by a maternal uncle. Marriage within the clan was forbidden. Wealth and lines of descent led to a hierarchy within the clan, and it became one of the objectives in social life to maintain the prestige of one's position, and to improve it by obtaining greater wealth or performing heroic deeds. One of the primary vehicles for so doing was the *potlatch*.

The potlatch was many things—a feast, a competition, a celebration of a marriage or a coming-of-age, a vehicle for the performing arts. Most of all it was a confirmation of status, because only a chief or clan leader could throw one. The host invited neighboring leaders of equal or greater wealth; fed, housed, and entertained them for weeks on end; then gave away much of his wealth, thereby climbing in social ranking. His wealth wasn't lost: it was an investment. Protocol demanded that his humbled guests invite him to future potlatches where he would be honored with even more riches than he doled out.

The Tlingit social system led to the development of an elaborate artistic culture to show off status and to portray the origin myths of the various clans. Most famous, of course, were the totem poles, which were carved to honor the dead, to document social events (as with the construction of a community house or holding of a potlatch), and to record history and oral tradition (for instance, to commemorate a military victory). Masks and house posts also gave woodcarvers opportunities to demonstrate their art. Ceremonial garments such as the famed Chilkat blanket (which could take a woman almost a year to weave from mountain-goat wool), spruce-root baskets, and alder bowls were other popular artistic pursuits.

ATHABASKANS

Alaska's "other" Indians, the Athabaskans, make their home in the middle and upper reaches of the vast Yukon River basin. Speakers of this family of languages include the Navajo, Apache, and Hopi; but unlike their cousins in the American Southwest, Alaska's Athabaskans are a people of subarctic scrub woodland.

Traditionally semi-nomadic hunters and trappers, the Athabaskans followed the caribou, moose, and bear by foot and birchbark canoe in the summer. In winter they settled in small villages from which they fished and watched their trap lines, traveling by snowshoes or dog sled. Each family kept a number of well-trained dogs;

from this the state sport of mushing evolved. With the arrival of the Europeans in the 18th and 19th centuries, the Athabaskans began to frequent trading posts and become exposed to Western culture.

The average winter village had six or fewer houses, each with a cache or store-house. The *kashim*, or community house, was the center of the village; the settlement's prosperity was judged by the grandeur of the kashim. Here the men did their carving and tool making, and practiced singing and dancing for ceremonial occasions. Young boys slept in the kashim. Extended families were the rule, old people often living with married children. Rules of proper marriage were not as stringent as with the Tlingits.

Men and women wore identical clothing, well designed for the climate: caribou-skin trousers (with moccasins attached) and long-sleeve shirts that draped to below the knees. They also wore heavy caribou-skin gloves or mittens and a hood with a small cape attached. Women did all the tailoring and sewing, often embroidering the garments with porcupine quills and natural or dyed colors. They also made birchbark and spruce-root baskets.

Men were involved in building houses and canoes, and creating their fishing and hunting gear. Those Athabaskans who lived in the northern and western Yukon basin, bordering Eskimo lands, also carved some masks for ceremonial purposes. Festive events, held in the kashim, included the bladder feast (in which animals killed during the year were honored in masked portrayals of hunting scenes), mask and doll ceremonies, and the partner's potlatch.

ESKIMOS

Alaska's Eskimos live on the state's northern and western coasts and islands, penetrating a short distance up the valleys of major rivers like the Kuskokwim, Yukon, Kobuk, and Noatak, and as far into the Gulf of Alaska as Kodiak Island. Their population is estimated at 34,000. Members of the Eskimo race, which extends from Siberia across northern Canada to Greenland, speak numerous dialects, but in Alaska there are only two—Inupiat in the Arctic and Yupik around the Bering Sea.

Hunters on land and sea, the Eskimo traditionally derive the materials for their tools and clothing from the same animals that provide their main sources of food. They are sometimes able to supplement their diet of fish, muktuk (whale blubber), seal meat, walrus, polar bear, caribou, and ptarmigan with seasonal roots, bulbs, and berries.

It is a popular misconception that Alaskan Eskimos live in dome-shaped ice-block shelters called igloos. Those were strictly used as emergency bivouac shelters by the Canadian Inuit. In fact, dwellings were mainly built partially underground and covered with sod. The extended family is the primary social unit, although polyandry was common in traditional society. Rules of hospitality and alliance building called for a host to offer his wife to an unrelated visitor, with the understanding that the favor would be reciprocated. There were no chiefs or headmen, but public ridicule and fear of blood fueds helped to enforce community solidarity.

Whaling has always been an important component of the economy, and remains so in many Eskimo communities today. The popular "Eskimo blanket toss" game originated as a means of lofting a member of the tribe as high as possible above the flat terrain to look seaward to spot whales. When one of the marine behemoths was seen, open sealskin boats called umiaks, outfitted with paddles, bailers, and harpoons, were launched from the shore or across the icepack. It required great knowledge and skill to harpoon a whale and tow it back to shore, where the entire community participated in the job of butchering the beast.

The midsummer salute to the now highly restricted whale harvest is still the biggest event of the year in Arctic Eskimo settlements. Other elaborate ceremonies stress the Eskimo link to the supernatural. Chief among them are the bladder feast and feasts for the dead. Neighboring villages may join together for these occasions.

Masks, more common along the Bering coast than in the Arctic, are the most memorable manifestation of Eskimo art. The spread of Christianity in the 19th and early 20th centuries curtailed the staging of many traditional religious festivals and thus the use of masks, but the recent growth of tourism has revived the art of mask making.

The Eskimo apply great artistry to everything they make, from wooden kettles to finely carved ivory bow-drill handles. The women specialize in sewing and weaving everything from watertight seal-gut parkas, to walrus covers for kayaks and umiaks, to a high grade of coiled beach-grass basketry decorated with bright floral or geometric patterns.

ALEUTS

When the Russians arrived in the mid–18th century, some 20,000 Aleuts inhabited the lower Alaska Peninsula and most of the 70 islands in the 1,100-mile-long Aleutian archipelago. Unalaska Island alone had 24 Aleut villages. Fewer than 100 years later intermarriage had so reduced the number of full-blooded Aleuts that only 15 islands were inhabited, the number of villages on Unalaska had fallen to 10, and most Aleuts had adopted a European lifestyle. Today about 8,000 Natives have at least one-fourth Aleut blood; perhaps 1,300 are full-blooded. Two of the few surviving settlements are on the Pribilof Islands, where the Aleuts are under government contract to handle seal herds.

Aleut villages were typically situated on the shore near river mouths, where spawning salmon were caught seasonally. The original dwellings were large communal homes for as many as 40 interrelated families. The role of the chief was hereditary, indicating prestige rather than formal authority. Occasionally one chief might have nominal power over several villages on one island. After the arrival of the Russians, the Aleut adapted to smaller family houses called *barabara*.

The traditional Aleut lifestyle resembled that of their Eskimo cousins in many ways, with even more dependence on the sea for survival. Sea otter and seal skins served as their clothing; these and other mammals, plus fish, shellfish, and sea birds, were their sources of food. Vegetable food was sparse, although seasonal blueberries and the bulbs of the Kamchatka lily were harvested.

Clothing was typically made of seal intestines sewn with sinew, making a watertight seam. The women's finest craftsmanship, however, was expressed in their baskets, mainly woven from a rye beach grass. The grass was collected and dried; the stems were trimmed into proper thickness by splitting with a fingernail, which the basket maker grew to a utile length. The baskets were often decorated with yarn and thread obtained in trade.

The art of Aleut males, such as the creation of stone knife blades by pecking and polishing, has not changed since the Stone Age.

The Aleut traveled between islands in one- and two-person skin boats called *bidarka* (kayaks) and large, open boats called *bidar* (umiaks).

WHITES

Alaska's white population is nearly as diverse as its indigenous population, albeit without the ancient heritage in this land. The descendants of early-19th-century Russian colonists, most of them of mixed Native blood, still worship at Orthodox churches; they can be found especially around Sitka, Kodiak Island, and the Kenai Peninsula. "Sourdoughs," many of whose grandfathers came to Alaska during the late-19th-century gold rushes, often shun the larger cities and make their lives in the bush; their name derives from the yeasty mix that early prospectors carried to make bread and hotcakes. More recent immigrants, the largest group of whom arrived during the Trans Alaska Pipeline construction in the 1970s, have made the Alaska population the second youngest in the union (average age: 27) and the most affluent (average per capita income: $18,230).

If you've never spent a full winter in Alaska, by the way—if you've never hung on until "breakup," when the ice thaws on the rivers—you're a "cheechako." If you make it, you can truly claim to be an Alaskan. If you don't, you're still an Outsider, as Alaskans call anyone from Down South—the Lower 48 and Hawaii.

---

3. The Natural Environment

Alaska is a young land. Its oldest rocks date back only about 600 million years. Because of its youth it's geologically volatile, as its volcanoes and earthquakes attest. It is also the most glacially active landscape in the inhabited world. Add to this the phenomena of permafrost and the aurora borealis (the "northern lights") and you can begin to appreciate the fascination many earth scientists have with Alaska.

Three major mountain ranges cross the state in roughly east-west strips. A coastal range arcs widely around the Gulf of Alaska, forming the Alexander Archipelago in the southeast, Kodiak Island in the southwest, and the St. Elias, Chugach, and Kenai Mountains in between. The massive Alaska Range, capped by Mount McKinley, rises in the middle of the state, continuing east to the Wrangell Mountains and to the southwest as the long, volcanic Aleutian Range. The considerably lower Brooks Range lies to the north of the Arctic Circle, giving way to the broad North Slope which descends gradually to the Beaufort Sea. Between the Brooks and Alaska Ranges, the vast plateau called "The Interior" is drained by North America's third-longest stream, the Yukon River, and its tributaries. Much of the terrain here is muskeg, deep bog-like areas favored by wildlife.

The Aleutian Trench, 25,000 feet deep along the archipelago's southern shore, marks the spot at which (according to the current theory of plate tectonics) the Pacific plate is sliding under the North American plate, causing tremendous geologic changes. More than half the state is seismically active—10% of the world's earthquakes occur annually in Alaska, most of them in the Aleutian Islands—and the Aleutian Range has 47 active volcanoes, the northernmost of which (10,197-foot Mount Redoubt) is visible from Anchorage. Mount Augustine, an island only 70 miles from Homer, was very active in 1986.

CLIMATE

Alaska's image as a snow-covered wasteland is a long way from being true. In a land mass that would stretch from Lisbon to Stockholm to Istanbul if superimposed on a map of Europe, the climatic range varies from temperate rain forest to continental to arctic desert.

Most weather fronts move off the warm Japan Current, which flows through the Gulf of Alaska. So the rainiest precincts of the state are those around the edge of the gulf. Most of southeastern Alaska and Prince William Sound are bathed in rainfall measuring 100 to 200 inches a year; Montague Island, at the southern entrance to the sound, recorded a North American record of 332 inches in 1976. Snowfall in this region also tends to be high—24 feet in one month and 81 feet in a winter at Thompson Pass, near Valdez—but temperatures are mild, with average summer temperatures in the 50s (Fahrenheit) and average winter temperatures in the 20s. High winds (100 miles per hour and more) whip the Aleutians with regularity and other coastal areas frequently in fall and winter, causing waves up to 50 feet in the Gulf of Alaska.

Anchorage, protected from most of the storms by the coastal mountains, lies in what is called the Transitional Zone. Much of the Kenai Peninsula and the Bering Sea coast also lie within this climatic belt. Precipitation averages about 15 inches a year, scattered through all months but highest in the late summer. The mean daily temperature in Anchorage is 58°F in July, 13°F in January.

Interior Alaska, entirely cut off from the effect of sea breezes and at the mercy of continental weather fronts, experiences great extremes of temperature. Fort Yukon, just north of the Arctic Circle, has recorded Alaska's all-time high of 100°F, and its low of −78°F is just two degrees from the lowest ever recorded in the state. Fairbanks, the largest city in the Interior, has average July highs of 62°F but suffers through three winter months in which the average daily temperature is around −12°F. Most of the ten inches of annual precipitation fall as summer rain.

The North Slope comprises the Arctic zone, a region marked by six months of subzero temperatures and midsummer highs which often don't exceed 40°F. Precipitation, however, is nearly as rare as a warm day. Barrow averages less than five inches of precipitation a year, though the few inches of snow that do fall stay on the ground for months.

Visitors seeking to tour the state during the time of least precipitation and warmest weather would do well to plan their trip in late May and early June. By July—in Anchorage and Fairbanks as well as Juneau—rainfall is almost double what it was a month earlier, and August is rainier still.

ICE AND SNOW

Because of its northern latitudes, an unusual feature of Alaska's terrain is permafrost, or permanently frozen ground. In the Arctic region, continuous permafrost underlies surface dirt to depths of 2,000 feet. Pockets of permafrost exist through the Interior to the southern slopes of the Alaska Range.

The nature of permafrost has created special problems for construction in much of Alaska. Because buildings and highways erected on permafrost can cause it to thaw and the structures to sink, layers of malleable gravel several feet thick are typically used as a foundation. Nevertheless the cracks in the Alaska Highway after spring thaw bear witness to the limited success of this technique. Other innovations, such as Styrofoam slabs, are being tried.

Glaciers are a far less permanent manifestation of the Alaskan climate. Only about 15,000 years ago, in the middle of the last Ice Age, all of Alaska was covered by ice and snow thousands of feet thick. As the cold weather gradually subsided, the ice receded, gouging fjords, lakes, and valleys as it went.

Today less than 5% of Alaska is covered by ice fields or glaciers. The 28,800-square-mile glacial area remaining is still larger than anywhere else in the world outside of Antarctica or the ice cap of Greenland. Two glaciers, the Malaspina and the Bering near Yakutat, are bigger than the state of Rhode Island, and several other of these moving rivers of ice approach them in size.

Glaciers are formed when the intense pressure of snow buildup on an alpine icefield causes underlying layers to compress into an almost plastic glacial ice—extremely hard, but able to flow like viscous water. This ice squeezes out between mountain peaks like toothpaste from a tube. Once started on its way, gravity keeps the glacier tumbling downward, grinding its way downhill at speeds that can reach several miles a day. Its terminus is the point at which the rate of melting equals the rate of accumulation. As these factors change, the glacier can advance or retreat.

The glacier may act like a giant conveyor belt as it moves down its valley, tearing rocks from mountain walls and depositing them as its terminus. These loads of debris, called moraines, tell geologists how far glaciers advanced before receding to current limits.

Often a glacier will tumble into the sea, calving huge icebergs into the frigid water with thunderous roars. This is known as a tidewater glacier; Columbia Glacier in Prince William Sound is the best known. Other glaciers end in lakes (like the Portage Glacier at Anchorage or the Mendenhall Glacier at Juneau) or simply end in a valley (like the Matanuska Glacier east of Palmer).

The great compression of glacial ice gives it a deep-blue appearance to the human eye, especially where it has fractured. This remarkable color is intensified on cloudy days. The glacial ice crystals are so dense that they act as prisms, absorbing all colors of sunlight except the blue wavelength, which is reflected back.

LONG DAYS, LONG NIGHTS

The Arctic Circle marks the point at which there is no sunrise on December 21, the winter solstice (shortest day of the year), and no sunset on June 21, the summer solstice (longest day). This gives rise to a unique phenomenon: when the sun rises on May 10 in Barrow, North America's northernmost city, it doesn't set until August 2. There are 84 days of continuous daylight. Yet when the sun sets on November 18, it doesn't rise again until January 24; thus Barrow residents tolerate 67 days of continuous darkness.

All Alaskans get used to long summer days and long winter nights, which are increasingly less so the farther south you go. Fairbanks has nearly 22 hours of daylight on June 21, but less than 4 hours on December 21, while days in Anchorage range from 19½ to 5½ hours in length and those in Juneau from 18½ to 6½ hours.

Many Alaskans will tell you that the best thing about long nights is that they give you more opportunity to view the aurora borealis, the "northern lights." This phenomenon is produced by protons and electrons, charged and released by sunspot activity, colliding with gas particles in the earth's upper atmosphere. Some of them are pulled by the planet's magnetic forces into the northern and southern latitudes, where they become visible to the naked eye. The colors and shapes of the magnetic waves vary greatly, from simple arcs of rainbow hues to hemispheric draperies.

WILDLIFE

For many Alaska visitors, the No. 1 reason to visit the state is to see its rich and varied wildlife. Land mammals take first spot on the list, though birds and marine life are not far behind.

Land Mammals

No matter where you go in the state, you'll be cautioned to beware of **bears.** Three principal species make their homes in Alaska. Polar bears are rarely troublesome—they spend most of their lives on the Arctic ice pack—but brown and black bears inhabit almost all the state's forested areas. The adult black bear, which typically weighs 200 pounds and stands four-and-a-half feet at the shoulder, is positively puny compared to the dangerous brown bear, also known as the grizzly. The brown bear can weigh over 1,200 pounds and stand eight feet tall on its hind legs. The Kodiak brown bear is the largest carnivore on earth. Unlike the black bear, adult brown bears don't climb trees . . . but then, they don't need to.

Many Alaskans, hunters or not, insist on carrying a high-caliber rifle or shotgun whenever they venture off a highway. It is legal to shoot a bear anytime in self-defense. The best way to deal with a bear in the wild is simply to avoid it, especially when cubs are involved. If a close encounter is unavoidable, don't surprise the bear. Make plenty of noise: hikers often tie bells or cans of rocks to their packs. If you face a bear, don't turn your back and run, for that can invite pursuit. Instead back away slowly. If you're planning a camping or backpacking trip, be sure to obtain the excellent pamphlet "The Bears and You" from any office of the U.S. Forest Service or the Alaska Department of Fish and Game.

Another animal that can be dangerous when irritated is the **moose.** This largest member of the deer family (up to eight feet at the shoulder) can frequently be seen crossing or grazing beside busy highways, especially in winter; every year commuter traffic leaving Anchorage on the Glenn Highway is inevitably backed up once or twice by a traffic accident caused by a moose. They are not the most intelligent of animals, and will stand their ground against a locomotive rather than give up a blade of grass between the rails. Moose appear ungainly, but they can run quickly and kick hard. Avoid approaching them too closely. Moose are found on the Alaskan mainland from Misty Fjords National Monument all the way to the North Slope, especially in birch forests.

Experts have identified at least 13 distinct herds of **caribou** on tundra-like grazing lands from the Aleutian Islands to the Kenai Peninsula to the Brooks Range and beyond. They number in the tens of thousands, but they shun civilized areas. Unless you're flying, Denali National Park is the best place to see them. **Reindeer** are caribou that have been domesticated for their milk, meat, and hides.

The **musk ox** was once native to Alaska, but none remained in 1929 when the woolly buffalo-like animal was reintroduced to Nunivak Island, in the Bering Sea. It has flourished since, and small herds now roam in several areas of western Alaska, including the Seward Peninsula near Nome. Basically docile animals, musk oxen were easy pickings for guns because of their behavior under attack: They form a circle with their young in the middle and challenge aggressors with their long horns. Some colonies have now been domesticated for their soft underwool, called *qiviut* by Eskimos.

Other large land animals in Alaska include the Dall sheep, found in all major mountain ranges except the southern Aleutian Range; the mountain goat, common in higher elevations south and east of Anchorage; the Sitka black-tailed deer, a denizen of dense rain forests in the Southeast, Prince William Sound, and Kodiak Island; and the American bison, several hundred of which graze near Delta Junction. Alaska also boasts many wolves, wolverines, foxes, beavers, and a great variety of smaller fur-bearing mammals.

Marine Mammals

There are few sights more spectacular than a **humpback whale** breaching—leaping high above the water and coming down with an explosive splash. These massive acrobats average 40 to 50 feet in length, weight 30 tons or more, and are found in all oceans. But they are an endangered species, their numbers today only about 7% of those of a few hundred years ago. The 850 or so that make their homes in the North Pacific might be spotted anywhere in the Gulf of Alaska, but especially in Prince William Sound or Glacier Bay. Alaskan waters boast nine other species of great whales and five smaller whales, plus porpoises and dolphins.

There are also eight species of **seals,** including the harbor seal so common at the foot of tidewater glaciers and the bearded seal (oogruk) whose meat the Eskimos love. The **Steller sea lion** and **Pacific walrus** are commonly found in the Bering and Chukchi Seas, with the sea lion's range extending to the Kenai Peninsula and through the Aleutians. The lovable little **sea otters,** whose fur almost caused their demise two centuries ago, have made a comeback, and now are frequent visitors to harbors and commerical fishing enterprises. You'll frequently see them far offshore, dining while floating on their backs.

Birds

According to the University of Alaska, documented sightings of 405 different species of birds have been made in Alaskan air space. Somewhat less than half of those make their homes in Alaska year round; the others migrate, some—like the arctic tern—from as far away as Antarctica.

In terms of sheer numbers, **sea birds** are by far the most common species. Ornithologists estimate there are more than 40 million here. Who doesn't love the colorful, big-beaked little puffin? Auklets, kittiwakes, murres, cormorants, and dozens of others have rookeries (nesting grounds and breeding places) along many of the Gulf of Alaska's rocky shores. The **trumpeter swan,** which has a major nesting colony in the Copper River Delta, has rebounded from endangered status in the past couple of decades and now numbers about 8,000.

And of course there's the **American bald eagle,** of which Alaska has nine times more in residence (an estimated 27,000) than all the other states combined. This magnificent bird, a national symbol of the United States of America, has a length of up to three feet, a wingspan of seven feet, and a lifespan in the wild of 20 to 30 years. It mates for life, and returns each year to the same treetop or cliffside to build its nest or reoccupy its old one. National law prohibits killing, injuring, or disturbing a bald eagle in any way.

No less a statesman than Benjamin Franklin, however, offered this honest assessment of the bald eagle in promoting the wild turkey as our national bird: "He is a bird of low moral character; he does not get his living honestly." Franklin was right in calling the bald eagle a scavenger. But fish, taken "honestly" from streams and rivers, is the main component of its diet. Visitors to the Chilkat River near Haines have in a single fall day counted as many as 3,000 eagles—that's 10% of the species —pursuing huge runs of spawning chum salmon.

Bald eagles don't get "bald"—that is, they don't develop their white head and tail feathers—until they reach an age of four years. Prior to that they're classified as immature and are not yet ready for breeding.

FISHING AND HUNTING

If an Alaska visitor learns nothing else about fishing during his stay, a basic knowledge of different types of salmon and commercial fishing vessels will probably seep in through osmosis. This is household language in Alaska—it's just assumed that you know.

Quickly, there are five species of **salmon** in Pacific waters: chinook, sockeye, coho, humpback, and chum. To complicate matters, chinook is commonly known as king salmon, sockeye as red salmon or kokanee, coho as silver salmon, humpback as pink salmon, and dog as chum. The king is the largest—it must be 50 pounds to be considered "trophy class." A trophy-class silver weighs 20 pounds; chum, 15 pounds; red, 12 pounds; and pink, 9 pounds.

Three different kinds of commercial boats go after the salmon. Don't make the mistake of pointing at a purse seiner or gill-netter and calling it a troller; you'll get merely headshakes and chuckles from the locals. Purse seiners are the largest boats in the fishing fleet, running to 58 feet. The six-member crew sets a large net in a circle, tightens it with a drawstring, and hauls the works aboard, sharks and seaweed along with salmon. Only the salmon are kept; because of the indiscriminate manner in which they are caught, they are invariably canned. You can recognize a purse seiner by the boom and circular power winch which hoist the net. Gill-netters unwind their net from a spool-like reel, usually mounted on the stern of the vessel. Weights and floats drop it like a curtain in front of swimming salmon. The net's mesh is designed so that medium-sized fish are snared by their gills, while smaller fish swim through the mesh and larger ones glance off it and go around. Trollers trail baited hooks through the water from several long poles extended on both sides of the vessel. Chinook and coho salmon taken by trolling command the highest market prices; they are killed, cleaned, and placed on ice immediately after they are caught, and thus kept fresh all the way to the restaurant.

After salmon, Alaska's most popular saltwater sport fish is the **halibut,** a large, flat bottomfish that can weigh 300 pounds or more. They more typically run 20 to 50 pounds. Alaskan **freshwater favorites** are rainbow trout, lake trout, cutthroat, Dolly Varden, arctic char, whitefish, grayling, burbot, sheefish, and northern pike.

You've got to have an Alaskan **sport-fishing license** to dip a line anywhere. Charter-boat operators usually include a $10 three-day nonresident sport-fishing license in their fee; otherwise, most sporting-goods stores are licensed as agents for the Alaska Department of Fish and Game. A 14-day nonresident license costs $20, and an annual license costs $36.

A nonresident **hunting license** will set you back $60. On top of that, you must buy a big-game locking tag (ranging in cost from $135 for Sitka black-tailed deer to $1,100 for musk oxen) for each animal you plan to take, and when hunting bear or sheep you are required to have a guide or be accompanied by a close relative Alaska resident over 19 years old. For more information on licensing regulations, contact the **Alaska Department of Fish and Game,** Division of Licensing, P.O. Box 3-2000, Juneau, AK 99802 (tel. 907/465-2376). There are a great many special rules governing both fishing and hunting, especially the latter; obtain a current copy of "Alaska Game Regulations" from any office of the Alaska Board of Game or Alaska Department of Fish and Game.

Strict laws prohibit the taking of marine and Arctic mammals—including whales, walruses, seals, sea otters, and polar bears—by anyone but native Alaskans traditionally dependent on them for subsistence. The restriction extends to the possession of walrus-tusk ivory, whale baleen, and sea-otter fur, until it has been crafted for sale as an authentic Native handcraft or article of clothing.

An enormous number of fishing and hunting lodges throughout the Alaskan bush entice outdoorsmen (and women) to challenge salmon with a rod or bear with a shotgun. The most popular fishing lodges are in the southwest around Bristol Bay, though those of the Panhandle are not far behind. The **Alaska Sportfishing Lodge Association,** 500 Wall St., Suite 401, Seattle, WA 98121 (tel. 206/622-3932), and **Alaska Sportfishing Packages, Inc.,** Fourth and Blanchard Building, Suite 1320, Seattle, WA 98121 (tel. 206/382-1051, or toll free 800/426-0603), are reputable marketing agencies. Including air fare from Anchorage, you can expect to pay anywhere from $1,200 to $3,000 for a week's fishing at one of these all-inclusive lodges. Most are open only from May to September.

Alaska has more than 600 businesses catering to the adventure travel industry, including some 250 outfitters, guides, air taxis, and boating operators registered to work in national parks and preserves. The Alaska State Division of Tourism's annual **"Vacation Planner"** (write P.O. Box E, Juneau, AK 99811; tel. 907/465-2010) and current monthly issues of *Alaska* magazine (write 808 E. St., Anchorage, AK 99501; tel. 907/272-6070) are two good places to shop for the lodge or outfitter best for you. A small percentage of them are flimflam operations, so whenever possible talk to someone who has previously stayed with them.

FEDERALLY PROTECTED LANDS

Approximately 40% of Alaskan land is protected under various categories by the federal government. This includes 76 million acres of national wildlife refuges, more than 54 million acres of national parks and preserves, and 23 million acres of national forests. Hunting and mining are permitted in national forests, wildlife refuges, and preserves, but not in national parks. Timber harvesting is also allowed in national forests, but not in the other divisions.

Alaska has 14 **national parks and preserves.** The most famous are Denali National Park, encompassing Mount McKinley, and Glacier Bay, with its great numbers of tidewater glaciers and impressive marine life. The others are Kenai Fjords and Wrangell–St. Elias in south-central Alaska; Yukon-Charley Rivers on the Canadian border in the Interior; Gates of the Arctic, Kobuk Valley, and Noatak in the Brooks Range; Cape Krusenstern and Bering Land Bridge on the Chukchi Sea; and Lake Clark, Katmai, and Aniakchak in the Aleutian Range. In addition there are two **national historic parks**—Sitka and Klondike Gold Rush. Each has its unique features; each is discussed in the regional chapters following.

Two enormous **national wildlife refuges,** each comprising more than 19 million acres, are included in the state's refuge system: Arctic National Wildlife Refuge and Yukon Delta National Wildlife Refuge. Alaska Maritime National Wildlife Refuge, though not the largest in land area, encompasses more than 2,500 headlands and offshore islands from Ketchikan to Barrow, including most of the Aleutian chain. Alaska's 13 other national wildlife refuges include the Kenai, which covers a large percentage of that peninsula, and the Kodiak, which takes in a good two-thirds of that island.

Alaska has only two **national forests,** but they are the two largest in the United States. Tongass National Forest, with its 16.9 million acres, covers the entire Panhandle with the exception of Glacier Bay National Park, small areas near the major towns, and a few other anomalies. It also encompasses Misty Fjords and Admiralty Island National Monuments, and 12 additional wilderness areas totaling 5.4 million acres. Chugach National Forest, with 5.9 million acres, includes all of Prince William Sound, the northeastern third of the Kenai Peninsula, and most of Afognak Island near Kodiak Island.

One of the unique and welcome features of Alaskan national forests is the system of **recreational cabins** for public use. Some 180 of these are located in the two national forests, 20% of them in Chugach National Forest and the rest in Tongass, in the Southeast. Few are accessible by road; they must be reached by floatplane, boat, and/or foot. They cost $15 a night, which can make for a very cheap vacation, even when adding the cost of an aircraft charter. Parties should reserve well in advance, especially during hunting season. You must carry all food, supplies, and bedding because none is provided. Make reservations by mail by writing Chugach National Forest, 201 E. Ninth Ave., Suite 206, Anchorage, AK 99501 (tel. 907/271-2599), or Tongass National Forest, P.O. Box 2097, Juneau, AK 99803 (tel. 907/586-8751).

The **Alaska State Parks** also manages about 3 million acres of recreational land in 85 units around the state, half of it accessible by road. The half that isn't is the primitive but beautiful 1.4-million-acre Wood-Tikchik State Park near Bristol Bay. Other major units include Chugach State Park abutting Anchorage, Denali State Park, Kachemak Bay State Park, and Chena River State Recreation Area, each with more than 250,000 acres. Many of the units have campsites, and there is talk of introducing a cabin system similar to that of the national forests.

ALASKA: A TOURIST SURVEY

This chapter contains a potpourri of information you should know *before* your departure for Alaska—odd bits and pieces like when to go, what to bring, where to stay, where to get further information, how to spend your time and money . . . and how much it will cost.

The best news about Alaska for U.S. citizens is that even though you'll have to travel overseas or cross foreign soil to get there, it isn't a foreign country—so you don't need any more identification than if you were driving to the next state. You don't even have to worry about changing your money—unless, of course, you're cutting across Canada or including the Yukon in your Alaska vacation. In that case, I strongly recommend that you also purchase the latest edition of *Frommer's Canada*.

1. Preparing for Your Trip

MONEY MATTERS
Well, I might as well start with the biggest worry. How much does Alaska cost, anyway?

As you already suspected, it's not cheap. If we decided to publish a "$-A-Day" guide to Alaska, we might get away with $50 and $75 a day—if two people were traveling together. If you're driving your own self-contained recreational vehicle or setting up a tent every night or staying in youth hostels whenever possible, you've greatly reduced the expense of accommodation . . . but you have the added expense of gasoline and vehicle maintenance. Package-tour operators can offer tempting options price-wise, so long as you don't mind having your freedom of movement somewhat abridged.

As an independent traveler planning a trip to Alaska and demanding moderate comfort, I wouldn't take less than $75 per day per person, not including my round-trip transportation expenses. Thus a couple planning a three-week Alaska vacation should figure on spending no less than $3,000 over and above the cost of getting there. It's worth it, believe me!

Now, $3,000 is an awfully large sum to be carrying as cash. And out-of-state checks are hard to cash in Alaska. I suggest purchasing traveler's checks—any kind will do—from your bank or other agent before you leave home. Remember, too, that since Alaska is the 49th state, there's no exchange rate to worry about when you use a credit card. MasterCard, VISA, and American Express are almost universally accepted in larger towns. Many off-the-beaten-track villages take only cash.

WHEN TO GO

If you've read the discussion of climate in the previous chapter (Section 3, "The Natural Environment"), you know a bit about the various climatic zones of Alaska —that you can expect rain any time of year in the southeast and along the coast of the Gulf of Alaska, and that you'll experience the state's highest and lowest daytime temperatures in the Interior. To a certain extent, the best time to visit is affected by where you plan to go and what you want to do there.

Alaska regards the visitor season as beginning on Memorial Day weekend and ending on Labor Day weekend; that's when the cruise ships and tour buses flood the state with package tourists from the Lower 48. In many instances that's the only time visitor attractions are open—as with the wildlife tours at Mount McKinley, the riverboat cruises in Fairbanks, the Russian dancers of Sitka, and almost everything in the gold rush–era city of Skagway. If you're traveling in Alaska at this time you'll have the warmest weather and the most receptive greeting committees. But you may be out of luck in finding a place to stay unless you've booked months in advance, and you'll be sharing the roads with thousands of others. July and August are the most heavily traveled months. May and June, on the other hand, are the driest months (on average) throughout the state, and temperatures are nearly as warm as later in the summer. They also offer the bonus of having less of the plague of giant mosquitoes that traditionally celebrate the Fourth of July with a feast . . . on visitors.

Of course Alaska's natural attractions don't go anywhere during the "off-season" for tourism. Some of them become less accessible when tourist concessions close for the season, but major roads are kept open year round. And those hardy folks who don't mind short days of snow find plenty of places to go in Alaska in the winter. Except in Fairbanks and other more northerly climes, where midwinter temperatures often fall to 30° or 40° below zero (Fahrenheit), the climate is a good deal warmer in Alaska than in Chicago or Minneapolis at that time of year.

WHAT TO PACK

No matter what time of year you're making your Alaska trip, you should include both warm clothing and rain gear in your luggage. In the middle of summer, temperatures in Fairbanks often climb into the 80s, but they can just as easily drop into the 30s or 40s at night. A warm sweater and an overcoat should be sufficient to combat the cold, unless you're taking a side trip to Barrow or Kotzebue, in which case you'll want to add a parka or other winter coat . . . and perhaps some gloves and a set of long underwear. Summer daytime temperatures in those towns are commonly in the 30s. The amount and durability of the rain gear you'll need will depend on how much time you plan to spend outdoors. I have never seen an Alaskan carrying an umbrella, except in downtown Anchorage. If hiking, fishing, or other outdoor pursuits are on the agenda, get yourself a good pair of high rubber boots.

In winter you'll naturally want to bundle up in layers of wool. Any time of year, a pair of sturdy and comfortable walking shoes—not just tennis shoes—is essential. Alaskans dress very casually. With the exception of major hotels in Anchorage, nowhere will anyone blink twice if you show up for a fancy dinner in corduroys and a plaid shirt. Men can bring along a tie for that one big night out.

It's sometimes like banging one's head against a wall to suggest it, but please, for your own sake, *travel as light as possible.* Except perhaps for underwear and socks, carry no more than two changes of clothing; keep your toiletries and beauty aids to a minimum; and try to avoid taking electric appliances unless you can't imagine doing without your hairdryer or electric razor for two weeks. Never carry more than you can handle by yourself without assistance: you won't find bellmen at most hotels except during the high tourist season, and you'll never see porters at smaller airports. Ideally you shouldn't have more than one suitcase and a small bag of essentials that fits neatly under your seat on the airplane.

That said, there are a few items you may not have considered that could prove priceless during your stay: (1) a travel alarm clock, so as not to be at the mercy of your hotel for wake-up calls; (2) a Swiss army knife, which has a multitude of uses, from bottle opener to screwdriver; (3) a small flashlight, especially in winter when it gets dark early; (4) a pair of eye shades, to help you sleep in the summer when it's still light outside; and (5) a small first-aid kit (containing an antibiotic ointment, bandages, aspirin, soap, a thermometer, motion sickness pills, and required medications) to avoid dependence on others in minor emergencies. Some travelers also appreciate: (6) a washcloth in a plastic bag, on the outside chance your hotel doesn't have one; (7) a pair of light wooden (not plastic) shoe trees to air out your footwear after you put in a hard day on your feet; (8) a magnifying glass to read the small print on maps; and (9) bug spray, to dissuade those six-legged pests so prevalent during the Alaska summer.

INFORMATION SOURCES

There's a good variety of material available on the state of Alaska. The single best source of information (other than, I hope, this book) is the **Alaska Division of Tourism,** P.O. Box E, Juneau, AK 99811 (tel. 907/465-2010). Write or give them a call and request their annual "Vacation Planner." It's free. You should also get in touch with local visitors and convention bureaus, mentioned in subsequent chapters of this book, for information on specific destinations.

The **Alaska Northwest Publishing Co.,** 130 Second Ave. South, Edmonds, WA 98020, publishes more books on Alaska—more than 100 are in print—than any other publishing house. Among them is *The Milepost,* an annual 530-page, softcover compendium ($15) that is almost requisite if you're driving to Alaska: the book covers all highways in Alaska and Canada's Yukon Territory, plus the Alaska Highway and major access routes through British Columbia and Alberta, in mile-by-mile detail. It also includes one of the better planning maps available for traveling in Alaska. Its major weakness is that hotels and restaurants are listed only if they buy advertising, so it's best used in concert with this volume.

Other good **maps** are published by oil companies—I especially like the one distributed by the Alaska-owned Tesoro stations—and by the Alaska Division of Tourism.

For general reading on modern Alaska, two of the more enjoyable **books** of the post-pipeline era are *Going to Extremes* by Joe McGinniss (Signet), and *Coming into the Country* by John McPhee (Bantam). James Michener's epic *Alaska* (Random House, 1988) starts "about a billion years ago" and continues to modern times.

AN INVITATION TO READERS

Like all the books in this series, *Frommer's Alaska* hopes to maintain a continuing dialogue between its author and its readers. All of us share a common aim—to travel as widely and as well as possible, at the lowest possible cost—and in achieving that goal, your comments and suggestions can be of tremendous aid to other readers. Therefore if you come across a particularly appealing hotel, restaurant, shop, or bargain, please don't keep it to yourself. And this applies to any comments you may have about the existing listings. The fact that a hotel or restaurant is recommended in this edition doesn't mean that it will necessarily appear in future editions if readers report that its service has slipped or that its prices have risen too drastically. Send your comments or finds to me, c/o Prentice Hall Travel, 15 Columbus Circle, New York, NY 10023.

It's helpful to providers of services, and therefore to me, to let them know you learned of them in the pages of this book. When possible, please, mention *Frommer's Alaska*.

2. Frommer's Dollarwise® Travel Club—How to Save Money On All Your Travels

In this book we'll be looking at how to get your money's worth in Alaska, but there is a "device" for saving money and determining value on *all* your trips. It's the popular, international Frommer's Dollarwise Travel Club, now in its 30th successful year of operation. The club was formed at the urging of numerous readers of the $-A-Day and Frommer guides, who felt that such an organization could provide continuing travel information and a sense of community to value-minded travelers in all parts of the world. And so it does!

In keeping with the budget concept, the annual membership fee is low and is immediately exceeded by the value of your benefits. Upon receipt of $18 (U.S. residents), or $20 U.S. by check drawn on a U.S. bank or via international postal money order in U.S. funds (Canadian, Mexican, and other foreign residents) to cover one year's membership, we will send all new members the following items.

(1) Any *two* of the following books
Please designate in your letter which two you wish to receive:

Frommer $-A-Day® Guides
Europe on $40 a Day
Australia on $30 a Day
Eastern Europe on $25 a Day
England on $50 a Day
Greece on $30 a Day
Hawaii on $60 a Day
India on $25 a Day
Ireland on $40 a Day
Israel on $40 a Day
Mexico (plus Belize and Guatemala) on $35 a Day
New York on $60 a Day
New Zealand on $40 a Day
Scandinavia on $60 a Day
Scotland and Wales on $40 a Day
South America on $35 a Day
Spain and Morocco (plus the Canary Is.) on $40 a Day
Turkey on $30 a Day
Washington, D.C., and Historic Virginia on $40 a Day
($-A-Day Guides document hundreds of budget accommodations and facilities, helping you get the most for your travel dollars.)

Frommer Guides
Alaska
Australia
Austria and Hungary
Belgium, Holland & Luxembourg
Bermuda and The Bahamas
Brazil
California and Las Vegas
Canada
Caribbean
Egypt
England and Scotland
Florida
France
Germany
Italy
Japan and Hong Kong
Mid-Atlantic States
New England
New York State
Northwest
Portugal, Madeira & the Azores
Skiing USA—East
Skiing USA—West
South Pacific
Southeast Asia
Southern Atlantic States
Southwest
Switzerland and Liechtenstein
Texas
USA

(Frommer Guides discuss accommodations and facilities in all price ranges, with emphasis on the medium-priced.)

Frommer Touring Guides
Australia
Egypt
Florence
London
Paris
Scotland
Thailand
Venice

(These new, color illustrated guides include walking tours, cultural and historic sites, and other vital travel information.)

Gault Millau
Chicago
France
Hong Kong
Italy
London
Los Angeles
New England
New York

San Francisco
Washington, D.C.
(Irreverent, savvy, and comprehensive, each of these renowned guides candidly reviews over 1,000 restaurants, hotels, shops, nightspots, museums, and sights.)

Serious Shopper's Guides
Italy
London
Los Angeles
Paris
(Practical and comprehensive, each of these handsomely illustrated guides lists hundreds of stores, selling everything from antiques to wine, conveniently organized alphabetically by category.)

A Shopper's Guide to the Caribbean
(Two experienced Caribbean hands guide you through this shopper's paradise, offering witty insights and helpful tips on the wares and emporia of more than 25 islands.)

Beat the High Cost of Travel
(This practical guide details how to save money on absolutely all travel items—accommodations, transportation, dining, sightseeing, shopping, taxes, and more. Includes special budget information for seniors, students, singles, and families.)

Bed & Breakfast—North America
(This guide contains a directory of over 150 organizations that offer bed & breakfast referrals and reservations throughout North America. The scenic attractions, and major schools and universities near the homes of each are also listed.)

California with Kids
(A must for parents traveling in California, providing key information on selecting the best accommodations, restaurants, and sightseeing attractions for the particular needs of the family, whether the kids are toddlers, school-age, pre-teens, or teens.)

Frommer's Belgium
(Arthur Frommer unlocks the treasures of a country overlooked by most travelers to Europe. Discover the medieval charm, modern sophistication, and natural beauty of this quintessentially European country.)

Frommer's Cruises
(This complete guide covers all the basics of cruising—ports of call, costs, fly-cruise package bargains, cabin selection booking, embarkation and debarkation and describes in detail more than 60 ships cruising the waters of Alaska, the Caribbean, Mexico, Hawaii, Panama, Canada, and the United States.)

Caribbean Hideaways
(Well-known travel author Ian Keown describes the most romantic, alluring places to stay in the Caribbean, rating each establishment on romantic ambience, food, sports opportunities, and price.)

Frommer's Skiing Europe
(Describes top ski resorts in Austria, France, Italy, and Switzerland. Illustrated with maps of each resort area. Includes supplement on Argentinian resorts.)

Guide to Honeymoon Destinations
(A special guide for that most romantic trip of your life, with full details on planning

and choosing the destination that will be just right in the U.S. [California, New England, Hawaii, Florida, New York, South Carolina, etc.], Canada, Mexico, and the Caribbean.)

Marilyn Wood's Wonderful Weekends
(This very selective guide covers the best mini-vacation destinations within a 200-mile radius of New York City. It describes special country inns and other accommodations, restaurants, picnic spots, sights, and activities—all the information needed for a two- or three-day stay.)

Manhattan's Outdoor Sculpture
(A total guide, fully illustrated with black-and-white photos, to more than 300 sculptures and monuments that grace Manhattan's plazas, parks, and other public spaces.)

Motorist's Phrase Book
(A practical phrase book in French, German, and Spanish designed specifically for the English-speaking motorist touring abroad.)

Paris Rendez-Vous
(An amusing and *au courant* guide to the best meeting places in Paris, organized for hour-to-hour use: from power breakfasts and fun brunches, through tea at four or cocktails at five, to romantic dinners and dancing 'til dawn.)

Swap and Go—Home Exchanging Made Easy
(Two veteran home exchangers explain in detail all the money-saving benefits of a home exchange, and then describe precisely how to do it. Also includes information on home rentals and many tips on low-cost travel.)

The Candy Apple: New York with Kids
(A spirited guide to the wonders of the Big Apple by a savvy New York grandmother with a kid's-eye view to fun. Indispensable for visitors and residents alike.)

The New World of Travel
(From America's #1 travel expert, Arthur Frommer, an annual sourcebook with the hottest news and latest trends that's guaranteed to change the way you travel—and save you hundreds of dollars. Jam-packed with alternative new modes of travel that will lead you to vacations that cater to the mind, the spirit, and a sense of thrift.)

Travel Diary and Record Book
(A 96-page diary for personal travel notes plus a section for such vital data as passport and traveler's check numbers, itinerary, postcard list, special people and places to visit, and a reference section with temperature and conversion charts, and world maps with distance zones.)

Where to Stay USA
(By the Council on International Educational Exchange, this extraordinary guide is the first to list accommodations in all 50 states that cost anywhere from $3 to $30 per night.)

(2) Any *one* of the Frommer City Guides
Amsterdam and Holland
Athens
Atlantic City and Cape May
Boston
Cancun, Cozumel, and the Yucatán

Chicago
Dublin and Ireland
Hawaii
Las Vegas
Lisbon, Madrid, and Costa del Sol
London
Los Angeles
Mexico City and Acapulco
Minneapolis and St. Paul
Montréal and Québec City
New Orleans
New York
Orlando, Disney World, and EPCOT
Paris
Philadelphia
Rio
Rome
San Francisco
Santa Fe, Taos, and Albuquerque
Sydney
Washington, D.C.

(Pocket-size guides to hotels, restaurants, nightspots, and sightseeing attractions covering all price ranges.)

(3) A one-year subscription to *The Dollarwise Traveler*

This quarterly eight-page tabloid newspaper keeps you up to date on fastbreaking developments in low-cost travel in all parts of the world bringing you the latest money-saving information—the kind of information you'd have to pay $35 a year to obtain elsewhere. This consumer-conscious publication also features columns of special interest to readers: **Hospitality Exchange** (members all over the world who are willing to provide hospitality to other members as they pass through their home cities); **Share-a-Trip** (offers and requests from members for travel companions who can share costs and help avoid the burdensome single supplement); and **Readers Ask . . . Readers Reply** (travel questions from members to which other members reply with authentic firsthand information).

(4) Your personal membership card

Membership entitles you to purchase through the club all Frommer publications for a third to a half off their regular retail prices during the term of your membership.

So why not join this hardy band of international budgeteers and participate in its exchange of travel information and hospitality? Simply send your name and address, together with your annual membership fee of $18 (U.S. residents) or $20 U.S. (Canadian, Mexican, and other foreign residents), by check drawn on a U.S. bank or via international postal money order in U.S. funds to: Frommer's Dollarwise Travel Club, Inc., 15 Columbus Circle, New York, NY 10023. And please remember to specify which *two* of the books in section (1) and which *one* in section (2) you wish to receive in your initial package of members' benefits. Or, if you prefer, use the order form at the end of the book and enclose $18 or $20 in U.S. currency.

Once you are a member, there is no obligation to buy additional books. No books will be mailed to you without your specific order.

3. Getting There

The fastest, most direct way to reach Alaska is by air. The slower, more scenic ways are by sea or by road. Your means of travel should depend on your time frame and the purpose of your trip. There are numerous options in all categories.

BY AIR

There's a reason Anchorage has become known as the "Air Crossroads of the World." Located roughly equidistant (via the polar great circle routes) from New York and Tokyo, and only slightly farther from London, Alaska's biggest city is a port of call for carriers from three continents and a midway stopover on numerous intercontinental flights.

Foreign carriers visiting Anchorage include Air France, British Airways, China Airlines, KLM Royal Dutch Airlines, Japan Air Lines, Korean Airlines, Sabena Belgian World Airlines, Scandinavian Airlines, and Swissair. Northwest also stops in Anchorage en route to Japan.

From the Lower 48 and Canada, flights arrive not only in Anchorage, but also in Fairbanks (via Anchorage), in many of the cities of the southeast (via Juneau or Ketchikan), and in Cordova (via Juneau).

The star of the skies, as far as travel to and from Alaska is concerned, is **Alaska Airlines** (tel. toll free 800/426-0333). Every year since 1975 Alaska Airlines has carried more passengers between Alaska and the Lower 48 than any other airline. And with good reason: its efficient service, frequency of flights, and network of routes around the state make it my preferred airline for travel to Alaska. The airline serves 14 cities in Alaska, 4 cities in Mexico, and 17 cities in Washington, Oregon, California, Arizona, and Idaho. Through an interchange with American Airlines, it also provides through-plane service from Alaska to Chicago, Washington, D.C., Dallas/Fort Worth, and Houston. Principal offices are in Seattle. The airline has applied to fly a route between Nome and Providenyia, in Soviet Siberia, pending government approval.

Alaska Airlines offers a special "Buy Alaska" fare that enables travelers to make one-way stops at any Alaskan cities along their routes for just $30 each. Passengers age 62 or older and children under 12 receive additional discounts on coach fares. Make reservations by calling their toll-free number.

Three other domestic airlines—**Northwest** (tel. toll free 800/225-2525), **United** (tel. toll free 800/241-6522), and **Delta** (tel. toll free 800/221-1212)— have nonstop flights to Anchorage from Chicago, Denver, Honolulu, Minneapolis, Portland, Salt Lake City, San Francisco, and/or Seattle; direct flights from Boston, Dallas, Los Angeles, New York, Oklahoma City, San Diego, and/or Washington, D.C.; and connections to almost every other town with an airport. United and Delta also have commuter flights between Anchorage and Fairbanks, and Delta makes stops in Juneau between Seattle and Fairbanks. **Morris Air** (tel. toll free 800/444-5660), a charter service associated with Braniff, flies daily between Seattle and Anchorage on the graveyard shift ($189 to $209 one-way). **Hawaiian Airlines** (tel. toll free 800/367-5320) recently began to fly twice weekly between Honolulu and Anchorage.

From Canada, Yukon-based **Air North** (tel. 907/789-3262) connects Fairbanks and Juneau with Whitehorse and Dawson, while **Trans Provincial Airlines** (tel. 604/627-1341) connects Prince Rupert, British Columbia, with Ketchikan.

You can save a lot of money by buying one of the special excursion fares that the airlines have available. These fares—which have varying advance-purchase and minimum/maximum-stay requirements—may offer discounts of close to 50% on regular economy fares. In mid-1989, for example, standard round-trip coach fare on Alaska Airlines from Seattle to Anchorage was $769 (tax included), but a 30-day advance-purchase fare, with a maximum stay of 21 days in Alaska, cost just $438.

BY SEA

The Alaska state ferry system, formally known as the **Alaska Marine Highway,** is among North America's best travel bargains. You can board the M/V *Columbia, Malaspina,* or *Matanuska* in Bellingham, Washington (weekly in winter, twice weekly in summer) and enjoy a 3½-day cruise through the beautiful Inside Passage to Skagway for as little as $389 ($320 between October and April), including overnight accommodations. The price is considerably less if you bring a sleeping bag and stretch out on the floor or in the solarium. For slight additional charges you can stop off at any cities on the southeastern route—Ketchikan, Wrangell, Petersburg, Sitka, Juneau, Haines, and smaller communities—and reboard on the ferry's next visit a few days or hours later. You can also board an Alaska Marine Hwy. vessel in Prince Rupert, British Columbia, en route to Alaska. The food served in the cafeteria is generally excellent, and boats also have cocktail lounges and gift shops.

Passenger fares are about 30% more between May and September than in the off-season, and staterooms are also priced higher. The schedule works like this. Everyone must pay a basic deck fare with a graduated scale based on distance of travel ($214 between Bellingham and Skagway in summer; $138 between Bellingham and Ketchikan). Children 6 to 11 pay approximately half price; younger kids go for free. Round-trip fares are twice the one-way price. Several types of staterooms are available on the major boats, ranging from two-berth inside cabins to four-berth cabin suites with complete toilet facilities. The fare for the latter is about three times that for the inside cabin ($299 vs. $175, summer rates).

If you're bringing a vehicle—perhaps with plans to ferry up to Skagway and return home via Whitehorse and the Alaska Highway—you'll be charged according to its overall length. You can take a 15-foot car from Bellingham to Skagway for $522, but a 50-foot RV will run you all of $2,535. Except for the largest vehicles, it appears to cost more to ship your car to Alaska in winter than in summer; in fact it's cheaper, because drivers travel free with vehicles in winter.

Anytime is a good time to take the ferry, but if you're traveling in summer, be sure to book well in advance. During the off-season months you'll not only get the best fares, but you're less likely to have any trouble getting a stateroom and far more likely to meet "real" Alaskans. During one December trip I had a chance to visit with the manager of an Alaska Peninsula fishing lodge, a gold-nugget jewelry maker from Juneau, and three-quarters of the student body from tiny (about 20 students) Hydaburg High School on Prince of Wales Island.

From October 1 to May 15 senior citizens travel free in Alaskan waters on the commuter vessels *LeConte* and *Aurora,* paying only the Bellingham–Ketchikan fare ($106 in 1989). For information or reservations, contact the Alaska Marine Highway, P.O. Box R, Juneau, AK 99811 (tel. 907/465-3941, or toll free 800/642-0066).

Alaska Marine Hwy. ferries departing from Bellingham don't make any stops in Canadian ports as they ply the waters of the Inside Passage, thus avoiding any need for Customs and Immigrations inspection. If you'd like to dawdle along the British Columbia coast, look into **B.C. Ferries,** 1112 Fort St., Victoria, BC, Canada V8V 4V2 (tel. 604/386-3431, or 206/441-6865 in Seattle). The *Queen of the North* and *Queen of Prince Rupert* operate an every-other-day 15-hour shuttle in summer between Port Hardy, at the northern tip of Vancouver Island, via the Queen Charlotte Islands or the Indian village of Bella Bella to Prince Rupert, where ferry connections can be made to Ketchikan. From October through May one or the other operates a twice-weekly shuttle over the same route via the Queen Charlottes.

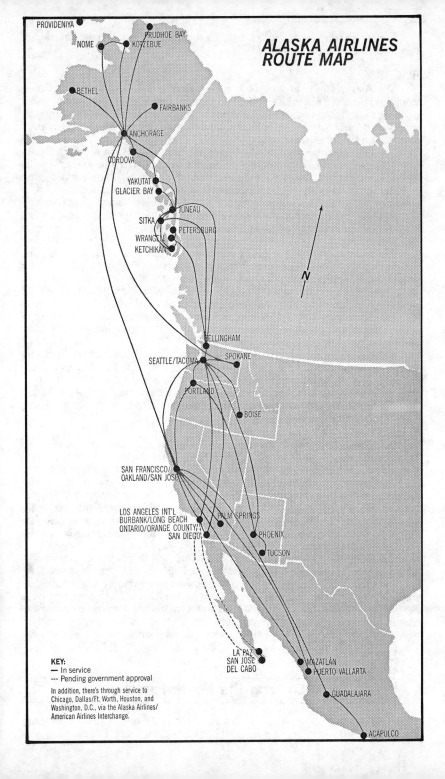

ALASKA AIRLINES ROUTE MAP

PROVIDENIYA
NOME
PRUDHOE BAY
KOTZEBUE
BETHEL
FAIRBANKS
ANCHORAGE
CORDOVA
YAKUTAT
GLACIER BAY
JUNEAU
SITKA
PETERSBURG
WRANGELL
KETCHIKAN

N

BELLINGHAM
SPOKANE
SEATTLE/TACOMA
PORTLAND
BOISE
SAN FRANCISCO/
OAKLAND/SAN JOSE
LOS ANGELES INT'L
BURBANK/LONG BEACH
ONTARIO/ORANGE COUNTY/
SAN DIEGO
PALM SPRINGS
PHOENIX
TUCSON

LA PAZ
SAN JOSE
DEL CABO
MAZATLÁN
PUERTO VALLARTA
GUADALAJARA
ACAPULCO

KEY:
— In service
--- Pending government approval

In addition, there's through service to
Chicago, Dallas/Ft. Worth, Houston, and
Washington, D.C., via the Alaska Airlines/
American Airlines Interchange.

For information on **cruise ships** plying Alaskan waters, see the next section of this chapter, "Cruising the Inside Passage."

BY CAR

The **Alaska Highway** may be the most famous road in North America—ironically, since it's not among the more traveled routes on the continent. But it does see much more traffic than some might imagine. Built in 1942 as a military supply road for U.S. bases in Alaska, it has outgrown its legend as a road guaranteed to ruin even the strongest vehicle.

The two-lane highway officially begins at Dawson Creek, in northern British Columbia, and ends 1,520 miles later in Fairbanks (though Delta Junction, 97 miles east of Fairbanks, also claims to be the end). Most of the road is now surfaced with asphalt. Segments of the highway (mainly in Canada) are unquestionably in poor condition, laced with loose gravel, potholes, and buckled pavement. But considering the effect that the freezing and thawing of permafrost has on any construction, it's a minor wonder that road crews are able to keep the highway open year round at all.

The Milepost, the bible of road travel to and within Alaska, recommends that drivers take their time and drive with their headlights on at all times. Watch out for wildlife in the road, road repair crews, flying gravel, and slippery stretches of ice or mud anytime of year. The highway is treated with calcium chloride, which keeps the dust down but corrodes paint and metal, so be sure to wash your vehicle as soon as it's practical to do so. If you're traveling in winter, include extra blankets and a survival kit. Last but not least, give your vehicle and tires a good mechanical checkup before you start on your journey.

Services—gas, food, and lodging—are found along the highway at regular intervals rarely exceeding 50 miles (though there's one stretch of 100 miles without services). Not all facilities are open year round or 24 hours a day, so try not to let your tank run down to its last gallon. Gas prices in Canada and most of Alaska (except the Anchorage area) are markedly higher than in the continental United States.

BY BUS

There are no direct bus routes from the Lower 48 to Alaska, save those operated by tour companies or on an irregular charter basis. It is possible, however, to travel in Canada by public transport to the Yukon and there transfer to a tour line in Alaska.

The most reliable means to reach Whitehorse from the south is with **Greyhound/Trailways.** There is scheduled service to Dawson Creek from Vancouver and Calgary, thence to the Yukon. Service is available most of the year, but is considerably reduced in winter. One-way fare to Whitehorse from Seattle (via Vancouver) is $149 (U.S. dollars). It's a 52-hour trip, including three transfers. For information, call Greyhound (tel. toll free 800/237-8211).

Three companies—two American, one Canadian—have regular summer-only service between Whitehorse, the Alaska Marine Highway ferry terminuses of Skagway and Haines, and Anchorage and other Alaskan communities. For schedule information on **Alaskon Express,** contact Gray Line of Alaska, 300 Elliott Ave. West, Seattle, WA 98119 (tel. toll free 800/544-2206). To find out more on **Alaska-Yukon Motorcoaches,** write Alaska Sightseeing Tours, 349 Wrangell St., Anchorage, AK 99501 (tel. 907/276-1305). Contact **Atlas Tours** at 609 W. Hastings St., Dept. 104, 5th Floor, Vancouver, BC, V6B 4W4 (tel. 604/669-1332).

4. Cruising the Inside Passage

It's easy to say you want to take a cruise to Alaska. Why not? Sit back, let someone else take the worry out of travel, and just enjoy the scenery. But there is a wide variety of different cruise options available, and not all are right for you. For example, are you looking for a small, informal boat that cuts down on the frills but maximizes the scenic opportunities? Or would you be more comfortable aboard a major cruise liner with a casino, nightly cabaret entertainment, and black-tie dinners? Both options, and many others, are available in Alaskan waters.

As a first step, get hold of a copy of *Frommer's Cruises,* a 400-page compendium of everything you need to know about travel on the high seas. And don't make a choice about which boat you want to take until you've consulted your travel agent.

Annie Scrivanich of Cruise Advisors, Inc., recommends that travelers plan their trips to Alaska as if they were only going once. "They should first select the itinerary that interests them most, then the ship," she says. "They should plan well in advance. I suggest making reservations in November or December for travel in the next year. This affords the best selection of cabins and sailings. Plus, most cruise lines offer substantial discounts to those who reserve early."

Cruise Advisors, Inc., whose annual "Alaska Discount Cruise Guide" lists a wide range of the lowest cruise fares available, can be contacted at 2442 N.W. Market St., Suite 367, Seattle, WA 98107 (tel. 206/784-9852, or toll free 800/544-9361).

CHOOSING A CRUISE LINER

Marylyn Springer and Donald A. Schultz, the authors of *Frommer's Cruises,* point out that a ship's personality is all-important in choosing your cruise. "They really do have personalities," Springer and Schultz write. "To be perhaps a bit more accurate about that, it's really the crew, the officers, and the philosophy of the ship's owners that impart 'personality' to the vessel. Food, entertainment, crew nationality, crew-to-passenger ratio, cruise length, and even historical factors all play a part [in establishing an] informal or formal atmosphere on board. That formality, or lack of it, is reflected in luxuriousness of accommodations, cruise price, on-board entertainment, and often in crew-to-passenger ratio."

The more you are willing to pay, in other words, the higher the standard of stateroom and entertainment you'll get, the more crew will be available to serve your every need, and the more you can expect older, more affluent and sophisticated fellow passengers. The inverse also follows: shorter, lower-cost cruises have comfortable but not ritzy quarters, on-deck parties instead of string quartets, and a younger group of passengers.

Don't forget to consider ports of call when making your choice of vessel. Is there a particular place you want to visit? Or is the cruise experience enough in itself? Many Alaska cruise lines offer package tours that enable you to combine a sea cruise with a land tour.

Every cruise ship has a range of prices. Normally the upper and lower figures indicate the luxury and location of your stateroom. Outside (ocean-view) cabins cost more than inside (no-view) cabins, and suites with separate sitting rooms and bedrooms are at the top end of the price spectrum. If you travel in the "value season," before mid-June or after Labor Day, you'll save about 10%. Meals and entertainment on board are included in the price you pay, but drinks, casino charges, tips, shopping, shore excursions, and land transportation are not.

Several cruise lines are becoming responsive to the needs of physically handicapped travelers. The following ships have cabins specially designed for the wheelchair traveler: Admiral's *Stardancer* (1), Crystal's *Crystal Harmony* (4), Holland America's *Westerdam* (4), and Princess's *Star Princess* (6).

THE CRUISE SHIP ROSTER

There are always new ships and cruise lines plying Alaskan waters and older ones placed in drydock, so don't regard the following list as definitive. Your travel agent should have up-to-date information.

Admiral Cruises

The *Stardancer* leaves Vancouver every Friday, Memorial Day to mid-September, on seven-day cruises to Juneau, Tracy Arm, Haines, Skagway, Ketchikan, and Misty Fjords. Cost is $1,315 to $3,235. This 1,400-passenger vessel with an international crew also has a gymnasium, jogging track, swimming pools, library, theaters, and several lounges with live entertainment. Contact Admiral Cruises, P.O. Box 010882, Miami, FL 33101 (tel. toll free 800/327-0271).

Costa Cruises

The *Daphne* leaves Vancouver every Friday, mid-May to mid-September, on seven-day cruises to Wrangell, Endicott Arm, Juneau, Skagway, Davidson and Rainbow Glaciers, and Ketchikan. Cost is $1,260 to $2,870. This spacious 450-passenger luxury yacht, with a casino, gymnasium, swimming pool, library, shopping arcade, theater, cabaret lounge, and discothèque, has Italian officers and a generally casual atmosphere. Contact Costa Cruises, World Trade Center, 80 S.W. 8th St., Miami, FL 33130 (tel. 305/358-7330, or toll free 800/462-6782).

Crystal Cruises

The *Crystal Harmony* departs on its inaugural voyage on July 24, 1990. The ship will leave San Francisco on 12 trips in 1990, sailing to Vancouver, Misty Fjords, Ketchikan, Wrangell, Tracy and Endicott Arms, Juneau, Skagway, Haines, Sitka, and Victoria. Cost is $2,940 to $11,400, including air fare within North America. The most spacious ship afloat, the 49,400-ton *Crystal Harmony* has eight passenger decks and 480 staterooms for 960 guests. All cabins have sitting areas, bathtubs, and mini-refrigerators, and more than 50% have large private verandas. Contact Crystal Cruises, 2121 Ave. of the Stars, Los Angeles, CA 90067 (tel. 213/785-9300, or toll free 800/446-6645).

Cunard/Norwegian American Cruises

The *Sagafjord* leaves Vancouver or Anchorage, June through late August, on 10- and 11-day cruises to Ketchikan, Endicott Arm, Skagway, Sitka, Yakutat, Hubbard Glacier, Valdez, College Fjord, Seward, Kenai Fjords, Homer, and Cook Inlet. The *Sagafjord* is the only ship to sail into Anchorage. Cost is $1,890 to $5,990. This is one of the top cruise ships in the world, with a rich wood-and-copper interior design. Handling 589 passengers, it has a complete health and exercise spa, swimming pool, shopping mall, ballroom and nightclub, and many other elegant touches. Contact Cunard Lines, 555 Fifth Ave., New York, NY 10017 (tel. 212/661-7505, or toll free 800/880-7500, 800/221-4800, 800/221-4444 in the Northeast, 800/522-7520 in New York State).

Holland America Line/Westours

The *Noordam, Westerdam,* and *Nieuw Amsterdam* leave Vancouver every Tuesday, Thursday, and Saturday, respectively, late May to mid-September, on three-, four-, and seven-day cruises to Ketchikan, Juneau, Glacier Bay, and Sitka. Cost is $999 to $3,699. The company's flagship, the *Rotterdam,* departs every other Sunday from Vancouver, B.C., for Seward on a seven-glacier route. Fare is $899 to $3,399. All four ships have Dutch officers, an Indonesian/Filipino crew . . . and a no-tipping policy. All have casinos, gymnasiums and weight rooms, swimming pools, tennis courts, libraries, shopping arcades, theaters, and several lounges and discothèques, with evening entertainment ranging from cabaret shows to sedate string quartets to discothèques. The *Nieuw Amsterdam* and its twin, the *Noordam,* are floating museums of historic art. They accommodate 1,214 passengers. The recently refurbished *Rotterdam*, ten decks high and three-quarters as long as the Empire State Building is tall, has cabins for 1,114. The new *Westerdam*, with a capacity of 1,300 passengers, is the Holland America Line's largest ship. (It was built in 1986 as the *Homeric*.) Contact Holland America Line/Westours, 300 Elliott Ave. West, Seattle, WA 98119 (tel. 206/281-3535 or 281-1970, or toll free 800/426-0327).

Princess Cruises

Six ships are in Alaska service during the summer season. Four of them—the *Pacific Princess, Island Princess, Dawn Princess,* and *Fair Princess*—leave Vancouver every other Thursday and Saturday, mid-May to mid-September, on seven-day Gulf of Alaska cruises to Whittier, with stops in Ketchikan, Juneau, Skagway, Glacier Bay, and Columbia Glacier. Itineraries are reversed on alternate weeks. Fares run $999 to $3,359. The *Star Princess* sails every Saturday from Vancouver on three-, four-, and seven-day cruises to Southeast Alaska, visiting Juneau, Skagway, Glacier Bay, and Ketchikan. Fares are $1,149 to $3,649. The *Sea Princess* sails round trip from San Francisco on a ten-day itinerary that features Ketchikan, Juneau, Skagway, Glacier Bay, Sitka, and Victoria. Fares are $1,769 to $4,939. All ships have British officers and staff, Italian dining room personnel, and an international crew. All have casinos, workout facilities, swimming pools, libraries, shopping arcades, and theaters. The *Dawn Princess, Fair Princess,* and *Star Princess* are very accommodating to children, with a wide variety of special areas and planned activities. Contact Princess Cruises, 2029 Century Park East, Los Angeles, CA 90067 (tel. 213/553-1770, or toll free 800/421-0522, 800/252-0158 in California).

Regency Cruises

The *Regent Sea* and *Regent Sun* leave Vancouver every other Friday and Sunday, mid-May to mid-September, on seven-day cruises to Whittier via Ketchikan, Juneau, Skagway, Sitka, and Prince William Sound (Columbia Glacier). The 725-passenger vessels return to Vancouver from Anchorage on alternate weeks. Cost is $1,195 to $2,525. The Panamanian-registered ships have seven passenger decks, a casino, sports deck and gymnasium, indoor and outdoor pool, library, shopping arcade, theater, and several lounges including a cabaret and discothèque. Write Regency Cruises, 260 Madison Ave., New York, NY 10016 (tel. 212/972-4774, or toll free 800/457-5566).

Royal Viking Lines

The *Royal Viking Sea* leaves San Francisco in July on an 11-day cruise to Seattle, Victoria, Sitka, Skagway, Haines, Glacier Bay, Juneau, and Ketchikan. In July and August it departs Vancouver on 11-day cruises to Juneau, Columbia Glacier, Valdez, Hubbard Glacier, Sitka, and Victoria. Fare is $2,890 to $9,510, including air fare within North America. The 750-passenger Scandinavian liner has a casino, gym and sports deck, weight room, tennis courts, swimming pools, shopping arcade, theater, and several lounges. Name entertainers and lecturers make these cruises especially popular. Contact Royal Viking Lines, 2 Alhambra Plaza, Coral Gables, FL 33134 (tel. 305/460-4700, or toll free 800/422-8000).

Special Expeditions

Sven-Olof Lindblad's M.V. *Sea Lion* is a one-class ship, carrying 74 passengers in 39 outside cabins. The 11-day cruise, with three departures a month, June to September, begins in Prince Rupert, British Columbia, and includes Agate Beach, Sumner Strait, Admiralty Island, Seymour Canal, Tracy Arm, Glacier Bay, Elfin Cove, Le Conte Glacier, and Misty Fjords. Ports of call are Sitka and Petersburg. Fare is $2,400 to $3,380. The *Sea Lion*'s shallow draft of eight feet allows access to waterways inaccessible on other vessels. These cruises, therefore, focus on Alaska's natural habitat. Each voyage carries a staff of naturalists who conduct informal lectures on natural history. Contact Special Expeditions, Inc., 720 Fifth Ave., New York, NY 10019 (tel. 212/765-7740, or toll free 800/762-0003).

TravAlaska Cruise Tours

The *Sheltered Seas,* a 65-foot charter yacht, leaves Ketchikan on Thursday and Juneau on Monday, late May to mid-September, on seven-day cruises through the Inside Passage. Cost is $895, including overnight accommodation in on-shore hotels at Petersburg, Juneau, and/or Ketchikan. This is an intimate, casual means of touring, with a maximum of 80 passengers on a trip. Contact TravAlaska Cruise Tours, Fourth and Battery Building, Suite 700, Seattle, WA 98121 (tel. 206/441-8687).

Windstar Sail Cruises

The *Windspirit* sails seven-day voyages from Prince Rupert, British Columbia, to Juneau between late May and early September. The itinerary includes Ketchikan, Misty Fjords, Petersburg, Tracy Arm, Sitka, and Skagway. Fare was unavailable at press time. A motorized sailing vessel that carries 144 passengers, the *Windspirit* travels at a relaxed, unstructured pace, much of it under sail. Contact Windstar Cruises, 300 Elliott Ave. West, Seattle, WA 98119 (tel. 206/286-3210, or toll free 800/258-7245).

World Explorer Cruises

The *Universe* leaves Vancouver every other Sunday, June through early September, on 14-day cruises to Juneau, Skagway, Glacier Bay, Valdez, Columbia Glacier, Seward, Wrangell, Sitka, Ketchikan, and Victoria. Cost is $1,595 to $3,395. This 550-passenger ship is a floating university for half the year, chartered to the University of Pittsburgh's semester-at-sea program, so it has one of the largest libraries afloat: 11,000 volumes! Academic lecturers and quality musicians make this a favorite cruise for professional people and educators. The *Universe* also has a swimming pool, shops, a theater, five lounges, and a nightclub. The ship has an American staff and a Chinese crew. Contact World Explorer Cruises, 555 Montgomery St., San Francisco, CA 94111 (tel. 415/391-9262, or toll free 800/854-3835, 800/222-2255 in California).

5. Getting Around

Unlike most other parts of the United States, you can't drive everywhere in Alaska. But between the road, rail, sea, and air networks, no area of the state is entirely inaccessible.

BY AIR

Alaskans fly more private planes than citizens of any other state—and perhaps more than any other nation as well. Statistics in 1986 showed that there were some 11,000 registered pilots in Alaska, one for every 49 residents, and about 9,600 registered aircraft, one for every 59 Alaskans. Those figures have no doubt risen. Compare those numbers to statistics for the entire U.S.: one pilot for every 250

Americans, one aircraft for every 650. There are about 1,000 airports, or one for every 500 Alaskans.

Certainly Alaska is so vast in area, and has so few roads, that the only practical way to reach most communities is by small plane. Indeed the exploits of many of Alaska's pioneer bush pilots are legendary. Twin-engine planes, which often must cope with notoriously poor runways, are frequently outfitted with floats for water landings or skis for snow landings.

Statewide service aboard larger aircraft is provided by **Alaska Airlines** (tel. toll free 800/426-0333) to Anchorage, Bethel, Cordova, Fairbanks, Glacier Bay, Juneau, Ketchikan, Kotzebue, Nome, Petersburg, Prudhoe Bay, Sitka, Wrangell, and Yakutat. Through subcontract agreements with other air carriers, Alaska Airlines also serves 60 bush villages.

MarkAir (tel. toll free 800/426-6784, 800/478-0800 in Alaska) is the state's largest Alaska-only carrier, with extensive passenger service throughout the western part of the state. Its fleet of Boeing 737s and smaller DeHavillands serves Anchorage, Aniak, Barrow, Bethel, Dillingham, Dutch Harbor, Fairbanks, Fort Yukon, Galena, Iliamna, King Salmon, Kodiak, McGrath, Prudhoe Bay, St. Mary's, Tanana, and Unalakleet. **Hermens/MarkAir Express** serves 110 more small rural communities from hub towns.

Reeve Aleutian Airways (tel. 907/243-4700 in Anchorage or toll free 800/544-2248) is Alaska's oldest airline, founded in 1932 by a Kansas barnstormer named Bob Reeve. It provides regular service on Boeing 727s from Anchorage to the weather-battered, 3,000-mile-long Aleutian chain, including Adak, Cold Bay, King Cove, Port Heiden, St. Paul (Pribilofs), Sand Point, and Shemya. It works closely with **Peninsula Airways** (same toll free number) to serve Unalaska (Dutch Harbor) and smaller communities.

Commuter service is provided by a plethora of small commuter airlines and air-taxi services. Among those exclusively serving the southeast are **L.A.B. Flying Service** (tel. 907/766-2222 in Haines), serving the northern Panhandle (Haines, Juneau, Skagway, and Glacier Bay); and **Temsco Airlines** (tel. 907/225-9810 in Ketchikan), with service between Ketchikan, Prince of Wales Island, and Misty Fjords.

In the Kenai Peninsula and Prince William Sound region, **South Central Air** (tel. 907/243-8791 in Anchorage) serves Homer, Kenai, Seward, and Soldotna from Anchorage, while **ERA** (tel. toll free 800/426-0333), the Alaska Airlines commuter line, flies from Anchorage to Homer, Kenai, and Valdez.

Among the many other air services to keep in mind are **Arctic Circle Air** (tel. 907/456-1166 in Fairbanks), which flies between Fairbanks and Anaktuvuk Pass, Bettles, Eagle, Fort Yukon, and other points; **Cape Smythe Air Service** (tel. 907/852-8333 in Barrow or 907/443-2414 in Nome), flying between Barrow, Kotzebue, Nome, Point Hope, Prudhoe Bay, Wainwright, and many other arctic and northwest Alaskan communities; and **Ryan Air Service** (tel. 907/248-0695 in Anchorage), with flights from Anchorage to communities throughout the Yukon–Kuskokwim Delta region.

Each community has its own local air-taxi services, and frequently helicopter service as well. At least once on your Alaskan trip, plan to invest $100 or so in a flightseeing excursion. It may be the highlight of your trip.

BY SEA

The **Alaska Marine Highway** (tel. 907/465-3941, or toll free 800/642-0066) has two ferry systems with nine boats in continual operation. The Southeast System serves 15 towns in Alaska's Panhandle, while the Southwest System stops in 12 towns in Prince William Sound, the Kenai Peninsula, and Kodiak Island, with seven trips a year to the Alaska Peninsula and the Aleutians.

The five boats that cover longer distances—the *Columbia, Malaspina, Matanuska, Taku,* and *Tustumena*—all have staterooms for overnight guests. The four smaller boats—the *Aurora, Bartlett, Chilkat,* and *LeConte*—ply shorter routes and have no staterooms, so those on overnight excursions must spread blankets or sleeping bags across lounge seats or on the floors. All boats but the *Chilkat* (which shuttles between Ketchikan, Metlakatla, and Hollis) have food service and a solarium; all but the *Chilkat* and *Bartlett* (the Prince William Sound commuter) have a cocktail lounge.

Sample fares in summer 1989 (not including stateroom): Juneau to Ketchikan, $60; Juneau to Skagway, $22; Juneau to Sitka, $20; Valdez to Homer, $116; and Homer to Kodiak, $38. Rates are 20% to 30% less from October to May.

BY CAR

Despite its immense size, Alaska has less than 16,000 miles of roads, of which perhaps one-third are paved. The main highway system runs through south-central Alaska and part of the Interior, connecting Anchorage and the Kenai Peninsula with Denali National Park, Fairbanks, and points east (Canada). In southeast Alaska, only Haines and Skagway, at the northern end of the Inside Passage, and tiny Hyder have road connections (via the Yukon) to the rest of Alaska.

The price of gas in Anchorage is comparable to the Lower 48, but elsewhere in Alaska it's considerably higher. As a general rule, the farther you get from major cities, the more you'll have to pay for gas. Sometimes it's hard to accept that you can be virtually straddling the pipeline but paying upward of $1.50 a gallon to fill your tank.

The frigid winter weather in many parts of Alaska, particularly the Interior, creates some unusual maintenance problems for motor vehicles. Throughout the state you'll see what appear to be electric plugs protruding through the front grills of cars. Outside hotels in Fairbanks and other inland towns, you'll see a line of what appear to be electric sockets in the parking lots. As you may have guessed, the plugs fit in the sockets. How else are you going to keep your vehicle charged in –40°F weather?

You should drive defensively at all times. The mandated speed limit on all highways, unless otherwise posted, is 55 mph.

Car Rentals

Most major car-rental agencies have outlets in Alaska, many of them in every town of size. Even in southeastern and arctic towns without connecting roads from outside, rentals are available for driving the local road system. You can also obtain recreational vehicle rentals on a weekly basis.

Rates change regularly. The only certainty is that they are higher during the summer tourist season. Most agencies also have reduced rates on weekends.

Use these rates as guidelines only: economy model, $35 to $39 daily, $190 to $230 weekly; full size, $45 to $49 daily, $260 to $310 weekly; van, $65 daily, $390 weekly.

BY BUS

Several regional bus lines operate specific routes in Alaska, mainly during the summer months. Their services are discussed in the appropriate chapters, following.

BY RAIL

First opened in 1923, the **Alaska Railroad** runs 470 miles from Seward and Whittier, the deep-water ports of south-central Alaska, through Anchorage to Denali National Park and Fairbanks.

The railroad now operates four basic routes: a daily express schedule between Anchorage and Fairbanks via Wasilla, Talkeetna, and Denali National Park; a twice-weekly Anchorage–Fairbanks "dayliner" service, stopping at every small station (including flag stops) on the route; a Thursday-through-Sunday summer run between Anchorage and Seward; and a shuttle service several times daily between Portage station (near Girdwood, east of Anchorage) and the Prince William Sound port of

Whittier. During the winter months the Anchorage–Fairbanks "dayliner" operates twice monthly—northbound on the first and third Tuesdays of each month, southbound on the following Wednesdays.

Not surprisingly, the most popular tourist excursion route is the daily summer express train, often called the Denali National Park route. From May 21 to September 16 the *Denali Express* leaves Anchorage at 8:30 a.m., and arrives in Denali Park at 3:45 p.m. and in Fairbanks at 8 p.m. The *Anchorage Express* leaves Fairbanks at 8:30 a.m., and arrives in Denali Park at 12:15 p.m. and in Anchorage at 8 p.m. The train is equipped with a dome car and full dining-and-beverage service. Reservations are required. One-way adult fares are $62 between Anchorage and Denali Park, $33 between Denali Park and Fairbanks, $88 between Anchorage and Fairbanks (with or without a Denali stopover). Children are charged half price; round trips are double the one-way fares. A ten-day unlimited-travel rail pass costs $209.

In addition to the Alaska Railroad's Vistaliner dome car, both Gray Line (Holland America Line/Westours) and Princess Tours own and operate several premium glass-domed cars—Gray Line with its *McKinley Explorer* cars, Princess with its *Midnight Sun Express*. The dome cars, which depart daily as part of the regular Alaska Railroad schedule from May 21 to September 20, allow passengers an unobstructed view of the tall trees and mountains along the route. Some passengers find the luxury of professional tour guides, gourmet cuisine, and entertainment provided by Gray Line and Princess to be well worth the extra cost. Gray Line charges $149 ($72.50 for children) from Anchorage to Fairbanks; Princess Tours, which includes an overnight stay in Denali National Park, is $295 for adults, $185 for children, one way. Others prefer the quieter, budget-priced ride in Alaska Railroad's own cars, with commentary and guitar playing by college students on summer vacation.

For reservations and further information, contact the Alaska Railroad, 411 W. First Ave. (P.O. Box 107500), Anchorage, AK 99510 (tel. 907/265-2623, or toll free 800/544-0552). For information on the luxury cars, contact Holland America Line or Princess Tours as listed below.

6. Tour Operators

Many travelers find it most convenient, and often (depending on their desired level of travel) less expensive, to leave their Alaskan visit in the hands of tour experts. These travel packagers handle a large percentage of Alaska tourists each year, most often through "cruise/tour" packages that combine a week's cruise up the Inside Passage with bus travel through the Yukon to Anchorage, Denali National Park, Fairbanks, and Prince William Sound. Tour options like Arctic excursions (to Barrow, Kotzebue, and/or Nome) may be thrown in. A few companies offer trips to the Kenai Peninsula, Kodiak Island, the Pribilofs, and the Aleutians. Your best bet is to shop around (or have your travel agent shop around) and determine which itinerary and price range best suits you. These were some of the major tour operators in 1989:

Alaska Sightseeing Tours, 808 Fourth and Battery Building, Seattle, WA 98121 (tel. 206/441-8687, or toll free 800/621-5557); 543 W. Fourth Ave., Anchorage, AK 99501 (tel. 907/276-1305).

Alaska Travel Adventures, 9085 Glacier Hwy., Juneau, AK 99801 (tel. 907/789-0052).

Atlas Tours, 609 W. Hastings St., Dept. 104, 5th Floor, Vancouver, B.C. V6B 4W4 (tel. 604/669-1332).

CampAlaska Tours, P.O. Box 872247, Wasilla, AK 99687 (tel. 907/376-9438).

Cruise Alaska Tours, 10518 N.E. 37th Circle, Kirkland, WA 98033 (tel. 206/827-7881, or toll free 800/426-2134).

Holland America Line/Westours–Gray Line of Alaska, 300 Elliott Ave. West, Seattle, WA 98119 (tel. 206/281-3535, or toll free 800/426-0327); 547 W. Fourth Ave., Anchorage, AK 99501 (tel. 206/277-5581, or toll free 800/544-2206); affiliated with **Leisure Tours,** at the same Seattle address (tel. 206/281-8210).

Midnight Sun Tours, P.O. Box 103355, Anchorage, AK 99510 (tel. 907/276-8687, or toll free 800/544-2235).

Princess Tours, 2815 Second Ave., Suite 400, Seattle, WA 98121 (tel. 206/728-4202, or toll free 800/647-7750); affiliated with **Tour Alaska,** 2555 76th Ave. SE, Mercer Island, WA 98040 (tel. 206/236-1592, or toll free 800/835-8907).

Then there's **Green Tortoise Alternative Travel,** an alternative that isn't for everyone. Twice a summer, in July and August, a refurbished school bus packed with shoestring-budget travelers takes a month-long trip from the Lower 48. Contact Green Tortoise at P.O. Box 24459, San Francisco, CA 94124 (tel. 415/821-0803, or toll free 800/227-4766 outside California).

---

7. Settling In

All right, so you've arrived in Alaska. Now what?

The nuts and bolts of traveling in Alaska—the type of accommodations you'll find, the food you'll come across, the liquor laws you'll encounter, and so forth—are laid out in this section. Here also you'll read some generalities about touring a state that puts a great value on the outdoors, and little on indoor activities.

Before we get started, you've got a right to ask: What time is it?

ALASKA TIME

Until 1983 Alaska had four different time zones. Juneau was in the same Pacific time zone as San Francisco; Anchorage was two hours earlier. Then Congress passed a bill to reduce the time zones from four to two, so that today it's the same time in Ketchikan as in Nome. Only the western Aleutians and some Bering Sea islands are on Hawaii time.

Alaska Standard Time is one hour earlier than Pacific Standard Time, four hours behind Eastern Standard Time. When it's noon in New York and 9 a.m. in San Francisco, it's 8 a.m. in Sitka, Anchorage, and Dutch Harbor (but 7 a.m. in Adak).

STATE SYMBOLS

Since you're in Alaska, you'd better learn a little Alaskana.

The **state flag**—"eight stars of gold on a field of blue"—was designed by a 13-year-old orphan in a territory-wide school contest in 1926. Simple in concept, it shows the constellation known as the Big Dipper pointing at the North Star. Wrote creator Benny Benson, now among the state's most decorated patriots: "The blue field is for the Alaska sky and the forget-me-not, an Alaska flower. The North Star is for the future state of Alaska, the most northerly of the Union. The dipper is for the Great Bear—symbolizing strength."

Other symbols are as follows:

State motto: "North to the Future."
State sport: Dog mushing.
State bird: Willow ptarmigan, a small arctic grouse that changes its plumage from brown in summer to white in winter.
State fish: King salmon.
State tree: Sitka spruce, a large tree (it grows to 160 feet high, 3 to 5 feet in diameter) and valuable timber resource found throughout the Gulf of Alaska region.

State mineral: Gold.
State gem: Jade, found in northwestern Alaska in the vicinity of Kotzebue.

LANGUAGE

English is, of course, the common tongue of nearly all Alaskans, with a smattering of Inupiat, Yupik, Tlingit, and other Native tongues thrown in. But that doesn't mean you'll understand every word an Alaskan says. The following vocabulary list is supplied to help you cope with uniquely Alaskan words:

akutak—Eskimo ice cream, traditionally made of whipped soapberries, seal oil, and snow.

baleen—The black, fringed, bone-like substance that lines the mouth of baleen whales, straining plankton and krill from the water. It is often used in Native crafts.

billiken—A smiling, pot-bellied good-luck charm with a pointed head, commonly carved from ivory by Yupik Eskimos.

blanket toss—Also called the *nalukataq,* this Eskimo game requires a dozen or more people to grasp the edges of a circular walrus-hide blanket and toss an individual as high as 20 feet into the air, as on a trampoline.

breakup—The end of an Alaskan winter, when the ice that has frozen the major rivers thaws, pounding its way downstream as the spring snows melt. It typically occurs in the Yukon River in early May. In the Nenana Ice Classic, Alaska's biggest lottery-style pool, Alaskans each year buy tickets to guess the exact minute of breakup of the Tanana River at Nenana, with over $50,000 paid to winners.

bush—Any part of Alaska not accessible by road or ferry.

cabin fever—What you get if breakup is late. Even sourdoughs, housebound during the long, dark, cold winter months, may suffer depression, discontent, and even fits of violence.

cache—A miniature log cabin storage bin, mounted on stilts and reached by a ladder, to keep food and other goods safe from animal invasions.

cheechako—A newcomer or "greenhorn," not unlike the Hawaiian word "malihini." Specifically, a cheechako is one who has not spent a full winter in Alaska, until breakup.

hooligan—Small smelt caught by dip-netting as they swim upriver to spawn.

ice fog—An unpleasant weather phenomenon that occurs in the Interior and arctic during winter. Clear skies allow heat to rise from the earth's surface, trapping ice crystals in a dry fog at lower elevations. In Fairbanks this may take the form of ice smog.

iceworm—A black, segmented worm, usually the size of a straight pin, that lives near the surface of glaciers and icefields. Its myth, perpetuated by the annual Cordova Iceworm Festival (see the "Prince William Sound" section in Chapter V), has outgrown its reality.

igloo—A traditional Eskimo dwelling made of sod, driftwood, and whalebone. The stereotypical ice-block igloo was built mainly by Canadian Eskimos as an emergency bivouac.

mukluks—Eskimo moccasins, very warm but lightweight. They are usually made with sealskin soles and caribou tops, and trimmed with fur.

muktuk—A favorite Eskimo delicacy: whale blubber, specifically the outer layers of skin.

muskeg—Bog-like areas underlain by permafrost or periodically frozen ground, where little vegetation except scrub trees, shrubs, and moss can grow.

North Slope—The frigid north side of the Brooks Range, where the oil and natural gas (and money) are. Also referred to merely as "The Slope."

no-see-ums—Almost microscopic in size, these tiny gnats are seen all too often in pesky swarms, especially in the summer. Good insect repellent and netting may deter them.

Outside—Anywhere but Alaska.

qiviut—The warm underwool of the musk ox, knitted into scarves, caps, and other clothing items.

Robert Service (1874–1958)—The most famous balladeer of the gold rush days. Though he was a Canadian, plays based on Service's epic poems "The Shooting of Dan McGrew" and "The Cremation of Sam McGee" are widely performed on Alaskan stages.

skookum—Strong or hearty, as in a skookum meal or a skookum baby.

skookum chuck—A narrow passage between the open sea and a tidal lagoon. It may take on the appearance of river rapids when the tide changes.

soapstone—Compact talc, an extremely soft and greasy-feeling mineral used in carving art objects.

sourdough—An Alaskan oldtimer, often someone whose granddaddy arrived during the gold rushes and stayed. The name comes from the high-yeast bread so popular in the bush.

squaw candy—Dried or smoked salmon, a staple winter food for bush Alaskans and their dogs.

the whole nine yards—All of it.

ulu—A traditional, fan-shaped Eskimo knife with a handle of bone or wood, used for scraping (mainly animal skins) and chopping.

umiak—A skin-covered Eskimo boat, lightweight but hardy for dragging across sea ice; usually made of walrus or oogruk (bearded seal) skin.

williwaws—Sudden windstorms that can exceed 100 miles an hour.

WHERE TO STAY

Alaskan accommodations are, as a general rule, excellent. Lodging in major cities, including Anchorage, Fairbanks, and Juneau, is on a par with that of similarly sized communities in the Lower 48. The farther from population centers you travel, the more rustic your lodging is likely to become.

During most of the year you'll have no problem arriving without reservations and walking into the room of your choice. That is decidedly *not* true during the peak summer season, when advance reservations are essential. It's important also that you check the local calendar: during festival periods rooms are also snapped up in a hurry.

Seasonal rates are the rule rather than the exception in most of Alaska. In some areas, like Anchorage, the difference between winter and summer rates may be only 10% to 20%. In other parts of the state, including Fairbanks, summer rates can be 50% or more above winter rates. The justification is that if the hotel or motel operators don't make their money during the brief visitor season, they'll go hungry all year.

Virtually every Alaskan community, no matter what size, has a **city or borough bed tax,** which may range from 2% to 8%. This is *not* included in the rates quoted in this book; the local tax is noted separately at the beginning of each "Where to Stay" section. Specific information about arranging for the various types of accommodations outlined below is also provided in the individual chapters.

Hotels

With the exception of some of those in Anchorage, major hotels are not of international standard, though many deserve a "first-class" label. They cater primarily to house guests, running their restaurants and bars as adjuncts. Bathrooms are excellent, containing not only ample towels and soap, but often an array of complimentary amenities—shampoo, hand lotion, and shoeshine and sewing kits among them. Room telephones and televisions are standard equipment in better hotels. Rates commonly run $80 a night and upward to the $130 range.

The second tier of hotel accommodation falls into the budget category, often in the $25- to $50-a-night range. Rooms here tend to be secondary to the bar and/or restaurant on the ground floor: they're frequently up a side stairs, with a shared bathroom down the hall. A few of the more respectable entries in this classification may be listed in this book as budget alternatives.

Motels

These are mainly located in cities and towns, with a rare few along the state's highways. Don't plan on driving on ahead with the intention of finding a vacant motel en route to your final destination. You may have a long drive.

Most motels are moderately priced, in the $50 to $80 range.

Roadhouses

First built along the routes that took turn-of-the-century fortune hunters from the seaports to the goldfields, these wayside lodges usually incorporate a good restaurant and small bar with a handful of rustic rooms. They normally have a sink in the room but a shared bath. Prices are quite reasonable. Though rarely modern, these take the place of motels along Alaska's highways.

Youth Hostels

Alaska has 12 youth hostels, all of them easily reached by road or ferry. Charges are typically $5 to $8.50 a night, depending in part on whether you're a member of the International Youth Hostel Federation. All have separate men's and women's dormitories and bathrooms, communal kitchens, and common rooms. Some have a family room set aside. Blankets and cooking utensils are provided; you must bring a sheet sack or sleeping bag, and food. To help keep maintenance costs to a minimum, you'll normally be assigned a cleanup chore.

Alaskan hostels are in or near Anchorage, Delta Junction, Fairbanks, Girdwood, Haines, Juneau, Ketchikan, Palmer, Seward, Sitka, Soldotna, and Tok. The Delta Junction, Fairbanks, Ketchikan, Palmer, Sitka, and Tok hostels are open summer only.

Annual adult memberships cost $20; individuals under 18 or over 55 pay $10. Write for information: Alaska Council, American Youth Hostels, P.O. Box 4-1461, Anchorage, AK 99509.

Bed-and-Breakfasts

This option allows you to stay in a private home, relax with hosts anxious to share their knowledge about Alaska, and enjoy a breakfast which may range from bran muffins and coffee to hearty sourdough pancakes. Most B&Bs don't have more than three or four guest rooms available for rent. Prices are typically $40 to $70 a night per couple.

Serviced Apartments

There aren't many of these around, although their numbers are increasing. They can be a great bargain for families, who get a two- or three-bedroom apartment with all bedding and cooking utensils provided, and maid service once or twice weekly. Long-term rentals are considerably cheaper than one- or two-night stays.

Camping Grounds

There are plenty of campgrounds along the highways all over the state. Most accommodate recreational vehicles as well as tent-campers. In the southeast and south-central regions, most are operated by the Forest Service and have a nominal usage fee of $5 or so. Facilities in state and national parks are likewise low-priced. Private campgrounds, especially those providing electric hookups for RVs, may cost up to $15.

Fishing and Hunting Lodges

With few exceptions, these are off the beaten path and must be reached by small plane, or in some instances, chartered boat. You normally visit the lodge on a three- to seven-day package which includes round-trip transportation, lodging (which can be rustic to contemporary), all meals, sporting equipment, and guide service. Prices run in the thousands of dollars. Look at the advertisements in *Alaska* magazine or any magazine catering to hunters or fishermen if you think you might be interested.

Forest Service Cabins

One of Alaska's truly unique travel bargains is its system of 180 primitive cabins scattered throughout Tongass and Chugach National Forests. Although prices have risen to $15 a night (per cabin, not per person) and may soon go up to $20, they still offer an opportunity for a cheap vacation. A few can be reached by trail off a main road, but most are in isolated locations requiring a fly-in or boat drop. Most have sleeping lofts for six people, wood stoves, tables, pit toilets, and a firewood cache. You must provide your bedding, food, and all other requirements.

Cabin permits are issued either on a first-come, first-served basis, or by drawing, with applications taken six months in advance. Cabins are open for use year round, but fill up quickly during fishing and hunting seasons and in the summer. For information and reservations, write Tongass National Forest, P.O. Box 1628, Juneau, AK 99802; or Chugach National Forest, 201 E. Ninth Ave., Anchorage, AK 99501.

EATING AND DRINKING

Alaska isn't the most gastronomically exciting of all states. For the most part the cuisine is rather ordinary and bland . . . unless you're a seafood lover. Then you might find yourself in seventh heaven.

Probably nowhere on earth will you fina better salmon or halibut, tiny Petersburg shrimp, king or tanner crab than is pulled from Alaskan waters. If you're a gourmet, you may learn the subtle taste differences between the five varieties of Alaskan salmon (many sourdoughs swear by the coho, or silver). You may also learn to love such freshwater fish as arctic char, grayling, and whitefish. Try it pan-fried, oven-baked, or alder-smoked—the way the Natives do it.

With its large Native population, of course, Alaska has a wide variety of unusual foods—though few of them ever make it onto a restaurant menu. You may occasionally find some wild game (like caribou steak) in a continental restaurant, and you'll assuredly encounter reindeer sausage on breakfast menus. But nowhere with the possible exception of Barrow, Kotzebue, and other Eskimo towns are you likely to see muktuk (whale blubber) on the menu, or oogruk (bearded seal meat), or even akutak (Eskimo ice cream, made with seal oil and snow). And you'd have to know the right places to go in Kake or Angoon to find gumboots or Chinese slippers, two varieties of chiton (a shellfish) favored by Indians of the Panhandle.

If the food fails to be unusual, the prices and the quantities usually are. The prices are guaranteed to be higher than what you pay in the Lower 48, and the quantities will ordinarily be larger than what you expect in a restaurant. Blame the former on shipping costs, and credit the latter to a frontier appetite.

Eating three square meals a day—a full breakfast, lunch, and dinner—can easily cost $30 per person, even without venturing well into the bush or eating in hotel penthouses. Figure $7 for a breakfast omelet and coffee, $8 for soup, sandwich, and soft drink at lunchtime, $15 for a three-course dinner, perhaps with a single glass of wine. I try to cut costs by doing my breakfast shopping at a late-night grocery and eating my main meal of the day at lunch. Even with that, I still have to plan on $20 a day for meals.

If you're a member of a fraternal organization, such as the Eagles, Elks, or Moose, you'll find these private clubs a great place to get an excellent meal at reasonable cost. In many smaller towns the club becomes "the only game in town" when it comes to dining in style. Out-of-town members are welcomed with open arms; nonmembers must find a local member to sponsor them.

The drinking age in Alaska is 21. State law allows bars, restaurants, liquor stores, and other licensed establishments to operate from 8 a.m. to 5 a.m. seven days a week. Anchorage, Juneau, and many other towns have passed local ordinances reducing the hours, usually to 2 a.m.; Fairbanks is among those cities clinging to 5 a.m. closing hours.

If you're a beer drinker, be sure to try Alaska's own Chinook label, brewed in Juneau. In 1987 and 1988, Chinook Alaskan Amber Beer was voted the most popular beer at the Great American Beer Festival in Denver, Colorado. A Porter-style beer and a pale ale are also manufactured.

In many bush communities, mainly because of the social misery alcohol has imposed on Alaska Natives, the sale and importation of alcoholic beverages has been banned. Barrow, Bethel, and Kotzebue have banned the sale of liquor, but allow its discreet importation.

Drunk-driving laws are getting tougher. Under a measure enacted in 1983, first offenders are subject to a mandatory 72-hour jail sentence and the 30-day loss of all driving privileges. Additional offenses bring increasingly stiff penalties.

WHAT TO SEE AND DO

Priority No. 1: *Don't stay indoors.* Alaska is a state that beseeches you to get out-of-doors and take part in whatever activities you are physically capable of. If you're young in body or spirit, indulge yourself in some river rafting, sea kayaking, or glacier skiing. If you've reached an age when the spirit is willing but the body is not, you can still go in for a fishing expedition, a hot-air balloon trip, or a flightseeing excursion.

Dog mushing is Alaska's state sport. If you plan to be in Alaska during the winter, it's something you can build a trip around—especially if you couple Anchorage's annual Fur Rendezvous winter festival, which incorporates the world-championship sled-dog races, with the great 1,000-mile Iditarod Race from Anchorage to Nome less than a month later. Even summertime visitors can savor some of the flavor of mushing by watching dry-land exhibitions (with wheels on sled runners) in Fairbanks, Nome, Tok, and other locations.

Alaska's rich wildlife is best seen by getting away from the highways, either by backpacking into the bush or arranging to be dropped off (and picked up later) by a small plane or chartered boat. The extensive national park and wildlife refuge system is set up to allow just such opportunities.

The towns and cities themselves have a modicum of attractions, such as museums and historic sites. Each has a character of its own. Sitka and Kodiak, for instance, have a rich Russian heritage; Skagway, Nome, and Fairbanks still ooze with the atmosphere of the gold rushes; frozen, isolated Barrow and rainy, bustling Ketchikan are as different as two towns can be. Part of the pleasure of Alaska is in discovering the tremendous variety that comprises the whole.

Nights Out

To begin with, you're not going to Alaska for its nightlife. The bawdy days of the gold rushes and the pipeline construction are now mere memories, and while most towns have their bars and every city its dance bands, they're hardly worth a trip in themselves. Many of the performers in hotels and small clubs are musicians from the West Coast who find competition in the Lower 48 so stiff that they're forced to book a series of gigs through Alaska.

There is one true Alaskan musician: the bush balladeer. You'll occasionally find this sourdough folk singer in small clubs in out-of-the-way locations, and occasionally in bigger towns like Anchorage, Fairbanks, and Homer. Accompanied just by a guitar and a sharp wit, he or she is worth seeking out.

Anchorage is a city with a growing reputation for the arts. Its beautiful new Performing Arts Center stands as testimony, and its symphony and theater are highly regarded. Sitka has an acclaimed Summer Music Festival which draws many of the world's leading classical instrumentalists, and Juneau has some fine dramatic troupes.

SAFETY

Whenever you're traveling in an unfamiliar city or area, stay alert. Be aware of your immediate surroundings. Wear a moneybelt and don't sling your camera or purse over your shoulder; wear the strap diagonally across your body. This will minimize the possibility of your becoming a victim of crime. Every society has its criminals. It's your responsibility to be aware and alert even in the most heavily touristed areas.

MEETING ALASKANS

If you stay on your cruise ship or tour bus, you won't meet any Alaskans unless they're looking for your money. If you wander off on your own, it won't take you longer than your first conversation to make a new friend. Ask the fellow sitting next to you at the lunch counter to tell you a bear story, or the lady in the bookstore to share some thoughts on how to identify authentic Native crafts. You'll find that the Alaskans, for all their informality, will go out of their way to be friendly.

SOUTHEAST ALASKA

1. KETCHIKAN
2. WRANGELL
3. PETERSBURG
4. SITKA
5. JUNEAU
6. GLACIER BAY NATIONAL PARK
7. HAINES
8. SKAGWAY

Alaska's Panhandle stretches some 600 miles along the eastern shore of the Pacific Ocean from Mount St. Elias to Dixon Entrance, near Prince Rupert, British Columbia. Over 90% of its land area—the 1,000 islands of the Alexander Archipelago and the adjacent North American mainland—is federal land. Tongass National Forest, with 16.9 million acres, is the country's largest. Two national parks (Glacier Bay and Wrangell–St. Elias) and two national monuments (Misty Fjords and Admiralty Island) occupy most of the rest of the territory.

The most remarkable feature of "Southeast," as it prefers to be known, is its waterways. The region has more than 10,000 miles of shoreline. Nearly all the major towns are located on sheltered straits and bays miles from open water. The state ferry system and most cruise ships take advantage of the calm waters of this Inside Passage. Some of the passages are of striking beauty, such as the Lynn Canal between Juneau and Skagway, and the Behm Canal ("Misty Fjords") near Ketchikan. Snow-clad mountains tower as much as 15,000 feet above these waterways, and dozens of glaciers pour their centuries-old rivers of ice directly into bays and inlets.

Only about 65,000 permanent residents have intruded upon this natural wonderland. The vast majority live in a handful of settlements which sprinkle the densely forested coastline. The state capital of Juneau, with a population of around 27,000, is the "yuppiest" of all Alaskan cities; its economy is built around government and service industries. But every town in the southeast has a distinct character. Ketchikan (pop. 14,000), Alaska's rainy southern gateway, is a fishing and lumber town with a rich Indian heritage. Sitka (pop. 8,500) is proud of its Russian history. Wrangell (pop. 3,100) has a frontier atmosphere, while Petersburg (pop. 3,300), founded by Norwegians, still has an affluent Scandinavian flavor. Haines (pop. 1,500), built in part around an old military barracks, boasts the largest concentration of bald eagles in the world. Skagway (pop. 800), jumping-off point for the Klondike gold rush, feeds on summer tourists who disembark from cruise ships to explore its turn-of-the-century community.

There's one drawback to the southeast: it rains a lot. Late spring and early summer are the driest times, but that's relative. Juneau gets an average annual precipitation of 53 inches, Petersburg gets 104 inches, and Ketchikan, a whopping 160 inches. Seattle, which has a reputation for wetness, by contrast averages only 34 inches a year. If you're going to southeast Alaska, don't forget your raincoat and boots! On the plus side, temperatures are mild, with July averages of 56°F in Juneau, 58°F in Ketchikan, and January averages of 22°F in Juneau, 33°F in Ketchikan.

For tourist information, contact the **Southeast Alaska Tourism Council,** P.O. Box 385, Juneau, AK 99802 (tel. 907/586-2989). Each major town has its own visitors' bureau or chamber of commerce to assist you in finding lodging and to provide other information.

GETTING THERE

There are only two practical ways to get to southeast Alaska—by sea and by air. But even though schedules will place a few limitations on your travel plans, you'll have no problem getting around.

By Air

From Seattle, **Alaska Airlines** has daily nonstop flights to and from Juneau and Ketchikan; direct flights to Sitka, Wrangell, Petersburg, and Yakutat; and three-times-weekly connections to Glacier Bay. All points connect with the rest of Alaska via three daily Juneau–Anchorage flights. Call for reservations and information (tel. 907/789-0600 in Juneau, 907/225-2141 in Ketchikan, 907/874-3308 in Wrangell, 907/772-4255 in Petersburg, 907/966-2266 in Sitka, 907/784-3366 in Yakutat, or toll free 800/426-0333).

Once you're in a gateway city, numerous local air-taxi services will carry you to any settlement or isolated bay. These include **Temsco** in the south and **L.A.B.** in the north. Specific information is presented in the sections on individual towns.

By Ferry

With no highways connecting the major settlements of the southeast, the state ferry system—properly called the **Alaska Marine Highway**—is the link on which most of the region's residents depend. Since becoming fully operational in 1963 the system has provided efficient and punctual service from Skagway to Ketchikan, and all the way to Seattle. In 1989 the southern terminus was moved to Bellingham, Washington.

The *Matanuska* and *Columbia* each provide weekly sailings from Bellingham in summer for Ketchikan, Wrangell, Petersburg, Sitka, Juneau, Haines, and Skagway. (There's one boat a week in winter.) The *Malaspina* and *Taku* provide similar twice-weekly service from Prince Rupert, British Columbia. The marine "milk run" operator is the *LeConte,* stopping at least once a week (and sometimes as often as three times a week) in Petersburg, Kake, Sitka, Angoon, Tenakee Springs, Hoonah, Juneau, Haines, and Skagway. The *Aurora* operates continually between Prince Rupert, Ketchikan, and Hollis (Prince of Wales Island), with a weekly side trip to Hyder; and the *Chilkat* runs a shuttle service between Ketchikan and Metlakatla.

Everyone pays a standard walk-on fare, not including meals or berths; children 6 to 11 pay half fare, and those under 5 sail free. If you take a cabin, you pay extra for that; prices are per cabin, not per person, and vary according to the cabin's size and location on the ship. If you're bringing a car, you'll also pay for its passage; costs vary with vehicle length.

The sample fares in the following table are for adult walk-on passage, a two-berth cabin with ocean view and complete facilities, and a vehicle from 10 to 15 feet in length.

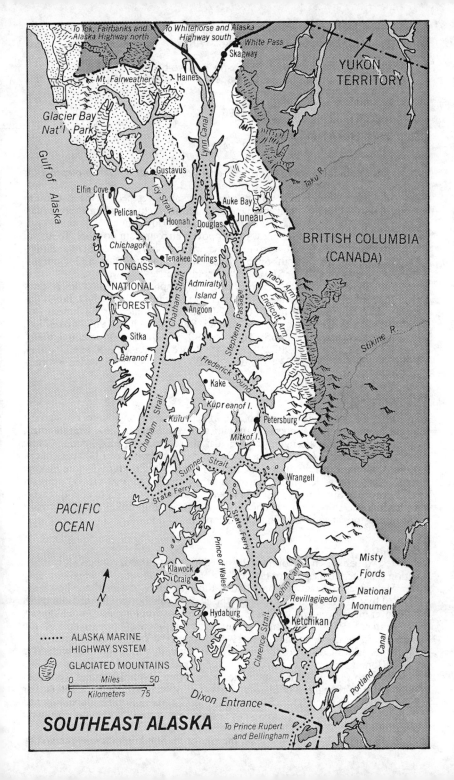

To Tok, Fairbanks and
Alaska Highway north

To Whitehorse and Alaska
Highway south

White Pass

Skagway

YUKON
TERRITORY

Mt. Fairweather

Haines

Glacier Bay
Nat'l Park

Gulf
of
Alaska

Gustavus

Lynn Canal

Taku R.

Elfin Cove

Auke Bay

BRITISH COLUMBIA
(CANADA)

Pelican

Icy Strait

Hoonah

Douglas

Juneau

Chichagof I.

TONGASS

Tenakee Springs

Chatham Strait

Tracy Arm

NATIONAL

Admiralty
Island

Stephens Passage

Endicott Arm

FOREST

Angoon

Stikine R.

Sitka

Baranof I.

Frederick Sound

Kake

PACIFIC
OCEAN

Kupreanof I.

Kuiu I.

Petersburg

Mitkof I.

Chatham Strait

Sumner Strait

State Ferry

Wrangell

State Ferry

Prince of Wales I.

Behm Canal

Misty
Fjords

Klawock
Craig

National

Revillagigedo I.

Monument

Clarence Strait

Hydaburg

Ketchikan

····· ALASKA MARINE
HIGHWAY SYSTEM

GLACIATED MOUNTAINS

Dixon Entrance

Portland Canal

0   Miles   50
0   Kilometers   75

SOUTHEAST ALASKA

To Prince Rupert
and Bellingham

STANDARD FARES

	Walk-on Passage	Two-berth Cabin	Vehicle (10–15 feet)
From Bellingham to:			
Ketchikan	$138	$123	$337
Juneau	$196	$164	$480
Skagway	$214	$175	$522
From Prince Rupert to:			
Skagway	$104	$80	$250

Thus a couple traveling from Bellingham to Skagway with their compact car and staying in a two-berth cabin would pay $1,125 for the four-day, one-way journey—$175 less if they brought their sleeping bags and stretched out in the solarium at night. But unless you're continuing to the Interior or returning home via the Alaska Highway through Canada, there's little reason to bring your car.

The ferry system used to allow free stopovers en route, but no more. To stop in Ketchikan, Sitka, and Juneau en route to Skagway, you'll have to pay $138 (Seattle–Ketchikan), $44 (Ketchikan–Sitka), $20 (Sitka–Juneau), plus $22 (Juneau–Skagway), a total of $224 or $10 over the straight Seattle–Skagway fare.

I've covered details of Alaska ferry service in Chapter II. For schedules, reservations, and other information, contact the Alaska Marine Highway, P.O. Box R, Juneau, AK 99811 (tel. toll free 800/642-0066). Local offices are in Juneau (tel. 907/465-3941), Ketchikan (tel. 907/225-6181), Wrangell (tel. 907/874-3711), Petersburg (tel. 907/772-3855), Sitka (tel. 907/747-8737), Haines (tel. 907/766-2111), Skagway (tel. 907/983-2941), Prince Rupert (tel. 604/627-1744), and in Seattle (tel. 206/623-1970 days or 206/623-1149 for recorded information).

By Cruise Ship

Twelve different cruise lines operate 21 separate ships on voyages through the Inside Passage and the numbers are growing each year. Some of these ships are small, carrying as few as 90 passengers (in particular, those operated by Exploration Cruise Lines); others are ocean-going behemoths which carry upward of 1,000 passengers. Peruse the section on "Cruising the Inside Passage" in Chapter II before making your decision on which ship, if any, is most appropriate for you. (If you insist on taking your car, Sundance Cruises' *Sundancer* is the only nonferry to offer that service.) All cruise ships stop in Juneau, most also pause in Sitka, and many make additional stops at southeast Alaska's other ports.

By Road

Yes, you can reach the southeast by paved highway . . . but your choice of destination is limited to Skagway or Haines.

Main access to Skagway is provided by Klondike Hwy. 2, which branches off the Alaska Hwy. at Mile 905, just south of the city of Whitehorse. The road climbs 98 miles over magnificent White Pass (3,290 feet) before dropping sharply to Skagway. The winter of 1986–1987 marked the first time this pass was kept open through the snow. Heading north on the Alaska Hwy. through the Yukon, you can turn off at Mile 866, Jake's Corner, onto gravel Yukon Hwy. 8, which connects with fully paved Klondike Hwy. 2 at Carcross.

To reach Haines, continue on the Alaska Hwy. about 100 miles west from Whitehorse to the village of Haines Junction at Mile 1,016. Here the spectacular Haines Hwy. turns south for 151 miles, skirting Canada's Kluane National Park and climbing over Chilkat Pass (3,493 feet). The road enters the U.S. 41 miles northwest of Haines. A little less than half of the highway is gravel.

Haines and Skagway—both on the Alaska Marine Highway—are served by

Alaskon Express buses (tel. toll free 800/544-2206), with twice-weekly service to Whitehorse, Fairbanks, and Anchorage. For information, call the toll-free number or contact **Gray Line of Alaska,** 300 Elliott Ave. West, Seattle, WA 98119 (tel. 907/983-2241 in Skagway, 907/766-2468 in Haines). **Alaska-Yukon Motorcoaches,** 349 Wrangell St., Anchorage, AK 95501 (tel. 907/276-1305, or toll free 800/637-3334), provides similar service.

For many years there has been talk about connecting Wrangell by road with British Columbia's Cassiar Hwy. It will remain mere rumor for the foreseeable future. Another rumor would connect Juneau with Haines by ferrying across the Lynn Canal. Tiny Hyder, alone in its isolation across the Portland Canal from Stewart, British Columbia, already is joined with Canada by highway bridge; its only connection with the rest of Alaska is a weekly ferry to Ketchikan.

1. Ketchikan

Long, skinny Ketchikan snakes for several miles along the southwestern shore of Revillagigedo Island, facing Tongass Narrows. Built partly on a steep hillside and partly on pilings driven into the narrows, it's the first town that travelers reach when ferrying northward—thus its monicker, "Alaska's First City." In fact it's the state's fourth-largest community after Anchorage, Fairbanks, and Juneau. Half of the 14,000-plus inhabitants live in the city proper, the others within commuting distance. In terms of economy and climate Ketchikan has more in common with Seattle, 650 miles south, than it does with Anchorage, 750 miles northwest.

Don't come to Ketchikan expecting clear skies. With an average annual rainfall of 160 inches, it's unlikely you'll get them. Even in the "dry" season (May, June, and July), Ketchikan averages 8 inches of rain per month. October, November, and December are the rainiest times—average October precipitation is 25 inches, and a record 43 inches once fell in November. Ketchikan also gets about 52 inches of snow a year, but it doesn't last long: the average January temperature is 33°F, so rain quickly washes the white stuff away . . . then freezes overnight, playing havoc with city plumbing! The steep stairs that climb many hillsides in place of streets were built by residents who didn't want to fight ice and mud to get home.

Ketchikan got its name from a Tlingit settlement, Kitschk-hin—*hin* meaning "creek" and *kitschk* meaning "thundering wings of an eagle." The town was established in 1887 with the construction of a salmon cannery at the mouth of Ketchikan Creek, which even today, citizens say, is so thick with spawning salmon in the fall that "you can walk across on their backs." Gold was discovered in the area in 1898, followed soon thereafter by silver and copper, and Ketchikan found its niche as a supply center. Though mining faded in importance, the fishing industry continued to boom. In the 1930s Ketchikan had a dozen canneries and was called the "Salmon Capital of the World." Overfishing eventually caused a drastic decline in fishing income, but the economy diversified so that today the timber industry (its most visible sign is the $80-million Louisiana-Pacific Corp. pulp mill at Ward Cove, north of the city) is on an almost equal footing with the fleet. The mining of molybdenum, essential as an alloy in stainless-steel production, has recently become important with the development of the huge Quartz Hill mine. 45 miles southeast of Ketchikan, by U.S. Borax and Chemical Corp. Three canneries survive.

Today Ketchikan is proud to show off its Native heritage. Situated at the conjunction of three cultures—Tlingit, Haida, and Tsimshian—Ketchikan features the Totem Heritage Cultural Center, the Totem Bight State Park, and the Saxman Totem Park, the latter at a Tlingit village just south of town.

There are about 40 miles of roads extending north and south of Ketchikan along the west coast of Revillagigedo Island. (The island was named by Spanish explorers for an 18th-century Mexican viceroy; locals just pronounce it "Ruhvilla.")

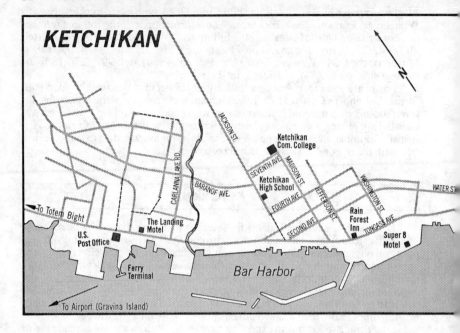

There are fishing camps and resorts at both ends of the road, although most wilderness camps are "fly-in" getaways.

Ketchikan is the gateway to Misty Fjords National Monument; to the numerous settlements on Prince of Wales Island, southeast Alaska's largest island; and to the Tsimshian town of Metlakatla on Annette Island, the only Indian reservation in the state of Alaska.

You'll find the flavor of Ketchikan decidedly blue collar, especially around the colorful waterfront. Fishermen and loggers contribute to a rowdy atmosphere in the cafés and bars along Front Street and out Tongass Avenue. During the summer months, when gift shops brighten their showcase windows for the throngs who arrive aboard cruise ships, this isn't quite as evident. But drop into town any other time of year and if you're not wearing a wool hat and "Ketchikan sneakers" (rubber mud boots), you'll feel out of place.

ORIENTATION

Ketchikan spreads in a northwest-southeast direction along the riverine Tongass Narrows. The ferry terminals — both for the Marine Highway System and Ketchikan International Airport—are at the north end of town, along with the post office; but most city buildings, as well as the heritage center and historic district, are 2½ miles south. Tongass Avenue is the sole artery connecting the two halves of town; as a result it's often congested with traffic. The Plaza Port West shopping mall (and its McDonald's restaurant) is situated about halfway between, in the Westend Commercial District.

Getting Around

The **airport** is a curiosity. It stands apart from the rest of the city on Gravina Island, across Tongass Narrows; until a bridge (still a hot topic of discussion) is

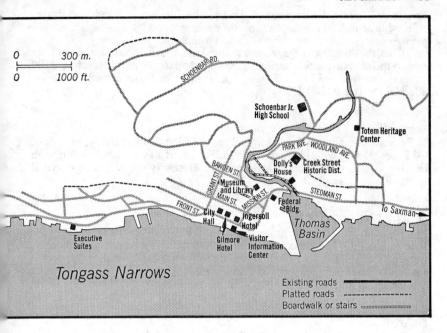

0   300 m.
0   1000 ft.

SCHOENBAR RD.

Schoenbar Jr.
High School

Totem Heritage
Center

PARK AVE. WOODLAND AVE.

BAWDEN ST.

GRANT ST.

Dolly's
House

Creek Street
Historic Dist.

Museum
and Library

MAIN ST.

MISSION ST.

STEDMAN ST.

FRONT ST.

City
Hall

Federal
Bldg.

To Saxman

Executive
Suites

Ingersoll
Hotel

Thomas
Basin

Gilmore
Hotel

Visitor
Information
Center

Tongass Narrows

Existing roads ————
Platted roads --------
Boardwalk or stairs ══════

built, it must be reached by ferry shuttle. The ferry crossing takes seven minutes and costs $2.50. Twin boats leave at 15-minute intervals from shore and airport; each carries nine cars and a couple of dozen foot passengers. In addition to **Alaska Airlines** (tel. 907/225-2141 or 225-3138), **Ketchikan Air Service** (tel. 907/225-6608) flies from the airport to local destinations.

An efficient **city bus** service runs between the ferry terminal and city center at half-hourly intervals from 6:45 a.m. to 6:45 p.m. daily except Sunday. The fare is $1. There's an **"Airporter" bus** service (tel. 225-2888), which will pick you up at your hotel, drive right onto the airport ferry, and deliver you and your luggage at the "departing passengers" door for $8. Taxis are $2 at flagfall, and cost about $7 to $8 from downtown to the ferry terminal; call **Alaska Cab** (tel. 225-2133), **Yellow Taxi** (tel. 225-5555), or **Sourdough Cab** (tel. 225-6651).

If you rent a car at the airport, you'll have to wait for the ferry after you rent the vehicle. **Budget** (tel. 225-9862) and **All Star Rent-a-Car** (tel. 225-2232) have outlets at the airport. All Star has a second office half a mile south of the ferry terminal at 2842 Tongass Ave. (tel. 225-5123). If you don't mind driving a slightly used car, their rates are excellent—$29 a day plus 20¢ a mile.

Motor scooters can be rented from **S.E.A. Skooters** at City Dock.

Information

Visit or write the **Ketchikan Visitors Bureau,** opposite the cruise-ship landing dock at 131 Front St., Ketchikan, AK 99901 (tel. 907/225-6166), for additional information. The visitors bureau maintains a "liquid sunshine gauge" to let you know exactly how much rain has fallen so far in the year.

If you plan to do any fishing or hunting, hiking, or boating in the Ketchikan area, you should also contact the **U.S. Forest Service Information Center,** in the Federal Building at Mill and Stedman Streets (tel. 907/225-3101). Open from 8 a.m. to 4:30 p.m. Monday through Friday, plus summer weekends and during cruise-ship arrivals, it has displays and slide programs on local forest and wildlife management, plus a variety of free maps and pamphlets.

Read the **Ketchikan Daily News** Monday through Saturday. Call 911 for **emergencies.** For medical assistance, visit **Ketchikan General Hospital,** 3100 Tongass Ave. (tel. 225-5171). A full-service bank is the **National Bank of Alaska,** 306 Main St. (tel. 225-2184).

Festivals

Special occasions in Ketchikan include the **King Salmon Derby,** over three weekends starting with Memorial Day; the **Fourth of July** weekend, featuring an exciting logging carnival and parade; and the **Blueberry Festival,** on the second weekend in August.

WHERE TO STAY

For a city geared to the summer tourist trade, Ketchikan has surprisingly few hotel rooms: only 244 of average standard at last count. The newest hotel, though a first-class facility, has only 14 rooms, which hardly remedy the situation. I expect to see a major new hotel project in Ketchikan soon.

Tax Note: Add 8% bed tax to all room prices quoted.

Deluxe

The new accommodation is the **Royal Executive Suites,** 1471 Tongass Ave. (P.O. Box 8331), Ketchikan, AK 99901 (tel. 907/225-1900), which opened in early 1986 on pilings extending into the Tongass Narrows. Owner Kirk Thomas, a former bush pilot, has designed a small luxury hotel to appeal to the business traveler. The 14 rooms have a pastel color scheme—slate-blue carpeting, lilac upholstery, natural wood trim—and rheostatic lighting. Each of six two-room suites contains a full kitchen, living room with telephone (local calls are 40¢) and 23-channel cable television, a spacious bedroom with clock-radio, and in-room Jacuzzi bath. Full-wall windows with blinds overlook the harbor; on the top floor, they extend to the ceiling.

Suites are $140 a night. There are four deluxe studios ($105 a night) with in-room Jacuzzis; standard studios cost $85. A ground-floor "spa" has a sauna, hot tub, and exercise treadmill, and there's a coin-op guest laundry. Room service meals are provided by a local caterer. Royal Executive Suites is located three-quarters of a mile from downtown and 1½ miles from the ferry terminal; courtesy car service is available.

Moderate

In the central downtown area are a pair of older lodgings. The three-story **Ingersoll Hotel,** 303 Mission St. (P.O. Box 6440), Ketchikan, AK 99901 (tel. 907/225-2124), was built of reinforced concrete in 1924 on the site of a fire-ravaged 1899 inn. Now under new management, its 60 fully renovated rooms are decorated in blue and rust tones with oak trim. A typical room has two double beds, a large dresser and desk, telephone (25¢ local calls), 13-channel cable TV, and Alaskan art prints on the walls. Full breakfasts are included. Many of the rooms—priced at $62 single, $72 double—have views over Front Street.

The **Gilmore Hotel,** 326 Front St., Ketchikan, AK 99901 (tel. 907/225-9423), has more of an antiquated feeling than the Ingersoll, a block and a half away. Built of concrete in 1928, the 42 rooms still have old hot-water radiators. But they also have ten-channel cable TV–radio, direct-dial phones, and other modern furnishings. Most rooms have full shower-baths, though eight have showers only and ten others share toilet and shower facilities down the hall. Rates range from $48 to $53 single, $53 to $62 double.

Adjacent to Plaza Port West shopping mall but set back off the highway on Tongass Narrows is the **Super 8 Motel,** 2151 Sea Level Dr. (P.O. Box 8818), Ketchikan, AK 99901 (tel. 907/225-9088, or toll free 800/843-1991). Each of the 82 spacious rooms has queen-size beds, double-insulated walls, ten-channel cable TV, and direct-dial phones. The motel has special no-smoking rooms and a conference room which holds up to 50 people. Other facilities include a guest laundry, video game room, complimentary freezers for successful fishermen, and a courtesy van. Rates are $68 single, $76 double, $83 twin, May through September; somewhat less in winter.

The horseshoe-shaped motel called the **Best Western Landing,** 3434 Tongass Ave., Ketchikan, AK 99901 (tel. 907/225-5166), is set against the hills directly across the street from the ferry terminal. The 46 rooms are simply but tastefully furnished with queen-size or double beds, combination desk-dressers, televisions, and direct-dial phones. Books and postcards are sold in the cozy lobby. Year-round rates are $53 for one person, $57 for two. An adjoining café (open daily from 6 a.m. to 10 p.m.) has lunches for about $6 and dinners in the $11 to $13 range. Try the locally famous corned beef hash. The Landing also has a spacious second-floor lounge.

Budget

On the lower end of the scale is the **Rain Forest Inn,** a block off Tongass Avenue at 2311 Hemlock St., Ketchikan, AK 99901 (tel. 907/225-9500). Eight rooms hold two to four people each: you can rent by the bed ($17) or by the room ($39 for two, $51 for four). Visitors staying more than a night or two get kitchen privileges. Showers and coin-operated laundry facilities are available, along with complimentary morning coffee.

Youth Hostel

A summer-only youth hostel is located in the **Methodist Church** at Grant and Main Streets (P.O. Box 8515), Ketchikan, AK 99901 (tel. 907/225-3319). Bring your own sleeping bag and stay in a gender-separated dorm room for $4 a night if you're an American Youth Hostels member, $7 if you're not. (AYH membership cards are on sale for $20, well worth it if you're hosteling through Alaska.) The hostel opens Memorial Day and closes Labor Day, and hours are strict: come and go as you please only from 6 to 8:30 a.m. and 7 to 11 p.m. Concessions are made for late ferry arrivals.

Bed-and-Breakfast

Don't forget this option. **Ketchikan Bed & Breakfast,** P.O. Box 3213, Ketchikan, AK 99901 (tel. 907/225-8550), is a reservation service for travelers who wish to stay in private homes, many of them within easy walking distance of downtown. Among the homes available are the Great Alaska Cedar Works, once the home of a salmon cannery foreman, and Kingfisher Marine, a two-bedroom beach house. Rates, including breakfast, range from $40 for a single to $65 for a luxury double.

Out-of-Town Resorts

A couple of fishing resorts outside Ketchikan also take guests. The **George Inlet Lodge,** Mile 12 on South Tongass Hwy. (P.O. Box 5077), Ketchikan, AK 99901 (tel. 907/225-6077, or 206/268-0950 for reservations), in a renovated cannery bunkhouse, offers all-inclusive packages starting at $990 per person for three days and two nights, May through September. Locals enjoy its "open-to-the-public" buffets (by reservation only) Tuesday through Sunday at 8 p.m., with a Sunday champagne brunch from 11 a.m. to 2 p.m.

Clover Pass Resort, Mile 15 on North Tongass Hwy. (P.O. Box 7322), Ketchikan, AK 99901 (tel. 907/247-2234), is the headquarters of the annual Salmon Derby. Open late March through September, it offers fishing charters, boat rentals, and fuel. Overnight rates for the 26 rooms and six cabins are $70 to $100. There's also an RV park with 30 hookups. The public restaurant/bar has an extensive menu specializing in seafood and steaks; it's open from 7 a.m. to 10 p.m. daily. Sometimes in the summer otters can be seen playing offshore.

Salmon Falls Resort, Mile 17 North Tongass Hwy. (P.O. Box 5420), Ketchikan, AK 99901 (tel. 907/225/2752, or toll free 800/247-9059), is an impressive new luxury fishing resort at the entrance to the Behm Canal. Its 36 units (plans are to double the number) appear rustic with peeled pine-log construction, but they've all got private baths, two double beds, phones, and other modern amenities. All-inclusive fishing packages are $295 a day self-guided (with a 19-foot skiff and gear) or $395 a day for a guided charter boat, with a minimum stay of two nights. Meals are served in the Hospitality Center, an octagonal beamed lodge with a 40-foot section of the Alaska Pipeline as its center support! Excellent dinners are priced in the $13 to $19 range.

Campgrounds

There's camping at several locations in the Ketchikan area. Nicest are the U.S. Forest Service's **Signal Creek** campground, 7½ miles north of the city on Ward Lake Road, with eight tent and 17 RV units; **Last Chance** campground, with 23 tent spaces two miles farther up the same road; and **Settlers Cove** state campground, 18 miles north of Ketchikan, with nine tent spaces and seven RV pads. All have tables, water, pit toilets, and a two-week camping limit. All areas charge $5 a night.

WHERE TO EAT

A huge etched-glass window, through which the long Alaskan twilight streams, sets the tone at **Charley's Restaurant** in the Ingersoll Hotel at 208 Front St. (tel. 225-5090). This is Ketchikan's favorite place for a meal or a quiet drink. Full dinners, not including wine, are priced from $14 to $27; especially popular is the Madagascar pepper steak. Lunch sandwiches are priced from $6.25 to $8.50; breakfasts range $5 to $8. Open from 6:30 a.m. to 3 p.m. and 5 to 10 p.m. daily.

Hanging plants and rattan furniture give the small **Gilmore Garden** restaurant, in the Gilmore Hotel, 326 Front St. (tel. 225-9423), a light, airy feeling. Its international menu features dinners priced from $11 to $20, including entrecôte marchand de vin, pollo alla cacciatora, enchiladas, cheese fondue, and Alaska shrimp Louie. There are sourdough pancakes for breakfast, luncheon sandwiches ($6 to $8), and a "pasta of the day." On Sunday there's a champagne brunch. The bar's showpiece La Cimbali espresso machine whips up such coffee specialties as "chantilly lace" and "Gilmore vintage 1928." Open from 7 a.m. to 10 p.m. daily.

After these two, gourmet offerings are limited. The **New Peking**, at 4 Creek St. (tel. 225-9355), has excellent Mandarin, Szechuan, and Cantonese cuisine with combination dinners from $10 per person and luncheon specials from $7. Open from 11:30 a.m. to 2:30 p.m. and 5 to 10 p.m. Monday through Friday, 4 to 10 p.m. on Saturday and Sunday. The **Harbor Inn**, 320 Mission St. (tel. 225-2850), is a local 24-hours-a-day hangout with filling breakfasts (three eggs, hotcakes, meat, and juice) priced at $5.50; a New York steak-and-fries dinner, only $10. **Kay's Kitchen**, 2813 Tongass Ave. (tel. 225-5860), open from 11 a.m. to 4 p.m. weekdays for lunch only, has homemade soups, deli-style sandwiches, and great desserts, plus a Norwegian gift shop.

You can get a good hamburger for $5.50 at **Latitude 56**, in the Ketchikan Bowling Center at 2050 Sea Level Dr. (tel. 225-9011), next to the Super 8. Open from 6 a.m. to 10 p.m. daily. **The Short Stop Café**, located in Gilmore Mall at 318 Front St. (tel. 225-2710), is a good choice for a light lunch. Open from 8 a.m. to 4 p.m. Monday through Saturday. **Grandeli's,** in the Plaza Port West Mall, is probably Ketchikan's best deli. Open from 10 a.m. to 9 p.m. Monday through Friday, to 6 p.m. on Saturday, and noon to 6 p.m. on Sunday. For pizza, try the **Pizza Mill** at 808 Water St. (tel. 225-6646), open from 11 a.m. to 11 p.m. Sunday through Thursday, to midnight on Friday and Saturday.

The **Sourdough Inn,** 834 Water St. (tel. 225-4545), is a popular café with a faithful clientele, while **June's,** 203 Stedman St., at Creek Street (tel. 225-4305), open from noon to 11 p.m. daily, is famous for its chili. The **Diaz Café,** 335 Stedman St. (tel. 225-2257), has Filipino and American food from 11 a.m. to 9:30 p.m. daily except Monday. When it comes to soda-fountain fare like banana splits, **Ohashi's,** at 223 Stedman St. near the Thomas Basin boat harbor (tel. 225-2278), is a Ketchikan institution. Open from 8 a.m. to 5 p.m. Monday through Saturday.

WHAT TO SEE AND DO

The first stop for many visitors is the **Creek Street Historic District,** formerly known as "The Line"—from 1902 to 1954 southeast Alaska's most notorious red-light district. This zigzagging boardwalk on pilings above Ketchikan Creek supported at least 30 "sporting houses" in its heyday. "It was the only place in Alaska where both fish and fishermen went upstream to spawn," one oldtimer told me, with tongue planted firmly in cheek. Territorial law said that no more than two women could live in a house or it could be considered an illegal brothel—so women like Frenchie and Black Mary merely lived alone and carried on. They observed a 4 a.m. curfew, had weekly health checkups, and agreed to shop downtown only on Wednesday. But not everything was above board: in Prohibition times Creek Street was the one place in Ketchikan where liquor was easily obtained, smuggled from Canada by boats which unloaded their cargoes through trap doors. Today the old houses are being spruced up and converted into small shops and businesses.

Dolly's House, a two-story green structure at 24 Creek St. (tel. 225-6329), has been preserved just as it was when "The Line" was done away with in 1954. Its colorful madam, Dolly Copeland Arthur, lived in the house from 1919 to 1970. Though she died in 1975 in a local nursing home, her house is now a period museum, open from 9 a.m. to 5 p.m. daily, mid-May through September. Admission is $2. In this five-room world of brass beds and floral wallpaper, with secret wall panels for bootleg whisky, you'll get a glimpse of the old times.

Several wooden platforms for viewing spawning salmon between June and August have recently been built as extensions of Creek Street. As many as 1,500 king salmon, weighing up to 50 pounds, return up Ketchikan Creek each year to deposit their roe. Ten times that many pink salmon, usually weighing no more than five pounds, also make the journey. Fishing is not allowed in the creek.

Native Heritage

Perhaps the best reason to spend a bit of time in Ketchikan is to absorb some of its Native Indian culture. This area is unique in Alaska because three separate tribes lived in close proximity. While Tlingit are predominant on Revillagigedo Island and throughout southeast Alaska, the southern half of Prince of Wales Island is principally Haida, and nearby Annette Island is a Tsimshian reservation.

The **Totem Heritage Center,** 601 Deermount Ave. (tel. 225-5900), was built by the city in 1976 to preserve and exhibit a unique collection of 33 original totem poles and house posts from nearby Tlingit and Haida villages, all abandoned around the turn of the century. Totem poles were never built to last: as they weathered away, new poles were carved and erected to honor the dead, to record history and oral tradition, and to document social events. The poles on display, carved from cedar between 1850 and 1900, were saved for posterity as an example of the work of master carvers.

The Heritage Center is open from 8 a.m. to 5 p.m. Monday through Saturday and 9 a.m. to 4 p.m. on Sunday, June 1 to September 30; winter hours are 1 to 5 p.m. Tuesday through Friday (times are extended when cruise ships are in port). Admission is $1 for adults, free for children under 18. Between October and May, classes in Native arts, crafts, and culture are taught by tribal elders from the Alaska Native Brotherhood/Sisterhood and the Southeast Alaska Indian Arts Council. Some of the classes' work is on sale in the center's small gift shop.

The center is administered by the **Tongass Historical Society Museum,** which shares the Centennial Building with the public library, overlooking Ketchikan Creek at 629 Dock St. (tel. 225-5600). The museum documents Ketchikan's Native and white history with photos and artifacts, including a renowned collection of Indian basketry and steamed bentwood boxes. Look for the work of local Tlingit artist Nathan Jackson. Open from 8:30 a.m. to 5 p.m. Monday through Saturday and 10 a.m. to 4 p.m. on Sunday, June through September; and from 1 to 5 p.m. Wednesday through Friday, 1 to 4 p.m. on weekends, October through May. Admission is $1. A short distance outside the building is a 1983 totem pole, carved by Dempsey Bob, which depicts the tale of "The Raven Stealing the Sun."

Jackson, Bob, and other carvers today teach their craft at the **Saxman Totem Park,** billed as "the world's largest collection of totem poles." It's located three miles south of downtown Ketchikan in the Tlingit village of Saxman, founded in the late 1800s by Natives who migrated from outlying villages, then returned to their original homes in the 1930s to recover 25 totems. Some poles were repaired, restored, and brightly painted; replicas were made of others. The spectacular totem pole at the entrance to the park is called the "Sun and Raven"; a native guide will tell you the story behind this and other poles. But you might recognize Abraham Lincoln immediately by his stovepipe hat.

While you're in Saxman, enjoy the Cape Fox Dancers and Naa Kahidi Theater, take in the craft demonstrations and village museum, and sample some Native cooking. Craftsmen will be happy to accept a commission to carve you a personal totem pole, by the way—at $5,000 a foot! Telephone 225-9038 for general information about Saxman tours and events.

There remains one other significant monument to Native culture in the Ketchikan area. On the site of a former Tlingit summer camp, in **Totem Bight State Historical Park,** ten miles north of the city on the Tongass Highway, you'll find replicas of a 19th-century clan house and 14 Tlingit and Haida totem poles. When the Civilian Conservation Corps took on the project in the 1930s they intended it to be a model village, but it was never completed. The setting is lovely: you must park your vehicle and walk a couple of hundred yards through rain forest (complete with interpretive signs) to reach the park clearing on a small coastal cove. A brochure identifies each pole. Bald eagles can often be seen atop trees and totem poles in this vicinity.

Walking Tour

If you're on foot in Ketchikan, the Visitors Bureau has a recommended two-hour walking tour which starts at its waterfront headquarters. Pick up the map/brochure. In addition to Creek Street, the museum, and the Heritage Center, it will lead you past.

St. John's Episcopal Church, on Mission Street. The town's oldest church was built in 1903 as part of a complex that included a hospital and school. Its interior paneling is original native cedar provided by early Saxman Indians.

Thomas Basin, one of the city's three major harbors, and possibly the most picturesque. Before it was dredged in 1931 this was a broad, sandy tidal flat where young Ketchikan folk had a baseball field. As the tide came in, oldtimers report, outfielders chased fly balls in a skiff! Today you can watch fishermen repair their nets and trawlers return with their catch.

Deer Mountain Fish Hatchery, across Ketchikan Creek from the Heritage Center, is open for public observation in the summer from 9 a.m. to 12:30 p.m. and

1:30 to 5:30 p.m. daily. Biologists from the Alaska Department of Fish and Game raise salmon here for release into the creek.

Sports

FISHING   No fewer than 19 charter-boat operators are registered in Ketchikan. Ask the Visitors Bureau for a list, or contact the **Ketchikan Marine Charter Association,** P.O. Box 7896, Ketchikan, AK 99901 (tel. 907/225-2628). You can take halibut, red snapper, sea bass, or cod through most of the year, king (chinook) salmon May through July, pink (humpback) salmon June through September, and silver (coho) salmon July through September. There's also trout fishing (rainbows, Dolly Vardens, and cutthroat) in inland lakes and streams.

Among the outstanding wilderness lodges in the Ketchikan area are the **Yes Bay Lodge** (write Yes Bay, AK 99950), and the **Rediscovery Lodge** (write 1113 Fifth Ave. South, Suite 108, Edmonds, WA 98020, in winter) at Bell Island Hot Springs. Both offer full-board packages. The U.S. Forest Service maintains numerous cabins in remote areas of Tongass National Forest for $15 a night. There are 16 on Revillagigedo Island alone. You only have to fly, boat, or walk in and supply your own food and bedding. Call 225-3101 for reservations.

The **Alaska Department of Fish and Game,** 2050 Sea Level Dr., Suite 205 (tel. 225-2475), can provide plenty of details. Don't forget to buy a license (a ten-day nonresident pass costs $15). If you're planning to rent a boat—**Knudson Cove Marina,** Mile 14.8 on North Tongass Hwy. (tel. 247-8500), can help you—be sure also to pick up a tide table. Respect the weather and the very cold water. A good fishing tackle dealer is **The Outfitter,** 3232 Tongass Ave. (tel. 225-6888).

HUNTING   The most common game animal in this part of Alaska is the Sitka black-tailed deer. Mountain goats are frequently spotted in the Misty Fjords, and black bears are common throughout the region. Brown bears (grizzlies) and moose are more unusual here. The **Alaska Department of Fish and Game** (tel. 225-2475) or sporting goods dealers—try **Deer Mountain Sports,** 1025 Water St. (tel. 225-2890)—can line you up with outfitters.

HIKING   No shortage of opportunities here. The Deer Mountain Trail, a steep three-mile climb through bear country to a spectacular overlook 3,000 feet above the Tongass Narrows, starts near the corner of Deermount Avenue and Fair Street. An easier walk is the one-mile nature trail circling Ward Lake north of Ketchikan. For more remote possibilities, contact the U.S. Forest Service Information Center (tel. 225-3101) in the Federal Building.

KAYAKING AND CANOEING   An outfit called **Outdoor Alaska,** 247 Bawden St. (tel. 225-6044 or 225-3498), has kayak rentals at $20 a day, and organizes sea kayaking expeditions for those with more time and adventurous spirit. Three days and two nights run about $160. Write Outdoor Alaska, P.O. Box 7814, Ketchikan, AK 99901. **Kayak Alaska,** which runs the Kayak Shop at 407 Stedman St. (tel. 225-1736) in the "Once in a Blue Moose" gift shop, offers sales, rentals, and instruction. Tours of the waterfront and Saxman Village cost $30 to $35 for 2½ to 4 hours.

Guided kayak trips are also operated by **Southeast Exposure,** P.O. Box 9143, Ketchikan, AK 99901 (tel. 225-8829).

Canoes can be rented from the **City Parks and Recreation Department** (tel. 225-3881).

WINTER SPORTS On almost any winter weekend you'll find a couple of hundred **ice skaters** on family outings at Ward Lake, eight miles north of Ketchikan. The Forest Service maintains picnic and barbecue shelters year round. Another eight miles inland up the Ward Lake Road is Harriet Hunt Lake, where the **Ketchikan Ski Club** has a pair of rope tows operating on weekends when there's sufficient snow. There's also cross-country skiing, snowmobiling, and ice skating at **Harriet Hunt recreation area.** Contact the Ketchikan Visitors Bureau for details.

OTHER SPORTS You can go **swimming** in the indoor pools at Ketchikan High School, 2610 Fourth Ave. (tel. 225-2010), or Valley Park Elementary School, 410 Schoenbar Rd. (tel. 225-4212). Call for schedules and information. The high school also has a sauna. There are also public **tennis courts** at the high school and at Schoenbar Junior High School, 217 Schoenbar Rd. (tel. 225-5138).

If you're a ten-pin enthusiast, **Ketchikan Bowling Center,** 2050 Sea Level Dr. (tel. 225-9011), has 16 lanes, a video game room, and an adjoining café and pub. The **North Star Athletic Club** in the midtown Tongass Commercial Center (tel. 225-9080) has a weight room and exercise equipment, racquetball and handball courts, and a sauna. Guest memberships are available.

Tours

Several companies offer Ketchikan city tours. From May 15 through September 25, **Gray Line of Alaska** (tel. 225-5930) takes ferry passengers for a 1¼-hour city tour ($10 for adults, $5 for children under 12), and those with more time can get a seat on the 2½-hour Totem Bight Tour ($20 for adults, $10 for children under 12), departing 8:30 a.m. daily. Gray Line also offers a unique two-hour bus/canoe tour to a mountain lake ($49 for adults, $30 for children under 12), departing at 9 a.m. and 3 p.m. daily. **Alaska Sightseeing Tours** (tel. 225-2740), located in the Ingersoll Hotel lobby, offers a three-hour daily Totem Bight Tour ($18 for adults, $9 for children 5 to 11), departing at 9:30 a.m. and 1:30 p.m. daily.

Outdoor Alaska (tel. 247-8444 or 225-6044) offers a unique two-hour historical harbor tour aboard the *Misty Fjord, Crystal Fjord,* or *Emerald Fjord* ($36 per person) and a 1½-hour tour of the fishing fleet and the Silver Lining Seafoods processing plant ($22 per person). Special sunset dinner charters can also be arranged. Check with Outdoor Alaska's 501 Water St. office.

SHOPPING

There are some excellent local artists and craftspeople. Whites as well as Natives frequently employ Indian motifs. Look for their work at 20 Creek St. at **Morning Raven** (tel. 225-5060). The **Scanlon Gallery,** 310 Mission St. (tel. 225-4730), has a fine collection of paintings, sculptures, and jewelry by Alaskan artists. Among the numerous gift shops near the cruise ship dock are **Tom Sawyer's Jewelry and Curios,** 304-306 Mission St. (tel. 225-4220), and **Authentic Alaska Craft,** 318 Dock St. (tel. 225-6925).

Need film? Try **Schallerer's Photo and Gift,** 218 Front St. (tel. 225-4210). A book? Among the most interesting bookstores in Ketchikan is the **Voyageur Book Store,** 405 Dock St. (tel. 225-5011), the place for new releases and gift books; I've got a soft spot for **Parnassus,** upstairs at 28 Creek St. (tel. 225-7690), where you can browse through used books while listening to classical music and sipping espresso. In addition to the independent bookstores in Ketchikan, **Waldenbooks,** the nationwide chain store, is represented at 103 Plaza Port (tel. 225-8120).

You can't tour **Silver Lining Seafoods,** 1705 Tongass Ave. (tel. 225-6664 or 225-9865), on your own, but you can visit the shop to sample and purchase fresh seafood, smoked salmon, or gift packs for shipment home at wholesale prices. Don't miss the large aquarium of native Alaskan marine life.

NIGHTLIFE

You won't want to miss *The Fish Pirate's Daughter,* a farcical melodrama staged at 7:30 p.m. every Friday from Memorial Day to Labor Day at the **Main Street Theatre,** 338 Main St. (tel. 225-2211). Admission is $7. Audiences boo villainous cannery owner Kurt Von Ohlsun, lust after Creek Street madam Violet LaRosa, and swoon for Sweet William Uprightly, the highly principled Commissioner of Fish. The First City Players have made this a Ketchikan attraction since 1967.

Generally speaking, nightlife in Ketchikan borders on the seedy. Granted, it's not as wild as when Creek Street was in its full glory, nor as brassy as when burlesque dancers from the late-lamented Shamrock Club accosted tour buses on Stedman Street well into the 1970s. Today the **Frontier Saloon,** 127 Main St. (tel. 225-9950), is the top club for dancing to a live rock 'n' roll band. The cozy **Pioneer Bar,** 122 Front St. (tel. 225-3210), always packed with locals until 5 a.m., features a country-and-western duo and a small dance floor. The **Rainbird Bar,** 114 Front St. (tel. 225-9905), is spacious but doesn't draw the crowds; it also has live weekend entertainment. There are at least half a dozen more watering holes along this two-block strip of Front Street. You might want to mosey into the **Sourdough Bar,** 301 Front St. (tel. 225-2217), to look at the photos of beached ships lining its walls.

For less boisterous entertainment, enjoy the solo lounge act at **Charley's** in the Ingersoll Hotel (tel. 225-5090), or sip a drink at **O'Dowd's Pub** (tel. 225-9011) in the Ketchikan Bowling Center building.

The local cinema is the **Coliseum Twin Theatre,** 405 Mission St. (tel. 225-2294), with two shows nightly and weekend matinees. Check the *Ketchikan Daily News* for listings. You can find out about other local entertainment by contacting the **Ketchikan Area Arts and Humanities Council,** 338 Main St. (tel. 225-2211).

SHORT TRIPS FROM KETCHIKAN

The quickest and easiest way to travel outside Ketchikan is by plane. Several air-taxi services operating seaplanes are located along the Tongass Avenue strip. I've been pleased in my experience with **Temsco Airlines,** 1249 Tongass Ave. (tel. 225-9810). Temsco reaches every community in the greater Ketchikan area, from Prince of Wales Island to Prince Rupert, with its fleet of Cessnas, DeHavilland Beavers and Otters, and Grumman Gooses. You might also check **Taquan Air Service,** 1007 Water St. (tel. 225-9668), or **Ketchikan Air Service,** 1719 Tongass Ave. (tel. 225-6608). Standard charter rates are $120 per person for a 90-minute flight.

Misty Fjords National Monument

Air is certainly the most efficient way to visit Misty Fjords National Monument, blanketing 3,570 square miles east of Ketchikan. Long fingers of water flanked by 3,000-foot granite cliffs extend east and west off long, narrow Behm Canal, a natural extension of the northeastern Pacific Ocean. Walker Cove and Rudyerd Bay are exceptionally picturesque. Active glaciers wind from 7,000-foot-plus peaks on the Canadian border, joining with the heavy southeastern Alaskan rainfall to feed the lush vegetation and myriad rivers, lakes, and streams. The area's great mineral wealth is coveted: when molybdenum was discovered a few years ago, part of the monument was set aside for mine development. There are large numbers of bears, deer, wolves, mountain goats, and bald eagles. The U.S. Forest Service has 14 rustic cabins throughout the national monument, most of them on inland lakes accessible only by floatplane or by a strenuous combination of boat and backpacking. National monument headquarters are at 1817 Tongass Ave. (P.O. Box 6137), Ketchikan, AK 99901 (tel. 225-2148).

Many of the air-taxi operators, including Temsco and Taquan, offer flightseeing tours over the Misty Fjords for competitive prices of $90 to $110 per person. You can book a 75- to 90-minute flightseeing trip with Gray Line (tel. 225-5930) or Alaska Sightseeing (tel. 225-2740) for $110. Alternatively, Outdoor Alaska (tel. 247-8444 or 225-6044) has 12-hour cruises into the national monument aboard the *Misty Fjords* for $120 ($90 for kids 3 to 11), leaving at 9:15 a.m. on Sunday, Wednesday, and Friday, June 5 through August 30. Meals are included. Outdoor Alaska also offers an exciting cruise/fly option for $169 ($129 for children). And it has dropoff and pickup service for kayakers, canoeists, and fishermen.

Prince of Wales Island

At 2,731 square miles, heavily forested Prince of Wales is the third-largest American island (after Kodiak Island and Hawaii's Big Island). Measuring roughly 130 miles north-south and 30 miles east-west, it has more than 700 miles of roads built for its thriving logging industry. Yet there's only one port of entry for vehicle traffic, a small one at Hollis (pop. 150), with no phones, restaurants, or visitor facilities. Passengers and vehicles can travel between Ketchikan and Hollis aboard the ferry *Aurora* daily in summer, two to four times weekly in winter. The passenger fare is $14. From Hollis, an all-weather road leads 31 miles to the communities of Klawock and Craig, 6 miles apart.

It's more convenient, if also more expensive, to fly from Ketchikan to Prince of Wales. All Ketchikan-based air taxis fly these routes; as an example, Westflight plies the Ketchikan–Klawock/Craig course four times a day for $50 one way.

Craig (pop. 900) sits picturesquely on a tiny island connected to the Prince of Wales mainland by a short causeway. In many ways the Prince of Wales nerve center, it's home to many loggers and a purse-seine fishing fleet. But it was made unfortunately famous by the 1983 *Investor* killings and 1986–1987 mass-murder trials in Ketchikan and Juneau. Accommodation can be found at the 16-unit **Haida Way Lodge,** P.O. Box 90, Craig, AK 99921 (tel. 907/826-3268). Rates start at $70 in summer, ($60 in winter), plus 4% tax, and it's even got television, not to mention five kitchenette units and a newly licensed restaurant. For fine seafood, go to **Ruth Ann's Restaurant,** on the waterfront (tel. 826-3377). For general information on the town, contact Craig City Hall (tel. 826-3275) or the U.S. Forest Service (tel. 826-3271).

Klawock (pop. 500) was the location of Alaska's first salmon cannery (1878). Today a newer cannery remains important, but a 20-year-old sawmill is also a big employer. For visitors, the most impressive attraction is the totem park on the hill overlooking town, containing 21 totem poles from the abandoned Tlingit village of Tuxekan, 25 miles north. Some are replicas, others restored originals. **Fireweed Lodge,** P.O. Box 116, Klawock, AK 99925 (tel. 907/775-9996), has 18 rustic rooms with private baths, family-style meals, complete fishing and hunting packages, and Budget rental cars. Nightly rates range from $74 to $129, including meals. The **Log Cabin Campground,** P.O. Box 54, Klawock, AK 99925 (tel. 907/755-2205), has rustic beach cabins with kitchens and baths, tent sites, and RV hookups. Boats and canoes are available for rent. The folks who run the Log Cabin Campground also run **Klawock Wilderness Adventure,** which takes overnight canoeing and kayaking trips from May to September.

There are only two other towns on Prince of Wales Island. **Thorne Bay** (pop. 350), on the east coast, is headquarters of the huge Louisiana-Pacific Corp. logging operation. You'll find a restaurant and gas station (open six hours a week), and lodging in cabins at **McFarland's Floatel,** P.O. Box 159, Thorne Bay, AK 99925 (tel. 907/828-3335), with rates starting at $55. The fishing town of **Hydaburg** (pop. 420) is the largest Haida Indian community in Alaska. A totem park contains numerous poles from three abandoned Haida villages. A hotel-restaurant is under construction.

With excellent freshwater and saltwater fishing in Prince of Wales' waters, it isn't surprising that the 19 cabins maintained by the U.S. Forest Service here are in high demand. There are also several fishing resorts, the best of which is **Waterfall Resort,** 13 miles southwest of Craig by floatplane. With the infusion of nearly $10 million into a historic 1912 cannery, Waterfall opened in 1982 as a jet-setters' luxury lodge. From mid-May through mid-September the resort accommodates 80 visitors in 26 bungalows, four luxury apartments, and ten lodge rooms. Each room has full bath, electric heating, wall-to-wall carpeting, and wood furnishings, plus a wet bar and refrigerator. Remember, you're in isolation. The dining room serves family-style meals. There's full bar service, and video movies and games in the recreation lounge, overlooking a lagoon, plus an exercise room and hot tub. There's a general store, and a trained naturalist on staff who leads nature hikes. The resort has its own water and sewage-treatment plant. It's in radiophone contact with Ketchikan. There are executive conference facilities.

Oh, the fishing? There are 22 cabin cruisers in the resort's fleet, and your guide's fee (but not his tip) is included in your package cost. It takes 72 full-time employees to keep the operation running smoothly. And what does all this cost you? For a minimum stay of three nights, $1,675 per person, double occupancy. If you remain a week, $3,655. That includes round-trip air transportation from Ketchikan. Contact Waterfall Resort, P.O. Box 6440, Ketchikan, AK 99901 (tel. 907/225-9461, or toll free 800/544-5125).

Metlakatla

Sawmilling and fish processing are the economic stabilizers in Metlakatla, a Tsimshian Indian town of 1,300 people some 15 miles south of Ketchikan. Metlakatla is the main community in the Annette Island Indian Reservation, the only such federal reserve in Alaska. The town was founded in 1887 when Father William Duncan led a migration of Tsimshians from nearby British Columbia to escape Anglican church interference with the community's affairs. At Duncan's urging, the U.S. Congress granted the Metlakatla Indians title to the entire 86,000-acre island in 1891.

The ferry *Chilkat* has two round-trip sailings a day, four days a week, between Ketchikan and Metlakatla (fare: $10), except for five weeks in April and May when the boat is undergoing its annual maintenance. Then you have no choice but to fly. Even when you can go by sea, you'll probably have to walk the mile from the ferry terminal to town, as there are no buses or taxis.

The **Duncan Cottage Museum,** where the community founder lived until his death in 1918, is a national historic site containing, among other of Father Duncan's possessions, a pioneer apothecary. It's open weekdays year round from 9:30 a.m. to 4 p.m., and on weekends by request. You can also see the **Duncan Memorial Church,** a replica built after the original burned down in 1948. Tours of the **Annette Island Cannery** can be arranged from June 15 to September 1. The **Tribal Longhouse** is the home of the colorful Metlakatla Indian Dancers.

For further information on these attractions, plus historic walking tours and a salmon barbecue, contact the **Metlakatla Division of Tourism,** P.O. Box 45, Metlakatla, AK 99926 (tel. 907/886-1216).

Hyder

About 90 people still make their home in this "Friendliest Ghost Town in Alaska," which has more in common with British Columbia than with the state it's in. Located at the edge of Misty Fjords National Monument (18 miles by trail) and at the head of the beautiful Portland Canal, Hyder is connected by road and bridge with Stewart, B.C. (pop. 1,000), two miles distant. Hyder briefly boomed after gold and silver were discovered in 1919, and mining is still a popular local avocation. But the real modus operandi today is obvious: the town is without a bank yet it has three bars, all of them open till 5 a.m.! There's a hotel in Hyder, and three more in Stewart. In 1986 the ferry *Aurora* began to visit on Friday mornings from Ketchikan.

---

2. Wrangell

Wrangell has a frontier air about it not observed in other towns of the southeast. You'll notice it the moment you step off the ferry to be greeted by a bevy of colorfully costumed "Shady Ladies." You'll see it in the false façades of the old wooden buildings lining the main street. You'll feel it in the independent spirits of the townspeople.

Wrangell (pop. 3,100) is located at the northern tip of 30-mile-long Wrangell Island, just seven miles from the mouth of the Stikine River—the only portal to the Canadian interior between Skagway and Prince Rupert. That geographical anomaly has shaped the town's past, present, and future.

Wrangell is the only town in Alaska to have been under three different national flags—Russian, British, and American. It was founded in 1833 by Russian fur traders who built Redoubt St. Dionysius to discourage intrusions by the British Hudson's Bay Company, which had navigation rights up the Stikine River to Canada. In 1840 the fort was leased to the British for other concessions and the Union Jack flew over the renamed Fort Stikine until the U.S. purchase of Alaska in 1867. The Americans named the site Fort Wrangell after Baron Ferdinand Petrovich von Wrangell, manager of the Russian-American company in the 1830s.

Furs and Canadian gold rushes nurtured the town's economy during its early decades. Bars, gambling halls, and brothels sprang up almost overnight; during the Cassiar Gold Rush of the late 1870s the population of Wrangell reached an estimated 15,000. When naturalist John Muir visited in 1879, he called Wrangell "the most inhospitable place at first sight I had ever seen," built with a "devil-may-care abandon." Steamship service up the Stikine began with the gold rushes and continued as far as Telegraph Creek, British Columbia, into the 1930s.

In the late 1880s Wrangell's first salmon cannery and Alaska's first sawmill were built on the island, and the economy (and population) became more stable. Today the Wrangell Forest Products sawmill, rebuilt six miles south of town in 1981, ships spruce and hemlock to Pacific Rim markets, and a fleet of trollers, seiners, and gill netters make fishing a major industry.

Wrangell's climate is mild. Summer temperatures average 60°F; winter temperatures are in the 20s and 30s. Although it's only 85 miles north of Ketchikan, Wrangell gets half the rainfall of its neighbor—a "mere" 80 inches a year.

ORIENTATION

The town of Wrangell curves around a small harbor at the northern tip of Wrangell Island. Most businesses and points of interest are found in a one-mile stretch from the ferry dock (in the north) to Shakes Island (in the Inner Harbor). **Front Street** is the main thoroughfare. Its eastern side retains a false-fronted frontier feeling, though its shoreward face was rebuilt twice after fires (in 1906 and 1952). The **Zimovia Highway,** extending from the ferry dock (via Church Street) south for 11 miles, is the chief artery on 15- by 30-mile Wrangell Island.

Getting Around

Wrangell Airport, about a mile northeast of the ferry terminal, is served by **Alaska Airlines** (tel. 907/874-3308), with two flights daily providing direct connections to Juneau, Ketchikan, and Seattle. **Wrangell Air** (tel. 874-2369) has several scheduled flights daily to Ketchikan and Petersburg, with half-price tickets for children 12 and under. **Diamond Aviation** (tel. 874-2319) offers charter air-taxi services. **Airporter service** is provided by the Roadhouse Lodge (tel. 874-2335) at $3 a head.

Alaska Marine Highway ferries arrive and depart most days (tel. 874-3711 for recorded information, 874-2021 for reservations). There's one taxi company, **Star Cab** (tel. 874-3622 or 874-3511), and one car-rental firm, **All Star** (tel. 874-3322). The **Roadhouse Lodge** (tel. 874-2335) also rents cars at $15 per day, plus gas.

Information

Drop into the **Visitors Center,** an A-frame structure on Outer Drive facing the harbor, for local information. Open from 10 a.m. to 4 p.m. weekdays in summer, and when cruise ships are in port, it's operated by the **Wrangell Chamber of Commerce,** P.O. Box 49, Wrangell, AK 99929 (tel. 907/874-3901). For information on outdoor activities, visit or write the offices of the **Wrangell Ranger District,** U.S. Forest Service, 525 Bennett St. (P.O. Box 51), Wrangell, AK 99929 (tel. 907/874-2323).

The weekly *Wrangell Sentinel,* begun in 1902, is the oldest continuous publication in Alaska. For medical help, a physician is always on call at **Wrangell General Hospital,** 310 Bennett St. (tel. 874-3356). You can do your banking at **National Bank of Alaska,** on Front Street (tel. 874-3341).

Festivals

The year's main celebration is the **Tent City Festival,** held the first weekend in February to recall the 19th-century "boom town" days when thousands of gold miners wintered here in tents. Everyone in town dons period clothing for the Shady Lady Ball; the other highlight is the John Muir Enduro, a race up Mount Dewey in mud or snow! The **Fourth of July** is also a major occasion, with a logging show, fireworks, a parade, and other events.

WHERE TO STAY AND EAT

In town, the most popular choice is the **Stikine Inn,** close to the ferry terminal and overlooking the waterfront at 107 Front St. (P.O. Box 990), Wrangell, AK 99929 (tel. 907/874-3388). Request a room in the 1982 addition, where you'll get a larger bed and won't have to cope with the live rock music booming from the Fireview Room cocktail lounge directly below. The 34 rooms are nicely appointed in an autumnal color scheme, with wall-to-wall carpeting, telephone, television, desk/dresser, and electric baseboard heating. The **Dock Side Restaurant** is a coffeeshop/dining room with full meal service from 6 a.m. to 10 p.m. daily (from 7 a.m. on Sunday). The hotel has a hair salon, a travel agency, and a 24-hour desk. Singles are $60, doubles run $65, twins cost $72, and there are two suites at $70 to $90. (Add 6% city tax to all prices.)

The older **Thunderbird Hotel,** 223 Front St. (P.O. Box 110), Wrangell, AK 99929 (tel. 907/874-3322), is somewhat depressing looking from the outside. But this one-story hotel has 14 spacious rooms with telephones and six-channel TV, clock-radios, desks, and three-quarter baths. Soda and ice machines are in the corridor, and there's a coin-op laundry next door to the hotel, which is open from 7 a.m. to 10:30 p.m. Rates: $45 single, $52 double, $59 twin. Room/car-rental packages are available.

Across the Inner Harbor from Shakes Island, on Shustack Point, is **Harding's Old Sourdough Lodge,** P.O. Box 1062, Wrangell, AK 99929 (tel. 907/874-

3613), a fishing lodge in a semi-urban setting. Lloyd and Dolores Harding, long-time Wrangellites, have instilled the 16 cozy rooms, each individually decorated, with a real family feeling. Toilets, showers, and a guest laundry—as well as a recreation room, television, and a sauna and steambath—are down the hall. Transportation is provided to the ferry dock and airport. Full-board rates are $75 per day for one person, $105 for two. Charters cost extra. If you're not a fisherperson—if you're satisfied with a bed and a logger-style breakfast—the tab is $53 per day per person ($45 without breakfast). All dining is family style, and Dolores's cooking is famous.

The rustic **Roadhouse Lodge,** P.O. Box 1199, Wrangell, AK 99929 (tel. 907/874-2335), is four miles south of town on the Zimovia Hwy. overlooking Shoemaker Harbor. Dick and Dottie Olson provide airport and ferry pickup service, and lodge guests can join their city tours (offered to cruise-ship and ferry arrivals) at no charge. Ten rooms and one suite have queen-size or twin beds, rocking chairs, and color satellite television. Singles are $48; doubles $54. Room/car packages, including tax and mileage, are $15 more. From the homey bar and **restaurant** you can often watch humpback whales and sea lions at play. Dinners, served from 5 p.m., include salad bar, potato, and dessert; try the shrimp sauteed in seasoned butter, for $16. Salmon and halibut bakes ($15 a head) are held for groups of ten or more. The lodge has an exercise room with sun bed, and arranges charter fishing packages.

Among Wrangell bed-and-breadfasts, **Clarke B&B** stands out. Marlene Clarke's A-frame home overlooks the Inner Harbor at 732 Case Ave. (P.O. Box 1020), Wrangell, AK 99929 (tel. 907/874-2125 or 874-3863). One of her units, an efficiency apartment, even has a private bath and a small kitchen with refrigerator. Singles are $35 a night; doubles, $45. Clarke's sourdough waffles make a great breakfast.

There's no charge for campers to erect their tents or park their RVs at **Shoemaker Bay** boat harbor, five miles south of Wrangell on the Zimovia Hwy. The undeveloped **Pat's Lake Campground,** 11 miles south of Wrangell, is popular with those who prefer a more rustic setting.

When you're ready for your evening meal, you might consider dining at the **Lodge of the Hungry Beaver,** 274 Shakes St. (tel. 874-3005), which claims to be on the original site of Russian Redoubt St. Dionysius. Located in the rear of the Marine Bar and Pizza Parlor, the Hungry Beaver features filet mignon ($18.50) and sauteed shrimp ($16) dinners accompanied by homemade soup and salad bar. It's open from 5 to 10 p.m. nightly.

Also popular are the **Diamond C Café,** 215 Front St. (tel. 874-3677), with daily lunch and dinner specials, homemade quiches, and desserts, open from 11 a.m. to 8 p.m. Monday through Friday, to 3 p.m. on Saturday; and **Maggie's and Son,** inside the Yamasaki Mall on Lynch Street (tel. 874-3205), with deli sandwiches, salads, pizza, and ice cream from 11 a.m. to 9 p.m. daily (4 to 9 p.m. on Sunday).

Wrangell grocery prices are the cheapest in southeast Alaska, by the way.

WHAT TO SEE AND DO

Tiny **Chief Shakes Island,** which divides the Inner and Outer Harbors, is a restored Tlingit settlement connected to Wrangell Island by a wooden footbridge off Shakes Street. Its centerpiece is the Tribal House of the Bear, an Indian community center originally built about 1800, reconstructed in 1939 by the Civilian Conservation Corps. Inside you'll find a central firepit, two tiers of wooden platforms where tribe members slept, and the chief's private quarters. Six house totems, two of them a century old, relate clan legends. Native dancers perform between 1 and 3 p.m. on Sunday in summer. Numerous totem poles stand outside, some original to the site, some moved from other locations, and some replicas. The most popular seems to have been the "Three Frogs Totem," constructed to ridicule three women of the Kiksadi clan who married three Shakes clan slaves. But it was vandalized and badly damaged in 1985, and its restoration is in doubt. The totems can be visited anytime, but the tribal house is open only during cruise-ship arrivals from mid-May to mid-September and by appointment. Contact the Wrangell Cooperative Association (tel. 874-3505 or 874-3747). A $1 donation is requested for admission.

You can visit the **grave of Chief Shakes V** two blocks away on the hillside across from Hansen's Boat Shop on Case Avenue. The plot, surrounded by a picket fence, is marked by two killer whale totems in ill repair. Shakes V was ruler from the 1830s to 1850s. (In all, there were eight chiefs named Shakes.)

If you become enamored with Wrangell history, head for the **Wrangell Museum,** in a 1906 schoolhouse at 2nd and Bevier Streets (tel. 874-3770), a block and a half from the ferry dock. The collection interprets local Native and white history and culture with artifacts, photographs—even tape recordings. A ceremonial Tlingit dance blanket, a turn-of-the-century linotype machine and printing press, and exhibits of 19th-century Stikine River fur trapping will tickle your fancy. The museum is open in summer from 1 to 4 p.m. Monday through Saturday, and for cruise ships and ferries daily; September 16 to May 14 it's open from 7 to 9 p.m. on Tuesday and 1 to 4 p.m. on Wednesday, or by appointment.

For ancient history, see the fascinating **petroglyphs** on a beach 20 minutes' walk (about half a mile) north of the ferry terminal. Visit at low tide: these mysterious prehistoric rock carvings are just above the 12-foot tide level. (Be sure to get a tide table, available locally.) A slippery boardwalk leads from the highway to the gravel beach. Turn to your right at the foot of the boardwalk and begin looking immediately for strange faces and spiral symbols on the larger rocks. Some scholars think these carvings may date from as much as 8,000 years ago! Their creators are completely unknown. Their purpose is likewise baffling, the only clue being that all but three of the 40-or-so known petroglyphs face out to sea. Local shops will sell you rice paper and other supplies to make rubbings. Ferns, crushed into balls, are better coloring agents than crayons or charcoal.

If you're the sort of person who likes to spend Sunday afternoons at garage sales and antique stores, then **Our Collections** (tel. 874-3646) might appeal to you. This eclectic exhibit of tools, furniture, and other bric-a-brac accumulated by Bolly and Elva Bigelow during their five decades of Alaskan residency is open during cruise-ship arrivals and by appointment. Look for the large metal barn-like building on the beach side of Evergreen Avenue, north of the ferry terminal near the petroglyph boardwalk.

Most of these sights and others, including several 19th- and early-20th-century churches, are included in the **Wrangell Walking Tour,** described in the annual "Wrangell Guide," published by the *Wrangell Sentinel* and distributed by the Visitors Center.

Shoppers might want to check out **Sylvia's Gift House,** 109 McKinnon St. (tel. 874-3852), and **Norris Gifts,** 124 Front St. (tel. 874-3810).

If you have a vehicle, you might like to drive five miles south of Wrangell down the Zimovia Hwy. for a look at the **Wrangell Institute,** an enormous Native boarding school on 140 acres of land facing Shoemaker Harbor. Formerly operated by the federal Bureau of Indian Affairs, it was closed in 1975 when the oil boom provided money for schools all over the state. Today the Cook Inlet Native Corporation has the long-vacant institute on the sales block. Aspiring resort developers can contact the City of Wrangell's Office of Economic Development for details.

Five miles northeast of Wrangell, opposite the mouth of the Stikine River, is a rock phenomenon to match the petroglyphs. This one, however, is natural and not man-made. The **Garnet Ledge** is the property of the Boy Scouts of America and is shared by all of Wrangell's children. You might meet kids peddling garnets at the ferry or cruise-ship dock, or you can buy the stones at the museum. Wrangell's garnets are said to have a unique crystalline structure. Though adults are forbidden from exploiting the semiprecious gems for commercial use, you can get a permit

($10 per day per person for two days) to work the ledge with hand tools only. Inquire at the museum. Access is by boat or floatplane.

Sports

FISHING Contact the **Wrangell Charter Boat Association,** P.O. Box 1078, Wrangell, AK 99929 (tel. 907/874-3800), to arrange for a boat. The association has a 24-hour dispatch service. Going rates are about $125 a day. Wrangell boats are fast and seaworthy, built scow-nosed for the treacherous currents, sand bars, and (in spring) floating ice at the mouth of the Stikine. It's important to have local navigational knowledge.

There are five major salmon-spawning streams within 20 miles of Wrangell, not counting the Stikine River. Kings run May to December; coho, August to October; humpbacks, mid-May to mid-September; sockeye and chum, June to September; and steelhead, April to May and September to December. Halibut season runs March through October. Crab and shrimp fishermen require pots. Freshwater fishermen will find Dolly Vardens and cutthroat trout at Pat's Lake, 11 miles south of Wrangell off the Zimovia Hwy. (Salmon spawn in September at the mouth of Pat's Creek, a short walk downstream.) Arctic grayling can be snared at Tyee Lake.

If the big one got away, don't fret: you can buy fresh or frozen local salmon, halibut, shrimp, and dungeness crab at **Sea Level Seafoods,** on the waterfront at the south edge of town (tel. 874-2401), or **Windjammer Seafoods,** next to the ferry terminal on Stikine Avenue (tel. 847-2351). Both companies welcome visitors for informal tours.

The annual **Wrangell King Salmon Derby** is held in May. Write P.O. Box 928, Wrangell, AK 99929, for full information.

HUNTING Brown bears (grizzlies) are in season from April to June and again from September to December; black bears, from April to December. Mountain goats are in season August to December. The season for ducks, geese, and other waterfowl is September to December.

The **Alaska Department of Fish and Wildlife** (tel. 874-3215) will issue you a hunting or fishing license and update you on regulations. Or you can go directly to a sporting goods dealer. Try **Angerman's,** across from the Stikine Inn at 6 Front St. (tel. 874-3640).

HIKING Trace John Muir's steps up the **Mount Dewey Trail,** beginning on 3rd Street a block above Wrangell High School. There's a clearing at the top where an observation tower once stood. You'll have a great view and see many bald eagles.

Opposite Shoemaker Harbor, five miles south of Wrangell, a one-mile trail leads to pretty **Rainbow Falls.** Come prepared for mud and rain.

Contact the **Wrangell Ranger District,** U.S. Forest Service, 525 Bennett St. (tel. 874-2323), for more detailed recommendations.

Tours

The **Roadhouse Lodge,** Mile 4 on Zimovia Hwy. (tel. 874-2335), and **C & E Bradley's,** 930 Zimovia Hwy. (tel. 874-3611), will escort Wrangell area tours. Contact them for specific routes and rates.

NIGHTLIFE

Live music, provided by young rock bands from the Lower 48, blares most nights at the **Fireview Room** in the Stikine Inn (tel. 874-3388). The **Totem Bar,** on

Front Street (tel. 874-3533), is a local favorite, with a waiting line at the pool tables. The **Shady Lady Brig Bar,** on Front Street near Shakes Street (tel. 874-3442), is popular with commercial fishermen. The real action in town is at the **Elks Lodge** (tel. 874-3716), next door to the Stikine Inn—but you've got to be a member, as most of the townsfolk are.

The best entertainment is provided by the several local dance and/or theater groups. They perform at festivals and frequently meet cruise ships, but other performances must be arranged in advance. Look for the **Shady Ladies** (tel. 874-3751), elegantly costumed like 19th-century saloon girls; the **Tent City Players** (tel. 874-2316); and the **Native Dancers** (tel. 874-3575). The **Wrangell Arts Council** (tel. 874-2027) can provide information about other activities.

SHORT TRIPS FROM WRANGELL

Air charter is the most efficient way to see the wilderness around Wrangell. **Diamond Aviation** (tel. 874-2319) offers combination tours of the lower Stikine River and the LeConte Glacier (see the "Petersburg" section, following) in five-passenger Beechcrafts or three-passenger Cessnas for $120. **Wrangell Air** (tel. 874-2369) has river-glacier tours for $180 in a six-passenger Cessna 207. Fill up the plane and the cost is minimal. Charter services are provided to other destinations by both carriers for about $190 an hour.

For boat travel, contact the **Wrangell Charter Boat Association** (tel. 874-3901).

Stikine River

The 330-mile-long Stikine (pronounced "Stick-*een*") is the fastest navigable river on the North American continent. Only 30 miles of it are in the United States, and these are preserved in the Stikine-LeConte Wilderness Area. No trails penetrate this wilderness, so boat and floatplane provide the only access. **Chief Shakes Hot Springs,** 22 miles from Wrangell, and the **Garnet Ledge,** five miles from town, are the two most popular local destinations.

River rats who make the 150-mile trip upstream to **Telegraph Creek,** British Columbia (pop. 300), will be awed by the variety of landforms flanking the river: lava flows and cinder cones, 10,000-foot mountains, glaciers hanging from alpine valleys. Above Telegraph Creek the surging waters have carved the impenetrable 55-mile-long Grand Canyon of the Stikine through 1,000-foot canyon walls. Below the town, kayakers, canoeists, and rafters can travel all the way to Wrangell, enjoying prolific wildlife.

The Stikine, however, is not categorized as a "wild and scenic river." It is heavily used by Canada for commercial purposes, and even in the most pristine stretch, kayakers might encounter barges or log rafts. Part-time Canadian Customs operates at a border house on the riverbank: visitors must clear there before proceeding upstream. River travelers returning to Alaska must report to U.S. Customs at Wrangell.

Tim and Terry Buness, who operate **Buness Bros.** sporting goods store at 64 Front St. (tel. 874-3811), offer motorized charter tours up the Stikine and to other wilderness destinations.

The U.S. Forest Service maintains 13 primitive **cabins** along the lower river and near its mouth. These can be reserved for $15 a day. Contact the Wrangell Ranger District, P.O. Box 51, Wrangell, AK 99929 (tel. 907/874-2323). The U.S. Forest Service also has a free map of Stikine River canoe/kayak trails.

Anan Creek

About 30 miles south of Wrangell, opposite the south end of Wrangell Island, Anan Creek flows from Anan Lake into Ernest Sound. In July and August some 200,000 spawning humpback salmon return to this creek, attracting huge numbers of seals, eagles, and bears. For these two months the Forest Service maintains a day-use **bear observatory** for photography buffs one mile upstream from its Anan Bay cabin. Bear watchers are advised to make plenty of noise until they reach the observatory, and to arm themselves in case of bear emergencies. The grizzly, one longtime observer told me, "is the *ursus* equivalent of a sumo wrestler. Black bears are basically more docile, but they're just as unpredictable."

You can reserve the Anan Bay cabin, or any of nine others in the southern part of the Wrangell Ranger District, for $15 a day. Eagle Lake and Marten Lake are favorites. Contact **Diamond Aviation** or **Wrangell Air** for air transportation; **TH Charters**, P.O. Box 934, Wrangell, AK 99929 (tel. 907/874-3455), for boat charters.

---

3. Petersburg

Alaska's Little Norway tries hard to perpetuate its reputation as a Scandinavian enclave on the Inside Passage. Colorful *rosemaling* designs decorate many of the houses and the venerable Sons of Norway Hall, and the Little Norway Festival in May is the highlight of the social calendar. Not as immediately evident is a clannishness and Scandinavian reserve among the residents of this town of 3,300. A large halibut and salmon fleet and related fish-processing industries are the economic mainstays.

Located on the beautiful Wrangell Narrows at the northern end of Mitkof Island, halfway between Ketchikan and Juneau, Petersburg was founded in 1897 by Peter Buschmann, a Norseman (of course). Buschmann found a natural harbor, lumber for building, ice from the nearby LeConte Glacier, and rich fishing grounds in easy reach, so he settled with his family and built a salmon cannery (now Petersburg Fisheries/Icicle Seafoods) and a sawmill. With Scandinavian practicality, Buschmann realized that slow, steady economic growth was healthier than the boom-and-bust cycle promised by gold rushes. So he began enticing Seattleites to work in his cannery for $35 a month. By 1925 the town was making more money from the seas than any other Alaskan town was from gold mines. That affluence has continued to the present day: a drive north from downtown along Nordic Drive and Sandy Beach Drive reveals an unusually large number of fine homes.

Petersburg averages 106 inches of rain annually, considerably more than Wrangell but far less than Ketchikan. Average temperatures range from the 60s in summer to the 30s in winter.

ORIENTATION
Petersburg is one of the few towns in southeast Alaska that doesn't straggle for miles along the coast, hemmed in by mountains and sea. Instead it lies comfortably upon muskeg at the northern end of densely forested Mitkof Island, over 200 square miles in size.

Nordic Drive is the main road through town (it becomes the **Mitkof Highway** south of the ferry dock). Numbered streets (1st through 8th) parallel Nordic to the east, while lettered streets (Balder, Charles, Dolphin, Excel, Fram, Gjoa, Haugen, etc.) intersect it at right angles from north to south. Harbor Way, Sing Lee Alley, and a couple of other lanes that don't fit the pattern are west of Nordic Drive, facing the harbor.

Getting Around
Petersburg Airport, built in 1969 on the muskeg east of town, is served by **Alaska Airlines** (tel. 907/772-4255), with direct connections daily to Juneau, Ketchikan, and Seattle, and nonstop flights to Sitka and Wrangell. **Wrangell Air** (tel. 907/874-2369) also has regularly scheduled commuter flights to Wrangell and

Ketchikan. **Alaska Island Air** (tel. 772-3130), **Kupreanof Flying Service** (tel. 772-3396), **Nordic Air** (tel. 772-3535), **Pacific Wing** (tel. 772-9258), and **Temsco Helicopters** (tel. 772-4780) have air-taxi and charter service.

Alaska Marine Highway ferries arrive and depart most days; call 772-3855 for information. **City Cab** (tel. 772-3003) handles most ground transportation; **All Star Rent-a-Car** (tel. 772-4281) has an outlet at Scandia House, and **Avis** (tel. 772-4716) can be found at the Tides Inn.

Information

You can get free maps and literature and get almost any question answered between 7:30 a.m. and 5 p.m. weekdays at the **Petersburg Chamber of Commerce** information center in the Harbormaster building on Harbor Way. Write P.O. Box 649, Petersburg, AK 99833 (tel. 907/772-3646). Another prime source of information is the **Petersburg Ranger District,** U.S. Forest Service, in the Federal Building at Nordic Way and Gjoa Street (P.O. Box 1328), Petersburg, AK 99833 (tel. 907/772-3871).

The *Petersburg Pilot* is published weekly. For medical assistance, visit **Petersburg General Hospital,** 201 Fram St. (tel. 772-4291), or dial 911 in an emergency. The **National Bank of Alaska** is on Nordic Drive at Fram Street (tel. 772-3833).

Festivals

The **Little Norway Festival** is held annually on the weekend closest to Norwegian Independence Day, May 17. There's folkdancing in national costume, "raids" from the Viking ship *Valhalla,* and feasting on typically Norse dishes.

The annual **Salmon Derby,** held four days over Memorial Day weekend, is the year's biggest event. The rest of the calendar includes a **Fourth of July** parade and an **October Arts Festival** with the Shakespearean Mitkof Dessert Theater. On December 24 local merchants and shopkeepers invite patrons into the "back room" to partake in **Julebukking**—Norwegian holiday punch and other delicacies.

WHERE TO STAY

The **Tides Inn,** 1st and Dolphin Streets (P.O. Box 1048), Petersburg, AK 99833 (tel. 907/772-4288), has 47 spacious rooms decorated in earth tones with 22-channel televisions, phones, and full baths. The new (1984) wing has harbor views, fresher décor, and baseboard heating, a step above the electric heaters in the older wing during the winter cold. The framed print of a salmon steak on the wall of your room may make you hungry but, sorry, there's no restaurant attached. One of the nicest features is a large lobby area with newspapers, magazines, and notebooks chock full of tourist information about all corners of southeast Alaska. Rates are $60 single, $75 double. Sales tax is 9% on top of that, including a 3% bed tax.

Original oil paintings of townspeople in Norwegian costume decorate the rooms and lobby of the **Scandia House,** a main-street landmark at 110 N. Nordic Dr. (P.O. Box 689), Petersburg, AK 99833 (tel. 907/772-4281). The 24 rooms of the former Mitkof Hotel, built in 1910 by immigrants, have been completely renovated with the local touch. A rose-color theme was given to second-floor rooms, evergreen to those on the third. All rooms have telephones and cable TVs with built-in clock-radios. Rates are $45 to $50 European Plan (bath down the hall), $60 to $65 American Plan (private bath), $68 double ($10 per extra person) for suites. Six kitchen suites are $73 double. All rates include a continental breakfast of coffee and pastries. The hotel also offers complete sport-fishing packages, from skiff rentals to charter trips, plus freezer space and shipment of your catch through its Aaristos agency.

The **Beachcomber Inn,** P.O. Box 570, Petersburg, AK 99833 (tel. 907/772-3888), is four miles south of town on the Mitkof Hwy. A cannery from 1912 to 1949, the Lodge now offers salmon- and halibut-fishing packages; nonfishing guests can watch eagles dive for fish from their windows. A van shuttles guests from the ferry dock and airport. Waterfront view units with private bath are $55 single, $65 double; without a view of the Wrangell Narrows, they're $10 less. The restaurant (open daily from 6 to 10 p.m.) is popular for its seafood and steak dinners, priced from $13 to $24. This is the place to sample Petersburg shrimp: a complete dinner is $16.75. There's live entertainment in the Cannery Lounge Wednesday through Sunday in summer.

Bed-and-breakfast is offered at two locations. Guests at **Hoelting Hus,** 107 Dolphin St. (P.O. Box 958), Petersburg, AK 99833 (tel. 907/772-3692), rave about the Norwegian pastries served for breakfast. The Norse home, which has a view of the harbor, prices rooms at $50 single, $60 double. The Hoeltings also offer a two-hour tour of the city. **Jewell's by the Sea,** 806 S. Nordic Dr. (P.O. Box 1662), Petersburg, AK 99833 (tel. 907/772-3620), is Petersburg's most notable gallery of locally produced arts and crafts. This beachfront home near the ferry terminal charges $40 single, $45 double.

There are two recreational vehicle parks in Petersburg. **LeConte RV Park** has ten full-service hookups and four open spaces near downtown at 4th Street and Haugen Drive (tel. 772-4680). **Twin Creek RV Park,** 7½ miles south on the Mitkof Hwy. (tel. 772-3282 or 772-3244), has 20 spaces with electricity and water. Both have rest rooms, showers, and dump stations, and both charge upward of $10 a night.

Tent campers can trek out to **Tent City,** the city campground, with 36 tent platforms, a central cooking area, and rest rooms near the airport on Haugen Drive (tel. 772-3003). The charge is $3 a night, with weekly reservations accepted. If Tent City is already full with summer cannery workers, there are two free but unimproved campgrounds south of Petersburg on the Mitkof Highway: **Ohmer Creek** (21 miles) and **Summer Strait** (26 miles). Bring water.

WHERE TO EAT

Petersburg's best restaurant is the **Beachcomber Inn.** But there's a variety of other choices for more budget-oriented tastes.

Harbor Lights Pizza, on a pier opposite the Sons of Norway Hall at 16 Sing Lee Alley (tel. 772-3424), is more than a pizza parlor. While you can get a 14-inch Viking Special (pepperoni, green pepper, and sausage) for $13.50, for example, or an oyster pizza for $3 less, you'll also find sandwiches, a full salad bar, a beer garden, and luncheon specials. Historic Petersburg photos decorate the walls. Open from 11 a.m. to midnight daily.

Deli fans have a couple of options. **Greens & Grains,** at North Nordic Drive and Excel Street (tel. 772-4433), offers the unlikely combination of sushi, hot dogs, and Norwegian cookies, as well as more typical deli foods. Open from 7 a.m. to 6 p.m. Monday through Saturday and 11 a.m. to 5 p.m. on Sunday. **Helse,** Sing Lee Alley and Harbor Way (tel. 772-3444), is a health-food deli with homemade soup and bread, and Mexican specials on Monday. Try the King Neptune sandwich: shrimp, avocado, sprouts, and tomatoes for $5.50. Open from 9 a.m. to 5:30 p.m. Monday through Saturday. **Tante's,** 11B Gjoa St. (tel. 772-4778), is Petersburg's favorite breakfast and lunch stop, renowned for its homemade soups and Norwegian pastries. Open from 7 a.m. to 5 p.m. daily except Sunday.

In the middle of downtown is the **Homestead Café,** 206 N. Nordic Dr. (tel. 772-3900), with steaks and an evening salad bar, closed only from 11 p.m. Saturday to 6 a.m. Monday. Next door, the **Twin Dragon,** 204 N. Nordic Dr. (tel. 772-3752), offers an excellent Chinese menu daily from 11:30 a.m. to 10 p.m. **Joan**

Mei, at 400 N. Nordic Dr. (tel. 772-3456), is a glorified hamburger stand open from 8 a.m. to 10 p.m. daily.

South of downtown, **Pellerito's Pizzeria,** 1105 S. Nordic Dr. (tel. 772-3727), makes its own pasta and pizza dough, and has gelato (Italian ice cream) too. It's open daily from 11:30 a.m. to 10 p.m.

WHAT TO SEE AND DO

The collection at the **Clausen Memorial Museum,** 2nd and Fram Streets (tel. 772-3598), stresses Petersburg's historic ties to the sea. Among the exhibits are two mounted world-record salmon (a 126½-pound king and a 36-pound chum), a re-created cannery office, displays of past and present fishing methods, and pioneer artifacts (including some brought by Peter Buschmann). On the lawn is Carson Boysen's 11-foot bronze sculpture and fountain, *Fisk* (Norwegian for "fish"). Open from 11 a.m. to 4 p.m. daily May through September; on Wednesday, Thursday, and Sunday only (or by appointment) the rest of the year, except Christmas and New Year's Days. No admission fee, but donations are welcomed.

A **walking tour** described in the annual "Viking Visitor Guide," published by the *Petersburg Pilot* and distributed by the chamber of commerce, will introduce you to a variety of fascinating nooks and crannies. **Petersburg Boat Harbor** has 489 stalls for Alaska's largest commercial halibut fleet and other fishing and pleasure boats. A boardwalk enables you to walk from end to end. The famous **Sons of Norway Hall,** on Sing Lee Alley (tel. 772-4575), declared a National Historic Site in 1979, was built in 1912 on pilings over picturesque Hammer Slough. It houses Fedrelandet No. 23 of the Sons of Norway, an international fraternal organization to preserve the Norwegian ethnic heritage, and was the home of all community gatherings in early Petersburg. Visit the **Husfliden** ("cottage industry") gift and handcraft shop on its second floor, especially if you'd like to know more about the *rosemaling* style of decorative house painting.

The Mitkof Hwy. takes you south to the **B. Frank Heintzleman Nursery** at Mile 9, operated by the Forest Service to nurture Sitka spruce seedlings for replanting on Tongass National Forest lands. The nursery, on the site of a former experimental fur farm, produces 800,000 young trees annually. For a tour (8 a.m. to 4:30 p.m. daily), contact the Petersburg Ranger District supervisor (tel. 772-3841). You can watch salmon climb the **Falls Creek Fish Ladder** (Mile 10.8) en route to the $2.2-million **Crystal Lake Hatchery** on Blind Slough at Mile 17 (tel. 772-4772), which welcomes the public for guided tours of its salmon and steelhead hatching and rearing facilities (8 a.m. to 4 p.m. daily). Nearby is a Forest Service **observatory** for watching the 60 to 80 trumpeter swans that winter at Blind Slough. All the while, look out on the Wrangell Narrows, the strait that separates Mitkof from Kupreanof island, for bald eagles, sea otters, porpoises, seals, and perhaps whales.

Sports

FISHING All waters, both fresh and salt, are open year round to sport fishing except near fish ladders and hatcheries. You can go after king salmon from May to July, silvers in August and September, pinks from mid-July through August, chum from July to September. Steelhead run in May and June. Rainbow, Dolly Varden, and cutthroat trout are best between May and October. The best time for halibut is June to October. You can also find cod, red snapper, flounder, herring, and tanner crab year round.

Charter operators—there are at least a dozen—include Dan O'Neil's **Secret Cove Charters** (tel. 772-4700), **Dick Hindman Charters** (tel. 772-4478), and Roald Norheim's **Keene Island, Inc.** (tel. 772-3659). **Aaristos,** 110 N. Nordic Dr.

(tel. 772-4281), can coordinate a full fishing package. Skiffs with outboard motors can be rented from Aaristos—$150 per 24 hours ($25 less for Scandia House guests)—or **Tongass Marine** (tel. 772-3905). Consult the U.S. Coast Guard near the ferry terminal for information on tides and currents. Petersburg shops sell marine charts, topographic maps, and tide charts. The **Petersburg Salmon Derby** is held Memorial Day weekend.

HUNTING   Black bear are in season September 1 through June 15. You can hunt mountain goat in August and September, and moose from September 15 to October 15. Go after waterfowl from September 1 to December 16, ptarmigan in August and September, grouse from August 1 to May 15. The **Alaska Department of Fish and Game,** P.O. Box 667, Petersburg, AK 99833 (tel. 907/772-3801), can give you full information on licenses and game regulations. The **Trading Union,** Nordic Drive at Dolphin Street (tel. 772-3881), and **Hammer & Wikan,** Nordic Drive at Excel Street (tel. 772-4246), have complete sporting-goods departments for hunting and fishing.

HIKING   Raven Trail, a 3½-mile walk beginning behind the airport, is the most popular trail on Mitkof Island. It leads to the Forest Service's Raven's Roost Cabin at 1,745 feet elevation, affording outstanding views of Petersburg and the Wrangell Narrows. About half the trail is boardwalk, but there are some very steep sections. A quarter-mile planked trail leads off the Mitkof Hwy. at Mile 16 to Blind River Rapids. Check with the Forest Service (tel. 772-3871) for current conditions and other trail information.

WINTER SPORTS   Travel by cross-country skis or snowshoes into Raven's Roost, where you can reserve the Forest Service **cabin** for $15 a night. Some alpine diehards have hired helicopters to ski the slopes in this area. Cross-country skiing and snowmobiling are also popular along the Three Lakes Loop Road, a logging road in the southeastern part of Mitkof Island. Icefishing is popular here (at Sand, Hill, and Crane Lakes) and at Petersburg Lake, on Kupreanof Island, nine air miles from Petersburg.

MISCELLANEOUS   The city **swimming pool** is at the elementary school on Dolphin Street between 3rd and 4th Streets (tel. 772-3304). Call for hours; admission is $1.50 for adults, 75¢ for children and seniors. There are exercise and weight machines in the high school's old **gym,** at the west end of 2nd Street, at Charles Street (tel. 772-4434), open weekday evenings; 50¢. This facility also has limited times scheduled for basketball, volleyball, and roller skating. Contact the city Parks and Recreation office (tel. 772-3392) for full information. **The Spa,** in Scandia House (tel. 772-4266), charges $7.50 per person for a private room with a hot tub. There are also saunas and tanning booths.

Complete information on all recreational pursuits can be obtained from the chamber of commerce (tel. 772-3646).

Tours

Any land and sea arrangements can be handled by **Viking Travel,** P.O. Box 787, Petersburg, AK 99833 (tel. 772-3818). Popular but expensive is Viking's half-day harbor tour aboard the F/V *Chan IV.* Syd Wright, who spends most of the year as principal of Petersburg High School, visits various types of fishing vessels and explains their functions, then pulls shrimp pots through Frederick Sound and provides wine with which to sample the fisherman's bounty. The price is a flat $320 for four to six people.

Aaristos, at the Scandia House, 110 N. Nordic Dr. (tel. 772-4281), has five-hour town and island tours including lunch. They're priced at $25 per person, with a four-passenger minimum.

SHOPPING

Hammer & Wikan, at Nordic Drive at Excel Street (tel. 772-4246), and the **Trading Union,** Nordic Drive at Dolphin Street (tel. 772-3881), stock many Norwegian gift items including pewter, crystal, and baking ware. Here you can also buy the "Norwegian Book of Knowledge"—40 pages, all of them blank. **Diamontes',** Nordic Drive at Fram Street (tel. 772-4858), has an excellent selection of both Alaskan and Norwegian gifts. **Jewell's by the Sea,** 806 S. Nordic Dr. (tel. 772-3620), three blocks north of the ferry dock, is the best place to check out local artists.

NIGHTLIFE

The action is at **Kito's Kave,** an otherwise nondescript red building at the decidedly un-Norwegian intersection of Sing Lee Alley and Chief John Lott Street (tel. 772-3207). A live band plays nightly except Monday from 9 p.m. to 2 a.m., unless preempted by special visitors—such as the Chippendale male strippers. Thursday night is Ladies' Night; Monday night there's a local jam session. The **Skoal Pub & Disco,** 1105 S. Nordic Dr. (tel. 772-3727), across from the ferry terminal, is new and equally popular. If you just want a quiet drink, your best bet may be the **Harbor Bar,** Nordic Drive near Dolphin Street (tel. 775-4526).

The **Viking Theater,** downtown on Nordic Drive (tel. 772-4204), has shows Thursday through Sunday nights. Look also for a community theater group known as the **Mitkof Mummers** (tel. 772-4859). The traditional **Leikaring dancers** sometimes perform for cruise ships at the Sons of Norway Hall. For information on these and other activities, contact the **Petersburg Arts Council** (tel. 772-4573).

SHORT TRIPS FROM PETERSBURG

The spectacular **LeConte Glacier,** 20 air miles east of Petersburg, is the southernmost active tidewater glacier in North America. As the glacier advances, large chunks of ice break off and tumble into LeConte Bay with a roar, creating icebergs such as those that once provided refrigeration for Petersburg's seafood shipments. One of a dozen glaciers that make up the huge Stikine Icefield surrounding 9,077-foot Devil's Thumb, the LeConte is believed to have retreated slightly in recent years. It was first observed by John Muir in 1879 and charted eight years later.

Local air services and charter boats offer excursions to the glacier. Check with air-taxi services listed under "Orientation" and charter operators listed under "Fishing" in this section.

Kake, a Tlingit community 40 miles from Petersburg on the northwest shore of huge (1,084 square miles) Kupreanof Island, is best known as the home of the "world's tallest totem pole" (124 feet), featured at the Expo '70 world's fair in Osaka, Japan. As is characteristic in southeast Alaska, the town's economy is fishing and logging based. Kake's 600 people are served every Monday (southbound) and Tuesday (northbound) by the ferry *LeConte.* There is accommodation at the **New Town Inn,** P.O. Box 222, Kake, AK 99830 (tel. 907/785-3472 or 785-3885), with singles priced at $71 and doubles at $79, including three meals. Tax is 5%. The inn is open year round.

There are 21 public-use U.S. Forest Service **cabins** in the Petersburg Ranger

District. Only one of them (Raven's Roost) is on Mitkof Island. There are 12 cabins on Kupreanof Island, four around Thomas Bay on the North American mainland, and two each on Kuiu and Woewodski Islands. They can be reserved for $15 a day; you must provide your own transportation, food, and survival equipment. Contact the Petersburg Ranger District, P.O. Box 1328, Petersburg, AK 99833 (tel. 907/772-3871).

There are no cabins in the **Tebenkof Bay Wilderness,** on the west side of Kuiu Island, 50 miles southwest of Petersburg. But wildlife abounds in this 66,800-acre expanse encompassing numerous broad bays and small islets. This is strictly for the adventurous: approach by floatplane or boat only. Amateur archeologists will find several historic Tlingit sites.

---

4. Sitka

Alaska's most historic city, and one of its most beautiful, looks out on the Gulf of Alaska and the Pacific Ocean, gazing westward toward the Russian behemoth that founded it nearly two centuries ago. Many of the sights of modern Sitka—St. Michael's Russian Orthodox Cathedral, the bishop's house, the old cemetery—harken to the days when Alexander Baranov and his men held sway from Castle Hill. But Sitka also has a rich Tlingit heritage, as evidenced by the exhibits in the Southeast Alaska Indian Cultural Center. And its cultural orientation is praiseworthy: the annual Summer Music Festival attracts some of the world's finest classical musicians, and the Sheldon Jackson Museum of Native artifacts is renowned.

Magnificent Fuji-like Mount Edgecumbe looms mysteriously across Sitka Sound from the town, which nestles along the sound's islet-filled eastern shore. About 8,500 people live here, making Sitka Alaska's fifth-largest city and the third largest in southeast. It's the only sizable community on 1,636-square-mile Baranof Island.

Sitka's location on the mild Japan Current has given it a climate that has been described as "perpetually autumn." Sitkans get used to morning fog. They expect about a month and a half of clear, crisp weather over the course of a year—the mean temperature in July is a scorching 54°F—and about eight months' worth of rain or snow. Average annual rainfall is 95 inches (October is the wettest month, June the driest), and average snowfall is about 70 inches—though it melts quickly in January's 35°F heat.

The history of Sitka is the chronicle of early Alaska, detailed in the first chapter of this book. A small fort called Redoubt Arkhangelsk Mikhailovsk was established in 1799 about six miles north of the modern town (the site is commemorated by Old Sitka State Park). The fort was burned to the ground, and most of its occupants slain, by hostile Tlingits in 1802; but two years later the Russians retaliated, bombarding the Native stronghold (on the site of modern Sitka National Historical Park) with cannons until the Tlingits fled. They didn't return to Sitka until 1821, and thereafter lived in an uneasy truce with the Russians. The colonists reconstructed the town, thereafter known as Novaya Archangelsk or "New Archangel," on its present site in 1804 and made it the capital of Russian Alaska until sovereignty passed to the United States in 1867.

Sitka (from its Tlingit name, "Shee-atika," meaning "by the sea") remained the Alaskan capital until mining income convinced the U.S. to transfer administrative headquarters to Juneau in 1906. Gold was never found in large quantities on Baranof Island, but fishing grew in importance after a salmon cannery was built in 1878. A Presbyterian mission school opened in Sitka the same year, eventually becoming a Native vocational school surviving today as Sheldon Jackson College.

Several thousand military personnel and civilian workers moved to Sitka immediately preceding and during World War II, occupying the army's Fort Ray and a

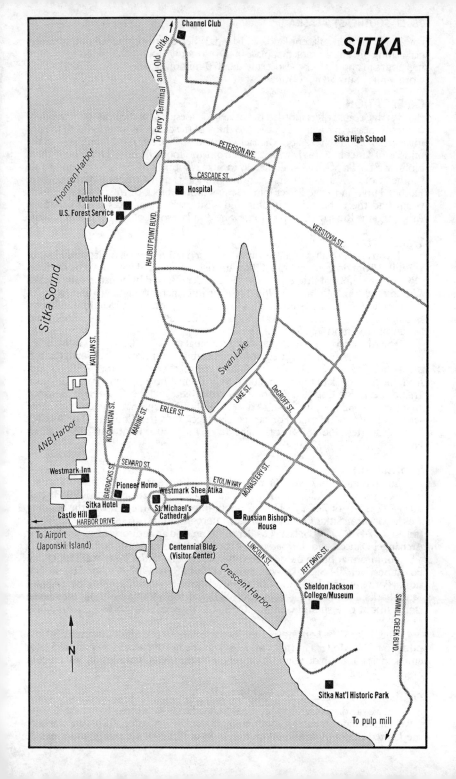

SITKA

naval air station on adjacent Japonski Island. When the troops pulled out, commercial fishing once again took first place in the economy. Today it's supported by summer tourism and timber—especially the $70-million Japanese-owned Alaska Pulp Corp. mill at Silver Bay, six miles east of town.

ORIENTATION

Partly because of its mottled history, Sitka doesn't have the neat street layout of other southeastern towns. It's easiest to think of the center of town as being the unmistakable onion spires of St. Michael's Cathedral. The cathedral is an island in the middle of **Lincoln Street,** which runs from the foot of Castle Hill (about three blocks west of St. Michael's) all the way to Sitka National Historical Site (a good mile southeast of the cathedral). Its main intersection is near **Crescent Harbor,** where Harbor Drive and Lake Street join. Here, within a block of the cruise-ship dock, you'll find the Centennial Building and Visitors Bureau offices, Westmark Shee Atika, and the Russian Bishop's House. Sheldon Jackson College is half a mile away.

Transportation

If you arrive by air, you'll land at the former naval air station on Japonski Island, 1.7 miles from downtown Sitka. **Sitka Airport** is connected with town by the John O'Connell Memorial Bridge, built in 1972. Sitka is served by nonstop daily **Alaska Airlines** (tel. 907/966-2266, 966-2261 for information) flights to and from Juneau and Ketchikan, and direct flights to Anchorage, Seattle, and San Jose and Long Beach, California. Local air-taxi services include **Bellair Inc.** (tel. 747-8636) and **Mountain Aviation** (tel. 966-2288).

The **Alaska Marine Highway ferry** terminal (tel. 747-8737, 747-3300 for information) is seven miles north of town on Halibut Point Road. The **Prewitt Enterprises** (tel. 747-8443) school bus will drop you off at your hotel for $2.50; taxi fare from the ferry dock to town runs about $12. There is no public bus system in Sitka. **Thlinget & Haida Cab** (tel. 747-6621), **Arrowhead Taxi** (tel. 747-8888), **Baranof Taxi** (tel. 747-3366), and **Sitka Taxi** (tel. 747-5001) don't have meters but charge set fares based on mileage. For car rentals, check **Avis** (tel. 966-2404) or **All Star Rent-a-Car** (tel. 966-2552) at the airport, or **AAA Auto Rental** at 2033 Halibut Point Rd. (tel. 747-8228).

Information

You'll want to make your first stop the **Sitka Convention and Visitors Bureau,** in the Centennial Building, 330 Harbor Dr. (P.O. Box 1226), Sitka, AK 99835 (tel. 907/747-5940, or 747-3739 for a 24-hour information line). Also in the building are the **Greater Sitka Chamber of Commerce,** P.O. Box 638, Sitka, AK 99835 (tel. 907/747-8604), the Isabel Miller Museum, and an auditorium where the New Archangel Dancers and the maestros of the Sitka Summer Music Festival perform.

For information on outdoor activities, contact the **Sitka Ranger District,** U.S. Forest Service, 204 Siginaka Way, Sitka, AK 99835 (tel. 907/747-6671); the **National Park Service,** P.O. Box 738, Sitka, AK 99835 (tel. 907/747-6281); **Alaska State Parks,** P.O. Box 142, Sitka, AK 99835 (tel. 907/747-6249); and the **Alaska Department of Fish and Game,** P.O. Box 510, Sitka, AK 99835 (tel. 907/747-6688).

The *Daily Sitka Sentinel* is published five days a week. **Sitka Community Hospital** is at 209 Moller Dr. (tel. 747-3241), at the north end of town. Call 911 for emergencies. You can do your banking at the **National Bank of Alaska,** 300 Lincoln St. (tel. 747-3226).

Festivals

Sitka's big day is October 18, **Alaska Day.** Each year a three- to five-day festival is woven around this date to commemorate the 1867 transfer of Russian Alaska to the United States. A memorial service at Sitka National Cemetery and a parade through town precede the Change of Colors Ceremony atop Castle Hill. There are military demonstrations, Native and Russian dancing, concerts, fun races, and the Lord Baranof Ball. You can get fined ($1) if you're male and not wearing a beard. For information, contact P.O. Box 102, Sitka, AK 99835 (tel. 907/747-8814).

Since 1972 the **Sitka Summer Music Festival** has attracted some of the world's leading chamber musicians for three weeks in June. The musicians, who have their transportation to Sitka paid but get no salary or expenses, play to sell-out crowds of 500 in Centennial Hall. Individual-performance tickets are $7 for adults, $4 for students and seniors. A summer writers' symposium is scheduled at the same time—and why not? Louis L'Amour wove his aptly named novel, *Sitka*, around the town, and James Michener lived here in 1985 and 1986 while writing *Alaska*. For information, contact P.O. Box 907, Sitka, AK 99835 (tel. 907/747-6774).

Sitka also hosts the **All-Alaska Logging Championships** in late June, featuring 17 events and $10,000 in prize money. Contact P.O. Box 1050, Sitka, AK 99835 (tel. 907/747-2225). **Russian Christmas** (January 7) is the biggest day of the Orthodox religious calendar. The Diocese of Alaska is one of two in America to celebrate it.

WHERE TO STAY

As elsewhere in Alaska, Sitka's hotel prices tend to be seasonal, though perhaps not as markedly as in other places. There's a 4% city tax and an additional 4% local bed tax on all room rates.

Deluxe

Sitka's best hotel, possibly the finest accommodation in southeast Alaska, is the **Westmark Shee Atika,** 330 Seward St. (P.O. Box 78), Sitka, AK 99835 (tel. 907/747-6241, or toll free 800/544-0970). Overlooking Crescent Harbor at the intersection of Lincoln and Lake Streets, it was built in 1978 by the Native-owned Shee Atika Corporation.

A Native art motif in stained wood runs throughout the hotel. Full wall murals depicting local Tlingit history and a grand piano add atmosphere to a sunken seating area which surrounds a lobby fireplace. Each of the 96 guest rooms is clean and spacious, featuring wood décor, rust-colored carpeting, and a Native wall mural. Each has a desk-dresser, table and chairs, and queen-size or double beds. You'll find 12-channel cable television with radio, direct-dial phone, and individually controlled baseboard heating. Shampoo and sewing kits are provided in the bathrooms. Some third-floor rooms have magnificent views of the harbor; others look out at the mountains backing Sitka. Vending machines are on each floor and in the lobby. Rates are $90 single, $98 double, in summer; $80 single, $84 double, in winter.

The interiors of the hotel's Raven Room and Kadataan Lounge, with their log beams and house poles, give you the feeling of being inside a modern Tlingit community house. The excellent restaurant, with seafood, pasta, and continental specialties in the $12 to $18 range, is open daily from 7 a.m. to 2 p.m. and 5 to 10 p.m. (on Sunday to 9 p.m.). There's room service daily from 7 a.m. to 10 p.m. A guest band plays light rock music for dancing in the lounge from 9 p.m. every night but Sunday.

The four-story **Westmark Inn,** Katlian Street at Totem Square (P.O. Box 318), Sitka, AK 99835 (tel. 907/747-6616, or toll free 800/544-0970), has recently been used as an annex by the Shee Atika. After extensive renovation, however, it may be ready to resume its previous role as Sitka's "other" first-class hotel. The lobby, decorated with planters and trimmed in brass, features wall-size sepia-tint photos of old Sitka. The 87 rooms, all with double beds, overlook Totem Square or the small-boat harbor. Original acrylic paintings of the harbor adorn the rooms' beige walls, accenting the ochre carpeting. All rooms have a cable TV, phone, baseboard heating, four-drawer dresser, and makeup table with shampoo and sewing kit. The rates are the same as the Shee Atika, above.

Moderate

The new **Super 8 Motel,** 404 Sawmill Creek Blvd., Sitka, AK 99835 (tel. 907/747-8804), is an imitation-Tudor structure near downtown. All 35 rooms offer cable TV, direct-dial phones (free local service), double or queen-size beds, and recliners. No-smoking rooms, a suite, and a waterbed are available, and pets are permitted. Free coffee is served in the lobby every morning. But unlike many other Super 8s, there's no courtesy van or guest laundry. Year-round rates are $61 single, $65 double, $67 twin.

The **Potlatch House,** 713 Katlian St., off Halibut Point Road (P.O. Box 58), Sitka, AK 99835 (tel. 907/747-8611), is a stiff walk from downtown, but its 24 remodeled motel-style units are pleasant. All are wood paneled and carpeted, and have 12-channel cable TV, phone, and baseboard heating. Four kitchenettes are available for no additional charge. Rates are $55 single, $63 double; $10 less in winter. The Canoe Club restaurant and lounge is open for lunch seven days a week, and for dinner daily except Monday until 9 p.m. (on Friday and Saturday until 10 p.m.).

Budget

The **Sitka Hotel,** 118 Lincoln St., Sitka, AK 99835 (no phone), will appeal to travelers who want a convenient location at the lowest possible price. This spartan inn has 50 rooms with single or twin beds, phones, and hot-water radiator heating. Rates are $40 single and $45 double with a private bath, $35 single and $40 double with facilities down the hall.

Bed-and-Breakfast

Karras B&B, 230 Kogwanton St., Sitka, AK 99835 (tel. 907/747-3978), is the most convenient bed-and-breakfast to downtown. Operated by a Greek man and his Tlingit wife well versed in Native legends, it has five pleasant rooms overlooking Mount Edgecumbe priced at $35 to $40 single, $50 to $55 double, plus tax. A full breakfast is served from 7:30 to 8:30 a.m. The family has a small library of Christian books, with reading space around a wood stove. No smoking, alcohol, pets, or unmarried couples allowed.

On the shore of Sitka Sound is **Helga's B&B,** 2821 Halibut Point Rd. (P.O. Box 1885), Sitka, AK 99835 (tel. 907/747-5497). This is an ideal choice for a family with a car or RV unit: it's about three miles north of the city toward the ferry dock, but one of the five rooms (with private baths) is a large family room with kitchenette, and Helga has two teenage daughters available for babysitting. From the deck, you can search for marine life in the sound. A full breakfast is served from 6:30 to 9 a.m. Rates are $40 single, $50 for couples; young children stay free with their parents. Half a block away is the Channel Club, Sitka's best-known restaurant.

Other B&Bs in Sitka include the **Creek's Edge Guest House,** 109 Cascade Creek Rd. (P.O. Box 2941), Sitka, AK 99835 (tel. 907/747-6484), with four rooms and year-round rates of $45 single, $50 double, and $65 for a suite; **Biorka Bed and Breakfast,** 611 Biorka St., Sitka, AK 99835 (tel. 907/747-3111), with two rooms at $45 single, $50 double, May 15 to September 15 ($5 less the rest of the year); **Hannah's Bed and Breakfast,** 504 Monastery St., Sitka, AK 99835 (tel. 907/747-8309), charging $40 single, $50 double; and **Mountain View Bed & Breakfast,** 201 Cascade Creek Rd. (P.O. Box 119), Sitka, AK 99835 (tel. 907/747-8966), charging $35 to $45 single, $40 to $50 double, and $75 for a one-bedroom apartment.

Youth Hostel

The **Sitka Youth Hostel** is located in the basement of the United Methodist church at 303 Kimshan St. (P.O. Box 2645), Sitka, AK 99835 (tel. 907/747-

8356), a stiff walk north of downtown. It has 20 beds in men's and women's dormitories, and showers but no cooking facilities. Open only from 8 to 9:30 a.m. and 6 to 11 p.m. June 1 to September 1. Rates are $5 for American Youth Hostel members, $8 for nonmembers; annual adult memberships are sold here for $20. You'll need a sleeping bag.

Campgrounds

There's overnight camping at the **Starrigavan Campground,** three-quarters of a mile north of the ferry dock, with 30 units; and at the **Sawmill Creek Campground,** six miles east of Sitka on Blue Lake Road, with nine units. Both sites have picnic tables, fireplaces, and toilets, but no water. Creek water should be boiled. Both are managed by the Sitka Ranger District, U.S. Forest Service, and accommodate RVs as well as tent campers. The overnight fee is $5 at Starrigavan, but free at Sawmill Creek. RVs can choose to stay closer to Sitka at **Sealing Cove,** across O' Connell Bridge on Japonski Island. The fee there is $5, and there's a 15-day limit.

WHERE TO EAT

For a not particularly cosmopolitan town of its size, Sitka has a surprising variety of cuisines. In addition to fine seafood restaurants and good hotel dining, Chinese, Filipino, Russian, Mexican, and Italian menus can all be found within a few short blocks of one another.

But novelty aside, there's little argument about which is Sitka's premier restaurant. All signs point to the **Channel Club,** on Halibut Point Road (tel. 747-9916), about halfway between downtown and the ferry terminal. Start with the 30-item salad bar, a meal in itself at $12 or included with your dinner. Then order from the items posted on the wall. The steaks are legendary—12-, 16-, and 20-ounce cuts for $15 to $19. If the nautical décor puts you in the mood for seafood, go for the halibut cheeks ($15). Fully licensed, with a good domestic wine selection, the Channel Club has won the prestigious Silver Spoon Award from the Gourmet Club of America on three separate occasions. Open nightly until 11 p.m.

Right in town, half a block from St. Michael's at 228 Harbor Dr., is **Staton's Steak House** (tel. 747-3396). Dimly lit in tones of orange and red, with miniature Native masks and totem poles on one wall and a giant king crab on another, Staton's is a steak-and-seafood house with a local following. Dinner prices range from $11 to $17, and include soup, salad, potato, and vegetable. Try the pepper steak or the gourmet halibut and chips. Daily lunch specials start at $6. Gold-nugget jewelry and other glittery delights are sold at the cashier's counter. Open Monday through Saturday to 9 p.m.

The **Marina Restaurant** (tel. 747-8840), formerly a Lincoln Street pizzeria, has moved into the second floor of a new building at 205 Harbor Dr. and enlarged its seafood menu. The wrought-iron railings and checkered tablecloths have been replaced by a pink-toned décor. But the menu still emphasizes Italian and Mexican cuisine, with many prices in the $10 to $13 range. If you don't feel like chicken cacciatore or linguine with clam sauce, consider a chimichanga. Homemade pizzas cost $8 to $16. The Marina is licensed for wine and beer, and has well-separated smoking/non-smoking sections. Open from 11 a.m. to 11 p.m. daily.

El Dorado, 714 Katlian St. (tel. 747-5070), is a *must* for south-of-the-border fanatics. Antonio and Dora Vasquez specialize in Mexican and South American cuisine, with full lunch entrees priced at $4.50 to $6.50 and dinners at $8 to $13. Try the chili verde con nopales (pork simmered in tomatilla sauce with cactus). Pizzas are also on the menu, starting at $8.50. Open from 10 a.m. to 11 p.m. daily.

The **Twin Dragon Chinese Restaurant,** 210 Katlian St. (tel. 747-5711), near the Sheffield House, has good Mandarin, Szechuan, and Cantonese food from $7 at lunch and $11 at dinner. The atmosphere is as Chinese as the immigrant management. Try the scallops in black-bean sauce. Open from 11:30 a.m. to 3 p.m. and 5 to 10 p.m. Monday through Saturday.

If you can't stand to be far from a **McDonald's,** look on Halibut Point Road at the north end of town. But if it's a special burger you want, try the **Bayview Restaurant,** upstairs in the Bayview Trading Company mall at 407 Lincoln St. (tel. 747-5440), with a view across Crescent Harbor. The Bayview has 25 varieties of burgers with prices ranging from $4.25 to $7. It's also got homemade soups, deli sandwiches, and desserts, plus borscht, pirozkis, and other Russian dishes that would have made Alexander Baranov feel right at home. Open Monday through Saturday from 11 a.m. to 7:30 p.m.

On the main downtown strip are two other restaurants very popular with locals —**Revard's,** 324 Lincoln St. (tel. 747-3449), open from 6 a.m. to 7:45 p.m. daily except Sunday; and the **Sitka Café,** 116 Lincoln St. (tel. 747-6488), at the Sitka Hotel, open from 6 a.m. to 7 p.m. Monday through Saturday and 7 a.m. to 3 p.m. on Sunday. Both serve standard coffeeshop fare, including dinners under $10. The Sitka Café also has Filipino specialties.

WHAT TO SEE AND DO

Sitka is a city of many attractions, but perhaps foremost is **Sitka National Historical Park,** P.O. Box 738, Sitka, AK 99835 (tel. 907/747-6281). Follow Lincoln Street south to where it ends near the mouth of the Indian River, and relive history at the site where Russians overran a Tlingit Indian stronghold and captured Sitka in 1804. A short trail winds past numerous totem poles to the actual battleground. The visitor center contains museum exhibits of southeast Alaska Indian culture, and offers an audio-visual presentation on Sitka's Russian history. You get an impressive sense of the continuity of Native culture when you visit the adjoining Southeast Alaska Indian Cultural Center, where craftspeople are at work on silver engraving, woodcarving, and beading projects. Here you can learn firsthand the legends behind their art. The park is open June through September from 8 a.m. to 5 p.m. daily, October through May from 8 a.m. to 5 p.m. weekdays. Native crafts are scheduled daily in summer only. Admission is free.

The **Russian Bishop's House,** facing Crescent Harbor on Lincoln Street between Monastery and Baranof Streets, is also administered by the National Park Service (tel. 747-6281). Built in 1842, it was the seat of power and authority for the Russian Orthodox church in Alaska until long after political sovereignty had passed to the United States. Its principal occupant, Bishop (now Saint) Innocent Veniaminov, was appointed metropolitan of Moscow in 1868. Restoration work based on the original plans and inventories have returned this building—the only complete Russian colonial structure standing in the Western Hemisphere—close to its original appearance. Ground-floor classrooms and priests' quarters hold museum displays of Russian history, while in the upstairs bishop's residence, National Park Service employees interpret the ecclesiastical lifestyle amid original furnishings. The old chapel was reconsecrated in October 1988. The Russian Bishop's House open from 8 a.m. to 5 p.m. June 1 to September 30, and by appointment the rest of the year. Free admission, but donations are accepted.

Other Czarist Memories

The gray-and-white-frame **St. Michael's Cathedral** you see today on Lincoln Street (tel. 747-8120) isn't the same one that stood on this spot during the Russian era. A downtown fire destroyed the original in 1966 . . . but the tragedy could have been much worse had not townspeople carried to safety many priceless icons and other art treasures. These works are now showcased on the inner walls of the new cathedral. An exact replica of the earlier building, it was completed in 1976 at a cost of $600,000. Take special note of Vladimir Borovikovsky's 18th-century painting of *Our Lady of Sitka,* to the left of the ornate altar screen. Thousands who pray to this "Sitka Madonna" regard her as a miracle healer. The image of St. Michael the Archangel, carried from Russia in 1816, represents the cathedral's patron saint.

Services are held at 9:30 a.m. every Sunday and at 6:30 p.m. on Wednesday throughout the year. Visitors are welcome, but must be prepared to stand through the service (there are no pews in an Orthodox church). The cathedral is also open for visitation from 11 a.m. to 3 p.m. (to noon on Sunday) June through September, from 9 a.m. on cruise-ship days, and by appointment the rest of the year. A $1 donation is requested.

There's not much to see anymore at **Castle Hill** except the view of Sitka Sound. Alexander Baranov's mansion ("Baranov Castle"), where the first American flag in Alaska was raised in 1867 during the transfer-of-power ceremony, stood here until it burned down in 1894. Before that the hill had been the site of a Tlingit village. A few Russian cannons still point out to sea, and there are a number of interpretive historical plaques. A short trail to the hilltop begins at the west side of the downtown post office on Lincoln Street.

There's a **Russian blockhouse** above the corner of Marine and Seward Streets, a solid-log replica of one of three 1805-era structures. Several Russian gravesites stand nearby, which may be of particular interest if you can read the Cyrillic alphabet. A couple of blocks east, if you turn off Seward and climb Observatory Street to where it disappears into the woods, you can explore an old **Russian cemetery** with its wooden double crosses slowly decaying back into the moss and soil. The Orthodox church still uses these grounds, which are being restored.

Sheldon Jackson College

The **Sheldon Jackson Museum,** P.O. Box 479, Sitka, AK 99835 (tel. 747-8981), a red octagonal building located just off Lincoln Street on the campus of Sheldon Jackson College, houses Alaska's oldest and one of its finest collections of Native artifacts. Jackson, a Presbyterian missionary who founded the school in 1878 and built this concrete museum in 1895, gathered most of the articles in the late 1800s during his travels through the Alaska territory and along the coast of Siberia. There is a fascinating display of Native vehicles: boats like the Eskimo umiak, Aleut bidarka, Athabaskan bark canoe, and Tlingit dugout, plus a reindeer sled and various dog sleds. Several are suspended from the ceiling; one wonders how Jackson carried them all back. There are excellent miniatures of fish traps and game snares. Clothing, weapons, ceremonial masks, and hundreds of other items representing Alaska's four main ethnic divisions are labeled and color coded for easy reference. The museum is open daily in summer (May 15 to September 15) from 8 a.m. to 5 p.m., and in winter from noon to 4 p.m. Tuesday through Friday and 10 a.m. to 4 p.m. on Saturday. Admission is $1 (for adults only).

Sheldon Jackson College, which served as author James Michener's home base in 1984–1987 while he wrote *Alaska,* is also the location of the all-volunteer **Alaska Raptor Rehabilitation Center** (call 747-8662 to reserve a time to visit) and a nonprofit **fish hatchery** on Lincoln Street, where daily tours are offered June through August.

Walking Tour

A mustachioed Cossack dancer named Little Droog ("friend" in Russian) is the symbol of the Sitka Convention and Visitors Bureau, and his image is on the cover of the walking-tour brochure distributed free at various places around the city.

Appropriately, the tour begins at the **Centennial Building,** on Crescent Har-

bor, where the visitors bureau and chamber of commerce offices, as well as the performing arts auditorium, are located. There is a wildlife display in the lobby, and a
summer sale by the Baranof Arts and Crafts Association. Under the same roof is the
Isabel Miller Museum (tel. 747-6455), operated by the Sitka Historical Society. Its
varied collection includes a full-scale model of Sitka under the Russians, ice saws
used in the 1850s to cut block ice for shipment to San Francisco, a facsimile of the
$7.2-million purchase agreement for Alaska signed in 1867 by Secretary of State
William Seward (the original is in the Smithsonian Institution), and one of the original copies of the Alaska State Constitution. Former Historical Society director Isabel Miller, 85 years young in 1989, still volunteers her time at the museum. Open in
summer from 8 a.m. to 5 p.m. Monday through Saturday, and 8 a.m. to 1 p.m. on
Sunday when a cruise ship is in port, and in winter from 10 a.m. to 4 p.m. Tuesday
through Saturday.
    As you walk toward downtown, you might notice a large home dominating a
small island in the sound just behind the Centennial Building. Connected to
Maksoutoff Street by a causeway, this private residence was built in 1915 on the
foundation of a Russian saltery. Its basement walls are eight to ten feet thick.
    Stop to look into **Sitka Lutheran Church,** packed into a downtown block fac-
ing St. Michael's Cathedral at 224 Lincoln St. (tel. 747-3338). A tiny museum explains that this was the first organized Lutheran congregation west of the Rocky
Mountains, founded in 1840 by Finns working for the Russian-American Company. Still in use is the West Coast's first pipe organ. This building, the third on the
site, was erected in 1967 after being destroyed by the same fire that razed St.
Michael's. Open from 8 a.m. to 5 p.m. Monday through Saturday; Sunday services
are at 10 a.m. in summer, at 11 a.m. in winter.
    Were it not for St. Michael's, the **Pioneer Home** at Lincoln and Katlian Streets
(tel. 747-3213) would be Sitka's dominant building. A huge red-roofed structure
built of yellow brick in 1934, it was the first state-supported long-term residence for
"sourdoughs" requiring some degree of medical care. There are now several such
homes around the state. The oldtimers love to talk story with visitors. A basement
arts-and-crafts shop sells handmade items between 8 a.m. and 4 p.m. weekdays, and
the garden is devoted to native Alaskan plants. In front of the home, on grounds
once used by Russian and American troops for parade drills, is a 13½-foot bronze
statue called *The Prospector,* sculpted in 1949 by Alonzo Victor Lewis.
    The Pioneer Home looks out on **Totem Square,** a park block containing a
1940 totem pole topped by a double-headed Russian eagle. On the north side of the
square is the Sheffield House; on the south, the post office and behind it Castle Hill.
    Southeast of town off Sawmill Creek Road, behind Sheldon Jackson College, is
Sitka National Cemetery. Open 24 hours, it's the oldest national cemetery west of
the Mississippi River.

Touring by Car

    Baranof Island doesn't have many miles of road—fewer than 30, in fact. But
there are a couple of points of interest. One is **Old Sitka State Historic Site,** administered by the state parks system (tel. 747-6249). About 7½ miles north of modern
Sitka on Halibut Point Road just past the ferry terminal, it was the location of the
original 1799 Russian settlement routed by the Tlingits. There's a small nature/
history trail; an interpretive center with exhibits recently opened, and evening programs are planned. Open 24 hours. Starrigavan campground is a quarter of a mile
farther north.
    Provided you aren't pulling a trailer, you can turn off Halibut Point Road on
Harbor Mountain Road four miles north of Sitka and wind your way three miles up
a narrow gravel road to a spectacular view at 2,100 feet elevation. A short, steep trail
climbs another 1,000 feet from a picnic area to a mountaintop lookout.
    Heading south, **Sawmill Creek Road** runs 13 miles to the Green Lake hydro-

electric plant (public access is not permitted). En route, 5¼ miles southeast of the city, you'll pass the Alaska Pulp Corp. mill.

World War II buffs can find gun emplacements and lookout stations on **Japonski Island,** site of the airport, the U.S. Coast Guard station, and Mount Edgecumbe High School.

Sports

FISHING   Some of Alaska's best fishing for salmon, halibut, and trout can be found in the waters around Sitka. Some 22 charter operators will be able to arrange a trip appropriate to your purpose; the Convention and Visitors Bureau can provide a comprehensive list. Typical rates are $90 to $150 per person for a full day of ocean fishing, $75 to $100 for half a day. Insurance costs keep driving prices higher.

Several state fishing records have been set in Sitka—including a 440-pound halibut, 93-pound king salmon, 26-pound coho, 47-pound lake trout, 17-pound Dolly Varden, and 8-pound cutthroat trout. Before you can catch them, though, you've got to have a license. If your charter operator doesn't make the appropriate arrangements for you, drop by **Murray Pacific Supply Corp.,** 475 Katlian St. (tel. 747-3171). Small skiffs are available for rent from the **Sitka Tool Shed** (tel. 747-3900). The Sport Fish Division of the **Alaska Department of Fish and Game,** 304 Lake St. (tel. 747-5355), will answer any questions you may have about regulations.

The Sitka Salmon Derby is held annually over the three-day Memorial Day weekend and the following two-day weekend in early June. A $5,000 grand prize is at stake. For entry information, rules, and regulations, write the Sitka Sportsman's Association, P.O. Box 1200, Sitka, AK 99835.

If you prefer freshwater to saltwater fishing, you can drive to Blue Lake—7½ miles east of Sitka near the pulp mill—populated by rainbow trout of two feet in length and larger. The big lake trout are in landlocked fjords like Redoubt Lake, only about 15 miles south of Sitka as the eagle flies, but a floatplane trip away or a rugged hike from the Green Lake Power Plant. Salmon runs on the Indian River and Starrigavan Creek are spectacular: it's hard to see the bottom of the foot-deep streams for the fish!

HUNTING   Sitka black-tailed deer are the favorite target of hunters in this region, but you can also go after brown bear, mountain goats, and a rich variety of waterfowl. Contact the Game Division of the **Alaska Department of Fish and Game,** 304 Lake St. (tel. 747-5449), for specific regulations and other information, and get your license from a good outfitter like **Mac's Sporting Goods,** 213 Harbor Dr. (tel. 747-6970).

HIKING   The **Sitka Ranger District,** U.S. Forest Service, P.O. Box 1980, Sitka, AK 99835 (tel. 907/747-6671), has published a superb "Recreational Opportunity Guide" detailing 33 separate hikes in its quadrant of the Tongass National Forest. Ten of the hikes are accessible from the Sitka road system, including a stroll through Sitka National Historical Park and the easy **Indian River Trail,** 5½ miles from its trailhead off Sawmill Creek Road to the Indian River Falls. Deer are frequently seen in the rain forest, and bear are often spotted as well. Plan accordingly. The three-quarter-mile **Beaver Lake Trail,** just above the pulp mill near Blue Lake, is steep but beautiful. If you take a skiff ten miles across Sitka Sound to Fred's Creek Cabin on the southeastern shore of Kruzof Island, you'll find the trail to the summit crater of dormant 3,201-foot **Mount Edgecumbe.** The 6.7-mile (one-way) trail is in good condition, but frequently muddy. Above 2,000 feet the ground is covered by a thick layer of red volcanic ash. On any of these hikes, insect repellent and rubber footwear are essential.

SAILING For boating, **Wyldewind Sail Charters,** P.O. Box 2264, Sitka, AK 99835 (tel. 907/747-3287 or 747-5734), will take up to six guests on short or extended sailing trips aboard a 37-foot yacht through southeast Alaska. Wilderness tours, wildlife photography, and whale watching are specialties. Rates are $65 per person per day, with a three-person minimum.

Waltzing Bear Charters, 4600 Halibut Point Rd., Sitka, AK 99835 (tel. 907/747-3608), charges $850 per week for longer sailing excursions.

KAYAKING **Baidarka Boats,** P.O. Box 2158, Sitka, AK 99835 (tel. 907/747-8996), has year-round rentals of ocean kayaks and will custom-organize a trip for you.

SCUBA-DIVING You can go out for the day with a certified dive instructor as your guide for $75 per person, gear rentals not included. Contact **Seafood Safaris,** P.O. Box 2585, Sitka, AK 99835 (tel. 907/747-5970), or **Myriad Adventures,** 203 Lincoln St., Sitka, AK 99835 (tel. 907/747-8279).

MISCELLANEOUS Sitka has two indoor **swimming pools,** including one at Blatchley Junior High School, Halibut Point Road (tel. 747-5677); call for hours and regulations. There are tennis courts, basketball and volleyball courts, softball fields, and a running track at various public schools. The visitors bureau can direct you. **Granite Creek Racquet Club,** 108 Granite Creek Rd. (tel. 747-6066), has athletic facilities. There are six lanes at the **Sitka Bowling Center,** 331 Lincoln St. (tel. 747-6310).

Tours

Prewitt Enterprises (tel. 747-8443) offers a three-hour historical tour of Sitka each morning and afternoon in summer, with hotel pickups; rates are $21 for adults, $10.50 for children. The same company has an abbreviated two-hour tour for ferry stopovers at $8 for adults, $4 for kids.

Allen Marine Tours (tel. 747-8941) has 2½-hour cruise tours to Silver Bay and Green Lake Falls, for views of the harbor, wildlife, pulp mill, and old mining sites, every Saturday, Sunday, and Monday evening June through August. Rates ($20 for adults, $10 for children) do not include dinner. Either the *St. Michael* or the *St. Aquilina* leaves Crescent Harbor at 6 p.m. sharp from the dock beside the Centennial Building. There's no need for reservations: each boat holds 300 passengers.

Sitka Wildlife Tours (tel. 747-5576), operated by Alaska Travel Adventures of Juneau, scours Sitka Sound by catamaran yacht and inflatable raft in a 3½-hour search for marine life, including whales. Fare is $75 for adults, $45 for children.

SHOPPING

The things to shop for in Sitka that you won't easily find elsewhere in Alaska are Russian items. Seek out hand-painted lacquer boxes and eggs, religious icons and etched plaques, Matrushka dolls, even antique brass samovars (tea urns). A good place to start your search is the **Russian-American Company** in MacDonald's Bay-view Trading Company mall, 407 Lincoln St. (tel. 747-6228), where you may be greeted by a store manager in a Russian hat and greatcoat. **Taranoff's Sitkakwan Gifts,** near the Sheffield at 208 Katlian St. (tel. 747-8667), has some remarkable antique Russian jewelry as well as some beautiful Tlingit silver and other artifacts. A wider selection of quality Native arts and crafts can be found at **Baranof Indian & Eskimo Arts,** across from St. Michael's at 237 Lincoln St. (tel. 747-6556).

Art collectors should visit the **Impressions Gallery,** 233 Lincoln St. (tel. 747-5502), for a wide selection of southeast Alaskan art, and **Foggy Island Fiberarts,** 104 Barracks St. (tel. 747-3444), for fine weaving. Among the most interesting bookstores in Sitka are **The Observatory,** 202 Katlian St. (tel. 747-3033), which carries new and used books, maps, and prints, specializing in Alaskana, and **Old Harbor Books,** 201 Lincoln St. (tel. 747-8808), with a selection of new books, topographical maps, and nautical charts. Businesses open between 8 and 10 a.m. weekdays and remain open until 5 p.m. or later.

CULTURE AND NIGHTLIFE

Every Sitka visitor should see the world-famous **New Archangel Dancers,** an all-woman troupe that performs whenever there's a cruise ship in town. Dressed in colorful folk costumes, these dancers have researched and choreographed their Russian leaps and twirls since 1969. All performances are at the Centennial Building auditorium; check with the visitors bureau for the dance schedule. Admission is $2. To find out about off-season performances, contact the dancers at P.O. Box 1687, Sitka, AK 99835 (tel. 747-5940). Occasionally Russian dinners (chicken Kiev) or salmon bakes are combined with evening dance performances for $16 to $18 per person, including wine. Call 747-3285 for information.

Other Sitka performing arts groups include the **Gajaa Heen** and **Noow Tlein** Tlingit dancers, who stage their shows at the Alaska Native Brotherhood hall on Katlian Street.

Sitka's best spot for loud rock 'n' roll is the **Kiksadi Club,** two miles south of downtown at 1516 Sawmill Creek Rd. (tel. 747-3285). There's a good dance floor in front of a well-positioned stage which frequently attracts California-based new wave bands. Music starts at 9 p.m. Tuesday through Sunday. Nondancers can play pool or video games.

Back in town, you can stroll down the road to **Ernie's Old Time Saloon,** 130 Lincoln St. (tel. 747-3334), a popular local watering hole whose interior walls are cloaked with mounted fish and game. The clientele is a bit crustier, but no less interesting, at the **Pioneer Bar,** 212 Katlian St. (tel. 747-3456).

The **Coliseum Twin Theater,** 315 Lincoln St. (tel. 747-6920), has first-run films nightly Wednesday through Sunday, plus a Sunday matinee.

SHORT TRIPS FROM SITKA

As the only sizable community for nearly 100 miles in any direction (Juneau and Petersburg are both over 90 miles by air), Sitka is understandably a major jumping-off point for wilderness excursions. Fewer than 500 people live in the tiny scattered settlements beyond Sitka on 1,636-square-mile Baranof Island. Even less populated is the west coast of 2,062-square-mile Chichagof Island, separated from Baranof by narrow Peril Strait. There are only two practical forms of transportation —charter boat and air taxi.

The U.S. Forest Service maintains 18 public-use cabins in the Sitka Ranger District. Six are on high lakes in the rugged, heavily glaciated **South Baranof Wilderness;** another four are in the forested lowlands of **West Chichagof–Yakobi Wilderness** north of Sitka. Three cabins are on Baranof Island, three on Kruzof Island around the base of Mount Edgecumbe, and two on the east side of Chichagof Island. The Lake Eva cabin on the northeast shore of Baranof Island has even been equipped with ramps to be handicapped-accessible. These 18 primitive cabins, which sleep four to six, can be reserved for $15 a night; book well ahead and supply all your own food and equipment. Contact the U.S. Forest Service, 204 Siginaka Way, Sitka, AK 99835 (tel. 907/747-6671).

Local air charters include **Bellair Inc.,** P.O. Box 371, Sitka, AK 99835 (tel.

907/747-8636), with rates from $219 per hour for a three-passenger Cessna 185 and $365 per hour for a seven-passenger Beaver; and **Mountain Aviation,** P.O. Box 875, Sitka, AK 99835 (tel. 907/966-2288), charges $200 per hour for a Cessna or $310 for a five-passenger Beaver.

Many of Sitka's charter operators offer overnight trips to wilderness areas and provide cabin and trail dropoff service. Try **Bluewater Charters,** P.O. Box 3107, Sitka, AK 99835 (tel. 907/747-3934); **Jolly Roger Charters,** P.O. Box 1801, Sitka, AK 99835 (tel. 907/747-3530); or **Sitka Total Vacations,** 310 Lake St., Sitka, AK 99835 (tel. 907/747-5460).

Steller Charters, 319 Peterson Ave., Sitka, AK 99835 (tel. 907/747-6711 or 747-3465), and **Alaska Naturalist and Photography Tours,** 9951 Sprucewood Park, No. 47, Juneau, AK 99801 (tel. 907/789-7429), specialize in natural history cruises. A "must" sight is the **St. Lazaria Island National Wildlife Refuge,** a 65-acre sanctuary 15 miles southwest of Sitka, just off the foot of Mount Edgecumbe. The island, shaped like a dumbbell with its long tidal flat connecting two steep forested bluffs, provides ideal breeding grounds for thousands of sea birds, including puffins, petrels, auklets, murres, guillemots, cormorants, and gulls.

Many visitors are surprised to find this stretch of southeast Alaska sprinkled with hot springs. About 20 miles south of Sitka, right on the coast, are the **Goddard Hot Springs.** There was a resort here once, but today bathhouses are the only facilities. Halfway up the east coast of Baranof Island, about 20 miles due east of Sitka (but a 120-mile boat trip), the community of Baranof lies on Warm Springs Bay. The **Baranof Warm Springs Lodge,** 9720 Trappers Lane, Juneau, AK 99801 (tel. 907/789-5070 or 789-9345), is open May through September, with individual cabins built around 110°F springs and family-style meals served in a central lodge. A third set of hot springs, these on the west coast of Chichagof Island some 65 air miles northwest of Sitka, are the **White Sulphur Springs.** There's a coveted U.S. Forest Service cabin here with a hot tub looking out on the Pacific Ocean.

If you make it all the way to White Sulphur, you might decide to continue through the Lisianski Strait and Lisianski Inlet to **Pelican,** a commercial fishing and crabbing village with a population of about 200. The ferry *LeConte* makes a stop in Pelican—for two hours every other Thursday. The main road is no more than a boardwalk built on pilings. The **Harbor Bed and Breakfast,** P.O. Box 717, Pelican, AK 99832 (tel. 907/735-2257), has a TV, laundry, and open kitchen for $65 double. **Rosie's Bar and Grill,** P.O. Box 754, Pelican, AK 99832 (tel. 907/735-2265), has four rooms available for overnights ($65, single or double) and a reputation for ribaldry known throughout Alaska. There are no pelicans in Pelican, by the way: it was named after a Finnish fish packer's boat in 1938.

The **Lisianski Fishing Lodge,** P.O. Box 776, Pelican, AK 99832 (tel. 907/735-2227), has a guest cabin that sleeps five for $240 apiece per day, full board. It's operated by Paul and Gail Corbin, who also operate fishing and sightseeing charters between Pelican and Sitka on the 53-foot ketch *Demijohn*. From September to May, contact 617 Katlian St., A-3, Sitka, AK 99835 (tel. 907/747-6273).

At the southern tip of Baranof Island, **Port Alexander** is an abandoned whaling port which only half a dozen fishing families still call home. The only real distinction this remote area now has is its weather—it's laced by 100-mph winds in the fall, and a weather station at **Little Port Walter** records an average annual rainfall of 221 inches, the most in southeast Alaska.

---

5. Juneau

Steep cliffs and mighty glaciers provide a startling backdrop for what may be the most beautiful state capital in America.

Waterfalls tumble down the walls of the near-vertical slopes. Residents of houses reached only by stairways can feel their summer spray—and in winter, know the threat of avalanches. Turn-of-the-century gold mines, bored deep into the mountain rock, impart a sense of history and sudden wealth.

The whisker-thin Gastineau Channel separates Juneau, on the North American mainland, from mountainous Douglas Island. The two are connected by bridge. Cruise boats anchor only a few hundred yards south, allowing their passengers to disembark and wander through the city's historic South Franklin district.

For all its natural beauty and tourist appeal, Juneau is first and foremost a government town. Most of its 30,000 citizens are directly or indirectly involved with state administration or supportive services. The people of Juneau, in fact, speak of three distinct "seasons." From January to April the state legislature is in session and several thousand temporary residents—lawmakers' staffs, lobbyists, and so forth—move into the city. From May through mid-September it's the tourist season, when thousands of visitors disembark from cruise boats in a single day. But from mid-September to December the city is suddenly quiet and townspeople go about their lives in a sort of hush.

Juneau hasn't always been a political percolator. Mining provided the early economic base. On October 4, 1880, a pair of struggling prospectors, Richard Harris and Joe Juneau, guided by Chief Kowee of the Tlingit Auk clan, discovered quartz outcroppings heavily streaked with gold along upper Gold Creek. Within 15 days they had written a code of laws for the newly created Harris Mining District and staked a 160-acre townsite along the channel. First called Harrisburgh, the town's name was changed the following May to Rockwell, after a U.S. naval commander, and a few months later to Juneau City. Many turn-of-the-century buildings still stand today along South Franklin Street.

By the spring of 1881 Gold Creek was crawling with prospectors—some exultant, all expectant. But even more lucrative was Douglas Island, across the channel. A San Francisco carpenter named John Treadwell made a lucky strike near Ready Bullion Creek and established a company which produced more than $70 million in gold over the next four decades. Indeed, consolidated companies that could afford large-scale hard-rock mining were the ones that achieved success here; the solo shovel-and-sluice-box technique was more suited for Nome or the Klondike than for Juneau. But the two biggest companies—Treadwell and Alaska-Gastineau—closed down within a few years of each other (in 1917 and 1922), and their heir apparent, Alaska-Juneau, constructed in 1916, had its finale written by the war in 1944.

By this time Juneau's economy had diversified. The capital was transferred here from Sitka in 1906 because of Juneau's growth and location on the Inside Passage, and because of Sitka's decline after the departure of the Russian fur traders and whalers.

When gold's tides ebbed, those of commercial fishing were on the rise. A salmon and halibut fleet, canneries, and cold-storage facilities boomed in the 1930s. The fleet remains, but the canneries have disappeared and only one tiny cold-storage plant survives in Douglas.

Since statehood in 1959, the city's administrative role has increased many-fold. Government directly employs every other Juneau resident. Since the mid-1970s there have been attempts by upstate Alaskans to move the state capital to Willow, a small town in the Susitna Valley, north of Anchorage. But until the state's voters approve funding for such a move—they have thus far refused—Alaska's political heartbeat will remain in Juneau.

Without question, Juneau has become the most highbrow community in southeast Alaska. Conversations in fern-endowed restaurants tend toward music and literature rather than hunting or logging. There's a small university (Alaska-Juneau), a professional theater group, a cinema that shows foreign films on a regular basis, and a world affairs council that sponsors lectures by a variety of internationally

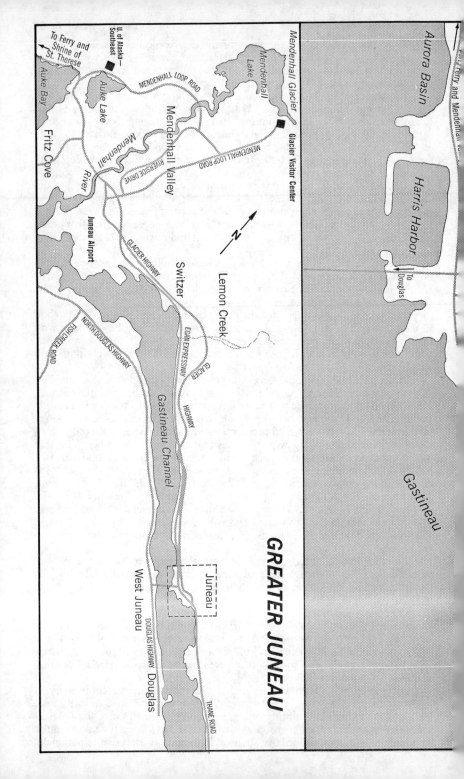

GREATER JUNEAU

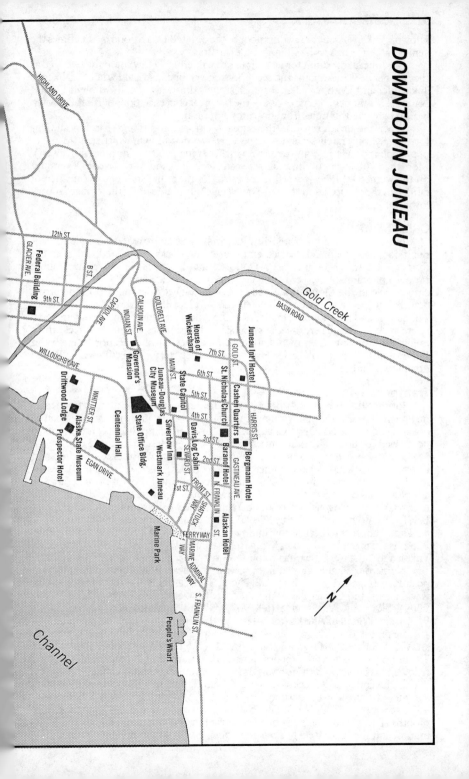

DOWNTOWN JUNEAU

Channel

People's Wharf

Marine Park

S. FRANKLIN ST.

MARINE ADMIRAL WAY

FERRY WAY

MARINE WAY

SHATTUCK WAY

FRONT ST.

1st ST.

Alaskan Hotel

N. FRANKLIN ST.

Prospector Hotel

Alaska State Museum

Driftwood Lodge

WHITTIER ST.

EGAN DRIVE

Centennial Hall

State Office Bldg.

Westmark Juneau

SEWARD ST.

Davis Log Cabin

2nd ST.

3rd ST.

Baranof Hotel

Gastineau Hotel

GASTINEAU AVE.

WILLOUGHBY AVE.

Governor's Mansion

CALHOUN AVE.

INDIAN ST.

Silverbow Inn

Juneau-Douglas City Museum

MAIN ST.

State Capitol

4th ST.

5th ST.

St. Nicholas Church

Baranof Hotel

GOLD ST.

Cashen Quarters

Bergmann Hotel

HARRIS ST.

Juneau Int'l Hostel

GOLDBELT AVE.

House of Wickersham

7th ST.

6th ST.

9th ST.

12th ST.

GLACIER AVE.

Federal Building

B ST.

CAPITOL AVE.

HIGHLAND DRIVE

Gold Creek

BASIN ROAD

N

known speakers. Even the sawdust floor of the old Red Dog Saloon is sometimes the venue for performances by Chicago blues artists.

But Juneau folk don't forget their ties to wilderness. How could they wedged as they are between mountains and sea? Spectacular cliff-constricted waterways like the Taku Inlet and Lynn Canal are barely a stone's throw away, and Admiralty Island National Monument, home of one of the last great concentrations of Alaskan brown bear, is barely ten air miles from downtown Juneau.

When the clouds separate, there are few cities more striking than Juneau. Unfortunately, they rarely separate—especially over downtown, which gets 92 inches of precipitation a year (compared to 56 inches at the airport, nine miles northwest). More than 100 inches of snow fall between November and April. (*Note:* Depending on the wetness of the snow, 10 to 12 inches of the white stuff equals one inch of rainfall in the precipitation count.) The average July high is 63°F; the average January low is 20°F.

ORIENTATION

Juneau is divided into three distinct parts. The **downtown,** where the government complex, historical district, and cruise-ship docks are located, clings to the foot of 3,819-foot Mount Roberts. **Douglas Island,** site of the old Treadwell mine, is now a pleasant suburb across the Gastineau Channel. And fully half of Juneau's citizens live in the **Mendenhall Valley / Auke Bay** district, nestled in the broad delta below spectacular Mendenhall Glacier, 9 to 13 miles northwest of downtown. The airport and big shopping malls are in the valley; the ferry terminal and university are at Auke Bay. There are a few homes and businesses at Salmon Creek, three miles northwest of downtown, and at Lemon Creek, five miles northwest. Egan Drive, which turns into Glacier Hwy., is the sole artery connecting Auke Bay to downtown Juneau.

Transportation

Juneau International Airport (yes, there are flights into Canada) is frequently maligned. There's nothing wrong with its facilities—it's just that thick fog banks, crushing down the Gastineau Channel, may cause some late fall and winter flights to be shelved for hours. If you do get stuck, the Glacier Restaurant and Lounge (tel. 789-9538), open from 6 a.m. to 11 p.m. daily, plus a well-stocked gift shop and newsstand, will keep you entertained. **Alaska Airlines** (tel. 907/789-0600) flies directly to Seattle seven times daily in summer, four times the rest of the year. The airline also has three daily flights to Anchorage and Ketchikan, two to Sitka, one each to Petersburg, Wrangell, Cordova, and Yakutat, and a daily summer flight to Glacier Bay. **Delta Airlines** (tel. toll free 800/221-1212) has a daily nonstop flight to Fairbanks and another to Seattle continuing to Los Angeles. **Air North** (tel. 907/789-3262) is a Canada-based carrier flying to Fairbanks, Whitehorse, Dawson, and other Yukon and Northwest Territories communities.

Numerous smaller air-taxi lines serving southeast Alaska are based at the airport. I have enjoyed trips with **L.A.B. Flying Service** (tel. 907/789-9160) to Skagway, Haines, and Glacier Bay. Others include **Glacier Bay Airways** (tel. 907/789-9009), **Skagway Air Service** (tel. 907/789-2006), **Ward Air** (tel. 907/789-9150), and **Wings of Alaska** (tel. 907/789-0790).

Be prepared for surprises in Juneau's air space. In early 1987, believe it or not, an Alaska Airlines Boeing 737 collided with a *fish* in mid-air shortly after takeoff! This is no tall tale: the pilot reported that he had startled a bald eagle with the finny fellow in his talons, and the fish was dropped onto the cockpit.

Eighteen ferries a week—nine northbound, nine southbound—stop during summer at the Auke Bay terminal of the **Alaska Marine Highway System** (tel. 907/465-3941 or 789-7453). The schedule is cut back somewhat during the winter months. The weekly *Columbia* or *Matanuska* ferry connects to Bellingham, Washington, and the twice-weekly *Taku* and *Malaspina* go as far as Prince Rupert. The

LeConte stops at every small port between Juneau and Petersburg three times a week. The terminal is 14 miles northwest of downtown, but there's a city ticket office at 1591 Glacier Ave. Taxis meet all scheduled ferry arrivals. Shuttle service is provided by the vans of **Mendenhall Glacier Transport** (tel. 789-5460).

As befits a capital city of 30,000, Juneau has an excellent **municipal bus** system. Visitors may be interested in the hourly service connecting downtown Juneau with the valley and Auke Bay (from 7:05 a.m. to 11:45 p.m.) and with Douglas (from 7 a.m. to 11:30 p.m.) for only 75¢. The Auke Bay route stops 1¾ miles short of the ferry dock. There's also a downtown–Auke Bay express bus, operating from 7:30 a.m. to 6 p.m., which makes an airport stop. Alas, Capital Transit takes Sunday off. For complete schedule information, visit 155 S. Seward St. (tel. 789-6901).

There are two cab companies, and their rates are similar. **Taku Glacier Cab** (tel. 586-2121) and **Capital Cab** (tel. 586-2772) both charge $11 to $12 between the airport and downtown ($1.50 at flagfall and 60¢ a mile).

Although Juneau isn't endowed with road connections to other cities on the North American mainland, there are about 100 miles of paved road in the area, so a vehicle is useful.

The Glacier Hwy., in fact, runs for 40 miles, from downtown Juneau past Auke Bay to Echo Cove on the Lynn Canal. (A proposed Juneau–Haines road-and-ferry link remains mere rumor.) Several major American car-rental firms have Juneau airport counters—**Avis** (tel. 789-9450, or toll free 800/331-1717), **Budget** (tel. 789-5186, or toll free 800/527-7000), **Hertz** (tel. 789-9494, or toll free 800/654-8200), and **National** (tel. 789-9814, or toll free 800/227-7368). If price is more important than convenience, check these other agencies: **Chrysler Rent-a-Car,** 8345 Old Dairy Rd. (tel. 789-1386); **Evergreen Ford,** 8895 Mallard St. (tel. 789-9386); **Holiday Payless,** 5454 Jenkins Dr., Lemon Creek (tel. 780-4118, or toll free 800/237-2804); **All Star Rent-a-Car,** Airport Mall, Auke Bay (tel. 789-9000, or toll free 800/426-5243); or **Rent-a-Wreck,** 1910 Alex Holden Way, Juneau (tel. 789-4111, or toll free 800/421-7253 outside Alaska). Cars are generally available, but it's wise to book ahead during the summer.

You can also find "Cruisin' Juneau" mopeds at the **Alaska Trading Post,** 479 S. Franklin St. (tel. 586-6861 for reservations). Bicycle paths or lanes parallel the Glacier Hwy., Mendenhall Loop Road, Douglas Hwy., and several other main arteries.

Information

The **Davis Log Cabin Information Center,** 134 3rd St., at Seward Street, Juneau, AK 99801 (tel. 907/586-2284), can tell you everything you'd ever want to know about Juneau, and then some. An attraction in its own right—it's a Juneau centennial re-creation of an 1881 cabin that was the city's first church and later a school, carpentry shop, and brewery office—its staff provides brochures, maps, tour schedules, and information on clubs and events, and will arrange guides and foreign-language translators for those who require them. There are also city information centers at the airport terminal and (in summer only) on the waterfront at the Marine Park kiosk and the cruise-ship terminal, 470 S. Franklin St. A 24-hour recorded schedule of events and activities is on the telephone line: 586-JUNO.

The **Juneau Convention & Visitors Bureau,** 76 Egan Dr., 3rd Floor, Juneau, AK 99801 (tel. 907/586-1737), provides assistance to state, national, and international organizations planning trade shows, conventions, seminars, or group tours. Its main facility is the Centennial Hall Convention Center, 101 Egan Dr. (tel. 586-5283), which boasts seating for more than 1,300 people and 11,000 square feet of exhibit space. Within Centennial Hall is the **U.S. Forest Service Information Center** (tel. 586-8751), open from 9 a.m. to 6 p.m. weekdays and summer weekends. The Forest Service has more than a dozen films, videotapes, and slide programs on wildlife, history, and lifestyles in Tongass National Forest, that it will show upon request. This is also the place to find out about backcountry travel and wilderness-cabin rental.

Other helpful contacts include the **Juneau Chamber of Commerce,** 1107 W. 8th St., Juneau, AK 99801 (tel. 907/586-6420); the **Alaska Division of Tourism,** P.O. Box E, Juneau, AK 99811 (tel. 907/465-2015); and the **National Park Service,** P.O. Box 1089, Juneau, AK 99802 (tel. 907/586-7937).

Miscellany

There are **public phones** and rest rooms in the Municipal Building, across Egan Drive from Marine Park, open from 8 a.m. to 6 p.m. Monday through Friday, 7 a.m. to 6 p.m. on Saturday and Sunday. **The Phone Connection,** 171 Shattuck Way and 275 S. Franklin St. (tel. 463-5828), provides a long-distance call station plus temporary rental of office space and equipment.

The local newspaper is the *Juneau Empire,* published Monday through Friday afternoon. You can usually also find a copy of the *Anchorage Daily News* or the *Seattle Post-Intelligencer* at a premium. **Bartlett Memorial Hospital,** Mile 3½ on Glacier Hwy. (tel. 586-2611), provides complete medical services. Dial 911 for emergencies. Several banks have branches both downtown and in the valley; the **National Bank of Alaska,** for instance, is at 123 Seward St. (tel. 586-3324) and 9150 Glacier Hwy. (tel. 789-9550).

Festivals

The most important date on the Juneau calendar of events is July 4. The **Fourth of July** agenda, in fact, lasts a full month, beginning with summer solstice! Events may include car rallies; softball and pool tournaments; a triathlon and fun runs; navy air and sea shows; watermelon-eating, pie-throwing, and sand-castle-building contests; and in keeping with the city's gold-mining heritage, even sluice races. The big day itself is highlighted by parades through downtown Juneau and Douglas, followed by carnivals and barbecues. For more information, contact the Juneau Festival Association (tel. 364-3346).

Other festive occasions include the **Ski-to-Sea Relay,** first weekend of April; **Alaska Folk Festival,** second week of April; **Golden North Salmon Derby,** in mid-August; the University of Alaska–Juneau's **Tuxedo Junction,** a formal "Monte Carlo" night at Centennial Hall in early November; and **Open House at the Governor's Mansion,** one weekday evening about a week before Christmas.

WHERE TO STAY

There are over a dozen tourist-class hotels in Juneau, ranging from plush new accommodations to turn-of-the-century classics. Most of them are in the downtown area, but several of the newer motels are near the airport at the foot of the Mendenhall Valley. All are subject to a whopping 11% tax: 4% city tax plus 7% bed tax.

Deluxe

A huge eagle, painstakingly carved from wood by the newest techniques of laser art, greets you as you enter the **Westmark Juneau,** across from the waterfront at 51 W. Egan Dr., Juneau, AK 99801 (tel. 907/586-6900, or toll free 800/544-0970). More such artwork adorns the walls overlooking the aptly named Woodcarver restaurant, while green carpeting and standing plants lend a foresty feeling to the lobby. The hotel has 105 rooms decorated in green and mauve or shades of blue, with all-modern furnishings, cable TV, phone, and thermostat-controlled forced-air heating. Complimentary shampoo and sewing kit are provided in the bathrooms. As you might expect of a hotel so near the convention center and State Office Building, the clientele is heavily business and government oriented. The Woodcarver is open daily from 6:30 a.m. to 2 p.m. and 5 to 9:30 p.m., and the adjoining lounge has bar service daily from 4:30 p.m. to midnight, with a "Munchie Bar" from 5 to 7 p.m. Room rates run from $128 single and $140 double, May 15 to September 15; $84 single and $94 double in the low season; and upwards of $150 for suites.

Moderate

When I'm in the Alaskan capital, I like to stay at the **Westmark-Baranof Hotel,** 127 N. Franklin St., Juneau, AK 99801 (tel. 907/586-2660, or toll free 800/544-0970). This classically elegant nine-story hotel, which celebrated its 50th anniversary in 1989, is convenient to all Juneau attractions yet enough removed from the busiest streets to be relatively quiet. On the walls of the subtly lit lobby—redone after a devastating 1984 fire that began in a hotel restaurant—are original oil paintings by Sydney Lawrence, Fred Machetanz, and other noted Alaskan artists. The Bubble Room piano bar, which opens directly on to the lobby, is *the* place for after-work "work" in Juneau—some claim more legislation has been determined in this lounge than at any other place in Alaska!

The sophisticated Gold Room, tastefully decorated with a jade/marble theme, is famous for its exclusive dinners and attentive service. If you start with vichyssoise or wilted-spinach flambé, then feast on chateaubriand complemented by a bottle of fine French burgundy, you can expect to pay about $70 for two. Open from 5 to 10 p.m. nightly. The Capital Café is open for three meals, seven days a week.

The hotel has 202 rooms, including 14 efficiency units and 10 one-bedroom suites. One of the Baranof's eccentric charms is that each floor and every unit is different, both in layout and décor! But all rooms have modern furnishings, cable TV, phone, baseboard steam heating, and such amenities as shampoo and sewing kit. The uppermost have double-paned windows and fine views. Summer rates are $92 to $96 single, $102 to $106 double, with prices 10% to 15% lower in winter. A gift shop, beauty parlor, travel agency, and Alaska Airlines office are on the ground floor.

Don't be deceived by the cozy lobby at the **Prospector Hotel,** 375 Whittier St., Juneau, AK 99801 (tel. 907/586-3737, or toll free 800/331-2711), located next to the Alaska State Museum. The rooms are huge! Each one is decorated in pastel shades of purple and gray with rust carpeting. The modern furnishings include full-length drapes, a large closet, electric baseboard heating, cable television, and telephone (local calls are free). Seaside rooms look across Egan Drive to the Gastineau Channel. Of the 59 rooms, 10 are suites and 20 more have efficiency kitchens. Summer rates are $79 single, $89 double, with efficiencies and suites marginally higher. Winter rates are $5 less.

The Diggings restaurant/lounge is open from 7 a.m. to 10 p.m. Monday through Saturday, with Sunday brunch from 9 a.m. to 3 p.m. Roast prime rib, cooked 4½ hours in rock salt, is the specialty of the house ($17.75). A live band plays light pop music for dancing nightly except Sunday. The Prospector is owned by the Native Shaan Seet corporation.

A nautical theme dominates the friendly **Breakwater Inn,** a mile from downtown at 1711 Glacier Ave., Juneau, AK 99801 (tel. 907/586-6303, or toll free 800/544-2250, 800/478-2250 in Alaska). As you enter, you'll notice on your left a large woodcut depicting the achievements of sailors. Glass floats are suspended by ropes over the reception desk, and more ropes direct you upstairs to the restaurant and lounge, which offer a wide-angle view across the highway to Gastineau Channel. The restaurant is open for three meals a day from 7 a.m. to 10 p.m. Lunches range from about $7 to $10; dinners, from $16 to $20.

The rooms are beautifully appointed, with solid wood furnishings and imitation leather trim. Thermostat-controlled heating is by forced air; each room has cable TV and telephone (local calls are 25¢). It's a good choice for families. Rates are $59 and $69 single, $69 and $79 double, in summer; $49 single and $52 double in winter.

The **Driftwood Lodge,** 435 Willoughby Ave. West, Juneau, AK 99801 (tel.

907/586-2280, or toll free 800/544-2239), qualifies as Juneau's most centrally lo-cated motel. Close to the State Museum and government complex, adjoining an ex-cellent restaurant (the Fiddlehead), and sharing a parking lot with a grocery and liquor store, it is a three-story private-entrance facility with no elevators but lots of staircases! There are 62 rather ordinary but well-kept rooms, including 21 standard units ($49 single, $62 double), 21 with kitchens ($59 single, $66 double), and 10 one-bedroom ($72) and 10 two-bedroom ($89) suites. Kitchens are stocked with pots, plates, and silverware. All rooms have cable TV, phone (local calls are free), and electric baseboard heating. A guest laundry is open from 7 a.m. to 10 p.m., but irons are hard to come by.

The **Silverbow Inn,** 120 2nd St., Juneau, AK 99801 (tel. 907/586-4146), one of southeast Alaska's finest restaurants (see the "Where to Eat" section, below), also has accommodations on its second and third floors. There are six cozy rooms, all with private baths but a European feel; owner Richard Lee eventually hopes to in-crease that number. Each room has an antique desk and wardrobe, double bed, elec-tric heating, telephone, and clock-radio. There are no TVs, but light jazz is sometimes played downstairs. The price of $85 single, $95 double, includes a conti-nental breakfast. Ask for an end room: they're larger.

Three hotels in the Mendenhall Valley, near the airport, are designed to offer a high level of service to the traveler. The four-story **Airport TraveLodge,** 9200 Gla-cier Hwy., Mendenhall Valley (P.O. Box 2240), Juneau, AK 99803 (tel. 907/789-3636), opened in 1986 with 84 rooms, an indoor swimming pool, whirlpool, exer-cise room, gift shop, and beauty parlor. Room rates were set at $75 single, $80 dou-ble. Fernando's, a popular Mexican restaurant, is attached (see the "Where to Eat" section, below).

The Best Western **Country Lane Inn,** 9300 Glacier Hwy., Juneau, AK 99801 (tel. 907/789-5005, or toll free 800/528-1234, 800/334-9401 in Alaska), has 58 rooms, an indoor pool, and a Jacuzzi. The management did not show me a room, however, so all I saw was the complimentary coffee, tea, and fruit in the lobby, and the courtesy van to the airport and ferry terminal. Room rates are $66 single, $72 double, and include a continental breakfast.

Super 8 Motel, 2295 Trout St., Juneau, AK 99801 (tel. 907/789-4858, or toll free 800/843-1991), gives you a lot for your money. Though a bit spartan in atmos-phere, with nothing but a mirror and a print on the cream-colored walls, each of the 75 rooms contains everything you need to be comfortable: queen-size bed, built-in desk/dresser/luggage rack, ample lighting, electric baseboard heating, cable TV, and telephone (local calls are free). There are vending machines on the second floor, a guest Laundromat, and a computerized elevator. A courtesy van is available to take you to the airport and ferry, and to downtown if you're ready to leave at 7:30 a.m. or 4:30 p.m. The lobby coffee is complimentary. Summer rates are $60 single and $66 double; rooms are somewhat less in winter.

Budget

There's probably nowhere you could stay in Alaska to get a better feeling for the gold-rush era than at the **Alaskan Hotel & Bar,** 167 S. Franklin St., Juneau, AK 99801 (tel. 907/586-1000, or toll free 800/327-9347). From the moment you step off historic South Franklin Street and walk through the hotel's swinging door, you'll feel as though you've been transported back to Victorian times. Oak antiques, stained glass (including a Tiffany window), and hanging plants adorn the small lob-by, which leads back to the bar (see the "Nightlife" section, below). The 40 rooms are on two upstairs floors (no elevators) whose corridors are lined with old photos of historic Juneau.

Each of the small rooms is decorated in turn-of-the-century bordello style, with an antique oak headboard, desk, and chair, and a combination wardrobe/dresser. Even the toilets and sinks are antique, whether you opt for one of the ten rooms with private bath or share a facility in the hall. The walls are papered with a yellow floral pattern; the carpet and drapes, which, sorry to say, don't help to keep out the late-night music from neighboring saloons, are chocolate brown, red, or royal blue. There's hot-water radiator heating and a guest Laundromat, cable TVs, and antique-style oak wall phones. Some kitchenettes are available. Rooms with bath are $45 and $50 single, $50 and $55 double; without bath, $36 single, $41 double. If you feel like using the hot tub or sauna, they're in the basement: rental is $20 an hour. Built in 1913, the Alaskan Hotel is on the National Register of Historic Places.

The **Inn at the Waterfront,** 455 S. Franklin St., Juneau, AK 99801 (tel. 907/ 586-2050), is another restoration project. In 1986 Bill Cullinane and Ann House bought the vintage-1898 brothel-turned-flophouse hotel across from the cruise-ship terminal. Two years later they opened with 21 intimate rooms, including six two- and three-bedroom suites. All have antique wardrobes and/or desks, modern beds, and a soothing color scheme of taupe carpets and blue bedspreads and curtains. They have direct-dial phones and cable hookups (TVs on request). Eleven standard rooms are priced $47 to $67 single, $56 to $76 double, with higher rates for water-front views. Four economy rooms with shared baths are $34 to $49 single, $43 to $58 double. The suites, each with hideaway couches in the sitting rooms, run $81 to $124 double.

Not only did the restoration introduce all-new heating, electrical, and plumb-ing systems, insulation, and siding, but it enabled the hotel to reopen the long-lost Crystal Baths, where up to eight people at a time can bask in steam for $10 an hour.

The Summit Restaurant and Lounge, which remained open through the hotel's overhaul, has long been considered one of Juneau's premier spots for steaks. Folks flock to the intimate, low-lit dining room for a wide range of beef, chicken, and sea-food dinners. Prices range from $15 to $27. There's also an extensive wine list. It's open from 5 to 10 p.m. daily.

To get to the **Bergmann Hotel,** 434 3rd St., at Harris Street, Juneau, AK 99801 (tel. 907/586-1690), you must climb a steep drive or a direct (but long) flight of stairs. The Bergmann is on the side of a hill in a residential district overlooking downtown. Listed, like the Alaskan Hotel, on the National Register, it was built shortly before its rival in 1913 by an immigrant German widow named Marie Bergmann. At the time it was considered Juneau's finest hotel, with electric lights, steam heat, hot and cold water in every room, and baths and showers on every floor.

After major renovation in the late 1980s, the hotel has 36 rooms, including six suites. Each is adorned differently, with modern furnishings, antique photographs, and flowers. All rooms have sinks, but there are no private baths. The rooms are quiet, with wall-to-wall carpeting, TV, and phone. Guests share a laundry. Rates are $45 single, $55 double, in summer; $35 single, $45 double, in winter. A little pub with a dedicated following is in the basement.

Cashen Quarters, 315 Gold St., Juneau, AK 99801 (tel. 907/586-9863), consist of five housekeeping units in a refurbished home at 303 Gold St., on the corner of 3rd. Clean and spacious, with stoves and refrigerators, forced-air heating, double beds, and easy chairs, they appeal mainly to families and older visitors. Toilet facilities are basic, there's no TV, and the only phone is the one in the office next door. Still, they're a bargain at $35 single, $45 double; $5 less in winter. Cash only, please.

Bed-and-Breakfast

The **Alaska Bed & Breakfast Association,** Southeastern Alaska, P.O. Box 21890, Juneau, AK 99802 (tel. 907/586-2959), is a central booking agency for B&Bs in the Juneau area. An effort is made to place visitors with compatible families —smokers, pet lovers, and so forth. Most rooms run $45 to $50 double.

Dawson's B&B, 1941 Glacier Hwy., Juneau, AK 99801 (tel. 907/586-9708), and Julie Isaac's **Windsock Inn B&B,** 410 D St. (P.O. Box 223), Douglas, AK 99824 (tel. 907/364-2431), advertise courtesy-car pickups at the airport and ferry termi-nal. There are numerous other such accommodations. Closest to downtown is

Crondahl's B&B, 626 5th St., Juneau, AK 99801 (tel. 907/586-1464), five blocks from the Capitol. Farthest is the **Lost Chord B&B,** 2200 Fritz Cove Rd., Juneau, AK 99801 (tel. 907/789-7296), in a secluded cove 14 miles from downtown. **Grandma's Feather Bed,** 2358 Mendenhall Loop Rd., Juneau, AK 99803 (tel. 907/789-5566), has large suites with Jacuzzis on the upper floor of a popular restaurant. Rates are $105 with Jacuzzi, $90 without.

Youth Hostel

The **Juneau International Hostel,** 614 Harris St., Juneau, AK 99801 (tel. 907/586-9559), is not just for youth. All ages are welcome to stay, provided they conform willingly to the hostel's somewhat restrictive rules. You're only able to use the hostel or check in from 7 to 9 a.m. and 5 to 10:30 p.m. Smoking and alcohol are taboo. You share eight-bed dormitory rooms and common bathrooms (segregated by sex), pay 50¢ if you want a shower, and limit your stay to three days. Blankets are supplied, but you must have your own "sheet sleeping sack" or buy one for 75¢. A community kitchen, laundry, and common room (for reading and conversation) make this easier to take. The overnight charges at this three-story yellow house are $7 for American Youth Hostels members, $9 for nonmembers. If you plan to do a lot of hosteling in Alaska, you can buy an annual membership here for $20.

Campgrounds

There are two Forest Service campgrounds near Auke Bay. The **Auke Village Campground,** Mile 15.8 on Glacier Hwy., has 11 sites; the **Mendenhall Lake Campground,** off Montana Creek Road five miles from the ferry terminal, has 60, including ten for trailers and seven specifically for backpackers. Both have wood and water, but Auke Village has flush toilets while Mendenhall Lake has mere pit facilities. Units cost $5 per night. No reservations are taken. Contact the Juneau Ranger District, U.S. Forest Service, P.O. Box 2097, Juneau, AK 99803 (tel. 907/789-3111), for more information.

Recreational vehicles are best served at the **Auke Bay RV Park,** 11930 Glacier Hwy. (P.O. Box 210215), Auke Bay, AK 99821 (tel. 907/789-9467), which takes reservations for its 25 spaces with electric, water, and sewer hookups. In a pinch, consider the **Tides Motel and Camper Park,** 5000 Glacier Hwy., Lemon Creek, Juneau, AK 99801 (tel. 907/780-4622), which reserves its 40 spaces with electric and water hookups, dump station, Laundromat, and showers. Be aware, however, that many spots at both these parks are taken up by permanent residents.

WHERE TO EAT

Probably because of its role as Alaska's governmental center, Juneau has as good a choice of restaurants as any city in the state, with the exception of Anchorage. It also has a heavy business turnover. Several fine restaurants, including excellent Italian and Chinese establishments in the downtown area, closed during the year this book was researched. There's no guarantee the ones mentioned here will still be operating when you visit. Of course you're guaranteed excellent food and service—for rather high prices—at the Baranof Hotel's Gold Room, the Westmark's Woodcarver, and the Prospector's Diggings, described in the "Where to Stay" section, above.

Downtown

Two Juneau restaurants in particular stand out. The **Silverbow Inn,** 120 2nd St., between Main and Seward (tel. 586-4146), has a menu and atmosphere reminiscent of a European country inn. The renovated building it occupies was known during Juneau's wild-and-woolly gold-rush days as the San Francisco Bakery; owner Richard Lee refurbished it with antiques in 1984. The food is a delightful surprise. Lunches, such as roast chicken with wild-rice stuffing and crab quiche with soup and salad, vary in price from $6.50 to $11. Candlelit dinners, which include salad, vegetable, French bread, and potato, rice, or pasta, are priced at $17 to $21: try the rosemary lamb chops, raspberry chicken, or salmon Florentine. There's an outrageous dessert selection, with taste tempters like sour cream–pecan cheesecake and homemade ice cream, and a brief but provocative international wine list. Vegetarian meals and light dinners (from $12) are available. Smokers are accommodated in a separate lounge. Open Monday through Friday from 7 to 10 a.m. for full breakfasts, from 11:30 a.m. to 2:30 p.m. for lunch, and from 5 to 9 p.m. for dinner. On Saturday, brunch is served from 9 a.m. to 2 p.m., and dinner, from 5 to 9 p.m. In winter, the restaurant serves continental breakfast weekdays at 9 a.m. and closes Sunday.

My other favorite is **The Fiddlehead,** at the Driftwood Lodge, 429 Willoughby Ave. West (tel. 586-3150). Live jazz and classical piano nightly, handcrafted stained-glass windows, and the work of local artists and photographers on the walls create an artsy atmosphere in this local standby, now in its second decade in business. The emphasis is on wholesome foods. You might opt for a breakfast of granola with yogurt, or for a heartier appetite, huevos grandes (fried eggs on rice with cheese, guacamole, sour cream, sprouts, and fried potatoes, for $8.50). Homemade soups, salads and burgers run $5 to $8 for lunch. Dinner entrees, priced at $13 to $19, include lamb curry, eggplant parmesan, chicken teriyaki, and smoked-salmon Caesar salad. As might be expected of a restaurant with its own bakery, desserts are superb: chocolate cake, ice cream pie and crème brûlé, for instance, accompanied by espresso coffee. There's a menu of domestic and imported wines and beers. Open Monday through Friday from 6 a.m. to 10 p.m., on Saturday and Sunday from 7 a.m.

The atmosphere of a turn-of-the-century mining camp is recalled at **The Cook House,** 200 Admiral Bay, next to the Red Dog Saloon (tel. 463-3658). At the front entrance stand a steam engine and stamp mill, and within the building, crafted to have a rustic, half-finished look, is a 20-part photomural of Juneau-area mining operations, courtesy of the State Historical Library. The open kitchen goes hand-in-hand with the scaffold and noose in one corner: "The cooking has never killed anyone, but the miners have hung more than one cook" reads a sign. The lunch menu offers a Texas-size burger for $5.75, salmon filet with fries or beans for $10. Dinner selections (with soup and salad, potatoes, and beans) include halibut broiled with lime cilantro butter for $13, a 16-ounce grub steak for $18. Dessert is homemade ice cream. The Cook House has a full liquor license. Open from 11 a.m. to 10 p.m. Sunday through Thursday, to 11 p.m. on Friday and Saturday.

Juneau's best Italian food may be served downstairs at **Luna's,** 210 Seward St. (tel. 586-6990), where even grownups are provided crayons to scribble on their butcher-paper tablecloths over the lunch hour. That lunch might be minestrone with Luna's famous homemade bread ($3.50), pasta (from $6.50) or pizza (from $11), or something more international, like Thai beef salad ($7.50) or Japanese udon with shrimp and chicken ($8). Dinners—chicken, steak, veal, or fresh seafood—run $12 to $18, including soup or salad, bread, vegetable, and pasta. Lighter eaters can get calzone (from $8) or a pasta entree (from $9). Gelato and espresso top off the meal. Wine and beer are served. Open from 11 a.m. to 9:30 p.m. Monday through Friday, with dinner from 5 p.m., and 5 to 9:30 p.m. on Saturday; closed Sunday.

For standard Chinese and American fare amid sometimes heated political "discussions" between customers, try **Taguchi's Fine Chow,** at 258 S. Franklin St. (tel. 586-3889). Combination dinners, priced at $8.25 to $9.50, include wonton soup, sweet-and-sour pork or ribs, chow mein, and more. Tempura and sukiyaki dishes, as well as seafood and hamburger steak, are in the same price range, but you can't wash them down with a beer because Taguchi's is unlicensed. Open from 6 a.m. to 8:30 p.m. daily except Sunday.

You can also find Asian food, along with usual American offerings, at the **City Café**, 439 S. Franklin St. (tel. 586-4180), an old Juneau standby. Breakfasts start at $3.50, daily lunch specials are $5.25, and a Chinese-Filipino combination dinner, perhaps including Mongolian beef and pork adobo, costs around $15. The City Café is licensed for wine and beer and is open 24 hours in summer, 6 a.m. to 10 p.m. daily in winter.

South Franklin has two friendly spots to satisfy lovers of hot, spicy Mexican food. **El Sombrero**, 157 S. Franklin St. (tel. 586-6770), is of course extensively decorated with a variety of sombreros. It has two-item combination dinners (enchilada and chile relleno, for instance) for $7 and full three-item dinners (including complimentary chips) for $10. Carta Blanca and Dos Equis are on the beer menu. Open from 11 a.m. to 10 p.m. Monday through Saturday, plus 4 to 10 p.m. on Sunday in summer (closed Sunday in winter).

Chips and salsa are free with all meals at the **Armadillo Tex-Mex Café**, 431 S. Franklin St. (tel. 586-1880), where you place counter orders beneath the casual glances of armadillo miniatures. Prices range from $4.75 for a bowl of Texas chili to $14 for a large order of barbecued ribs with potato salad, beans, and cornbread. Or you can build your own fajita—a gourmet steak taco—for $10. Once a month or so there's a comedy night featuring local talent. Mexican import beers are only $1.50 between 4 and 6 p.m. Open from 11 a.m. to 9 p.m. Monday through Saturday. Sunday brunch, with jalapeño and chorizo sausage omelets, is served from 9:30 a.m. to 5 p.m.

The **New Orpheum Café**, 245 Marine Way (tel. 463-5655), has taken over where the late lamented New Orpheum Theater left off. Foreign and vintage films are no longer shown at this counterculture center, but the espresso bar and café still have a '60s coffeehouse atmosphere. It's a place to look at art exhibits and listen to classical music while perusing reading material such as *Rolling Stone*. Light lunches are served weekdays from 11:30 a.m. to 2 p.m., desserts and quiches at all times: 11 a.m. to midnight Sunday to Thursday, until 1 a.m. Friday and Saturday.

For pizza, the place to go is **Bullwinkle's**, near the State Office Building at 318 Willoughby Ave. East (tel. 586-2400). Prices run $9 to $17. For a bargain, come on Friday night when imported beers are $1.50. Open from 11 a.m. to midnight Monday through Thursday, to 1 a.m. on Friday and Saturday, and from noon to midnight on Sunday. Try to ignore the blips and blurps from the bleeping video machines.

Two excellent salmon bakes just outside downtown offer bus service from major hotels. **Thane Ore House**, four miles south of town at 4400 Thane Rd. (tel. 586-3442), serves all-you-can-eat salmon, halibut, or barbecued ribs for $15 in a replica of a 19th-century miners' mess hall near the tailings of the old Alaska-Gastineau mine. You can pan for gold or see an exhibit of historic photos and artifacts. Open May 15 to October 15 from noon to 9:30 p.m. daily.

The **Gold Creek Salmon Bake** (tel. 586-1424), near the site of Harris's and Juneau's first gold discovery, is at the end of Basin Road east of the city. You get all the alder-smoked salmon, salad, bread, and lemonade you can consume for $19 (kids pay half price), and your first beer is free. Open June 1 to September 15 from 5:30 to 9 p.m. nightly. From here you can take a short hike to explore the remnants of the Alaska-Juneau Mining Company, now incorporated in the Last Chance Basin Historic District. (Pick up a walking tour brochure at the Juneau Douglas City Museum.)

Mendenhall Valley

A country favorite in the valley is **Grandma's Farmhouse Restaurant**, 2358 Mendenhall Loop Rd. (tel. 789-5566). You'll really feel like you're in grandma's house, with calico patterns on cushions and armchairs, and antique toys mounted on shelves. Dinners, from $12 to $17, include salad bar, homemade soup, vegetable, potato, and bread; the 14-ounce prime rib is a favorite. Luncheon sandwiches are $5 to $7, and a huge Petersburg shrimp Louie is $9.50. The bakery sells fresh bread and pastries, while a gift shop specializes in quilts and country handcrafts. Grandma's is open for breakfast and lunch from 7 a.m. to 3 p.m. weekdays, from 8 a.m. on weekends (including Sunday brunch). Dinner is served Sunday through Thursday from 5 to 9 p.m., to 10 p.m. on Friday and Saturday. Grandma's is licensed for wine and beer only.

Canton House, in the Capital Plaza Building at 8588 Old Dairy Rd. (tel. 789-5075), is probably Juneau's most authentic Chinese restaurant. Traditional, melodic Far Eastern music filters through trailing ivy draped over chandeliers. The simple blue-and-white color scheme and rattan-backed chairs are in stark contrast to the tendency of many Chinese restaurants to overdecorate in gaudy hues. Here the food does the talking. Cantonese and Szechuan are the featured cuisines, with entrees priced from $7.50 (almond chicken) to $16 (sliced abalone in black-bean sauce). If there are quite a few of you, you can order a nine-course family-style dinner ($13.50 per person) with crispy duck, Four Happiness, and Sam Sing in the Nest. Lunch specials ($5.25 per person) include your choice of two items (such as egg foo yung and chicken chow mein) plus soup, rice, and tea. On weekends there's an all-you-can-eat brunch. Open from 11:30 a.m. to 10 p.m. Monday through Thursday, to 11 p.m. on Friday, and from 10:30 a.m. to 10 p.m. on Saturday and Sunday.

Two of Juneau's classier Mexican restaurants are here in the valley. **Fernando's,** 9200 Glacier Hwy. at the Airport TraveLodge (tel. 789-3636), has great salads (the ensalada suprema has shrimp, two types of cheese, eggs, tomato, avocado, and lettuce on a tortilla shell) and full dinners (try the enchiladas suizas) in the $10 range. It also has a popular cantina. Open daily from 6 a.m. to 10 p.m.; Sunday brunch is on from 10 a.m. to 2 p.m.

Jovany's, 9121 Glacier Hwy. (tel. 789-2339), serves Italian and Greek food in generous portions. There are all-you-can-eat spaghetti and pizza specials ($4 from 5 to 8 p.m. daily), fish-and-chips lunches from $5, prime-rib dinners from $10. Open from 11 a.m. to 11 p.m. Monday through Thursday, to midnight on Friday, from 4 p.m. to midnight on Saturday, and 2 to 11 p.m. on Sunday.

The **Vintage Fare Café,** in the Nugget Mall (tel. 789-1865), boasts the only espresso bar in the Mendenhall Valley. Shoppers and others like its soups, salads, sandwiches, and desserts. Daily breakfast specials are priced under $3, and lunch specials under $5. Open from 9 a.m. to 8 p.m. Monday through Friday, 9 a.m. to 6 p.m. on Saturday, and 11 a.m. to 5 p.m. on Sunday.

Douglas

No restaurant in Juneau has survived longer than **Mike's,** 1120 2nd St. (tel. 364-3271). Mike Pusich opened his original Douglas saloon in 1914 and—except for the years of Prohibition (when he survived by selling clothes and groceries)—it has been going strong ever since. A 1937 fire destroyed the Dreamland nightclub, as it was known; but Mike's Place soon reappeared on the site. That was 50 years ago. Mike's eldest son, Rudy Pusich, took over upon his father's death in 1953 and still holds forth.

As you enter the restaurant, you'll have a chance to study several photos of the early-20th-century boom times of the Treadwell Mine here in Douglas. Then you'll descend the stairs to an elegant room on a hill above the Gastineau Channel. It's quiet during the week, but on weekends a band plays light rock and contemporary standards to dance to. Dinner prices run about $13 to $16, with seafood—especially halibut and Petersburg shrimp—high on the list of suggestions. Lunch specials cost about $5. Open from 11:30 a.m. to 1:30 p.m. and 4 to 10 p.m. daily except Monday.

The informal art deco décor re-creates a later Alaskan era at Douglas's other prime eating establishment, **Beauty and the Feast,** 916 3rd St. (tel. 364-3307). Omelets and burgers are standard fare here, at prices from $6 to $9.25, including soup and salad bar. Open from 1 to 8 p.m. Monday through Friday, 9 a.m. to 8 p.m. on Saturday (breakfast until 3 p.m.), and 10 a.m. to 2 p.m. for Sunday brunch. The restaurant's Billikin Bar does a booming business during Monday Night Football.

WHAT TO SEE AND DO

Juneau's attractions can be divided into two categories—those of the man-made variety, focused in the downtown area, and those of great scenic beauty, including the great Mendenhall Glacier.

The Ruling Class

Just as government and bureaucracy command Juneau's lifestyle and economy, government buildings dominate its skyline. Free tours of the unpretentious **State Capitol Building,** at 4th and Main Streets (tel. 465-3854), are offered every half-hour from 8:30 a.m. to 5 p.m. daily in summer. The governor and members of the legislature have their offices in this building. It is perfectly acceptable during session (January to May) to take a seat in the second-floor visitor's galleries of the Senate or House of Representatives. Built in 1931 as the Federal and Territorial Building, the Capitol's most notable architectural features are the four columns at its entrance, fashioned of marble from Prince of Wales Island. The corridors of the third and fifth floors contain historic photos of early Juneau.

Most Juneau visitors doing government business spend at least some time in the **State Office Building** (tel. 465-2111 for information), indecorously known by some as the "S.O.B." Because of its hillside location, the building has two main entrances. One, the less conspicuous, leads from a Willoughby Avenue parking lot to ground-floor elevators; another, off 4th Street opposite the Capitol Building, provides direct access to the eighth floor. Casual visitors should head straight for the eighth-floor Grand Court, where brown-bag lunch concerts are presented at noon every Friday on a fully restored 548-pipe theater organ. A century-old Haida totem pole called the "Old Witch" towers above. Inveterate readers will find the State Library and Alaska Historical Library on this floor.

A short distance uphill from the State Office Building is the **Governor's Mansion,** at 716 Calhoun Ave. Although this impressive white colonial-style structure can be seen high on a hill from most locations in downtown Juneau, it can't be visited by drop-in individuals except during an annual one-day open house in the week before Christmas. If you happen to be around, you'll be impressed by the well-kept original period furnishings dating from the time of the house's construction in 1912.

Perhaps the greatest statesman of Alaska's territorial era was Judge James Wickersham. Historian and anthropologist, mountaineer and environmentalist, congressman and federal judge, he did much to establish the credibility of rough-and-ready Alaska in the eyes of Washington, D.C., 5,000 miles distant. Wickersham died in 1939, but today his Juneau home—the **House of Wickersham,** 213 7th St. (tel. 586-9001)—is a state historic site. Now operated by the State Division of Parks, it holds a remarkable private collection of Native, Russian, and pioneer artifacts, books, and documents, including the judge's 47-volume handwritten diary. It is open from noon to 5 p.m. daily except Saturday, June through August; other times by appointment. A donation is requested.

The Museums

An essential stop is the two-story **Alaska State Museum,** on Whittier Street just north of Egan Drive (tel. 465-2901), where you can develop an understanding of Alaskan history, from ancient to modern. On the first floor are extensive displays of Native artifacts and lifestyles. As you climb a spiral ramp to the second floor, you'll circle a museum highlight, complete with sound effects: a family of eagles in their aerie high atop a tree, with brown bears resting at its foot. Exploration, Russian heritage, Alaska purchase, gold mining, maritime history, and the Alaska pipeline are featured on the upper floor. There's also a gift shop and rooms for temporary exhibitions. Open in summer from 9 a.m. to 6 p.m. weekdays, 10 a.m. to 6 p.m. weekends; in winter from 10 a.m. to 4 p.m. Tuesday through Saturday. Admission is $1.

The **Juneau-Douglas City Museum,** now permanently located at 114 W. 4th St., at Main Street (tel. 586-3572), has historical exhibits that emphasize the local mining industry, including lifestyles and working conditions. The museum also has a gallery of changing community exhibits from all over Alaska, and a hands-on Discovery Room for children. Brochures will start you on self-guided walking tours of the Juneau Historic District, totem poles, the Treadwell Mine, and Last Chance Basin. There's a small research library and video theater, as well as a gift shop. Open June to mid-September from 10 a.m. to 5 p.m. weekdays, 11 a.m. to 5 p.m. weekends; the remainder of the year, noon to 4:30 p.m. Monday and Thursday through Saturday. Closed during January and February. Donations are requested.

A Walking Tour

A tour of downtown Juneau attractions suggested by the folks at the Davis Log Cabin (see the "Orientation" section, above) begins in the relaxed waterfront atmosphere of Marine Park, where cruise-ship passengers arrive. Across Egan Drive in the **Municipal Building,** the assembly chambers contain an 8- by 50-foot photomural of the Mendenhall Glacier.

The **People's Wharf** neighborhood along South Franklin Street is Juneau's most historic district. Through the first half of this century it was the focus of commerce, with its municipal wharf, sawmill, and gold mill, and its entertainment, including bars, pool halls, and a red-light district. Many turn-of-the-century buildings remain. In 1986 their proud tenants launched a long-term project aimed at full renovation of the district as a tourist attraction. Building plaques have been designed to explain how ladies of the evening flaunted their wares from "cigar store" display windows between the 1920s and 1950s, and how police visited such dens of iniquity as the Occidental Bar, known to locals as the "Bucket of Blood," to hand unruly patrons one-way "blue tickets" to the next boat out of town.

The new **Juneau City Library** opened in 1989 atop a five-story parking garage at South Franklin Street and Admiralty Way. From the top there's a panoramic view across the Gastineau Channel to Douglas Island.

Several blocks north is **St. Nicholas Russian Orthodox Church,** 326 5th St. (tel. 586-1023), the oldest original Orthodox church building in southeast Alaska. The tiny (20-foot diameter) octagonal structure was erected in 1894. Priceless icons and church treasures, some dating to the 18th century, adorn the walls. Open changing hours daily, mid-May through September; other times by appointment. If you're interested in standing through services (remember, there are no pews in an Orthodox church), you can attend vespers at 7 p.m. on Saturday or divine liturgy at 10 a.m. on Sunday.

One of the most impressive of the city's several totem poles is visible from the church. If you can "read" the 45-foot **Four Story Totem,** a Haida pole carved in 1940, it will tell you about a monster frog, a bear with a fish trap, a shaman who captured an otter, and an octopus and halibut. It's in a park block at 6th and Seward Streets.

For history diehards, the graves of city founders Joe Juneau and Richard Harris, as well as the Tlingit chief Kowee who led them here, are in **Evergreen Cemetery,** on the west side of 12th Street near B Street. Juneau actually died in the Klondike and Harris in a sanitarium in Oregon, but their bodies were returned here for burial. There's a **monument** to them where Glacier Avenue crosses Gold Creek east of the **Federal Building,** at Glacier and 9th Street. In the Fed, by the way, the Bureau of Indian Affairs has created a fine Native arts display outside its third-floor offices.

Mendenhall Glacier

If you have time to see just one attraction in Juneau, make it the Mendenhall Glacier. There are certainly bigger, more majestic glaciers in Alaska, but none is as accessible as the Mendenhall. In fact thousands of Juneau residents have built their houses in the broad valley this glacier occupied little more than two centuries ago.

The **Mendenhall Glacier Visitor Center,** P.O. Box 2097, Juneau, AK 99803 (tel. 907/789-0097), overlooks the foot of the glacier where it drops 100 feet into icy Mendenhall Lake. Here you can observe what makes this and other glaciers what they are—perpetually moving rivers of ice, flowing from alpine terrain where they are fed by a continual supply of snow. Conditions of high overcast are ideal for glacier-watching because they bring out the cobalt blues of recently exposed, condensed ice, but the sight can be fascinating anytime.

The Mendenhall Glacier is located about five miles inland from Juneau Airport. In 1750 it was only about 2½ miles from the coast of the Gastineau Channel. But long-term climatic trends and other factors create cycles of glacial advance and retreat. The half mile of bedrock between the visitor center and the glacial face, in fact, has all been exposed since 1940. Several well-marked trails provide a rare opportunity to study natural transition in an unusual ecological habitat. Tongass National Forest naturalists regularly lead interpretive walks on these trails in summer.

The visitor center is open from 9 a.m. to 6:30 p.m. daily in summer (May to September), 10 a.m. to 4 p.m. on Saturday and Sunday only in winter. Its facilities include scale models of the glacier, one of them a cross-section, and an audio-visual room where films and slide shows are presented.

You can only see the foot of the Mendenhall Glacier from the visitor center. To fully appreciate its 12-mile length and 1½-mile girth you've got to board a plane or helicopter and hover over—or better yet, land on—the **Juneau Icefield.** At an elevation of 5,000 to 6,000 feet, it's about 1,500 square miles in area, larger than the state of Rhode Island. One hundred feet of snow falls each year, enough to nourish 36 glaciers.

Outstanding air tours of Mendenhall Glacier and the Juneau Icefield are offered by **Temsco Helicopters,** 1873 Shell Simmons Dr. (tel. 789-9501). The 45-minute, $115 Mendenhall Glacier Tour and the 75-minute, $189 Glacier Explorer both provide passengers with an opportunity to disembark onto the glacial ice. There you'll be met by professional glaciologists who will warn you that glacial crevasses are akin to river rapids and many times more dangerous: don't go leap-frogging. Heli-tours at similar rates are also offered by Anchorage-based **ERA Helicopters,** 6910 N. Douglas Hwy. (tel. 586-2030). Seeing a glacier in this way is a humbling experience, an unforgettable memory. I highly recommend it.

Another way to experience the glacier's output is to take a river-rafting trip, dodging small icebergs in Mendenhall Lake and floating down the Mendenhall River toward the sea. Exciting but certainly not perilous, these trips are operated daily May through September by **Alaska Travel Adventures,** 9085 Glacier Hwy. (tel. 789-0052). The price is $65 for adults, $40 for children 12 and under.

The tidal lands and estuaries at the end of the glacial valley, surrounding the airport and on both sides of the Gastineau Channel, have been designated the **Mendenhall Wetlands Refuge.** Principally a habitat for waterfowl and migratory birds, it also attracts numerous small mammals like muskrats. Bald eagles and bears are common visitors during salmon-spawning season. The refuge is administered by the Alaska Department of Fish and Game. There are six public access points to the refuge, including three along Egan Drive between downtown Juneau and the Mendenhall Valley. Wear rubber boots.

Auke Bay

The Auke Bay neighborhood, just northwest of the Mendenhall Valley and north of Douglas Island, is built around a busy public boat harbor and serene Auke Lake. The small **University of Alaska Southeast** (tel. 789-4458), a branch of the state institution (with headquarters in Fairbanks), opened its lakefront campus in 1971. Nearby, the United Presbyterian church's **Chapel by the Lake** (tel. 789-7592), constructed of spruce logs in 1958, has a picture window with a stunning view across Auke Lake to Mendenhall Glacier. Volunteers will show you around during the summer or you're welcome to attend Sunday services, at 8:30 and 10 a.m. in summer, 9:30 and 11 a.m. the rest of the year. **Auke Bay Fisheries Laboratory** (tel. 789-7231), a joint venture of UAS and the National Marine Fisheries Service, is on the bay at Mile 12 on Glacier Hwy.; visitors enjoy its saltwater aquarium.

The Alaska Marine Hwy. ferry terminal is on the north side of Auke Bay at Mile 14 on Glacier Hwy. A mile farther, **Auke Village Recreation Area** marks the original site of the Auk Tlingit winter village with a beach, picnic area, and campground. The unusual Yax-te totem pole with its raven crest was a 1941 gift to the Auk clan from Tlingits on Prince of Wales Island. Don't return to town until you've driven out to Mile 23, where the memorable Roman Catholic **Shrine of St. Therese** sits among trees on an island connected to the mainland by a quarter-mile causeway. Hand-hewn from rock by a Jesuit priest in 1938, the picturesque chapel, open daily, is a popular location for weddings. The site is worth a visit if only to sit on the rocks and watch local fishermen casting their lines while marine mammals and birds play offshore.

Douglas Island

There are only about 21 miles of road on Douglas Island, and they are without the attractions of the mainland. The town of Douglas is pleasant but unremarkable, with few surviving remnants of the great Treadwell mine. The best reason to go to Douglas Island in summer used to be a visit to Eaglecrest, a winter ski resort that once offered daily trips up its mile-long chair lift to spectacular views and a self-guiding nature trail through alpine meadows at 3,000 feet. Summer trips have been halted, and as of this writing, there are no plans to start them again.

Sports

FISHING Dozens of sport-fishing charters operate out of Juneau. The **Juneau Sportfishing Association** (tel. 586-1887, or toll free 800/544-2244) can make all arrangements for you. Or ask the folks at the Davis Log Cabin (see the "Orientation" section, above) to provide you a list of local charter operators. Expect to pay $100 per person for a half day, $150 for a full-day (eight-hour) charter. The best fishing coincides with the May-to-September tourist season, when all five salmon species plus halibut, cutthroat, steelhead, and Dolly Varden thrive. Most freshwater lakes and streams are fertile grounds for salmon and trout, the latter even in winter when ice fishing is popular.

The **Alaska Department of Fish and Game,** 802 3rd St., Douglas (tel. 907/465-4270), has a weekly fishing report line: call 465-4116. You can obtain a license from most charter operators, from the **Department of Revenue,** 1170 W. 8th St., Juneau, AK 99801 (tel. 907/465-2376), or from sporting goods dealers like **Ace Hardware,** 205 Front St. (tel. 586-2920), or **Orsi's Custom Rods & Tackle,** 4445 Mendenhall Rd. (tel. 789-3537). If you prefer not to book with a charter operator but to rent a skiff and motor instead, check **Auke Bay Marine** at the Auke Bay Boat Harbor (tel. 789-2913).

The **Golden North Salmon Derby,** held over three days in early or mid-August, has been staged annually since 1947. There was $106,000 in prizes last year! The biggest-ever winner weighed in at more than 59 pounds; the smallest, barely under 30 pounds. If you're a potential contestant, call the Territorial Sportsmen (tel. 789-2399).

Among the many wilderness hunting and fishing lodges in the Juneau area is the **Taku Glacier Lodge,** 2 Marine Way, Suite 228, Juneau, AK 99801 (tel. 907/586-1362), 30 air miles east near the top end of the Taku Inlet. The lodge, open May 15 to October 1, has six units with private baths, and holds a daily salmon bake. Three-hour flight tours over the Juneau Icefield, which include a salmon bake at the Taku Lodge, can also be arranged. **Adlersheim Lodge,** on the Lynn Canal 35 miles north of Juneau, is directly accessible by road via the Glacier Hwy. Six-day all-inclusive summer fishing packages start at $1,400. Full-board winter rates are $60 nightly. Contact P.O. Box 210447, Auke Bay, AK 99821 (tel. 907/780-4778). Other lodges on Admiralty and Chichagof Islands will be mentioned later in this chapter. There are 36 primitive U.S. Forest Service **cabins** in the Juneau Ranger District of Tongass National Forest, available by reservation for $15 a night. Visit the Forest Service at the Centennial Building or call 586-8751 for information.

HUNTING   Sitka black-tailed deer and waterfowl are the most highly sought species. Black and brown bears, mountain goats, moose, and wolves are also tracked. Many charter boats and air services serve the needs of hunters. Check regulations with the **Alaska Department of Fish and Game,** Game Division, P.O. Box 3-2000, Juneau, AK 99802 (tel. 907/465-4190). A professional guide must accompany nonresidents on bear hunts. You can obtain a list of registered guides by writing the Division of Occupational Licensing, Guide Licensing and Control Board, P.O. Box D, Juneau, AK 99811 (tel. 907/465-2542).

HIKING   Every hiker's first step should be through the doors of the Centennial Building to the U.S. Forest Service information office. There, ask to purchase the 61-page "Juneau Trails" guide, a bargain at $2. If you're in reasonably good shape, a popular hike is the steep climb up 3,665-foot **Gastineau Peak** (2¾ miles), continuing to 3,820-foot **Mount Roberts** (4½ miles). It begins up a wooden stairway at the end of 6th Street in downtown Juneau. At the end of Gold Creek Basin, you can retrace the steps of Joe Juneau and Richard Harris up the 3½-mile **Perseverance Trail** to several old mining excavations. Another 25 trails are detailed in "Juneau Trails." Remember that the weather can change quickly, and bears can be encountered on any trail. Be prepared.

Guided hikes are offered by **Alaska Rainforest Treks,** P.O. Box 210845, Auke Bay, AK 99821 (tel. 907/463-3466). The **Juneau Parks and Recreation Department,** 155 S. Seward St. (tel. 586-5226), also conducts free day hikes on Wednesday and Saturday. Visitors are welcome to join.

KAYAKING AND CANOEING   At **Alaska Travel Adventures,** 9085 Glacier Hwy. (tel. 789-0052), you can rent single and two-person kayaks and canoes for $5 an hour, $25 to $30 a day. The firm also offers numerous canoe and kayak trips of four to seven days in duration, June through August, for $475 to $850—including all meals, equipment, insurance, guide service, and plane or boat charter costs. From Juneau, most trips include Tracy Arm or Admiralty Island. Write or call for a brochure.

SAILING   At least three Juneau charter operators specialize in sailing trips of various lengths and descriptions. Consider the early-evening "Attitude Adjustment

Cruise," priced at $40, offered by **Marine Adventure Sailing Tours**, Aurora Basin D-33 (tel. 789-0919); the "Sunday Brunch and Fishing Sail," at $60, with **Windwalker Charters**, 800 F St., Suite L4 (tel. 586-6569 or 789-7495); and the 8½-day "Week Cruise" to Glacier Bay, Skagway, and Admiralty Island, at $2,000, with **58°22' North Sailing Charters**, Aurora Basin H-6 (tel. 789-7301). American Sailing Association courses, from a basic introduction to bareboat charter, are also offered by 58°22' North.

WINTER SPORTS Alaska's No. 2 winter resort is the **Eaglecrest** ski area on Douglas Island; only Mount Alyeska near Anchorage has more facilities. Eaglecrest has a 1,400-foot vertical drop from its 3,000-foot summit and 640 acres of open bowl, glade, and trail skiing. Two chair lifts (one a mile long) and a platter pull serve 32 trails marked beginner to expert. The day lodge houses a professional ski school and ski patrol, a rental and repair shop, and a snackbar. Depending on snow conditions, the area operates Thanksgiving to mid-April, from 9 a.m. to 4 p.m. Wednesday through Sunday, with night skiing until 7:30 p.m. on Thursday. Full-day all-lift tickets cost $19 for adults, $14 for youth (13 to 17) and seniors, $10 for children. A bus covers the 12 miles from downtown Juneau on weekends and holidays. Eaglecrest has a city office at 155 S. Seward St., Juneau, AK 99801 (tel. 907/586-5284), and recorded up-to-date snow reports on a message phone (tel. 586-5330).

Eaglecrest has six miles of cross-country trails track-set for nordic skiers as conditions warrant. Tickets are $5 for adults, $4 for youth. Other popular no-cost cross-country trails are on Forest Service land. The **Dan Moller Trail** on Douglas Island leads 3.3 miles from West Juneau up Kowee Creek to the Douglas Ski Bowl, where skiers schussed before Eaglecrest opened in 1976. The 3-mile **Spaulding Meadows Trail** at Auke Bay is closed to snowmobiles, while the 3½-mile **Windfall Lake Trail**, beginning at Mile 27 of Glacier Hwy., leads to a lake which attracts ice-fishermen for cutthroat and Dolly Varden. You can rent ski equipment at the **Foggy Mountain Shop**, 171 Shattuck Way (tel. 586-6780).

If you prefer company, you can join a free **Juneau Parks and Recreation Department** cross-country hike on Wednesday or Saturday in winter (tel. 586-5226 for information).

Real adventurous? Contact **Alaska Travel Adventures**, 9085 Glacier Hwy. (tel. 789-0052), about their summer heli-skiing tours on the Juneau Icefield.

OTHER SPORTS The **Juneau Parks and Recreation Department**, 155 S. Seward St. (tel. 586-5226), has an outstanding variety of programs for Juneau residents and visitors. You can go **swimming** every day of the week at the Augustus Brown Pool, 1619 Glacier Ave., next to Juneau Douglas High School (tel. 586-5325). Open times vary, but the pool is normally open for public lap swimming between noon and 1:30 p.m. daily and from 5:30 to 6:30 p.m. weekdays. Adult fees are $2.50 an hour.

The **Juneau Racquet Club**, 2841 Riverside Dr., near the Mendenhall Shopping Center (tel. 789-2181), has racquetball courts, four full-size tennis courts, basketball and badminton courts, an aerobics room, saunas, and whirlpools. By paying a guest fee, out-of-town visitors are entitled to use club facilities. There are outdoor **tennis courts** at Cope Park near downtown, at Adair-Kennedy Park in the valley, and at Robert Savikko Recreation Area in Douglas. The last also has a jogging track and an unusual (for southeast Alaska) sandy beach.

Inquire at the Log Cabin Information Center about possible bicycle rentals. There were none in Juneau at this writing. If you can obtain a bicycle, a 15-mile bike path running all the way to the Mendenhall Glacier begins near the Federal Building at 12th Street and Glacier Avenue.

Contacts for other sports: body-building, **Southeast Body Building Gym,** 5720 Glacier Hwy. (tel. 780-4800); bowling, **Channel Bowl,** 608 Willoughby Ave. West (tel. 586-1165); diving, **Scuba Crafts,** 4485 N. Douglas Hwy. (tel. 586-2341); golf, **Mendenhall Golf** (9 holes, par 3), 2101 Industrial Dr. (tel. 789-7323); indoor golf, **Par-T-Golf,** 5459 Shaune Dr. (tel. 780-6986); and shooting, **Hank Harmon Memorial Rifle Range,** 6200 Montana Creek Rd. (tel. 789-5920).

Tours

The "Big Three" of Alaska tourism all are busy in Juneau from mid-May through September. Packages offered by **Gray Line of Alaska,** 127 N. Franklin St., in the Westmark-Baranof Hotel (tel. 586-3773 or 586-9625); **Alaska Sightseeing Tours,** 51 W. Egan Dr., in the Westmark Juneau (tel. 586-6300); and **Royal Highway Tours** (tel. 463-3900) are comparable. All, for example, offer a two-hour Mendenhall Glacier–Auke Bay tour priced at $21 ($10.50 for children under 12). Times may vary slightly, but there are always morning and afternoon departures. Gray Line also has a two-hour city tour for $16.50 ($8.25 for children), while Alaska Sightseeing has a glacier tour for $20 ($10 for children), including the Shrine of St. Therese.

The itineraries of locally owned tour companies may be more appealing. **Alaska Up Close,** P.O. Box 32666, Juneau, AK 99803 (tel. 907/789-9544), and **German Connection Fototour,** P.O. Box 32925, Juneau, AK 99803 (tel. 907/780-4911), jointly operate a three-hour Mendenhall Glacier and city sightseeing tour for $25, and three-hour Juneau and Douglas Island nature photo tours for $49 including lunch, with departures at 9 a.m. and 2 p.m. **Mendenhall Glacier Transport,** P.O. Box 21594, Juneau, AK 99802 (tel. 907/789-5460), meets cruise passengers dockside to offer a 2½-hour city tour (including 30 minutes at the glacier) for $9. Its other tours include a visit to the Chinook Brewery ($15) and a meal at the Thane Ore House salmon bake ($25).

Alaska Travel Adventures offers a 90-minute Orelove Brothers historic tour hearkening back to the gold-rush era for $25. A prospector-guide leads the trip through the historic district to the Alaska-Juneau Mine site, where participants are given gold-panning lessons in Gold Creek. Book at 9085 Glacier Hwy. (tel. 789-0052).

SHOPPING

It seems as though half the storefronts on historic South Franklin Street are gift shops selling Alaskan souvenirs made in Taiwan. Take time to browse and spend your money cautiously. One outstanding shop in this area is **Objects of Bright Pride,** 165 S. Franklin St. (tel. 586-4969), which displays exclusive museum-quality works by Native and non-Native artisans—and prices them accordingly. **Golden Jade,** 240 S. Franklin St., **Latitude 58,** 170 S. Franklin St., and **George's Gift Shop,** 194 S. Franklin St., have a good selection of standard gift items at reasonable prices.

Many fine artists make their homes in the Juneau area. Among the best known is Rie Munoz, whose colorful paintings and murals with Native Alaskan themes can be found in galleries, museums, and commercial establishments all over the southeast and elsewhere around the state. The **Rie Munoz Gallery** is near Marine Park at 210 Ferry Way (tel. 586-1212). **Kaill Fine Crafts/Gallery** on Front Street has an especially fine collection of limited-edition prints by Alaskan artists John Fehringer and Byron Birdsall. **Artists' Cove Gallery,** 291 S. Franklin St. (tel. 463-3771), and **Deroux Terzis** in Merchant's Wharf, 14 Marine Way (tel. 463-3349), have outstanding contemporary collections. **Roy Windfree,** 289 S. Franklin St. (tel. 463-3909), has a unique studio/gallery featuring elaborate paper sculpture.

If your plans don't take you to Sitka, you can get a taste of Russia at the **Russian Shop,** on the second floor of the Senate Building at 175 S. Franklin St. Here you can find a wide selection of Orthodox religious icons, lacquer boxes, samovars, stacking

Matrushka dolls, and other items. In the same building, on the first floor, is the **Christmas Store,** merchandiser of specialty Alaskan ornaments and other gifts.

If you need film or camera repair, visit **Southeast Exposure,** at 216 2nd St. **Big City Books,** 100 N. Franklin St. (across from the Baranof Hotel), and **Hearthside Books,** with shops at 254 Front St. and in the Nugget Mall, Mendenhall Valley, are Juneau's only bookstores.

A unique Alaskan gift is fresh or smoked salmon. Several firms can ship it home for you, including the **Salmon Shoppe,** 201 S. Franklin St. Check at the Davis Log Cabin (see the "Orientation" section, above) for other suggestions.

CULTURE AND NIGHTLIFE

If you think of Juneau as a wild-and-woolly town in terms of nightlife, you're right. But you'd be just as right to call it a cultural oasis.

Nearly every visitor sooner or later ducks his or her head into the **Red Dog Saloon,** 278 S. Franklin St. (tel. 463-3777). The sawdust floor, bearskins, and collection of old firearms—including a gun that Wyatt Earp supposedly deposited for safekeeping in the 1880s and never returned to pick up—are straight out of the last century. There's frequently live music, including small rock combos, blues, and Alaskan bush balladry, but mainly this is just a friendly main-street saloon. Add your business card to the thousands of others tacked, pinned, or stapled to the wall. Like most Alaskan bars, the Red Dog opens at 11 a.m. and doesn't close until 2 in the morning.

If the Red Dog is typical of the miners' turn-of-the-century watering holes, then the **Alaskan Hotel & Bar,** next door at 167 S. Franklin St. (tel. 586-1000), was where the privileged class drank. Many of them still swap pleasantries here today. Reminiscent of a bygone era, this lounge is truly elegant, with its upholstered furnishings, stained wood and brass décor, imitation stained glass, upstairs balcony, and long bar. The piano is 19th century, but the beautiful Wurlitzer and big-screen television are admittedly of more recent vintage. Live entertainment is featured on a new stage.

The place to see and be seen in Juneau at this writing is **The Penthouse,** on the top floor of the Senate Building at 175 S. Franklin St. (tel. 586-5656). A huge ballroom divided into two sections—a disco dance floor with an enormous video screen, and a four-sided bar surrounded by high stools—the Penthouse is frankly un-Alaskan: it's a place where you dress to impress. Special events like singles auctions are sometimes held here.

Elsewhere downtown, you'll find a light rock combo playing dance music at **The Diggings** in the Prospector Hotel; a lounge singer in the Westmark-Juneau's **Woodcarver Room;** and a piano bar in the Baranof Hotel's **Bubble Room.** There's also a proliferation of skid-row bars along South Franklin and Front Streets—you'll quickly recognize them by the inebriated locals stumbling as they exit. If you *must* absorb some of this local flavor, the **Triangle Club,** 251 Front St., is the most infamous.

Out in the Mendenhall Valley, where half of Juneau's population makes its home, there are a few more lounges. **The Sandbar,** 2055 Jordan Ave. (tel. 789-3411), is Juneau's best blue-collar country-western venue, with Stetson-hatted musicians playing most nights and occasional strip shows during the after-work happy hour. The **Landing Strip Lounge,** 9121 Glacier Hwy. (tel. 789-2820), is a neighborhood "meet-market" where young construction workers are loath to stop playing pool or take off their pipeline hats to dance with bored secretaries to a live hardrock band.

Performing Arts

If you like live theater, or even if you don't, you'll enjoy the melodramatic **Lady Lou Revue** staged mid-May through mid-September in the Elks Hall at 109 N. Franklin St. Based on a pair of Robert Service ballads, "The Shooting of Dan

McGrew" and "The Cremation of Sam McGee," this rollicking 75-minute show re-creates some of the romance and excitement of the 1898 Klondike Gold Rush. There are shows at 2 and 8 p.m. almost daily; admission is $10 (children pay $5).

The *Lady Lou Revue* is a production of the **Perseverance Theater,** a nationally respected professional company which has toured to New York, France, and Guam, as well as throughout Alaska. Between September and May the company stages five separate productions, each for four-week runs, at its 150-seat theater, 914 3rd St., Douglas (tel. 364-2421). Productions range from Shakespeare to Tennessee Williams to Theater of the Absurd during the 1988–89 season. Inquire at Big City Books or Hearthside Books (see the "Shopping" section, above) for tickets and schedule information. Performances are on Thursday, Friday, and Saturday at 8 p.m., with Sunday matinees at 2 p.m.

The **Juneau Arts and Humanities Council,** 206 N. Franklin St. (tel. 586-ARTS), presents an annual winter-spring concert season which in the past has included jazz artists such as Dizzy Gillespie, dance troupes like the Theatre Ballet of Canada, and European performers like the Vienna Choir Boys and the Warsaw Philharmonic Orchestra. The council can also inform you of the activities of other local performing arts groups, such as the **Juneau-Douglas Little Theater** and the **Juneau International Folkdancers.** And they can tell you about a Juneau-based nonprofit organization called **Cama'i,** involved in a cross-cultural exchange program with Soviet Siberia.

If you're in the mood for a movie, the **20th Century Theater,** 222 Front St. (tel. 586-4055), and **Glacier Cinema,** 3303 Mendenhall Loop Rd. (tel. 789-9191), both have twin theaters showing first-run movies nightly, with weekend matinees.

The *Juneau Empire*'s Friday "Preview" section includes a calendar of arts, entertainment, gallery exhibits, and special events in the Juneau area for the following week.

SHORT TRIPS FROM JUNEAU

One voyage most visitors thoroughly enjoy is a trip south down the Stephens Passage to **Tracy Arm,** a long, finger-like fjord 50 miles from Juneau. The inlet, contained within the Tracy Arm–Fords Terror Wilderness Area, is fed by spectacular glaciers and is a good place to spot seals, whales, and porpoises. **Phillips' Cruises and Tours,** 76 Egan Dr., Suite 130 (tel. 907/463-5310), includes a seafood dinner and cocktails in its six-hour "Glacier Express" itinerary for $79 (children pay $39) plus tax. Many of the larger tour companies book their clients on these tours, which are available from mid-May through mid-September.

Nature cruises to Tracy Arm, Sitka, and Elfin Cove are offered by **Alaska Naturalist and Photography Tours,** 9951 Sprucewood Park, No. 47, Juneau, AK 99801 (tel. 907/789-7429), for $95 to $175 per person per day.

If you plan to head north from Juneau to Skagway, consider Westours' **Lynn Canal Tour** aboard the *Fairweather.* The 4½-hour cruise, offered mid-May to mid-September, is available one way ($119) or round trip ($179), with return to Juneau via air. Note that the ferry makes the same Juneau–Skagway trip, without the luxury frills, for $18 one way.

Admiralty Island

Admiralty Island National Monument, encompassing all but a small northern spur of the 1,709-square-mile island across Stephens Passage from Douglas Island, preserves the land Tlingit Indians know as Xootsnoowu ("hoots-new-woo")—the Fortress of Bears. On densely forested Admiralty Island the huge Alaskan brown bear outnumbers its most dangerous foe, man. Some naturalists estimate, in fact, that there is one bear per square mile of land area. A great variety of other wildlife also populates this pristine wilderness.

The U.S. Forest Service, while discouraging overuse of the fragile ecosystem, has improved access to the island's natural wonders by creating the **Admiralty Lakes**

Recreation Area, 110,000 acres accessible by canoe or kayak on lakes, rivers, and portages. Seven primitive Forest Service cabins, out of 16 on the island, are within the recreation area. They must be reserved in advance (at $15 a night) by visiting the Forest Service at Juneau's Centennial Building or writing P.O. Box 2097, Juneau, AK 99803. Access is generally by small-plane charter from Juneau. Visitors are warned that the risks of bear attack, exposure to storms, and geographical disorientation are very real on Admiralty Island.

Within the recreation area is the **Thayer Lake Wilderness Lodge,** perhaps the best known of several fishing lodges on the island. Located about 50 air miles due south of Juneau, it offers all meals and lodging plus fully guided lake and stream trout fishing for $130 per day (children 3 to 8 pay half price), two-day minimum, transportation not included. Private cabins are also available at $90 (with a wood stove) and $105 (with a gas stove) per day. Contact the lodge at P.O. Box 211614, Juneau, AK 99821 (tel. 907/789-5646) or P.O. Box 5416, Ketchikan, AK 99901 (tel. 907/225-3343).

Whalers' Cove Sport Fishing Lodge in Killisnoo Harbor at Angoon, about ten air miles south of Thayer Lake, accommodates up to 24 guests in 11 units, including five beachfront cabins. They're served by a fleet of charter boats. The spacious lodge also has a lounge and hot tub. All-inclusive package rates, including full board and daily guided fishing trips, are $2,495 per person for seven days and seven nights. For more information: P.O. Box 101, Angoon, AK 99820 (tel. 907/788-3123, or toll free 800/423-3123).

A third lodge, at Funter Bay on the northwest edge of Admiralty Island, is the **Admiralty Inn,** which serves a maximum of eight people interested in salmon and halibut fishing, crabbing, and photography. Rates start at $1,750 for five nights, with discounts for early booking. Contact the lodge at 1414 Mary Ellen Way, Juneau, AK 99801 (tel. 907/789-3263).

There's only one town on Admiralty Island, the Tlingit village of **Angoon** (pop. about 640). The ferry *LeConte* stops here twice a week; otherwise transportation is by floatplane or charter boat. Angoon is situated on the west coast of the island at the mouth of scenic but turbulent Kootznahoo Inlet, a maze of wooded islets, reefs, and channels that leads to Mitchell Bay and the cross-Admiralty canoe trail. Salmon fishing supplements subsistence hunting and gathering (shellfish, seaweed, and berries) to support the population in this most traditional of Tlingit communities in southeast Alaska. Angoon means "village on the beaver trail."

If you intend to stay in Angoon, a bed-and-breakfast establishment called the **Favorite Bay Inn,** P.O. Box 101, Angoon, AK 99820 (tel. 907/788-3123, or toll free 800/423-3123), will accommodate you for $49 single, $59 double. The owners operate a booking service for guides and transportation services. There is also a small motel: the **Kootznahoo Inlet Lodge,** P.O. Box 134, Angoon, AK 99820 (tel. 907/788-3501), with a dining room and 11 units including six kitchenettes priced at $56 single, $66 double. Local tax is 2%. You'll find a public **campground** near the ferry landing, three miles from town.

There is one café in town, **The Surf** (tel. 788-3535). Angoon is a dry community, which means you cannot purchase liquor locally.

If you appreciate Native crafts, Angoon is a good place to buy blankets, moccasins, and homemade beadwork. Many of these items are for sale at a shop in the Municipal Building. The nearby Community Services Building contains the headquarters of Admiralty Island National Monument (tel. 788-3166).

Chichagof Island

The Chatham Strait separates Admiralty Island from Chichagof Island. (Together with Baranof Island, south of Chichagof, they comprise the "ABC islands.") **Tenakee Springs,** on the north side of Tenakee Inlet near the island's east coast, has a permanent population of about 140, most of them retirees who regularly take advantage of the therapeutic hot (106° to 108°F) sulfur spring for which the town is named. A bathhouse on the waterfront was reconstructed after a devastating Thanksgiving 1984 storm. There's no mixed bathing—women use the spring from 9 a.m. to 2 p.m. and 6 to 10 p.m., and men all other hours—which discourages honeymooners.

Tenakee is intentionally remote. Only a fire truck and an old oil truck are allowed on the one street, Tenakee Avenue, two miles long and 4 to 12 feet wide. But the *LeConte* ferry stops twice a week, and if you want to stay over, you could do worse than the **Tenakee Inn and Tavern,** a lovely Victorian-style hotel between the ferry terminal and boat harbor, opened in 1985 by the same Adams family that operates the Alaskan Hotel & Bar in Juneau. Singles with shared bath are $40, and doubles run $45, plus 3% tax; rooms with private bath are $5 to $10 more. All rooms have kitchenette facilities. Bunkhouse beds go for just $15. Write 167 S. Franklin St., Juneau, AK 99801 (tel. 907/736-9238 or 586-1000, or toll free 800/327-9347). You can also rent efficiency cabins on the beach (bring your own sleeping bag) for $25 a night from **Snyder Mercantile Co.,** P.O. Box 505, Tenakee Springs, AK 99841 (tel. 907/736-2205). There's a primitive **campground** at Indian River, two miles east of town, but you'll have to share it with bears. The **Blue Moon Café,** next to the dock, serves meals.

The sheltered village of **Hoonah**—literally, "place where the north wind doesn't blow"—is a Tlingit settlement in Port Frederick on the north shore of Chicago Island, closer to Glacier Bay than to Juneau. About 860 people, most of them involved in fishing or logging, make their homes here. According to Tlingit tradition, Hoonah was founded centuries ago by tribespeople fleeing the advance of ice into Glacier Bay.

The *LeConte* stops three times a week. You can stay at the comfortable **Huna Totem Lodge,** P.O. Box 320, Hoonah, AK 99829 (tel. 907/945-3636), which has 28 units with private bath priced at $55 single, $70 double, plus a restaurant and lounge. **Mary's Inn** (tel. 945-3228) is a popular local café. Local tax is 4%.

Ask directions to the **Hoonah Indian Association Cultural Center** (tel. 945-3600), a small hillside museum containing Tlingit artifacts donated by local residents. Open from 9 a.m. to 5 p.m. Monday through Friday and by request. The **Glacier Winds** gift shop has excellent local craft items.

Tiny **Elfin Cove,** population 28 (at last count), is located near Chichagof Island's northwest extremity. The ferry doesn't call here, but for those who charter boats or planes or have their own transportation, there are several lodges with weekly fishing packages May to September. Contact the **Elfin Cove Sportfishing Lodge,** Glacier View, Elfin Cove, AK 99825 (tel. 907/239-2212), in summer, or P.O. Box 4007, Renton, WA 98057 (tel. toll free 800/422-2824), in winter, which hosts 10 to 12 guests at $2,650 per person for six nights; the **Tanaku Lodge,** General Delivery, Elfin Cove, AK 99825 (tel. 907/239-2205), a new cedar lodge with a hot tub, priced at $1,195 for five nights; or **Louie's Place,** P.O. Box 704, Juneau, AK 99802 (tel. 907/586-2032), a vacation home which accommodates four to six at $350 per week.

6. Glacier Bay National Park

A trip through Glacier Bay is a trip through natural time, a brief but powerful glimpse of the irrepressible forces of creation.

Only two centuries ago, the blinking of an eye in geologic terms, massive glaciers up to 4,000 feet thick occupied the modern bay's entire 800-foot-deep channel, all the way to its outlet on Icy Strait opposite Chichagof Island. In 1794 an exploration party sent by Capt. George Vancouver found an impassable wall of "compact solid mountains of ice" blocking what is now the entrance to the bay; yet by the time of naturalist John Muir's first visit in 1879, the ice had retreated over 45 miles. Since then glacial regression has unveiled a 65-mile-long, Y-shaped bay . . . and still the retreat continues. Geologists believe this is but the latest phase of a cycle of relentless progress and regress which has been going on for four million years.

As receding glaciers uncover land cloaked for centuries by ice, nature reclaims it. Glacier Bay visitors who travel up the bay by water, northward toward the existing great tidewater glaciers, have a unique opportunity to observe this reclamation process. The most popular trip, aboard the motor vessel *Spirit of Adventure,* begins in dense spruce forest at Bartlett Cove, where park headquarters is located. Voyagers traverse 200 years in time as they travel first past hardwood forest of alder and willow, then sedge and horsetail tundra, and finally to barren rock and glacial moraine. Here, where the Muir or Riggs or Grand Pacific Glacier spews enormous chunks of ice into the frigid water while hundreds of seals bark their approval, it's difficult not to feel awed, even humbled, by the might of nature.

The glaciers, of course, are the primary reason that people visit Glacier Bay. The national park and preserve contain 16 tidewater glaciers (those whose faces reach the sea) and myriad other, mostly nameless glaciers sliding down the flanks of 15,320-foot Mount Fairweather and other high peaks. Not all of them are retreating; those on the stormy Gulf of Alaska coast, west of the Fairweather Range, are slowly advancing.

Glaciers are frigid rivers formed when heavy snowfall compresses under its own weight to form ice, which then is caused by temperature, slope, and gravity to flow downhill. The face of a glacier where it reaches the water dwarfs even large cruise ships: it can be a few hundred yards to several miles wide, and is commonly 150 to 200 feet high. Many times each day large chunks of ice break off the face—the process is called "calving"—and float away as small icebergs.

The ice floes attract harbor seals by the hundreds and bald eagles by the dozens. Elsewhere in Glacier Bay, humpback whales breach with thunderous claps and colorful puffins flutter around their burrows on bird-filled islets. Some 40 varieties of mammals and more than 220 species of birds have been recorded in the park; naturalists recommend that serious animal and birdwatchers come armed with binoculars.

Binoculars don't help much, though, in pouring rain and dense fog. Glacier Bay gets its share of both. What Harry Fielding Reid wrote during an 1892 expedition to Glacier Bay still applies today: "We have concluded that there are many infallible signs of rain in this region. If the sun shines, if the stars appear, if there are clouds, or if there are none; these are all sure indications. If the barometer falls, it will rain; if the barometer rises, it will rain; if the barometer remains steady, it will continue to rain."

Annual rainfall, depending on which part of the park you're in, varies from 55 to 125 inches, with an additional 12 feet of snowfall. Bartlett Cove experiences summertime highs in the 60s, winter lows in the 20s, but the upper reaches of the bay can be 20°F cooler in both seasons. You can expect some rain to fall, on average, 228 days a year. Your chances of clear skies are best in May and June: as summer progresses into autumn, the probability of bad weather grows.

ORIENTATION

Glacier Bay was among the first of Alaska's federally protected lands, established in 1925 as Glacier Bay National Monument. In 1980, when Congress passed the Alaska National Interest Lands Conservation Act, it increased the protected area to 3.3 million acres (4,400 square miles) and changed its status to "national park and preserve." (The preserve, where hunting, trapping, and subsistence agriculture are allowed, comprises 57,000 acres at the mouth of the Alsek River in the park's northwest corner.)

The only access to Glacier Bay is by air or private boat. Airport and boat docks are in the hamlet of Gustavus (pop. 150), ten miles from Bartlett Cove via a graded gravel road. (No ferries run to this corner of the southeast, at least until local Gustavus politics allow.)

Alaska Airlines (tel. 697-2203 in Gustavus, or toll free 800/426-0333) flies between Juneau and Gustavus daily in summer for $94 round trip, but not at all the rest of the year. **Glacier Bay Airways,** P.O. Box 1, Gustavus, AK 99826 (tel. 697-2249, or 789-9009 in Juneau), has daily scheduled service between Juneau and Gustavus, with flightseeing tours and connections anywhere between Skagway, Elfin Cove, and Angoon. **L.A.B. Flying Service** (tel. 766-2222 in Haines) and **Skagway Air Service** (tel. 983-2219 in Skagway) are reliable carriers.

A shuttle bus operates between the Gustavus airport and the Glacier Bay Lodge at Bartlett Cove (for $7.50), and will let you off at any intermediate point. **TLC Taxi** (tel. 697-2239) charges $18 for the first person, $3 for each additional person, between town and Bartlett Cove. Some of the accommodations in Gustavus also provide transportation to and from the cove. And there's the option of bicycle rental from the Gustavus Inn.

The residents of Gustavus live in small wood houses scattered amid pasture and meadows sprinkled with wildflowers in early summer. The community has a post office, chapel, school, grocery store, and two cafés. But there is no bank, so Glacier Bay visitors should plan on taking care of their financial needs before arrival.

The **Gustavus Visitors Association,** P.O. Box 167, Gustavus, AK 99826, will send a free brochure, with a map and a listing of local businesses, on request. For park information, contact **Glacier Bay National Park and Preserve,** Park Headquarters, Gustavus, AK 99826 (tel. 907/697-2231). Maps, nautical charts, and brochures are available at the Visitor Center opposite the Bartlett Cove dock.

WHERE TO STAY AND EAT

All package tourists and many independent travelers park their bags at the **Glacier Bay Lodge,** P.O. Box 199, Gustavus, AK 99826 (tel. 907/697-2225). Located at Bartlett Cove, this is the only lodging available within the park. Open mid-May to mid-September, the lodge offers deluxe accommodations overlooking the bay— with prices to match.

The lodge, constructed of natural wood, is set in a spruce and hemlock rain forest. Boardwalks lead to the 55 rooms, which amount to interconnected cabins. These rooms are adequate for the location: most visitors will want to spend their time out-of-doors. Each room has a private bath, table and chair, and beds for two to four, but no TV or phone. Rates begin at $126 single, $136 double. A few dormitory beds are available at $20.

The busy restaurant in the main lodge building has a diverse menu. A buffet-style breakfast is served from 6 to 7 a.m. for $7.50 (or $4 for a continental), and a regular breakfast menu is available from 7:30 to 9 a.m. Lunches, served from 11:30 a.m. to 1:30 p.m., include sandwiches and salads priced from $5 to $10, while full steak or seafood dinners, served from 5:30 to 9:30 p.m., are in the $17 to $20 range. Budget and weight watchers are disappointed to find, however, that lunch offerings are unavailable at dinner—and the next closest restaurant is ten miles away in Gustavus.

Also in the main lodge, next to the reception desk, is a gift shop. Between the restaurant and Icebreaker Lounge (open 5:30 p.m. to midnight) is a plush seating area around a large fireplace. An information board stands by the door, announcing nature walks and other activities. Upstairs, next to a National Park Service wildlife exhibit, films and lectures are presented nightly. The boat dock is about a 300-yard walk south on a well-lit path.

Reservation requests should be directed to 523 Pine St., Suite 203, Seattle, WA 98101 (tel. 206/623-7110, or toll free 800/622-2042).

Visitors who consider it important to be at the center of action will be very happy at the Glacier Bay Lodge. But there are several more moderately priced options.

The **Gustavus Inn,** P.O. Box 31, Gustavus, AK 99826 (tel. 907/697-2254), takes the bed-and-breakfast concept one step further, offering full-board packages in an original Alaskan homestead April to November. David and JoAnn Lesh's big gray farmhouse has been totally refurbished to include 12 comfortable guest rooms, most with private baths, a homey dining room, a six-seat wine bar, and a library. Outside, on the five-acre property, are a children's playground in a big grassy field, a large vegetable garden and greenhouse, and a huge wine and root cellar.

The food at the inn is famous—so much so that Juneau residents frequently charter a plane to fly in just for dinner. Local catches of salmon, halibut, and crab are supplemented by home-grown vegetables and wild berry pies. Those visitors pay $24 for a full-course dinner. Inn guests have three meals included in the daily rate of $100 per adult (double occupancy), $50 for children 4 to 12. The rate also includes transfers to and from the airport and Bartlett Cove, and use of bicycles and fishing poles. The inn is 100 yards from the Salmon River, on the main airport road.

Al and Annie Unrein's rambling **Glacier Bay Country Inn,** P.O. Box 5, Gustavus, AK 99826 (tel. 907/697-2288), is in the center of a 160-acre farmstead reached by a one-mile detour off the Bartlett Cove road, about four miles from the airport and six from Park Service headquarters. Opened in June 1986, the home was built by Al himself as a labor of love—he even milled his own wood! It has log-beam ceilings, large porches, and dormer windows. A circular staircase leads from the library to a turret with a sitting room. There's a telescope in the lounge. Outside, the root cellar is covered by sweet hybrid strawberries. Eventually the Unreins plan to have their own airstrip.

Seven of the nine rooms, decorated with a garden, nautical, or forestry theme, have thermopedic beds with flannel sheets. All but two have private baths. Daily rates—$89 per person for adults, $54 for children 3 to 12—include $6 for breakfast, $8 for lunch, and $18 for dinner, prices that will be deducted if meals are not taken. But the Unreins are certain that the gourmet chef, a graduate of the Culinary Institute of America, will convince most folks to dine here. The lodge has its own boat, a 42-foot Sunnfjord, to take guests on sightseeing and fishing trips.

If you visit the oddly named **W. T. Fugarwe Lodge,** P.O. Box 27, Gustavus, AK 99826 (tel. 907/697-2244), owner J. L. "Doc" Bailey will relate the so-called Indian legend after which he named his inn. Suffice it to explain that "W.T." stands for "where the." If the name strikes your funny bone, you'll be ready for the back-slapping humor shared by Bailey and other former airline pilots who frequently visit.

The lodge, featured on the Outdoor News Network, resembles nothing so much as a hangar. Eight large but simply appointed rooms accommodate two to four guests in double beds or bunks. Private toilets are attached, but showers are down the hall. Hearty meals are served family style in a cozy dining room, including homemade breads and soups.

The Fugarwe specializes in fishing packages. Several world records have been set by guests fishing off the lodge's three salmon and halibut boats. Basic rates are $105 a day ($60 for lodging and $45 for meals), plus $100 per half day (4½ hours) for charter fishing. The lodge also offers flightseeing charters on a private Cessna for $140 an hour, and rents bicycles. Open June 1 to September 15. In the off-season, contact P.O. Box 486, Georgetown, CO 80444 (tel. 303/623-7108 or 303/569-2255).

The budget alternative is **Salmon River Rentals,** P.O. Box 13, Gustavus, AK 99826 (tel. 907/697-2245). Bring your own sleeping bag to spread on a bed or couch in one of the ten rustic housekeeping cabins. Each cabin has a wood stove, a gas camp stove or electric hotplate, a table with four chairs, a sink, and kitchen utensils. Rest-room facilities and showers are in a central building. Cabins rent for $40 a night or $200 a week. Open mid-May to mid-September.

Several bed-and-breakfast establishments have sprung up in Gustavus in recent years. Of particular note is **The Puffin,** P.O. Box 3, Gustavus, AK 99826 (tel. 907/697-2260 mid-April through September, 907/789-9787 all other times). Owner

Sandy Schroth has two modern cabins with wood heat and electricity in the center of town, priced at just $30 single, $10 per additional adult, half price for kids 2 to 12. The homestead has a private bathhouse. Schroth offers free pickup service and willingly makes all sightseeing and kayaking arrangements for guests. Glacier Bay Puffin Charters offer fishing trips and sightseeing aboard a 21-foot yacht.

Pleasant Enterprises, P.O. Box 58, Gustavus, AK 99826 (tel. 907/697-2328), has one room available at $35 single, $50 double, with laundry facilities and hot showers. **Goode Riverbed & Breakfast,** P.O. Box 37, Gustavus, AK 99826 (tel. 907/697-2241), has guest rooms and full baths available year round in a spacious log home. Rates are $40 single, $60 double.

Backpackers and kayakers can set up tents and camp free of charge at the **Bartlett Cove Campground,** about half a mile south of the Glacier Bay Lodge. A bear-proof food cache, wood, and firepits are provided, but there's a 14-day limit on stays. You can shower and use the laundry facilities at the lodge, where you must go for check-in and orientation.

Outside of the lodges, there is one choice for dining. The **Open Gate Café,** on Dockside Road (tel. 697-2227), has homemade breads and pastries, deli sandwiches, and burgers from $4, and light dinners (including stir-fry vegetables and pepper steak) from $9. Open from 6:30 a.m. to 4 p.m. on Monday, Wednesday, and Thursday, to 9 p.m. on Tuesday, Friday, and Saturday; closed Sunday.

WHAT TO SEE AND DO

A **boat cruise** is the highlight of any visit to Glacier Bay. Accompanied by a National Park Service ranger/naturalist (and 100-or-so other passengers), you'll cruise up the bay past island bird rookeries and floating icebergs to enormous tide-water glaciers. With luck, you'll see some whales along the way.

The *Spirit of Adventure* leaves the Bartlett Cove dock May 24 to September 20 promptly at 7:30 a.m. daily and returns at about 3:30 p.m. after voyaging up the eastern Muir Inlet. Tickets are $136.50 for adults or $68.25 for children ages 2 to 11. Separate lunch tickets can also be purchased; they're a less expensive option than filling up on the buffet breakfast in the lodge before departure. Beer and wine are also cheaper (by 50¢) on the boat than at the lodge. The vessel is heated, but most passengers like to spend a fair amount of time with camera or binoculars on deck, so dress warmly.

Sometimes these trips can get more exciting than advertised. In June 1986 a tour boat actually collided with a humpback whale that suddenly surfaced about 15 feet from the boat. There were no injuries either to the whale or to passengers.

Some private operators offer overnight sightseeing trips up Glacier Bay's 65-mile west arm to Tarr and Johns Hopkins Inlets. **Grand Pacific Charters,** P.O. Box 5, Gustavus, AK 99826 (tel. 907/697-2288), has two staterooms on its deluxe 42-foot yacht. **Fairweather Fishing and Guide Service,** P.O. Box 164, Gustavus, AK 99826 (tel. 907/697-2335 or 735-2253), specializes in whale watching and wild-life photography.

Many of the Gustavus innkeepers, including the Gustavus Inn, the Glacier Bay Country Inn, and the Puffin, offer packages that include lodging, cruise, meals, and transfers.

Sports

FISHING The Bartlett and Salmon Rivers and some small inland lakes can be good for Dolly Varden and cutthroat trout, and river-run salmon in season. Halibut and salmon are the main game fish in Glacier Bay and Icy Strait. Remember that an Alaska fishing license is required even though the park is federally operated.

Gustavus Marine Charters, P.O. Box 81, Gustavus, AK 99826 (tel. 907/ 697-2233), and **Mike Mills Charter Service,** P.O. Box 151, Gustavus, AK 99826 (tel. 907/697-2236), operate private charters from Glacier Bay, providing all tackle and bait. Their seasons run May through September. Rates vary according to number of people and size of boat; figure $90 per person (minimum of two) for a half day, $160 for a full day, including preparing and freezing your catch.

HUNTING Capturing, injuring, or killing animals is strictly prohibited in the park. Firearms are allowed only in the backcountry, and then for emergency use only. Special regulations apply to the preserve along the Alsek River, where sport hunting for moose and bear is permitted in late summer and fall. Consult a ranger or write the park superintendent for details.

HIKING AND BACKPACKING There are only two formal trails in Glacier Bay National Park, both at Bartlett Cove. The **Beach and Nature Trail** winds through a spruce rain forest and returns to the lodge via the rocky bay shore. A naturalist leads a tour along this mile-long trail at 2 p.m. daily. The **Bartlett River Trail** skirts a tidal lagoon, then cuts through the forest to the river estuary, 1½ miles from the lodge. Birds and small mammals are usually seen on this route.

Outside of Bartlett Cove, steep rocky slopes, dense underbrush, glacial streams, and tides that fluctuate as much as 25 feet daily make backpacking treacherous. Be sure to read the Forest Service publication "Hazards Ashore and Afloat." No open fires are permitted; you must carry your own portable stove and white-gas fuel bottle, as well as water. Be sure to include warm clothing, raingear, and insect repellent in your pack. Park rangers sell topographical maps on backcountry areas. Bring a compass and know how to use it.

The *Spirit of Adventure* will drop you off or pick you up anywhere along the shore of Glacier Bay for a per-stop charge of $10 over and above the normal tour cost. Other private charter-boat and floatplane operators can also provide backcountry transportation.

Backpacking expeditions are sometimes arranged by **Alaska Travel Adventures,** 9085 Glacier Hwy., Juneau, AK 99801 (tel. 907/789-0052). The same group also leads occasional cross-country ski trips in winter.

KAYAKING Among outdoor types, this is the most popular way to see the park. Kayaks are preferable to canoes because they ride lower and therefore can buck wind and waves more easily. Keep your distance from floating ice and tidewater glaciers, whose calving can create waves that will swamp a small craft and throw you into 34°F water. Park rangers at Bartlett Cove can provide nautical charts, tide tables, and local knowledge of hazardous areas.

Five saltwater wilderness areas have been designated within the park for the use of self-propelled boats only. These areas are unique in the national park system; rangers will direct you to them.

As with backpackers, kayakers can be dropped anywhere by the park boats for a small charge; there is no additional fee for carrying a kayak or other equipment.

You can rent two-person kayaks for $30 a day from **Glacier Bay Sea Kayaks,** P.O. Box 26, Gustavus, AK 99826 (tel. 907/697-2257). **Spirit Walker Expeditions,** P.O. Box 122, Gustavus, AK 99826 (tel. 907/697-2266), offers guided trips through Icy Strait and along the coast of Chichagof Island from mid-May to mid-September. Day trips are $70 per person, including lunch; all-inclusive overnight trips of three to seven days average $170 per day per person.

Alaska Travel Adventures (see above) operates thrilling week-long river-raft float trips down the Tatshenshini and Alsek Rivers from the Yukon Territory. If you've never been on a raft before, this is probably not the place to start!

YAKUTAT

The small town of Yakutat (pop. 450) is a gateway both to the Dry Bay/Alsek River edge of Glacier Bay National Park and Preserve, 50 miles southeast, and to the Yakutat Bay/Malaspina Glacier precincts of Wrangell–St. Elias National Park and Preserve, fewer than 20 miles northwest.

A Tlingit fishing town, it was overrun by the American media in September 1986 when a team of wildlife biologists from the states of Washington and California arrived to save dozens of harbor seals and porpoises trapped when the rapid advance of Hubbard Glacier, at the head of Yakutat Bay, dammed the entrance of Russell Fjord and created Russell Lake. The locals were baffled: they couldn't understand why anyone would want to save creatures they themselves kill for interfering with their fishing nets.

Yakutat has much to attract sport fishermen and nature lovers. You can rent a car and drive to the acclaimed trout grounds of the Situk River and Harlequin Lake, where there are U.S. Forest Service primitive **cabins** ($15 a night). More cabins are at Dry Bay, abutting Glacier Bay National Preserve. Contact the U.S. Forest Service (tel. 784-3359) for full information. **Gulf Air Taxi**, P.O. Box 37, Yakutat, AK 99689 (tel. 784-3240), can fly you there. Halibut and salmon, crab, and scallops are the most commonly taken ocean fish. **Yakutat Bay & River Charters** (tel. 784-3415) will arrange trips, and the Alaska Department of Fish and Game (tel. 784-3222) can offer additional information.

Yakutat is the home of the rare glacier or "blue" bear. Believed to have become isolated from other black bears during the Ice Ages, this creature adapted to its treeless situation by acquiring a protective pale-bluish color. Snow geese and trumpeter swans are frequently seen along this stretch of shoreline.

Across Yakutat Bay, the Malaspina Glacier covers 850 square miles, making it the largest in North America—in fact, it's larger than the entire state of Rhode Island. A miner's route to the Klondike gold fields actually crossed this glacier, but few of those who tackled it survived, and even fewer survived sane. The glacier is within the **Wrangell–St. Elias National Park,** which maintains a Yakutat District office (tel. 784-3295).

Alaska Airlines (tel. 784-3366) flies through Yakutat twice daily—in the late morning from Juneau, en route to Cordova and Anchorage, and in the late afternoon from those same destinations en route to Juneau. If the skies are clear, the view of the Malaspina Glacier is spectacular.

There are two places to stay in Yakutat, both open year round with restaurants and lounges. My choice is the **Glacier Bear Lodge,** P.O. Box 303, Yakutat, AK 99689 (tel. 907/784-3202), which has 30 rooms with private bath. Rates vary from $70 to $130, depending on whether a full meal package is desired.

---

7. Haines

Most Inside Passage travelers choose to bypass the quiet town of Haines and head directly for bustling Skagway. That's a shame. Even though they're only 15 miles apart, the two communities are almost as different as Paris and London.

Skagway is a tourist town through and through. Haines, whose 1,700 people don't depend very much on seasonal business, is proud of its natural history and Native traditions. The Chilkat Valley is the site of the world's largest American bald eagle preserve, where as many as 3,500 of the national symbol gather in the autumn months to feast on a late run of chum salmon. There is a tribal arts center at historic Fort William H. Seward where the Chilkat clan of Tlingit Indians carve totem poles and perform tribal dances. A network of rivers and trails cater to fishermen, hikers, and cross-country skiers. Together with Skagway, Haines is unique in southeast Alaska for having both a ferry terminal and a road connection to the Alaska Hwy. in Canada's Yukon Territory.

Set against a backdrop of forested peaks and glaciers, Haines occupies a narrow portage in a peninsula at the head of the Lynn Canal, between the mouths of two rivers—the Chilkat and the Chilkoot. Visited many times in the 19th century by white traders and trappers, it was established as a mission town in 1881 after Presbyterian missionary S. Hall Young and naturalist John Muir conferred with local Tlingit chieftains to determine an appropriate site. Called Dehshuh ("end of the trail") by Tlingits, Chilkoot by traders, it was renamed Haines in honor of the Presbyterian home missions secretary.

Haines's economy grew on fishing and gold mining. Several salmon canneries were operating here by the 1890s. The Porcupine Mining District produced thousands of dollars of gold in the early 1900s, and the Dalton Trail—named after the notorious Jack Dalton, who charged an outrageous fee to guide people over the trail to the Klondike and posted armed guards to prevent nonpayers from using it—began in Haines. Lumber and tourism have replaced gold mining as key industries, but fishing (mainly gill-net salmon and halibut) remains important.

Fort Seward was built by the U.S. Army as a permanent military post half a mile south of Haines at Port Chilkoot in 1904. It was renamed Chilkoot Barracks in 1922, and until the outbreak of World War II was the only army base in Alaska. After the war it was deactivated and sold to individual veterans. Port Chilkoot merged with Haines in 1970; two years later the post was designated a National Historic Site.

Haines is drier than most other southeastern towns, with an average annual precipitation of about 60 inches. The average July high temperature is 66°F (with extremes in the 80s); the average January low is 17°F (with extremes below −10°F). Spring and fall drizzle and winter snowfall are the norms.

ORIENTATION

There's no easy way to remember which is which, other than to memorize: Chilkat is west; Chilkoot is east. The Chilkat River empties into the Chilkat Inlet, on which is Chilkat State Park. The Chilkat Range is south, bordering Glacier Bay National Park, while Chilkat Lake is west of the village of Klukwan. The Chilkoot River empties out of Chilkoot Lake into the Chilkoot Inlet, on which is Chilkoot State Park. North of Skagway, the Chilkoot Trail climbs over Chilkoot Pass.

Most of Haines faces east. It looks out on Portage Cove and the Chilkoot Inlet, which is the eastern arm of the Lynn Canal. The Haines Hwy. separates Haines proper (downtown) from Port Chilkoot (the fort); each is on its own low hill, with downtown a half mile north of the fort. Many businesses, including motels and restaurants, are within a couple of blocks' walk of Second Avenue and Main Street. The principal exceptions are those around the parade grounds at Fort Seward. Front Street (Beach Road), Second Avenue, and Third Avenue (Mud Bay Road) connect the two parts of town.

Transportation

The airport is an exception to the "facing east" rule. It's 3½ miles west of downtown, on Chilkat Inlet. Alaska Airlines doesn't fly here, but many smaller outfits do. I've had nothing but fine service and comfortable flights in my travels with the Haines-based **L.A.B. Flying Service,** 480 Main St. (P.O. Box 272), Haines, AK

99827 (tel. 907/766-2222), whose routes cover the Lynn Canal area from Juneau to Skagway to Glacier Bay. **Haines Airways,** P.O. Box 61, Haines, AK 99827 (tel. 907/766-2646), and **Wings of Alaska,** Second Avenue and Willard Street, Haines, AK 99827 (tel. 907/766-2030), have similar routes. **Skagway Air Service,** P.O. Box 357, Skagway, AK 99840 (tel. 907/983-2218), and **Glacier Bay Airways,** P.O. Box 1, Gustavus, AK 99826 (tel. 907/697-2249), also fly into Haines. The various carriers will provide transportation to motels.

The **Alaska Marine Highway ferry** terminal (tel. 766-2111) is 4½ miles north of downtown Haines on Lutak Road, just before the cruise-ship dock. Each week seven northbound boats (to Skagway) and seven southbound boats call.

The **Haines Hwy.** connects Haines with the Alaska Hwy. at Haines Junction, Yukon Territory, 150 miles or four hours' drive northwest. The all-weather road (over three-quarters of it is paved) follows the old Dalton Trail to the Klondike. It's maintained year round. Car rentals are available from **Hertz** at the Thunderbird Motel (tel. 766-2131), from **Avis** at the Halsingland Hotel (tel. 766-2733), and from **Eagle's Nest** at the Eagle's Nest Motel (tel. 766-2352). The Eagle's Nest is also the agent for **No. 1 Motorhome Rental.**

Sockeye Cycle & Tours, located in the alley off Main Street, between Second and Third Avenues (tel. 766-2869), rents and services bicycles and runs bike tours for all ages.

Haines Street Car Co. (tel. 766-2819) runs a shuttlebus service from town to the ferry terminal, meeting all arrivals and departures. The charge is $5 one way. **Haines Taxi** (tel. 766-3138) is the best alternative.

Alaskon Express connects Haines with Anchorage, Fairbanks, Skagway, and Whitehorse, Yukon Territory, twice a week in summer (May 27 to September 13). Buses leave Haines at 8:15 a.m. on Friday and Tuesday and make afternoon connections at Haines Junction. Buses arrive in Haines at 6:30 p.m. on Sunday and Friday. The trip to Anchorage takes 34 hours (at a cost of $173, not including overnight lodging at Beaver Creek, Yukon Territory); to Skagway, 12 hours ($117); to Whitehorse, a little over 8 hours ($72). Purchase tickets in Haines at Wings of Alaska, Second Avenue and Willard Street (tel. 907/766-2030). Alaskon Express is associated with Gray Line of Alaska (tel. toll free 800/544-2206).

Information

Haines's very helpful **Visitor Information Center** shares a small wood cabin with the chamber of commerce, just off Second Avenue on Willard Street. Contact P.O. Box 518, Haines, AK 99827 (tel. 907/766-2202 or 766-2234). Open from 8 a.m. to 8 p.m. daily.

The Chilkat Valley is not a part of Tongass National Forest, so there is no Forest Service office in Haines. For outdoor information, try the **Alaska Division of Parks** in the Gateway Building on Main Street (tel. 755-2292). If you plan to cross into Canada from Haines, you may want to contact **U.S. Customs** (tel. 766-2374) or **Canadian Customs** (tel. 766-2541).

Haines's *Chilkat Valley News* is published weekly. The **Chilkat Valley Medical Center** is on 1st Street adjacent to the Visitor Information Center (tel. 766-2521). Call 911 for emergencies. The **post office** is on the Haines Hwy. near Second Avenue. The **First National Bank of Anchorage** maintains a branch on Main Street (tel. 766-2321).

Festivals

The year's big event in Haines is the **Southeast Alaska State Fair,** held on the third weekend of August. What began as a Strawberry Festival in the early 1900s evolved in 1969 into the premier fair for all of southeast Alaska and Canada's Yukon. It includes a five-day horse show, a logging carnival, miniature train rides, and outdoor entertainment of all types. Contact P.O. Box 385, Haines, AK 99827 (tel. 907/766-2478), for information. The 21-acre fairgrounds are on the south side of the Haines Hwy. near its junction with Main Street, about halfway between downtown and the airport.

There's also a **Winter Carnival** in late January or early February featuring the Alcan 200 international snow machine rally. And the **Fourth of July** is a big day, with raft races, logging events, parades, and a carnival atmosphere.

WHERE TO STAY

Haines offers a variety of accommodations, nearly all of them in the moderate price range. City tax of 5% should be added to all quoted rates.

Moderate

My favorite place to stay in Haines is the **Hotel Halsingland,** P.O. Box 158, Haines, AK 99827 (tel. 907/766-2000, or toll free 800/542-6363, 800/478-2525 in Alaska). That's not because it's the newest, or the best maintained, or the most centrally located—it's none of those. What it has is charm and ambience. Directly facing the Fort Seward parade grounds, the hotel has taken over what were the commanding officers' quarters in the days before World War II. The big white houses were purchased in 1947 by Clarence and Hilma Mattson; Hilma came from the Swedish province of Halsingland, and so the name. A huge hand-woven tapestry from Halsingland still hangs above a landing on the stairs. Hilma's nephew, Arne Olsson, and his wife, Joyce, operate the hotel today.

No two of the Halsingland's 60 rooms are alike. Many contain such unusual touches as a settee and a hanging lamp over the bed. All rooms have thermostat-controlled hot-water heating and wall-to-wall carpeting. Wildlife photographs decorate the walls. The rooms have no TV or phone, although two pay phones are available for use in the lobby. Rates with private bath are $59 single, $64 double, $70 twin. The Halsingland also has ten small "economy" rooms with shared bath for $29.50 single, $33.50 double. Open May through November only.

The hotel's Commander's Room Restaurant is popular among Haines residents for its local seafood dinners and generous portions of all meals. Full dinners such as halibut Humboldt (in white wine and cheese sauce) or sautéed prawns are priced at $15.50 and $16.50, while the "Stars and Stripes" special—steak and scallops—goes for $24.50, including salad bar. Dinner is served from 6 to 10 p.m. daily. Lunch (11 a.m. to 2 p.m.) and breakfast (7 to 10 a.m.) are in the $6 range. The bartender at the cozy Officer's Club lounge will try to convince you to order a "Fort Seward Howitzer" while you watch the ball game on TV.

The Halsingland also operates a licensed salmon bake, the Port Chilkoot Potlatch, from 5 to 8 p.m. daily (June through August) at the Totem Village Tribal House in the Fort Seward parade grounds. This all-you-can-eat-for-$15 feast is as good as any of its genre, and better than most.

The **Captain's Choice Motel,** Second Avenue and Dalton Street (P.O. Box 392), Haines, AK 99827 (tel. 907/766-3111, or toll free 800/247-7153, 800/478-2345 in Alaska), has many of the things the Halsingland lacks, including cable TV with HBO, room phones (with free local calls), courtesy coffee, and a downtown location. A natural-wood nautical theme is carried from the lobby into the 40 rooms, many of which overlook Portage Cove. Earth-toned carpeting, drapes, and bedspreads complement the wood décor in the rooms, which have all-modern touches including electric baseboard heat and desk-dresser combinations. Rates are $60 single, $70 double, $75 twin; slightly less during the off-season. Three deluxe suites with kitchenettes rent for $90 to $100 double. Pets are allowed in some rooms.

You'll feel welcome at the **Eagle's Nest Motel,** adjacent to the state fairgrounds at Mile 1 on Haines Hwy. (P.O. Box 267), Haines, AK 99827 (tel. 907/766-2352), as soon as you see the big stone fireplace in the lobby. Each of the nine quiet rooms has a white calico bedspread to go with rust-colored carpets, a queen-size bed, desk-dresser, couch or easy chair, 12-channel cable television, thermostat-controlled hot-water heating, and courtesy coffee. There's a pay phone in the lobby. Singles are $52; doubles, $59; twins, $69. Rates are slightly less in winter. This is the closest motel to the airport and the eagle preserve.

The **Thunderbird Motel,** Dalton Street at Second Avenue (P.O. Box 910), Haines, AK 99827 (tel. 907/766-2131, or toll free 800/327-2556), ushers you into the lobby on Astroturf carpeting, then announces your arrival to front-desk clerks with a loud buzzer. Bright floral bedspreads brighten the otherwise dreary wood-paneled rooms. Six units have kitchenettes; all 30 feature electric baseboard heating, 12-channel cable TV, and telephones (local calls are 25¢). Year round, singles are $52; doubles, $62. Kitchenette units rent for $72 double.

The **Mountain View Motel,** P.O. Box 62, Haines, AK 99827 (tel. 907/766-2900), has eight units—all with small kitchenettes—on Mud Bay Road at the Second Avenue entrance to Fort Seward. Each room has a dining table, two double beds, couch, dresser, and cable TV. The décor is uninspired, with brown carpeting and white trim; and what is the painting of the Arizona Indian village doing on the wall? Singles are $47.50; doubles, $52.50.

The **Fort Seward Condos,** Nos. 2 and 3 Officers' Row, Fort Seward (P.O. Box 75), Haines, AK 99827 (tel. 907/766-2425), are fully furnished one- and two-bedroom apartment units, some with fireplaces, in a historic residence. Owners Ted and Mimi Gregg request a three-day minimum stay. Rates start at $65 a day, $390 per week, including utilities and parking (but no phone or television).

Bed-and-Breakfast

Haines's original B&B is the **Fort Seward Bed & Breakfast,** No. 1 Officers' Row, Fort Seward (P.O. Box 5), Haines, AK 99827 (tel. 907/766-2856), and it's a good one. Owner Norm Smith, a 25-year resident of Haines, has worked hard to renovate this former chief surgeon's quarters, a grand Victorian (1904) structure in the classic Jeffersonian architectural style. Art students will appreciate its cross-gabled slate roof, decorated box cornices, and original leaded- and beveled-glass china cabinets. Selections from Smith's personal print and historic photo collection adorn the walls of the rooms and corridors, while an open veranda looks across the parade grounds to the Lynn Canal. Belgian tile fireplaces warm the three spacious bedrooms, which share a main-floor bathroom and rent for $55 single, $62 double, including tax. One flight up the oak-bannistered staircase are two fully furnished suites with private bath. They go for $85 for two, $95 for four. All rates drop $20 after September 30. Prices include an Alaska-size breakfast of sourdough pancakes and fresh-ground coffee. Open May 1 to December 15 only.

The **Summer Inn B&B,** Second Avenue between Dalton and Union Streets (P.O. Box 1198), Haines, AK 99827 (tel. 907/766-2970), opened in another historic home in 1987. Rates are $45 single, $55 double.

Budget

Haines's best budget accommodations are the economy rooms at the Hotel Halsingland. After that, the **Fish'n Lodge,** Mile 1 on Mud Bay Road (P.O. Box 1045), Haines, AK 99827 (tel. 907/766-2375), has two primitive fishing cabins on Chilkat Inlet with cooking facilities and a smokehouse. Singles are $30; doubles, $35. Open March to November and upon request.

Bear Creek Camp and Youth Hostel, 2½ miles from Haines at Mile 1 on

Small Tract Road (P.O. Box 334), Haines, AK 99827 (tel. 907/766-2259), has sourdough-type cabins—one step above a tent, with canvas stretched over a wood frame—at $30 a night including tax. The year-round hostel is basic; nonmembers are charged $12 a night, while members pay $7.

I would opt for **Noah's Art,** P.O. Box 804, Haines, AK 99827 (no phone), before the youth hostel. At this artists' community in an old barge at Mile 9 on Lutak Road (near Chilkoot Lake), you can throw your sleeping bag in a shared room by the week or month and cook in a community kitchen for less than the hostel charges. Or you can camp free on Noah's beach. The barge houses an art school and gallery, and sells fishing supplies and licenses.

Campgrounds

These may be one of Haines's strongest attractions. There are numerous private RV or camper parks and several public campgrounds in the immediate surrounding area.

The **Port Chilkoot Camper Park,** P.O. Box 473, Haines, AK 99827 (tel. 907/766-2755), on Mud Bay Road in Fort Seward between the Hotel Halsingland and the Mountain View Motel, has 60 spaces for $9 a night with electricity, $6.50 without. Tent sites are $3.50 a night. A Laundromat and coin-op showers are also available. The **Eagle Camper Park,** P.O. Box 28, Haines, AK 99827 (tel. 907/766-2335), closer to downtown on Union Street near Main, has 62 units with full hookups at $14, tent sites at $3.50, and showers. The **Haines Hitch-Up RV Park,** on Haines Hwy. at the entrance to town (tel. 907/766-2882), has 92 spaces at $14 a night for full electric, sewer, and water hookups. It also has a gift shop, Laundromat, and showers. **Ten Mile Camper Park,** Mile 10 on Haines Hwy. (tel. 907/766-2800), and **Oceanside RV Park,** Front Street at the foot of Dalton Street (tel. 907/766-2444), also cater to recreational vehicles.

Backpackers without vehicles won't find a better place to set up their tents than the **Portage Cove Campground,** three-quarters of a mile south of downtown Haines on Beach Road. On a small promontory extending into the Chilkoot Inlet, the campground provides picnic tables, water, and toilets. Farther away from town, there are 33 sites at **Chilkat State Park,** 7 miles south on Mud Bay Road, and 32 sites at **Chilkoot Lake Wayside,** 11 miles north of Haines but only 4 miles from the ferry terminal.

WHERE TO EAT

Haines won't be mistaken for the gastronomic capital of southeast Alaska. But there are several excellent restaurants, beginning with the Commander's Room at the Hotel Halsingland (see the "Where to Stay" section, above).

The **Fort Seward Lodge,** in the old PX on Totem Road at Fort Seward (tel. 766-2009), offers diners a beautiful evening view across the Lynn Canal, especially from its second-floor balcony. A hardwood floor and tasteful wood décor give it a spacious yet cozy feeling. The steak-and-seafood menu includes Chilkoot Inlet salmon for $12 and a 12-ounce sirloin steak for $13. The restaurant is open from 5 to 10 p.m. nightly.

The **Chilkat Restaurant & Bakery,** on Fifth Avenue north of Main Street (tel. 766-2920), is a country kitchen that greets families with open arms. From the embroidered welcome sign on the front door to the daintily curtained windows in the dining room, you'll feel as if you're at Aunt Millie's place. Dinners like roast beef and Hawaiian ham are reasonably priced at $10. Luncheon sandwiches, such as a reuben grill or halibut steak sandwich, are in the $6.50 range, while big breakfast omelets run $6. Homemade pastries are a favored dessert. Friday has been "Mexican Night" since 1981; the top price is $7.50, and reservations are suggested. The Chilkat has chosen not to apply for a liquor license. Open in summer from 7 a.m. to 8 p.m. Monday through Saturday; in winter from 7 a.m. to 5 p.m. Monday through Thursday, to 8 p.m. on Friday, and 8 a.m. to 4 p.m. on Saturday; closed Sunday.

A sign at **The Catalyst,** Main Street between Third and Fourth (tel. 766-2670), bears the following message: "The people you meet here will surprise you, delight you—even at times disturb you. And change forever the way you think." I wasn't at all disturbed. In fact I was delighted to discover this tiny European-style café. You can't get steaks or burgers here, but you will find seafood dishes, quiches, enchiladas, homemade soups, a 43-item salad bar, delicious chocolate torte, and an espresso coffee bar. Nothing on the menu is priced higher than $10. Open from noon to 9 p.m. daily except Sunday.

It's only appropriate that the **Lighthouse Restaurant** (tel. 766-2442), located at the foot of Main Street extending into the small boat harbor, should be decorated in nautical fashion. Fishing floats and greenery hang from the beams beside windows showcasing the harbor's busy activity. Dinner specials, such as barbecued spareribs and eastern oysters, are priced from $14.50 up; they include salad bar, potato, and bread. Lunches range from $5.25 for a burger and fries to $13 for a big fish-and-chips platter with salad, and three-egg breakfast omelets start at $5. Open from 8 a.m. to 10 p.m. daily, March through November.

The **Bamboo Room,** on Second Avenue between Main and Dalton Streets (tel. 766-9101), is the local standby. An informal, down-home café, it's open from 6 a.m. to 10 p.m. daily. Hotcakes and coffee are $3.50 for breakfast, quarter-pound burgers run $3.75 for lunch, and fried chicken is $10.25 for dinner. The house special is hot apple pie with brandy cinnamon sauce, at $1.50.

If you're in the mood for pizza, **Porcupine Pete's,** at Second Avenue and Main Street (tel. 766-9199), might satisfy your appetite. In a natural-wood, ice-cream-parlor atmosphere with video games blaring away, the open kitchen prepares grinders and hoagies for $3.25, and pizza for $2 a slice. Its pride and joy is the "kicking horse combo," four meats and nine vegetables on a 15-inch crust for $23.50. Open 11 a.m. to 11 p.m. Monday to Saturday, noon to 9 p.m. Sunday. A couple of doors away in the rear of the Fogcutter Bar, **Pizzacutter** (tel. 766-2420) has 13-inch pizzas from $10 and make-your-own sandwiches from $5.75. Open 11 a.m. to 10 p.m. Sunday to Thursday, until 11 p.m. Friday and Saturday.

WHAT TO SEE AND DO

Fort William H. Seward, otherwise known as Port Chilkoot, was the army regimental headquarters for all of Alaska from 1904 to 1942. Two full companies plus detachments of headquarters and quartermaster personnel were assigned here. After the fort's deactivation in 1946, a group of American veterans bought the fort with the idea of creating a small-business cooperative. That idea faltered, but many of the families involved have succeeded in Haines as artists and entrepreneurs.

Pick up a walking-tour map of the fort from the visitors center or museum. And don't expect a walled fortress with sentries posted. Signs are being placed to commemorate many of the individual buildings, and there are plans to renovate some of the structures for tourist visitation.

In particular, you should visit the former hospital building, No. 13, on the south side of the fort. Restored with historical site funds from the Alaska Division of Parks, it now houses the **Alaska Indian Arts Skill Center** (tel. 766-2160), where Tlingit artists tutor students in traditional arts like mask and totem pole carving, silver jewelry making, and blanket weaving. Visitors are welcome daily except Sunday from 9 a.m. to noon and 1 to 5 p.m. There is a display and sale room with excellent prices on quality wood crafts.

Immediately behind No. 13 is the **Chilkat Center for the Arts** (tel. 766-2160), a barn-like building that was formerly the army's recreation hall and, before that, a cannery warehouse on another site in the 1890s. Completely renovated in 1967, it now has a modern 350-seat theater and ample meeting rooms and facilities for conventions. In summer the colorful Chilkat Dancers share the auditorium with a melo-drama (*Lust for Dust*). See the "Culture and Nightlife" section, below.

The parade ground, at the center of the fort, is now the site of a replica of a small Tlingit community, **Totem Village.** This has never been thoroughly developed, al-though the Hotel Halsingland's nightly salmon bake is served in the Indian Tribal House. There's also a replica of a trapper's cabin, several totem poles, and a rack for drying and tanning pelts.

You can learn more about Haines's history at the **Sheldon Museum and Cultural Center,** on Main Street just above the boat harbor (tel. 766-2236). The museum has a fine collection of Tlingit artifacts, exhibits of Presbyterian mission and pioneer history, free Russian tea, and a book and gift store. I like the recon-structed shop of the pioneer who reputedly wore several pairs of glasses at once with this reasoning: "If one pair helps me see a little, more will help me see a lot." If you can't visit Haines between November and January, be sure to see the film *Last Stronghold of the Eagles.* Hours vary, but you can be certain to find the museum open from 1 to 5 p.m. daily in summer, plus some mornings and evenings, with a limited schedule the rest of the year. Admission is $2; children under 18 are free if accompa-nied by an adult. The museum is named for longtime resident Steve Sheldon (1885–1960), who willed much of his collection to the museum.

The Eagles

For centuries, as far back as Native man's earliest memories, eagles by the thou-sands have gathered on the Chilkat River in the fall and winter months to feast on a late run of chum salmon. To help protect them, the state in 1982 created the 48,000-acre **Alaska Chilkat Bald Eagle Preserve.** Visitors can park their vehicles in turnouts at the side of the Haines Hwy., 18 to 22 miles north of town at the "coun-cil grounds," and scan the trees and riverbanks with binoculars and cameras.

A particularly good time to scout for eagles is in mid- to late November, when the resident population of about 200 eagles soars to as many as 4,000—some com-ing from as far away as the state of Washington. Upwelling warm water keeps a three-mile stretch of the river free of ice, and it is here the eagles gather to feed.

Serious nature lovers won't be content with the side-of-the-road approach. Cer-tainly the best way to see the eagles is to float slowly down the river. **Chilkat Guides,** P.O. Box 170, Haines, AK 99827 (tel. 766-2409), lead one or two four-hour raft trips daily downriver at a charge of $45 for adults, $25 for children under 14. **Alas-ka Cross Country Guiding and Rafting,** P.O. Box 124, Haines, AK 99827, also offers eagle preserve tours.

A future note: The American Bald Eagle Foundation has plans to build a major interpretive visitor center and research facility in Haines.

Other Driving Trips

Mud Bay Road leads south nine miles from Fort Seward, halfway out the Chilkat Peninsula. The glaciers tumbling from rocky peaks across the Chilkat Inlet originate over the mountain crest in Glacier Bay National Park. Only one, **Davidson Glacier,** is a tidewater iceflow; you'll also see a spectacular hanging glacier known as **Rainbow Glacier.** Near the end of the road, at Letnikof Cove, is a 1917 salmon can-nery. **Chilkat State Park,** reached down an 11% grade on a two-mile gravel side road, is southeast Alaska's largest and newest state park. It offers picknicking, camp-ing, beachcombing, and fishing, plus whale and seal watching in Chilkat Inlet. The Parks Division hosts coffee klatches, campfire talks, and slide shows at a centrally located log cabin.

Northeast of Haines, the **Lutak Road** runs past the ferry terminal and cruise-ship dock to Chilkoot Lake and **Chilkoot State Park,** 11 miles from downtown. The lake is a popular venue for boating, fishing, and picknicking, as well as camping. At a fish weir on the Chilkoot River, two miles south of the park, toward town, you can watch salmon struggling upstream to their spawning ground.

Sports

FISHING The waters of the Chilkoot and Chilkat Inlets are rich in salmon and halibut. Troll for kings in the upper Lynn Canal in early summer—the Haines King Salmon Derby is held the last weekend of May and the first weekend of June. Pinks proliferate in the Chilkoot and Lutak Inlets in July and August. Chums and coho are excellent in the Chilkat Inlet and Chilkat River from September to early November. Trout fishermen go after Dolly Varden in Lutak Inlet and Chilkoot Lake June through November, or fly-fish for cutthroats in the Chilkoot and Chilkat Rivers.

You can get licenses and tackle at the **Alaska Sport Shop,** Fourth Avenue and Main Street (tel. 766-2441), or **Haines Tackle Company,** FAA and Battle Roads just south of Fort Seward (tel. 766-2255). Fishing charters carry four to six passengers and provide all bait and gear. Try **Lynn Canal Charter Service** (tel. 766-2254), at $15 per person per hour, minimum of two passengers and three hours. There's also a wilderness fishing camp on Chilkat Lake, accessible only by floatplane or riverboat. Contact **Don's Camp,** P.O. Box 645, Haines, AK 99827 (tel. 907/766-2303).

For additional information on fishing in the Haines area, contact the Alaska Department of Fish and Game, Division of Sport Fish (tel. 766-2625), or the Division of Fish and Wildlife Protection (tel. 766-2533).

HIKING AND BACKPACKING Pick up the green "Haines Is for Hikers" brochure at the Visitors Center. This short guide to local trail systems suggests numerous day trips of varying length and difficulty.

The shortest and easiest trip is the 2.4-mile **Battery Point Trail,** beginning at the end of Beach Road on the south side of Haines. It offers beautiful views across the Lynn Canal. There are three trails to the summit of 1,760-foot **Mount Riley,** ranging from a steep 2.1-mile hike off Mud Bay Road to a more gentle 5½-mile hike from Portage Cove. The peak of 3,920-foot **Mount Ripkinsky** is a difficult all-day climb from the top of Young Road overlooking Lutak Inlet. On clear days there's a view all the way to Admiralty Island south of Juneau. The **Seduction Point Trail** follows the west side of the Chilkat Peninsula 6.8 miles south from the Chilkat State Park visitor center to spectacular viewpoints across the Davidson Glacier. You might encounter bear or moose on any of these trails.

The more adventurous might enjoy an outing with **Ice-Field Ascents,** P.O. Box 170, Haines, AK 99827 (tel. 766-2097 or 766-2409), which specializes in "the art of negotiating variable terrain." Under director/artist John Svenson, the agency offers unusual guided hiking and glacier-walking trips, such as Haines-to-Skagway (10 to 14 days for $500). Experience with an ice axe and crampons is essential, but novices who sign on for a longer trip can pay half price for a weekend crash course at the Davidson Glacier, normally $135. Outings are strenuous, but the client-to-guide ratio is kept at 2 to 1.

RIVER RAFTING Besides the half-day trip down the Chilkat River, through the eagle preserve, there are numerous other rafting opportunities—many of them breathtaking both in their scenery and their waterborne adventure. **Alaska Cross Country Guiding and Rafting,** P.O. Box 124, Haines, AK 99827, flies visitors into its Tsiruku River wilderness lodge, then rafts them out through the preserve on two-day trips. **Chilkat Guides,** P.O. Box 170, Haines, AK 99827 (tel. 907/766-2409), also has two-day Tsiruku trips, which include a walk on the LeBlondeau Glacier (price: $225). Chilkat Guides' 11-day epic voyage down the Tatshenshini and Alsek Rivers has been called one of the last great adventures on the planet: starting at Dalton Post, Yukon Territory, it cuts a swath through the St. Elias Mountains, and at one point disappears into the eight-mile-wide Alsek Glacier. The trip ends at Dry Bay in Glacier Bay National Park/Preserve. Trips are seasonal, from June 1 to October 1.

WINTER SPORTS With average snowfall of eight to ten feet and a six-month cold season lasting from mid-November to mid-May, Haines appeals to many winter-sports enthusiasts—especially after February, when daylight hours are longer.

Cross-country skiers and snowshoers enjoy trails down the Chilkat River through the eagle preserve, and on the many other lakes and trails in the area. Telemarkers often head for Chilkat Pass, just across the Canadian border in British Columbia. **Telemark Line,** P.O. Box 491, Haines, AK 99827 (tel. 907/766-2876), a nordic ski shuttle and outfitting service, has daily charters for trailhead pickups and dropoffs along the Haines Hwy. and into the Yukon Territory.

There's a 100-strong local **snow machine** club, the Chilkat Snowburners, who sponsor the Alcan 200 rally in late January, with over $20,000 in prize money. **Ice fishermen** often strike it big at Mosquito Lake, while **dog-sled teams** practice along the lower Chilkat River and Chilkoot Lake.

OTHER SPORTS The Haines High School **swimming pool** is open to the public, with open swims scheduled from 1 to 3 p.m. and 7:30 to 9 p.m. Monday through Saturday. A $2 fee is charged. The high school also has free **tennis courts** and a **jogging track. Bicycles** can be rented from the Bike Shop (tel. 766-2249), in the basement of the Gateway Building. A **miniature golf** course has been set up on Second Avenue behind the Visitor Center.

Tours

Haines Street Car Co., P.O. Box 703, Haines, AK 99827 (tel. 907/766-2819), offers various three-hour tours of Haines, the Chilkat River valley, Chilkat Park, and Chilkoot Lake. All are priced at $15 (children 7 to 11 pay half price; under 7, free). A dinner and theater tour lets you take in the salmon bake and a show at the Chilkat Center, for $30, all-inclusive. Drivers meet all ferry arrivals, and will transport you to your hotel (one way, $3.50) or give you a whirlwind tour of Haines and get you back to the dock before departure for $6.

Alaska Sightseeing Co., based locally at the Hotel Halsingland (tel. 766-2435), also conducts three-hour local tours, including the fort and museum, for $16 ($8 for kids 5 to 11). This is offered May 15 to September 30 only, and departure times vary.

Among the unusual local tour options are guided photo tours of the bald eagle preserve, offered by **Eclipse Alaska,** P.O. Box 698, Haines, AK 99827 (tel. 907/766-2670), and **Alaska Nature Tours,** P.O. Box 491, Haines, AK 99827 (tel. 907/766-2876); and four-wheel-drive excursions to Glory Hole Spring at the head of Chilkoot Lake, led by **Chilkat Guides,** P.O. Box 170, Haines, AK 99827 (tel. 907/766-2409).

All local air-taxi operators offer flightseeing over Glacier Bay National Park and surrounding areas. See the "Orientation" section, above, for a listing.

SHOPPING

Haines is an artists' town, so it's no accident that there is a proliferation of fine art galleries around the Chilkat Valley.

At the **Northern Arts Gallery,** on Second Avenue behind the post office, look for Pete Andriesen's pen-and-ink drawings (and silkscreen reproductions thereof), Jenny Lyn Smith's silver- and woodcarvings in totemic designs, and Linda

Matthews's pottery. At the **Art Shop,** in the old Fort Seward telegraph building on Beach Road, note mountaineer John Svenson's watercolor and wood-block illustrations, and Gil Smith's paintings of mountain scenery. **The Sea Wolf,** on the Fort Seward parade grounds, and **The Whale Rider,** at Second Avenue and Willard Street, by the Visitors Center, are both operated by Tresham Gregg III, who has made his name as a multimedia artist by applying Tlingit themes to metal and wood sculptures. **Knute's Shop,** No. 5 Officers' Row in Fort Seward, is the studio-gallery of custom woodworker Lowell Knutson. You can see Sue Folletti's silver- and woodcarvings at **Chilkat Valley Arts,** 307 Willard St.

There are numerous gift shops along Main Street. I especially like **Hummingbird Arts Unlimited,** on Second Avenue not far from the Visitors Center. You can handle your photographic needs at **Bell's Store** on Second Avenue, and buy books on Second between Dalton and Union Streets at the **Gutenberg Dump,** which is worth a visit if only for the name.

CULTURE AND NIGHTLIFE

You will, of course, see the **Chilkat Dancers,** who perform throughout the summer at the Chilkat Center for the Arts on the following schedule: on Monday at 7:30 and 8:30 p.m.; on Wednesday, Thursday, and Saturday at 8:30 p.m. This troupe, comprised of white and Native adults and children performing tribal dances in traditional costume, has won international acclaim—they put on a great show. Adult admission is $5; children 5 to 18, $3.50; under 5, free. Call 766-2160 for more information.

On many nights that the dancers are not doing their thing at the Chilkat Center, the **Lynn Canal Community Players** are. From June to August, characters like the notorious Jack Dalton, miner Porcupine Pete, Sergeant Justin Time, and sweet Patience Steadfast take the stage on Friday and Sunday at 8:30 p.m. in a melodrama known as *Lust for Dust.* Tickets are $5 for adults, $3 for children. The theater group also presents several short-run plays at the Chilkat Center in the winter months, and hosts the biennial State Drama Festival of the Alaska State Community Theater Association in April of odd-numbered years. You can get more information by calling 766-2540.

Night lights are much dimmer in Haines than in Skagway or Juneau. The large lounge at the **Lighthouse Restaurant,** Front Street at Main (tel. 766-2442), occasionally books live bands. A good-size dance floor, jukebox, and pool tables will keep you hopping in any event. The **Pioneer Bar,** on Second Avenue between Main and Dalton Streets, and the **Fogcutter Bar,** on Main Street between First and Second Avenues, are popular local watering holes.

THE HAINES HIGHWAY

The Alaska Chilkat Bald Eagle Preserve is not the only point of interest on the Haines Hwy. as it heads north 40 miles to the Canadian border. The mountain scenery is equally spectacular.

The highway weaves its way up the Chilkat River valley as it leaves Haines. Locals frequently drive the first ten miles to the **10 Mile Steakhouse** (tel. 766-2800) for the Wednesday-night prime rib buffet or for horseshoe and volleyball tournaments. The restaurant is open from 3 p.m. Monday through Thursday, from 11 a.m. Friday through Sunday. It also has 26 camping sites without hookups.

In the middle of the eagle preserve, just past Milepost 21, there's a bumpy dead-end turnoff to the Tlingit village of **Klukwan** (pop. 100). This was once the main village of the Chilkat clan, famous for their blankets woven from cedar-bark fibers and mountain-goat hair. Today there's little to see—some newer houses, a handful of ramshackle older ones, and a log tribal house with a faded eagle-and-raven design painted on it. There are no facilities, and the Indians don't enjoy being subjects of photographic curiosity. Things may change if a cultural center, now under consideration, is built here.

The final miles to the border ascend through the Klehini River canyon, surrounded by snow-covered peaks. At Milepost 27, pristine **Mosquito Lake** (don't let the name scare you) has a campground and other facilities. Historic **33 Mile Roadhouse** (tel. 766-2979) is the last gas station before the border; open daily, it serves light meals and is licensed for beer and wine. A couple of miles farther, look across the Klehini River to pick out the remnants of the once-flourishing **Porcupine Mine ghost town,** destroyed by a flood in 1906.

Time your travels so you arrive at the border when Customs is open, or you could be in for a long wait. **Canadian Customs** is open from 7 a.m. to 10 p.m. May through September, 8 a.m. to 8 p.m. October through April. If you are coming from the north, be aware that **U.S. Customs** is open from 8 a.m. to midnight year round.

8. Skagway

Skagway is the end of the trail . . . and the beginning of it.

Skagway is the final stop of Alaska's Inside Passage for ferry or cruise-ship passengers. For the gold-seekers of 1898 who shed their sea legs here en route to the Klondike, and for modern-day adventurers who seek to retrace that adventure, it's the take-off point for the famed Chilkoot Trail.

But don't get the idea that Skagway is merely a stopping-off point. It isn't the sort of town where you can spend just a couple of hours, visit a museum and see a show, then depart, feeling as though you've "done" the town. It's a community that begs you to become immersed in its history and unique atmosphere, right down to the soap on Jefferson Smith's grave and the honky-tonk piano at the Red Onion Saloon.

Broadway, Skagway's main drag, looks almost the same today as it did eight decades ago. The boardwalks are still there; the biggest difference is that the dust and potholes have been paved over. More than 30 buildings along a five-block stretch were built between 1897 and 1903, and nearly all of them are still active places of business. In fact downtown Skagway is now a unit of the Klondike Gold Rush National Historical Park, a designation that aids with its preservation and adds to its interest.

Some folks claim—with some justification—that Broadway is "rolled up" in winter. Indeed, Skagway's permanent population of 600 more than doubles during the May-to-September tourist season. Temporary hotel workers (most of them college students from the Pacific Northwest and California) and other part-time residents flock in to cater to the lucrative cruise-ship crowd, whose numbers often reach 3,000 or more a day. Local merchants even make it a point to don period costumes on days of major cruise-ship arrivals.

Visitors who arrive in Skagway between October and April will find only two hotels and two bed-and-breakfasts open for business, representing but 70 of the town's 315 summer rooms. The 1987 decision to open the Klondike Hwy. to Whitehorse, Yukon Territory, year round has given the winter population a boost. Still, Skagway by winter doesn't have the excitement of the town in June, July, and August.

Skagway is located at the northern extreme of the Inside Passage, on a long finger of the Lynn Canal called the Taiya Inlet. The town was built where the Skagway River, tumbling from the 7,000-foot heights of the Canadian boundary ranges, flattens into a narrow plain nestling between high ridges.

Because of its extremely sheltered location, Skagway has a much drier climate than the rest of the southeast. The average annual precipitation is only 29 inches—less than half that of Haines, only 15 miles south. Temperatures average 57°F in July, 23°F in January. The north wind can be biting.

But it was more than climate that attracted Capt. William Moore in 1887 to build a homestead in the valley the Indians called Skagua, "Home of the North Wind." Moore was a riverboat skipper who had amassed a small fortune delivering miners and goods to British Columbia's Cassiar goldfields in the 1870s, and who now was convinced the Klondike would yield the next great lode. With the vision of a seer he began platting city streets, planning a wharf, and even musing about a railroad in preparation for the coming gold rush.

And come it did, in 1897 and 1898. Over 20,000 anxious fortune hunters boarded ships in Seattle and disembarked at this boom town at the mouth of the Skagway River, en route to Dawson City. The first boatload landed in July 1897 and overran Moore's settlement with a tent city. By October Broadway was lined with frame buildings and three new wharves were under construction. By 1899 the tracks of the White Pass & Yukon Route railroad were snaking over the mountains. Moore's vision of a metropolis had been no pipe dream.

Many of the new arrivals were less interested in panning streams or sluicing mud than in stripping the golden fleece from those who had already done so. Thousands remained in Skagway; Moore had not foreseen the proliferation of saloons and gambling halls (80 at one count), the thriving red-light district, the wolfpacks of thieves and con men. Skagway became known as "the roughest town on earth." Certainly it was among the most lawless.

Jefferson Randolph "Soapy" Smith was the most nefarious of all the wolves. Surrounding himself with a cadre of compliant lieutenants, he launched scam after unpunished scam to relieve the miners of their hard-won gold dust. His reign finally ended in a shootout with town surveyor Frank Reid on the city dock in July 1898, a duel that left both men dead. Their graves are found in Skagway's Gold Rush Cemetery; their story is recounted daily in summer in Gold Rush Productions' *Skaguay in the Days of '98* show at the Eagles Hall.

It wasn't long thereafter that the strike-it-rich miners heard about a new gold find—this one in Nome, in 1899—and all but abandoned the Klondike. Only the existence of the railroad shuttling freight between Whitehorse and the Inside Passage kept Skagway alive at all. The population shrank to a few hundred people, except for a few years during World War II when a couple of thousand federal workers channeled goods and personnel through Skagway to build the Alaska Hwy. Skagway's economy staggered in October 1982 when the railroad was shut down, forcing most of the population out of work. When it reopened as a summer tourist attraction in 1988, it gave the economy a shot in the arm.

ORIENTATION

Skagway's streets are laid out in a straight grid pattern. Paralleling Broadway on the east is Spring Street; on the west are, in order, State, Main, and Alaska Streets. These five thoroughfares are crisscrossed by numbered streets, from 1st Avenue to 23rd, which crosses the Skagway River and turns north as the Klondike Hwy.

Transportation

The 3,300-foot airstrip runs along the west side of Alaska Street, with the terminal on 12th Avenue. **L.A.B. Flying Service** (tel. 983-2471) has its office at the airport; associated with Alaska Airlines, this commuter service flies Pipers, a Navajo Chieftain, and two Britten-Norman Islanders to Juneau, Haines, Glacier Bay, and Hoonah. Skagway is also served by **Wings of Alaska,** with offices at the Golden North Hotel (tel. 983-2451 or 983-2294), and **Skagway Air Service,** at 4th and Broadway (tel. 983-2218). You can't miss the latter's colorful logo (a high-kicking dance-hall girl) or slogan ("We can can can.").

The ferries of the **Alaska Marine Hwy. System** (tel. 983-2229) visit Skagway eight times a week in summer, remaining in port for anywhere from 45 minutes to

9¼ hours before heading back south. The ferry dock empties directly onto Broadway. Cruise ships anchor in Taiya Inlet and unload passengers next to the Pullen Creek Park small-boat harbor, where Congress Way, an extension of Second Avenue, turns south.

Whitehorse, the capital of Canada's Yukon Territory, is 110 miles north on the Klondike Hwy. This bustling town of 17,000 is traditionally regarded as the midway point of the Alaska Hwy. There's daily bus service from Skagway to Whitehorse, Fairbanks, Anchorage, and points between on Gray Line's **Alaskon Express** (tel. 983-2241), May 27 to September 15, leaving the Klondike Hotel at 7:30 a.m. on Sunday, Tuesday, Wednesday, and Friday, at 9 a.m. other days. The fare is $51 to Whitehorse (4 hours), $169 to Fairbanks (32½ hours), and $185 to Anchorage (35½ hours). Journeys to Fairbanks and Anchorage require overnight stays at Beaver Creek, on the Yukon-Alaska border. Contact Gray Line of Alaska, 300 Elliott Ave. West, Seattle, WA 98119 (tel. toll free 800/544-2206). **Alaska-Yukon Motorcoaches** (tel. 983-2828) also has a scheduled run to Whitehorse. Inquire at the Golden North Hotel.

A novel way to get from Skagway to Whitehorse is aboard the **White Pass & Yukon Route** railway (tel. 907/983-2217, or toll free 800/343-7373). There's through service daily, late May to late September, from Skagway to Fraser, B.C., with bus connections to Whitehorse. The trip takes 4½ hours. Trains leave Whitehorse at 8:30 a.m. daily Yukon Time (one hour earlier than Alaska Time), and Skagway at 1 p.m. daily. Fare is $89 for adults, half price for kids. Chilkoot Trail hikers can be picked up at Lake Bennett, B.C., at 9:15 a.m. daily from mid-June to mid-September. The fare to Fraser, B.C., is $22; to Skagway, $67.

You can rent cars in Skagway from **Avis** (tel. 983-2247) at the Klondike Hotel, or privately at **Service Unlimited Chevron** (tel. 983-2595).

For local taxi service, try **Goldies** (tel. 983-2321) or **Frontier** (tel. 983-2512).

Information

Your single best source of information is the **Klondike Gold Rush National Historical Park Visitor Center,** in the old White Pass & Yukon Route railroad depot, at Second Avenue and Broadway (tel. 907/983-2921). The park rangers will give you a sheaf of printed materials, answer your questions, and steer you to the daily schedule of films, lectures, and historical walks. The **Skagway Convention and Visitors Bureau,** P.O. Box 415, Skagway, AK 99840 (tel. 907/983-2854 or 983-2297), is located at City Hall, on Seventh Avenue east of Broadway. You might also try the **Skagway Chamber of Commerce,** P.O. Box 194, Skagway, AK 99840 (tel. 907/983-2297).

If you have any questions before heading into (or after arriving from) Canada, check with the **U.S. Customs and Immigration Service,** at Second Avenue and Spring Street (tel. 983-2325 for Customs, 983-2377 for Immigration).

The *Skagway News* is published biweekly from May to October, monthly the rest of the year. There's a **medical clinic** on 11th Avenue between Broadway and State Street (tel. 983-2255; in an emergency, 983-2301). The **post office** and **National Bank of Alaska** (tel. 983-2264) share a building at Sixth Avenue and Broadway.

Festivals

The year's big party is on the **Fourth of July.** Four days before his death, Soapy Smith rode his tall white horse up Broadway as the grand marshal of the 1898 Independence Day parade. The twice-around parade, featuring the Bigger Hammer Marching Band, is still a tradition.

The cast of the *Days of '98* show honors Smith on July 8 with a wake at his grave in the Gold Rush Cemetery, beginning about 10 p.m. (after the last show). Smith's grandson, a resident of California, provides champagne for the party each year!

Other summer events (remember, Broadway is rolled up in winter) include the **Skagway Windfest,** with competition in ore-truck pulling and chain-saw throwing in mid-March (very early spring); the **Summer Solstice** street party, June 21; the **Eastern Star Flower Show** and Skagway Garden Club competition, August 17 to 20; and the **Klondike Trail of '98 Road Relay** from Skagway to Whitehorse, the third weekend in September.

WHERE TO STAY

With well over 300 rooms available in a town of 800, you might expect to have no problem finding accommodations. That's not always true. Because so many disembarking cruise-ship passengers stay overnight in Skagway before making onward connections, midsummer reservations are essential. Add 6% room tax to all prices quoted.

Deluxe

Two-thirds of the rooms in Skagway are at the **Westmark Inn,** P.O. Box 515, Skagway, AK 99840 (tel. 907/983-2291), owned and operated by Seattle-based Holland America Line/Westours, primarily for the benefit of its tour clientele. The interior décor of this rambling inn, which spills over two city blocks on either side of Third Avenue between Broadway and Spring Street, is evocative of the gold-rush era of the Gay '90s. Red carpets and red-velvet wallpaper, brass fixtures, and historical photos are its earmarks.

The gold-rush theme, including carpeting and wallpaper, is carried over into the "100" and "200" rooms in the main hotel building north of Third. An oval brass mirror hangs above the desk in each room; white loge-style drapes hide the midsummer midnight sun from the two double beds. There are thermostat-controlled electric baseboard heating, a clock-radio, and complimentary shampoo and vanity kit in the bathroom, but no TV or phone. The "300" through "600" rooms south of Third Avenue are more like motel units with outside entrances; although quite nice, they're smaller and less atmospheric than the lower-numbered accommodations. Rooms are $112 single, $126 double.

In the lobby are a gift shop, travel agency, Gray Line tour desk, and scale model of one of the Holland America Line cruise vessels. You'll also find courtesy-car service and a guest laundry. And for those who just can't stand to be away from the news any longer than necessary, *USA Today* and the *Seattle Post-Intelligencer* are available on weekdays a day late.

As you enter the spacious Chilkoot Dining Room adjoining the main lobby, take note of the mounted 126-pound king salmon—a world-record catch. Then try the salmon baked with brown sugar, an entree acclaimed by the press all the way to New York. If you're not a fish eater, the apple-almond chicken is a house specialty. All dinner entrees, served from 5 to 9 p.m. daily are priced at $11 to $20. Breakfast is on the table from 5:30 to 10 a.m., and there's a generous all-you-can-eat seafood buffet luncheon (priced at $8) from 11:30 a.m. to 1 p.m. The Chilkoot Room's garden-trellis atmosphere is given gold-rush flavor by historical photos on the walls.

Turn-of-the-century photos also adorn the Westmark's informal Sourdough Café. Checkered tablecloths and painted benches may make you feel that you're in an Italian diner—as indeed you are. Spaghetti dinners, including bread and salad, run $6.50 to $7.25, while veal parmigiana is a little higher at $8.50. Wine is $1.50 by the glass. Cafeteria-style lunches include a by-the-pound salad bar. Open from 11:30 a.m. to 3 p.m. and 5 to 8 p.m. daily.

To reach the Bonanza Lounge, open from 4 p.m. to midnight, you must climb a circular staircase from the lobby. Here you can sit in a red-velvet-cushioned chair and sip a Yukon Jack on the rocks as you lean over a black wrought-iron railing and enjoy the best live musical show in southeast Alaska . . . inevitably with a Gay '90s theme, like everything else in Skagway.

The Westmark is open only from May 15 to September 30. For off-season information or reservations, write or call Holland America Line/Westours, Inc., 300 Elliott Ave. West, Seattle, WA 98119 (tel. 206/281-3535, or toll free 800/544-2206).

Moderate

Whereas the Westmark Inn has re-created Skagway's heyday in its décor and atmosphere, the **Golden North Hotel,** at the corner of Broadway and Third Avenue (P.O. Box 431), Skagway, AK 99840 (tel. 907/983-2294 or 983-2451), doesn't have to pretend. This angelic relic, one of only two accommodations in Skagway that remain open year round, is believed to be the oldest hotel in Alaska in continuous operation since it opened (in 1898). It's a living museum of Victoriana—beginning with the lobby, whose reception desk, display sideboard, and even the settees facing the fireplace hail from another time.

A small plaque dedicates each of the 33 rooms to a different gold-rush–era family. Contained within are the original furnishings of that family: beds with oak or brass frames, hardwood dressers, portraits on the walls. Although each room has red carpeting and gaily patterned wallpaper, no two are the same. There are no TVs or phones, by the way. The rooms have three-quarter baths, and heating is done the old-fashioned way: with hot water. Singles are $60; doubles, $70; twins, $75. Three economy rooms with shared baths go for $35 single, $40 double. There's an access room for the handicapped on the ground floor.

The Golden North Restaurant is open from 6 a.m. to 9 p.m. daily. Breakfast omelets cost $5.25; lunch sandwiches or soup-and-salad bar, $6; dinner entrees (steak and seafood), $12.50 to $20. The adjacent lounge has live solo entertainment periodically.

At the north end of Skagway, the **Wind Valley Lodge,** P.O. Box 354, Skagway, AK 99840 (tel. 907/983-2236), caters as much to motorists and business travelers as to the short-term tourist. Like many ex-railroadmen, owner Les Fairbanks, a former brakeman on the White Pass & Yukon Route, couldn't stand to be far from the tracks. So he built across the street from the old railroad yard at 22nd Avenue and State Street, and even decorated his 30 spacious rooms with railroad photographs he took in the 1950s. Each room contains a queen-size bed or two twin beds, table and chairs, desk and dresser, electric baseboard heating, and cable television. Six rooms are designated no-smoking, and one is available for disabled travelers. Public phones are in a vending room, and there's a coin-operated guest laundry. The lodge provides courtesy transportation to those who need it, but it's a pleasant one-mile walk into town. Prices are $45 to $48 single, $55 to $57 double; kids under 6 stay free in their parents' room. Open April through November.

The **Gold Rush Lodge,** Alaska Street at Sixth Avenue (P.O. Box 514), Skagway, AK 99840 (tel. 907/983-2831), has 12 rooms, all with outside entrances. The rooms are comfortable but hardly flamboyant: orange carpet, twin beds, electric baseboard heating. To some it's important that the cable television features Home Box Office. There's no phone, though; you'll have to use the booth outside. A courtesy car provides service to the ferry terminal and downtown. Prices are $55 single, $65 twin. Open May 15 through August 31. In the off-season, contact P.O. Box 924, Alturas, CA 96801 (tel. 916/233-4677).

Never mind that the TV character of the 1950s was a member of the Royal Canadian Mounted Police. Sergeant Preston and his lead sled dog, King, did make occasional trips into Skagway. **Sgt. Preston's Lodge,** Sixth Avenue at State Street (P.O. Box 538), Skagway, AK 99840 (tel. 907/983-2521), reminds you of those legendary Mounties with buttons that read: "I Slept With Sgt. Preston!" The 22 rooms, decorated in autumn colors, vary in spaciousness, bed size, and amenities.

All have cable TV with HBO. They are kept warm by central forced-air heating. A continental breakfast and courtesy-van service are included, but there's no phone in the rooms. Prices are $55 single, $65 double, with private bath; $45 single, $55 double with shared bath. Open year round.

Budget

Irene's Inn, Broadway at Sixth Avenue (P.O. Box 538), Skagway, AK 99840 (tel. 907/983-2520), is under the same ownership as Sgt. Preston's but attracts a more budget-conscious type of guest. There's no reception desk: check in first at the good sergeant's or step down off the boardwalk, enter Irene's door, climb the red-carpeted stairs, and find the telephone, which will connect you with the room clerk. Irene's ten rooms are small and spartan, with only two twin beds, a towel rack, and a nightstand with a lamp. Venetian blinds and lace curtains are on the windows, a hot-water baseboard heater against a wood-paneled wall. The bathrooms are down the hall. But what did you expect for $30 single, $35 double? Open May 15 to September 15.

Bed-and-Breakfast

The **Skagway Inn,** P.O. Box 500, Skagway, AK 99840 (tel. 907/983-2289), was built in 1897 as a rooming house for women. Today its 14 rooms are named in remembrance of those hardy gals who survived rough-and-ready Skagway. There was Alice, for example, Essie, Flo, and Grace. Each of them was a little bit different —and so are each of the period-style rooms. Everyone shares the charming living room, however, with its couches and easy chairs, piano, and television. And breakfast is the same for all: cereal and yogurt, fruit and muffins, coffee and tea. Miss Emily's Tearoom offers a buffet of soups, salads, and sandwiches from 11 a.m. to 7 p.m. daily. There's courtesy-car service to the airport and ferry dock. The Skagway Inn is located on Broadway near Seventh Avenue. Rates are $48 single, $55 double, mid-April to early October.

Mary's Bed & Breakfast, Tenth Avenue and State Street (P.O. Box 72), Skagway, AK 99840 (tel. 907/983-2875), has three bedrooms. Rates are $40 single, $50 double, in summer; $30 single, $35 double, in winter. **Gramma's Bed & Breakfast,** Seventh Avenue and State Street (P.O. Box 315), Skagway, AK 99840 (tel. 907/983-2312), charges $40 single, $45 double.

Campgrounds

All three city campgrounds are run by the same enterprise—**Hoover's,** P.O. Box 304, Skagway, AK 99840 (tel. 907/983-2454). Hanousek Park, at 14th and Broadway, has ten tent sites and 40 RV spaces. Pullen Creek Park, on Congress Way near the small-boat harbor, has 42 RV sites. Hoover's 4th and Main campground has 20 RV sites. Rates are $5 for tents to $12.50 for RVs. Showers are available.

There's also a small National Park Service campground for backpackers at **Dyea,** near the Chilkoot Trailhead, nine miles by dirt road from Skagway. This one is free—but it will cost you $5 or more to get there by local taxi.

WHERE TO EAT

The Chilkoot Dining Room and Sourdough Café at the Westmark Inn, and the Golden North Restaurant at that hotel, are often considered the "best" restaurants in Skagway. But for their nights out, Skagway's sourdoughs commonly shun the tourist-heavy hotels in favor of the **Prospector's Sourdough Restaurant,** Broadway between Fourth and Fifth Avenues (tel. 983-2865). Oil paintings of mountain scenery hang on the walls of this spacious coffeehouse, open from 6 a.m. to 9 p.m. daily. It's the only place in town where you can get a fresh salmon dinner for $10, including soup or salad, potato, and vegetable. Steak sandwiches are $8.75 for lunch; Goldie's Grubstake, an Alaska-size breakfast with three hotcakes, two eggs, meat, and coffee, goes for $6.75.

Just up the block in an old log building is the **Northern Lights Café,** also on Broadway between Fourth and Fifth (tel. 983-2225). An informal coffeeshop, it has hearty breakfasts from $3.75, lunch burgers from $4 with fries, full porterhouse steak dinners for $15. Open daily from 6 a.m. to 10 p.m. in summer, shorter hours in winter.

Kountry Kitchen, at Fourth Avenue and State Street (tel. 983-2667), open from 6 a.m. to 10 p.m. daily (from 10:30 a.m. on Sunday), also offers a full menu. The **Sweet Tooth Saloon,** Broadway at Third (tel. 983-2405), open from 6 a.m. to 6 p.m. daily, is tiny (only seven tables) but has great cinnamon rolls and the cheapest eggs in town. There's an ice-cream parlor, the **Kone Kompany,** on Broadway at Fifth (tel. 983-2370), and a popular street stall, **Broadway Espresso,** which vends coffee, muffins, and sandwiches at its permanent location on Fifth Avenue just east of Broadway. **Dee's Salmon Bake,** Second Avenue off Broadway, offers just what the name implies in an indoor-outdoor seating area—plus halibut, steaks and burgers.

WHAT TO SEE AND DO

The **Klondike Gold Rush National Historical Park** comprises many of the buildings of the Historic District of Skagway, as well as the nearby ruins of Dyea, the Chilkoot and White Pass Trails, and a museum in Seattle commemorating the fortune-hunters' seaborne departure for the Klondike.

Start your visit at the park headquarters and visitor center, open from 8 a.m. to 6 p.m. daily May through September in the recently restored White Pass & Yukon Route depot building, Second Avenue and Broadway (tel. 983-2921). There's something happening every hour, from films to slide presentations to lectures to a permanent exhibit. Especially recommended are the movie *Days of Adventure, Dreams of Gold,* and the 45-minute guided walk, the latter usually starting at 11 a.m. and 3 p.m. For more information, write the National Park Service, P.O. Box 517, Skagway, AK 99840.

It would be hopelessly long-winded to describe each of the circa-1898 city structures visited in the walking tour. But one that's worth more than a passing glance is the **Arctic Brotherhood Hall** on Broadway between Second and Third. With a façade assembled from more than 20,000 pieces of tideflat driftwood, the headquarters of this now-defunct fraternal order (the last person initiated was President Warren Harding in 1923) is easily the most-photographed building in Skagway. Today the hall has become a mini-theater where *The White Pass Railroad Story* is recounted in photo, word, and song. It's presented daily in summer from 9 a.m. to 9 p.m. Admission is $2.50.

The other most-visited building is **City Hall,** one block east of Broadway on Sixth Avenue. Built in 1899 as McCabe Methodist College, Alaska's first, if short-lived, institution of higher education, it is also the state's oldest granite structure. From 1901 to 1956 the building was a federal courthouse. Today the ground floor contains city offices.

City Hall's second floor is occupied by the **Trail of '98 Museum** (tel. 983-2420). The most interesting items in the collection are the odds and ends from early Skagway—stampeders' sleds and snowshoes, settlers' Victorian-era appliances, casinos' roulette wheels and game boards. You can also peruse a multitude of old scrapbooks with historical photos and documents, a taxidermy display of local wildlife, and a variety of native artifacts. Open from 8 a.m. to 8 p.m. daily, June through September; 9 a.m. to 5 p.m. in May; closed October to April. Adult admission is $2; children, $1.

The narrow-gauge **White Pass & Yukon Route** railway was built at the turn of the century to handle the shipment of goods between here and the Yukon. It was closed down in October 1982, but reopened in May 1988 as a tourist attraction.

Today old Steam Engine No. 73 pulls the 1890s parlor cars 1½ miles through town, from the dock to the railroad yards off 23rd Avenue, where regular diesel engines take over for the 2,885-foot climb to the summit of White Pass. The 41-mile round trip spans spider-web trestles over gorges like Dead Horse Gulch, past cataracts like Bridal Veil and Pitchfork Falls, to panoramic spectacles like Inspiration Point.

The train operates daily from late May to late September, with irregular service at other times. Trains leave Skagway at 9 a.m. and 1:30 p.m. for the 2¾-hour round-trip run to White Pass. Fare is $67 for adults, half price for children 12 and under.

For full information, contact White Pass & Yukon Route, P.O. Box 435, Skagway, AK 99840 (tel. 907/983-2217, or toll free 800/343-7373).

If you're feeling energetic, you can walk another half mile up the tracks from the railyards to the **Gold Rush Cemetery.** The graves of Jefferson "Soapy" Smith and Frank Reid are here, as well as those of a multitude of other early settlers. It's ironic that Smith, a rather pathetic character in his time, has been raised to hero status in the 1980s while Reid, an upstanding citizen, has been vilified. An inscription on Reid's grave reads "He gave his life for the honor of Skagway," and an epitaph on the headstone of a prostitute named Ella Wilson is inscribed "She gave her honor for the life of Skagway."

You should also make it a point to stroll the numbered avenues off State and Main Streets to see some of Alaska's finest **Victorian architecture.** Despite the short season, many of these homes have magnificent gardens that have helped give Skagway the nickname "Garden City of the North."

Touring by Car

Skagway was not the only township on the Taiya Inlet in 1898. Nearby **Dyea**— 2½ miles by water, 9 miles by road—rivaled Skagway as the largest community in Alaska. Dyea was the gateway to the Chilkoot Trail, and like Skagway, had its share of hotels, banks and stores, saloons, casinos, and brothels. But when the railroad from Skagway opened up an easier route to the Yukon in 1899, Dyea abruptly died. It was a quiet death, but a certain one. Within a few years the abandoned buildings had been torn down, their lumber used for new construction elsewhere. Today there is little to be seen—scattered ruins of building foundations, rotting pilings of old wharves extending into the inlet, and the Slide Cemetery where 60 victims of a tragic Chilkoot Pass avalanche are buried.

The dirt road to Dyea branches west off the Klondike Hwy. about 2½ miles north of Skagway. It also leads to a National Park Service campground and to the **Chilkoot Trailhead,** about 6½ miles from the junction.

Prospectors had the option of two trails to reach the Klondike—the easier 40-mile White Pass Trail from Skagway or the shorter, steeper 33-mile Chilkoot Trail from Dyea. Naturally, most of them chose the latter. It was a costly mistake. The final half-mile climb over the snow-covered 3,739-foot pass took a severe toll on men and horses, all of whom were required to ascend 20 to 30 times to tote their ton of food and gear (enough for a year's prospecting, stipulated by the Canadian government) over the top.

For more specific information on the trail today, read the section on "Hiking and Backpacking," below.

Back on the Klondike Hwy., there's one more point of interest before the rapid climb to White Pass begins. Take a turnoff to the east about half a mile past the Dyea Road and you'll discover **Tent City,** a recent attempt by the proprietor of the famed Red Onion Saloon to re-create the atmosphere of the first few gold-rush months in old Skaguay (as it was originally spelled). Among the canvas-covered "buildings" are a cookhouse, general store, saloon, Chinese laundry, miner's home, and harlot's crib. The store contains a private collection of antique furnishings and ladies' wardrobes from the Red Onion, which was in fact a brothel. Summer visitors are given a chance to pan for gold from a sluice box. They are treated to refreshments in the mess hall and serenaded with gold-rush ballads and stories.

The 15 miles on the **Klondike Highway** from downtown Skagway to the Canadian border at White Pass (3,290 feet) afford one of the most beautiful drives in Alaska, with spectacular waterfalls, gaping chasms, and even a unique cantilever bridge for engineering students to appreciate. Canadian Customs is another eight miles past the summit. Returning south, U.S. Customs is just six miles out of Skagway. Both are now open 24 hours.

Sports

FISHING You can angle for silver and pink salmon from Skagway's beaches and wharves, but you'll need a boat to get deep enough for the big king salmon. Local lakes and streams contain rainbow trout, Dolly Vardens, and arctic char. **Skagway Sports Emporium,** on Fourth Avenue between Broadway and State Street (tel. 983-2480), and **Skagway Hardware,** at Fourth and Broadway (tel. 983-2233), sell fishing equipment and licenses.

HIKING AND BACKPACKING The 33-mile **Chilkoot Trail** follows the path of the gold seekers of 1898 over the Chilkoot Pass to Lake Bennett, Canada, from which they could travel down the Yukon River to Dawson City. A unit of the Klondike Gold Rush National Historical Park, this difficult but well-maintained trail is used by about 1,500 modern-day adventurers a year. The trip takes three to five days. Gold-rush ruins and relics (all of them federally protected) are scattered along the route; bear and moose are frequently encountered.

The trailhead is in Dyea. From May to mid-September taxis will carry you and your gear the nine miles from Skagway for $10. At the Canadian end you must hike an additional eight miles from Lake Bennett to Log Cabin on the Klondike Hwy., and catch the bus there to Whitehorse ($36) or Skagway ($15). For additional information and trail conditions, contact the National Park Service, P.O. Box 517, Skagway, AK 99840 (tel. 907/983-2921). Ask for their detailed brochure on the trail.

There are several fine day hikes closer to Skagway. The **Dewey Lake Trail System** starts in downtown Skagway across the railroad tracks from the Klondike Ho tel. Nine miles of trails connect numerous lakes, waterfalls, and historic sites. The five-and-a-half-mile **Denver Glacier Trail** begins about three miles up the railroad right-of-way, ascending 2,000 feet up the east fork of the Skagway river to the glacier.

OTHER SPORTS There are **tennis courts** at Skagway Public School, on State Street between 11th and 13th Avenues, and **softball** diamonds at 12th and Main and at 16th and Alaska. Skagway's slow-pitch teams have games every Monday through Thursday night, May through August.

Tours

My personal favorite among the numerous Skagway tour operators is the **Skagway Street Car Co.,** P.O. Box 400, Skagway, AK 99840 (tel. 907/983-2908). Steve and Gayla Hites have set out to re-create the early-20th-century tours hosted by Martin Itjen, a Skagway prospector, hotelier, undertaker, roulette spinner, and Ford dealer. Conductors dressed in period costume now squire visitors around Skagway in a fleet of antique automobiles—a 1923 Dodge screenside, a 1927 Dodge Laundalet convertible limousine, and a 1932 Ford paddywagon. The tour takes in historic Skagway from the waterfront, where the prospectors arrived, to the Gold Rush Cemetery, where the unlucky ones were laid to rest. Steve Hites, himself a talented musician once known as the "Singing Conductor" of the White Pass & Yukon Route, concertizes on guitar and harmonica in the Arctic Brotherhood Hall at the conclusion of the trip. The tour takes 2¼ hours and costs $34 (children under 12, $17). It operates from 9 a.m. to 9 p.m. daily, mid-May through September.

Also with a period flavor is **Skaguay Hack** (tel. 983-2472), which gives horse-drawn carriage rides and town tours. The Soapy Smith Excursion, which winds up at the cemetery, leaves Third Avenue and Broadway at 10 a.m. and 3 p.m. daily, mid-May to mid-September.

Similar historical tours by van or motorcoach are offered in the summer by **Gray Line** at the Klondike Hotel (tel. 983-2241), **Alaska Sightseeing Co.** at the Golden North Hotel (tel. 983-2828), **Atlas Tours** at Fourth and Broadway (tel. 983-2402), and **Royal Hyway Tours** (tel. 983-2895). Typical tours last 2 to 2½ hours and cost $16 for adults, $8 for children 5 to 11.

Alaska Sightseeing also offers a 3½-hour tour including Dyea and the Chilkoot Trail for $32 (children pay $16). Royal Hyway operates a 2½-hour Dyea tour, including gold panning and a visit to a sled-dog camp, for $35 (children pay $25).

Flightseeing tours over Chilkoot Pass (45 minutes) and to Glacier Bay (1½ hours) are offered by all local air charters, usually with a passenger minimum and on advance request. Check with **Skagway Air Service** (tel. 983-2219) or **L.A.B. Flying Service** (tel. 983-2471). The Glacier Bay tour costs $95 per person. Even more exciting than Pipers and Cessnas are helicopters: **Temsco Helicopters** (tel. 983-2909) depart from the ferry dock for glacier and gold-rush tours.

SHOPPING

Attracted by the historic atmosphere and the potential for sales to tourists, many artisans have chosen to make Skagway their home. You can find good buys in gold and silver jewelry, scrimshaw, woodcarving, ivory sculpture, paintings, and photography. The boardwalks of Broadway are lined with gift shops from Second to Sixth Avenue. My favorites are a couple of long-established businesses: **Kirme's Curio Shop,** at Fifth and Broadway (tel. 983-2341), and **Corrington's Alaska Ivory Co.,** on Broadway between Fifth and Sixth (tel. 983-2452). I'm also impressed by the fine ivory work at the **David Present Gallery,** at Third and Broadway (tel. 983-2873).

The best place in Skagway to get your photo and reading requirements handled is **Dedman's Photo Shop,** on Broadway between Third and Fourth (tel. 983-2353).

NIGHTLIFE

There aren't a lot of places to choose from, but those that do exist can really get wild when the ships are in port. Everyone—tourist, local, and seasonal worker—seems to gravitate to Madame Jan's **Red Onion Saloon and Gold Rush Brothel,** at Second Avenue and Broadway (tel. 983-2222). It's no longer a house of ill-repute, but you can buy a monogrammed garter and pretend you were there when it was. The Red Onion has live jazz frequently, honky-tonk piano and jukebox always, and dancing wherever you can find empty floor space. Great lunch sandwiches too.

Don't spend all your evening hours in the Red Onion, though. Take a break for *Skaguay in the Days of '98,* staged daily from mid-May to mid-September in the Eagles Hall, Sixth Avenue and Broadway. A musical production on a Gay '90s dance-hall set, the show recounts the flamboyant career and demise of Soapy Smith during Skagway's heyday. **Gold Rush Productions** has been presenting this show since 1926! The box office is open daily from 10 a.m. to 9 p.m.: adult tickets are $10; kids pay $5. An hour of casino-style gambling (with phony money) precedes the 9 p.m. evening curtain—the winner earns an opportunity to remove a garter from a dance-hall queen. A matinee schedule is geared to cruise ships. The Eagles Hall also has a musical slide presentation, *History of Skagway,* with ragtime music and Robert Service ballads, on a rotating schedule from 10 a.m. to 9 p.m. Inquire at the box office.

The **Westmark Inn** books seasonal entertainment from June 15 to September 1 into its Bonanza Lounge. These are often follies or circa-1900 musical shows, and are always highly professional. In addition, solo performers appear at the **Golden North Hotel** lounge several nights a week.

If you're merely looking for a cold beer and a pinch of conversation, **Moe's Frontier Bar,** on Broadway between Fourth and Fifth (tel. 983-2238), does a thriving business with the local crowd.

ANCHORAGE

Half of all Alaskans live in Anchorage, the state's largest city and commercial center. Its 250,000 people make their homes within sight of Mount McKinley, on a large, flat triangle of land bounded on the east by the rounded peaks of the Chugach Mountains, on the northwest and southwest by the tidal fluctuations of the Cook Inlet.

While the sourdoughs who live outside this northern metropolis insist that "Anchorage is not Alaska," the "new Alaskan" seems to prefer the comforts of a large city to the rigors of the bush. The people of Anchorage are mainly young (average age: 26) and affluent (average annual income: $28,000). They like sophisticated restaurants, shops, music, and theater. They like to live in suburbia, drive to a secure job in the morning and return home in the evening, and take their weekends to visit the wilderness.

That wilderness is never far away: moose frequently stroll through backyards and beluga whales frolic in the inlet. Within an easy day's trip are rugged mountains, mighty glaciers, and wild rivers.

Anchorage's climate, thanks to the warming Japanese Current, is surprisingly mild for a city at 61° North Latitude. Its winters have been compared to those of Innsbruck, Austria, with temperatures commonly in the teens and 20s; its 60°F and 70°F summers are like those of San Francisco. Summer days last over 19 hours in mid-June. Winter nights, kept bright by the aurora borealis, can seem almost interminable in the days before Christmas. Average annual precipitation is only about 15 inches, much of that falling in the form of winter snow (60 inches average).

A SHORT HISTORY

Once an Athabaskan Indian fishing camp, the site of Anchorage was first visited by the ubiquitous Capt. James Cook in 1778. Miners en route to rich inland goldfields used the deep-water anchorage at the mouth of Ship Creek before the turn of the 20th century. But it wasn't until 1914 that the town was established as a tent city for Alaska Railroad workers. The first permanent buildings were constructed the following year on the bluff overlooking the creek.

Anchorage remained primarily a rail headquarters, with its population stagnated at around 2,000, until World War II military spending gave impetus to the local economy. With the opening of Fort Richardson and Elmendorf Air Base, and the construction of the Alaska Hwy., the city became directly linked to the outside world. By 1950 some 40,000 people called themselves permanent residents.

No one who lived in Alaska in 1964 will ever forget the Good Friday earthquake. No one who has moved here since can ignore it. At 5:36 p.m. on March 27, the largest tremor ever felt on the North American continent devastated large sections of the city. Seismographs measured it between 8.4 and 8.6 on the Richter scale. Only nine people died, but property damage was estimated at over $300 million. With federal disaster aid, Anchorage quickly rebuilt. Earthquake Park and museum displays today graphically recall nature's wrath.

Anchorage owes its current stature to the building of the Trans Alaska Pipeline. The largest private construction project in history brought tens of thousands of new workers to Alaska in the 1970s. Many of them chose to remain and build their lives in the Anchorage area after the 779-mile pipeline was completed in 1977.

Because of its unique geographical location—roughly equidistant between Tokyo and New York, only slightly farther to London—Anchorage has become an international crossroads city and a world trade center. In the past decade 76% of all Alaskan exports have gone to Japan, the major consumer of Alaska's seafood, petroleum products, and timber. Korea and China are increasingly important markets.

---

1. Orientation

When locals talk about the Anchorage Bowl, the subject isn't a New Year's Day football game or a ten-pin alley. That's the name given to a mountain- and sea-ringed swath of land on which the city is built. Sprawling for some ten miles north-south, from Elmendorf Air Force Base to Rabbit Creek, and ten miles east-west, from Chugach State Park to Point Campbell, Anchorage city encompasses about 75 square miles of land. The Municipality of Anchorage, stretching over 50 miles from the Portage Glacier to the head of Cook Inlet, covers 1,955 square miles.

Despite this vastness, it's easy to find your way around downtown Anchorage. All numbered avenues run east-west, and all lettered streets run north-south. The city is divided neatly in two by **A Street.** West of it, streets proceed alphabetically, B through U. Eastward, they're also alphabetical, but with names—Barrow, Cordova, Denali, Eagle, Fairbanks, Gambell, Hyder, Ingra, and so on through Orca. Fifth Avenue, going one-way west, and Sixth Avenue, running one-way east, are extensions of the **Glenn Highway,** which runs east and north to Eagle River and beyond. Gambell Street, going one-way south, and Ingra Street, running one-way north, connect with the **Seward Highway,** the main thoroughfare to the Kenai Peninsula.

Downtown is generally defined as that area west of Merrill Field between Ship and Chester Creeks. The **main business district** runs from Third to Sixth Avenues between A and L Streets. **Midtown,** a growing business and restaurant area, lies west of the Seward Hwy. and south of Chester Creek as far as International Airport Road. **Spenard,** the city's traditional (and often notorious) entertainment district, weaves along Spenard Road connecting midtown with the international airport. Large parks and suburban shopping malls speckle the outlying areas to the south and east.

GETTING TO AND FROM ANCHORAGE

As Alaska's transportation hub, Anchorage is easily accessible by air and road, less readily by scheduled ship.

By Air

Well over 100 flights a day originate or terminate at **Anchorage International Airport.** The international terminal serves 16 airlines, many of them foreign flag carriers which consider Anchorage an ideal stopover and refueling point between the Orient and Europe or the U.S. East Coast. The domestic terminal handles all flights arriving and departing within Alaska and between Anchorage and the Lower 48 (plus Hawaii). The Anchorage Convention and Visitors Bureau staffs **information desks** on the ground floors of both terminals. There are also numerous restaurants or quick-serve cafés, lounges, and gift shops, and prominent displays of Alaskan wildlife and art in both terminals. The two terminals, about 500 yards apart, are connected by a free shuttle bus, operating at 15-minute intervals from 5:30 a.m. to 2:30 a.m. daily.

Here are the Anchorage addresses and phone numbers for leading airlines serving domestic traffic: **Alaska Airlines,** 4750 W. International Airport Rd. (tel. 243-3300, or toll free 800/426-0333), and also in the Anchorage Hilton and Sheraton Hotels; **Northwest Airlines,** 4300 W. International Airport Rd. (tel. 243-1123, or toll free 800/225-2525), and also in the Anchorage Hilton Hotel; **United Airlines,** at the airport (tel. 562-4020, or toll free 800/241-6522); **Delta Airlines,** 3830 W. International Airport Rd. (tel. 243-1311, or toll free 800/221-1212), and also at 509 W. Third Ave. and in the Hotel Captain Cook; and **MarkAir** (which flies in Alaska only), 4100 W. International Airport Rd. (tel. 243-6275, or toll free 800/426-6784, 800/478-0800 in Alaska).

GETTING TO AND FROM THE INTERNATIONAL AIRPORT   Anchorage International Airport is located about five miles southwest of downtown. If you've just arrived and are driving a rental car, the easiest way to reach the city center by road is to head east on International Airport Road to a cloverleaf intersection with Minnesota Drive, then turn left (north) and proceed until, after a big S-curve, you find yourself entering downtown on I Street. The drive takes 15 to 20 minutes.

There are three alternatives. The most expensive, as always, is by **taxi,** around $12 to downtown. An airport limousine service, **Ace Limo** (tel. 248-5114), meets incoming flights and delivers arrivals to downtown hotels for just $5. It also has pickup service once an hour. June 1 to September 30, Ace limos run daily from 5:30 a.m. to 11:05 p.m. The winter schedule is abbreviated; call for information.

The city bus, known as the **People Mover** (tel. 264-6543 weekdays from 7 a.m. to 6 p.m.), also serves the airport. Route 6 stops hourly on the lower level and plies the byways to downtown via Minnesota Drive. The adult fare is 75¢. Students pay 25¢; preschoolers and senior citizens ride free with a pass.

SMALLER AIRPORTS   In a state with eight times the national average number of pilots and 15 times the average aircraft per capita, it isn't surprising to learn that Anchorage International is not the only airport in the city (there are 17). In fact, International is not even the busiest. **Merrill Field** (tel. 276-4044), east of downtown between 4th and 15th Avenues, ranks as the 33rd-busiest airport in the United States, with 375,000-plus takeoffs and landings a year. If you're flying to an airstrip in the bush, chances are you'll do so from here.

If you're traveling to a fishing lodge, there's a good chance you'll visit **Lake Hood Air Harbor,** said to be the world's busiest floatplane base, with about 85,000 flight arrivals and departures annually. Most of those are in summer, of course, but don't be surprised to see ski-equipped planes taking off and landing on the winter ice. Lake Hood is immediately north of the international airport.

By Car

Contrary to popular belief, Anchorage is not the end of the Alaska Highway That's up north, in Delta Junction. But the Glenn Highway, which originates in An-

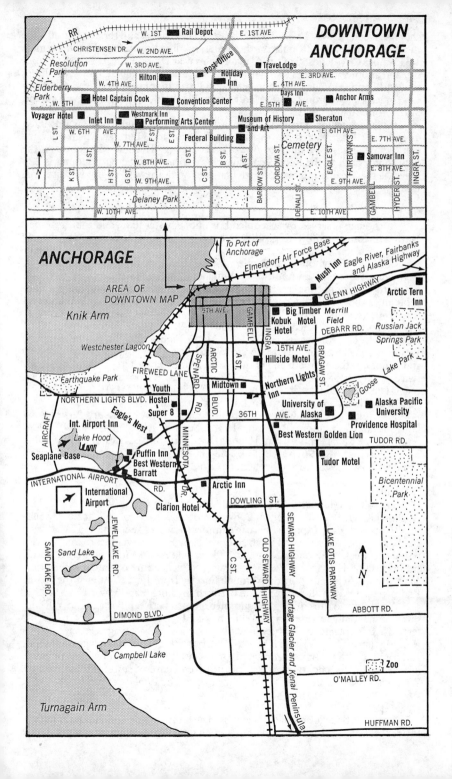

chorage, wends its way 180 miles northeast to Glennallen, and the Tok Cutoff joins the Alaska Highway 138 miles farther on at Tok junction. From there it's a mere 1,311 miles to Milepost 0 of the Alaska Highway at Dawson Creek, British Columbia, and another 712 miles to the nearest U.S. border crossings at Sumas, Washington, and Babb, Montana. Anchorage is 2,463 road miles from Seattle, 3,608 from Los Angeles, 3,690 from Chicago, 4,285 from Houston, 4,499 from New York, and 5,074 from Miami.

If you're heading north to Fairbanks, take the Glenn Highway as far as Palmer, 40 miles northeast; then turn west onto the George Parks Highway, which will carry you the remaining 335 miles to Alaska's second city. The Seward Highway is the only route south to the Kenai Peninsula. It's 126 miles to Seward. Homer is 225 miles via the Sterling Highway, which branches off the Seward Highway near Kenai Lake.

By Bus

Anchorage is served by scheduled bus lines, charter lines, and tour-bus lines. During the summer only, it's possible to travel by bus from the Lower 48 all the way to Anchorage.

Canadian Greyhound Lines operates year round, six times a week in summer, from Vancouver and Edmonton to Whitehorse, capital of the Yukon Territory. From there, connecting service to Anchorage is available mid-May to mid-September aboard **Alaska-Yukon Motorcoaches,** 349 Wrangell Ave., Anchorage, AK 99501 (tel. 907/276-1305, or toll free 800/637-3334), or **Alaskon Express,** 547 W. Fourth Ave., Anchorage, AK 99501 (tel. 907/279-0761, or toll free 800/544-2206). The former is operated by Alaska Sightseeing Tours, the latter by Westours and Gray Line. In addition to Whitehorse, the Alaskan towns of Skagway and Haines, at the northern end of the Alaska Marine Hwy. ferry system, are served twice weekly. It's $134 one way from Whitehorse to Anchorage, $185 from Skagway. **Alaska-Denali Transit,** P.O. Box 4557, Anchorage, AK 99510 (tel. 907/276-6443), provides connections to Anchorage from Fairbanks.

Scheduled bus lines with more localized itineraries are **Seward Bus Line,** at Fourth and Washington (P.O. Box 1338), Seward, AK 99664 (tel. 907/224-3608), to the Kenai Peninsula; and **Denali Overland Transportation Co.,** P.O. Box 330, Talkeetna, AK 99676 (tel. 907/733-2384), between Anchorage, Talkeetna, and Denali Park, March 15 to September 15 only.

By Rail

The **Alaska Railroad,** 411 W. First Ave., on Ship Creek (P.O. Box 7-2111), Anchorage, AK 99510 (tel. 907/265-2494 or 265-2623, or toll free 800/544-0552), operates daily express service in summer (May 24 to September 13) between Anchorage and Fairbanks via Denali National Park. From September to May, service is twice a week. The one-way fare is $88 for adults, $44 for children 5 to 12. Additional local service between Anchorage and Denali Park operates twice a week, May through September. Friday through Sunday from June to August the Alaska Railroad operates an all-day excursion between Anchorage and Seward.

A rail shuttle runs during the summer months between Portage and Whittier several times daily to serve Prince William Sound ferry arrivals and departures (the ferry doesn't operate to Whittier in winter). Unless an Anchorage–Portage train is running (it usually isn't), you'll have to buy a bus ticket at the Anchorage train depot and connect with the train at Portage, 40 miles east. Pray that it isn't raining or snowing, because there's no town, no station, not even a covered seating area at Portage. What settlement existed was wiped off the map by the 1964 earthquake.

By Ship

There's little regularly scheduled passenger-ship service to Anchorage. The fickle tides of the Cook Inlet ebb and neap over 38 feet in the springtime—second only to Nova Scotia's Bay of Fundy (43 feet) on the North American continent. An occasional cruise liner (Cunard's *Sagafjord* in 1989) puts the city on its schedule, but the vast majority dock at the deep-water port of Whittier and carry their passengers overland to Anchorage.

Although the Alaska Marine Highway system operates to Valdez, Whittier, and Seward, all of which have direct road or rail access to Anchorage, there is no interconnecting ferry to southeast Alaska and beyond.

If you really want to travel to Anchorage from the Lower 48 by ship, you may have to check with freighter companies or join a West Coast fishing crew.

GETTING AROUND

Bus, taxi, and rental cars are the preferred ways to get around Anchorage. The more energetic travel by foot or bicycle, or—in season—on cross-country skis.

Buses

The Anchorage public bus network—properly called the **People Mover Mass Transit System**—operates 22 routes to all corners of the city, providing easy access to most visitor attractions and activities. Regular service is available Monday through Friday from 5:30 a.m. to 11:05 p.m., on Saturday from 7:30 a.m. A few routes also have Sunday service from 9:30 a.m. to 6:30 p.m. Fares (exact change, please) are 75¢ for adults, 25¢ for students, free for preschoolers and senior citizens. For further information, contact P.O. Box 6-650, Anchorage, AK 99502 (tel. 907/264-6526).

The downtown **Transit Center** at Sixth Avenue and G Street has free information and maps of all routes from 6 a.m. to 10 p.m. daily. Every route but one makes a stop here. Until you get familiar with the route system, you can call the People Mover's **"Ride Line"** (tel. 264-6543 from 7 a.m. to 6 p.m. weekdays) and tell the operator where you are, where you'd like to go, and at what time of day. There's even "Ride Line" for the hearing impaired (tel. 276-6633).

One of the most useful services is the **Double Decker** sponsored by Anchorage hotels and businesses. The bus runs continually between downtown, Spenard, the international airport, and the university district, taking 75 minutes for one loop. It operates from 11 a.m. to 9:45 p.m. weekdays, 11 a.m. to 7:15 p.m. on Saturday, and noon to 7 p.m. on Sunday. Best of all, it's free!

Taxis

They're expensive but often indispensable, especially if the weather's bad or you have to get somewhere in a hurry. Try **Alaska Cab** (tel. 563-5353), **Checker Cab** (tel. 276-1234), or **Yellow Cab** (tel. 272-2422). All have similar rates. It's about $12, for example, from downtown to the international airport, a distance of five miles. Some folks insist they get the fairest fares from **Eagle Cab** (tel. 694-5555).

Car Rental

All major car-rental firms, and many privately owned local companies, are represented at Anchorage International Airport and downtown offices. I have had good service and fair prices renting from **National,** 521 W. Third Ave. (tel. 274-3695, or toll free 800/227-7368), and at the airport (tel. 243-3406). Other large rental agencies include **Avis,** Fifth Avenue and B Street (tel. 243-4300, or toll free 800/331-1212), and at the airport (tel. 243-2377); **Budget,** at the airport (tel. 243-0150, or toll free 800/527-0700); and **Hertz,** also at the airport (tel. 243-3314, or toll free 800/654-8200). Among cut-rate agencies, **Thrifty,** 3730 Spenard Rd. (tel. 276-2855, or toll free 800/FOR-CARS), offers free pickup and delivery service for clients. Check the Anchorage phone directory's *Yellow Pages* or the Anchorage Convention and Visitors Bureau for a complete list.

As availability of rental vehicles decreases in summer, rates increase. It's wise to make advance reservations at that time. Expect to pay $40 to $50 a day, limited mileage, for a compact model.

For information on current **road conditions,** call 243-7675; for **weather forecasts,** call 936-2626.

Bicycles

Try **Bicycle R&R,** 908 W. Northern Lights Blvd. (tel. 561-5246), or **Goose Lake Bike & Boat,** 2818 Aspen Court (tel. 276-2960), to discuss rentals. Bicycling is very popular in Anchorage, and the city has catered to its young population by installing a lengthy network of bicycle trails.

TOURIST INFORMATION

The best source of information in Anchorage is the **Anchorage Convention and Visitors Bureau,** 201 E. Third Ave., Anchorage, AK 99501 (tel. 907/276-4118). On arrival, don't fail to visit the ACVB's **Log Cabin Information Center,** at Fourth Avenue and F Street (tel. 907/274-3531), for full information on all area attractions, right down to restaurant menus. It's open daily from 7:30 a.m. to 7 p.m. June to August, 8:30 a.m. to 6 p.m. in May and September, and 9 a.m. to 4 p.m. the rest of the year. There's also a 24-hour **events** line with recorded information on current attractions, including cultural and sports events (tel. 276-3200). The **Anchorage Chamber of Commerce** is at 415 F St., Anchorage, AK 99501 (tel. 907/272-2401). For statewide tourist information, contact the **Alaska Division of Tourism,** 3601 C St., Suite 722, Anchorage, AK 99503 (tel. 907/563-2167).

The new glass-paned **Egan Civic and Convention Center,** 555 W. Fifth Ave. (tel. 263-2800), has nearly 100,000 square feet of space for meetings and exhibits.

For information on outdoor pursuits, try the **U.S. Forest Service** (Chugach National Forest), 201 E. Ninth Ave., Suite 206, Anchorage, AK 99501 (tel. 907/261-2500); the **Alaska Division of Parks and Outdoor Recreation,** 3601 C St. (P.O. Box 7001), Anchorage, AK 99510 (tel. 907/561-2020); and the **Alaska Public Lands Information Center,** Fourth Avenue and F Street, Anchorage, AK 99501 (tel. 907/271-2737).

AAA Alaska is affiliated with the American Automobile Association. Members can call 24 hours for emergency road service (tel. 907/337-6921) or during weekday office hours for travel assistance (tel. toll free 800/367-7020). For up-to-date information on winter road conditions, dial 337-9481.

For foreign visitors, the ACVB maintains a language bank of 26 languages, from Armenian to Indonesian, Inupiat to Serbo-Croatian. In addition, there are two foreign consulates (Japanese and Korean) and 11 honorary consulates in Anchorage.

USEFUL INFORMATION

The two major daily **newspapers** are the *Anchorage Daily News* (morning) and the *Anchorage Times* (evening). For **emergency assistance** from police, fire department, or ambulance, dial 911. The major **hospitals** are Providence Hospital, 3200 Providence Dr. (tel. 562-2211), and Humana Hospital, 2801 DeBarr Rd. (tel. 276-1131); there are also several out-patient emergency clinics, including FirstCare, 3710 Woodland, in Spenard (tel. 248-1122), or 1301 Huffman, in South Anchorage (tel. 345-1199). An emergency **dental** line is available 24 hours (tel. 279-9144). **Banks,** generally open from 10 a.m. to 6 p.m. Monday through Friday, are easily located in the downtown area and major suburban shopping areas. For **one-hour dry cleaning,** try Alaska Cleaners, with 15 locations in greater Anchorage, including Fourth Avenue and I Street (tel. 274-7753), open from 7:30 a.m. to 6 p.m.

daily. Need a **babysitter**? Call Rent-a-Mom, 3605 Arctic Blvd., Suite 1222 (tel. 349-4463).

SPECIAL EVENTS

The **Fur Rendezvous,** Anchorage's annual ten-day winter carnival, is Alaska's biggest party. Its reputation stems from days long past when fur trappers and gold miners, escaping winter's grip, came to the "big town" to replenish their supplies and get rowdy for a few days. They'd race their sled-dog teams, auction off their caribou skins and otter pelts, and grab a saloon girl for a fling. Revived in 1936, it has been held annually ever since.

"Rondy," as it is known locally, usually begins on the second Friday of February. In 1989 it ran from February 10 to 19; in 1990 the tentative dates are February 9 to 18; in 1991, February 8 to 17. Some 140 different events are scheduled, from snow-sculpture contests to snowshoe softball, sled-dog races to dog weight-pulling, Telemark ski races to hot-air ballooning, snowmobile races to auto rallies, beer-drinking contests to the Eskimo blanket toss. The first weekend highlight is the Miners and Trappers Ball, a gigantic masquerade party which limits tickets to 4,000 lucky Alaskans (or visitors). On the final weekend the big Rondy Parade is held through downtown.

Don't worry about snow. On the rare occasions when it's been in short supply, the city fathers have stockpiled enough of the white stuff to stage events. The Anchorage Fur Rendezvous office, at 327 Eagle St. (tel. 907/277-8615), is the clearinghouse for information on that annual event.

As befits a city of a quarter of a million people, Anchorage has a full slate of happenings throughout the year. After Rondy, the most important is the start of the **Iditarod Sled Dog Trail Race** (about 1,100 treacherous miles to Nome) the first Saturday in March (call 907/376-5155 for information). Other popular occasions are the three-day **Renaissance Festival** at Tudor Center in mid-June; the **Mayor's Midnight Sun Marathon** on June 21, the longest day of the year; **Spirit Days,** with Native story telling and a potlatch, the last weekend of June; the **Freedom Days Festival** over the July 4 weekend; **Quiana Alaska,** a festival of Native singing, dancing, and storytelling in mid-October; and the **Christmas Tree Lighting Ceremony** in early December. There are many more events throughout the year; check with the Log Cabin Visitor Information Center for a full events calendar.

---

2. Where to Stay

With more than 4,000 guest rooms available in Anchorage, one might expect no shortage of space for travelers. Not necessarily so! During the height of the summer tourist season, in July and August, rooms are at a premium. No matter that most hotels and motels increase their rates, some by small increments, others by giant steps; they're almost guaranteed of full houses every night. So it's essential to book ahead.

If you do get stuck without a room, the Anchorage Convention and Visitors Bureau sometimes operates a **lodging hotline** (tel. 276-7655) during the summer months and other peak periods. Contact the **Log Cabin Visitor Information Center** (tel. 907/274-3531) if the line is not connected.

In the pages that follow I have categorized hotels and motels according to location and price. **Downtown** is between Ship Creek and Chester Creek, from Ingra Street (Seward Hwy.) to the Cook Inlet's Knik Arm. **Midtown/Spenard** includes everything south of Chester Creek and west of Seward Highway as far as International Airport Road—as well as the airport itself. **South Anchorage** is everything else along the Seward Highway corridor, heading toward the Kenai Peninsula. **East Anchorage** comprises all lodgings along the Glenn Highway, heading toward the Matanuska Valley.

The price breakdown for a double room—8% room tax *not* included—is roughly as follows: luxury, $110 and up a day; upper bracket, $85 to $110; middle bracket, $60 to $85; bargain basement, under $60. Because rates often vary considerably according to season, I have based my categories on summer charges.

DOWNTOWN

Most of the downtown hotels are concentrated between Third and Sixth Avenues, and Gambell and L Streets.

Three at the Top

The finest accommodation in Alaska is the **Hotel Captain Cook,** at Fifth Avenue and K Street, Anchorage, AK 99501 (tel. 907/276-6000, or toll free 800/323-7500). This landmark hotel, whose three gold-colored towers are easily seen from anywhere in downtown Anchorage, is owned by former U.S. Secretary of the Interior Walter J. Hickel and managed by his son, Wally Jr. It's a member of the independent Preferred Hotels group that also includes such prestigious names as the Imperial Hotel in Tokyo, the Dorchester in London, the Stanford Court in San Francisco, and the Breakers in Palm Beach.

The coordinating themes of the Captain Cook are its rich décor of teakwood and polished brass, and its art, reflecting Hickel Sr.'s fascination with the famous 18th-century English navigator who explored this coast of Alaska and most of the South Seas. Original oil paintings of James Cook's voyages are located throughout the hotel corridors and in many guest rooms, along with woodcarvings, charts, and other 18th-century nautical regalia.

The Cook has 600 guest rooms in its three towers (10, 17, and 20 stories, respectively), connected by a spacious ground level of restaurants, shops, and guest services. The shops, which number about 20, include furriers, jewelers, boutiques, art galleries, florists, and confectioners, as well as a sundry shop and newsstand. You'll also find a barbershop, beauty salon, and concierge service on the main floor. There are 13 meeting rooms, banquet seating for 1,000, and guest parking in a covered lot.

The finest of the Cook's four restaurants is the elite Crow's Nest, serving French cuisine, fresh Alaskan seafood, and wild game in a rooftop room designed like the underdeck of a ship. For $50 a person, not including wine, you can enjoy a "menu gastronomique prix fixe," a seven-course gourmet dinner, while you're pampered by waiters who speak French, Italian, Spanish, German, and Danish (remember, Vitus Bering was a Dane). All entrees are priced at $24 à la carte, from crevettes à la "dry martini" to poussin rôti aux truffes. Open from 6 to 11 p.m. Tuesday through Sunday (7 p.m. to midnight in summer). The lounge opens at 4 p.m. A popular Sunday champagne brunch is served from 10 a.m. to 2 p.m.

Among the Cook's other restaurants, I like Fletchers, an informal businessmen's pub in the lobby level of Tower III. The hand-molded copper ceiling, Italian marble floor and bar, and mahogany walls contrast with the simple menu of gourmet pizzas (Fletchers' special has duck sausage and goat cheese, at $8), fresh pastas, salads, and sandwiches. The bar features 31 imported beers and a world-class selection of 28 cognacs. Open from 11 a.m. to midnight Monday through Friday, from 5 p.m. on Saturday. The Quarter Deck, on the tenth floor of Tower I, is a private club for members and hotel guests only. Guest chefs prepare regional dishes and nouvelle cuisine surprises like brazil-nut chicken salads, wild mushroom omelets, and grilled scallops with hazelnuts. Lunch items, served from 11 a.m. to 2 p.m. Monday through Friday, run $7 to $12.75; full dinners, offered from 6 to 10 p.m. Monday through Saturday, will cost about $30 per person, including wine. How does "chocolate decadence" strike you for dessert? The Quarter Deck's lounge and reading library, in a teakwood room decorated with Native Pacific artifacts, are open from 10 a.m. to 1 p.m. Monday through Saturday. Don't bother to bring cash or credit cards to dinner; your room will be billed directly.

Also in the lobby is the Pantry, open 24 hours a day. It's a pleasant coffeeshop, but priced on the high side: a BLT sandwich is $6.25; two eggs with bacon, $7.75. A children's menu is available.

Just off the lobby is the Whale's Tail, with live entertainment—usually a small top-40 combo for dancing—nightly except Sunday until 1 a.m. Tapa tablecloths and lampshades add to the Polynesian atmosphere. Fondue and hors d'oeuvres are served beginning at 5 p.m.

When you finish your meals and drinks, you can work off the extra calories at the Captain Cook Athletic Club. This private membership club is open to guests for $10 a day or $35 a week. Facilities include a five-lane swimming pool, three racquetball courts, Nautilus weight room, sauna, Jacuzzi, steamroom, solarium, tanning parlor, and masseur. All towels and exercise clothing are provided to both men and women.

Guest rooms are typically masculine in tone, decorated in muted shades of maroons, browns, and beiges. Teakwood furnishings and rattan lamps add to the effect. All rooms have queen-size beds, plush chairs or couches, desk/dressers, large closets, and individually controlled electric baseboard heating. Local phone calls cost 50¢. Television is local reception only, though satellite pickup is being contemplated. There's an alarm clock, plus shampoo, soaps, and a sewing kit in the bathroom.

Year-round room rates start at $120 single, $130 double. For $135 to $160 you can get an executive suite in the 17th-floor penthouse of Tower II, with such special touches as a velour bathrobe, a shoeshine machine, and complimentary breakfast in a private lounge. There are also deluxe two-bedroom suites with parlors for up to $500 a night. Room service is available 24 hours.

The 407-room **Sheraton Anchorage Hotel,** 401 E. Sixth Ave., Anchorage, AK 99501 (tel. 907/276-8700, or toll free 800/325-3535), calls itself a "showcase for Alaska art." The spacious lobby, with its giant sun roof, certainly has a museum feel to it. The theme is drawn from the art of all five major Native groups—Athabaskans, Aleuts, Tlingits, and Haidas, as well as Eskimos.

Look around the lobby. The free-standing marble staircase has genuine jade tiles from Alaska's southwest. The huge columns are decorated in the fashion of Yupik Eskimo arrow cases. The etched-marble murals—one shows a caribou migration, another a man being carried to the moon by an eagle—are Native designs which depict the kinship between animal and hunter.

A departure from the Native theme is Josephine's, the Sheraton's highly regarded continental restaurant in the 15th-floor penthouse. The décor here is Napoleonic: it's named after Bonaparte's empress. Why? Well, as it turns out, Josephine's emblem was the trumpeter swan, a bird frequently seen migrating in Alaska. You'll find the symbol embossed in crystal here. You'll also find six French Empire–style chandeliers, and magnificent carpets and fabrics patterned after those in Napoleon's last palace. Cuisine, of course, is French provincial. A favorite is potpourri Napoléon —medallions of veal, Scottish red deer, and stuffed quail, served with fresh linguine. If you start with steak tartare or escargots bourguignons, and have a bottle of wine with your meal, you'll pay about $80 for a dinner for two. Open for dinner from 5 to 10 p.m. Tuesday through Sunday, and 10 a.m. to 2:30 p.m. for Sunday brunch.

More down to earth is the Bistro, adjoining the lobby. With its wood-beamed ceiling, potted ficus trees, and awning, its Mediterranean look is appropriate to the southern European cuisine served here. Pastas and other dishes are $6 to $12. Open from 6 a.m. to 10 p.m. daily. On the other side of the lobby, behind the heavy door with the Tlingit totemic shark carved in it, is the Paimuit Lounge. Paimuit ("pie-a-mute") is Yupik for "gathering place," and that's what this is. I don't see how the brass-topped tables, stainless-steel dance floor, and general glass-and-chrome hi-tech look re-creates "the feeling experienced from the inside of a glacier," as the hotel would have us believe . . . but then, I've never been inside a glacier. Hot hors d'oeuvres are served from 5 to 7 p.m. nightly, and a disk jockey spins top-40 records Wednesday through Saturday nights.

Other guest facilities include a small health club, with weight equipment, a sauna, and a Jacuzzi, and a gift and sundry shop in the lobby. The Sheraton's meeting facilities are the best in the city: the Grand Ballroom seats up to 1,300.

Dark winter days are made brighter by a pastel color scheme of peaches and lime greens in the rooms and corridors. Business travelers are pleased to find a writing desk, modem jack (for laptop computers), and two phones in every room (local calls are 50¢). Each room has a queen-size bed or two double beds and an armoire. AM/FM radio and an alarm clock are built into the remote-control cable television, and in-house films can be viewed for an additional charge. Bathroom amenities include a hairdryer, three soaps, shampoo, lotion, shoe polish, and a sewing kit. Room rates begin at $139 single, $159 double, in summer; from $130 in winter.

The **Anchorage Hilton,** 500 W. Third Ave. (P.O. Box 100520), Anchorage, AK 99510 (tel. 907/272-7411, or toll free 800/245-2527), is owned by a Native Alaskan group, the Bristol Bay Native Corporation. But other than the snarling grizzly rearing above the main entrance from his glass box, there's little in the décor of this 600-room hotel to remind one of the Alaskan bush.

Anchorage oldtimers can tell you the long history of this hotel, beginning with the construction of the Anchorage Hotel in 1916. They'll tell you how the hotel was for decades the hub of city social life, even serving as a Red Cross station when it survived the 1964 earthquake unscathed. A 22-story tower replaced the old hotel in 1972, and Hilton assumed management in 1977. In 1986 the hotel completed a $30-million renovation and expansion program, which included a new 15-story tower and a shopping mall with gift shops, art galleries, boutiques, a hairstylist, and a newsstand.

You'll get a feel for the loving luxury lavished on the Hilton when you see the reception desktop of solid Alaskan jade. There's plenty of plush seating in the large lobby; the reception floor also houses Alaskan and Northwest airline desks, a restaurant (the Berry Patch), and a lounge (Sydney's). The hotel also has a health club, free to guests, with a heated swimming pool, Universal gym, sauna, Jacuzzi, and health-food bar.

Atop the new 15-story Westward Tower is the Top of the World restaurant, already famous locally for its Sunday champagne brunches and its 360° view. Enjoy, too, the art deco setting, with its pastel tones: lilac carpeting, blue-green chairs, brass railings, etched-glass dividers, huge pots of silk flowers. Dinner entrees, priced at $18 to $28, include such innovative recipes as breast of duckling with juniper berry sauce and apples, and fresh Hawaiian mahimahi (fish) with macadamia-nut butter sauce. In seasons with long days and warmer weather, a rooftop terrace is open for drinks and hors d'oeuvres.

On the ground floor, the Berry Patch coffeeshop, decorated in shades of pastel peach with modern-art prints, serves omelets, salads, sandwiches, pastas, and half a dozen dinner entrees. Lunch runs $7 to $11; dinner, $10 to $16. The days of the old Anchorage Hotel are recalled in the festive decor of Sydney's, which features a deli buffet lunch and a compact-disc sound system.

The new guest rooms in the Hilton's Westward Tower sport a proud burgundy-and-jade color scheme. The older rooms, in the taller Anchorage Tower, have a similar mauve look. All rooms are spacious and well lit, with handsome stained-wood furniture, including six-drawer dressers. Limited-edition prints hang over the queen-size beds. The very large closet has floor-to-ceiling mirrors. Heating is thermostat-controlled electric baseboard. The television, with built-in AM/FM radio, has cable pickup and in-house movies ($6.25). Beside the bed are a direct-dial phone (local calls are 75¢) and an alarm clock. In the bathroom you'll find an array of hair-care products, lotion, soaps, and a sewing kit. Room rates begin at $99 off-season, $120 single and $140 double in-season. Suites are priced at $185 to $900.

The Upper Bracket

Perhaps no hotel in Anchorage has a more central location than the **Westmark Anchorage,** 720 W. Fifth Ave., Anchorage, AK 99501 (tel. 907/276-7676, or toll free 800/544-0970, 800/274-6631 in Alaska). The fact that it's near the new Performing Arts Center isn't lost on business travelers, who comprise a hefty portion of the regular clientele.

Small trees (in planters), rock pillars, and woolen tapestries surround deep couches in the cozy lobby. A 24-hour garden-style coffeeshop, the Manor House, has an entrance right off the lobby, and beyond it is a gift and sundry shop with an entrance on G Street. A 14th-floor cocktail lounge, the Penthouse, also serves businessmen's lunches on weekdays (11:30 a.m. to 2 p.m.).

But the hotel's pride and joy is the House of Lords restaurant, an elegant candlelit establishment featuring large private booths with rich red leather upholstery. Service is outstanding, and the continental offerings—seafood, meat, and pasta—are superb. Entrees are priced between $14 and $23; I recommend the chateaubriand au pistachio, at $19.50 per person for a minimum of two people. Daily except Sunday, lunch is served from 11:30 a.m. to 2 p.m.; dinner, from 6 to 11 p.m. The adjoining Library Lounge is a good place for an apéritif or after-dinner drink.

The Westmark has 200 spacious rooms, newly renovated with a beige or navy-blue color scheme. They have rich wood furnishings, queen-size beds, blue serge chairs, an armoire, and landscape paintings on the walls. There's cable television with Showtime and ESPN, and direct-dial phones (local calls are 35¢). Heating is by electric baseboard. Sinks, outside the bath, are provided with shampoo and sewing kits. Summer rates are $100 single, $110 double; off-season rates drop to $75 single, $85 double. Courtesy-van service is available.

Under the same ownership but a step down in class is the **Anchorage TraveLodge—A Westmark Hotel,** 115 E. Third Ave., Anchorage, AK 99501 (tel. 907/272-7561, toll free 800/544-0970, 800/274-6631 in Alaska). Only 16 of the 90 rooms, for instance, have shower/bath combinations; the others have showers only. But the rooms are good-sized, and those on the ground floor even have private entrances. The carpets are gray, the drapes and bedspreads rustic in color. Rustic paintings hang on the walls. TVs have local reception plus a movie channel. Local calls are 35¢. Heating is electric baseboard. Shampoo and a sewing kit are provided in the bathroom. Summer rates (mid-May to mid-September) are $93 single, $108 double; off-season rates are about $15 less.

The Coach House Restaurant and Lounge have a nice warm feeling, with lots of greenery and a big fireplace. Try the pecan chicken at $7.25 for lunch or dinner. Open from 6 a.m. to 9 p.m. daily (to 10 p.m. in summer) for food, to 11:30 p.m. for drinks.

The **Holiday Inn of Anchorage,** 239 W. Fourth Ave., Anchorage, AK 99501 (tel. 907/279-8671, or toll free 800/465-4329), the only member of that chain in Alaska, is a great place for families. Its heated indoor swimming pool (open from 10 a.m. to 11 p.m. daily) is a favorite among kids, who can purchase swimsuits from the hotel if they didn't bring their own!

The modern lobby features Native Alaskan art on one wall. But the Native theme doesn't carry beyond the lobby. The corridors are so long and spartan, in fact, that they look like bowling alleys. They do give access to a coin-op guest Laundromat and a sauna.

No such atmosphere problem besets the Greenery restaurant on the second floor. Here the décor features hanging plants and works of modern art—all in green. You can't miss the impressionistic full-wall mural of wildflowers on the North Slope as you enter. A homemade soup and salad bar complements the standard coffeeshop fare of omelets (from $5), sandwiches (from $4.50), and several entrees

($11 to $15). Open from 5 a.m. to 2 p.m. and 5 to 11 p.m. daily in summer, 7 a.m. to 2 p.m. and 5 to 10 p.m. in winter. Lucy's Lounge adjoins the restaurant. Across the hallway, for fast-food junkies, is Eats.

Each of the 252 rooms has queen-size or double beds with reading lamps, a long dresser, chairs, and table. The carpets are rust colored, the walls beige, the bedspreads carmine. Prints decorate the walls. There's satellite television and direct-dial phones (local calls are 35¢). Room rates in summer (May 23 to September 8) are $97 to $105 single, $112 to $120 double; off-season, they're $60 to $65 single, $65 to $70 double.

The Middle Bracket

Anchorage's closest approximation of intimate European-style lodging is the **Voyager Hotel,** 501 K St., Anchorage, AK 99501 (tel. 907/277-9501, or toll free 800/247-9070). Located across Fifth Avenue from the Hotel Captain Cook, its cozy lobby, tastefully decorated in lavenders and charcoal grays, immediately speaks of its international flavor. There's an antique barometer on the wall, an antique chest with coffee service, a lighted globe, and a big world map.

Owner Stan Williams, who was born in Anchorage when the population was 2,100 and has never left, bought an old boarding house in 1979 and totally transformed it. Each of the Voyager's 38 clean, spacious rooms is a mini-suite, complete with kitchen facilities. The rooms are tastefully appointed with mauve carpets, blue upholstery, and light floral bedspreads. Modern-art prints adorn the walls. Each room has a queen-size bed, lamps that turn on at the touch of a finger, a large desk, four-drawer dresser, divan, and wheeled chairs. There's also cable television, plenty of closet space, and electric baseboard heating. Local phone calls are free. The office will provide a "kitchen kit," with pots, dishes, and silverware, on request. Soft drinks, snacks, and sundries are sold from machines on the second floor. Room rates are seasonal, ranging from $65 single, $70 double, in winter, to $89 single, $99 double, in summer. Senior citizens can get discounts.

In the basement of the Voyager is the privately owned Corsair restaurant, one of Anchorage's finest (see the "Where to Eat" section, below). The Derrick Lounge, with a street entrance, adjoins the lobby.

It's away from the business district at the southwest corner of downtown, but it's hard to miss the towering 14-story **Inlet Towers,** 1200 L St., Anchorage, AK 99501 (tel. 907/276-0110, or toll free 800/544-0786). And you shouldn't miss it, because this former residential apartment building is one of Anchorage's best hotel bargains.

The lobby features a five-panel mural of the Cook Inlet. There are men's and women's saunas and exercise rooms and a beauty salon on the premises, and a coin-op guest Laundromat in the basement. But that's not why you should come here. You should come because you can get a full one-bedroom or two-bedroom suite, complete with kitchenette, for less than the price of a standard first-class hotel room elsewhere.

Of the Inlet Towers' 138 clean, spacious, well-kept rooms, 70 are one-bedroom suites. The balance are either two-bedroom units or studios—which, loosely translated, means "standard." All rooms decorated in tones of brown and beige with floral upholstery and rustic wall paintings, have double beds with reading lamps, dressers, armchairs, cable TV (with VCR and videotape rental in lobby), direct-dial phones (local calls are 25¢, and a 10% surcharge on long-distance calls), and electric baseboard heating. Kitchenettes have electric stoves, refrigerators, toasters, and coffee percolators. Suites have extra closet and shelf space, and large living rooms with couches and dining tables.

Summer rates: two bedrooms, $110 to $120; one bedroom, $90 to $95; studio, $80 to $90. Winter rates are $20 less.

The **Days Inn** (formerly the Plaza Inn), 321 E. Fifth Ave., Anchorage, AK 99501 (tel. 907/276-7226, or toll free 800/544-2240, 800/478-2240 in Alaska), is built in the shape of a square, three-story doughnut. That's not as strange as it sounds, because the central courtyard is used for parking.

The 118 rooms typically have maroon carpeting, gray drapes, orange or blue bedspreads, and bare white walls. The hotel is soundproofed, but its lighting could be improved. Each room has double beds, a long desk/dresser, table and chair, electric baseboard heating, and free local telephone calls and cable television. On the negative side, three floors are served by a single slow elevator—but while you wait, you can take advantage of the soft drinks and ice on each floor. Courtesy-van service is offered. Rates are $99 single, $109 double, in summer; $54 single, $59 double, off-season.

The 24-hour Daybreak Coffee Shop is reasonably priced, with eggs Benedict for $5.50, cheeseburgers at $5, and a full steak-and-prawns, $12.50. The Plaza Lounge is open until 2 a.m.

Picture this, if you can: a motel room with one wall covered by orange wool, a second by a green-and-beige tartan fabric, a third by a velvety batik-style print, and a fourth of simple plaster painted lime green. Add a double Jacuzzi and a few antiques, like a love seat and early-20th-century headboard, and (presto!) you've got a deluxe room at the **Alaska Samovar Inn,** 720 Gambell St., Anchorage, AK 99501 (tel. 907/277-1511).

The pleasant lobby, with plush couches, potted plants, and rich wood décor, doesn't give any hint of what's ahead. Neither does the central parking area, despite the huge satellite dish towering over the picnic tables. Indeed, most of the Samovar's 68 rooms are not this eclectic. But some are more so. That's a trademark of motels owned by Kendall Family Enterprises, which has three more on Anchorage's east side.

The only unusual touches in the standard units are the small Jacuzzi bath, the full double mirror beside the dressing table, and the peach-colored walls. Two of those three are nice additions. These rooms are furnished with queen-size beds, desk/dressers, electric baseboard heating, small fans, telephones (free local calls), and TV-radios with three movie channels. Amenities include packs of liquid laundry soap and shampoo.

At the other end of the spectrum is the Jade Suite, whose centerpiece is a giant Jacuzzi surrounded by mirrors and hanging plants. In case you wanted to know, it comes with a split of champagne that will stay chilled in the room refrigerator until you're ready for it. The color scheme is green, of course: olive-green carpeting, forest-green patterned walls and bedspread. The bed, love seat, dresser, chairs, and table are all antiques. If green isn't to your liking, inquire about the Oak, Empress, and Gay '90s suites.

Standard units are priced at $65 to $70; deluxe units are $80. The four suites start at $105.

The **House of Bernard's** restaurant, with French chef Michel, is open from early till late for breakfast (Swedish pancakes are $3.25), lunch (king crab Louis is $11.75), and dinner (Cornish game hen, stuffed with wild rice, pistachio nuts, brandy, and crabmeat, runs $16).

The Uptown, 234 E. Second Ave., Anchorage, AK 99501 (tel. 907/279-4232 or 349-2513), is a converted apartment building with simple but clean one-bedroom suites. Each unit has a full kitchen, cable TV, and telephone; some also have sofa beds and fireplaces. A laundry is open to all guests. Rates are $60 to $65 in summer (June through November), $50 to $55 in winter (December through May). Weekly rates are $375 to $425 in summer, $300 to $325 in winter.

In the same block as the Westmark Inn is the Korean-managed **Inlet Inn,** 539 H St., Anchorage, AK 99501 (tel. 907/277-5541). Built in 1952, it's still well maintained. The narrow wood-paneled corridors lead to 93 small, sparsely furnished rooms with double or twin beds and desk/dressers. Wildlife prints accent the dark-wood walls. All rooms have phones (free local calls), satellite TV (with built-in radio), and private baths, but the baseboard heating is centrally controlled. Rates are

$50 single, $60 double, $65 twin, in summer; $40 single, $45 double, $48 twin, in winter.

The Bargain Basement

The **Anchor Arms Apartments,** 433 Eagle St., Anchorage, AK 99501 (tel. 907/272-9619), are another "find." Formerly the crew lodgings for Lufthansa Airlines, these 46 one-bedroom suites, just around the corner from the Sheraton, are clean and spacious. All are furnished with double beds and dressers, couches, coffee tables, and dining tables. The kitchen has a refrigerator and stove with oven; dishes and pots are provided. There's a full bath, TV (local reception only), and electric baseboard heating. The apartments also have a coin-op guest Laundromat. If you can do without a phone in your room and don't mind yellow-brick walls, you can't beat the price: $40 a night or $245 a week, year round.

The **Anchorage International Hostel,** 700 H St., Anchorage, AK 99501 (tel. 907/276-3635), has 60 beds in separate male and female dormitories, plus a few family rooms for parents with children. It also has a full kitchen, showers, and a laundry room. Bring your own sleeping bag or bedroll, or rent linens at the hostel. Blankets are free.

The hostel is open all year for maximum stays of three consecutive nights. You must check in between 5 and 9 p.m., check out between 7 and 9 a.m., and vacate the hostel during the day. An 11 p.m. curfew is strictly enforced. Smoking, alcohol, illegal drugs, and pets are forbidden. Rates: $10 for American Youth Hostels members, $13 for nonmembers. AYH memberships, sold here, are $20 a year for adults, $10 for juniors (under 17) and seniors (60 plus), $30 for families.

MIDTOWN/SPENARD

This area includes the midtown business district, the Spenard Road entertainment strip, and the international airport. Geographically, it comprises the section of Anchorage west of the Seward Hwy. and south of downtown as far as International Airport Road.

The Luxury Leader

Without a lot of hoopla, the **Clarion Hotel Anchorage,** 4800 Spenard Rd., Anchorage, AK 99517 (tel. 907/243-2300, or toll free 800/544-6553, 800/478-2100 in Alaska), has combined the best of two worlds. It's a city hotel, barely five minutes' drive from the international airport (with 24-hour courtesy-car service), yet it has many of the attributes of an opulent wilderness fishing lodge, including a private dock for chartered seaplanes on adjacent Lake Spenard.

The low-ceilinged lobby is casually elegant. The first thing you'll notice as you enter is the wide, red-carpeted staircase with the mahogany banister leading to the third-floor ballrooms. Reception is to your left; the concierge, an expert in booking "Alaskan experience" wilderness trips, has a desk to your right, near the gift shop. In the far corner, surrounded by plush seating, is a big fireplace shared with the Fancy Moose Lounge.

A long, key-shaped hotel of modular construction, the Clarion opened in June 1986. Its odd shape, which makes the farthest rooms a very long walk from the lobby, was dictated by airport-area building codes, which kept the height to three stories, and by a desire to give the restaurant and bar lake frontage.

You'll realize how appropriately named is the Flying Machine Restaurant as you watch seaplanes land on Lake Spenard and adjacent Lake Hood. The décor emphasizes the aeronautic theme: Byron Birdsall watercolors and prints depict the seaplane in Alaska, and there are historical aviation photos, an antique aviator's jacket, aerial topographical maps, and other curiosities. But the cuisine is more California than

Alaska. Consider a healthy breakfast of granola and yogurt parfait ($4.25), a lunch of halibut and chips ($8.50), and a national-award–winning dinner of salmon filets in yellow-and-blue cornmeal with a shrimp hollandaise ($19). In warm weather, food and beverage service are available on an outdoor patio. Open from 6 a.m. to midnight.

Next door is the Fancy Moose Lounge, which calls itself an "Alaskan-style saloon" but, with its palm-leaf ceiling fans, doesn't look the part. The dance floor doesn't get much use, but the video jukebox and three television screens, usually tuned either to music videos or ESPN, do.

Athletes who eschew the armchair can work up a thirst by lifting weights in the health club or renting a bicycle and going for a ride on the lakeside trails.

The Clarion's 248 rooms contain many special touches that can't be found in other Anchorage hotels. Every room has track lighting with dimmer switches, a mini-refrigerator built into the dressing table, a hairdryer, a working desk of a design patented by the Clarion chain, and Stonington Gallery art on the walls. In addition the hotel virtually guarantees that noise from the nearby airports won't disturb your slumber: the double five-inch-thick walls are separated by a one-inch air gap. A pastel color scheme—blue-green carpeting, pink-and-brown covers on the queen-size beds—enhances the units. Each room also has an easy chair, entertainment console with nine-channel cable television, clock-radio, thermostat-controlled hot-air heating, and direct-dial telephones (local calls are 50¢). Bathroom amenities include shampoo, conditioner, and hand cream. The Clarion also has three rooms for the handicapped, three hospitality suites, and two large rooms with fireplaces.

Summer rates for singles are $150 to $165; doubles run $165 to $180. In winter (October through May), singles go for $115 to $130; doubles are $130 to $145.

The Upper Bracket

The closest accommodation to the airport is the **Anchorage International Airport Inn,** 3333 International Airport Rd., Anchorage, AK 99502 (tel. 907/243-2233, or toll free 800/544-0986, 800/478-2233 in Alaska). Don't get lost trying to find the entrance: you must turn left off the airport road onto Spenard Road, and take the first left again to Aviation Drive. It's easiest just to call for the courtesy-car service, offered 24 hours. With six clocks in the lobby giving the current time in New York, Seattle, Honolulu, Tokyo, and London, as well as Anchorage, you'll always know what hour it is.

A hunting-lodge theme, with Alaskan big-game animal heads mounted above the lobby fireplace, carries into the Trophy Room lounge. The International Dining Room, open from 6:30 a.m. to 11 p.m. daily, serves a weekday luncheon buffet at $9 and a wide range of dinner courses, priced $12 to $22, including salad, dessert, and coffee. A gift shop sells sundries as well as *USA Today* and the *Wall Street Journal*.

The Airport Inn has 141 rooms impressively appointed with rich wood furnishings on gray carpets, lavender bedspreads, and wildlife prints on the white walls. Each room has a king- or queen-size bed, dresser, easy chair, electric baseboard heating, cable TV with built-in radio, and direct-dial telephone (free local calls). The dressing table has a lighted makeup mirror and hairdryer. Shampoo, conditioner, and mouthwash are provided.

Rates are $86 single, $91 double, $96 twin. For a few dollars more, the inn's "suite deal" gives you a mini-refrigerator stocked with beverages, complimentary coffee with your morning paper, and other special touches. Seven no-smoking rooms are available. Room/car packages in conjunction with National Car Rental are priced at $106, single or double, $116 twin.

The **Best Western Barratt Inn,** 4616 Spenard Rd., Anchorage, AK 99517 (tel. 907/243-3131, or toll free 800/221-7550, 800/478-7550 in Alaska), offers a real choice of accommodation styles in its 216 units. Each of the four separate buildings —on opposite sides of busy Spenard Road, but connected by a tunnel—houses a different category of room: standard, medium, superior, and deluxe.

The standard unit (Building I), with its blue-gray color scheme, is relatively small. There's room enough for a queen-size bed, two armchairs, desk/dresser, satellite TV with built-in radio, direct-dial phone (free local calls), electric baseboard heating, and hairdryer. The superior unit (Building III), at the other end of the spectrum, is very spacious. Its extras include a king-size bed, sofa, easy chairs, dresser, clock-radio, TV stand with drop-leaf desk, and refrigerator. Shampoo, lotion, and cold-water detergent are provided in the bathroom, along with a hairdryer. The color scheme is unusual: pastel carpets, chocolate ripple chairs, and a bright, multicolored bedspread.

The Barratt also offers 24-hour courtesy-car service to and from the airport and a coin-operated guest laundry. The modern Susitna Restaurant, open from 6 a.m. to 10 p.m. daily, has good food at good prices: try the blueberry pancakes ($6) for breakfast or a mushroom burger ($5.25) for lunch. Most dinners are priced from $9 to $11; a specialty is fresh seafood.

Rates for standard rooms are $59 single, $69 double; medium and superior rooms run $90 and $100; deluxe units (often fully booked by Alaska Airlines in summer) are $110.

The newly renovated **Northern Lights Inn,** 598 W. Northern Lights Blvd., Anchorage, AK 99503 (tel. 907/561-5200), doesn't depend on the aurora borealis for an Alaskan atmosphere. Early dog-sledding photos are reproduced on the walls of the spacious lobby, and foods like sourdough pancakes and reindeer stew highlight the menu at its Cama'i Restaurant.

The 126 rooms on eight floors are nicely appointed, with a heavy use of wood paneling. All rooms have queen-size or double beds, satellite TV with built-in radio, and direct-dial phones (local calls are free). Rates are $76 single, $82 double, in summer; slightly less the rest of the year.

The restaurant, open daily from 6 a.m. to 2 p.m. and 5 to 10 p.m., uses imaginative curves in the design of its booths and partitions. Daily luncheon specials, including prime rib, London broil, and baked salmon, are priced at $7. Dinner runs from $9 for chopped sirloin to $15 for tempura prawns.

Hotel guests get a complimentary membership in the nearby GreatLand Gold Health Club. The club's facilities include an indoor track, Nautilus equipment, sauna, and Jacuzzi.

The Middle Bracket

The **Super 8 Motel,** 3501 Minnesota Dr., Anchorage, AK 99503 (tel. 907/276-8884, or toll free 800/843-1991), has a big double entranceway where you can stomp the snow off your boots on winter days. Throughout the year it offers 24-hour courtesy-van service to and from the airport, baggage-storage facilities, and a coin-operated guest Laundromat.

The 84 rooms have queen-size beds, a built-in desk and luggage rack, cable television, direct-dial phones (local calls are free), and electric baseboard heating. Watercolors on the walls complement brown carpets and autumn-pattern bedspreads. Soft drinks and snacks are sold in the second-floor vending room. Some no-smoking rooms and a room with facilities for the handicapped are available. Pets are permitted with a deposit.

Rates in the summer are $68 single, $76 double, $83 twin. Winter rates are less. Guests who join the Super 8 VIP Club get a 10% discount effective immediately.

If you enjoy watching the black-and-white birds who swoop and dive around Alaskan ferries and cruise ships, you'll love the **Puffin Inn,** 4400 Spenard Rd., Anchorage, AK 99517 (tel. 907/243-4044). Everything here pursues the puffin theme, from the pictures in the guest rooms to the gift items sold at the front desk—stuffed toy birds, etched ulus (Eskimo knives), cards, jewelry, cups, potholders, etc.

The 42 rooms, including 16 newer units, are simple but nice, with a light beige-and-red décor. All rooms have queen-size beds, desk/dressers, local TV with two cable channels, and telephones (local calls are 25¢). The older rooms, slightly cheaper, have hot-water rather than electric baseboard heating, and shower instead of shower/bath combinations.

Summer rates are $69 single, $74 double, $79 twin. Winter rates are $47 single, $52 double, $57 twin, and they even include a complimentary continental breakfast—muffins, coffee, and the morning paper—in your room. Courtesy-car service is available to and from the airport.

One of the nicer touches at the **Anchorage Eagle Nest Hotel,** 4110 Spenard Rd., Anchorage, AK 99503 (tel. 907/243-3433 or toll free 800/478-3433 in Alaska), is an enclosed summer wildflower garden with a pair of barbecue pits. In the lobby of this rustic-looking, two-story lodging are a gift shop, selling Native crafts and jewelry, and a snack corner, complete with freezer and microwave.

The 26 well-lit rooms, decorated in dark earth tones, include standard units as well as one- and two-bedroom suites. All contain queen-size beds, round tables, two comfortable chairs, 40-channel cable TV, direct-dial phones (free local calls), courtesy coffee, and electric baseboard heating. Wildlife or scenic photos hang on the walls. Each suite has a full-size kitchen with stove and oven, refrigerator, dishwasher, toaster, and coffeemaker. A coin-op guest Laundromat is available. Summer rates for standard units are $72 to $81; one-bedroom suites, $80 to $90; two-bedroom suites $110. Rates run about $25 less in winter.

Budget Accommodations

The **Hillside Motel,** 2150 Gambell St., Anchorage, AK 99503 (tel. 907/258-6006), has a lovely location: just southeast of downtown, adjacent to Chester Creek park which has seasonal bicycle, jogging, and cross-country trails. The 26 quiet, wood-paneled units have double beds, desk/dressers, local television, telephones (free local calls), in-room coffee, and electric baseboard heating. There's also a coin-op guest laundry and a gift counter in the spacious lobby. Year-round rates are $50 single, $60 double. Six large kitchenettes are available for families at $65 a night.

The **Arctic Inn Motel,** 842 W. International Airport Rd., Anchorage, AK 99518 (tel. 907/561-1328), has 23 units next door to the Cup 'n' Saucer café and the popular Flight Deck Lounge country-and-western bar. Each room has a double bed or two twin beds, desk/dresser, local TV, telephone (free local calls), and electric baseboard heating. Rustic prints decorate the walls. Rates run $47 single, $52 double, in summer; $40 single, $45 double, in winter.

Some folks have lived in the **Midtown Lodge,** 604 W. 26th Ave., Anchorage, AK 99503 (tel. 907/258-7778), since 1968! Budget travelers who don't require a private bath will be comfortable here. The 65 carpeted units are uninspired in décor, but most contain a small refrigerator and TV, and all have a private phone (local calls are free) as well as a bed, nightstand, desk/dresser, and chair. Electric heating is centrally controlled. Towels and soap are provided to guests, who share a central men's or women's lavatory. There's also a coin-op laundry and a kitchen for those who bring their own utensils. You can watch in-house movies in the TV lounge. Drinks, snacks, and cigarettes are sold. Year-round rates are $28 single, $32 double or twin; weekly rates are available on request from the hotel.

SOUTH ANCHORAGE

These lodgings are located close to the Seward Highway as it heads south out of Anchorage en route to the Kenai Peninsula.

Upper Bracket

The only lion in the state of Alaska may be the big African cat poised, with fangs bared, just inside the lobby doors at the **Best Western Golden Lion Hotel,** 1000 E.

36th Ave., at the New Seward Highway, Anchorage, AK 99508 (tel. 907/561-1522, or toll free 800/528-1234). Don't worry: it's stuffed. But it's an imposing sentinel as it guards the wide, red-carpeted stairway leading to the Lion's Pride Restaurant and Lion's Den lounge on the second floor.

Pictures of lions decorate the walls of both dining room and lounge. The restaurant, open from 6:30 a.m. to 2 p.m. and 5 to 10 p.m. daily, has a very popular Sunday brunch ($10). Regular dinner entrees range in price from $6 for teriyaki chicken to $21.50 for Australian lobster tail. Top-40 dance music is played in the lounge several nights a week.

The 83 spacious rooms are decorated in orange and brown, with autumn-pattern bedspreads and drapes, and prints of forest scenes on the walls. The orange-and-white striped wallpaper in the bathrooms is almost too dazzling. Each sound-proofed room has two queen-size beds (or a queen-size and a sofa), a big desk/dresser, table and chairs, individual heating and air-conditioning, cable TV, and direct-dial phone (free local calls). In the lobby you can buy snacks, sundries, and cigarettes; pick up local papers plus *USA Today* and the *Christian Science Monitor;* or visit a hair stylist or gift shop.

Summer rates are $92 single, $98 double. In winter, rooms cost $77 single, $83 double.

Middle Bracket

It's nothing fancy, but **Alaska's Tudor Motel,** 4424 Lake Otis Parkway (at Tudor Road), Anchorage, AK 99507 (tel. 907/561-2234), formerly a small apartment complex, has 15 reasonably priced one-bedroom house-keeping units with private entrances.

The full kitchenettes come with cooking utensils provided. Furnishings include double beds, dressers, 17-channel cable televisions with built-in radios, phones (local calls are 25¢), tiled baths, and covered electric baseboard heating. Pets are permitted, but keep in mind that maid service is only offered twice weekly (or upon departure).

Summer rates start at $49 single, $54 double, going up to $83.25 for four people in a suite. Winter rates are $10 less. If you stay a week, the seventh day is free. The office is open for check-ins only from 8 a.m. to 10 p.m.

EAST ANCHORAGE

This area includes all accommodations east of the Seward Highway and north of Chester Creek . . . mainly the Glenn Highway corridor, heading east from Anchorage toward Eagle River.

Budget Accommodations

Kendall Family Enterprises' flagship is the **Mush Inn,** 333 Concrete Ave., Anchorage, AK 99501 (tel. 907/277-4554), half a block north of the Glenn Hwy. near Merrill Field. It's easily identified by its sign, which depicts sled-dog musher "Sourdough Jake" behind his team of eight dogs, a lone tethered bear in the lead. Watercolors of historic Russian Orthodox churches, the only such collection in Alaska, cover one wall of the lobby. Sandwiches, soft drinks, and cigarettes are sold, and there's a coin-op guest laundry.

The 94 rooms are located in four separate two-story buildings of wood or concrete-block construction. They vary considerably in size and furnishings. The smallest rooms have little more than a bed and shower; the large family rooms contain a queen-size bed and two twin beds, plus full kitchenettes. Standard units have a red-brown color scheme and contain two double or queen-size beds, desk/dresser, satellite TV with built-in radio, phones (free local calls), and electric baseboard heating. Many have small kitchens with a stove, refrigerator, and table.

Among the "specialty rooms" are the Korean Room, with Oriental antiques, a colorful butterfly collection, and a dragon lamp hanging over the Jacuzzi; the bright 1890s Room, with brass-trimmed antiques, white lace bedspread, and wall-size photographs of movie stars (John Wayne, Mae West, Clark Gable, and Humphrey Bogart); and the Sweetheart Room, with a heart-shaped waterbed and Jacuzzi.

Year-round rates are $54 to $60 for standard rooms, $75 to $95 for specialty rooms. Pets are permitted.

The **Big Timber Motel,** 2037 E. Fifth Ave., Anchorage, AK 99501 (tel. 907/272-2541), is the smallest of the three Kendall Family Enterprises establishments on the east side of the city.

Most of the 23 clean, spacious, well-maintained rooms have paneled walls and red carpets. They come furnished with king- or queen-size beds, desk/dressers, large closets, satellite TVs, phones (free local calls), electric baseboard heating, portable fans, and in most cases, small Jacuzzi/steambath combinations. About half a dozen are family rooms with kitchenettes.

Twelve "specialty" rooms have large Jacuzzis and/or waterbeds. The Monte Carlo Room has night tables fashioned like giant dice, face-card murals on the walls, and a tape deck built into the velvet headboard on the bed. The Cave Room has imitation flagstone walls and a Neanderthal fur chair. The intimate Islander Room is all green, from the fern-frond wallpaper to the hibiscus bedspread, reflected in an overhead mirror. Use your imagination in picturing the 1800s Room, the Lotus Blossom Room, and the Rose Room (which has a private fireplace).

Year-round rates are $50, single or double, and $55 for a family room; specialty suites are $75 to $100.

Historical photos hang in the rooms and line the walls of the narrow corridors of the **Kobuk Hotel-Motel,** 1104 E. Fifth Ave., at Karluk Street, Anchorage, AK 99501 (tel. 907/274-1650). Its 56 rooms are decorated in earth tones, 38 of them in the newer annex. All are appointed with double beds and reading lamps, desk/dressers, chairs, cable televisions, phones (free local calls), and electric baseboard heating. Many rooms have a Jacuzzi/steambath, and five kitchenettes are available. Rooms on the second floor of the annex are slightly larger, though all have small, awkwardly located wardrobe closets. One specialty room straight out of Rudyard Kipling has a tiger on the waterbed blanket, a forest-green carpet, jungle-décor wallpaper, and a big vase of dried plumes, grass, and peacock feathers.

Year-round rates run $47 to $50, single or double; $52 to $54 with kitchenette, $55 with Jacuzzi, $69 for specialty rooms.

Specialty rooms notwithstanding, for my money I haven't found a more pleasant small motel for a tight budget than the **Arctic Tern Inn** (formerly the Wonder Park Motel), 5000 Taku Dr., Anchorage, AK 99508 (tel. 907/337-1544). Access is via Boniface Parkway to the Glenn Hwy. frontage road.

You'll register in the pleasant, carpeted lobby with a small snackshop. The new management will tell you how to find the coin-op guest laundry, then direct you down the well-lit, carpeted corridors to your room.

The motel's four small studios and 33 spacious one- and two-bedroom suites have wood-paneled walls and orange or chocolate-brown carpeting. Utensils for the kitchenette are furnished for a small deposit. Each nice, clean room has a double or twin beds, desk and dresser in the bedroom, a hideaway couch, chair, coffee table, and kitchen table with chairs in the main room. You also get cable TV, phone (free local calls), and thermostat-controlled hot-water baseboard heating.

Summer rates are $50 for one bedroom, $60 for two bedrooms, $40 for a studio. In winter, they're $5 less.

BED-AND-BREAKFAST

Weary of hotel rooms? Anchorage is proud of its bed-and-breakfast associations, which pair visitors with local families for $40 to $75 a night, including breakfast (which could be anything from continental to a full sourdough meal). At last count, there were 171 B&Bs in Anchorage. Most give discounts to guests staying longer than one night. In all cases, whether through a private owner or an association, it's essential to book ahead.

The two principal associations offer similar services. **Alaska Private Lodgings,** P.O. Box 200047, Anchorage, AK 99520 (tel. 907/258-1717), has private rooms, suites, and apartments available downtown, in the suburbs, or out of town in Fairbanks, Healy, Homer, Palmer, Seldovia, Seward, Soldotna, Talkeetna, Valdez, Wasilla, and Willow. Car-rental discounts can be arranged. Singles are priced $35 to $55; doubles, $45 to $60.

Accommodations Alaska Style: Stay With a Friend, 3065 Arctic Blvd., Suite 173, Anchorage, AK 99503 (tel. 907/344-4006), has guest rooms for prices ranging from budget ($35 single, $45 double) to luxury ($90 double). There are also some one- and two-bedroom suites starting at $45, with TVs or recreation rooms, hot tubs, saunas, or Jacuzzis; and fully furnished apartments starting at $55. Statewide, 112 B&B operators list with this agency, including those with homes in Denali Park, Fairbanks, Girdwood (Alyeska), Gustavus (Glacier Bay), Hatcher Pass, Homer, Juneau, McCarthy, Palmer, Seward, Sitka, Soldotna, Talkeetna, Valdez, and Wasilla.

There are far too many B&Bs in the Anchorage area to mention each individually, but here are a couple of my personal favorites:

Patt and Frank Schlehofer's **A Log Home B&B,** 2440 Sprucewood St., Anchorage, AK 99508 (tel. 907/276-8527), displays the "Early American" heritage the hosts carried from New England when they moved to Alaska a few years ago. Three rooms, priced at $50 and $65, can accommodate solo visitors, two singles, or couples. A large modern bath is shared. A continental breakfast of fresh fruit, pastries, juice, and gourmet coffee or tea is served daily. Guests have access to laundry, storage, and freezer facilities. Smoking is permitted only on an outside deck.

Sixth & B Bed & Breakfast, 145 W. Sixth Ave., Anchorage, AK 99501 (tel. 907/279-5293), is a downtown oasis just one block west of the Anchorage Museum of History and Art. Seven spruce trees surround the 1930s home, once a Lutheran parsonage; a 25-foot flagpole declares it the world headquarters of the Far From Fenway Fan Club, an organization founded by B&B owner Peter Roberts for displaced Boston Red Sox baseball fans. Two double rooms with shared bath cost $45 single, $55 double, a night, and a third-floor penthouse with private bath runs $70, single or double. Bicycles come with the rooms. Roberts's basement is occupied by PeTees Quality T-shirts, featuring his own designs.

Among the dozens of other B&Bs in Anchorage are these, recommended by friends: **All the Comforts of Home,** 12531 Turk's Turn, Anchorage, AK 99516 (tel. 907/345-4279); **The Cassel,** 1040 W. 27th Ave., Anchorage, AK 99503 (tel. 907/277-7746); **The Green Bough,** 3832 Young St., Anchorage, AK 99508 (tel. 907/262-4636); **Heart of Anchorage,** 725 K St., Anchorage, AK 99501 (tel. 907/279-7066 or 276-7703); and **Hillcrest Haven,** 1449 Hillcrest Dr., Anchorage, AK 99503 (tel. 907/274-3086). Each undoubtedly has its charms. I suggest writing ahead for information.

CAMPING

Two areas are open to tent and RV campers, both in East Anchorage. **Russian Jack Springs Park,** off the Boniface Parkway, just south of the Glenn Hwy., contains Lion's camper park, with 50 RV spaces, ten tent sites, rest rooms, hot showers, and pay phones. Facilities at Russian Jack Springs Park include picnic grounds, hiking trails, a nine-hole golf course, softball fields, and tennis courts.

Centennial Park has 89 campsites, with picnic tables and fire pits, suitable for either RV or tent camping. There are rest rooms, hot showers, and pay phones. Access is from Muldoon Road and Boundary Avenue, just south of the Glenn Hwy. Rates at both parks are $12 a night, with stays limited to seven nights.

For further information, write or call the **Anchorage Parks and Recreation Department,** 2525 Gambell St., Room 404, Anchorage, AK 99503 (tel. 907/264-4474).

---

3. Where to Eat

It wasn't too many years ago that a mention of Anchorage restaurants would have brought a chorus of guffaws. "What are they serving today?" someone might have asked. "Whale blubber? Reindeer stew?" Though *that* sort of diet has traditionally been the exclusive fare of Eskimo communities in the far north and west, it is true that Anchorage cuisine was pretty much of the steak-and-potatoes variety.

As the city has grown more cosmopolitan, however, so have the tastes of its citizens. Anchorage is a long way from becoming the fine-food capital of North America, but it's no longer difficult to find sushi or coquilles St-Jacques, linguine or a big chimichanga.

Anchorage is *not* so cosmopolitan, though, as to require a coat and tie everywhere you go. In fact about the only places where you might be looked at cross-eyed if you arrive in clean, ironed jeans and a wool sweater are the premier establishments in the big international hotels—the **Crow's Nest** at the Cook, **Josephine's** at the Sheraton, the **Top of the World** at the Hilton, and the **House of Lords** at the Westmark. In general, you can feel good about being casual.

The restaurants listed below are categorized like the accommodations, by area of the city and approximate price. As a rule of thumb, figure $25 and up per person for a complete dinner at a "Deluxe" restaurant, $13 to $25 at a "Moderate" restaurant, and $5 to $13 at a "Budget" restaurant. I will frequently save on my personal expenses by having my main meal at lunch at a better restaurant, when prices are much lower than at dinnertime.

DOWNTOWN DELUXE RESTAURANTS

Aside from the hotel restaurants, described above, there are a handful of truly outstanding independent dining establishments.

Some say the best continental cuisine in Anchorage is served in the basement of the Voyager Hotel at **The Corsair,** 944 W. Fifth Ave., across from the Hotel Captain Cook (tel. 278-4502). European chef Hans Kruger's establishment is elegantly designed like a ship's hold, with rigging above each intimately secluded table. The service is timed to allow you to savor your meal, not rush through it. You might start with oysters Corsair (baked on the half shell with foie gras, at $7.50), followed by roast duckling Madagascar (with red wine and green-peppercorn sauce, at $20.50) or rack of lamb Armenonville ($28), and topped off with strawberries Devonshire ($6). Entrees, priced from $15.75 to $32, also include a wide selection of seafood, steaks, and veal dishes. *Wine Spectator* magazine says the Corsair has one of the top 100 wine lists in the United States. Kruger recommends the trockenbeerenausleses, perhaps because he likes to hear patrons try to say the word. Open for dinner from 5 to 11 p.m. Monday through Saturday.

Ask an Anchorage resident to name his or her favorite restaurant, and chances are he'll say "The Marx Brothers." He's not talking about Groucho, Chico, and Harpo, but **The Marx Bros. Café,** 627 W. Third Ave. (tel. 278-2133). Squeezed into a refurbished 1916 wood-frame house a block from the Hilton, this culinary tribute to the famed family of comedy is nothing to joke about. The menu changes regularly to offer a variety of gourmet specialties such as seafood mousse and venison. You can open with Dungeness crab ravioli with lemon-basil-beurre sauce ($7.50), then enjoy grilled shrimp with papaya-mint salsa ($18.50), black-horned antelope with smoked caribou-ham sauce ($16), or New York steak with black-bean sauce ($25) for a main course. Entrees range in price from $15 to $35. The dessert menu features the Marx Bros. Café's homemade cheesecake. There's also an extensive wine cellar. Open Monday through Saturday from 6 to 9:30 p.m.

Don't let the less-than-sophisticated façade of **Club Paris,** 417 W. Fifth Ave. (tel. 277-6332), fool you: it's famous for its char-broiled steaks. In the rear of a dimly lit cocktail lounge, in a plush booth or at a table, you can feast on a dinner of escargots ($9), filet mignon ($24.50), sautéed mushrooms ($6), crème de menthe parfait ($5.50), and a bottle of châteauneuf du pape for two ($22.50). Open daily except Sunday for lunch from 11:30 a.m. to 2:30 p.m., and for dinner Monday through Saturday from 5 to 11 p.m., on Sunday to 10 p.m.

DOWNTOWN MODERATELY PRICED RESTAURANTS

Seafood
Simon and Seafort's Saloon and Grill, 420 L St. (tel. 274-3502), goes to great lengths to re-create the atmosphere of a circa-1900 grand saloon. Not only is there white marble and brass trim throughout, the restaurant also offers a great view across Cook Inlet. Scan the 14-page dinner menu, then ask for the fresh fish list (entrees run $11 to $15). You might go for the baked Alaska halibut in dill sauce, or something more exotic like Hawaiian ono with hazelnut butter or toasted almonds. Simon's also makes its own pasta daily, and offers a superb selection of desserts like New Orleans pear-bread pudding with bourbon sauce ($2.75). At lunchtime the price ceiling is $7.75; consider the sesame chicken salad ($7) or a bowl of homemade clam chowder ($3.25). Open from 11:30 a.m. to 2 p.m. and 5:30 to 10 p.m. daily (for dinner only on Sunday). The bar, a popular gathering place for Anchorage singles, features gourmet beer and 70 different brands of scotch.

If you're looking for the sunset view that Simon's offers, but with a little less glitz and a little more Alaskana, walk just one block down L Street to the **Kayak Seafood Grill,** 510 L St. (tel. 274-7617). Historical photos, wildlife murals, and unique caribou-horn chandeliers lend atmosphere to this fine eatery, whose full picture windows stare across Cook Inlet from Mount Iliamna to the "Sleeping Lady." Sit at plush booths upholstered in shades of brown with red overtones, or at separate tables, with piped-in music by Paul Simon, James Taylor, and Maria Muldaur in the background. Dinner entrees, priced between $10 and $16, range from brewbattered halibut to broadbill swordfish to fresh steamer clams, with a few beef and fowl dishes thrown in for good measure. The restaurant also has a well-attended singles bar. Open for lunch from 11 a.m. to 3 p.m. Monday through Friday; for dinner from 5 to 10 p.m. Sunday through Thursday, to 11 p.m. on Friday and Saturday; and for Sunday brunch from 9:30 a.m. to 2 p.m.

Bob Sparks, owner of **Elevation 92,** 1007 W. Third Ave. (tel. 279-1578), once owned a Sun Valley restaurant called Elevation 6000. When he moved to Alaska in the mid-1970s and started this restaurant overlooking the inlet, it was only natural that he adapt the name to his new elevation. There's a garden feel to the dining room, with hanging ferns and tall potted plants beside stained-wood trellises with cut-glass panels. Local salmon, halibut, and king crab headline the summer menu: seafood selections change according to availability and season. You can start with crab-stuffed mushrooms ($5), then follow with Cajun-style king salmon ($17). If seafood isn't your kettle of fish, try the tournedos bordelaise ($18). Praline cheesecake ($4) makes a tasty dessert. Lunch prices range from $5.75 to $8.75. A popular wine and seafood bar serves as a lounge. Open from 11:30 a.m. to midnight weekdays, 5 p.m. to midnight on weekends.

There's a re-created "Tent City" at the **Old Anchorage Salmon Bake,** at Third Avenue and K Street (tel. 279-8790). A gift shop, Alaskan products store, and gold-panning exhibition occupy other tent structures. Lunch (11 a.m. to 2 p.m.) offers an Alaskan salmon burger for $6.25, including salad bar and barbecue beans; and dinner (4 to 9 p.m.) gives you a feast of salmon, halibut, snow crab, reindeer sausage, and an all-you-can-eat salad bar for $17. Open daily June 1 to mid-September. There's seating for 400, including 150 under cover in case of rain.

Mexican

If you've visited **La Mex** at the Royal Hawaiian Center in Waikiki, you may be pleased to know that two other members of the family are here in Anchorage, at 538 I St. (tel. 274-7678) and at 2556 Spenard Rd. (tel. 274-7511). The downtown outlet is a showcase of sorts, a two-story hacienda in pueblo style. The courtyard is painted in traditional pottery designs—blood reds and turquoise blues on ochre—and an enormous sun mobile with various cryptic signs hangs from the ceiling above the waiting area. Taco-enchilada combination meals are $5.75 for lunch, $6.75 for dinner. More gourmet selections featuring shrimp and chicken run to $12. You can dine well at the bar with a "grande," the house specialty giant margarita, and a plate of tostaditos ($6.25), chips smothered in beans, cheese, lettuce, jalapeños, and house dressing. The I Street Mex is open from 11 a.m. to 10:30 p.m. Tuesday through Thursday, to 11 p.m. on Friday and Saturday; closed Sunday and Monday. Spenard hours are 11 a.m. to 11 p.m. Monday through Thursday, to midnight on Friday and Saturday, to 10 p.m. on Sunday.

Oriental

From the rich leather-and-wood counter at the **Tea Leaf** restaurant, 313 E St., across from the Hilton (tel. 279-0134), you can watch your meal being prepared. It's a real production when owner-chef Pyong Sun Yi is in the open kitchen: meat and vegetables chopped, marinated, and stir-fried in a wok. This long and narrow but elegant restaurant has plush private booths and a spacious lounge, in addition to ten high-backed chairs for solo diners. The 172-item menu (which proudly states: "We add no MSG to our cooking!") offers recommendations on the best way to order Chinese dinners: a foursome might start with drunken chicken and sizzling rice soup, followed by a quartet of entrees in the beef, pork, fowl, and/or seafood categories. A spread like that will run about $50 for four. Luncheon specials—two dishes with fried rice—are a bargain at $6.50. Open from 11 a.m. to 2:30 p.m. and 4 to 10 p.m. Sunday through Thursday, to 11 p.m. on Friday and Saturday.

Ah Ka Hi Hana, 930 W. Fifth Ave. (tel. 276-2215), adjacent to the Fifth Avenue parking lot across from the Cook, has a delightful sushi bar as well as full Japanese meals. It's open daily except Sunday for lunch and dinner. Two-bite servings of tuna, shrimp, octopus, and sea-urchin sushi run between $3.10 and $3.60 each.

DOWNTOWN BUDGET RESTAURANTS

At these establishments you can enjoy dinner for less than $13 per person.

Alaskan

When Native Alaskans come to Anchorage, they often gather at the Alaska Native Medical Center to visit with friends, infirm or not. The center's **Tundra Club** café, 250 Gambell St. (tel. 278-4716), has therefore become the city's most popular spot for authentic Native cuisine, including sourdough pancakes, berry dumplings, fish pie, reindeer sausage, Indian fry bread, and akutak (Eskimo ice cream). Lunch, usually meat, potatoes, and vegetables, is served on a paper plate and is still only $5. Perhaps nowhere else in Alaska can you dine while surrounded by the simultaneous voices of Inupiat, Yupik, and Athabaskan speakers. Don't expect a lot of atmosphere, though: the building, with its thick, wooden government-issue doors, survived the 1964 earthquake without major damage but has worn out at least two dozen coats of paint. Open Monday through Friday from 7 a.m. to 3 p.m.

Delis

Anchorage's former mayor, Tony Knowles, is a part-owner of the **Downtown Deli & Café,** 525 W. Fourth Ave. (tel. 276-7116), Anchorage's closest approximation of a New York deli. This is where the visitor can come for lox and bagels, pickled herring, matzohs, and other noshes. Breakfast is served anytime: try the cheese blintzes ($4.75) or bagel Benedict ($7.50). The seafood melt, a heaping open-face sandwich for $7, and fresh spinach salad at $6.50, are popular lunches. Dinner entrees, ranging from chicken Florentine to seafood pasta primavera, are priced from $10 to $13. The atmosphere is at once casual and campus-like, with ivy hanging over smoked-glass room dividers and seating on wooden benches. Open daily in summer from 6 a.m. to 11 p.m.; in winter, Monday through Saturday from 7 a.m. to 10 p.m. and on Sunday from 9 a.m. to 4 p.m.

New American

The owners of **Sacks Fifth Avenue Café,** 625 W. Fifth Ave. (tel. 276-3546), may have had their tongues firmly in cheek when they named their little restaurant, but there's nothing false about its quality for price. Homemade pastas and deli sandwiches are served in a bright, airy garden atmosphere, with Scandinavian-style furnishings and large potted plants. Light jazz is piped in, and there are changing art and photo exhibitions on the walls. For lunch you might try an Alaskan reindeer-sausage sandwich with melted cheese and red onions for $6.75, or a Japanese noodle salad (udon noodles and shiitake mushrooms in a spicy sauce) for $6.75. Popular dinner entrees include chicken, shrimp, and vegetables in a light ginger cream sauce ($13), and tournedos of beef in chili butter ($15.50). There's an extensive wine list. Open from 11 a.m. to 9 p.m. Monday through Saturday, and 11 a.m. to 2:30 p.m. for Sunday brunch.

Literary

This is an odd category for food, but this is an unusual café. **Cyrano's,** 413 D St. (tel. 274-2599), in the center of downtown Anchorage, serves light meals—soups, salads, and sandwiches—with wine and cappuccinos beside the stacks of one of Alaska's thought-provoking bookstores. The name honors 17th-century French writer Savinien Cyrano de Bergerac, legendary for his love of word play and fine cuisine. Book reviews, poetry readings, and light musical performances are frequent evening events; an improvisational theater group often performs Saturday nights. Open Monday through Thursday from 10 a.m. to 6 p.m., on Friday to 9 p.m., on Saturday to midnight, and on Sunday from noon to 5 p.m. in winter; Monday 10 a.m. to 6 p.m., Tuesday through Friday 10 a.m. to 6 p.m. (Saturday and Sunday hours don't change) in summer.

READER'S RESTAURANT SELECTION: "**Muffin Man** has great muffins, coffee, and juice, with sandwiches available" (Margaret Cushum, North Caldwell, N.J.). *Author's Note:* The Muffin Man is at 529 I St. (tel. 279-6836). It's open from 5 a.m. to 3 p.m. Monday through Friday.

Mexican

La Cabaña, 312 E. Fourth Ave., at Cordova Street (tel. 272-0135), was Alaska's first Mexican restaurant when the Torres family opened it in 1953 at another location. It may not be in the same place, but it's still in the same family. The décor is unpretentiously south-of-the-border, with curtained alcoves, wrought-iron railings and chandeliers, colorful cloth flowers, sarape-style drapes, and wall murals. Piped-in mariachi music completes the feeling. Two-item luncheon specials are priced at $4.75 to $5.25; dinners are $7.75 to $9.75. Complimentary chips come with all meals. There's a full bar which serves excellent margaritas. Open for lunch weekdays from 11:30 a.m. to 3 p.m., and for dinner Monday through Friday from 3 to 11 p.m., on Saturday from 5 to 11 p.m., and on Sunday from 5 to 10 p.m.

Oriental

Where do Japanese visitors eat when they're in town? Many of them head for **Kumagoro,** 533 W. Fourth Ave. (tel. 272-9905), open from 10 a.m. to 10 p.m. daily. It's a casual Japanese eatery with shoji screens and bamboo dividers. Champon ramen, at $8, is a stew of vegetables and seafood (shrimp, squid, octopus) which is a full meal in itself.

MIDTOWN/SPENARD MODERATELY PRICED RESTAURANTS

Anchorage's fastest-growing concentration of restaurants and nightspots is in this district.

Alaskan

The **Garden of Eatin',** 2502 McRae Rd., at Arkansas Drive, in Spenard (tel. 248-FOOD), could almost qualify for the "deluxe" category were it not for its very reasonably priced lunches and the difficulty of taking seriously a restaurant lodged in a World War II quonset hut. The light-hearted management of the Garden obviously sees dining as a time for amusement: its "calor'o'fare" menu for weight-watchers offers items like shredded egg skin, mosquito knuckles sautéed in vinegar, and boiled tablecloth stains. Fortunately, you're not locked into that regimen. In this garden setting of hanging plants you can enjoy an elegant dinner of prime rib ($18) or crab imperial ($25). Open for dinner from 6 to 10 p.m. Tuesday through Saturday.

Steaks

Stuart Anderson's Cattle Company, 300 W. Tudor Rd., at C Street (tel. 562-2844), is like all others in this chain of western steakhouses—a low-lit, intimate restaurant with comfortable private booths, and a noisy, bustling disco lounge. Sound-proofing is guaranteed. Full steak dinners start at $9, including soup or salad, potato or rice, and bread. Prime rib and lobster run $21. Chicken dinners start at $10, while fresh catches of the day, like rainbow trout ($10) and Hawaiian thresher shark ($13), are based on market price. Open Monday through Thursday from 11 a.m. to 10:30 p.m., on Friday and Saturday to 11 p.m., on Sunday from 4 to 10:30 p.m. The lounge stays open into the wee hours, with DJ entertainment nightly.

Greek

Athenian music sets the pace at **The Greek Corner,** 302 W. Fireweed Lane (tel. 276-2820). Spanakopita (spinach pie), dolmades (stuffed grape leaves), and lamb dishes, as well as baklava (a honey-and-walnut pastry), highlight the menu here, supplemented by a variety of pastas. Lunches are priced in the $5 to $7 range; full dinners, $9 to $15. Open from 11 a.m. to 2 p.m. Monday through Friday for lunch, 4:30 to 11 p.m. daily for dinner.

Italian

Romano's, 2415 C St., at Fireweed Lane (tel. 278-1414), is Anchorage's No. 1 choice for a romantic trattoria dinner with fine wine and candlelight. You can listen to Pavarotti belt out a Puccini aria as you dine in a Venetian atmosphere, complete with arches and a wall-size mural of gondoliers on the canals. Dinners, priced from $9.50 to $13.50, include chicken cacciatore and veal dishes like scaloppine piccata. Pastas—spaghetti, ravioli, linguine—start at $8. There's also a selection of seafoods and steaks. Escape to the Vesuvio Room for after-dinner cocktails. Open Sunday through Thursday from 5 to 11 p.m., to 11:30 p.m. on Friday and Saturday.

Vegetarians will enjoy **One Guy from Italy,** 3020 Minnesota Dr., in the Z Plaza at Benson Boulevard (tel. 277-9231). The service isn't the speediest, but the food is good—including an extensive menu of meat-free items like eggplant parmigiana. Veal parmigiana ($13.75) and seafood cannelloni ($11) are popular meals at this spacious neighborhood restaurant on two red-upholstered levels. Spaghetti dinners, including soup or salad and garlic bread, run $6.25 to $9.25. Licensed for wine and beer. Open daily from 11 a.m. to 11 p.m.

Oriental

In authentic Chinese fashion, the atmosphere at **Ah Sa Wan,** 560 W. Tudor Rd. (tel. 562-7788 or 563-0044), is so elaborate as to perhaps appear ostentatious. But as Chinese opera fans know, that's as it should be. Colorfully painted opera masks are the unifying theme in this elegant Mandarin and Cantonese restaurant. (You'll recognize it immediately: it looks like a temple gate from the outside.) Lunch specials are priced at $4.50 to $6, and dinner combinations at $9 to $15 per person. For $12 per person you can have a Mandarin feast of sizzling rice soup, eggroll, Mongolian beef, sweet-and-sour pork, shrimp with lobster sauce, and fried rice. The kung pao chicken ($8.50) is also excellent. Adventuresome? Try moo goo gai pan ($8.50), sautéed sea cucumber ($12.50), or Ma-po's tofu ($9). Open from 11:30 a.m. to 10 p.m. Sunday through Thursday, to 11 p.m. on Friday and Saturday.

A fine Japanese restaurant, **Daruma,** adjoins Ah Sa Wan at 550 W. Tudor Rd. (tel. 561-6622 or 561-6633). A *daruma* is a religious hermit of sorts, a roly-poly, big-eyed good-luck charm. You'll see several on a shelf behind the sushi bar. Traditional Japanese prints decorate the walls of this restaurant, which is as simple in décor (natural-wood chairs, a large aquarium) as its Chinese cousin is ornate. Lunch entrees are priced from $5.50 to $12, including donburi, yaki soba, and tsukimi udon. A good choice might be the special, which for $10 includes miso soup, salad, three kinds of nigiri sushi, shrimp tempura, sesame chicken, rice, and azuki (red bean) ice cream. Dinner entrees are $8.50 to $23.50. For $15 per person you can feast on beef or chicken sukiyaki, chicken teriyaki, shrimp tempura, miso soup, salad, rice, and tea. Wash it down with hot sake or plum wine. Open from 11 a.m. to 11 p.m. Monday through Saturday, to 10 p.m. on Sunday.

In Spenard, the **Tempura Kitchen,** 3826 Spenard Rd. (tel. 277-2741), is a popular local Japanese restaurant and sushi bar ($2.75 to $3.25 an order), with three chefs chopping, slicing, and rolling. Lunch is served from 11:30 a.m. to 2 p.m. Monday through Friday, and dinner, from 5 to 10 p.m. daily.

READERS' RESTAURANT SELECTION: "**Peking Palace** has excellent food with complete dinners for two starting at $10.50" (Einar and Lilyan Anderson, Sisters, Ore.). *Author's Note:* Peking Palace is at 500 E. Benson Blvd. (tel. 274-5236).

MIDTOWN/SPENARD BUDGET RESTAURANTS

Alaskan

No restaurant in Anchorage can boast the pioneer atmosphere of **Gwennie's Old Alaska Restaurant,** 4333 Spenard Rd., in Spenard (tel. 243-2090). A spacious two-story cabin of log and stone, Gwennie's is chock full of every kind of Alaskana you can think of, from photos of Anchorage in 1915 and after the 1964 earthquake to Eskimo sleds made of whale baleen and a 45,000-year-old bison skull. Dug into the middle of the ground floor is a wishing well, 3 feet deep and 12 feet across, whose proceeds are periodically donated to charity. There's an old Wurlitzer in the lounge, and lots of hanging plants everywhere. Breakfast is served anytime; try the reindeer sausage omelet ($8). A bowl of chili ($3.75) makes a great lunch, and barbecued ribs ($12) are popular at dinner. You don't need to ask for ice water: every table gets a big pitcher. Open Monday through Saturday at 6 a.m., on Sunday at 8 a.m., until 10 p.m. daily.

Also in Spenard, the **Hogg Bros. Café,** 2421 Spenard Rd. (tel. 276-9649), is an Anchorage breakfast institution, sharing a saloon-style building with Chilkoot Charlie's nightclub. It's only open eight hours daily—from 8 a.m. to 4 p.m., seven days a week—but as the management proclaims, "Everything else is just eggs" compared to the generous and unusual breakfasts offered here, like 20 different omelets, the Hogg McKinley and El Breakfast de Roberta. For lunch, try an asparagus burger. But the food actually takes second place to the people-watching. You'll have to drop in to see what I mean.

American

Harry's, 101 W. Benson Blvd., in the Alaska Pacific Bank Building (tel. 561-5317), is dedicated to the memory of Harry R. Truman, the old man who refused to leave his Spirit Lake lodge when Washington's Mount St. Helens erupted in 1980. "Though Harry never came to Alaska," explains a plaque, "his outlook on life and his rugged individualism would have been right at home here on the Last Frontier." A life-size statue of Truman with binoculars, sitting on a barrel surrounded by wildlife, greets guests who can look past the video games. Photos of him and the mountain are hung by the fireplace. The highest price on the menu is $12, for a rib-eye or top sirloin steak. There's a wide selection of soups, salads, burgers, and baked potato entrees from $6.

Harry's does good business as a singles bar. The numerous specialty drinks include the Griz Killer ($3.25), "a drink that'll stop a rampaging bear dead in its tracks, lights out, forever." The restaurant is open from 11 a.m. to 11 p.m. daily.

Deli/Bakery

A personal favorite is the **Café Europa,** 601 W. 36th Ave., between C Street and Arctic Boulevard (tel. 563-5704). This spacious café has garden-style décor, with potted ferns and pandanus plants standing on the light-green carpet, ivy accenting the abstract watercolors on the walls, and fresh flowers on the white linen tablecloths. All prices are in the $6 to $8 range, including croissant sandwiches ($6.50), salads (like bay shrimp for $7), pastas (like Cajun chicken fettuccine for $8), quiche with soup or salad ($6.25), London broil ($7), and broiled halibut ($7.25). Weekend champagne brunches are superb: you can have a gourmet egg or crêpe dish with fruit compote, fresh croissant, and juice for $10, or an additional $3 if you want a split of champagne. The Europa also has an espresso bar and its own bakery, open evenings. The café is open weekdays from 7 a.m. to 6 p.m. Brunch only is served on Saturday (8 a.m. to 6 p.m.) and Sunday (10 a.m. to 4 p.m.)

Seafood

You're guaranteed fresh fish—and only fresh fish—at the **Sea Galley,** 4101 Credit Union Dr., between 40th Avenue and C Street (tel. 563-3520). The fish menu and daily blackboard specials list only the day's catches, either from Alaskan waters or flown in (often from Hawaii). Prices vary from $9 to $12 for a full fish meal, and up to $21 for a pound of king crab legs. The Sea Galley also has steaks and salads ($7 for an unaccompanied salad bar), plus a children's menu. An oyster bar attached to the lounge serves the misshapen shellfish for $6 to $6.50 the half dozen. Nets and other nautical décor hang from the ceilings and walls over the rustic, light-wood construction. Open Monday through Thursday from 11 a.m. to 10 p.m., on Friday and Saturday to 11 p.m., and on Sunday from 11 a.m. to 10 p.m.

Mexican

There's always a fiesta at **Garcia's of Scottsdale,** 4140 B St. (tel. 561-4476). Multicolored balloons dangle from the ceiling of this vibrant hacienda garden, giving it a permanent party feel. As befits a party, the portions are generous. At lunch, you might have a taco salad ($6.25) or the pollo fundido ($6.50)—a deep-fried flour tortilla filled with chicken, covered with melted cheese, and served with rice. Dinner combinations start at $7.75, but if you want a little of everything— enchilada, taco, tostada, rice, and beans—it will come on two plates (Garcia's calls it "el supremo sampler") for $10. Open from 11 a.m. to 10 p.m. Monday through Thursday, to midnight on Friday and Saturday, and noon to 10 p.m. on Sunday.

Natural Foods

Daily vegetarian casserole specials, just $4 a plate, make the **Natural Pantry,** 300 W. 36th Ave. (tel. 563-2727), one of Anchorage's best bargains. There are also a variety of soups, sandwiches, and quiches in the $3.50 to $4.25 range. Open from 11 a.m. to 7:30 p.m. weekdays, to 6:30 p.m. on Saturday; closed Sunday.

SOUTH ANCHORAGE RESTAURANTS

Most of these restaurants are within shouting distance of the Seward Highway as it heads out of town toward Girdwood and the Kenai Peninsula.

Alaskan

Did you ever want to dine at a gold mine? The **Sourdough Mining Co.,** 5200 Juneau St., off International Airport Road between the Old and New Seward Highway (tel. 563-2272), is a replica of the abandoned mill house at Independence Mine on Hatcher Pass. Enter through a mining tunnel to a collection of 1890s antiques and hunting and fishing trophies. Mesquite-grilled baby back ribs are the house specialty at $19 for a full rack, $12 for a half rack. Other choices include Alaskan-style catfish rolled in cornmeal and spices ($11), New Orleans pepper steak ($18), and king crab ($20). Arctic lime pie is $2. The Creekside Saloon overlooks Campbell Creek, where you can watch spawning salmon in season. Folk and ballad singers frequently perform on weekend nights. Open seven days a week from 11 a.m. to 11 p.m.

American

Yesterday's, 1300 E. Dimond Blvd., at New Seward Highway (tel. 344-1115), has eclectic early-20th-century décor and a 20-page, tab-divided menu that reads like a catalog. Here's where you can come for deli salads (like taco salad, at $8), gourmet hamburgers (from $6), or unusual croissant, baguette, or pita sandwiches ($6 to $8). There's a limited selection of seafood and meat entrees for under $14. Ice creams and coffee drinks are specialties. Open daily except Sunday from 11 a.m. to midnight. The lounge is open to 2:30 a.m.

Eastern European

Alaska's only glimpse behind the Iron Curtain is afforded by the **Warsaw Restaurant,** 7550 Old Seward Hwy. (tel. 344-8193). Polish sausage, stuffed cabbage, pirozhkis, and wienerschnitzel dinners are some of the offerings, priced from $4 to $7 for lunch, $8.50 to $16.50 for dinner. Open from 11 a.m. to 3 p.m. and 5 to 10 p.m. Monday through Saturday and 4 to 10 p.m. on Sunday.

Italian

Armen's Mazzi's, 2052 E. Northern Lights Blvd. (tel. 279-9547), bills itself as "the best little Italian restaurant this side of New York." Owner Armen Kevrekian claims to be the first Anchorage Italian restaurateur to serve deep-dish Sicilian pizza, calzone, and homemade pasta, and the first to offer a no-smoking room. Though those points may be in doubt, the richness of the décor is not. Enjoy the Persian carpets, fine carved wooden chairs, stained glass, wrought-iron work, and reproductions of Michelangelo's *David* and other classic sculptures. You have your choice of pastas à la carte or as full dinners, with soup or salad and garlic bread. Spaghetti and fettuccine (full dinners are $10) and manicotti (full dinners for $13) are favorites. Veal dinners—parmigiana, francese, marsala, Tuscany, and contadine—start at $14. There's a highly palatable wine list, and an espresso bar. Open for lunch from 11 a.m. to 2 p.m. on weekdays, and for dinner from 5 to 10 p.m. Sunday through Thursday, to 11 p.m. on Friday and Saturday.

Mexican

Anchorage residents insist, and with good reason, that **Mexico in Alaska,** 7305 Old Seward Hwy. (tel. 349-1528), is the most authentic Mexican restaurant in the city—maybe in Alaska. Its chefs come straight from the state of Michoacan. Sure, you can get your tacos and enchiladas here, but why not step out and have huachinango à la veracruzana (red snapper, Veracruz style), pollo en mole (chicken in a spicy chocolate sauce), or lengua en salsa de aceituna (beef tongue in olive sauce)? Most entrees are in the $10 to $12 range. Open from 11 a.m. to 9 p.m. weekdays, noon to 10 p.m. on Saturday, and 4 to 9 p.m. on Sunday.

ANCHORAGE EAST RESTAURANTS

These are just a few of the restaurants along the Glenn Highway heading east from downtown.

American

Peggy's, 1675 E. Fifth Ave. (tel. 258-7599), calls itself Alaska's oldest family restaurant. Anchorage residents know it best for its fruit and cream pies. But Peggy's offers generous portions of all meals. There's a working man's breakfast—three eggs, ham, potatoes and gravy, two pancakes, and toast—for $6.75; a nine-ounce sirloin luncheon steak with salad and fries for $8.50; and a jumbo prawns dinner for $10. Open daily from 6 a.m. to 10 p.m.

Hamburger lovers will find Anchorage's best at the **Red Robin Burger & Spirits Emporium,** 3401 Penland Parkway, in the Northway Mall (tel. 276-7788). The only Alaskan installment of a Seattle-based chain that has recently expanded into Japan, the Red Robin couples a party atmosphere with an imaginative variety of gourmet burgers in the $7 price range. Open Monday through Thursday from 11 a.m. to midnight, on Friday and Saturday to 2 a.m., and on Sunday from 10 a.m. to 11:30 p.m. (brunch until 2 p.m.).

Chinese

The **Imperial Palace,** 400 Sitka St. (tel. 274-9167), is arguably the best Chinese restaurant on the east side of Anchorage. Lunch specials, consisting predominantly of San Francisco–style chop suey, chow mein, and egg foo yung, run $4.25 to $5.50. Spicy Mandarin and Szechuan specialties make tasty dinners for $9 to $13.50 per person. Open Monday through Saturday from 11 a.m. to 10:30 p.m. and on Sunday from noon to 10:30 p.m.

FAST-FOOD RESTAURANTS

Like any good-sized American city, Anchorage has its share of McDonald's (nine), Burger Kings (seven), Kentucky Fried Chickens (five), Arby's (three), and other national chain fast-food restaurants. I'm not a big fan of slap-on-the-cheeseburgers, but I will admit that it's occasionally essential to eat on the run.

In Anchorage my favorite spot for that sort of mobile behavior is the 24-hour **California Roll** restaurant and bakery, 2960 C St., at Benson Boulevard (tel. 563-8522). The décor is tastefully done, with large plants in a planter at the counter. The menu offers a variety of sandwiches, none more expensive than the California tuna ($7), plus salads, quiches, and an espresso bar.

For a local quick-chicken fix, you might drop in at **Wings 'n' Things,** 529 I St. (tel. 277-6257), where $16 will buy you a bucket of 50 chicken wings (smaller quantities are available too, of course). Submarine sandwiches here cost $4.50 to $6. Open from 11 a.m. to 10 p.m. Monday through Saturday; closed Sunday.

For those late-night pizza deliveries, Anchorage has numerous hole-in-the-wall parlors. I like **Hollywood All Night Pizza,** 343 W. Benson Blvd. (tel. 562-3666). You'll pay $10.50 (for a small 14-inch pizza with a single ingredient) to $24 (for an 18-incher with the works). Ask about the Mexican pizza, with chorizo sausage and ortega chiles. Hollywood Pizza isn't really open all night, by the way. Its hours, daily, are 4 p.m. to 4 a.m.

Ice-cream fans will find six Baskin-Robbins parlors in Anchorage. But don't miss **Larsons Homemade Ice Cream and Yogurt Garden,** 425 E. Fifth Ave. (tel. 338-6054). Jim and Pete Larson make their own gourmet ice cream, using a 16% fresh-cream base. And they give you full quarter-pound scoops. Open from 11 a.m. to 11 p.m. Monday through Saturday, from noon on Sunday.

4. What to See and Do

Many Anchorage visitors are under the impression that while the city has lots of guest facilities, it doesn't have a whole lot to see and do.

Granted, the more spectacular sights and activities—the Portage Glacier, for example—are at least a two-hour drive from downtown Anchorage. But there's more than enough in the central city to fill up two or three days' time.

A good way to get oriented in Anchorage is to take a downtown walking tour. The one assembled by the Anchorage Convention and Visitors Bureau, included in the city's annual visitors guide, is considerably longer and more detailed than the one suggested here.

A DOWNTOWN WALKING TOUR

Start at the Anchorage Convention and Visitors Bureau's sod-roofed **Log Cabin Visitor Information Center,** at the southeast corner of Fourth Avenue and F Street. A milepost in front stresses Anchorage's location as the "Air Crossroads of the World." You may be surprised to find the mileages from East Asia, Western Europe, and the eastern and southern United States almost identical. Also outside are a 5,114-pound jade boulder from the Kobuk River area of northwestern Alaska and a "peace pole" erected in 1985 by a Japanese group.

Immediately to the east, on the grounds of the **Old City Hall,** is a white sculpted memorial to former Secretary of State William H. Seward, who engineered the purchase of Alaska from Russia in 1867. The first floor of the former municipal building, now occupied by the Alaska Pacific Bank, has a rotating exhibit of historical photos of Anchorage.

Many of the buildings along this stretch of Fourth Avenue date from the early days of the city's history. The entire façade of the **Old Federal Building and U.S. Courthouse,** between F and G Streets, was covered by a gigantic 49-star American flag with the passage by the U.S. Congress of the Alaska Statehood Bill in 1958. The building, dating from the late 1930s, is on the National Register of Historic Places. So is the **4th Avenue Theater,** across the street. Built in 1947 by a redoubtable Alaskan millionaire named Cap Lathrop, it was the venue of many stage productions until completion of the new Performing Arts Center in 1988. It was reverted to a role of small playhouse and cinema. The interior is handsomely designed, with handcrafted woodwork, bronze and silver murals, and ceiling lights outlining the North Star and Big Dipper of Alaska's flag.

Turn north (left) on E Street. Between Second and Third Avenues you'll see a small **Bureau of Land Management monument,** with a bronze memorial plaque commemorating the original 1915 townsite survey. Four etchings depict the first land auction, the original tent city, an aerial view of Anchorage, and a 1985 street map. This is a good viewpoint from which to see the **Alaska Railroad Depot** at the foot of the hill, Ship Creek just behind it, and the military bases in the near distance.

If you wind your way down to the train station on First Avenue, you can see Engine No. 1, a small locomotive first used in the construction of the Panama Canal in the early 1900s. There are also some Native totem poles outside and historical photos inside the station. Anchorage was built as a railroad town, the headquarters of a line connecting the port of Seward with the gold-rush city of Fairbanks.

Ship Creek was the historic site of Tanaina Indian summer fishing camps and the small native village of Zludiat. Upstream to the east are an interpretive salmon-viewing platform and a waterfowl-nesting area in a pond beside a power plant. One of the nine people who lived by Ship Creek in 1914, when federal railroad surveyors arrived, was the ranger for the 5.8-million-acre Chugach National Forest, established in 1907 by President Theodore Roosevelt.

Government Hill, on the other side of Ship Creek, is an isolated residential district where federal employees were housed in the city's early days. Californians, take note: Hollywood and Vine run parallel here, not at right angles as in Los Angeles. The **Port of Anchorage** (tel. 272-1531) is at the north end of Government Hill. Built in 1951, the port handles more than 400 tanker and container ships bearing two million tons of cargo a year. A new visitor observation deck is a great place for spotting small, white beluga whales in the Cook Inlet during the spring and fall. Tours of the port can be arranged.

Along Second Avenue are a series of old Anchorage homes. Noteworthy are no. 542, the **Andrew Christensen House,** former home of the General Land Office director who auctioned the original townsite; no. 605, the **Leopold David House,** built by Anchorage's first elected mayor; no. 610, the **William Edes House,** built for the former Alaska Engineering Commission chairman; and no. 618, **Cottage 23,** built in 1917 for an AEC storekeeper and occupied from the 1930s to 1950s by noted Alaskan artist Mildred Hammill.

Follow Christensen Drive to H Street, then turn west (right) on Third Avenue. Two blocks down, you'll find the **Boney Memorial Courthouse,** with its main entrance on K Street. There are numerous fine examples of Native arts on display inside, including a totem pole, a steel wall panel engraved to show an Eskimo dance ceremony, and a teak wall panel carved to represent 19th-century scrimshaw on walrus ivory. There are more carvings on the doors. Across K Street, in front of the office building at no. 310, is a fiberglass statue titled *The Last Blue Whale* by Anchorage sculptor Josef Princiotta.

Resolution Park is at the westward end of Third Avenue, where it joins L Street. The **Captain Cook Memorial,** featuring a statue of the great English navigator looking seaward, was built in 1978 to commemorate the 200th anniversary of Cook's exploration of the inlet bearing his name. George Vancouver and William Bligh, later to gain their own degree of fame (or notoriety), were with him on the voyage. On a clear day Resolution Park is a good place from which to see the mountains on Anchorage's flanks: Mount McKinley and Mount Foraker to the north, volcanic Mount Spurr and the Sleeping Lady to the west.

Downhill and west one block from Fifth Avenue and L Street is **Elderberry Park.** The chief point of interest here is the **Oscar Anderson House,** at 420 M St. (tel. 274-2336), a well-preserved example of a 1915 wood-frame home. Anderson, a coal company executive, lived in the house until 1969. His widow donated the house to the city in 1976 and it was completely restored in 1982. Open May through September from 1 to 4 p.m. Wednesday through Friday and noon to 4 p.m. on Saturday and Sunday; other times by special arrangement. Admission is $2 for adults, $1 for senior citizens and children 6 to 12.

Head back toward downtown, traveling east on Fifth Avenue. At the corner of H Street is the **Holy Family Cathedral.** A plaque beside the front door commemorates a visit in 1981 by Pope John Paul II. Over and down a block, at Sixth Avenue and G Street, is the **People Mover Transit Center,** the hub of Anchorage public transportation. The **Hill Building,** at 632 W. Sixth Ave., is the site of all major municipal government offices.

Across the street is the **Alaska Center for the Performing Arts.** The $67-million facility, ten years in the making, opened in September 1988. The exterior features New York artist Eric Staller's *Visual Music,* a $100,000 light sculpture hooked up to a pair of computers. Various other commissioned works of over $120,000 value, including impressive Native masks, are within. The multilevel, gaily carpeted center has three main theaters: the 2,100-seat Evangeline Atwood Concert Hall, the 800-seat Discovery Theatre for dramatic performances, and the 350-seat Sydney Laurence Theatre. The lobby is open from 11:30 a.m. to 6 p.m. Monday through Saturday and prior to all events.

Town Square, a three-quarter-block landscaped park with picnic tables, is between Fifth and Sixth and E and F. At Fifth Avenue and F Street, across the mezzanine balcony of the **National Bank of Alaska** building, stretches a 160-foot-long mural depicting 200 years of Alaskan history, from Russian colonization to the construction of the Trans Alaska Pipeline. During the summer months, free concerts are held Friday at noon in the plaza in front of the building. The **William A. Egan Civic and Convention Center** stretches from E to F Street along Fifth Avenue. Named after Alaska's first governor, it's a common site of national and regional conventions and trade expositions. In the lobby are examples of modern Native artworks.

If you've walked enough, the Log Cabin lies immediately to the north of the Egan Center. Otherwise, turn south on E Street and proceed four blocks to **Delaney Park,** better known to Anchorage citizens as, simply, "The Park Strip." A block wide and a mile long, it extends west from A Street all the way to P, between Ninth and Tenth Avenues. Once the site of the city's first airfield, it now contains ball fields, skating rinks, tennis courts, picnic tables, the Delaney Community Center, a centennial rose garden (on N Street), and several monuments and memorials—the most impressive of which is a veterans' memorial flanked by an American flag atop a huge spruce tree. A 50-ton bonfire was held here to mark statehood in 1959, and Pope John Paul II celebrated outdoor mass here in 1981. Across the street from the park at Tenth Avenue and I Street is the **Anchorage Pioneers Home,** built for senior Alaskans who have lived in the state for at least three decades, and also the home of **Star the Reindeer,** probably the most photographed individual of the species. The current "Star" is the fourth one. No. 2 was kidnapped (to much public indignation) and was never heard from again. He presumably became sausage. No. 3 choked on the plastic wrappers of "goodies" he was thrown by wellwishers.

The **Federal Building,** U.S. Courthouse, and the Federal Building Annex are on either side of Eighth Avenue between A and C Streets. The main entrance to the **Anchorage Museum of History and Art** (see the "Museums" section, following) is at Seventh and A. Due east, between Cordova and Eagle, is the **Anchorage Cemetery,** where several famous Alaskans are buried. Artist Sydney Laurence's tombstone is marked by a painter's palette. Upright whalebones identify the graves of notable Eskimos, while crosses with extra diagonals denote Russian Orthodox plots.

MUSEUMS

The **Anchorage Museum of History and Art,** 121 W. Seventh Ave. (tel. 264-4326), has Alaska's premier permanent display of art, from prehistoric to contemporary. Since opening in 1968, it has twice been expanded, and now has 93,000 square feet of floor space plus underground parking for 100 cars.

Galleries on the west side of the ground floor exhibit holdings of the permanent collection, with noted Alaskan artists like Sydney Laurence, Fred Machetanz, and

Eustace Ziegler well represented. The east-side galleries have temporary special exhibits (sometimes from the Smithsonian Institution) as well as an excellent children's gallery and activity rooms. Also on the ground floor are a museum shop and café, and an auditorium for the presentation of public programs, often including lectures, film series, and jazz performances.

A large second-floor gallery contains a comprehensive display of Alaskan history, from Native cultures through Russian occupation up to the present day. The museum offices and a research library, containing many valuable books and more than 150,000 historical photos of Alaska, are also upstairs.

The museum is supported by the Municipality of Anchorage, but donations are accepted to develop educational programs and temporary exhibits. Open daily June to August, Monday through Saturday from 9 a.m. to 6 p.m. (until 9 p.m. on Tuesday and Thursday), on Sunday from 1 to 5 p.m.; from September to May, daily except Monday from 9 a.m. to 6 p.m., with the same Sunday-afternoon hours.

The **Alaska Wildlife and Natural History Museum,** 317 E St. (tel. 272-3519), is a taxidermist's delight. Some of the dioramas of the state's animals, birds, and fish (in "natural" habitat) are quite amusing, such as the two black bear cubs raiding a trapper's cabin for honey. More valuable, perhaps, are the excellent half-hourly nature films. Still, the $5 admission charge ($3.50 for senior citizens, $1.50 for children 3 to 12) is rather stiff. There's a gift shop if you want to spend more. Open from 8 a.m. to 8 p.m. daily in summer, 10 a.m. to 6 p.m. in winter.

Downtown, the **Imaginarium,** 725 W. Fifth Ave., is a hands-on science discovery center for children. It's open from 1 to 8 p.m. Tuesday through Saturday and noon to 5 p.m. on Sunday in summer, noon to 6 p.m. Tuesday through Saturday and noon to 4 p.m. on Sunday in winter. Admission is $4 for adults, $2 for kids under 12. The **Visual Arts Center,** at Fifth and G, is open daily except Sunday with local and national arts exhibits, workshops, and studios for visiting artists.

There are exhibits of pioneer bush aircraft at the **Alaska Aviation Heritage Museum,** 4721 Aircraft Dr., on Lake Hood (tel. 248-5325), open from 9 a.m. to 7 p.m. daily. The **Reeve Aviation Picture Museum,** 343 W. Sixth Ave., has a collection of over 1,100 photographs.

There are excellent mounted displays of Alaskan wildlife at the **Elmendorf Air Force Base Wildlife Museum,** Building 4-803 (tel. 552-2282), open year round Monday through Friday from 9 a.m. to 4 p.m. and on Saturday from 10 a.m. to 3 p.m.; and the **Fort Richardson Alaskan Fish and Wildlife Center,** Building 600 (tel. 863-8113), open year round Monday through Friday from 9 a.m. to 5 p.m., on Saturday from 10 a.m. to 4 p.m., and on Sunday from noon to 4 p.m.

In midtown, the National Bank of Alaska's **Heritage Library and Museum,** 301 W. Northern Lights Blvd. (tel. 265-2834), has an outstanding private collection of rare books, paintings, photographs and Native artifacts. It's open noon to 4 p.m. Monday through Friday, and admission is free.

The $17-million **Z. J. Loussac Public Library,** 36th Avenue and Denali Street (tel. 261-2846), is an architectural fantasy of cylindrical shapes and geometric forms. In addition to Alaska books, it houses the Anchorage municipal council chambers and a public auditorium. Numerous fine paintings and bronze sculptures are located inside. Open Monday through Thursday from noon to 8 p.m., Friday and Saturday from 10 a.m. to 6 p.m., and Sunday from noon to 6 p.m.

THE ALASKA ZOO

I personally find it much more interesting and educational to see real animals, not stuffed ones. At the 13-acre Alaska Zoo, 4371 O'Malley Rd. (tel. 346-3242), in the southeast quadrant of Anchorage, there are no lions and tigers, no monkeys and giraffes. In fact this zoo's only concession to a traditional wild-animal park is the inclusion of Indian and African elephants. Otherwise, every animal and bird represented here is indigenous to Alaska. Come and learn the difference between black, blue, and brown bears, between reindeer and caribou. Observe moose and musk oxen in their natural habitat, and see seals and otters frolic in an aquarium. The zoo is also a sanctuary for the rehabilitation of injured or orphaned animals and birds that are being prepared for return to the wild. There is a gift shop near the entrance. Open from 9 a.m. to 6 p.m. daily May through September, from 10 a.m. to dusk every day but Tuesday the rest of the year. Admission is $3.50 for adults, $3 for students, $2.50 for senior citizens and children 3 to 12.

PARKS

Wildlife lovers can see multitudes of birds at the **Potter Marsh Waterfowl Nesting Area** and the **Westchester Lagoon Waterfowl Sanctuary.** Potter Marsh is at the city's southernmost extreme, along the Seward Hwy. as it heads along the Turnagain Arm. When waterfowl migrate in late April and early May, it's alive with over 130 species, from teal and geese to whistling swans. Many birds remain through the summer. Look for small mammals like muskrat, mink, and beaver as you walk the interpretive boardwalk. Westchester Lagoon, a broadening of Chester Creek at the southwest end of downtown, has a half-mile marked nature trail starting on 19th Avenue off Spenard Road.

Nearby **Potter Section House and Historic Park** (tel. 345-2631) has guided tours of an old railway building from 10 a.m. to 8 p.m. daily, May to September, and 10 a.m. to 4 p.m. Thursday through Sunday the rest of the year.

If you continue south on Spenard Road to Northern Lights Boulevard, then turn west and follow it about three miles, you'll come to **Earthquake Park,** arguably the best place in Anchorage to still get a picture of the damage done by the Good Friday quake of '64. From a pavilion of photographs and geological diagrams you can get a good idea of the disaster. On a clear day you can see all the way to Mount McKinley.

Other parks in Anchorage include **Bicentennial Park,** 5,000 acres south of Tudor Road, including 18 miles of trails for summer hiking and winter dog mushing; **Centennial Park,** 78 acres at Glenn Hwy. and Muldoon Road, with camping, sledding, and skiing; **Kincaid Park,** site of the 1983 World Cup cross-country championship, west of the international airport at Point Campbell; and **Russian Jack Springs Park,** with a wide range of sports and recreation facilities (including a municipal greenhouse) on either side of DeBarr Road off Boniface Parkway.

You shouldn't be surprised to find wildlife—of the large variety—in these parks. In fact you might even expect it, especially in winter, when big game descend from the surrounding mountains. Moose reports regularly punctuate midwinter traffic reports on Anchorage radio stations, and bear tales occur and recur in residential districts. City jail inmates once complained of a bear wandering outside their fence because it made them feel as if they were in a zoo.

If you're planning to look for wildlife in Denali National Park or other federal lands, you might benefit from a visit to the **Alaska Public Lands Information Center,** Fourth Avenue and F Street (tel. 271-2737). You can talk to a ranger, pick up brochures and maps, look at some displays, and see free films.

UNIVERSITIES

Anchorage is the home of two four-year universities, the **University of Alaska, Anchorage** and **Alaska Pacific University.** All are located on "College Row," beside Providence Hospital along Providence Drive and University Drive, east of midtown.

Privately owned Alaska Pacific (tel. 561-1266), formerly Alaska Methodist University, was the site of the 1971 convention of the Alaska Federation of Natives, which approved the Alaska Native Settlement Act passed by Congress. The U.S. Geological Survey has an office on campus which sells topographical maps.

UAA (tel. 786-1800), one of several campuses of the state institution (the main campus is in Fairbanks), has a performing arts center and sports complex which may be of interest to visitors.

The university campuses lie next to **Goose Lake,** with bicycle and cross-country ski trails, swimming and ice skating, picnic areas, and a playground. Dog-sled tours are offered in winter.

SPORTS

A great variety of summer and winter, indoor and outdoor sports are available for participants and spectators in the Anchorage area.

BALLOONING Have a yen to go around the world in 80 days . . . or around the Anchorage Bowl in 80 minutes? Contact **Hot Air Affair,** 3605 Arctic Blvd., Suite 1575 (tel. 349-7333), or any of nine other operators listed in the *Yellow Pages.* Prices are typically $150 per person for a one-hour flight in a ten-passenger balloon. Launch sites vary according to weather conditions.

BASEBALL Two semi-pro teams—the **Anchorage Glacier Pilots** (tel. 274-3627) and the **Anchorage Bucs** (tel. 272-2827)—play in the six-team Alaska League that attracts some of the nation's top college players from June through August. Many current big-league stars played in this local league. Home games are at Mulcahy Ball Park, East 16th Avenue and Cordova Street. Check local papers for schedules.

BASKETBALL The **Great Alaska Shoot-Out** is one of the nation's leading pre-season major college tournaments. Since this eight-team confrontation began in 1978, North Carolina, Louisville, Indiana, and many other nationally ranked teams have performed at the George M. Sullivan Sports Arena in late November. The tourney is hosted by the NCAA Division II University of Alaska/Anchorage Seawolves. In February the UAA women's team sponsors its own tournament, the Northern Lights Invitational. Some of the finest university teams in the country participate, and some of the great players, such as former UCLA Olympian Cheryl Miller.

BICYCLING There are 121 miles of bike trails in the city of Anchorage, not including outlying areas of the municipality. Inquire at the Log Cabin Visitor Information Center about the "Earth Cycle" summer program for free use of bikes. Or rent all-terrain bikes or ten-speed touring bicycles from **Goose Lake Services,** East Northern Lights Boulevard at the University of Alaska (tel. 276-2960). **Engle Expeditions,** P.O. Box 90375, Anchorage, AK 99509 (tel. 907/563-0706), organizes tours.

BOATING Cook Inlet waters are treacherous because of tides, mud flats, and silty waters. Local knowledge is essential. Turnagain Arm is off-limits for all boats, *period.* The best motorboating is in Big Lake and other Susitna Valley lakes north of Anchorage. You can rent boats and trailers from **Big Boy Toys,** 5610A Old Seward Hwy. (tel. 563-0660).

BOWLING Downtown, the public can strike down the tenpins at **Elks Anchorage Lodge No. 1351,** 717 W. Third Ave. (tel. 276-1351). The closest major bowling alley to the city center is **Center Bowl,** 3717 Minnesota Dr., at Spenard Road (tel. 562-2695), with 30 lanes, a restaurant, and lounge.

DIVING Tours are available through **Underwater Safaris–Alaska,** 6161 A St. (tel. 562-3483). For equipment, supplies, and personalized instruction, try **Dive Alaska,** 3002 Spenard Rd. (tel. 276-6479).

DOG SLEDDING Mushing is the official state sport, and throughout the winter months you'll see teams training and racing. Even in summer you'll often see dry-land training runs, with sleds having converted their runners to wheels.

The two biggest races in Anchorage (with purses valued in thousands of dollars) are the World Sled Dog Championships during the Fur Rendezvous in February and the grueling Iditarod Sled Dog Race, an Anchorage-to-Nome marathon, in early March (an Iditarod is about 1,100 miles). Every Sunday from January to March the Tudor Sled Dog Track of the **Alaska Sled Dog Racing Association,** off East Tudor Road near Bragaw Street (tel. 248-5796), hosts races at 10 a.m. and 1 p.m.

Chugach Express (tel. 783-2266), which takes visitors on three-hour dog-sled tours near Girdwood (see the "Short Trips from Anchorage" section, below), also offers various mushing options at Kincaid Park, starting with a 30-minute excursion costing $25 for adults, $15 for children. You're guaranteed some time behind the sled. Short loops of the Delaney Park strip near downtown are also possible, especially during Rondy.

FISHING Within the Municipality of Anchorage there are 19 creeks, four rivers, and numerous lakes. Many of the smaller lakes within the city are stocked with rainbow trout, a species popular with winter ice fishermen.

In the waters of the Cook Inlet, of course, are a great many saltwater varieties. Numerous fishing charters are registered in Anchorage; consult the Log Cabin Visitors Information Center for recommendations. Most charters operate out of towns on Prince William Sound or the Kenai Peninsula.

King salmon run from May to July, reds in June and July, pinks and chums in July and August, and silvers from July to November. Steelhead are commonly caught between September and November. Halibut fishing is best May to September; cod, May to October. Trout and grayling are year-round species.

For information on regulations on other questions, contact the **Alaska Department of Fish and Game,** 333 Raspberry Rd. (tel. 344-0541). The department also has a recorded message of current fishing conditions (tel. 349-4687). Nonresident licenses cost $10 for 3 days, $20 for 14 days, and $36 for one year.

A good place to buy or rent equipment is **Angler's Habitat,** 700 E. Benson Blvd. (tel. 276-7847). **Sport Fishing Alaska,** 1401 Shore Dr. (tel. 344-8674), charters trips year round.

GOLF There are currently four courses in Anchorage open to the public. **Eagle Glen Golf Course,** Elmendorf AFB (tel. 552-2773), has 18 holes, open June to October. **Moose Run Golf Course,** Fort Richardson (tel. 428-0056), is Alaska's oldest; it also has 18 holes and is open May to October. Rentals are available at both; civilian greens fees are $12 weekdays, $15 on weekends. **Russian Jack Springs Park,** on Boniface Parkway south of DeBarr Road (tel. 333-8338), has a nine-hole, par-30 course open mid-May to mid-September, from 7 a.m. to 10 p.m. Adult greens fees are $6 weekdays, $8 on weekends. **O'Malley's on the Green,** 3651 O'Malley Rd. (tel. 522-3322), recently opened with 18 holes and a restaurant.

HEALTH CLUBS Numerous fitness centers in the Anchorage area offer weight rooms, aerobics programs, saunas, and Jacuzzis, and a variety of other services. They include: the **Alaska Athletic Club,** with two locations, at 745 W. Fourth Ave. (tel. 274-4232) and 630 E. Tudor Rd. (tel. 562-2460); **The Alaska Club,** 5201 E. Tudor Rd. (tel. 337-9550); **Gold's Gym,** 5011 Arctic Blvd. (tel. 561-2214); and **GreatLand Golden Health Club,** 360 W. Benson Blvd. (tel. 561-5535).

HIKING Hiking is a year-round activity in Anchorage. When snow covers the ground, die-hard hikers don their snowshoes. The entire Anchorage Bowl and neighboring Chugach Mountains are crisscrossed by trails, and the network is well worked by local hiking clubs and individuals. The Log Cabin Visitors Information Center has trail maps and information on scheduled hikes.

Of special interest within the city are the Westchester Lagoon nature trail, off 19th Avenue between Arctic Boulevard and Spenard Road, with facilities for the handicapped; and a fitness trail in Muldoon Park, starting at the corner of Muldoon Road and East Northern Lights Boulevard.

A good day hike for families is the 3½-mile (round-trip) climb of 4,050-foot Rendezvous Peak. The trail begins at about 2,500 feet elevation in the parking lot of Arctic Valley Ski Area, 15 miles east of downtown. Allow three to five hours for the climb.

For a longer trip, consider the 27-mile Iditarod Trail segment between Crow Creek Road in Girdwood and the Eagle River Visitor Center of **Chugach State Park.** You can get full information from park headquarters in the Frontier Building, 3601 C St. (tel. 561-2020, or 694-6391 for a recorded message on current trail conditions). Park officials offer a planning service for overnight backpackers. Make sure you know how to deal with bears, should you encounter any. You can get additional help from the **Chugach National Forest** office at 201 E. Ninth Ave., Suite 206 (tel. 261-2500).

HORSEBACK RIDING   The **Wallace Brothers Mountain Ranch,** Wallace Mountain Road (P.O. Box 670632), Chugiak, AK 99567 (tel. 907/688-2161), is the nearest location, about a half-hour drive north of downtown. The ranch is open from 8 a.m. to 9 p.m. daily, year round.

HUNTING   Within the Municipality of Anchorage there are seasons (some by permit only) for sheep, goat, moose, black bear, waterfowl, and small game such as rabbit and ptarmigan. Nonresident hunting licenses cost $60, plus tag fees for species hunting. Call the **Alaska Department of Fish and Game,** 333 Raspberry Rd. (tel. 344-0541), for full information.

ICE HOCKEY   The University of Alaska/Anchorage is a leading hockey power in national collegiate competition, regularly scheduling matches against large schools from the Midwest and Northeast. Home contests (admission is $4 for adults, $2 for seniors and children) are played in the **UAA Sports Center,** 2801 Providence Dr. (tel. 786-1233). Local high schools and community groups also have teams.

The annual Nissan/Jeep Hockey Classic, an international college tournament, is held at Sullivan Arena in mid-December.

ICE SKATING   Eight outdoor skating rinks are maintained by Anchorage Parks and Recreation. Some have skate rentals. Closest to downtown is the **Delaney Park Community Center,** Tenth Avenue and E Street (tel. 264-4291), with warm-up facilities.

Ben Boeke Ice Arena, 334 E. 16th Ave. (tel. 274-5715), has two year-round rinks, skate rentals, and instruction. Times are also set aside for public use at **Dempsey Anderson Ice Arena,** 1741 W. Northern Lights Blvd. (tel. 277-7571), and the **UAA Sports Center,** 2801 Providence Dr. (tel. 786-1233).

Serious skaters can get instruction and training with the **Anchorage Figure Skating Club,** P.O. Box 4-2222, Anchorage, AK 99502 (tel. 345-6325).

RACQUETBALL   The **Alaska Athletic Club,** 630 E. Tudor Rd. (tel. 562-2460), has 13 racquetball/handball courts, weight equipment, and various other facilities.

The **Anchorage Racquet Club,** 700 S. Bragaw St. (tel. 278-3621), has three racquetball/volleyball courts and eight tennis courts (five indoor), a weight room, and pro shop.

RIVER RAFTING   In the greater Anchorage area, float trips are offered on the Eagle and Portage Rivers. Contact **Alaska Whitewater,** P.O. Box 142294, Anchorage, AK 99514 (tel. 338-0471). The trip down the Eagle River, only about a 15-minute drive from downtown Anchorage, costs $69. This is an excellent river for wildlife viewing.

ROLLER SKATING   You can put wheels on your feet at **Anchorage Great Skate,** 2809 Arctic Blvd. (tel. 561-5848); **Dimond Skateland,** 8100 Homer Dr. (tel. 349-8825); and **Royal Roller Rink,** 6411 DeBarr Rd. (tel. 333-1413).

SAILING   Small boats can test on Westchester Lagoon and Jewel Lake, although serious sailors usually head for Prince William Sound. Check with **Pilot Rock Sailing Charters,** 2220 Paxson Dr. (tel. 338-2401). **Sailing Inc.,** 8125 Jewel Lake Rd. (tel. 243-7649), offers instruction.

SHOOTING   The Alaska Department of Fish and Game (tel. 344-0541) maintains the **Rabbit Creek Rifle Range** at Potter Marsh, Mile 10 of the Old Seward Hwy.

SKIING   Remember all those bicycle trails? Some 21 miles of them are groomed as cross-country ski trails during the winter. **Kincaid Park** (tel. 264-4365), proposed as the nordic site for the 1994 Winter Olympics, has 19 additional miles of trails, including five miles lit for night (or short winter day) skiing, and warmup facilities. **Russian Jack Springs Park** (tel. 337-4444) has 6½ miles of nordic trails (three miles lit), a beginners' rope tow, and a chalet with ski rentals.

Most of the summer hiking trails are also appropriate for nordic skiers.

The **Nordic Ski Association of Anchorage,** P.O. Box 103504, Anchorage, AK 99510 (tel. 277-0827), can get you together with other cross-country skiers for day and weekend outings. There's also a recorded nordic ski report number: 277-5114.

The best-known (and rightly so) downhill ski resort in the Anchorage area is Alyeska, at Girdwood (see the "Short Trips from Anchorage" section, below). But there are a couple of other smaller areas in the Chugach Mountains nearer to the city center.

To reach **Alpenglow at Arctic Valley** (tel. 522-3645), head five miles northeast on the Glenn Hwy., then take the Arctic Valley turnoff as it winds another ten miles uphill. The resort has two chair lifts, a T-bar, and three rope tows, plus a ski school and a day lodge with a cafeteria. Shuttle buses run from downtown Anchorage. Open weekends and holidays December through April. Call 349-SNOW for up-to-date information on conditions.

Hilltop Ski Area (tel. 346-2165) is ten miles south of downtown on Abbott Road in Hillside Park, four miles east of the Seward Hwy. near Service High School. Hillside operates daily from 9 a.m. to 10 p.m., November to mid-April, as snow permits. Facilities include a chair lift and three lighted runs, plus some cross-country trails. Rates are $11 for a full day (9 a.m. to 5 p.m.), $9 for night skiing (5 to 10 p.m.). Instruction is offered daily. Hillside is on the People Mover bus route. Call 346-1446 for ski conditions.

You can buy or rent ski equipment in Anchorage at **Gary King Sporting Goods,** 202 E. Northern Lights Blvd. (tel. 279-7454), or **Sunshine Sports,** 1231 W. Northern Lights Blvd. (tel. 272-6444). **Recreational Equipment, Inc.** (REI), 2710 Spenard Rd. (tel. 272-4565), and **Barney's Sports Chalet,** 906 W. Northern Lights Blvd. (tel. 561-5242), are strong in nordic, ski mountaineering, and Telemark gear. **The Rental Room,** 5905 Lake Otis Parkway (tel. 562-2866), deals strictly in rentals.

Call the **Avalanche Forecast Center** (tel. 271-4500) for a recorded message of backcountry avalanche danger before setting out on a cross-country tour.

SLEDDING There's a special sledding hill with warm-up facilities maintained by Anchorage Parks and Recreation in **Centennial Park** (tel. 264-4365). It's limited to plastic sleds, cardboards, or inner tubes. With an 80° vertical drop and 600-foot outrun, it's a challenge. Of course, wherever there's a hill with snow on it, kids will be sledding.

SNOW MACHINING The World Championships Cross-Country Snow Machine Race, a two-day, 200-mile challenge from Talkeetna to Anchorage, is an integral part of the Fur Rendezvous. Most winter weekends, snowmobilers frequent Bicentennial Park or Connors Lake. Chugach State Park trails are more popular. Contact the **Alaska Motor Mushers Club,** 3931 Edinburgh Dr. (tel. 243-0888), for full information.

SOCCER Municipal Parks and Recreation (tel. 264-4365) operates the **Anchorage Metro Soccer leagues.** You can write ahead for information to P.O. Box 196650, Anchorage, AK 99519.

SWIMMING Five indoor pools—four at **local high schools,** plus the **UAA Sports Center**—have public schedules. Admission is $3.50 for adults (over 18), $2 for children and students, 75¢ for senior citizens. Call 264-4474 for locations and hours.

YMCA members can visit the **Anchorage YMCA,** 5353 Lake Otis Parkway (tel. 563-3211), and get discounts.

Supervised public swimming is offered outdoors in summer at three city lakes, administered by Anchorage Parks and Recreation (tel. 264-4365). All have lifeguards (noon to 8 p.m.), picnic areas, and playgrounds. **Goose Lake** (Northern Lights Boulevard and Providence Drive) also has tennis courts and a bathhouse. The others are **Jewel Lake** (Jewel Lake Road and Dimond Boulevard) and **Spenard Beach** (Spenard Road and Lakeshore Drive).

TENNIS No fewer than 49 public courts are maintained by Anchorage Parks and Recreation, including five courts in the **Delaney Park** strip at Ninth Avenue and C Street. For further information, call 264-4365.

Private clubs include the **Anchorage Racquet Club,** 700 S. Bragaw St. (tel. 278-3621), and **Four Seasons Sports Center,** 1133 N St. (tel. 279-4189).

TOURS

Numerous agencies operate half-day tours of Anchorage. Each company covers similar ground—everyone seems to hit Earthquake Park and the Lake Hood seaplane base—but itineraries vary depending on whim or weather conditions.

I personally feel that locally owned and operated tours cover the city better than larger brokers, which emerge from the woodwork only during the summer months. You won't find the little guys operating out of the big hotels, but you will find their makeshift booths outside the Log Cabin Visitor Information Center at Fourth Avenue and F Street.

Eagle Custom Tours, 614 W. Fourth Ave. (tel. 258-2901 or 349-6710), offers a variety of trips year round, from bus tours to winter activities. The three-hour city tour departs the Log Cabin daily at 9 a.m., makes hotel pickups, and costs $15 for adults, $10 for children. A 5½-hour southern tour, including Portage Glacier and Alyeska, leaves at noon and costs $30 for adults, $20 for children. A northern tour ($40) takes in the Independence Mine at Hatcher Pass. In winter, there are ski packages, dog-sled rides, and snowmobile and ice-fishing tours.

A 2½-hour walking tour offered by **Back Trails Tours** (tel. 276-5528) leaves from the Log Cabin twice daily in summer, at 8:30 a.m. and 1 p.m. Monday through Friday. The $14 price includes a snack and drink. This tour puts its emphasis on views and natural attractions, such as salmon and wildflowers. Hikes and cross-country ski excursions in the greater Anchorage area are specialties of this little company. Write them at 2316 Galewood St., Anchorage, AK 99508.

You might also check with **Personalized Tours of Alaska** (tel. 344-1458).

Among the larger companies, **Alaska Sightseeing Tours,** 543 W. Fourth Ave. (tel. 276-1305), or at the Sheraton and Westmark Hotels, operates a three-hour city tour May 15 to September 30, with daily departures at 3 p.m. The fare is $22 for adults, $11 for children 5 to 11. This tour includes the Museum of History and Art, the universities, military bases, railroad, and port. There's also a full-day tour, leaving at 8 a.m. daily, which, at $48 for adults, $24 for children, combines the city tour with a trip to Alyeska and the Portage Glacier (see the "Short Trips from Anchorage" section, below).

Gray Line of Alaska, at Fourth Avenue and F Street (tel. 277-5581), and in the Hilton lobby, operates a 2½-hour tour with emphasis on Anchorage history and Cook Inlet views. Tours depart twice daily at 8 a.m. and 3 p.m. May 15 to September 15. Tickets are $20 for adults, $10 for children.

Royal Hyway Tours, 329 F St. (tel. 276-7711), and at the Hotel Captain Cook, offers a 2½-hour Anchorage tour May 1 to September 30, departing at 9 a.m. This tour, priced at $20 for adults, $10 for children under 12, stops at the wildlife museum.

Yukon-based **Atlas Tours,** 411 W. Fourth Ave. (tel. 276-1909), and at the Holiday Inn, also includes the wildlife museum, as well as Lake Hood and Earthquake Park, in its 2½-hour city tour. The excursion departs at 9 a.m. and 3 p.m. daily, June 1 to September 10. Tickets are $20 for adults, $10 for children.

Flightseeing

A large number of local flightseeing services offer trips over the Anchorage Bowl. **Airlift Alaska** (tel. 276-3809), departing from Merrill Field, charges $85 per person for a 75-minute look at the Anchorage Bowl and Knik Glacier. **J&M Alaska Air Tours** (tel. 276-5422), also from Merrill Field, charges $95 to fly over Anchorage and the Matanuska-Susitna Valleys. Other carriers include **Anchorage Air Center** (tel. 278-9752), at Merrill Field, and **Regal Air** (tel. 243-8535), at Lake Hood.

Helicopters have some advantages over fixed-wing aircraft. They have a much larger window area, and can hover in one spot for an extended period of time. **HeliTour Alaska,** P.O. Box 190283, Anchorage, AK 99519 (tel. 243-1466), offers three tours, including a 3½-hour picnic-lunch trip into the Chugach range ($235 per person) and a 2½-hour excursion to Mount Alyeska ($139 per person). Round-trip transportation from Anchorage hotels is offered by HeliTour and other flightseeing firms.

---

5. Shopping

As the state's largest market, it stands to reason that Anchorage has the greatest variety of Alaskan merchandise of any community in the state.

NATIVE ARTS AND CRAFTS

Most visitors are first attracted by the handcrafted work of Eskimos, Aleuts, Athabaskans, Tlingits, and other indigenous peoples. Here are some crafts to keep an eye out for:

Walrus-tusk ivory, used in scrimshaw (etching) work, jewelry, and figurines. Only Alaskan Natives are permitted to harvest or possess unworked ivory; it can be sold only after it has been crafted.

Gold, jade, and hematite jewelry. Gold is synonymous with Alaska, but few people realize that green jade is quarried near Kotzebue, and hematite (a shiny black semiprecious stone) is native to iron ore deposits.

Soapstone sculptures, varying in color from dark green to brown and gray. This easily carved stone must be waxed or oiled to preserve its appearance.

Woodcarvings. Southeast Alaska Indians carve colorful masks, totem poles, and boxes from yellow cedar. Athabaskans, from the Interior, employ birch in manufacturing a variety of household utensils. Eskimos and Aleuts, who rarely see trees in their home regions, nevertheless craft driftwood into masks and other items.

Baskets, woven with all manner of material from marsh grasses to willow roots to birch bark, and sometimes whale baleen or sealskin.

The **Alaska Native Arts & Crafts Association,** 333 W. Fourth Ave., in Post Office Mall (tel. 274-2932), is a good place to start your search for something "typically Alaskan." Prices on the broad selection of items sold here are set by the Native artists themselves, with no additional retail markup by the shop itself. Even if you choose not to buy something here, you'll have a good idea of competitive pricing when you browse elsewhere. Open from 10 a.m. to 6 p.m. Monday through Friday and 10 a.m. to 5 p.m. on Saturday.

Natives own and operate **Alaska Heritage Arts,** 400 D St. (tel. 278-4787); you can watch and talk to carvers as they create works of ivory, soapstone, bone, horn, and wood. Open from 10 a.m. to 7 p.m. Monday through Saturday and noon to 5 p.m. on Sunday.

Other shops in Anchorage with good selections of authentic Native crafts include the **Alaska Ivory Exchange,** 700 W. Fourth Ave. (tel. 272-2215), and **Lamebull's Lodge,** 621 A St. (tel. 277-8935).

FURS AND QIVIUT

Anchorage's winter festival wouldn't be called the Fur Rendezvous if there weren't furs. Trappers throng to the big city in February with hundreds of pelts from animals large (bear) and small (beaver), and all sizes in between. The big fur auctions, well advertised, are worth attending if you're in the market for furs.

From June through September you can get free guided tours at the **Anchorage Fur Factory,** 105 W. Fourth Ave. (tel. 277-8414), to see how pelts are treated in preparation for garment making. The factory outlet sells parkas, fashion coats, Eskimo mukluks (boots), and other fur garments. Open from 9 a.m. to 7 p.m. daily.

The finest-quality furs (and the most expensive) are sold at **A. C. Bang,** in the Hotel Captain Cook (tel. 258-6334). Two other excellent furriers are **David Green & Sons,** 130 W. Fourth Ave. and 423 W. Fifth Ave. (tel. 277-9595), and **Martin Victor Furs,** 428 W. Fourth Ave. (tel. 277-7683).

Furs, of course, are not unique to Alaska, although the state's climate makes it a natural market for them. *Qiviut* is.

Qiviut is the soft, warm underwool of the musk ox—known to Eskimos as oomingmak, "the bearded one." **Oomingmak,** the establishment, is the principal outlet for the Alaskan Musk Ox Producers' Co-operative. The little shop at 604 H St. (tel. 272-9225) markets *qiviut* garments hand-knit from the yarn of domesticated musk oxen in isolated Unalakleet, on the Bering Sea. It's not cheap: scarves are priced at $135 to $175; caps, $60 to $90.

FINE ARTS

There is no shortage of artisans or art galleries in the Anchorage area. Perhaps best known is the **Stonington Gallery,** on the ground floor of the Hunt Building, at 550 W. Seventh Ave., at E Street (tel. 272-1489). If you're shopping for paintings or small sculptures, you should also visit **Stephan Fine Arts,** 600 W. Sixth Ave., at F Street (tel. 278-9555); and **Artique Ltd.,** with a downtown gallery at 314 G St. (tel. 277-1663) and a Town & Country Square gallery in midtown at 570 E. Benson Blvd. (tel. 277-5658). Artique features the work of watercolor specialist Byron

Birdsall, and of Jon Van Zyle, a part-time sled-dog musher best known for his acrylics of Iditarod scenes. Another local favorite is John Tennant, a specialist in silver miniatures.

Less well-known, but equally interesting galleries are **Lefors Academy Fine Arts,** 2823 E. Tudor Rd. (tel. 562-1066), which features classes and the quaint LaPalette Café; **Amniote Egg,** 1123 F St. (tel. 272-9072), with an interesting array of "alternative" artwork; and the **Alaska Art Print Company,** 1236 W. Tenth Ave. (tel. 278-4975), with a collection of silkscreened and limited-edition prints.

There are many excellent **photographers** whose work is represented in these and small private galleries. Two whose work I especially like are Myron Rosenberg, who does some intriguing cultural studies, and Johnny Johnson, a superb wildlife photographer.

CAMERAS AND BOOKS

At 531 W. Fourth Ave., **Stewart's Photo Shop** (tel. 272-8581) is one of the city's oldest and best photographic equipment stores. For repair work, I'm partial to **Dan's Camera Repair,** 735 W. Fourth Ave. (tel. 277-7214).

Among the most interesting bookstores in Anchorage is **The Book Cache,** with 11 locations, including downtown at 436 W. Fifth Ave. (tel. 277-2723). Also check out **Cyrano's,** a bookshop and café at 413 D St. (tel. 274-2599). In addition to the independent bookstores in Anchorage, the following nationwide chain stores are well represented: **B. Dalton** and **Waldenbooks.**

GIFTS

One of the first items you'll see in any souvenir shop is a fan-shaped knife with a wooden handle in "the wrong place." This is an ulu. Traditionally made of bone and used by Eskimos for skinning and fileting seals and whales, the tourist ulu of today has a stainless-steel blade and a walnut handle. Many of the ulus sold at Anchorage gift shops for $14 to $20 are made at the **Ulu Factory,** 298 Warehouse Ave. (tel. 276-3119).

You'll be confronted by gift shops on nearly every block in downtown Anchorage. There's really no one "best" one, but I like the selection at the **Caribou Trading Company,** 326 E St., near the Hilton (tel. 276-3960); **The Rusty Harpoon,** 411 W. Fourth Ave., in the Sunshine Plaza (tel. 278-9011); and **Arctic Artisans,** in the Northway Mall on Glenn Highway (tel. 272-8835).

READER'S SHOPPING SUGGESTION—GIFTS: "We found **J. C. Penney** stores especially price-wise in shopping for T-shirts and ulus" (Kay Siebrass, Mankato, Minn.).

SEAFOOD AND GAME

Seafood gift packs, with salmon, crab, halibut, and other treats, make great items to carry home or to ship to friends overseas. The **Alaskan Food & Gift Cache,** 419 D St. (tel. 279-3912), and **Tenth and M Seafoods,** 1020 M St. (tel. 272-3474), can handle all arrangements.

If you have more of a taste for wild game, contact **Indian Valley Meats,** P.O. Box 8809, Indian, AK 99540 (tel. 907/653-7511), off the Seward Hwy. south of Anchorage. The folks there will cut, grind, wrap, label, freeze, box, and/or can moose, mountain goat, dall sheep, caribou, and deer meat.

6. Culture and Nightlife

The residents' penchant toward yuppiedom in recent years has resulted in the rapid growth of a variety of cultural attractions. Anchorage has its own symphony, ballet, modern dance, and opera companies and theatrical troupes.

When the **Alaska Center for the Performing Arts,** 621 W. Sixth Ave. (tel. 263-2900), opened in September 1988, its facilities immediately became the focus of Anchorage cultural life. The $67-million structure, ten years in the making, contains the 2,100-seat Evangeline Atwood Concert Hall, the 800-seat Discovery Theatre, and the 350-seat Sydney Laurence Theatre, and other facilities. Tickets for all events are sold in the lobby from 11:30 a.m. to 6 p.m. Monday through Saturday, and immediately prior to events.

Ticket prices vary, but typically range from $10 to $25. For schedule and ticket information, call 343-ARTS.

But performances take place all over the city, in the suburbs as well as downtown. To keep up on the action, pick up the Thursday-morning *Anchorage Daily News* and turn to its 24-page "Weekend" tabloid section. The *News* and the evening *Anchorage Times* both have complete daily events calendars. The Anchorage Convention and Visitors Bureau has a daily recorded listing of doings around town (tel. 276-3200), while the **Anchorage Arts Council** announces visual and performing arts events (tel. 276-ARTS).

Tickets to many events can be purchased from **Tickets, Inc.,** kater-corner from the Log Cabin in the lobby of the Alaska Pacific Bank Building, 524 W. Fourth Ave. (tel. 279-9695).

THEATER

The **Alaska Repertory Theater** (tel. 276-5500) may not be active in 1990, but other fine troupes will be. The **Anchorage Light Opera Theater** (tel. 561-7515) is among those performing at the ACPA. Look also for the **Anchorage Community Theater** (tel. 344-4713), which presents four major shows annually; the **Theater Guild** (tel. 276-2008), with a September-to-May season; and **Way-Off Broadway Productions** (tel. 563-3075). Some of these groups may use the University of Alaska/Anchorage Performing Arts Center. Contact the Log Cabin Visitor Information Center for specifics.

Synergy, Seventh Avenue and A Street (tel. 276-2825), offers an entertaining series of comedies throughout the year. The curtain usually goes up at 8 p.m. Thursday through Saturday and at 1 p.m. on Sunday. Wednesday night is improvisational comedy night. Synergy also has a restaurant open for lunch (Tuesday through Friday) and pre-show dinners.

Many summer visitors are drawn to the most typically Alaskan of Anchorage's theater offerings—**Larry Beck's Alaska Show** (tel. 278-3831), presented by the Alaska Heritage Review at 8 p.m. every night from June 1 to September 13 at the Egan Convention Center, 555 W. Fifth Ave. A polished narrator, singer, and showman, Beck assumes various personae in offering a stirring 90-minute tribute to the Alaskan Gold Rush and the poetry of balladeer Robert Service. Admission is $12 for adults, $8 for children 6 to 12.

CINEMA

Perhaps because its winter nights are so much longer, Anchorage appears to have a greater population of regular moviegoers than other cities its size. As long as the Fourth Avenue Theatre is hosting the Alaska Rep, no first-run films are shown downtown; elsewhere, however, movie theaters are prolific. At last count, there were 34 in Anchorage. The largest is the eight-screen **Fireweed Cinemas,** Fireweed Lane at Gambell Street (tel. 277-3825). Slightly farther from downtown is the six-screen **University Cinemas,** 3901 Old Seward Hwy. (tel. 562-1250). You can see recent movies for $1 at the **Capri Cinema,** 3425 E. Tudor Rd. (tel. 562-2478); and at 7 p.m. on Tuesday only, foreign films and revivals are shown at the **Anchorage Museum,** 121 W. Seventh Ave. (tel. 264-4326). The **Campus Center Cafeteria** at the University of Alaska/Anchorage (tel. 786-1204) has a Saturday-night film program, and two universities—UAA (tel. 786-1731) and Alaska Pacific (tel. 564-1266)—have Sunday-night discount shows.

There is one downtown theater. It's the domed **Alaska Experience Theater,** 705 W. Sixth Ave., at G Street (tel. 272-9076), and its breathtaking 40-minute presentation of *Alaska the Greatland* in three-dimensional Omnivision is definitely worth the price of admission. Filmed from helicopters, rafts, and trains, the movie makes you feel a part of all you see. It's shown hourly, every day of the year, from 9 a.m. to 10 p.m. in summer, 11 a.m. to 8 p.m. in winter. Adjoining the theater is an Alaska Earthquake Exhibit which uses newsreels to re-create the Good Friday 1964 quake in a room that rumbles and shakes. Adult tickets are $6 for the movie, $5 for the quake exhibit, or $10 for both. Children and seniors pay about 30% less.

If you were inspired by Larry Beck's Alaska Show, you can visit Beck's **Alaskana Theater,** 711 W. Fourth Ave. (tel. 276-0712), to watch a series of free films on the state's history, hourly from 10 a.m. to 8 p.m. daily.

CLASSICAL MUSIC, OPERA, DANCE

Even before Anchorage had a paved street it had an orchestra. The first music teacher arrived here by ship in 1928 and immediately began organizing a choir and producing an operetta.

The **Anchorage Concert Association** (tel. 272-1741) and **Anchorage Symphony** (tel. 274-8668) were both founded in the late 1940s, and they've been going strong ever since. The Concert Association brings "name" performers to Anchorage for two series of shows—Discover Dance and the Celebrity Series—during an October-to-April season. The symphony plays an October-to-May season, performing everything from the European masters to traditional Eskimo chants. A Winter Classics series, in October and February, brings many top-name musicians who perform at the Sitka Summer Music Festival. A mid-June Basically Bach Festival highlights the music of Johann Sebastian and other composers like Mozart and Haydn, and a Viennese Waltz Night is hosted by the Anchorage Symphony League in early May.

The **Anchorage Opera** (tel. 279-2557) has a short March-and-April season of lavish productions, with guest artists boosting local talent in classic tales, plus a wintertime dinner opera. **Ballet Alaska** (tel. 279-2871), the **Alaska Contemporary Dance Company** (tel. 276-2088), and the **Alaska Dance Theater** (tel. 562-5707) get lots of support. The ballet's big event is Tchaikovsky's popular *Nutcracker Suite* during Thanksgiving weekend.

Many of these concert and dance groups use the fine auditorium at **West High School,** 1700 Hillcrest Dr. (tel. 274-2502).

NIGHTCLUBS

Nightlife in Anchorage hotels tends toward penthouse cocktails and champagne music. If you're looking for more excitement than that, you'll have to leave downtown.

Spenard Road is the butt of many local jokes because of its large number of highly visible "escort agencies" and "massage parlors." But it's the area where nightlights burn the brightest and longest.

Most stereotypically "Alaskan," with sawdust floors, padded tree-stump stools, and gold rush–era décor, is **Chilkoot Charlie's,** 2435 Spenard Rd., at Fireweed Lane (tel. 272-1010). Once a rowdy saloon where no self-respecting young man would take a date, strict management measures have toned down that image, with the result that "Koot's" may now be the most popular club in Anchorage.

The club is actually six separate rooms strung together. Between them are three bars, including an upstairs wine lounge; a snackbar; an enclosed courtyard with horseshoe and barbecue pits; a big slate fireplace; a game room for pool and darts; and two stages for live music. One of them vibrates to the beat of high-decibel rock music for dancing, starting at 9:30 p.m., 365 days a year. The other features mainly country, folk, and ballad singers starting at 6 p.m. weekdays. The bar is open till 2:30 a.m. nightly, to 3 a.m. on Friday and Saturday.

Drink prices are reasonable; the bar's slogan, in fact, is: "We cheat the other guy and pass the savings on to you!" If you're there on your birthday, you can get a free pitcher of beer or a mixed drink.

Chilkoot Charlie, by the way, was a legendary sourdough (immortalized by balladeer Ruben Gaines) who performed feats that could be ascribed only to an Alaskan. He once, for instance, staved off starvation on an ice floe by eating the tail of a polar bear and giving the bear the bone to chew on. That's why the modern polar bear has only a stump for a tail.

Perhaps because I'm a person who appreciates a little eccentricity and subtle, tongue-in-cheek humor along with good music, my personal favorite nightspot in Anchorage is the **Fly by Night Club,** 3300 Spenard Rd. (tel. 279-7726). The whimsical owner, a jazz musician known only as Mr. White Keys, serves his guests Spam hors d'oeuvres—half price with champagne by the glass, free with Dom Perignon (the club's phone number can be read 279-SPAM). But he slaps a 50¢-per-bottle tax on Budweiser beer because, as he explains: "In spite of our attempt to offer a tremendous selection of little-known but excellent American and Canadian beers, you nitwits continue to drink nothing but Budweiser. . . ."

The musical selection here is as enigmatic as Mr. White Keys. Slapstick revues like *The Whale Fat Follies* are normal fare at 8 p.m. Tuesday through Saturday; tickets are $9.50 and $11.50. Dance music starts at 10:30 p.m., featuring the owner's own Spamtones on Tuesday and Wednesday, while some of the state's best rock bands (seek out Waldo while you're in town) play Thursday through Saturday. The Fly by Night is closed Sunday and Monday. Special occasions—and there are more than you might imagine—are times for celebration. Fats Domino's birthday, for example, calls for a '50s party.

Rock 'n' Roll

A generation has passed since Little Eva set the nation on fire with "The Locomotion," but trains remain big in the Anchorage rock scene. Colorful locomotives light up the walls of the glittery disco-style showroom at **Grand Central Station,** 549 W. International Airport Rd. (tel. 562-4934). Contemporary rock groups and occasional touring stars play to crowds numbering up to about 300 at this spacious cabaret. Dancing begins at 9:30 p.m. Tuesday through Saturday. If you come early, Pedro's Mexican restaurant, adjoining the Station, has south-of-the-border dinners starting at $7. The railroad theme carries to the **Midnight Express,** 2612 Spenard Rd. (tel. 279-1861), across the street from Chilkoot Charlie's. Less ostentatious than the Station, the Express attracts solid rock and country-western bands; it also has two big-screen TVs for afternoon sports events. The dance floor is advertised as Alaska's largest.

Downtown, **The Hub,** 122 E. Fourth Ave. (tel. 276-9347), draws new-wavers and rough-and-tumble working-class folk who try to converse over the sound of heavy-metal acts. The **Keyboard Lounge,** 939 W. Fourth Ave. (tel. 276-8131), beside the Hotel Captain Cook, draws an older blue-collar crowd to listen to top-40 rock bands Tuesday through Sunday nights.

Country and Western Music

The **Sawmill Club,** 6119 Old Seward Hwy., at Dowling Road (tel. 562-2135), has begun to capture a younger generation of C&W fans with dinner buffets and nightly entertainment that's frequently of national caliber. Colored flags, draped across the ceiling, add atmosphere to this large theater-style establishment. Free country dance lessons are offered every Tuesday and Thursday at 7 p.m.

Jazz

Anchorage doesn't have a lot to offer jazz enthusiasts on a regular basis. Some clubs, like the above-mentioned Fly by Night, have jazz nights, and the Anchorage Museum has occasional Sunday performances.

Another possibility is **The Office,** 545 E. Northern Lights Blvd. (tel. 276-9150), a small second-story cocktail lounge with a circular bar, small dance floor, and frequent solo jazz artists.

Folk

Although Alaskan bush ballads are a unique form of folk music, opportunities to hear them are catch-as-catch-can. Chilkoot Charlie's occasionally features ballad-eers, as do other small taverns around town. Try the **Creekside Saloon** at the Sourdough Mining Co. restaurant, 5200 Juneau St., off International Airport Road. Alaskan balladeers like Doc Schultz often perform here Tuesday through Saturday nights. And if you're into bluegrass, you'll be pleased to know about the Bluegrass Festival in late July at the State Fairgrounds in Palmer, sponsored by radio station KSKA.

Comedy

Check out the **Cama'i Lounge** at the Northern Lights Inn. There's also **P.J.'s,** 3608 Spenard Rd. (tel. 561-9017), a smoky, low-ceilinged local watering hole which follows its Thursday Ladies Only nights (male strippers) with a Friday- and Saturday-night Comedy Alley. "Name" West Coast talents are frequently on stage.

Burlesque

Anchorage's best-known evening attraction is the **Great Alaskan Bush Co.,** with two locations. The scantily clad dancers at these twin strip clubs aren't shy about dancing on a patron's table or trading a conversation for a drink—especially if the patron has just come in from the Bristol Bay fishing grounds or North Slope oil fields with a wad of bills in his pocket. Strict licensing laws prevent the meeting from going beyond conversation . . . in the club, at least. Visitors without bucks can sip on a beer and enjoy the show from a distance.

The original sawdust-floored Bush Company is half a block from the Sheraton at 531 E. Fifth Ave. (tel. 276-5504). It has been one-upped by a saloon-theater at 631 E. International Airport Rd. (tel. 561-2609). This new Show Room is designed like a high-class, Old West saloon with wagon-wheel chandeliers and full balcony.

There are other strip clubs around Anchorage, but none of them holds a candle to the Bush Company.

Downtown Bars

Media folks hang out at **Darwin's Theory,** 426 G St. (tel. 277-5322), a "local tavern" that is more evolutionary than revolutionary. **F Street Station,** 325 F St. (tel. 272-5196), is more fashionable, with round wooden tables, brass fittings, and oysters on the half shell.

Two bars patronized by Anchorage's gay men and women are **The Raven,** 618 Gambell St. (tel. 276-9672), and the **Blue Moon,** 530 E. Fifth Ave. (tel. 277-0441).

Rock Concerts

When headliners come to town, they draw capacity crowds to the 8,000-seat **George M. Sullivan Sports Arena.** Call the arena's recorded event information line (tel. 279-2596), read the newspapers, or consult Tickets, Inc., to find out who if anyone will be in Anchorage during your visit.

---

7. Short Trips from Anchorage

Many of Anchorage's quarter-million residents think of urban life as a necessary evil. The city, to them, is not a place where they want to be "cooped up" any longer than necessary. With spectacular scenery and many wilderness attractions within easy driving distance, why stay in the Big Smoke?

Within the Municipality of Anchorage there are two directions to travel: southeast on the Seward Highway, along the Cook Inlet's Turnagain Arm; and northeast on the Glenn Highway, through Eagle River toward the Matanuska Valley. We'll head south first.

TURNAGAIN ARM

Heading out of downtown Anchorage you'll cross Rabbit Creek Road, then descend to this long bay at the aforementioned Potter Marsh state game refuge. You'll trace the shoreline of Turnagain Arm all the way to Portage, a distance of about 37 miles. As the story goes, Turnagain Arm got its name in 1778 when Capt. James Cook took the *Resolution* up the inlet just far enough to realize it wasn't the fabled Northwest Passage, then told his crew to "turn again." Don't be foolish, however, and get out of your vehicle to scavenge on the mudflats. For one thing, some of it is quicksand. For another, when the tide comes in you might not have time enough to run to safety. Turnagain Arm has the second-greatest tide range in North America—nearly 39 feet in the spring, regularly 25 to 30 feet—and watching the bore tide rushing in can be a memorable experience from a safe spot.

Twelve miles from downtown Anchorage you enter **Chugach State Park.** McHugh Creek State Wayside, three miles farther, is a nice place to stop for lunch beside a pretty waterfall. You'll pass several trailheads, the tiny community of Indian, the Bird Creek State Campground with 19 sites, and (27 miles from downtown Anchorage) the renowned **Bird House Bar,** a collapsing log shanty half-buried in sod. You'll know it by the large blue bird's head protruding from its outer wall. The interior is, in a word, bizarre. Everything slants in a different direction—floors, walls, bar, you name it. Some say you've had too many to drink when things begin to look normal! The walls are covered with business cards, photos, and expired driver's licenses, and the bartender may insist that you cannot leave until you leave something behind from your own person. Ask about calling the ptarmigan.

GIRDWOOD

Ten miles farther, at the Girdwood Station shopping center, turn left on the Girdwood/Alyeska Access Road. This three-mile paved road leads to the community of Girdwood and Mount Alyeska, Alaska's No. 1 ski resort. Girdwood's full-time population is only around 300, but that figure mushrooms into the thousands on winter weekends and holiday periods with the influx of Anchorage snow-lovers to privately owned condominiums.

Mount Alyeska

When Anchorage bid for the 1994 Winter Olympic Games, the **Alyeska Resort,** P.O. Box 249, Girdwood, AK 99587 (tel. 907/783-2222), was proposed as the site for all alpine ski events. It's a challenging mountain with excellent facilities —five chair lifts (including a high-speed quad) handling over 5,000 skiers an hour, a 2,900-foot vertical drop, two rope tows for novices, a 60-acre snowmaking capability, National Ski Patrol, equipment rental-repair shop, professional ski school, and NASTAR racing program. A tramway is planned for the 1993 season. Timberline on this 3,939-foot mountain is just 1,500 feet, so there's plenty of open snow for experts. If there seem to be a surprising number of Japanese skiers, that may be because Alyeska is owned by the Seibu Group, a Japanese hospitality industry conglomerate.

Though snow conditions vary from year to year (tel. 783-2121 for daily reports), the ski resort typically opens in mid-November on a Wednesday-through-Sunday schedule, then expands to a full seven-day (10:30 a.m. to 5:30 p.m.), four-night (Wednesday through Saturday, 4:30 to 9:30 p.m.) format from mid-December to mid-March. Spring skiing, on a reduced schedule, may last until June. Tickets are $27 for adults, $15 for children (to 12) and seniors (over 59), $13 for all ages for night skiing. Full ski-boot-pole rental packages cost $18 all day for adults, $10 for those 12 and under. If the children are too young to ski, plant them for the day at the nearby Little Bear's Playhouse child-care center (tel. 783-2116).

You don't have to be a skier to appreciate Alyeska. Nonskiers are welcome, in summer, to ride 1¼-mile-long Chair 1 to the glass-enclosed **Skyride Restaurant.** From the sundeck at 2,350 feet elevation, you get an eagle's-eye view of Girdwood's Glacier Valley and, if you're lucky, of the bore tide steaming in on Turnagain Arm. The restaurant is open daily during lift hours, serving homemade soups, deli sandwiches, wine, and beer. There's also a special summer sightseeing package (10:30 a.m. to 5 p.m. daily, mid-June to mid-September) that gives you the lift and lunch at $15 for adults, $10 for children.

Crow Creek Mine

One of the first gold strikes in Alaska was made here in Glacier Valley in 1888, and while it didn't become anything enormously big, argonauts are still pursuing the dream. You can too . . . at Crow Creek Mine, P.O. Box 113, Girdwood, AK 99587. The mine's 19th-century buildings—a blacksmith's shop, bunkhouse, mess hall, barn, icehouse, and meat cache—have all been preserved, and are in fact still lived in. You'll see here a fine example of a turn-of-the-century placer mine as well as the first non-Native settlement in the Anchorage area; as such, the mine has been included in the National Register of Historic Places. Crow Creek Road, on which the mine is located (3½ miles off the Girdwood–Alyeska road), was part of the original Seward-to-Nome Iditarod Trail through Crow Pass.

Previously owned by Arne Erickson, the mine was bought by the Toohey family in 1974. Cynthia Toohey estimates that more gold remains on the site than was recovered during the life of the mine (1898 to 1940), when it was producing an average of 700 ounces a month. If you want to try your hand at panning or sluicing, the Tooheys will be glad to provide you with a pan, shovel, cup, and guaranteed bag of gold for $4 a day. "Look in the side of the hill for gold, not in the creek," cautions Cynthia, who should know: the 2½-ounce gold nugget she wears on a chain around her neck was found in the side of a Crow Creek hill. Other finds, many crafted into jewelry, are sold in the gift shop. Admission for sightseeing alone is $2. Open from 9 a.m. to 6 p.m. daily from Memorial Day to October 1. Primitive overnight camping adjacent to the mine costs $2 per unit.

If you're here in the winter, by the way, although the mine is closed, the Tooheys still live here—without electricity, without well water, without a telephone. They communicate with the outside world by citizens band radio, keep warm around a wood stove and kerosene lantern, and go shopping in a snowmobile or on cross-country skis.

Incidentally, the open meadows of Glacier Valley are the best place in the Anchorage area to try your hand at mushing, if you're here in the winter. Contact **Chugach Express,** P.O. Box 261, Girdwood, AK 99587 (tel. 783-2266), and ask them about their dog-sledding trips, which range in duration from 30 minutes to three days.

There are two big annual events in the valley, aside from the Alyeska-sponsored spring carnival (in April) and occasional World Cup races. The **Girdwood Forest Fair,** a two-day craft, food, and entertainment fair, is held in early July. The **Alaska Festival of Music,** a Labor Day weekend bash, has folk, rock, jazz, country, classical, and big-band music ringing throughout the valley, from outdoor amphitheaters to indoor stages.

Where to Stay in Girdwood

Alyeska's **Nugget Inn** lodge, at the foot of the mountain (tel. 907/783-2222), has 29 spacious hotel rooms and several condo units. Hotel rooms are furnished with queen-size beds, desk/dressers, and special closets for skis and ski boots. The rooms have televisions, and you can phone Anchorage without charge. Rates on winter weekends and holiday periods are $80 single, $90 double (plus 8% bed tax). Midweek and off-season rates are $70 and $80.

The Nugget Inn restaurant on the second floor is open daily from 8 a.m. to 10 p.m. You can have blueberry hotcakes ($4) for breakfast or an eight-ounce steak dinner ($13). Burgers and pizzas are good too. Enjoy a hot rum toddy at the adjoining Sitzmark Lounge and dance to live bands on weekends and holidays. The Bake Shop (tel. 783-2831), with an entrance on the lodge's exterior shop row, has superb soups, sandwiches, and pastries.

Alyeska's Japanese owners plan a new $50-million hotel project on 76 acres in Girdwood for 1993. The new hotel, with 297 beds, would be three-quarters of a mile from the slopes, but would be connected by a special access lift.

Several condominium-rental agencies are active in Girdwood, providing temporary tenants for the expensive condos owned mainly by Anchorage professional people. These homes are scattered along the lower slopes of the mountain on narrow streets bearing the names of famous ski resorts: Cortina, Davos, Garmisch, Kitzbuhel, Megeve. Some of the nicest units are offered by **Alyeska Vacations,** a division of H. J. Gellert & Associates, 715 L St., Suite 5, Anchorage, AK 99501 (tel. 907/277-3752 or 783-2283 in Girdwood). Every one is different but fully furnished, often with a fully equipped kitchen, television, and VCR (rent videos at the Girdwood mercantile), stereo system, telephone, laundry facilities, hot tub and/or sauna, even waterbeds. Property manager Janet Gellert takes great pains to match an individual's requirements to the appropriate unit. Rates vary, but start at $55 a day and $210 a week for studios, $85 and $355 for two-bedroom suites, $180 a night and up for luxury chalets.

There are a handful of bed-and-breakfasts, including Austrian natives Heinrich and Emmy Gruber's **Alyeska View B&B,** P.O. Box 234, Girdwood, AK 99587 (tel. 907/783-2747). The home is off Vail Drive, but you'll have to call or write for directions. The Alyeska View has two deluxe guest rooms, one of them with a Jacuzzi, TV loft, ski waxing area, and lots of *Gemütlichkeit.* Summer rates (May 15 to September 30) are $45 single, $60 double; winter rates (November 15 to April 15) are $45 and $65.

And there's a year-round youth hostel at Girdwood, the tiny **Alyeska International Youth Hostel,** P.O. Box 10-4099, Anchorage, AK 99510 (tel. 907/277-7388). Located on Alpina Way half a mile from the ski lifts, it has four beds and an outdoor sauna.

Where to Eat in Girdwood

Apart from the ski slopes, though, there is one reason why Anchorage residents regularly make the 75-mile round-trip drive to Girdwood. That reason is the **Double Musky Inn,** on Crow Creek Road (tel. 783-2822). Many faithful patrons insist that this Cajun restaurant, decorated with mirrors and harlequin masks, has the best cuisine in Alaska.

Cajun cooking, as owner Bob Persons explains, is "400-year-old French country food adapted to the locally available game, seafood, vegetables, and spices." All the food is spicy, but it's cooked to order, hot or mild, depending on the diner's preference. The specialties of the house are 16-ounce pepper steak in a burgundy sauce ($21) and blackened redfish (salmon) à la (chef Paul) Prudhomme ($20). Meals include vegetable, salad, and rolls.

By 6 p.m. on a Friday or Saturday the Double Musky bar is already packed with people willing to wait two hours or longer for a table. In spite of its reputation, however, I found the Double Musky a bit too snobbish for my pedestrian tastes. Oh, the food was superb. But if I'm paying $80 for a dinner for two—as you can easily do here with appetizer, dessert, and wine—I do not expect such less-than-gracious service as I received here.

The Double Musky is open from 5 to 11 p.m. Tuesday through Thursday, 4 to 11 p.m. Friday through Sunday; closed Monday.

Back near Girdwood village center, behind the post office and near the fire station, is the **Chair 5** restaurant (tel. 783-2500). The scene here is Alaskan rustic, with a big wood stove heating up the room. Rock 'n' roll and country-western music add a little life, while the menu lists 54 beers from all over the world. Dinner is served from 5 p.m. to midnight daily; big burgers cost $5 with fries, a large pizza with the works is $16.50, and a steak-and-seafood menu (meals include salad, potato, vegetable, and bread) is priced $7.50 to $15.50. Every night features an all-you-can-eat special; on Monday, for instance, it's Mexican food.

Back up at Alyeska, the Tyrolean A-frame a few steps below the lodge is the **Edelweiss Gasthaus** (tel. 783-2526). Pretend you're at Garmisch or Innsbruck and enjoy home-cooked German food, like grilled Bratwurst mit Sauerkraut ($6) or Wiener Schnitzel mit Kartoffelsalat ($12). The menu is written on skis behind the bar, which serves beer and wine. A variety of German-Austrian gifts, from steins to lederhosen, are sold here. Open from 10 a.m. to 10 p.m. daily.

PORTAGE GLACIER

This natural wonder isn't as awe-inspiring as the glaciers of Glacier Bay or Prince William Sound, but it has an attribute shared by only one of Alaska's other great glaciers: easy accessibility by road from a metropolitan center. (The other is Juneau's Mendenhall Glacier.) Portage Glacier is, in fact, the most visited attraction in the state of Alaska. The access road is off the Seward Hwy. 48 miles from downtown Anchorage, 11 miles from the Girdwood junction.

Portage Glacier and four others—Byron, Middle, Explorer, and Placer—overhang or drop into the Portage Valley, a historically important pass connecting Prince William Sound with Turnagain Arm. When the Pleistocene Age ended 10,000 years ago, they were all part of a single massive glacier that covered the entire valley. What you see now are but remnants. Portage is the most spectacular because it terminates in a photogenic three-mile-long lake, speckled with small icebergs throughout the year.

All visitor activity at Portage Glacier focuses on the $8-million **Begich, Boggs Visitor Center** (tel. 907/783-2326), opened in 1986 in memory of Reps. Nick Begich of Alaska and Hale Boggs of Louisiana (who died in a 1972 plane crash in this area). The picture windows of the center's 400-seat theater look directly on the lake and glacier, underscoring every point made by Chugach National Forest rangers as they explain the geology of the region. They also show a 20-minute movie (charge: $1). Excellent exhibits and displays introduce the flora and fauna of the area, including the obscure iceworm, a tiny invertebrate that lives between glacial ice crystals and feeds on pollen and algae.

A short nature trail interprets natural and geologic history on the terminal moraine where the visitor center is built. Another three-quarter-mile-long trail leads to Byron Glacier. Three campgrounds with 55 campsites and six picnic sites are located in the valley.

Within snowball-throwing distance of the lake is **Portage Glacier Lodge,** where you can enjoy soup, sandwiches, and pie while sitting around a warm fireplace. The lodge also has a gift shop.

Another 1¼ miles up the shore of Portage Lake, the **M.V. *Ptarmigan*** departs seven times daily from May to September, on a more-or-less hourly basis, to take visitors on a cruise through the iceberg-studded lake. The boat is the only way to reach the foot of Portage Glacier unless you come equipped with winter mountaineering gear. The *Ptarmigan,* an 80-foot vessel which carries up to 200 passengers, is owned and operated by Holland America Line/Westours. Tickets are $18.50 for adults ($9.50 for children under 12).

Gray Line of Alaska (tel. 277-5581) offers twice-a-day shuttle tours from Anchorage, including the Portage Lake cruise. The tours leave at 7:15 a.m. and 3:30 p.m. and are priced at $32 (children pay $16). Gray Line's standard six-hour Portage Glacier bus tour, including a "no-host" lunch and "optional" chair-lift ride (you pay extra) at Alyeska Resort, runs $28 for adults, $14 for kids, although the lake cruise can be tacked on. **Royal Highway Tours** (tel. 276-7711) and **Alaska Sightseeing Tours** (tel. 276-1305) run similar tours.

My favorite Portage Glacier tour is the one operated by a unique service called **Bed and Meals on Wheels,** P.O. Box 190411, Anchorage, AK 99519 (tel. 248-3747). John Regan, Jr., puts four adults (and perhaps a child or two) in a 25-foot motorhome for a full-day spin around Turnagain Arm. The trip starts in Anchorage at 9 a.m., takes about nine hours, and costs just $30 per person, including lunch.

Oh, if you're wondering what happened to the town of Portage, or even if there was one, it was inundated by the inlet during the 1964 earthquake and abandoned. You can still see its foundations near the depot-less Alaska Railroad loading dock for the Whittier shuttle, about a mile on the Anchorage side of the glacier access road.

HOPE

A minor gold-rush town in the late 19th century, a virtual ghost town by the second decade of the 20th, Hope (pop. about 100) is 88 road miles from Anchorage but only about 15 air miles. Built on the south side of Turnagain Arm opposite Indian, it is today an isolated weekend getaway destination at the mouth of Resurrection Creek.

Perhaps modern gold-rush bravado is to blame for Hope's best-known citizen's becoming more of a tourist attraction than the one he built. Tom Williams, whose replica 1800s mining camp, **Paystreke,** is five miles upstream from Hope on rutted Resurrection Creek Road, placed a newspaper ad for "mail order brides" for his all-male crew in September 1985 and drew nearly 4,000 responses. He wound up as a national media hero, even making an appearance on "The Phil Donahue Show," and lived with one of the responding women for several months until she tired of an Alaskan winter without running water or electricity. But although the relationship fizzled, he couldn't have asked for better national publicity for his enterprise.

Williams, a burly man in his early 40s, mined an 18-acre claim on Resurrection Creek for several years before deciding to seek his fortune in the tourism industry. He started work in 1984 and now has 17 buildings. They include a general store, gold-nugget jeweler, leather shop, antique photo studio, and the Grubstake Café, with salmon bakes ($9), steaks, and great sourdough pancakes. Coffee is on the house. He also has a gold-panning school, and hopes to introduce a fly-fishing academy. Lodging is presently only in tent cabins that sleep four for $20 a night (bring your own sleeping bag), but long-range plans are for 50 to 60 self-contained units, including a handful of honeymoon cabins. Also in the works is a saloon-style can-can show. All this is coming about, Williams told me, "with PMA and OPM—a positive mental attitude and other people's money."

The brides are not forgotten in this hoopla. Paystreke's first wedding was performed in July 1986, its second in September. Vows were taken in period costume, which in one case meant long johns and flannels.

Williams has at least one built-in market. His camp is at the trailhead of the 38-mile **Resurrection Pass Trail** across the northern Kenai Peninsula, a pathway used by some 8,000 backpackers a year. There are seven public-use cabins along the trail, where hikers can stay for $15 a night. Permits can be obtained from the Chugach National Forest supervisor's office, 201 E. Ninth Ave., Anchorage (tel. 271-2599).

Hope township itself has few buildings remaining. Most of the old streets, since abandoned, were absorbed by the 1964 earthquake. Joyce and Don Ohr's **Seaview Café,** on Main Street (tel. 782-3364), built in 1896, is the center of what activity remains in town. The Ohrs are also experts on local history, and will sell you a walking guide map to the townsite. Across Main Street from the café are a small gift shop and ice-cream parlor.

If you plan on staying overnight in Hope, I recommend the **Bear Creek Lodge,** P.O. Box 90, Hope, AK 99605 (tel. 907/782-3141), at Milepost 15.9 of

the Hope Highway. The lodge has seven log cabins nestled around a pond frequently visited by geese. The cabins are charming, each with a double bed and hideaway
couch, wood stove, radio, table and chair, and frilly drapes on the windows. A central bathhouse is clean and well maintained. Rooms go for $50 a night.

The tiny restaurant seats but 12 at three tables, but it's good home-style cooking, and you can't beat the price—steak dinner and champagne for two, including
after-dinner coffee and dessert, just $27.50! The restaurant is open from 8 a.m. to 8
p.m. daily except Tuesday.

For campers, the U.S. Forest Service **Porcupine Creek Campground,** with 24
tent sites, toilets, and firepits, is at the end of the Hope Highway, two miles past Bear
Creek. Overnight fee is $5.

EAGLE RIVER

This community of about 9,000, 12 miles northeast of downtown Anchorage
on the Glenn Hwy., has become a well-to-do bedroom community for Alaska's metropolis. For the visitor, it's the primary gateway to 495,000-acre **Chugach State
Park.**

The park's **Eagle River Visitor Center** (tel. 694-2108) is a beautiful 12½-mile
drive east of town, up the Eagle River Valley. The first white man to encounter this
valley, U.S. Army Capt. Edwin Glenn, in 1897, was so impressed that he called it "a
miniature Yosemite." Eagles, bear, moose, and other animals populate the densely
forested valley floor, and dall sheep can often be seen on the sheer mountainsides.

From the veranda of the visitor center, you can study those sheep through telescopes and gaze out on the glaciated Chugach Mountains. Excellent wildlife displays include a "hands-on" exhibit for children. The center also has a three-quarter-
mile interpretive nature trail, accessible to the handicapped, a beaver pond, and a
salmon-spawning area. There are other short trails from the center and a series of
ranger-led hikes and naturalist programs. Eagle River Visitor Center is open in summer from 11 a.m. to 7 p.m. Thursday through Monday, and in winter from 11 a.m.
to 5 p.m. Friday through Sunday.

The visitor center is the northern trailhead for the popular 25-mile **Old Iditarod
Trail** segment connecting Eagle River and Girdwood over Crow Pass. Get full information on trail conditions from Chugach State Park headquarters, 2601 Commercial Dr., Anchorage, AK 99501 (tel. 907/694-6391), and file a trip plan with park
rangers (tel. 907/279-3413).

Eagle River itself is a Class II white-water trip for canoers, kayakers, and rafters.
Canoe trailheads are at miles 7.5 and 9 of the Eagle River Road. A five-hour paddle
excursion from Anchorage is offered May to September and costs $69 (minimum
age is 13). Contact **Alaska Whitewater,** P.O. Box 142294, Anchorage, AK 99514
(tel. 907/338-0471).

Eagle River, of course, isn't the only point of access to this huge state park.
About ten miles north of town, look for signs on the Glenn Hwy. pointing to **Thunderbird Falls.** This twin cataract, hidden in a canyon near a picnic area, is an easy
one-mile hike from road's end. Turquoise-green **Eklutna Lake,** a ten-mile drive east
from Glenn Hwy. Milepost 26, is the largest lake in Chugach State Park. Seven miles
long and one mile wide, it gets its color from glacial silt. It's a popular spot for fishing, camping, swimming, and hiking.

Near the lake turnoff, just west of the highway, is the tiny Indian village of
Eklutna. Its St. Nicholas Russian Orthodox Church, which dates from the 1860s, is
almost certainly the oldest surviving building in the Municipality of Anchorage. A
hand-hewn log prayer chapel stands nearby, surrounded by dozens of "spirit
houses"—family graves brightly painted in traditional colors. Most Tanaina Indians, Athabaskans who have lived along the Knik Arm of Cook Inlet since the mid–
17th century, were converted to Russian Orthodoxy 150 to 200 years ago by mis-
sionaries.

If you've been too long in the park to return to Anchorage, don't despair: Eagle

River has ample visitor services. For a bed, check out the comfortable **Eagle River Motel,** Monte Drive, Eagle River, AK 99577 (tel. 907/694-5000). **Garcia's Cantina,** in Valley River Center (tel. 694-8600), has excellent Mexican food and a convivial atmosphere.

Further information on the area is available from the **Chugiak–Eagle River Chamber of Commerce,** P.O. Box 353, Eagle River, AK 99577 (tel. 907/694-4702).

SOUTH-CENTRAL ALASKA

1. KENAI PENINSULA
2. PRINCE WILLIAM SOUND
3. COPPER RIVER BASIN
4. MATANUSKA-SUSITNA VALLEYS

All of south-central Alaska is within a day's trip of Anchorage. That said, it's a wildly diverse region. It incorporates the halibut fleets of Homer, the seal and bird rookeries of Kenai Fjords National Park, the awesome splendor of the great Columbia Glacier thundering into deep-blue Prince William Sound, oil tankers steaming fully loaded out of the port of Valdez, white-water rivers plummeting from the high peaks of Wrangell–St. Elias National Park, and gentle agricultural colonies in the Matanuska Valley.

Each portion of the region demands separate treatment.

1. Kenai Peninsula

Were it not for the narrow isthmus between Portage and Whittier, the Kenai Peninsula would be an island. That geographical anomaly is responsible for its unique character. Connected by road to Anchorage and interior Alaska, it hasn't suffered for 20th-century influence; yet its semi-isolation has allowed it to evolve in its own way, and in its own time. Happy to be a vacation playground for Anchorage sportsmen and women, it has nevertheless fallen comfortably into a slower, more casual lifestyle.

That's not to say that every corner of the Kenai Peninsula is alike. Far from it. Some 150 miles long and 60 to 110 miles wide, larger than Vermont, this protrusion is almost a microcosm of the entire state of Alaska in its variety. From the low-lying lake and river country of the Kenai National Wildlife Refuge to the rugged shoreline of the Kenai Fjords, from the enormous ice fields cloaking the Kenai Mountains to the halibut banks and clam beds of Kachemak Bay, there's something for everyone here.

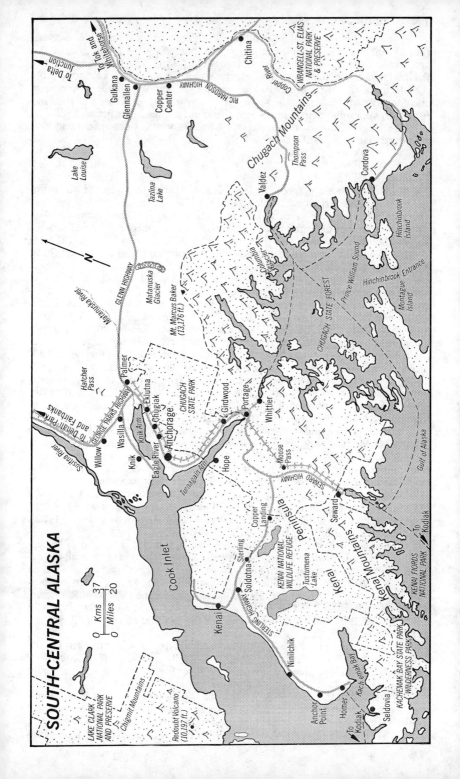

SOUTH-CENTRAL ALASKA

The towns of the Kenai Peninsula are as different as the topography. **Seward** (pop. 3,200) is a growing industrial center, a deep-water port and fishing community surrounded by snow-covered mountains. **Kenai** (pop. 6,500) has emerged from a fascinating Russian history to become an important oil town. **Soldotna** (pop. 3,800), founded only in the 1940s, has become the seat of peninsula government and a sportsman's heaven on the Kenai River. **Homer** (pop. 4,100) is an artists' and fishermen's community in a spectacularly beautiful setting on Kachemak Bay.

For detailed information, contact the **Kenai Peninsula Convention and Visitors Bureau,** P.O. Box 497, Kenai, AK 99611 (tel. 907/283-7989).

GETTING THERE

The two main highways on the Kenai Peninsula are fully paved and well maintained. The **Seward Highway,** which covers the 127 miles from Anchorage to Seward, climbs through the Kenai Mountains after leaving Turnagain Arm, and then drops through scenic lake and river country to Resurrection Bay on the Gulf of Alaska. The **Sterling Highway,** which branches west off the Seward Highway 38 miles north of Seward, runs across the middle of the peninsula to Soldotna, then down the coast of the Cook Inlet to Homer, 225 miles from Anchorage.

Each of the main communities on the peninsula has a small airport and is served by regional airlines. A surprising number of Kenai residents, in fact, commute to Anchorage daily in private planes. I like flying **South Central Air,** with reservations offices in Anchorage (tel. 243-8791), Seward (tel. 224-3268), Soldotna (tel. 262-9820), Kenai (tel. 283-7343), and Homer (tel. 235-6171). Serving only the Kenai Peninsula, its 12-seat twin-engine aircraft give passengers a great fly-over view. My second choice is **ERA,** the Alaska Airlines commuter line; you can call toll free (tel. 800/426-0333) or contact reservations offices in Anchorage (tel. 243-3300), Kenai (tel. 283-3168), or Homer (tel. 235-5205). ERA flies larger jets several times daily between Anchorage, Kenai, and Homer, as well as Valdez. **Harbor Air,** based in Seward, flies two nonstop round trips a day to Anchorage; call them in Anchorage (tel. 243-1167) or Seward (tel. 224-3133).

Seward, Homer, and tiny Seldovia are also served by the southwest sector of the **Alaska Marine Highway System.** The M.V. *Tustumena* runs between these ports, Kodiak Island, and Prince William Sound twice weekly throughout the year, except for a one-week-long trip to Dutch Harbor in the Aleutians each month between May and September, and a ten-week maintenance period in Seattle beginning January 1. The passenger fare between Seward and Homer is $80. For specific schedule and fare information, contact the Alaska Marine Highway, P.O. Box R, Juneau, AK 99811 (tel. toll free 800/642-0066) or call the ferry office in Anchorage (tel. 272-4482), Seward (tel. 224-5485), or Homer (tel. 235-8449).

The final travel alternative to the Kenai Peninsula is rail. From May 27 to September 4 only, Thursday through Sunday, the **Alaska Railroad** runs an all-day excursion from Anchorage to Seward and return. The train leaves Anchorage at 7 a.m., reaching Seward at 11 a.m., and departing Seward at 6 p.m., getting back to Anchorage four hours later, for a fare of $60 round trip or $35 one way. For information, contact the railroad at P O Box 7-2111, Anchorage, AK 99510 (tel. 907/265-2494 or 265-2623, or toll free 800/544-0552), or in Seward at P.O. Box 330, Seward, AK 99664 (tel. 907/224-8001).

Package tours of the Kenai Peninsula are offered from Anchorage. **Gray Line of Alaska,** 547 W. Fourth Ave., Anchorage, AK 99501 (tel. 907/277-5581, or toll free 800/544-2206), offers a 12-hour Kenai River fishing trip, leaving Anchorage daily at 8:30 a.m. June 1 through August 15. Fare is $135.

Trails North, P.O. Box 923, Seward, AK 99664 (tel. 907/224-3587), offers two-day tours from Anchorage to Seward via Portage Glacier, with adventure travel options, for prices starting at $196 per person. **Bed and Meals on Wheels,** P.O. Box 190411, Anchorage, AK 99519 (tel. 907/248-3747), will take you on a two-day tour to Seward and Portage Glacier for $150 (shared party) to $200 (private party). Sleeping bag and mosquito repellent are provided.

SEWARD

High, snowy peaks surround Seward, nestled at the head of lovely Resurrection Bay. Founded in 1902 as the starting point for the federally financed Alaska Railroad, it was named after William Seward, the secretary of state who arranged the purchase of Alaska from Russia in 1867. Even before that the year-round ice-free harbor was the southern terminus of the Iditarod Trail, the overland route to the Nome goldfields. Seward attracted adventurers of all kinds—miners, trappers, loggers, and fishermen—who thronged to the town for business dealings, supplies, and entertainment.

Despite several devastating setbacks, including the 1964 earthquake and tidal wave (which destroyed over 90% of the town's economy), Seward has shown great resiliency. It has fisheries and shipping industries, a Pacific Rim coal port, a lumber mill, marine research center, vocational training center, and the new state penitentiary.

The climate is mild—average summer highs in the 60s, average winter lows in the 20s. Precipitation is moderate, about 60 inches annually, including seven to eight feet of snow.

Orientation

Seward is the only community on the Kenai Peninsula with a traditional "downtown." The Seward Highway enters town three miles from Milepost 0 when it crosses the Resurrection River near the airport. As you continue into town, you'll see Mount Marathon towering above you on your right, and on your left, the Suneel Alaska coal terminal, Alaska Railroad depot, and small-boat harbor. When you pass a lagoon and cross Van Buren Street, the highway becomes Third Avenue, and you're in downtown Seward.

Downtown streets are laid out in a traditional grid pattern. Starting on the mountain slopes, First to Sixth Avenues run north-south; the beachside Seventh Avenue has been renamed Ballaine Boulevard after a turn-of-the-century city father. Railway Avenue fronts the ferry dock (at the end of Fourth Avenue). From there, the east-west streets are first presidential (Washington, Adams, Jefferson, Madison, Monroe)—and then alphabetical (A, B, C, and D). The main business district is on Fourth Avenue between Washington and Jefferson Streets.

The **Visitor Information Center** is housed in an early-day Alaska Railroad car permanently resting at Third Avenue and Jefferson Street. Open mid-May to mid-September from 9 a.m. to 5 p.m. daily, it's operated by the **Seward Chamber of Commerce,** P.O. Box 749, Seward, AK 99664 (tel. 907/224-8051). Other seasons, you can drop in at the chamber's second-floor office in the Ray Building at Fifth and Adams during weekday business hours.

Seward has a taxi service, **Yellow Cab** (tel. 224-8788), and a car-rental agency, **National,** at the New Seward Hotel (tel. 224-8001). **Seward Bus Lines,** Fourth Avenue and Washington Street (tel. 224-3608), runs a regular service to Anchorage. During the summer, the **Alaska Trolley Car Co.** (tel. 345-1017) offers daily $1-a-ride service from 7 a.m. to dark between downtown, the harbor, and the airport.

The town has as many institutions of higher learning as it has banks (two). The University of Alaska Institute of Marine Research and the Alaska Vocational Technical Center are located here. There's a weekly newspaper (the *Seward Phoenix Log*) and the 33-bed **Seward General Hospital,** at First Avenue and Jefferson Street (tel. 224-5205).

As for special events, July 4 is the big occasion in Seward. All eyes focus on the **Mount Marathon Race,** an annual trudge up and down the 3,022-foot mountain that began in 1909 as a wager between two sourdoughs. Today hundreds of runners from all over the world compete in three divisions—junior, women's, and men's. If you're not a runner, you can enjoy a Fourth of July parade, street carnival, softball tournament, and more.

Seward also plays host to the largest fishing derby in the state of Alaska, the annual **Silver Salmon Derby.** Held continuously from the second through the third weekend of August, it offers over $40,000 in prizes, including $5,000 to the grand champion. The 1990 derby will be the 35th annual.

The third week of January, the **Polar Bear Jump-Off Festival** features a couple dozen costumed citizens plunging into Resurrection Bay in an American Cancer Society benefit during a full weekend of activities.

Where to Stay

I enjoy staying downtown at the **New Seward Hotel,** 217 Fifth Ave. (P.O. Box 675), Seward, AK 99664 (tel. 907/224-8001), because of its central location and its European-style ambience. Owner-manager Brad Snowden advertises that "we pamper you," and that's no empty boast. There aren't many hotels where the front-desk staff will call you by name after check-in.

The 58 rooms are red carpeted and wood paneled, with paintings on the walls, drapes on the windows, nice wood furnishings, and hot-water radiator heating. They aren't particularly large, and there's no elevator to the second floor, but here the "little things" truly make a difference—such as remote-control cable TVs with 24-hour in-house movies, free local phone calls, and amenity packs (with razor, comb, shampoo, sewing kit, etc.) in every room. The lobby has courtesy coffee and a well-stocked little gift shop. Huge moose and dall sheep heads, and Native crafts, add atmosphere. Ask about the "cat-in-the-can." There's a game room with a pool table and darts in the basement.

Shuttle-van service is provided between the hotel, harbor, ferry dock, and train station. The New Seward also serves as a National Car Rental agent and as a booking point for Kenai Fjords tours.

The cozy hotel saloon, decorated in turn-of-the-century San Francisco style, is easily spotted by the antique gargoyle street lamps on the sidewalk outside. It's downtown Seward's most popular after-work gathering place. A seafood bar offers light meals, and solo guitarists frequently perform.

Standard rooms in the main hotel are $74 single, $87 double, with private bath; $56 single, $69 double, with shared bath. Budget-watchers can stay in the cozy "bargain basement" for $48 single, $58 double.

A new wing, which may be given franchise status by a major national hotel chain in 1990, has 20 luxury rooms, all with refrigerators and coffeemakers. Rates are $90 to $111 single, $103 to $124 double.

Because of the large number of oil-spill clean-up workers in town through 1990, early reservations are recommended here and at all Seward hotels.

There's real history at the **Van Gilder Hotel,** 308 Adams St. (P.O. Box 775), Seward, AK 99664 (tel. 907/224-3079). The city's oldest building (1909), listed on the National Register of Historic Places, has been extensively restored. The 26 pleasing rooms are furnished with European antiques. The rooms lack phones, but all have double beds and cable TVs. The 11 rooms with private baths cost $75 single, $85 double; 15 "pension rooms" with shared bath run $50 a night. Guided tours of the hotel, including a slide show and recitation of Robert Service balladry, begin at 10 a.m. and 3 p.m. daily, and are free for hotel guests.

The Sourdough Bar and Grill is open from 7 a.m. to 10 p.m. daily, with specialty seafood dinners priced from $12 to $20. Try the Resurrection Bay seafood Napoléon, a house chowder, for $4.

The **Breeze Inn,** on Third Avenue facing the boat harbor (P.O. Box 935), Seward, AK 99664 (tel. 907/224-5238), has been refurbished under new management. The 49 rooms of this three-story motel are clean and spacious, with décor in shades of brown and gray. There's cable television; local phone calls are 25¢. If being at the marina is important to you, this may be the place to stay. A coffeeshop serves breakfast plus lunch and dinner buffets daily, and an adjoining lounge features top-40 bands weekend nights. Summer rates are $64 single, $61 double; winter rates are $5 less.

There are two pleasant small motels in town. Flower boxes greet guests at the **Marina Motel,** 1603 Seward Hwy. (P.O. Box 1134), Seward, AK 99664 (tel. 907/224-5518). The 18 wood-paneled rooms are decorated in earth tones and furnished with double beds, cable TVs, and phones with free local calls. There's courtesy coffee and juice in the rooms. One kitchenette is available. A small library in the office lends magazines and paperbacks, and there are adjacent picnic grounds for summertime feasts. Phone ahead for a courtesy car. Rates are $65 single, $75 double, in summer; less in winter.

Murphy's Motel, 911 Fourth Ave. (P.O. Box 736), Seward, AK 99664 (tel. 907/224-8090), has 11 cozy rooms done in shades of brown. All have double beds, cable television, free local phone calls, and courtesy coffee. The reception area is a private museum of beautiful antique furniture. Courtesy-car service is offered. Rates are $52 single, $64 double, in summer; $45 single, $55 double, in winter.

The Visitors Information Center has a listing of local residents offering **bed-and-breakfast** facilities.

Camping is possible at several locations around Seward, including the Resurrection Bay beachfront, downtown along Ballaine Boulevard. Rates are $5 a night per campsite. Contact City of Seward, P.O. Box 167, Seward, AK 99664 (tel. 907/224-3331). Miller's Landing at Lowell Point, down an unpaved road south of town, offers primitive camping at $3 per night. Contact P.O. Box 81, Seward, AK 99664 (tel. 907/224-5739). There are three Chugach National Forest campgrounds 17 to 25 miles north of town on the Seward Hwy.

Recreational vehicles can stay overnight at **Olsen's Salmon Creek Trailer Park,** Salmon Creek Road (P.O. Box 1858), Seward, AK 99664 (tel. 907/224-3433), for $15 a night with utilities; **Bear Creek Mobile Home Park,** Bear Lake Road, Mile 6.6 on Seward Hwy. (P.O. Box 386), Seward, AK 99664 (tel. 907/224-5725); or at **Seward Tesoro,** Mile 2 on Seward Hwy. (P.O. Box 656), Seward, AK 99664 (tel. 907/224-3569), for $12 a night with hookups, $5 without.

Where to Eat

The **Harbor Dinner Club,** 220 Fifth Ave. (tel. 224-3012), has a long-established reputation as Seward's best restaurant. Light nautical décor—model ships, fishermen's floats, and driftwood—decorates the walls. The cuisine is likewise maritime: try the seafood special, a cornucopia of deep-fried, sautéed, and/or poached prawns, scallops, and halibut for $16.50, including vegetable, potato, and soup or salad. The lunch menu features 57 different sandwiches priced from $4 to $6.50. Open for lunch weekdays from 11 a.m. to 2:30 p.m., on Saturday and Sunday from 11:30 a.m. to 5 p.m. Dinner hours are 5 to 11 p.m. daily.

The atmosphere at the new **Ray's Waterfront,** 1316 Fourth Ave. (tel. 244-5606), is enough to inspire any would-be fisher to toss a line into the briny. Ray's is built on pilings in the small-boat harbor, so diners can watch vessels carry their catch right to the docks. On the cedar walls are 55 mounts of fish from local waters, including a 300-pound halibut and a beluga whale. Lunches, priced from $5 to $10, feature burgers, seafood pastas, and halibut and chips. Dinners, $9 to $17, include broiled or blackened salmon and halibut, prime rib, and steaks. It's open daily in summer from 11 a.m. to 11 p.m., though the lounge remains active until 2 or 3 a.m. Winter hours are limited, and the restaurant may be closed in December and January, so call ahead. Dinner reservations are recommended anytime.

Thorn's Showcase Lounge, 208 Fourth Ave. (tel. 224-3700), is big among local steak lovers. In a bar atmosphere of dim red lighting you can get a 13-ounce New York steak with potato and salad for just $14. Dinner is served from 5:30 to 11 p.m. nightly.

The **Frontier Restaurant,** Fifth Avenue and Washington Street (tel. 224-3161), has a coffeeshop atmosphere but offers large quantities of good food at reasonable prices. Halibut in a cheese sauce, with vegetable, roll, and soup or salad, is $11.50.

The **Peking Restaurant,** 338 Fourth Ave. (tel. 224-5444), gets an "A" for atmosphere—hanging lanterns, bronze Oriental casts, and a prevailing phoenix-and-dragon theme. The meals are Americanized Cantonese, Szechuan, and Mandarin, with lunches priced from $5.50, and dinners from $9.50. Open daily from 11:30 a.m. to 10:30 p.m.

What to See and Do

There aren't a lot of attractions in Seward itself. The Visitor Information Center will try to inspire you with their walking tour, but I find these to be the only spots of significant interest:

The **Resurrection Bay Historical Society Museum,** Third Avenue and Jefferson Street, is open from 11 a.m. to 4 p.m. daily, June 15 through Labor Day. Visit to see what destruction nature wrought on Seward in the 1964 quake, and to learn about Russian Gov. Alexander Baranov's late-18th-century shipyard near modern Seward. Admission is 50¢ for adults, 25¢ for children.

The earthquake is also of abiding interest at the **Seward Community Library,** opposite the City-State Building at Third Avenue and Adams Street. A slide program called *Seward Is Burning!* is presented June to Labor Day, and free films are shown at 7:30 p.m. on Friday. The original Alaska flag, signed by the designer, is on display. Open from 1 to 8 p.m. Monday through Friday and 1 to 6 p.m. on Saturday.

Why is Alaska's first flag in Seward? Because a 13-year-old orphan named Benny Benson was a Seward schoolboy when his "eight stars of gold on a field of blue" was unanimously chosen the territorial flag in a 1926 contest. A **Benny Benson Memorial** stands today in a small park opposite the boat harbor at Milepost 1 of the Seward Hwy.

The University of Alaska's **Institute of Marine Science,** on Third Avenue between Washington Street and Railway Avenue, is open summers from 1 to 5 p.m. Monday through Friday (except holidays), and by special arrangement at other times. Look at the marine display, see slide shows and films, and ask about aquaculture projects and oceanographic research.

Iditarod Trailhead Park, near the ferry terminal at the foot of Fourth Avenue, contains the Mile "0" monument of the Iditarod National Historic Trail, which ends in Nome. An Iditarod is about 1,100 miles.

Sports

FISHING Resurrection Bay is a saltwater fishery, one of Alaska's most popular. Boats are nearly gunwale to gunwale in August during the annual Silver Salmon Derby. Chum salmon, pink salmon, and Dolly Varden are also prolific in summer. Red snapper, halibut, and cod thrive on the sea floor. Locals say the best fishing is off Lowell Point or Fourth of July Creek.

The consensus choice as Seward's most complete fishing supply and information center is **The Fish House,** P.O. Box 1345, Seward, AK 99664 (tel. 907/224-3674), facing the harbormaster's house at the small-boat harbor, open from 6 a.m. to 9 p.m. daily. Dale Clemens and his staff can make charter arrangements for you on any of 14 different boats. Some 20 charter operators work out of Seward, and most maintain dockside booths where you can make your own decision about which one to fish with. Typical full-day rates for salmon or halibut fishing are $90 per person, including all bait and equipment.

The most popular nearby freshwater holes are at **Grayling Lake,** 13 miles north, where you can fly-fish for grayling May to October; and **Grouse Lake,** eight miles north, with excellent winter ice-fishing for Dolly Varden.

Thirty-one miles north of Seward on the Seward Highway, the **Trail Lakes Hatchery,** operated by the Alaska Department of Fish and Game, will show you where many of Resurrection Bay's salmon get their start. The visitor center here is open daily from 8 a.m. to 4:30 p.m. in summer. When the hatchery reaches capacity operation in 1992, it will raise 4 million king salmon, 6 million coho, and 30 million sockeye each year.

HIKING A wide variety of trails—short and long, level and steep—are open for hiking in **Chugach National Forest.** Check with forest headquarters, 334 Fourth Ave. (P.O. Box 275), Seward, AK 99664 (tel. 907/224-3374), for complete trail information. Among the more popular trails in the Seward area are the **Two Lakes Trail,** a one-mile loop along the base of Mount Marathon, beginning behind the VoTech at Second Avenue and B Street; and the gently sloping **Johnson Pass Trail,** a 23-mile segment of the Old Iditarod Trail connecting Upper Trail Lake (Mile 33 on Seward Hwy.) with Granite Creek (Mile 64). Wildlife, especially black bear, is common.

The Forest Service also maintains 11 walk-in **cabins** for public use at $15 per night in the Seward district of Chugach National Forest. You can book up to 180 days in advance.

If you're adventurous, consider a 7½-mile (one way) beach walk from Lowell Point south to Fort McGilvray in the **Caines Head State Recreation Area,** but be sure to check the tide tables first, though. Built by the U.S. Army in 1942 as an artillery command post against a possible Japanese attack on Resurrection Bay, Fort McGilvray was abandoned in 1944 and was quickly reclaimed by the forest. History buffs find it a fascinating place to visit, either by foot or boat.

HUNTING Black and brown bear, moose, mountain goat, and dall sheep roam the Chugach National Forest around Seward. Small game such as snowshoe hare, ptarmigan, and grouse are also hunted. Waterfowl hunting can be some of the best in Alaska. For details, contact the **Alaska Department of Fish and Game** at 333 Raspberry Rd., Anchorage, AK 99502 (tel. 907/344-0541, or 224-3017 in Seward).

KAYAKING AND CANOEING The sheltered inlets of Resurrection Bay and the Kenai Fjords are ideal for small man-powered craft. Seward is the home base of **Alaska Treks 'n' Voyages,** P.O. Box 625, Seward, AK 99664 (tel. 907/224-3960 in summer, 907/288-3610 in winter), the foremost purveyor in the area of three- to eight-day sea kayak voyages in the Kenai Fjords.

SAILING Skippered day sails ($50 to $100 per person) and weekend trips (from $600 per couple) are offered by several operators, including **Seward Sailing Company,** Pouch 6577, Box 737, Anchorage, AK 99502 (tel. 907/248-4635), and **Resurrection Bay Sails,** 3210 Lark Court, Anchorage, AK 99507 (tel. 907/561-2249). The Fish House (see "Fishing," above) has a complete list.

WINTER SPORTS Cross-country skiing, snowshoeing, and snow machining are popular on trails frequented by hikers in the summer. **Turnagain Pass,** at Mile 68 on Seward Hwy., reserves the west side of the road for snow machiners and the east side for skiers. Another good bet is **Summit Lake,** at Mile 46. Owners Marty and June Arnoldy, who fled the madness of running an Oregon singles bar, can fix you a meal or put a rustic roof over your head at the log **Summit Lake Lodge,** Mile 45.8 on Seward Hwy., Moose Pass, AK 99631 (there are no phone lines in this remote locale).

OTHER DIVERSIONS The Visitor Information Center will give you directions to Seward's swimming pool, ice skating rink, gymnasium, tennis courts, and softball fields. **Dreamland Bowl,** Fifth Avenue at Railway Avenue (tel. 224-3544), is a town social center. **Liberty Theater,** 305 Adams St. (tel. 224-5418), has first-run movies.

Tours

Trails North, P.O. Box 923, Seward, AK 99664 (tel. 907/224-3587), has the local monopoly on land tours. You can hop aboard their buses at Pier 34 in the small-boat harbor for a 1½-hour town tour at 11 a.m. on Thursday, Saturday, and Sunday. The cost is $7.50 per head. At 4 p.m. on those same days they'll give you a sled-dog-mushing demonstration (one hour, $7.50), and if you care to join them at 1 p.m. on Thursday, Saturday, or Sunday, they'll take you to the Exit Glacier (see "Kenai Fjords National Park," below) and combine it with a sled-dog demo for $12.50. Family rates are available. **Seward Bus Lines** (tel. 224-3608) and **Gray Line of Alaska** (tel. 277-5581 in Anchorage) also offer local charter tours.

KENAI FJORDS NATIONAL PARK

Encompassing steep-sided ocean fjords and a vast wilderness of ice, this 580,000-acre park, established in 1980, is home to thousands of sea birds and marine mammals. Stretching for about 50 miles along the southeastern shore of the Kenai Peninsula, just south and west of Seward, it's one of Alaska's most dramatic protected landscapes.

Visitors can reach the seacoast by chartered boat from Seward, the icefield by foot, and either by small plane. But your first stop should be at the Kenai Fjords National Park **headquarters and visitor center,** located in Seward at the small-boat harbor: P.O. Box 1727, Seward, AK 99664 (tel. 907/224-3175). From Memorial Day to Labor Day, it's open daily from 8 a.m. to 7 p.m.; the rest of the year it's open weekdays from 8 a.m. to 5 p.m. The visitor center has a photo exhibit, slide programs, and a variety of publications and maps.

The park's most accessible corner is about 12 miles from downtown Seward. Head north to Mile 3.7 on Seward Hwy., then turn west onto a gravel road which leads nine miles up the Resurrection River to the **Exit Glacier Ranger Station.** Open daily in summer, it has exhibits, weekend campfire programs, and naturalist-led hikes.

Exit Glacier is but a remnant of a much larger glacier that once extended all the way to Resurrection Bay. As it retreats, it reveals the process of plant succession from lichen to hemlock and spruce. A half-mile walk from the visitor center gives you a chance to reach out and touch the highly compacted ice. But be cautious: a California woman was killed here by calving glacial ice in 1987. There is access for the handicapped to within a quarter-mile of the glacier.

A steep three-mile trail follows the flank of the glacier to the top of the **Harding Icefield,** 35 miles long and 20 miles wide. This alpine desert, 4,000 feet above sea level, wasn't even discovered until the early 1900s when surveyors realized several coastal glaciers were part of the same system. Only a few isolated mountain peaks, called *nunataks* by Eskimos, interrupt its rolling surface.

Harbor Air, based at Seward Airport (tel. 224-3133), offers dramatic one-hour flightseeing tours of the icefield for $70 per person (minimum of three people). Landings can be arranged for one-day or long-term winter expeditions. **Alaska Treks 'n' Voyages** in Seward (tel. 224-3960 in summer) leads overnight icefield expeditions, with optional glacier skiing, three times a week in July and August priced from $155 per person.

Some 35 to 65 feet of snow falls annually on the icefield. Its increasing pressure slowly forces fingers of ice—glaciers—in all directions. Eight of them are tidewater glaciers which tumble into the Kenai Fjords, producing myriad icebergs.

Harbor seals, pups as well as adults, love the icebergs. They share the waters of the fjords with sea lions, sea otters, porpoises, and several species of whales. Thousands of puffins, kittiwakes, murres, and gulls nest on the steep cliffs and rocky islands of the fjords.

The best way to see the maritime portion of the park is by charter boat from Seward. **Kenai Fjords Tours, Inc.,** P.O. Box 1889, Seward, AK 99664 (tel. 907/ 224-3668), operates eight-hour trips to the Holgate Arm and Chiswell Islands, the latter a division of the Alaska Maritime National Wildlife Refuge, for $70 per person (children pay half price), mid-May to early September. Half-day wildlife cruises in Resurrection Bay are $45. **Quest Charters,** 510 W. Tudor Rd., Suite 5, Anchorage, AK 99503 (tel. 907/562-2628, or 907/224-3025 in summer in Seward), has similar excursions from May to September for $70 per person, half-day trips for $45.

SOLDOTNA

The youngest town on the Kenai Peninsula was just a fork in the road as recently as 1947. When the area was opened to homesteading in that year, Soldotna boomed. It has since become the major commercial and recreation center of the central peninsula. For a stretch of several miles down the Sterling and Kenai Spur Hwys., you'll see nothing but shopping malls, motels, and small restaurants.

But there's plenty of wilderness just off the "strip." Soldotna is headquarters for the nearly two-million-acre Kenai National Wildlife Refuge, covering most of the western half of the peninsula, and is the main stepping-off point for fishing expeditions on the Kenai River, Alaska's best king salmon stream.

Located a few miles upstream from the mouth of the Kenai River, Soldotna gets slightly warmer in summer (68°F average high) than neighboring Kenai town, but still has chilly winters (19°F average daytime high) and minimal precipitation (18 inches annually, most of it as snow).

Orientation

The easiest place to orient yourself is the "Y" junction, at the east end of the downtown, where the Kenai Spur Hwy. branches northwest toward Kenai town while the Sterling Hwy. continues in a northeast-to-southwest direction. The residential district lies west of here, along with most of the Kenai Peninsula Borough government buildings (on Binkley Street). Kalifornsky Beach Road intersects the Sterling Hwy. south of the Kenai River bridge and leads west to Kenai Peninsula Community College and Kenai town. Funny River Road winds east two miles to the airport.

The **Greater Soldotna Chamber of Commerce,** P.O. Box 236, Soldotna, AK 99669 (tel. 907/262-9814), maintains a **Tourist Information Center** from May 15 through Labor Day in a new building on the Sterling Hwy. just south of the Kenai River bridge. The chamber is open year round from 9 a.m. to 5 p.m. weekdays.

Central Peninsula General Hospital, off Mary Dale Drive (tel. 262-4404), is staffed 24 hours a day for emergencies. To get around town, you can either call **Soldotna Cab** (tel. 262-3222) or rent a car from **Peninsula Ford,** 43925 Sterling Hwy. (tel. 262-5491), or **Hutchings Chevrolet,** 44055 Sterling Hwy. (tel. 262-5891).

The town's two biggest annual events are focused on the Soldotna Rodeo Grounds off Kalifornsky Beach Road. **Soldotna Progress Days,** held since 1961 on the last weekend of July, include a horse show and rodeo, parade, air show, races, dances, and arts and crafts exhibits. The **York Winter Games** take place at the rodeo grounds the third weekend in January.

Where to Stay

Of all the motels in the central Kenai Peninsula, I am most impressed by the **Soldotna Inn,** 35041 Kenai Spur Hwy. (P.O. Box 565), Soldotna, AK 99669 (tel. 907/262-9169). The management is very friendly, the 28 rooms spacious and thoughtfully maintained; there's a refrigerator in every room, and there's no charge for local phone calls. There's also a guest laundry, and special amenities—shampoo, conditioner, and lotion—in the bathrooms. A red-brown color scheme decorates most rooms, which have queen-size beds, nature pictures on the walls, cable TV, and hot-water heating. Four lovely suites contain full kitchens. Some rooms have waterbeds, and two rooms have been set aside for nonsmokers. In the lobby, mounted moose and dall sheep heads overlook a small gift and sundry shop. Rates start at $55 single, $65 double, $70 twin, $80 for a small suite, $112 for a luxury suite (plus 5% tax). The hotel includes Mykel's restaurant (see the "Where to Eat" section, below).

The **Kenai River Lodge,** 393 Riverside Dr., Soldotna, AK 99669 (tel. 907/262-4292), is like a fishing lodge in the city. Nestling on the riverbank beside the Sterling Hwy. just west of the Kenai River bridge, it was built in the early 1970s by June and Bob Green, who wanted a permanent home on the river. (Bob charges $125 per person per trip for king salmon fishing and $85 for silver salmon fishing; if you want a permanent record of your catch, he'll videotape it.) The crowded, eclectic lobby has a small tackle shop and Alaskan gifts. The 30 motel units have queen-size beds with red covers, black or orange carpets, nature photos on the walls, cable TVs, phones (local calls are 50¢), and electric heat. Each room has a view of the river, and private frontage is available. The Sea Wind Restaurant, open from 7 a.m. to 10 p.m. daily, offers a seafood-and-steak menu, including a 16-ounce T-bone with potato, salad, and roll, for $13.50. There's an outdoor deck for summer barbecues. The Upper Deck Lounge is open late for after-dinner drinks. Singles are priced at $65; doubles, $70.

Of the 49 units in the **King Salmon Motel,** 35545 Kenai Spur Hwy. (P.O. Box 430), Soldotna, AK 99669 (tel. 907/262-5857 or 262-6106), 24 have kitchenettes, and the office provides dishes and pans on request. The balance have refrigerators, and all have coffeemakers. Each spacious, nicely appointed room has plush brown carpeting, queen-size beds, satellite TV, telephone (local calls are 15¢), and hot-water baseboard heat. There's always a pot of coffee on in the pleasant lobby. Single or double, rates are $81 to $89 in summer, $55 to $60 in winter.

The **Bunk House Inn,** 44715 Sterling Hwy., Soldotna, AK 99669 (tel. 907/262-4584), is one more place to hang your hat. The 34 spacious rooms are decorated in earth tones, with framed mosaics on the walls, satellite TVs, phones (local calls are 50¢), electric heat, and tiny bathrooms. Two units have kitchenettes with gas stoves. Standard rates are $75 single, $100 double, including tax. The attractive lobby has plenty of potted and hanging plants. The Bunk House Restaurant, open from 4 a.m. to 10 p.m. in summer, from 7 a.m. to 10 p.m. the rest of the year, has burgers for $5 and full dinners for $10 to $16.50, including catfish ($14.50). The unfinished-wood décor carries to the Brand X Lounge, where country-and-western singers perform on weekends.

There's also a youth hostel in Soldotna, the **Soldotna International Youth Hostel,** 444 Riverview Dr. (P.O. Box 327), Soldotna, AK 99669 (tel. 907/262-5549). Open all year, it has 16 beds in male, female, and family dorms.

The city of Soldotna runs two **campgrounds,** both in wooded settings on the Kenai River. **Swift Water Park,** off East Redoubt Avenue, east of the Sterling Hwy., on the north side of town, has 45 campsites. **Centennial Park,** at the south end of Soldotna off Kalifornsky Beach Road, has 170 units, 32 of them for tents. The charge is $6 a day. No reservations.

Where to Eat

Soldotna has the best selection of restaurants on the peninsula. The finest of all is concealed in a grove of trees just north of the Y junction of the Sterling and Kenai Spur Hwys. A short boardwalk leads from a parking area to the **Four Seasons Restaurant** (tel. 262-5006). Classical music, hanging ferns, and solid-wood décor have you feeling as if you're in the Vienna Woods, or at least taking a walk in the Black Forest. Everything is made from scratch here. The chefs specialize in new variations on old favorites, like chicken teriyaki ($15), halibut Florentine ($15.25), and a 12-

ounce New York steak with mushrooms ($19). All dinners include homemade soup and hors d'oeuvres, vegetable, and potato. There's also a full wine list. For a lighter meal, try the spinach salad with imported cheeses, olives, eggs, dried fruit, almonds, and garlic mustard dressing, served with soup and bread ($11).

During the summer, lunch is served from 11 a.m. to 3 p.m., and dinner is from 5:30 to 10 p.m. Monday through Saturday. A breakfast buffet is offered on Sunday from 9:30 a.m. to 1 p.m. Closed Monday in the winter and annually for four weeks beginning at Christmas.

Mykel's, in the Soldotna Inn on Kenai Spur Road (tel. 262-4305), is a low-lit, fully licensed restaurant with red décor and private booths. The soup-and-salad bar is very popular. Daily luncheon specials are priced at $5 to $7. For dinner, you can have prime rib ($17) or halibut any of three different ways (try it sautéed with mushrooms in white wine, at $15). Open from 6 a.m. to 11 p.m. Monday through Saturday and 7 a.m. to 10 p.m. on Sunday.

Sizzler Family Steak House, 44900 Sterling Hwy., at the corner of Kalifornsky Beach Road (tel. 262-1005), is not much different from all those Sizzlers in the Lower 48. Place your order at the counter, pick it up when your number is called, and enjoy steaks, seafood, and combination plates for $9 and $10. The salad bar is $5.70 by itself, $2.25 with meal. Solid-wood décor, hanging lamps, and historical Alaska photos give this Sizzler a little character. Open Sunday through Thursday from 11 a.m. to 10 p.m., to 11 p.m. on Friday and Saturday.

Other worthwhile Soldotna restaurants include **Pizza Pete's,** 35320 Kenai Spur Hwy. (tel. 262-5306), for 29 varieties of pizza, plus Italian food, seafood, steaks, and shish kebab; **Golden Dragon** restaurant, 36102 Kenai Spur Hwy. (tel. 262-6366), for Chinese and American food; and **D & D Taco,** Kenai Spur Hwy. (tel. 262-1717), for Mexican food.

What to See and Do

Soldotna isn't a town you can "do." It's the center of a region you must "see."

Start your exploration at the headquarters and visitor center of the **Kenai National Wildlife Refuge,** P.O. Box 2139, Soldotna, AK 99669 (tel. 907/262-7021), on Ski Hill Road one mile south of the Kenai River bridge. Signs on the Sterling Hwy. will point you in the right direction. Open daily throughout the year, it has lifelike wildlife dioramas, a bookshop, and free brochures. Nature films are shown hourly from noon to 5 p.m. on weekends.

Formerly the Kenai National Moose Range, this is the most accessible of all Alaskan wildlife refuges. It stretches 110 miles north-south from Turnagain Arm to the 6,600-foot heights of the Kenai Mountains, and another 40 miles west-east from Soldotna to the Chugach National Forest. Over two-thirds of this expanse is designated wilderness. It includes 15 campgrounds (most of them improved), 15 hiking trails, two canoe trails—and of course, a great deal of wildlife.

In particular, the animal that many people come here to see is the moose, the largest antlered deer on earth. Alaskans are a bit jaded when it comes to moose sightings, but it's very exciting to watch a 1,400-pound bull moose grazing by the side of a road. Calves are born in the late spring; you'll often see them with their mothers in swampy areas during the summer. But don't approach them too closely; the bull in particular can be dangerous when feeling protective.

You're likely to spot dall sheep on mountainsides in the rugged Kenai River canyon terrain along the Sterling Highway on the east boundary of the refuge. Black bears often visit campsites, and brown bears congregate at salmon-spawning streams. Mountain goats are found mainly in the glaciated Kenai Mountains; caribou and wolves are relatively scarce. You may see many small mammals, including beaver, lynx, and wolverine; the trumpeter swan and a variety of other waterfowl; and 146 species of resident and migratory birds. The visitor center has checklists for amateur ornithologists.

Apart from the Sterling Highway, there are two pleasant drives for car-bound travelers. The **Swanson River Road** (turn off the highway at Mile 83) leads 30 miles through an area of low lakes and marshland rife with wildlife. Even more scenic is the **Skilak Lake Loop Road,** a 19½-mile side road that follows a ridge overlooking deep valleys, lakes, and rivers.

Sports

FISHING The Kenai River boasts 11 different sport fish, but the one everybody comes for is the king salmon, which averages 23 pounds but grows to 85 pounds or larger. The world-record king, a 97-pounder, was taken out of the river in May 1985 by a Soldotna fisherman. Kings usually peak in mid-June, although the season continues through July. Red salmon run in June and July, pinks in August, silvers from July to October. The river also yields trophy-size rainbow trout, Dolly Varden, arctic char, grayling, and others. Big Eddy's Jetty and Poacher's Cove, both on the river near Soldotna, are among the most popular fishing holes.

Many fishing services operate out of the Soldotna area, and I hesitate to recommend one over any other. Full-time Kenai River residents are usually more reliable than "weekend guides" from Anchorage. Rates vary from $80 to $140 per person for a day's excursion. Many guide services have packages with area motels. Write the chamber of commerce and ask for a current list of guides or inquire at the **Sports Den,** 44176 Sterling Hwy. (tel. 262-7491), where you can not only get up-to-the-minute fishing information, but also rent equipment, including boats and canoes. Some say that **Big Sky Charter and Fish Camp,** near Sterling, is a sterling operation. Rates for a private cabin with kitchen are $100 a day, $600 per week. Charter fishing costs $125 per person for a half day. Contact them at 13120 Saunders Rd., Anchorage, AK 99516 (tel. 907/345-5760 in winter or 907/262-9496 in summer).

Because the Kenai River is the most heavily used freshwater fishery in Alaska, the Alaska Department of Natural Resources has established the Kenai River Special Management Area to protect the spawning grounds and wildlife habitat of this 80-mile stream. The **Alaska Department of Fish and Game,** P.O. Box 3150, Soldotna, AK 99669 (tel. 907/262-9368), is keeping a close watch on human impact: fishing is subject to suspension on 48-hour notice.

Nonresident sport-fishing licenses cost $10 for 3 days, $20 for 14 days, $36 for a year.

You must also have a fishing license to dig for clams. Razor clams are in season along the shore of Cook Inlet from April to October. Clam Gulch, on the Sterling Hwy. 40 miles south of Soldotna, is the most popular location, although anywhere from Kasilof to Anchor Point is regarded as prime clamming ground during low tide. The bag limit is 60 clams, regardless of size.

HIKING There are more than 200 miles of trails and routes in the wildlife refuge. Hikers should have staunch rubber boots for the marshy lowland muskeg, and should be in reasonably good shape for more strenuous hill climbs; you can get a map of the area at the Kenai refuge visitor center. Nearest to Soldotna is the **Funny River Trail,** which climbs nearly 21 miles (with an elevation gain of 2,000 feet) into the Kenai Mountain foothills. The trailhead is near the municipal airport.

A plus for hikers is the proliferation of wild berries free for the picking. Look for blueberries, cranberries, lingonberries, raspberries, strawberries, rose hips, and currants, and ask someone to describe cloud, crow, salmon, service, and nagoon (!) berries.

HUNTING Hunting is permitted throughout the Kenai National Wildlife Refuge in accordance with state game regulations. Big-game animals plus snowshoe hare, ptarmigan, spruce grouse, and waterfowl are the most sought species.

KAYAKING AND CANOEING Two canoe routes in the northern lowlands of the Kenai

National Wildlife Refuge have been designated as National Recreational Trails: the **Swanson River Route,** 80 miles long, connects 40 small lakes with 46 miles of stream; and the **Swan Lake Route,** 60 miles long, connects 30 small lakes with 33 miles of stream. The longest portage on either route is less than a mile. Either circuit can be traveled leisurely in a week or less, and portions thereof make good weekend trips. You're guaranteed relative isolation: no more than 15 people are permitted within the canoe system lakes at any one time. Contact headquarters in Soldotna for route maps and complete canoeing regulations.

Rent canoes for $25 a day from **Kenai Paddle Excursions,** Mile 81.7 on Sterling Hwy. (P.O. Box 588), Sterling, AK 99672 (tel. 907/262-2942 in summer, 717/354-7190 in winter). They'll also provide shuttle service to the Swan Lake trailhead. From June 15 through August 31 the firm operates guided camping tours for rates starting at $180 for two days, $225 for three days.

RIVER RAFTING For river rafting, **Action Alaska,** 440 L St., Anchorage, AK 99501 (tel. 907/279-1406), will take you on a six-hour float trip down the Class IV white water of the Kenai River canyon to Skilak Lake for $69 per person. The outing begins at 11 a.m. near Cooper Landing, 45 miles east of Soldotna, and includes a gourmet picnic lunch of smoked salmon, reindeer sausage, and champagne.

Alaska Rivers Co., P.O. Box 827, Cooper Landing, AK 99572 (tel. 907/595-1226), offers a similar canyon trip plus a less rigorous three-hour scenic float ($39 per person) and a variety of custom white-water trips. Canoe and kayak instruction is available.

Alaska Wildland Adventures, P.O. Box 26, Cooper Landing, AK 99572 (tel. 907/595-1279, or toll free 800/478-4100), has three-hour Kenai River floats for $39, seven-hour trips for $69, and five-hour fishing trips for $85. It also has a salmon bake ($15 for adults, half price for kids) daily at noon at its headquarters, Mile 50.1 on Sterling Hwy.

Rafting season is mid-May to mid-September, depending on the water level in the river.

WINTER SPORTS Cross-country skiing, snowshoeing, ice fishing, and skating on frozen lakes are all popular cold-weather pursuits on the Kenai Peninsula. And add dog sledding to that list: Soldotna hosts the state championship sled-dog races the last weekend of February (after the Anchorage Fur Rendezvous). The start and finish lines are at the airport. Soldotna has outdoor ice-skating rinks and a new Olympic-size hockey rink in the sports center on Kalifornsky Beach Road.

OTHER SPORTS The Kenai Peninsula's first golf course (nine holes) is east of downtown on the Sterling Hwy. (There's now a new course in Kenai.) The town also has its requisite bowling alley, tennis courts, softball fields, and high school swimming pool, open to the public during scheduled hours. Further information can be obtained from the Greater Soldotna Chamber of Commerce (tel. 262-9814).

The **Central Peninsula Sports Center,** 538 Kalifornsky Beach Rd. (tel. 262-3150), has racquetball courts and an indoor jogging track. It's open from 7:30 a.m. to 9 p.m. weekdays and 9 a.m. to 6 p.m. on Saturday; closed Sunday.

Nightlife

Nightwatch, on Sterling Hwy. at Funny River Road (tel. 262-7020), occupies a new building overlooking the Kenai River on the southeast side of the bridge. This popular lounge and bar features local entertainment on weekends. About half a mile north on the Sterling Hwy. is the **Maverick Club,** a tavern with live and loud rock 'n' roll several nights a week. Area residents often go to the nearby town of Kenai to dance (see the Kenai nightlife entries, below), just as many Kenai citizens prefer to shop and dine in Soldotna.

The **Orca Twin Theaters,** in the Red Diamond Center on Kalifornsky Beach

Road (tel. 262-7003), regularly show first-run movies. Tickets are $4 for adults, $2 for children.

Sterling Highway East of Soldotna

Sterling, a small town 13 miles east of Soldotna, is the location of the **Izaak Walton State Recreation Site** at the confluence of the Kenai and Moose Rivers. Archeological excavations in this area have revealed that Eskimos had fishing settlements here more than 2,000 years ago. Interpretive displays will help you find the ancient house sites.

Cooper Landing (pop. 350) stretches along the banks of the upper Kenai River for nearly 10 miles, 39 to 49 miles east of Soldotna. Aside from its fishing and rafting lures, it's a nesting place for bald eagles and the site of the **Charley Hubbard Gold Mining Museum,** Mile 51 on Sterling Hwy. The museum, with artifacts and photographs, is open daily from Memorial Day through August. The Resurrection Pass and Russian River trailheads are nearby.

Princess Tours expects to open its luxury wilderness inn, the **Kenai Princess Lodge,** at Cooper Landing in time for the 1990 visitor season. The 28-unit lodge, 47 miles east of Soldotna, is located on a 35-acre plot in Kenai National Wildlife Refuge. The old Resurrection Lodge is being resurrected to become the 8,500-square-foot main lodge, with a dining room and bar, gift shop, and huge stone fireplace. Seven quadriplex log buildings, spread along 1,900 feet of the Kenai River, will contain 24 regular rooms and four mini-suites, all with wood stoves, vaulted ceilings with skylights, screened veranda decks, and private entrances. The suites will have Jacuzzis. Rates will be $145, single or double, $200 for mini-suites; $10 each for a third and fourth person.

Guests will participate in a variety of activities, including fishing (in season), guided and independent hikes, horseback riding, river rafting, and a salmon bake. The lodge also will have a 25-space RV park with full water, sewage, and electric hookups, plus Laundromat, showers and toilet, and grocery.

For reservations and information, contact Princess Tours, 2815 Second Ave., Suite 400, Seattle, WA 98121 (tel. 206/728-4202, or toll free 800/647-7750).

Worthy of mention is **Vinton's Alpine Inn Motel,** Mile 48.2 on Sterling Hwy. (P.O. Box 801), Cooper Landing, AK 99572 (tel. 907/595-1212). Twelve modern units with full kitchenettes and TV are priced at $65 single, $75 double, a night ($45 and $55 in the off-season). A gold-nugget jewelry shop is attached.

If you're passing through at lunchtime, grab a famous cheeseburger ($6.50 with a Pepsi and fries) at **Gwin's Lodge,** Mile 52 on Sterling Hwy. (tel. 595-1266), open from 8 a.m. to 5 a.m. daily.

KENAI

The peninsula's largest town can lay legitimate claim to being both its oldest and its most progressive. In 1791 Russian fur traders built a fort, Nikoaevsky Redoubt, near a Tanaina Indian village on a low bluff overlooking the Cook Inlet and the mouth of the Kenai River. In 1869, two years after the American purchase of Alaska, the U.S. Army erected Fort Kenay. A replica of the fort and an early Russian Orthodox church stand today in Old Town. Commercial fishing came into prominence in the late 19th century, and remains of major importance today: Kenai is Alaska's third-largest fish-processing center.

The boom that built modern Kenai began in 1957 when oil was discovered in the Cook Inlet. The companies exploiting the field—Amoco, Atlantic Richfield, Marathon, Mobil, Phillips, Shell, Standard, Union, and Tesoro Alaska—could be a *Who's Who* of the oil industry. Several of them have built refineries at Nikiski, 12 miles north of Kenai town, in an industrial area where two liquefied natural gas plants and an ammonia-urea chemical factory are also in operation. Fifteen offshore platforms are now producing 200,000 barrels of crude oil and 800 million cubic feet of natural gas per day.

Kenai's climate is cool and dry, with average summer temperatures in the low 60s and winter in the mid teens. Extremes can be up to 80°F and down to −40°F. Only about 20 inches of precipitation falls a year, much of it as snowfall (an annual average of 69 inches).

Orientation

Located on the west shore of the Kenai Peninsula at the mouth of the Kenai River, Kenai township comprises a fistful of residential pockets mainly along the Kenai Spur Hwy., between 4 and 15 miles from the Sterling Hwy. junction in Soldotna. The central business district and civic center, 11 miles from Soldotna, is focused around the junction of the Spur Hwy. and Main Street Loop. Old Town is on the south side of the highway beside the river.

The **Greater Kenai Chamber of Commerce,** P.O. Box 497, Kenai, AK 99611 (tel. 907/283-7989), has its offices and visitor center in an old log cabin at 402 Overland St., facing the Kenai Spur Hwy. at the corner of Main Street. It's open year round from 9 a.m. to 5 p.m. weekdays.

There is hourly air-taxi service to and from Anchorage, 30 minutes away by air, as well as to Homer and Kodiak. **Kenai Airport,** the peninsula's largest, is a 15-minute walk north of downtown at 305 N. Willow St. **City Cab** (tel. 283-7865) can transport you from there to your destination, or you can get transportation from one of the four car-rental agencies that have outlets at the airport—**National** (tel. 283-9566), **Avis** (tel. 283-7900), **Hertz** (tel. 283-7979), and **A1-Auto Rental** (tel. 283-7865).

The *Peninsula Clarion,* a tabloid newspaper, is published five times a week (Monday through Friday) in Kenai. There are four banks and a medical clinic, the **Kenai Medical Center,** at 11355 Kenai Spur Hwy. (tel. 283-4611). The nearest hospital is in Soldotna.

Where to Stay

The **Uptown Motel,** 47 Spur View Dr. (P.O. Box 1886), Kenai, AK 99611 (tel. 907/283-3660), has 52 rooms in two barrack-like buildings. Decorated in reds, each contains a satellite TV, telephone (local calls are 15¢), and electric heat. Ten rooms are set aside for nonsmokers, and one suite contains a Jacuzzi. The Back Door Mexican restaurant has taco-enchilada dinners from $7, and Louie's Restaurant (which welcomes children till 10 p.m.) serves steak-and-seafood dinners, mostly in the $10 to $12 range. Published room rates are $79 single, $89 double, plus tax.

King Oscar's Motel, P.O. Box 1080, Kenai, AK 99611 (tel. 907/283-6060), on the Spur Hwy. just as it enters Kenai from the east, opened in 1987. The motel has 52 rooms with queen-size beds, satellite TVs, and phones, as well as a guest laundry. It provides airport service as well as fish cleaning and freezer space. Mr. D's restaurant and lounge features live entertainment. Rooms are priced at $79.50 single, $89.50 double; $10 less during winter season.

The **Katmai Motel,** at the junction of Kenai Spur Hwy. and Beaver Loop Road (P.O. Box 2840), Kenai, AK 99611 (tel. 907/283-6101), was once the belle dame of Kenai. A 1986 renovation with Scandinavian-style furniture helped revive its image a bit, but the necessary additional noise-proofing wasn't installed in the 30 rooms. Local TV and phone are free. The Katmai Restaurant (open 24 hours daily) serves lunch sandwiches for $5 to $7, and steak and seafood dinners in the $14 to $17 range. The Katmai Lounge, a popular country-and-western bar with dancing, may be the best reason to visit. Room rates are $69 single, $74 double.

If you have a car at your disposal, there are several excellent options. My nod goes to the **Daniels Lake Lodge** bed-and-breakfast, P.O. Box 1444, Kenai, AK 99611 (tel. 907/776-5578). It's a bit of a drive—about 20 miles north of downtown Kenai on Drift Circle, off Halbouty Road—but well worth it if you value waking up to the sight of the sun rising over a pristine woodland lake. Karen

Walters has turned over her entire downstairs to guests. Three bedrooms open onto a large living room with a big wood stove. The walls are decorated with photos of the same wildlife you're likely to see on the lakeshore, including moose and bears. For lonely evenings, there's a TV, radio, and tape player, and local phone calls are free. The shared bathroom has a large sunken shower and a sauna. Laundry facilities are off the kitchen. You cook your own meals, but Karen will keep you supplied with duck eggs, goat milk, and other country fixings. Rates are $46 single, $58 double, $104 for a two-bedroom suite.

River guide Herman Fandel and his educator wife, Irene, have turned their spacious, antique-furnished home into **Irene's Lodge,** 702 Lawton Dr., Kenai, AK 99611 (tel. 907/283-4501), a year-round bed-and-breakfast located a block off Kenai Spur Hwy. just east of town. Two of the five guest rooms have private baths and entrances. The Fandels prepare a full Alaska-size breakfast for guests, and enjoy making tour arrangements. Rates are $75 for two.

Families who like an unhurried place to stay and enjoy doing their own cooking would find it hard to beat **Country Apartments** (tel. 907/262-7881). The four lovely one-bedroom log cabins and two apartment units (a duplex and a triplex) are near Soldotna and the Kenai River on College Road. The mailing address is 10819 Spur Hwy., Suite 349, Kenai, AK 99611. All are completely furnished with towels, linens, kitchen utensils, and TV. Rates are $50 single, $75 double, $100 for three people.

Kenai Municipal Campground, on Forest Drive overlooking the Cook Inlet, has 40 units on a wooded site which also features a children's playground. Stays are limited to three days. Contact the chamber of commerce (tel. 907/283-7989) for information.

Recreational vehicles can hook up south of Kenai at the **Kenai RV Park,** at 912 Highland Ave. (tel. 283-2665), with 30 spaces, or **Overland RV Park,** at 410 Overland St. (tel. 283-4227), with 18 spots. Both parks, with full hookups, are off Kenai Spur Road.

Where to Eat

The local favorite is the new **Windmill Restaurant,** 145 S. Willow St. (tel. 283-4662). Fresh seafood is the specialty, with lunches priced from $6 to $8, and dinners at $8 to $20. "It's kind of European," says bed-and-breakfast operator Karen Walters. "It's great, in my opinion." Open daily except Sunday from 11 a.m. to 10 p.m.

Outside the motels, other popular small restaurants include the **Unique P'tea't** coffeeshop in Carr's Mall, just north of town on Kenai Spur Road (tel. 283-7007), with homemade sandwiches, soups, and salads; **Sourdough Sal's II,** 51805 N. Kenai Spur Rd. (Mile 26) in the Nikishka Mall (tel. 776-5489); and **Pizza Paradisos,** Frontage Road and Main Street, downtown (tel. 283-7008).

Possibly the nicest restaurant in the immediate vicinity of Kenai town is **The Albatross,** Mile 13.1 on Kalifornsky Beach Road (tel. 283-7052), six miles south of downtown near the Whalers Bluff subdivision. This low-lit steakhouse has an excellent domestic and imported wine list, and a full menu of seafood and beef specialties: snow crab ($17), halibut and scallops ($16), and steaks ($11.50 to $18). Open for dinner only, from 5:30 to 10 p.m. Monday through Thursday, to 11 p.m. on Friday and Saturday, and from 4 to 8 p.m. on Sunday.

What to See and Do

Most of Kenai's visitor attractions are in Old Town. Pick up a walking-tour map from the chamber of commerce information center and begin there. Among the stops you will make are:

Fort Kenay, Mission Street at Overland Avenue (tel. 283-7294), a 1967 reconstruction of the circa-1869 U.S. Army stockade, houses the one-room **Kenai Historical Museum** of local and natural history. Open daily June 1 to September 14 from 10 a.m. to 5 p.m. weekdays, to 3 p.m. on Saturday, and noon to 4 p.m. on Sunday.

The **Holy Assumption of the Virgin Mary Church,** opposite the fort on Mission Street, is a National Historic Landmark. This sky-blue, onion-domed but spartan Russian Orthodox church is still actively used as a place of worship. The adjacent **St. Nicholas Chapel** is a shrine; its first resident priest, Igumen Nicholai, and other church leaders are buried under the floor. If you want a tour, contact Father Targonsky at the parish house (the oldest building in Kenai), next door to the fort (tel. 283-4122).

The **Kenai Fine Arts Center** and Olde Towne Gallery, 816 Cook St., near Main (tel. 283-7040), is a combination art school, studio, and shop. You'll see here the work of some outstanding central Kenai artists, especially in pottery and fiber crafts. Open from 10 a.m. to 4 p.m. Monday through Saturday.

Twenty-five miles north of Kenai, as far as the fully paved North Kenai Spur Road will take you, the 4,000-acre **Captain Cook State Recreation Area** nestles by the mouth of the Swanson River. Many local folks come out here to picnic, to look for wildlife, or to walk the beach in search of agates. Canoeing in the river, swimming in Stormy Lake, fishing, and (in winter) cross-country skiing are also popular. Camping facilities are provided for RVs, tent campers, and boaters. State park rangers are based in Soldotna (tel. 262-5581).

Sports

FISHING   More than a dozen outfitters call Kenai home. A five-hour morning or afternoon outing to the banks of the Kenai River, including transportation to and from a Kenai motel, typically costs $125 per person, all inclusive. Check with **Kenai River Fishing** (tel. 262-5097), or **Fred Braun Sport Fishing,** 405 Overland St. (tel. 283-2665 or 283-4648).

WINTER SPORTS   There's a lighted outdoor rink for ice skating in Kenai, and an Olympic-size indoor arena (with an extended season) at the North Peninsula Recreation Area in Nikiski. Cross-country skiers have hundreds of square miles of flat, treeless terrain to lay their tracks across.

OTHER SPORTS   Kenai's **Peninsula Oilers,** who play in the Alaska Baseball League, are *the* game in town in the summertime. They play a 54-game June-to-August schedule against teams from the Anchorage and Fairbanks areas, including 27 home games at their park on Tinker Lane. Among their alumni are current major-league pitchers Dave Stieb of the Toronto Blue Jays and Frank Viola of the New York Mets.

There's golf at the new 18-hole **Kenai Golf Course,** 1420 Lawton Dr. (tel. 283-7500), with a pro shop and driving range.

The **swimming pools** at Kenai Central High School and Nikiski's North Peninsula Recreation Area are open to the public during scheduled hours. The **Kenai Recreation Center** has weight and exercise rooms, as well as racquetball, volleyball, and basketball courts. It's open from 6 a.m. to 10 p.m. Monday through Saturday and 1 to 10 p.m. on Sunday. Softball is a popular summer activity. For information, call **Kenai Parks and Recreation** (tel. 283-3855).

Nightlife

The **Rainbow Bar,** on Main Street at Overland, is cramped, crowded, smoky, and at this writing, the most popular rock 'n' roll club on the peninsula when there's live music (Tuesday through Saturday nights).

Larry's, on North Kenai Spur Road a couple of miles north of downtown, has live country-and-western music seven nights a week. This is a place where men still wear their Stetsons when slow-dancing.

The **Katmai Lounge,** in the Katmai Motel, downtown, has live C&W and rock oldies. A big, well-lit room, it has lots of seating and a friendly crowd.

First-run movies and occasional revivals are shown on the three screens at the **Kambe Theater,** 215 Willow St. (tel. 283-4554), downtown. Wednesday and matinee presentations cost just $2.

NINILCHIK

About 750 people live in the old Russian fishing village of Ninilchik, halfway between Soldotna and Homer. The new town on the Sterling Hwy. doesn't look like much more than a wide spot in the road, but seek out the winding road that turns downhill toward the shore of Cook Inlet, just past the Ninilchik River bridge. A handful of ramshackle log houses are still occupied by about two dozen descendants of 19th-century Russian colonists. Most today are commercial set-net beach fishermen who worship at the turn-of-the-century Russian Orthodox church overlooking the community from the top of a bluff. Visitors to the village and church are encouraged to park their cars in designated areas, travel on foot, and avoid cutting through private property.

It seems like an out-of-the-way location, but Ninilchik is the site of the annual **Kenai Peninsula State Fair** on the third weekend of August. There's a parade, horse and livestock shows, garden produce and flower exhibits, arts and crafts displays, and carnival entertainment—everything you'd expect of a small state fair.

HOMER

Few if any sights in Alaska surpass the arresting first view of Kachemak Bay one gets upon rounding the last big turn before Homer on the southbound Sterling Hwy. The heavily glaciated peaks of the Kenai Range rise dramatically above the deep-blue waters of the bay, while the Homer Spit—said to be the second longest in the world—paints a curlicue pattern from the forested foreshore. Off to the west you may see volcanic Mount Augustine island steaming away.

About 225 road miles (and half that many air miles) southwest of Anchorage, Homer has in recent years gained a reputation as the "Acapulco of Alaska"—for all the right reasons. It has great natural beauty, a warm mild climate (by Alaskan standards), numerous fine artisans, a fleet of deep-sea fishing boats, and a booming tourist industry.

Established in 1895 and named after an early gold prospector, Homer owed most of its turn-of-the-century settlement to the Cook Inlet Coal Fields Company, which built a town and dock on the 4½-mile-long spit and a railroad to the mines, seven miles away. Coal production dwindled, but fishermen and homesteaders arrived in the 1920s. Today fishing and seafood-processing are the most important industries. The construction of a $355-million hydroelectric project at Bradley Lake, just east of Kachemak Bay, began in 1986 and is expected to bring more people and money to the town. The population of 4,100 swells with summer tourists and fishery workers.

Moderated by the warm Japan Current, summer temperatures in Homer hover in the balmy 60s and low 70s, while midwinter temperatures are commonly 10°F to 20°F. The Kenai Range protects Kachemak Bay from the storms of the Gulf of Alaska; average annual precipitation in Homer is only 23 inches.

Orientation

For purposes of getting acquainted, Homer can be divided into four sections: Homer Bluffs, downtown, Ocean Drive, and the Spit. Entering Homer, the Sterling Hwy. forks, with the upper (left-hand) road becoming **Pioneer Avenue**, the main drag of downtown, and the lower road, the **Homer By-Pass,** heading directly toward the Spit. Above downtown rise the bluffs, peppered with residences. **Lake Street** intersects both Pioneer Avenue and the By-Pass at their eastern ends and crosses a lagoon known as Beluga Lake to reach **Ocean Drive.** This east-west strip of motels, restaurants, and businesses ends at the **Homer Spit Road,** which turns straight out to sea for nearly five miles.

Homer Airport (tel. 235-8588), served by two commercial carriers and several smaller air-taxi services, is on Kachemak Bay Drive, which runs east from Homer Spit Road just below its intersection with Ocean Drive. Beluga Lake is used by float-planes in summer, skiplanes in winter. The **Alaska Marine Hwy. System** (tel. 235-8449) connects Homer with Kodiak and Seldovia, as well as Seward and Valdez; the M/V *Tustumena* ties up at Ramp Two on the Spit.

A Smile Taxi (tel. 235-6995) or **Lynx Taxi** (tel. 235-5969) can meet you at the ferry or airport and shuttle you to your hotel. There are also several car-rental agencies, all with airport offices. They include **Avis** (tel. 235-9802) and **Hertz** (tel. 235-6614).

A small log cabin houses a **tourist information center** on Homer Spit Road opposite the Fishing Village. For advance arrangements, contact the **Homer Chamber of Commerce,** P.O. Box 541, Homer, AK 99601 (tel. 907/235-7740).

Homer has a weekly newspaper, the *Homer News;* a 38-bed hospital, the **South Peninsula Hospital,** on Bayview Avenue (tel. 235-8101); four banks; 19 churches; and numerous community organizations.

There are three festival periods. The town awakens from the frozen doldrums when the three-day **Winter Carnival** is staged beginning the first Friday of February. It opens with the Miss Homer pageant at the high school, picks up steam with a Saturday parade down Pioneer Avenue, and climaxes on Sunday with stock-car races —on frozen Beluga Lake. It includes such diversions as cherry-pit spitting and out-house racing, iceboat and cross-country ski races, a seafood-chowder-cooking contest, and arts-and-crafts exhibits.

The **Spring Arts Festival,** held over several weeks in late April and early May, is an annual "coming-out" for area artisans to show what they've produced in the winter. Painters and photographers, craftspeople and musicians, dancers and dramatists are all featured.

Memorial Day is the official opening of the tourist season, and the starting date of the **Homer Jackpot Halibut Derby,** which runs until Labor Day weekend. There are also the September (Labor Day weekend) **Taste of Homer,** an opportunity to snack on a variety of foods; October (Columbus Day weekend) **Kachemak Appreciation Days,** which honor the commercial fishing community and area pioneers; and a small arts-and-crafts-oriented **Renaissance Faire** the second weekend of December.

Where to Stay

There are numerous motels and other accommodations in Homer and its immediate vicinity. You can pay as much as $135 for an oceanfront suite or as little as $35 for a comfortable room if you're willing to share a bath. Camping, of course, is much cheaper yet. Summer rates apply from Memorial Day to Labor Day. All rates are subject to a 5% city bed tax.

MODERATELY PRICED ACCOMMODATIONS Much of the summer activity in Homer is centered on the Spit, so it's natural for many visitors to be attracted by its location to the **Land's End Resort,** 4786 Homer Spit Rd., Homer, AK 99603 (tel. 907/235-2500). Land's End is the last stop on the Spit: beyond here, in all directions but the one from which you came, it's all water. Sea otters, seals, and bald eagles frolic in the water and ashore, within easy sight of the hotel. Woodcarvings of a fisherman and mermaid stand on the roof over the entrance, luring you in.

There's a beautiful view of Kachemak Bay from the picture windows of the Chart Room restaurant, open from 6 a.m. to 10 p.m. daily. Seafood dinners are in the $14 to $19 range, and include mesquite-broiled salmon and halibut, and fresh Dungeness crab. The wine list has 50 domestic and foreign selections. The adjoining Wheelhouse Lounge has live entertainment Thursday through Sunday. It can get loud and boisterous during both shows and football games (the big-screen TV is a popular attraction). The Captain's Quarters, on the upper deck, is a quieter, more intimate lounge. It has a walk-out deck, wine by the glass, and oysters on the half shell.

The 40 rooms, decorated in blues or browns, have twin beds, dressers, satellite TVs, individually controlled heat, and new lighting. Fourteen have full baths; the others have showers but no tubs. All but 12 rooms have private decks facing the ocean. Six suites have queen-size beds and sofa beds to sleep additional guests. Rates for one or two are $65 to $95 from mid-March to mid-September, 30% less in the off-season. Land's End is closed from November to mid-March.

If staying on the Spit isn't essential, the **Best Western Bidarka Inn,** 575 Sterling Highway (P.O. Box 1408), Homer, AK 99603 (tel. 907/235-8148, or toll free 800/528-1234), might satisfy you more. Located on the Sterling Highway as it enters town, this may be Homer's finest mid-priced accommodation. The 74 spacious rooms, with orange carpets and cream trim, are furnished with queen-size beds, satellite TV-radio, direct-dial phone, and electric heat. There is a guest laundry, and shuttle service is available. A fitness center includes exercise equipment and hot tubs. Service can be abrupt, however.

A marine display hangs on the walls of the small lobby, through which you enter the Bidarka Inn's Periwinkle Gardens restaurant (open from 5 a.m. to 10 p.m. daily) and lounge.

Summer rates are $68 single, $76 double; in winter they drop slightly. Six units with kitchenettes are $10 more. A bidarka, by the way, is a sealskin Aleut kayak.

The **Lakewood Inn,** 984 Ocean Dr., Homer, AK 99603 (tel. 907/235-6146), is built on a bluff overlooking Beluga Lake with its waterfowl population and winter ice racing. The inn has 25 rooms, including five suites with kitchenettes. The cozy standard rooms, decorated in pastel tones against bare white walls, contain cable TVs, direct-dial phones (local calls are free), and electric heat.

From the windows of the restaurant, you can watch the ducks as you enjoy a continental breakfast (from 7 to 10 a.m.) or a buffet lunch for $6.75 (from 11 a.m. to 2 p.m.) or dinner for $9 (from 5 to 9 p.m.). The buffet includes a salad bar and ice-cream bar. The Mallard Lounge has specialty drinks plus non-alcoholic beverages "for the driver." Upstairs, the Raven's Nest sometimes has live music on weekends.

Summer rates (June through August) are $65 single, $70 double, $120 for suites. In the off-season, singles are $50 to $55; doubles, $55 to $65; suites, $70 to $85.

BUDGET ACCOMMODATIONS Entering the **Driftwood Inn,** 135 W. Bunnell Ave., Homer, AK 99603 (tel. 907/235-8019), is like walking into someone's living room. Jeff Murphy's 20-room guest mansion in old Homer has a stone fireplace surrounded by couches and chairs, a well-lit library alcove, hanging plants, and a big fish tank. To your left as you walk in is the reception desk and a community kitchen, with tables, a refrigerator, microwave, and complimentary coffee and tea for all.

The rooms vary considerably in size and furnishings, but two main themes prevail. The upstairs "Grandma's Place" rooms have calico curtains, patchwork quilts on double beds, wood and brass fittings, and other touches reminiscent of the '20s and '30s; most have private baths. The small downstairs "Ship's Quarters" units are like cabins on the Alaska ferry, with nautical décor and outside entrances; they share baths. All rooms have a desk and dresser, hot-water baseboard heat, color TV with in-house movies, and AM/FM radio.

There's also a TV in the living room, a community phone in the kitchen area, laundry facilities, and a courtesy car. On a deck facing Bishop's Beach are a picnic table and barbecue. The inn also has a playground for kids, five dog kennels (available by advance arrangement), conference facilities for up to 40 people, and fish-cleaning, shellfish-cooking, and freezing facilities.

Young, budget-conscious travelers love the Driftwood Inn. Rates are $50 to $75 single in summer, $40 to $65 in winter, plus $5 per additional person.

There's but one hotel on Homer's downtown strip: the log-construction **Heritage Hotel,** 147 E. Pioneer Ave., Homer, AK 99603 (tel. 907/235-7787). Its homey front lobby, with couches, chairs, and lots of green plants, gives you a comfortable feeling right away. The 36 rooms include 11 with shared bath, 5 with private bath, in the original (1946) building; and 20 with private bath in the 1980 annex. Rooms are decorated in earth tones and have a queen-size bed or two doubles, radio, phone (free local calls), electric heat, and courtesy coffee or tea. Newer rooms have color TVs with in-house movies.

Summer rates: with bath, singles are $50 and $60, and doubles run $55 and $65; without bath, singles are $45, and doubles, $50. Winter rates: with bath, singles go for $45 and $50, and doubles run $50 and $55; without bath, singles cost $40, and doubles are $45. The hotel's one suite (with a kitchenette) goes for $80 in summer, $70 in winter.

Remember that staggering view as the Sterling Hwy. turns toward Homer? From your room at the **Bay View Motel,** three miles west of downtown at 2851 Sterling Hwy. (P.O. Box 804), Homer, AK 99603 (tel. 907/235-8485), you can wake up to that scene every day. The 12 units are decorated in Cape Cod gray with white trim and furnished with double beds, desks, private facilities with showers (no baths), TVs, and hot-water heating. A phone is available in the office. Five rooms have kitchenettes, and there's a honeymoon suite with a fireplace and a separate guest cottage with a loft. Summer visitors can use the barbecue pit and picnic tables on the lawn; for winter visitors, a five-kilometer (three-mile) cross-country ski track begins across the highway. Room rates start at $59 single, $64 double, $89 for the suite or cottage, in summer; 25% less in winter.

BED-AND-BREAKFAST A large number of these home-stay establishments, encouraged by the boom in tourism, have been born in Homer in recent years.

Nearest to downtown is the **Brass Ring Bed & Breakfast,** 987 Hillfair Court, Homer, AK 99603 (tel. 907/235-5450). Guy and Renée Doyle are your hosts in this beautiful home custom-built of white spruce in late 1984 specifically as a B&B. Each of the five guest rooms is furnished with antiques and decorated with Norwegian country stenciling. Breakfasts are made to order in the big kitchen, and guests are encouraged to make themselves at home in the living room and den (with TV/VCR and library). The house has 2½ baths, a wood stove and electric heat, laundry facilities, and freezer space for fish. No smoking, please.

The Brass Ring is located on a cul-de-sac about two city blocks from the intersection of Pioneer Avenue and Lake Street. Rates in summer are $50 single, $60 double; in winter, $45 single, $55 double.

Moose occasionally wander through the yard of **Seekins' Bed & Breakfast,** Race Road (P.O. Box 1264), Homer, AK 99603 (tel. 907/235-8996), high on Homer Bluffs overlooking the city and bay. There's a variety of accommodation here—a one-bedroom cabin, a three-bedroom guesthouse atop a garage, a single room, and a family room in the main house. All but one of the units has its own kitchen; all have color TVs and warm décor. You're invited to share a big continental breakfast with hosts Floyd and Gert Seekins, who probably know Homer as well as or better than anyone: they also operate Homer Tours (see the "Tours" section, below) and arrange fishing charters. Call 235-8998 for referral to other B&Bs if Seekins' is full. Room rates are $40 and $45 single, $50 to $60 double.

Inquire at the tourist information center about other B&Bs in Homer. One that gets consistently good reports is the **Magic Canyon B&B,** 40015 Waterman Rd., at Mile 5 on East End Road (tel. 907/235-6077), where guests are invited to share in guided nature walks and lectures on Alaskan history and anthropology. The 75-acre homestead has a sundeck with a hot tub and a library of Alaskana.

Farther out of town, at Mile 9.9 on East End Road, is **Pavik's B&B** (tel. 907/

235-7383), lodged in a historic log cabin. Rooms are just $35. For those who want to rough it, a sheepherder's covered wagon is available for $25.

CAMPING First-time summer visitors are always stunned by the sea of tents and RVs set up just above the high-water mark on the Spit. The **Homer Spit Campground,** P.O. Box 1196, Homer, AK 99603 (tel. 907/235-8206), is open May to September and accepts reservations. For payment of a $9 fee, campers get rest rooms, tap water, hot showers, and a dump station. Electrical hookups for recreational vehicles are $13.50. The maximum stay is 14 days.

The City of Homer (tel. 907/235-8121) operates the 40-acre **City Campground** on Mullican Drive, near the hospital on the slopes overlooking town, and sells permits for camping on city land on the Spit. The fee for city camping is $4.

Where to Eat

Aside from the hotel eateries, particularly those at the Lakewood Inn and the Land's End Resort, there exist an ample handful of good restaurants at all price levels.

The more elegant among them offer a similar range of steak and seafood dishes. Out on the Spit, with second-story picture windows giving a full view of harbor activity, is the **Porpoise Room,** Fish Dock Road (tel. 235-7848). Its summer special is an all-you-can-eat seafood buffet, offered daily from 5:30 to 10 p.m. For $17 you can fill up on crab, shrimp, prawns, scallops, halibut, and salad bar. Most entrees are priced from $13.50 to $18. Open year round from 7 a.m. to midnight daily.

The Waterfront, Bunnell Avenue near Main Street in old Homer (tel. 235-8747), is known as the oldest restaurant in town. Today its lack of décor makes it more reminiscent of a local bar. But Homerites keep coming back for its steaks (from $15), its filet Oscar (with asparagus and crabmeat; $17), and its prime rib with Yorkshire pudding ($16). Lunch sandwiches are priced from $5 to $6.25.

East of Homer on East End Road are two popular steak-and-seafood spots. **T's Homestead,** eight miles out in Fritz Creek (tel. 235-8723), features a 22-ounce T-bone steak special for $23. Reservations, please. Dinner is served from 5 to 10 p.m. daily except Monday, and there is often Alaskan bush entertainment on weekends. The **Putter Inn,** overlooking Kachemak Bay, 4½ miles east of Homer (tel. 235-8644), offers a steak-and-teriyaki-shrimp special for $20. Open daily from 5 p.m. to the wee hours.

Homer's favorite lunch stop is the **Fresh Sourdough Express Bakery,** 1316 Ocean Dr. (tel. 235-7571). The Express began in 1982 as a green bakery van on the Spit; now the owners grind their own flour daily for 19 varieties of sourdough breads and five yeast breads. Breakfasts are typically stuffed savory croissants ($4), pastries, muffins, and sourdough waffles. Deli-style sandwiches cost $4 and $5 for lunch. There are homemade soups and an espresso bar. Take a number and get in line with the locals. Open year round from 6 a.m. to 10 p.m. daily. The bakery has a branch on the Spit, called **The Sourdough Connection** (tel. 235-8701), open from 6 a.m. to 8 p.m. daily.

Homer isn't rich in ethnic cuisine, but **Don Jose's,** 127 W. Pioneer Ave. (tel. 235-7963), is the place to come for Mexican and Italian food. A wrought-iron fence and hanging ivy divide the split-level restaurant in two. Oil-on-black-velvet paintings hang on the walls, and mariachi music is piped in. Have a full burrito grande dinner for $9 and wash it down with a raspberry margarita, or dine on lasagne with sausage for $7.25. Lunch specials (served until 2 p.m.) are priced from $5 to $7.25. Open from 11 a.m. to 11 p.m. Sunday through Thursday, until midnight on Friday and Saturday.

Don Jose's also has pizzas, but for that most Homerites gravitate to **Pizza Nick's,** 565 E. Pioneer Ave. (tel. 235-7312). A small pepperoni pizza costs $8; an extra-large (19-inch) "Nick's special" is $19.50. You can also enjoy a generous cannelloni for $9 or order any of several dinner entrees in the $6 to $9 range. Open from 11 a.m. to midnight Sunday through Thursday, to 1 a.m. on Friday and Saturday.

Homer's only Chinese restaurant is one of the most aptly named I've seen: **Chow's,** 435 E. Pioneer Ave. (tel. 235-6226). Enter through the rear of this small café to a virtual greenhouse of potted plants and cacti. There are a few booths and tables, plus counter space. Place your order at the window and wait for your name to be called. Oriental plates, like sweet-and-sour pork, broccoli beef, and teriyaki chicken, are $7 including eggroll, rice, and cookie. Full stir-fry shrimp-and-vegetable dinners with rice are $10. Diners with allergies will be pleased that the chefs refuse to use monosodium glutamate. Open Monday through Friday, 11 a.m. to 8:30 p.m.

On the Spit you'll find numerous seasonal fast-food hamburger and fish-and-chips shops. The consensus favorites seem to be the **Glacier Drive-In** and **Boardwalk Fish and Chips.** There's also a **McDonald's** on Lake Street.

What to See and Do

So much of Homer's summertime activity centers on the Spit that it might be a good idea to take a downtown walking tour before you head for Kachemak Bay.

DOWNTOWN HOMER Start at the west end of Pioneer Avenue where it branches off the Sterling Hwy. On your left, just before the intersection of Barlett Street, you'll see the hexagonal headquarters offices of the **Alaska Maritime National Wildlife Refuge,** 202 W. Pioneer Ave. (tel. 235-6546). Open from 8 a.m. to 5 p.m. weekdays, the building contains a visitor center with displays, interpretive exhibits, maps, and literature on the birds and sea mammals of the refuge. Alaska Maritime refuge comprises more than 2,500 islands, islets, rocks, reefs, and headlands of the Alaskan coast, from the southeast rain forest to Arctic Ocean tundra. Most of the Aleutian Islands and the smaller islands of the Gulf of Alaska and Bering Sea are part of the 3.5-million-acre refuge. Some 15 to 30 million birds of 55 species nest in the refuge, as well as thousands of sea lions, seals, walruses, and sea otters. Closest to Homer are designated shore areas and islands of Kachemak Bay and the Cook Inlet.

Just around the corner at 3779 Bartlett St. is the **Pratt Museum** (tel. 235-8635) of the Homer Society of Natural History. One of Alaska's finest museums, the Pratt has two floors of exhibits of nature and anthropology. There are dioramas of large land animals, mounted bird displays, two saltwater aquariums which show the deep-sea life of Kachemak Bay, exhibits of prehistoric tools, artifacts of modern industry, and a botanical garden of Alaskan wildflowers. A museum shop sells gifts and publications. The museum also has a reference library and media collection, functions as a Marine Mammal Information Center, and hosts adult education workshops. Admission is $3 for adults, $2 for seniors, $1 for students 18 and under, free for children under 6. Open daily in summer from 10 a.m. to 5 p.m.; in winter, closed Monday and for the month of January.

Farther east on Pioneer Avenue is the **Homer Public Library,** the Tourist Information Center, and—just past Pizza Nick's restaurant—**Ptarmigan Arts,** 471 E. Pioneer Ave. (tel. 235-5345). Of the numerous galleries in Homer, this is probably the single best place to survey the work of the town's artists. Ptarmigan Arts is a co-op, and each of the 45 to 50 member artisans contributes time and energy to run the shop and studios. They work in many media, including painting, sculpture, pottery, basketry, weaving, leatherwork, woodcarving, stained glass, metalsmithing, jewelry, scrimshaw, and photography. Open from 10 a.m. to 7 p.m. daily. Across Pioneer Avenue is a new co-op gallery, the **Arctic Wolf Gallery.**

Don't miss a visit to **Alaska Wild Berry Products,** 528 E. Pioneer Ave. (tel. 235-8858). Homer's most famous shop and "factory" gathers the numerous tasty berries from the meadows and hillsides of the Kenai Peninsula, then juices, pulps, and blends them into natural jams, jellies, and sauces. No preservatives are used in the process, which visitors can watch from beginning to end through showcase windows. Sample the jams, homemade fudge, and candies in a tasting room. Wild Berry Products has an excellent gift shop of various souvenir items as well as their own gift packs, and a mini-museum of local pioneer and prehistoric artifacts. Open daily from 10 a.m. to 5 p.m.

THE HOMER SPIT   The very existence of a commercial community on the Spit represents an uneasy truce between man and nature. Turned into a tidal island by the '64 earthquake, rebuilt but again washed out by a storm in 1979, the Spit has been resurrected by steel bulkheads and concrete blocks. As a visitor, you'll travel about 3½ miles out on the Spit before you see much of anything but sand, rocks, and water. Then, suddenly, you're right in the middle of the action.

Businesses are built around the newly enlarged **Small Boat Basin**. Located on the Spit's east (leeward) side, this is the home of the 98 boats operated by 60 charter-boat firms, as well as a great many private fishing and pleasure craft.

As you drive out the Spit, two boardwalk "villages" on your right are sure to catch your eye. Both are populated by fishing-charter operators, gift shops, and small cafés. The **Fishing Village** is built high above the waterline on pilings, while the **Cannery Row Boardwalk** has a collection of gray Cape Cod–style shanties.

The ramshackle lighthouse across Spit Road from the Boardwalk is the **Salty Dawg** (tel. 235-9990). Built in 1897, it has somehow survived all Spit catastrophes as a school, a post office, a grocery store, a railroad station, a coal-mining office, and an oil company headquarters. Today it's a saloon, famous statewide as a sometimes-rowdy hangout for fishermen and "tent city" denizens.

On the grounds of the Homer Spit Campground is a rustic sign that reads: **"The Eagle's Spot:** Keep Out." From late January to May, before the campground opens for the season, you may see more American bald eagles in this one spot than you have collectively seen in your entire life up until then. I counted more than 100 on the beach in a five-minute sitting. But if you picture a bald eagle as a perpetually majestic raptor, your romanticism may be shattered by the scavenger practices of these birds of prey.

Seward Fisheries, 842 Fish Dock Rd. (tel. 235-8107), near the end of the Spit, will give tours of its processing facilities on request. Inquire at **Icicle Seafood Market** on the west side of the fisheries building.

HALIBUT COVE   Halibut Cove, with its spruce-cloaked islet and peninsula surrounding a deep green lagoon, is beyond doubt one of the most charming small communities in the state of Alaska. It is kept that way in part because it cannot be reached by road—only by boat or floatplane.

Between 1911 and 1928 this isolated location was the site of a thriving herring fishery, with 36 salteries (fish-curing plants) supporting a population of nearly 1,000. After waste pollution drove the fishermen out of business, bootleggers concealed their stills here during Prohibition times.

In its late-20th-century incarnation the community of Halibut Cove owes its existence to Clem Tillion, who bought Ismailof Island as a young man in 1943 and established it as a family estate. Tillion, who retired as speaker of the Alaska House of Representatives but remains a member of the North Pacific Fisheries Commission, is the father figure for a tightly knit artists' community of about 65 year-round residents, swelling to about 125 in summer.

About a mile of boardwalks connects the boat dock with the large green Tillion home—you'll recognize it by the birdhouses for nesting swallows (they eat the mosquitoes) under the eaves—and the cove's first and only restaurant, **The Saltry** (tel. 296-2223). The fare here is exotic seafood like sushi, salmon caviar, ceviche, black cod, and sable fish chowder. Queasy stomachs can get a cheese plate. Prices range from $5 to $12. The ample wine list includes sake, and Black Hook Premium Ale is on tap. Dinner is served from 2 to 9 p.m.; reservations are required.

Clem's wife, Diana Tillion, an artist renowned for her octopus-ink paintings, operates the **Cove Gallery.** Within this geodesic dome structure you can see the paintings and sculptures of many of Halibut Cove's artisan residents.

If you feel you'd like to stay a while, there are several accommodation options in the cove. The **Quiet Place Lodge,** P.O. Box 6474, Halibut Cove, AK 99603 (tel. 907/296-2212), has five guest cabins with a full bath in the main lodge building, and a separate sauna. Daily bed-and-breakfast rates are $100 per cabin for two people ($150 for four adults). For extended stays, full board and guided boating, fishing, or hiking excursions run $175 per person per day, all inclusive. The **Ishmalof Island Lodge,** P.O. Box 6430, Halibut Cove, AK 99603 (tel. 907/296-2217), charges $195 per day (all inclusive) for four or more guests. Unless you have your own boat you must arrange to be picked up at the Saltry. Artist Sydney Bishop's two cozy **Halibut Cove Cabins,** P.O. Box 1990, Homer, AK 99603 (tel. 907/296-2214 in Halibut Cove or 235-8110 in Homer), are situated at the east end of Ismailof Island. Bring your own food and bedding; cushions, kitchen appliances, a wood stove, well water, and showers are provided. Rates are $70 a day or $350 a week for two.

The **Kachemak Bay Ferry** (tel. 235-7847 in Homer, 296-2223 in Halibut Cove) is the 34-passenger *Danny J,* a fishing boat-cum-shuttle service. It leaves the Spit daily at 1 p.m. for Halibut Cove via Gull Island (more on which later). After a 1½-hour layover it departs the cove at 4 p.m. for the return run to Homer. The round-trip fare for this tour is $30. The ferry leaves again for the cove at 5 p.m., returning at 10 p.m.; on this trip it carries only cove residents or visitors with dinner reservations at the Saltry. Fare is $15.

KACHEMAK BAY   This long inlet's entire south shore—not just Halibut Cove—is a world unto itself.

Most of the land here, from the bayshore over the crest of the Kenai Mountains to the Gulf of Alaska, is part and parcel of **Kachemak Bay State Park** or the adjoining **Kachemak Bay State Wilderness Park.** Together they comprise some 350,000 acres of primitive mountain and fjord terrain. There are only three short hiking trails in the preserves, two of them from near Halibut Cove (to the Grewingk Glacier and to Leisure Lake). Hunting, fishing, and trapping are allowed in the parks, but horses and motorized vehicles are not. The *Danny J* offers dropoff service to adventurous hikers and campers. The Alaska Division of Parks (tel. 235-7024) has detailed information.

Of chief interest to Homer visitors are several coastal enclaves. The first of note is a community of birds. **Gull Island,** about three miles off the Spit, is a major bird rookery and a part of Alaska Maritime National Wildlife Refuge. An estimated 8,000 puffins, guillemots, kittiwakes, murres, cormorants, and gulls nest on this barren, rocky outcropping, and numerous other species frequently visit.

Nearby, in Peterson Bay, is the **Center for Alaskan Coastal Studies** of the non-profit China Poot Bay Society (tel. 235-6667). Kachemak Bay has a unique marine ecosystem, which the society was established to protect. An astonishing variety of invertebrate species, mollusks, and crustaceans make their homes in the tidepools of Peterson and China Poot Bays, two small inlets on opposite sides of a peninsula just west of Halibut Cove. The entire bay is rich in fish, marine mammals, and sea, shore, and woodland birds. Visitors to the marine research center are treated to explorations of tidepools, subarctic rain forest, and prehistoric archeological sites.

Rainbow Tours, on Homer's Cannery Row Boardwalk (tel. 235-7272), offers daily tours to Gull Island and Peterson Bay departing from the Spit at 9 a.m., noon, and (Gull Island only) 4 p.m. The fare is $30 (children pay $15) to the Center for Alaskan Coastal Studies, or $15 ($10 for children) for Gull Island alone. Plan on spending all day at the center.

China Poot Bay is also the site of the **Kachemak Bay Wilderness Lodge,** P.O. Box 956, Homer, AK 99603 (tel. 907/235-8910). Acclaimed in the pages of *The Hideaway Report* newsletter as "America's best wilderness lodge," it offers days of leisure spent in a beautiful natural environment.

Host Mike McBride is a member of the prestigious Explorers Club and is a registered guide and naturalist, a licensed skipper, and a former bush pilot. His wife, Diane, a biologist and emergency medical technician, is the lodge's gourmet chef. Together with a staff of eight, they have created an experience that begs to be embraced—for those who can afford it.

Everything is provided, from hip boots to French wine. The lodge has its own electric generator, a sod-roofed Finnish sauna, and a community bath and shower. A maximum of eight to ten guests at a time stay in private cabins with wood stoves and electric lights. Family-style meals are served in the huge main lodge. The ingredients are seafood from the bay, fruits and berries from the hills, vegetables from a backyard garden, and homemade bread from a wood oven.

The minimum stay is five days. All-inclusive package rates are $1,750 per person, including round-trip transfer from Homer. The lodge is open to guests from May to mid-December.

A few miles west are two long, finger-like fjords, Sadie Cove and Tutka Bay. Each has a lodge of its own. Keith Iverson's **Sadie Cove Wilderness Lodge**, P.O. Box 2265, Homer, AK 99603 (tel. 907/235-7766), has three four-person cabins; rates are $200 per day per person, with a two-day minimum. John and Nelda Osgood's **Tutka Bay Lodge**, P.O. Box 960, Homer, AK 99603 (tel. 907/235-8163), has deluxe accommodations for up to 15 guests with rates from $200 per day, room and board, per person, including transportation from Homer and guide service.

Near the Tutka Bay Lodge is one of the Alaska Department of Fish and Game's most remote facilities, the **Tutka Lagoon Hatchery** (tel. 235-8191 in Homer). Built in 1976, it has a capacity of 30 million salmon eggs, mainly pink and chum. Visitors are welcome.

SELDOVIA Spread across a low promontory, completely surrounded by water and mountains, Seldovia's secluded charm makes it a popular destination for many visitors.

This fishing village of about 700 people was settled by the Russians in the late 18th century as a year-round harbor and coal port. Salmon and crab processing are the main industries. Seldovia was once famed for a half-mile boardwalk which served as its main street; this was destroyed when the land mass dropped about four feet into the bay during the 1964 earthquake. Only a small portion of the boardwalk was preserved when the town was rebuilt. Some of the town's past does remain intact, however: **St. Nicholas Russian Orthodox Church,** long the social hub of Seldovia, was built in 1891 on a hill overlooking the harbor. Restored in 1981, it's still in use today.

Visitors come to Seldovia not to visit indoor attractions, but to enjoy fishing, hiking, birdwatching, and cross-country skiing. For information, contact the **Seldovia Chamber of Commerce,** P.O. Drawer F, Seldovia, AK 99663 (tel. 907/234-7816).

Seldovia is served by the **Alaska Marine Highway System** (tel. 234-7868). The ferry M/V *Tustumena* operates between Homer and Seldovia twice weekly in summer, leaving Homer at 2:30 a.m. on Tuesday (with immediate return) and 11:45 a.m. on Wednesday (with a 3¼-hour layover). In fall and early spring, service is once weekly (leaving Homer Tuesday at 1:15 p.m., returning from Seldovia at 3:30 p.m.); there's no service while the *Tustumena* is in maintenance from January to mid-March. One-way fares are $12 for adults, $6 for children 6 to 11.

Daily year-round ferry service is offered by **Rainbow Tours** (tel. 235-7272 in Homer), leaving Homer at 1 a.m., returning from Seldovia at 4 p.m. Adult fares are $30 round trip, $20 one way; children pay $20 and $10.

Where to stay in Seldovia? Annie McKenzie's **Boardwalk Hotel,** P.O. Box 72, Seldovia, AK 99663 (tel. 907/234-7816), has modern rooms on the waterfront for $58 single, $84 double. **Stamper's Bayview Lodge,** Drawer A, Seldovia, AK

99663 (tel. 907/234-7631), has furnished one- and two-bedroom condominium units from $40. **Seldovia Lodge,** P.O. Box 136, Seldovia, AK 99663 (tel. 907/234-7654), changes rates from $36 to $48 for rooms with satellite TV; the restaurant has a salad bar, Saturday barbecue, and live music in the lounge weekends. You can also dine at the **Kachemak Kafé** (tel. 234-7494), open daily from 7 a.m. to 5 p.m., and the **Centurion Restaurant** (tel. 234-7676), a seafood-and-steak spot facing the boat harbor.

MOUNT AUGUSTINE Seventy miles west of Kachemak Bay, on the west side of the Cook Inlet, is a volcanic island that may rumble or send up smoke plumes during your visit to Homer. Mount Augustine was very active as recently as the spring of 1986, sending ash clouds over Homer and Seldovia, grounding planes, and sending citizens running for dust masks and air filters. During a volcanic eruption a tsunami (tidal wave) is always a danger. If you hear sirens, head for high ground!

AIR TAXIS AND FLIGHTSEEING The fastest way to the wilderness, including the maritime wilderness, is by air. Whether you're sightseeing or on a fishing or hunting expedition, there are numerous charter-flight operators in Homer. **Kachemak Air Service,** P.O. Box 1769, Homer, AK 99603 (tel. 235-8924), offers scenic flights in DeHavilland Beavers and Otters at a rate of $50 per seat. Other flight operators include **Cook Inlet Aviation,** 2060 Kachemak Dr., Homer, AK 99603 (tel. 235-8163); **Homer Air,** P.O. Box 302, Homer, AK 99603 (tel. 235-8591); and **Beluga Lake Float Plane Service,** P.O. Box 2072, Homer, AK 99603 (tel. 235-8256).

ANCHOR POINT This small community on the Sterling Hwy., 16 miles northwest of Homer, has one chief claim to fame: it represents the most westerly point on the North American continent that can be reached by a continuous road system. (The easternmost is Cape Breton, Nova Scotia.) A marker designates the spot.

The town's population of 226 swells in the summer with the arrival of hordes of fishermen seeking the steelhead and silver salmon that run in the Anchor River.

Four miles east of Anchor Point is the **Norman Lowell Studio and Gallery** (tel. 235-7344), billed as Alaska's largest private art gallery. Lowell, an artist who has made his home here since 1959, also shares his original homestead and garden with visitors. Open Monday through Saturday from 9 a.m. to 9 p.m. (to 6 p.m. on Wednesday) and from 1 to 5 p.m. on Sunday.

The **Anchor River Inn,** P.O. Box 154, Anchor Point, AK 99556 (tel. 907/235-8531), has 20 comfortable rooms with queen-size beds, TVs, and electric heat. The spacious newer units are priced at $55 single, $60 double, year round; the cozy older rooms are a budget bargain at $30 single, $35 double. A restaurant is open for three meals a day.

Inland from Anchor Point, up the North Fork road, is a unique community of Russian-Americans known in Homer as "The Old Believers." In their settlement of **Nikolaevsk,** they pursue the original lifestyles of their 17th-century ancestors who refused to conform to mandated changes in their traditional Orthodox faith. While the people don't appreciate curious visitors in their isolated village, they can frequently be seen in their colorful costumes in Anchor Point and Homer.

Sports

FISHING Many Anchorage residents and other Alaskans come to Homer specifically for the fishing. There's no shortage of craft here to take them out into Kachemak Bay and the Cook Inlet looking for halibut and other species: at last count, 60 charter-boat firms had 98 vessels available.

One good way to choose your boat and skipper is to wander around the small-boat harbor on the Homer Spit as charters are coming in with their catches, and see who has been most successful in snaring the "big ones." I had good luck with **North Country Halibut Charters,** P.O. Box 889, Homer, AK 99603 (tel. 235-7620). They have an office on the Cannery Row Boardwalk. **Central Charters Booking Agency,** 4241 Homer Spit Rd., Homer, AK 99603 (tel. 235-7847), will be happy to line you up quickly with any available boat. Typical rates are $100 per person for a 12-hour excursion (starting at 7 a.m.) or until you've caught your limit.

Summer fishermen and women can buy $2 tickets and enter the **Homer Jackpot Halibut Derby,** running from Memorial Day to Labor Day. The largest fish caught during the summer wins a jackpot of between $5,000 and $10,000; it usually takes a 350-pounder to capture the prize. Daily bonuses are offered for the big fish of the day.

You can get licenses and buy tackle, or camping gear from sporting goods shops. Try **Sportsman Marine Supply** (tel. 235-8918) or **Kachemak Gear Shed** (tel. 235-5562), both on the Spit.

If you do catch that big one, **The Exchange** on the Spit (tel. 235-6241), will vacuum-pack, smoke, freeze, and/or ship it to your home.

DIVING Given Kachemak Bay's rich underseas life, this is a natural. **Marine Service and Diving,** on the Cannery Row Boardwalk (tel. 235-7643), gives diving tours, lessons, and recommendations, and will help you with equipment rental. Windsurfing and waterskiing lessons can also be arranged daily except Monday from 9 a.m. to 5 p.m.

HIKING Most of it is across the bay in Kachemak Bay State Park. Nearer to Homer, the **Diamond Creek Trail,** opposite Diamond Ridge Road west of town, winds down a creek valley to a lonely stretch of beach. Figure 45 minutes each way.

One Homer agency can arrange almost any wilderness experience, from dog sledding to horse packing to glacier skiing. Check with **Kachemak Wilderness Adventures,** 4306 Homer Spit Rd., Homer, AK 99603 (tel. 235-6094), and specify the type of adventure you're looking for. The shop also provides guide service and rents equipment.

HORSEBACK RIDING **Kachemak Bay Horseback Adventures,** 58335 East End Rd. (tel. 235-7850), will take you for country lopes to historic homesteads and archeological sites, and will provide all your meals, from a farm breakfast to a ranch-style dinner.

HUNTING The place to go for bear, sheep, goats, moose, and other animals is Kachemak Bay State Park. Contact the Alaska Department of Fish and Game, 2355 Kachemak Dr. (tel. 235-6564), for regulations and other information.

KAYAKING For rentals, contact **Yak Treks,** 53970 Canyon Rd. (tel. 235-8302). They'll also take you on six-hour lunch tours to Gull Island and Halibut Cove, or multiday trips into Kachemak Bay State Park, including all food and equipment. **Quiet Sports,** on Pioneer Avenue (tel. 235-8620), rents single kayaks for $30 and $35 a day, doubles for $50.

Ageya Kayak Tours, P.O. Box 141506, Anchorage, AK 99514 (tel. 907/248-7140, or 235-8345 in Homer), offers guided voyages into the state park as well as kayaking seminars and wilderness studies courses. Ageya also takes remote seven-day paddles into the Kenai Fjords (about $725 per person) and around Shuyak Island, off Kodiak Island (from $825 per person). Prices include equipment, food, air transportation, and a guide/instructor.

WINTER SPORTS If you're not into ice-racing stock cars, you can at least put on a pair of **skates** and glide around Beluga Lake. Downhill **skiers** will find a rope tow on Ohlson Mountain; cross-country skiers enjoy the terrain out East End Road. **Snowmobilers** usually head farther afield, into the Caribou Hills or 20 miles out East End Road. Inquire at Quiet Sports, Pioneer Avenue (tel. 235-8620), about possible equipment rentals.

MISCELLANEOUS SPORTS **Kachemak Bowl,** Pioneer Avenue at Lake Street (tel. 235-8666), has eight lanes. **Bicyclists** can rent wheels from **Quiet Sports,** on Pioneer Avenue across from the library (tel. 235-8620). A one-mile public **orienteering** course starts behind Homer High School at the wooden bridge. **Roller skaters** will find a rink at Lakeside Mall. The **Kachemak Bay Gun Club** (tel. 235-7442 or 235-6894) has a pistol range and trapshooting. The public can use the **swimming pool** and **tennis courts** at the high school (tel. 235-7416 or 235-6090). **Weightlifters** will find Nautilus equipment at Hot Tub Emporium, on Pioneer Avenue in the basement of the Acropolis Building.

For information on these and other sports activities, contact the **Homer Recreation Department** (tel. 235-6210).

Tours

Gert Seekins's **Homer Tours,** P.O. Box 1264, Homer, AK 99603 (tel. 235-8996), takes visitors high above Homer on Skyline Drive for superb views of the city, Spit, and bay. They also stop at the Pratt Museum, the Norman Lowell Art Studio and other galleries, and Wild Berry Products, and finish up with a tour of the Seward Fisheries processing plant. Custom trips can also be arranged. Standard rates are $25 per person for a four-hour tour.

Nightlife

Homer's hot spot is **Alice's Champagne Palace,** a big barn-like building on Pioneer Avenue (tel. 235-7650). Alaska's best rock bands play here, unless they're preempted by national or international recording artists. Dance to the live music from 10 p.m. Wednesday through Sunday, and continue until 5 a.m. There's also a pool table, pinball machines, and video games. Margie's Kitchen serves burgers, tamales, and other fast food from 11:30 a.m. to midnight Sunday through Wednesday, until 2 a.m. Thursday through Saturday.

Two other downtown spots also do a brisk business. **Hobo Jim's Alaskan Bar,** on Pioneer Avenue across from Alice's (tel. 235-9932), has been remodeled since Hobo Jim, a noted bush-ballad and sea-shanty singer, bought what previously was Jack's Other Place. The **Bayside Lounge,** adjoining Mama Mia's at 445 E. Pioneer Ave. (tel. 235-6921) features solo country guitarists. Some 4½ miles east of Homer on East End Road, the **Putter Inn** (tel. 235-8644) has a big dance floor with local rock or country-and-western bands.

Out on the Spit, the **Wheelhouse Lounge** at Land's End Resort (tel. 235-6178) always does good business. But for real Spit atmosphere you must visit the ramshackle **Salty Dawg** (tel. 235-9990). It's nearly a century old, and looks it, with a sawdust floor, initials carved into all the counters and tables, and flags, lifebuoys, and T-shirts hanging from the ceilings and walls. This saloon is famous throughout Alaska as a fishermen's den. When it's stormy out, some of them come at 11 a.m. when the Salty Dawg opens and stay till closing around 5 a.m.

The bar scene aside, Homer has a very active performing arts schedule throughout the year. Dance troupes, theatrical companies, musicians, and others frequently visit the town. Contact the **Homer Council on the Arts,** P.O. Box 1764, Homer, AK 99603 (tel. 235-5675), for this year's schedule.

Pier One, Homer's community theater group, presents a series of summer plays in an old warehouse on the Spit. It also has a regular season running October to May, featuring contemporary and classical drama and comedy. A new group called **Fresh Produce** specializes in improvisational theater, and there are several small local dance companies.

Homer Family Theater, at Main Street and Pioneer Avenue (tel. 235-6728), has first-run films. The **Pratt Museum,** 3779 Bartlett St. (tel. 235-8635), offers an educational film series from June to August, with showtime at 7 p.m. on Thursday at the museum.

2. Prince William Sound

The sparkling blue waters of forest-shrouded, isle-studded Prince William Sound are a playground both for Anchorage boaters and myriad marine mammals. The fjords and inlets of this magnificent expanse see a regular traffic of pleasure boats and cruise ships, ferries and oil tankers, trollers and kayaks. They also see a wealth of humpback and other whales, seals and sea lions, porpoises and sea otters.

Many Alaska visitors venture into Prince William Sound specifically to view the Columbia Glacier. Truly, it's worth the trip. This massive tidewater glacier, 5 miles wide at its terminus and 41 miles long, covers as much ground as does the city of Los Angeles. To moor among harbor seals a short distance from the roar of the glacier's calving ice, or to hover over it in a helicopter, is an experience not easily forgotten.

But the sound is more than one glacier, of course. In all, well over a dozen glaciers tumble into its waters. Almost completely encompassed in Chugach National Forest, there are 15 public-use cabins and numerous other recreational opportunities on the shores of the sound. Each of its three main settlements has a character all its own—tiny Whittier (pop. 330), the jumping-off point for Anchorage visitors; Valdez (pop. 3,700), Alaska pipeline oil port and center of a thriving tourist trade; and Cordova (pop. 2,600), a laid-back fishing town near the mouth of the Copper River.

Shielded from Gulf of Alaska storms by two large islands at its southern entrance, Montague and Hinchinbrook, Prince William Sound enjoys a mild if wet climate. Summer temperatures are usually in the 50s and 60s Fahrenheit, while the midwinter average is in the 20s. But precipitation in different corners of the sound ranges from 60 to 180 inches annually. Good raingear is essential.

For general information on Prince William Sound, contact the offices of **Chugach National Forest,** 201 E. Fourth Ave., Anchorage, AK 99501 (tel. 907/ 271-2500), the Valdez Convention and Visitors Bureau, or the chamber of commerce in Cordova.

GETTING THERE

The only town on Prince William Sound with road access is Valdez. The Richardson Hwy. connects Valdez with Glennallen, 121 miles north via snowy Thompson Pass; from there it's a straight drive to either Anchorage (another 181 miles west) or Fairbanks (250 miles north). Various tour buses ply the six-hour route regularly in summer.

Valdez and Cordova both are served by regularly scheduled flights. Cordova, in fact, is a daily stop (each way) for **Alaska Airlines** on its Anchorage–Juneau run. Call the airline's toll-free number (tel. 800/426-0333), or the offices in Cordova (tel. 424-7151), Anchorage (tel. 243-3300), or Juneau (tel. 789-0600). Valdez is served twice daily to and from Anchorage by **ERA,** an Alaska Airlines commuter line; call toll free (tel. 800/426-0333), or in Valdez (tel. 835-2636) or Anchorage (tel. 243-3300). Within the area of the sound itself there are air-taxi lines based in all three towns. (In Whittier there are float planes only.)

Unquestionably the best way to see Prince William Sound is by sea. The ferries of the **Alaska Marine Highway System** do it most often and for the least cost. The M/V *Bartlett* is a permanent fixture in the sound, shuttling back and forth between Cordova and Valdez (a six-hour voyage) several times a week. From mid-May through mid-September the route is extended to include Whittier and the Columbia Glacier five times weekly; as an added bonus, a U.S. Forest Service naturalist accompanies these trips as a narrator. When the *Bartlett* goes into port for nine weeks' annual maintenance in mid-March, travelers must depend on the weekly visits of the M/V *Tustumena,* which connects Valdez and Cordova with Seward, Homer, Kodiak, and occasionally, other points west. Typical deck-class fares are: Whittier–Valdez, $54; Valdez–Cordova, $24; Cordova–Seward, $54. For further information, contact the Alaska Marine Hwy. System, P.O. Box R, Juneau, AK 99811 (tel. toll free 800/544-2251, 800/551-7185 in Alaska), or call the terminal in Valdez (tel. 835-4436) or Cordova (tel. 424-7333).

The only practical way to reach Whittier from Anchorage is by train via Portage. The half-hour Whittier Shuttle runs four to six times daily in summer, less often in winter. The fare is $9 from Portage or $18 one way from Anchorage; passengers are usually bused from the **Alaska Railroad** station in Anchorage (tel. 265-2685) to meet the shuttle.

Most major Alaskan tour companies offer Prince William Sound cruises via the Columbia Glacier. I like the service and narration provided by **Columbia Glacier Cruises,** 547 W. Fourth Ave. (P.O. Box 479), Anchorage, AK 99510 (tel. 907/276-8866), aboard the M/V *Glacier Queen II.* The *Queen* is a luxury yacht with two seating decks, a full bar and galley. (Gray Line of Alaska obviously likes the boat, because they book their Columbia Glacier tours on it.) The tour can be taken as a one- or two-day trip, either eastbound or westbound, with road or air connections between Anchorage and Valdez. The one-day fly/cruise price is $208; the standard two-day trip, including overnight shared accommodation in Valdez, is $249. Tours operate from the Memorial Day holiday to mid-September.

Alaska Sightseeing Tours, 543 W. Fourth Ave., Anchorage, AK 99501 (tel. 907/276-1305), offers one- and two-day cruises in the sound aboard the sleek M/V *Glacier Seas.* The tour operators promise gourmet meals and more scenery aboard this luxury yacht than others can provide. The one-day fly-cruise price is $248; the two-day drive/cruise price, including hotel in Valdez, is $299 single, $249 twin. If you travel between mid-May and June 15 or after September 1 (until September 15), you'll pay just $275 single, $225 twin. Children 5 to 11 get a discount.

WHITTIER

Tour brochures say Whittier is "unique . . . even in Alaska." How right they are. Well over half of the town's population lives in a single building, the 14-story Begich Towers, which also contains the city hall, post office, library, grocery store, café, museum, and art gallery. Most of the others live in a private condominium.

If the community is reminiscent of a military camp, well, that's what it was. Whittier was a prime debarkation point for cargo and troops of the Alaska Command after the Portage–Prince William Sound railroad spur was completed in 1943. About 1,200 people lived here until 1960, when the command was deactivated. The Buckner Building, now a hollow concrete skeleton awaiting renovation, was then the primary residence: a city under one roof, it held 1,000 apartments, a hospital, school, library, bank, restaurants, shops, radio station, theater, bowling alley, gymnasium, swimming pool, jail, and morgue.

Although ferries and summer cruise ships tie up in Whittier, the community really cannot be considered more than a jumping-off place. Most activities in Whittier are of the outdoor variety, mainly hiking and boating. But these are often put on hold by days on end of wind gusting to 90 mph (chiefly in winter) and an average annual precipitation of 173 inches, including 22 feet of snow.

If you are inclined to tarry in Whittier, you can get information at the **City Office** in Begich Towers (tel. 472-2327). The **Whittier Historical & Fine Arts Museum,** on the first floor of the Towers, is open from 1 to 6 p.m. daily except Tuesday and Thursday.

The two visitor accommodations are *not* in Begich Towers. The **Sportsman's Inn,** P.O. Box 698, Whittier, AK 99693 (tel. 907/472-2352), is on a low bluff overlooking the sea-train terminal. It has a pleasant restaurant and bar, with rooms for $43 single, $49 double. The **Anchor Inn,** P.O. Box 746, Whittier, AK 99693 (tel. 907/472-2354), is located between the railroad shop and Begich Towers. It has a coffeeshop and rooms ($35 double) which belie the somewhat weathered outward appearance of the building.

Most visitors to Whittier, however, restrict their wanderings to the shoreward area between the railroad tracks, ferry dock, and small-boat harbor. Numerous fishing and cruise boats and sailing charters operate out of the harbor, frequently run by weekend sailors commuting from Anchorage. The **Harbor Office** (tel. 472-2330) can give you a full list and make recommendations depending on your needs and desires.

One outfit in particular deserves special note. **Alaskan Wilderness Sailing Safaris,** P.O. Box 701, Whittier, AK 99693, or P.O. Box 1313, Valdez, AK 99686 (tel. 907/338-2134 in summer or 907/835-5175 in winter), offers a variety of sailing options, from open cruises to special-interest trips. The latter, operating on a predetermined schedule, have in the past included a women's sailing week, guided naturalist tour, marine resources, wilderness and glacier photography, and songs and lore of the sea. A week's trip costs $550, including food and skipper service. Voyages are planned from mid-May into September. Write for details.

Whittier is also the point of departure for **Alaska Sea Kayaking,** 211 S. Bailey St., Palmer, AK 99645 (tel. 907/745-3487). Folks aged 12 to 70 have enjoyed paddling through the quiet coves and bays of the sound from May until September. Trips are three to seven days in duration, and cost an average of $80 to $90 per person per day.

The world's largest **kittiwake rookery** is just across Passage Canal from Whittier, beside a glacier-fed cascade. For many boaters, including ferries and cruise liners, the rookery is the first or last stop before arriving in, or after departing from, Whittier.

COLUMBIA GLACIER

The Columbia Glacier is so large—440 square miles in area—that to see the entire ice flow you'd have to be a good distance above it in a plane or helicopter. Cruise boats can approach the glacial terminus to within about half a mile; even from there, the thunder of ice chunks falling from its 200-foot cliff face is almost deafening. Ferries are restricted from approaching within 3½ miles.

At the face of the glacier, Columbia Bay is teeming with life. Great numbers of sea mammals and birds are drawn by an abundance of plankton, microscopic animal and plant life swarming amid the glacial debris. Harbor seals are the most photographed: adults and young pups are seen by the hundreds swimming in the near-freezing water or reclining on ice floes. There are also a great many bald eagles, kittiwakes, and gulls, and an occasional sea otter.

The glacier starts just beneath the summit of 12,023-foot Mount Witherspoon in the Chugach Mountains. The weight of 100 feet of annual snowfall squeezes it out of its icefield much like toothpaste from a tube, and gravity does the rest. The ice is so densely compacted that it absorbs every color but blue, which is reflected back when the glacier is fractured.

But after nearly two centuries of remarkable stability, the glacier began to retreat in the 1970s. As it recedes deeper back into its fjord, an increased number of icebergs break off into the sound—about 10 million tons of ice daily, geologists estimate. At its current rate of retreat, the Columbia Glacier may be only 25 miles long (instead of the present 41) by the third decade of the 21st century.

VALDEZ

They call it the "Switzerland of Alaska," though in many regards Valdez (say "Val-*deez*") is more reminiscent of Norway. Surrounded on all sides by steep mountains dropping into fjord-like Port Valdez Bay, it is at once a gateway to the marine world of Prince William Sound and the alpine wonderland of Thompson Pass and the Chugach Mountains. Since the mid-1970s it has also been a busy oil port, the southern terminus of the Trans Alaska Pipeline.

A Hispanic name was pinned on Valdez in 1790 when Spanish-Mexican caravels discovered the inlet, but no real effort was made to settle the fjord until the Klondike gold rush of 1897 and 1898 sent thousands of stampeders scampering through Thompson Pass toward the Yukon. After a road was pushed through to Fairbanks at the turn of the century, Alaskans quickly established the value of Valdez's deep-water, ice-free port. The town grew and flourished.

Then came the 1964 earthquake. Valdez was literally wiped off the map by the tremor and a series of tidal waves. Few buildings were left standing as the surviving population fled to higher ground. There was little question in their mind but to rebuild the town, though the old site at the tip of the bay was no longer appropriate. A new townsite was chosen four miles up the north shore. With the construction of the pipeline terminal across the bay and the growth of tourism in Prince William Sound, the economy again boomed. Recently the town has added a $51-million terminal and a $7-million civic center.

Valdez's climate is quite mild, with midsummer temperatures in the 50s and 60s, midwinter temps in the 20s. Rainfall is fairly heavy in the spring and summer (though not as heavy as in Whittier), while snow falls from October to April.

Orientation

As the Richardson Highway enters Valdez from the east, it becomes **Egan Drive,** the town's main street, at the intersection of Meals Avenue. (William Egan, Alaska's first state governor, was born and raised in Valdez.) At the other end of downtown, two long blocks away, **Hazelet Avenue** runs north-south toward the Mineral Creek. The ferry terminal is near the south (bay) end of Hazelet. The boat harbor faces North Harbor Drive, which runs parallel to Egan Drive two blocks south via Meals. **Valdez Airport** is about four miles east of town, near the old townsite. The Alyeska Pipeline Terminal is south across Port Valdez Bay, about 4 miles by boat and 13 by road.

The **Valdez Convention and Visitors Bureau,** P.O. Box 1603, Valdez, AK 99686 (tel. 907/835-2984), has its main offices at 200 Chenega Ave., across from City Hall. The bureau also operates a **visitor information center** (tel. 835-INFO) during the summer months. There is a 24-hour recorded **"hotline"** for parks and recreation information (tel. 835-2555). You can get city information from the **Valdez Chamber of Commerce,** P.O. Box 512, Valdez, AK 99686 (tel. 907/835-2330).

There's one taxi service in town, **Valdez Yellow Cab** (tel. 835-2500), and three car-rental outfits: **Avis** (tel. 835-4774) and **Hertz** (tel. 835-4402), both at the airport, and **Budget** (tel. 835-4445), at the Village Inn. In addition to **ERA** (tel. 835-2636), Valdez Airport is served by **Valdez Aero Service** (tel. 835-2453). Many people arrive in town by ferry on the **Alaska Marine Highway System** (tel. 835-4436) or by bus aboard **Valdez-Anchorage Bus Lines** (tel. 835-5299).

Valdez has a weekly newspaper, the *Valdez Vanguard;* a hospital, **Valdez Community Hospital** (tel. 835-2249); 14 churches; and numerous fraternal organizations (the most prominent of which are the American Legion and the Elks).

Aside from fishing derbies, there are two important annual festivities. **Gold Rush Days,** held for five days through the second weekend of August, includes a parade, dance, casino night, and community fish fry. **Winter Carnival,** lasting five days in March, takes advantage of the heavy snowfall while celebrating the beginning of spring. Other special occasions include the **Ice Climbing Festival,** in February over President's Day weekend, and the **Whitewater Weekend** in early June.

Where to Stay

The hospitality industry in Valdez is highly seasonal. Hotels jack their prices up from $30 to $50 a room during the summer season—and they get it, no problem. All room charges are subject to a 6% local bed tax.

The town's largest hotel, and the one located nearest the small-boat harbor, is the **Westmark Valdez,** 100 Fidalgo Dr. (P.O. Box 468), Valdez, AK 99686 (tel. 907/835-4391, or toll free 800/544-0970, 800/478-1111 in Alaska). Don't be deceived by the small lobby and reception desk; the hotel contains 100 rooms, guaranteed full most of the summer. Each room has two double beds, a four-drawer dresser, dressing table, cable TV, phone (free local calls), and thermostat-controlled hot-water heating. The rooms, with brown carpets, red-purple bedspreads (it works), and cream-colored fabric walls, are well lit.

The Captain's Table restaurant, overlooking the harbor, offers breakfasts and lunches in the $5 to $9 range, and full dinners for $12 to $21. Open daily from 6 a.m. to 11 p.m. in summer, from 6:30 a.m. to 9 p.m. in winter. The adjoining Wheelhouse Lounge has a nautical theme underscored by a collection of oil supertankers' lifebuoys. It's open from 11 a.m. to 1 a.m. daily.

Room rates are $114 single, $125 double, May to September; $78 single, $88 double, in the off-season.

The **Westmark Inn,** 208 Egan Dr. (P.O. Box 1915), Valdez, AK 99686 (tel. 907/835-4485, or toll free 800/544-2206), is a seasonal property with a clientele of 80% tour groups, most of them booked with Westours. It has several things in its favor, not the least of which is a spacious, comfortable lobby—the only one in Valdez. The 40 rooms are nicely appointed in orange tones with white trim and prints of watercolors on the walls. Each room has two double beds and other standard furnishings, plus 16-channel cable television, telephone (free local calls), and electric heating. Amenities include shampoo, hand lotion, and a vanity kit.

The restaurant, open for three meals daily, specializes in fresh seafood, with dinners priced in the $15 range. There's also a bar and a deli.

Rooms are $114 single, $125 double. Opening dates vary from year to year, but generally they are late May to mid-September.

A step down in standard, but not in facilities, is the **Village Inn,** Meals Avenue at the Richardson Hwy. (P.O. Box 365), Valdez, AK 99686 (tel. 907/835-4445). There are 60 standard units with two double beds and the usual furnishings in a décor of earth tones and natural wood. Each room has cable TV, phone (free local calls), and electric heat. Eighteen economy units are slightly smaller and more worn, without a private bath. There are also 16 six-person cottages. Within the building are the Body Works Spa and Fitness Center, offering hotel guests a reduced rate; two electronic Par-T-Golf courses; sauna; and courtesy car. Alaska Sightseeing Tours books its clients at this hotel.

Next door, under the same management, the Mining District restaurant (summer only) has all-you-can-eat breakfasts for $5.75 and dinners for $10. The Sugarloaf Saloon has frequent solo entertainers.

Standard rooms are priced at $98, single or double, in summer, and $68 in winter. Cottages are $75, flat rate. Economy rooms are $62 in summer, less in winter. The Village Inn also has two-bedroom condominium units just outside town available for $125 a night.

Valdez's best bargain for dollar watchers may be the **Totem Inn,** Mile 0.2 on Richardson Hwy. (P.O. Box 648), Valdez, AK 99686 (tel. 907/835-4443). With big-game heads mounted on the walls surrounding the restaurant-cum-reception area and a big fireplace to one side, it looks for all the world like a hunting lodge. Aquariums and totem poles add interesting touches to the dimly lit main room. The 27 guest rooms are richly decorated in blues and whites; each has a queen-size bed, comfortable furnishings, cable TV, phone (free local calls), electric heat . . . and a small refrigerator in each private bathroom. A guest laundry is free of charge; bring your own soap. Dinners in the fully licensed restaurant are priced from $8 to $32, with most dishes in the $12 to $16 range. Local seafood is a specialty.

Room rates are $85, single or double, in summer; $35 single, $40 double, the rest of the year.

The **Valdez Motel,** 136 Egan Dr. (P.O. Box 65), Valdez, AK 99686 (tel. 907/ 835-4444), is Valdez's oldest-existing accommodation (it had been the Port of Valdez Hotel in the old town prior to the quake) and its least expensive during the tourist season. The 15 wood-paneled rooms contain two twins or a king-size bed, essential furnishings, cable TVs, phones (local calls are 15¢), courtesy coffee, and steam heating. Three rooms have small kitchenettes. Rates are $80 single, $85 double, in summer; $50, single or double, in winter.

One bed-and-breakfast establishment is **The Lake House,** Mile 6 on Richardson Hwy. (P.O. Box 1499), Valdez, AK 99686 (tel. 907/835-4752). Bob and Marilyn Walker, who declare they are "dedicated to the independent traveler," offer six rooms in their spacious home overlooking beautiful Robe Lake. Each room is a little different: two have solarium windows, another has a fireplace, and another has a balcony looking out on the lake as it reflects the surrounding mountains. The six rooms share three baths. Guests are shown the fixings for continental breakfasts and told to help themselves. Rates are $60 single, $70 double. So rapidly has the bed-and-breakfast business burgeoned in Valdez that the visitors bureau now lists 13 B&Bs.

Two Valdez camper parks are near the small-boat harbor. **Sea Otter RV Park,** on the South Harbor Drive spit (P.O. Box 947), Valdez, AK 99686 (tel. 907/835-2787), has rest rooms, showers, a Laundromat, and dump station. Full hookups are $15 a day; electric only, $12. **Bearpaw Camper Park,** North Harbor Drive (P.O. Box 93), Valdez, AK 99686 (tel. 907/835-4558), has similar facilities and rates, but without the sea life that visits the end of the spit.

The city operates the 101-site **Valdez Glacier Campground,** six miles from town at the end of the airport road. You'll find tap water, firepits, picnic tables, and outhouses.

Where to Eat

When Valdezans go out for dinner, it's likely they'll dine at one of the hotels— commonly the Westmark Valdez or the Totem Inn. One other establishment that stands out is the **Pipeline Club,** 112 Egan Dr. (tel. 835-4891). Adjoining the Valdez Motel but maintaining a separate identity, it is first and foremost a steakhouse, with red upholstery and brick walls, and atmospheric dim lighting. Steak and eggs costs $8.75 for breakfast; a steak sandwich is $8.25 for lunch. For dinner, the management recommends flambé specialties: you can start with coquilles aux lardon ($9); follow with steak Diane flamed in brandy, with baked potato and soup or salad ($19); and conclude with cherries jubilee ($9 for two) or peaches Véronique ($8 for two). There are also cheaper meals like lasagne ($8) and chop suey ($10). Open from 4:30 a.m. to 2 p.m. and 5 to 11 p.m. daily. The lounge, which keeps kicking till 5 a.m., is a great place to meet some local Valdezans and hear some impromptu musical talent.

Pizza Palace, North Harbor Drive opposite the small-boat harbor (tel. 835-2365), is a lot of fun simply for the décor—old newspapers on the walls, photos of the earthquake, a fine doll collection, and more. The food is good too: pizzas, calzone, Mexican food, Greek food—most in the $9 to $12 range. It shares a building with the Harbor Club, still Valdez's favorite haunt for live music and dancing, but a mere shade of its wild-and-woolly pipeline-construction days when hookers who worked the bar lived in RVs parked outside.

Nearer the center of town, the **Alaska Halibut House,** at Meals and Pioneer Avenues (tel. 835-2788), has seafood-and-chips baskets for prices around $7.

The **Hideaway Café** in Valdez Center Mall (tel. 835-2393) is a traditional Valdez stop for breakfast or lunch.

What to See and Do

A major attraction in downtown Valdez, and one of the best small museums in Alaska, is the **Valdez Museum,** Egan Drive at Chenega Avenue (tel. 835-2764). Even if you think you have little interest in local history, go. Valdez senior citizens have volunteered to make three of the exhibits come alive—a woodcarver in a sportsman's display, a seamstress in a sewing room, and a bartender (serving apple juice) across a bar rescued from the Pinzon Hotel in old Valdez. Other exhibits include early-20th-century fire trucks and firefighting equipment in almost mint condition; mining tools in an old cabin; a scale model of the pipeline terminal across the bay; and earthquake information and photos. The museum is open daily from 10 a.m. to 6 p.m. mid-May to mid-September, and Tuesday through Saturday the rest of the year. There is no formal admission charge, although donations to maintain the museum are requested.

The Valdez **walking tour** brochure assembled by the chamber of commerce is out of print, but ask at the museum or visitor information center to peruse an old copy. It pinpoints some of the 50-or-so buildings that were moved from the old townsite after the '64 quake. Other points of interest include:

A **native head** sculpted from wood, standing in front of Prince William Sound Community College on Pioneer Avenue, is one of a planned series in all 50 states of sculptures on a native theme by Peter Toth.

Valdez Civic Center, overlooking the ferry dock on Clifton Avenue near Hazelet (tel. 835-4440), is a state-of-the-art convention and performing arts center. Nearby is a **U.S. Coast Guard Station,** 105 Clifton Dr.

Not including the Columbia Glacier, Valdez's most popular attraction is the **Alyeska Pipeline Terminal.** Drive seven miles east on the Richardson Hwy., then turn west (down the south shore of Port Valdez Bay) on Dayville Road for another six miles. The terminal has a visitor information office (tel. 835-6283) at its outer gate where interpretive displays and brochures are available for the non-engineers among us, and where almost any question regarding the pipeline and oil shipment can be answered. It's open daily Memorial Day to Labor Day from 8 a.m. to 8 p.m., and weekdays the rest of the year.

When crude oil arrives at the terminal after completing its 800-mile journey from Prudhoe Bay, it is temporarily stored here in 18 tanks (each with a capacity of 510,000 barrels) until it's loaded onto tankers. That's a total storage capacity of 378 million gallons of oil. Tankers of 50,000 to 265,000 deadweight tons dock at four berths; oil is gravity-fed to them through hydraulically controlled metal arms with loading rates up to 110,000 barrels an hour. The arms simultaneously pump out ship-ballast water.

You may be impressed to see the precautions taken to minimize the effects of man-made or natural disasters. There are oil-spill cleanup equipment, vapor recovery systems, facilities for the treatment of sewage, water and ballast water, firefighting equipment, and more. (After the 1989 *Exxon Valdez* oil-spill, however, many question whether these precautions are sufficient.)

Even more fascinating is the Operations Control Center, from which the entire 800-mile pipeline system is monitored and directed by remote control. Computer consoles with data displays and pushbutton controls enable pipeline controllers to initiate actions at every working level, including emergency procedures where necessary. The system depends on a microwave communications network with satellite backup.

Only 300 men and women are currently employed at the marine terminal, down from 3,500 who occupied the Alyeska barracks during mid-'70s construction. But the others haven't been forgotten. All the 70,000 people who worked on the pipeline are commemorated in the **Pipeline Monument,** a 13-foot bronze casting just outside the terminal gate. Sculptor Malcolm Alexander's acclaimed work, commissioned in 1977 and completed in 1980, depicts a surveyor, engineer, welder, teamster, and workman.

Two-hour tours of the Alyeska Pipeline marine terminal can be booked at the Gray Line desks in the Westmark Valdez or Westmark Inn. Offered daily at 10 a.m. and 7 p.m. mid-May to mid-September, the tour costs $15 for adults, $7.50 for children under 12.

Tours pass the **Solomon Gulch Salmon Hatchery,** on Dayville Road a mile east of the terminal. The Valdez Fisheries Development Association (tel. 835-2594) gives guided tours by appointment. Visiting hours are 8 a.m. to 5 p.m. daily.

There's little to be seen on the **Old Town Site.** A plaque, dedicated to those who lost their lives during the 1964 earthquake, is located at the end of the road.

Several drives can be recommended to visitors who appreciate alpine scenery. The narrow **Mineral Creek Canyon** road winds 5½ miles north to sites of gold- and copper-mining endeavors. Seven miles from Valdez, up the airport road, is the rapidly receding **Valdez Glacier.** The first miners' trail to the Copper River Basin and interior went over this glacier. Thirteen miles east of Valdez along the Richardson Hwy. is the beginning of sheer **Keystone Canyon** with its two beautiful waterfalls, Bridal Veil Falls and Horsetail Falls. **Thompson Pass,** 24 miles from (and 2,771 feet above) Valdez, has wildflower meadows in spring and summer, downhill skiing in winter, and always a fine scenic overlook.

Sports

FISHING   The waters of Valdez Arm are rich in fish life. Five species of salmon, halibut, red snapper, rock bass, ling cod, and gray cod are sought by fishermen in the salt water, while Dolly Varden and rainbow trout are pursued in Robe Lake and the Robe and Lowe Rivers. Shrimp and crab are also popular catches, and there are excellent clamming beaches. A halibut derby is held in late May or early June, a pink salmon derby is held over the Fourth of July weekend, and a silver salmon derby attracts fishermen from all over Alaska during the month of August.

More than a dozen private operators charter boats from the small-boat harbor for day trips and longer excursions; there's very little difference between them. You can either visit the boats in the harbor and book a trip right at the docks, or consult an outdoor store like **Hook, Line and Sinker** (tel. 835-4410) or **Beaver Sports** (tel. 835-4727). They can advise you on private boat rental and also sell licenses.

HIKING   The possibilities are almost endless. Two favorite areas are **Mineral Creek Canyon,** where a trail at the end of the rutted 5½-mile road leads an additional mile to an abandoned gold stamp mill, and 1½-miles farther to the foot of the Mineral Creek Glacier; and the **Worthington Glacier,** accessible by a short road and trail off Keystone Canyon.

RAFTING   This comes in two forms—motorized ocean rafting and white-water river rafting.

John Cotter's Alaska Waterways, P.O. Box 1881, Valdez, AK 99686 (tel. 835-5151), makes one-day trips for up to 25 people at a time on pontooned military rafts to Shoup Glacier, a small but impressive tidewater glacier several miles west of

Valdez on Port Valdez Bay. A 115-horsepower motor directs the craft past kittiwake and tern rookeries and an abandoned cliffside gold mine to Shoup Bay, where you can get out and wander for up to five hours before returning to Valdez. The price is $70, including lunch; children 12 and under are charged $52.50. Cotter also offers two-day Shoup Glacier weekends for $175 per person, including all meals and equipment. Departure times vary, depending on tides. Trips are offered from Memorial Day to mid-September, or by prior arrangement.

The favorite excursion offered by Mike Buck's **Keystone Raft & Kayak Adventures,** P.O. Box 1486, Valdez, AK 99686 (tel. 835-2606), is a short but spectacular run down the Lowe River, through the precipitous Class III Keystone Canyon. Rafters cover six miles of river past Bridal Veil and Horsetail Falls in one hour, starting 17 miles east of Valdez. There are five trips a day between June 10 and September 8, at a rate of $30 for adults, $20 for children. All transportation is provided, plus rubber boats, rainsuits, and lifejackets. Expect to get wet anyway.

WINTER SPORTS One thing there's never any shortage of in Valdez is snow. An average of 25 to 30 feet falls on the city annually (though not all at once). Thompson Pass once received 81 feet of snow in a winter, and 5 feet in a single 24-hour period. So the popularity of winter sports in Valdez comes as no surprise.

Cross-country **skiing** is probably No. 1 on the list. There are trails and meadows everywhere; the Mineral Creek Canyon road is kept groomed in winter. Just east of town, on Salmonberry Hill at Mile 5.5 on Richardson Hwy., is a short poma lift and warming hut for beginning skiers. Advanced skiers go to Thompson Pass: there are no lifts, but a 2,000-foot car shuttle works just as well, and the powder is always good. Thompson Pass is also popular for **snowmobiling** and **dog sledding,** while **ice climbing** is the domain of an adventuresome few in Keystone Canyon.

OTHER SPORTS For general information, call the 24-hour activity hotline sponsored by the **Valdez Parks and Recreation Department** (tel. 835-2555). The recorded information will include schedules for open **swimming** at Valdez High School on Robe River Drive; **racquetball** at Hermon Hutchins Grade School on West Klutina Drive; and many other activities, including the local **rifle range.** The Black Gold Park Strip on the west side of Valdez off Cottonwood Drive has **tennis, basketball,** and **volleyball** courts and some **horseshoe** pits. **Softball** fields are east of town at Mile 1.5 on Richardson Hwy. A **bicycle** path parallels the highway for several miles.

Tours

Valdez Sightseeing Tours (tel. 835-4776 or 835-2500) is the only agency giving land tours of the entire Valdez area. Day tours take in the old town, Keystone Canyon, and Worthington Glacier, while evening tours visit the Solomon Gulch Fish Hatchery.

Gray Line of Alaska, with travel desks in the Westmark Valdez and Westmark Inn, has two tours: the aforementioned visit to the pipeline terminal and a full-day Columbia Glacier cruise. The fare of $122.50 includes round-trip passage to Whittier via the Columbia Glacier, two light meals aboard the *Glacier Queen II,* and the separate pipeline terminal tour.

The most adventuresome local charter-boat operator is Stan Stephens, captain of the custom-built 80-foot *Glacier Spirit.* **Stan Stephens Charters,** P.O. Box 1297, Valdez, AK 99686 (tel. 835-4731), offers a wide variety of waterborne opportunities, from daily Columbia Glacier cruises (leaving the Westmark Dock at 1 p.m., Memorial Day to Labor Day), to chartered dinner parties and wildlife cruises up to ten days long. Hunting and fishing expeditions are available throughout the year, except February through April when Stephens operates cross-country ski charters to remote parts of Prince William Sound.

Local air taxis will fly you over the Columbia and other glaciers for rates beginning at $125 per person. An even more spectacular way to see the Columbia Glacier is aboard a helicopter. A 50-minute tour with **Solay Helicopters** (tel. 835-4999), piloted by longtime Alaska resident Bob Hites, costs $140 per person. My flight over the Columbia Glacier was one of the most awe-inspiring experiences I have had in Alaska, one that I highly recommend.

CORDOVA

The charming community of Cordova is nestled between dense evergreen forests and the rocky peaks of the Chugach Mountains at the eastern end of Prince William Sound. Surrounded by water—Orca Inlet is to the west, freshwater Eyak Lake to the east—it comes as no surprise that most of its 2,300 residents depend on fishing for their livelihood. About 20 miles east of town is the Copper River Delta, one of the richest salmon-spawning grounds in the world. Cordova is also a regional headquarters for the Chugach National Forest and a major wildlife-viewing destination.

Cordova's raison d'être was copper—the mineral and the river. The discovery in 1889 of a major copper vein on the Chitina River, a tributary of the Copper, created a need for an ice-free port and railroad center. A small Orca Inlet cannery site filled the bill. Construction of the Copper River & Northwestern Railway began in 1906 with the arrival of a steamship-load of materials at the new townsite. It was completed in 1911, running 196 miles up the Copper River to the Chitina and on to the great Kennicott mine.

Once Cordova was established as a railroad town, fishing gradually grew in importance. When the Kennicott mine shut down in 1938, fishing kept Cordova from becoming a ghost town. Miles of track were sold for scrap iron, and the Copper River Hwy. was laid on the old rail bed. Intended to link Cordova by road with the rest of the state, it was started from both ends, but before the ends could join, the '64 earthquake destroyed the Million Dollar Bridge across the Copper River (downtown survived the quake). Although the issue is frequently discussed, work on the road has never been resumed.

The climate is typical of Prince William Sound—mild and wet. Summer temperatures average in the 50s and low 60s, winter temperatures in the 20s. Average annual precipitation is 167 inches, much of it snow and most of it falling in the winter and spring, especially in March and April.

Orientation

It's hard to get lost in Cordova. **First Street,** the main drag through the two blocks of downtown, continues north about a mile to the state ferry dock and south (then east) to become the Copper River Hwy. It looks west, across the boat harbor to Orca Inlet and Spike Island. One block below it, running up against the harbor, is **Railroad Avenue.** Second Street is a block east and uphill. **Council Avenue** connects the three. Eyak Lake is half a mile east and a few hundred feet higher than downtown.

The **Cordova Chamber of Commerce,** P.O. Box 99, Cordova, AK 99574 (tel. 907/424-7260), has an office in the National Bank of Alaska Building on 1st Street that provides visitor information. When that office is closed, ask for assistance at the **Cordova Museum,** 1st Street near Adams Avenue (tel. 424-7443).

Club Taxi (tel. 424-3211) and **O & L Taxi** (tel. 424-3456) will get you around town. **Copper River Express** (tel. 424-5463) meets Alaska Marine Hwy. ferries and Alaska Airlines flights as a matter of course, and others by special arrangement. **Car rentals** are available from the town's major motel, the **Reluctant Fisherman** (tel. 424-3272).

Cordova Airport is 13 miles east on the Copper River Hwy. It's served from Anchorage and Juneau by **Alaska Airlines** (tel. 424-7151), from Anchorage by **North Pacific Airlines** (tel. 424-3777), and **Wilbur's Flight Operations** (tel. 424-5695 or 424-7102). Three air-charter services are based at the gravel city airstrip on Eyak Lake—**Fishing and Flying** (tel. 424-3324), **Chitina Air Service** (tel. 424-

3524), and **Cordova Air** (tel. 424-3289). Their prices run between $195 and $240 an hour.

For ferry arrival and departure times, call the **Alaska Marine Highway System** (tel. 424-7333).

Cordova has a weekly newspaper, the *Cordova Times;* a beautiful new 22-bed hospital, the **Cordova Community Hospital,** on Railroad Row near 2nd Street (dial 911 in emergency); two banks; 11 churches; and numerous fraternal organizations.

The year's big event is the **Cordova Iceworm Festival,** held Thursday through Sunday the first full weekend of February. Festivities include a boat parade and the blessing of the fleet, art exhibits, carnivals, square dances, and a grand parade highlighted by the annual appearance of the many-legged Cordova Iceworm. In fact, the rarely seen iceworm (*Mesenchytraeus solifugus*) is only slightly larger than microscopic in size. It feeds on pollen carried to the surface of glacial ice, but its legend is far greater than its reality. Turn-of-the-century sourdoughs frightened greenhorns with overblown tales about the worms, and poet Robert Service immortalized the creatures with a ballad about the iceworm cocktail.

Where to Stay

The **Reluctant Fisherman,** P.O. Box 150, Cordova, AK 99574 (tel. 907/424-3272), is Cordova's only first-class lodging. Located on Railroad Avenue overlooking the small-boat harbor, it has 44 rooms, a restaurant and coffeeshop, lounge, guest Laundromat, gift shop, and travel agency. The wood-paneled rooms, decorated in earth tones with floral bedspreads, are amply furnished and quiet—except when the fleet is in, but then tranquility has no meaning in Cordova. They've all got cable television, direct-dial phone (free local calls), dressing tables, and electric heat. Eighteen rooms with a view of the harbor are priced at $88 in summer, $60 in the off-season; other rooms are $65 in summer, $50 in the off-season. Three rooms with kitchenette are available for $5 more. Local sales tax is another 4%.

Cordova's rich history is reflected in the solid-copper ceilings of the dining room and lounge. The dining room is also a showcase of Alaskan native art, and its big picture windows gazing upon the small-boat harbor let diners ruminate on which boat their dinner came from. Meal prices are reasonable: $14 for a salmon dinner, including soup, salad, and potato; $6.50 for a lunch of halibut and chips. Note the copper bar top in the Bird House lounge; like many other hotel fixtures, including the "cage" at reception, it came from a late, lamented Cordova bank building. Solo entertainers frequently perform in the lounge at night.

The **Prince William Motel,** 2nd Street at Council Avenue (P.O. Box 848), Cordova, AK 99574 (tel. 907/424-3201, or 424-7406 after 8 p.m.), doesn't look like much from the outside, and the reception area isn't much bigger than a closet. But its 14 wood-paneled rooms are nicely decorated in tones of orange, yellow, and off-white. Each room has good-sized beds, a love seat, cable TV, phone (free local calls), dressing tables, and thermostat-controlled steam heating. Six rooms have kitchenettes with pots and utensils at no additional charge. There's also a guest Laundromat. Year-round rates are $65, single or double, plus tax. The Prince William is under the same ownership as the adjacent Windsinger Café and bar.

The **Cordova House,** on 1st Street (P.O. Box 700), Cordova, AK 99574 (tel. 907/424-3388), was recently redecorated and refurbished. Built in 1908, it has two floors of rooms above a bar. The 12 steam-heated rooms are small, but they have private baths (with showers) and satellite television. Rates are $62.50 single, $78 double.

The **Alaska Hotel,** 1st Street at Browning Avenue (P.O. Box 364), Cordova, AK 99574 (tel. 907/424-3288), hearkens back to an earlier day. Built in 1908, it is today a working-man's hotel with 11 budget-priced rooms. None of them has a phone or TV, but all have twin or double beds, wall-to-wall brown carpeting, and adequate furnishings, plus fluorescent lighting and radiator heating. Rates are $35 single without a bath, $45 with a bath (no shower), $5 per additional person. Cash only, please. The hotel is worth a visit if only to see the honky-tonk bar downstairs, featuring a backbar carried by boat from a hotel in the defunct coal-boom town of Katalla.

The only campground in town is the **Odiak Camper Park,** on Whitshed Road (P.O. Box 1210), Cordova, AK 99574 (tel. 907/424-7311). A private facility, it has 25 slots with rest rooms, hot showers, and a dump station.

Fifteen miles from town, on a Copper River Hwy. side road two miles north of the airport, **Cabin Lake Campground** has tent sites with tables, firepits, and garbage cans. Obtain a use permit from the offices of the Eyak Native Corporation, at the corner of LeFevre and Chase Avenues (tel. 424-7161).

Where to Eat

The **Windsinger Café,** on 1st Street, near Council Avenue (tel. 424-3206), isn't a 24-hour eatery, but it seems like it's never closed. Starting with breakfast at 6 a.m., it remains open until the last-callers depart from the bar well after the witching hour. Pleasant nautical décor is the café's trademark, with cork and rope lining the walls and the prow of the vessel *Windsinger* extending over the bandstand. Open daily for three meals, including steak and seafood specialties. Razor clams are a din-nertime favorite at $17. Every night but Sunday from 10 p.m., the lounge is Cordova's rocking-est spot with live bands and dancing.

A fine little Italian restaurant overlooks the harbor from the west side of 1st Street opposite Browning Avenue. The **Ambrosia Restaurant** (tel. 424-7175), housed in a former blacksmith's shop built in 1908, has a cozy wood-paneled décor of brown-checkered tablecloths and hanging ivy. Full spaghetti, lasagne, and other pasta dinners are $9.75 to $11.75; veal parmesan and chicken cacciatore are $13.50. Pizzas range in price from $9.75 (11-inch, with one topping) to $26.75 (17-inch, with the works). Licensed for beer and wine. Open daily from 11 a.m. to 11 p.m. No credit cards.

The **Sourdough Café,** in the back of the Cordova House on 1st Street (tel. 424-5494), gives generous portions of basic but tasty fare. It's open daily from 6 a.m. to 11 p.m. for breakfast, lunch, and dinner. T-bone and rib steaks are $17, in-cluding soup or salad, baked potato or fries.

Also on 1st Street are the **Killer Whale Café,** a lunch spot on a deck above the Orca Book and Sound Co., featuring deli-style sandwiches ($5), homemade soups ($2), desserts, gourmet teas, and coffees; and Stella Chung's **OK Restaurant** (tel. 424-3433), serving standard chop suey and chow mein lunches ($6.50 to $7.50) and a variety of Oriental dinners: Mandarin, Szechuan, Japanese, and Korean ($10 to $20).

I'd be suspicious of any mobile fast-food joint that declares in writing: "We move our buns for you." But locals swear by the $5 hamburgers made at **The Bea-con,** located in a camper beside the small-boat harbor on Breakwater Avenue, near the fishermen's rowdy Anchor Bar. Open from 11 a.m. to 7 p.m. daily.

A mile and a half up the Copper River Hwy., with a deck looking out on Eyak Lake, is the **Powder House** (tel. 424-3529)—which was once, in fact, a railway gun-powder warehouse. (You can buy a T-shirt that says "I got blasted at the Powder House.") The soup-and-sandwich bar provides light lunches in the $4 to $6.50 range. Dinner specials—moderately priced salmon barbecues and the like—are served on Wednesday, Friday, and Saturday nights. Entertainment in the bar runs the gamut from folk to country to bluegrass. Open daily from 10 a.m. until closing, whenever that may be.

What to See and Do

Start your visit to Cordova by following the **walking tour** compiled by the Cor-dova Historical Society. Brochures are available from the chamber of commerce or city offices.

The tour starts at the Centennial Building, 1st Street and Adams Avenue, built in 1967 to house the city museum and library. Before you begin, spend some time browsing in the **Cordova Museum** (tel. 424-7443). The eclectic collection has brought together many bits and pieces of memorabilia relating to local history, including some wonderful early-20th-century photographs. You'll also find a Native canoe, an enormous lighthouse lens, a beaver-paw tobacco pouch, a copper still, and a giant harmonica. You can learn all you'd ever care to know about the tiny iceworm and the festival created in its name in 1961. Open from 1 to 5 p.m. on Monday and Friday, to 9 p.m. on Tuesday and Thursday, 1 to 5 and 7 to 9 p.m. on Saturday.

Climb Adams Avenue to 2nd Street and the historic **Red Dragon Mission** and **St. George's Episcopal Church.** Founded in 1908 and 1919, respectively, to bring religion to the miners and railroad workers, they are still in active use today. Both are listed on the National Register of Historic Sites.

Just north on 2nd Street, in the Federal Building, is the Cordova district office of the **U.S. Forest Service,** P.O. Box 280, Cordova, AK 99574 (tel. 424-7661). Nearly 2.7 million acres of Chugach National Forest are administered from here. Wildlife habitat, waterfowl-nesting areas, and recreation lands are managed and protected. The rangers are happy to share their knowledge of recreational opportunities and wildlife viewing from 7:30 a.m. to 5 p.m. weekdays.

Directly west two blocks is the **small-boat harbor,** home of Prince William Sound's largest commercial fishing fleet. It's fun to browse down the docks and chat with fishermen. Near the Harbormaster's Office (tel. 424-3351) on the South Containment Field is the **Cordova Fishermen's Memorial,** a bronze statue by sculptor Joan Bugbee Jackson dedicated in 1985 to all Cordova fishermen who have lost their lives at sea. Called *The Southeasterly,* it depicts a raincoated pilot at the helm of his boat, shaking his fist at the weather with a look of frightened rage.

Facing the harbor on Breakwater Avenue is the **Fathom Gallery** (tel. 424-3116), Cordova's best art gallery and gift shop. The work of many local artists, sculptors, photographers, and writers is displayed and sold here.

On the north side of the harbor are several **canneries,** which will arrange tours on request. South of the harbor near Odiak Slough is the **Eyak Packing Company** (tel. 424-5300), a family-operated smokery which also offers tours.

Photographer Rose Arvidson and her husband, Bob, have taken their beachfront property on Whitshed Road and created a little park, **Odiak Gardens,** on a promontory jutting into Orca Inlet. You'll see it from several vantage points: a small lighthouse, ship's mast, and pavilion surrounded by flowers. Visitors are welcome.

Behind the city, at the end of Ski Hill Road off upper Council Avenue, is the **Eyak Ski Hill,** on the slopes of Mount Eyak. The views of Prince William Sound and downtown Cordova are outstanding here.

Eyak Lake, the beautiful glacier-fed lake on the east side of Cordova, is a real treat. Waterfalls cascade down the sides of surrounding mountains into its basin and trumpeter swans feed year round near the lake outlet. Brown bear can often be seen in early summer pursuing spawning salmon at the lake's north end, where it's fed by Power Creek. The Eyak River, which flows from the Y-shaped lake's east end to the Gulf of Alaska, is a popular scenic route for kayakers, canoeists, and hikers.

At the west end of Eyak Lake, nearest the city, is **Nirvana Park,** a meditative retreat built in the 1930s by eccentric Henry Feldman. The **Pioneer Cemetery** is across Lake Avenue. The **Eyak Village Building,** at Chase Avenue and LeFevre Road, which serves as headquarters for the Eyak Native Corporation, displays artifacts from 9 a.m. to 5 p.m. weekdays, and the coffee pot is always on.

DRIVING You can head out the Copper River Hwy. only as far as the Million Dollar Bridge, 48 miles from Cordova. But that's far enough to spend time in some of the finest birdwatching country in North America. Several million birds pass through here on their annual migrations, and more than 240 species of shorebirds, waterfowl, and other birds have been spotted on the **Copper River Flats,** including the largest-known concentration of trumpeter swans on the continent. You should also look for beavers, mink, otters, and brown and black bears in the vast tidal marsh that is the **Copper River Delta.** Moose wander down the highway as a matter of course, except during the short September moose-hunting season. There's superb berry picking here in the summer and fall, but it's best to ask first at the Cordova Sea Grant office for a guide to berries. There are some poisonous wild fruits in the area.

One lodge in this area caters exclusively to nature lovers. The **Goose Cove Lodge,** P.O. Box 325, Cordova, AK 99574 (tel. 907/424-7742), charges $1,195 to $1,895 for a variety of all-inclusive full-week packages, often featuring guest naturalists.

A mile and a half past the airport an access road leads four miles to a picnic ground with a view of **Sheridan Glacier.** It's a one-mile hike through bear country to the glacier's terminal moraine. At 41 miles on the Copper River Hwy. you'll have a beautiful view of the **Sherman and Goodwin Glaciers** flowing down 6,263-foot Mount Murchison.

The **Million Dollar Bridge** is at Mile 49, wedged between the spectacular **Childs and Miles Glaciers.** The 1964 quake toppled the bridge's north span into the Copper River and damaged the other spans. Makeshift repairs have been made, but travel beyond this point is strictly at your own risk; anyway, the road peters out in another mile.

CRUISING With its marine setting, this is a natural for Cordova. Humpback, killer, and minke whales are at home in Prince William Sound, and harbor seals, Steller sea lions, and porpoises frequent Orca Inlet. Sea otters can sometimes be seen from the docks or in the small-boat harbor, floating on their backs while feeding on crabs and clams.

Cordova is the home of some of the world's foremost fish hatcheries. The nonprofit **Prince William Sound Aquaculture Corporation** (tel. 424-7511), founded in 1974, operates the world's largest pink salmon hatchery at Port San Juan on **Evans Island,** near the southwest entrance to the sound between Cordova and Seward. A new hatchery on **Esther Island** east of Whittier will be three times larger and will eventually raise all species of salmon. The state of Alaska also operates two hatcheries in the Prince William Sound islands. All of these hatcheries love to give tours.

A few miles across Orca Inlet from Cordova is **Hawkins Island** with its Native village site of **Palugvik,** a national historic landmark. Palugvik marks the southeasternmost point of Eskimo settlement and a place of cross-cultural adaptation: when Tlingit and Eyak (Athabaskan) Indians migrated into the area, the Chugach Eskimos borrowed their tools and foods, and began to assume private ownership of objects, including slaves. This noncommunal social behavior had been unknown to most Eskimos.

Sixty-two miles southeast of Cordova is isolated **Kayak Island.** Captain Vitus Bering's landing here in 1741 is believed to have been the first European landfall on the west coast of North America. Today this remote 22- by 1½-mile island, administered as a part of Chugach National Forest, offers only beach and forest wilderness. The totally automated Cape St. Elias Lighthouse at the southwestern end of the island has been a beacon to sailors since it was built by the Coast Guard in 1916.

A majority of the 14 U.S. Forest Service public-use **cabins** in the Cordova Ranger District are located on Prince William Sound islands. Priced at $15 a night (but going up), these cabins go fast, so advance reservations are essential. From late August to October in particular they are heavily booked by hunters stalking the Sitka black-tailed deer. Contact the **U.S. Forest Service,** P.O. Box 280, Cordova, AK 99574 (tel. 907/424-7661), for reservations and assistance in trip planning.

Three charter-boat operators can be found in the small-boat harbor: **Tatonduk**

Outfitters (tel. 424-7742), **Prince William Sound Charter Service** (tel. 424-3532), and **Winter King Charters** (tel. 424-7170).

Alaska Seacoast Charters, P.O. Box 319, Cordova, AK 99574 (tel. 907/424-7742, or toll free 800/551-1769), runs a series of six-day natural-history and glacier cruises throughout the summer. Prices are $1,995 per person, double occupancy, including transportation to the *Discovery* from Cordova Airport.

Sports

FISHING   The possibilities are almost endless. Commercial fishermen gill-net for red and king salmon in the Copper River Delta, and purse-seine for pink and chum salmon in the sound. Silver salmon fishing is excellent right from the ferry dock. Halibut, herring, crabs, shrimp, and clams are other easily found seafoods.

Eyak Lake is closed to salmon fishing, but like many other freshwater lakes and rivers, is open year round to Dolly Varden and cutthroat trout fishing—including in winter for ice fishing.

One of Alaska's finest wilderness fishing-guide services is based in Cordova— **Alaskan Wilderness Outfitting Co.,** P.O. Box 1516, Cordova, AK 99574 (tel. 907/424-5552). Various packages can be arranged in fresh- and saltwater climes from June through September, at prices starting at $695 per person for six days, all-inclusive.

HIKING   Surrounded as Cordova is by national forest lands, there's no shortage of trails. Many folks enjoy walking the mile from road's end onto the **Sheridan Glacier.** The 3.7-mile **Lake Elsner loop trail** starts from Cabin Lake, at the Eyak Corporation campground near the airport. The **Crater Lake trail** up the steep slopes of Mount Eyak is one of the most accessible and worthwhile for day trekkers. About 2½ miles long, it begins at Skater's Cabin, just past the city airport on Power Creek Road.

When hiking on the Copper River Flats or other boggy areas, the terrain may demand the use of rubber boots as well as sturdier hiking shoes. No matter where you are hiking, be on the lookout for bears and know what to do if you encounter one.

HUNTING   Moose, bear, deer, mountain goat, ducks, and geese are the most commonly sought species. Get full information on license fees and hunting seasons from the **Alaska Department of Fish and Game,** P.O. Box 669, Cordova, AK 99574 (tel. 907/424-3215).

WINTER SPORTS   The **Eyak Ski Hill and Lodge,** at the top of Ski Hill Road off upper Council Avenue (tel. 424-7766), has a 3,600-foot chair lift that's a true relic: it formerly operated at Sun Valley, Idaho, where it was erected in the 1930s as one of the first ski lifts in the western United States. Today the city-owned lift runs up Tripod Hill on Mount Eyak. The small but challenging ski area also has a beginners' rope tow and ski school. There's ice skating on Lake Eyak, and cross-country skiing is great on the lake or in the Copper River Flats.

OTHER SPORTS   The **Bob Korn Memorial Swimming Pool,** a five-lane Olympic-size pool on Railroad Avenue (tel. 424-7200), has lockers and shower facilities, classes, and open swim times. **Eyak Community Center,** in the old city hall at 2nd Street and Council Avenue (tel. 424-7282 or 424-3277), has a weight room and gymnasium with public hours, equipment rentals, and aerobics classes. Usual hours are 2 to

10 p.m. daily except Sunday The **Cordova Trap & Gun Club** has a shooting range on Sheridan Glacier Road.

---

3. Copper River Basin

The dominant features of the Copper River Basin are not its towns but its geography. And that's what makes this region special.

Here are the Wrangell Mountains, their ice-covered masses starkly visible from nearly every point in the basin. Here are the Copper and Chitina Rivers, their white-water canyons challenging intrepid outdoorsmen. Weathered homesteaders share their domain with the ghosts of copper miners and a variety of wildlife. Fishermen rush to test their skills and patience against trout and salmon in the many small lakes and streams, while mountaineers relish the challenge thrown their way by the massifs of Wrangell–St. Elias National Park and Preserve. And right through the middle of it all runs the Trans Alaska Pipeline, a reminder of man's mettle in modern Alaska.

This land was the traditional home of the Ahtna Indians, a semi-nomadic clan of the Athabaskan tribe which hunted and fished and repelled Russian incursions. But the Indians couldn't keep back the horde of half-crazed gold seekers who traversed the basin en route to the Klondike in 1898.

Some of the newcomers, upon finding sizable veins of copper, stayed. Kennicott and McCarthy, on the southern slopes of the Wrangell Range, established huge copper-mining operations, and the river junction town of Chitina, a gateway on the railroad to Cordova, boomed as an outfitting center. By 1938, however, the expense of working the deposits had grown greater than the potential profits. Today Kennicott is merely a picturesque reminder of the boom-and-bust cycles, so much a part of Alaskan history.

Today only about 2,700 people live in the entire Copper River Basin. That's about one for every seven square miles of land area. About 1,000 of them are Ahtna Indians, many of whose elders still speak the ancestral language. Ahtna, Incorporated, the Native corporation, has been especially active in construction, mining, and tourism in the region.

The corporation makes its headquarters in the region's hub and largest town, Glennallen (pop. 500), at the junction of the Glenn and Richardson Highways. No other community in the basin has more than 200 permanent residents. That perhaps is not surprising in a virtual wilderness where temperatures are often 50°F below zero on long winter nights. Midsummer temperatures, on the other hand, frequently top 70°F (the mercury once hit 90°F). Annual precipitation is only about 10 inches, including 50 inches of snow accumulation.

GETTING THERE

The **Richardson Highway,** running south-north from Valdez to Fairbanks, and the **Glenn Highway,** running northeast-southwest from Tok to Anchorage, are the principal arteries of the Copper River Basin. They overlap for about 14 miles from Glennallen north to Gakona Junction. Seventeen miles south of Copper Center on the Richardson Highway, the **Edgerton Highway** follows the Copper and Chitina Rivers east 33 miles to Chitina, whereupon a summer-only dirt road continues 60 more miles along the old railroad bed to what remains of McCarthy. If work from the Cordova end is ever resumed, the Copper River Highway would join the Edgerton Highway at Chitina.

Private car is the most practical way to visit, though bus and small plane are also options. **Alaska-Denali Transit** (tel. 907/561-1078) has year-round service between Anchorage and Valdez; the fare to Glennallen is $33 from Anchorage, $22 from Valdez. **Alaska-Yukon Motorcoaches** (tel. 907/276-1305) run a similar service from May 27 to September 15. Once you're in the Copper River Basin, **Wrangell Mt. Bus Adventures** (tel. 907/822-5519) runs between Glennallen and McCarthy on Monday, Wednesday, and Friday from May 15 to September 15. The round-trip fare from Glennallen is $80 to McCarthy, $60 to Chitina.

Three air taxis serve the area. **Gulkana Air Service,** three miles north of Glennallen on the Richardson Hwy., and **Sportsman Flying Service,** at Tolsona Lake, 17 miles west of Glennallen on the Glenn Hwy., charter flights for fishing, hunting, and sightseeing at rates of about $200 an hour. Contact both at P.O. Box 31, Glennallen, AK 99588 (tel. 907/822-5532 or 822-3221). **McCarthy Air,** McCarthy, AK 99588, flies from McCarthy to Anchorage for $150 per person and to Glennallen for $75 per person (based on three passengers). For information, call the McCarthy Lodge (tel. 907/333-5402).

For information about the Copper River Basin, contact the **Greater Copper Valley Chamber of Commerce,** P.O. Box 469, Glennallen, AK 99588 (tel. 907/822-5555).

GLENNALLEN

The town proper is spread along the Glenn Hwy. about 1½ miles west of the Richardson Hwy. junction. Most services in the Copper River Basin are focused here, including a state trooper station and offices for the Bureau of Land Management and the Alaska Department of Fish and Game. There's also a seven-bed, two-doctor Cross Road Medical Center (tel. 822-5888, or 911 in emergencies). In lieu of a newspaper, personal messages are broadcast daily as "Caribou Clatter" on Christian-format KCAM radio (790).

Right in Glennallen, at Mile 187 on Glenn Hwy., the **Caribou Motor Inn,** P.O. Box 329, Glennallen, AK 99588 (tel. 907/822-3302), has 38 units—10 with private bath, 28 in former pipeline construction trailers with shared baths. The rooms are adequately furnished with double and single beds, and cable TVs, but no phones. They go for $35 to $43 single, $39 to $48 double, year round. The Caribou also has a café, and showers for $4.

North of Glennallen 12 miles, at Gakona Junction (where the Richardson Hwy. meets the Tok Cut-off), the **Gakona Junction Village,** P.O. Box 222, Gakona, AK 99586 (tel. 907/822-3664, or toll free 800/962-1933, 800/478-3665 in Alaska), has 18 pleasant units and a reasonably priced restaurant. You'll feel right at home when you enter the lobby: it's like a living room, with couches and a coffee table flanked by a grandfather clock, heated by a big fireplace. The rooms, appointed in beige and white, are spacious and amply furnished, with two double or three single beds, cable TV, dressing tables, and centrally controlled hot-water heating. There's a pay phone in the entryway and a guest Laundromat down the hall. Bunny's Café, open from 6 a.m. to 9 p.m., doubles as an art gallery. Have homemade pastries for breakfast, a hot turkey sandwich for lunch ($6), chicken fried steak ($8), or halibut Olympia ($13) for dinner. Room rates during high season (June 1 to September 15) are $57.50 single, $67.50 double; in the off-season, $8 less.

Two miles past the junction on the road to Tok is the **Gakona Lodge,** P.O. Box 285, Gakona, AK 99586 (tel. 907/822-3482), a historic way station that serves perhaps the best charcoal-grilled steaks between Anchorage and Whitehorse. The log Carriage House restaurant has hunting trophies mounted all over its walls, but it also has a touch of coarse elegance: dim lighting and red tablecloths. You'll get a 16-ounce New York cut here for $17, a 20-ounce T-bone for $19, or a Yankee pot roast dinner for as little as $8. There's a full bar and a nice wine list. Nine basic rooms with communal baths are available for overnights at year-round rates of $25 single, $45 double.

Midway between Glennallen and Gakona at Mile 118 on Richardson Hwy., the **Dry Creek State Recreation Site** has 58 campsites on 372 acres with well water and toilets. Its information center, housed in a sod-roofed log cabin, has displays on the region's geology, natural history, and recreational opportunities. The Copper

Basin district ranger for Alaska State Parks, P.O. Box 286, Glennallen, AK 99588 (tel. 907/822-5536), can inform you about other campsites and picnic grounds in the area.

LAKE LOUISE

Twenty-seven miles west of Glennallen on the Glenn Hwy. is the junction to Lake Louise, a popular summer-winter resort area. The gravel road leads 17 miles to a state recreation area with campsites and a boat launch. The lake is held to be especially good for lake trout, burbot, and grayling fishing. Ice fishing, snowmachining, and cross-country skiing are popular here in winter.

Several lodges accommodate long-term guests as well as overnight visitors. Two favorites are **Evergreen, The Lodge at Lake Louise,** Star Route C, Box 8867, Lake Louise, AK 99645 (tel. 907/822-3250), and the **Wolverine Lodge,** Star Route C, Box 8862, Palmer, AK 99645 (tel. 907/822-3988).

COPPER CENTER

Established as a trading post in 1896, turned into a mining camp by the 1898 gold rush, Copper Center grew to become a principal supply center for the entire region. The **George I. Ashby Memorial Museum,** operated by the Copper Valley Historical Society, has preserved many fascinating pioneer and Native artifacts, including telegraph, mining, and trapping articles. It's open summers only, Wednesday through Saturday from 1 to 4 p.m., and also on Friday from 6 to 8 p.m.

The museum is housed in a bunkhouse annex of the **Copper Center Lodge,** built in 1932 to replace the historic Blix Roadhouse constructed in 1898 but later destroyed by fire. A three-story log structure, it has 14 no-frills rooms with private bath priced at $40 a night single, $45 double. Write Copper Center, AK 99573 (tel. 907/822-3245).

CHITINA

Sixty-four miles southeast of Glennallen at the end of the Edgerton Cutoff, Chitina (pop. 42) has a couple of dozen homes, a National Park Service ranger station, minimal tourist facilities, and one public phone. Established in 1908, and once considered a likely candidate to become Alaska's capital, Chitina's star faded rapidly after the demise of copper mining in the Wrangell Range. The old town is still fun to walk through and reminisce. There's one motel/restaurant here: the **Copper Nugget,** P.O. Box 55, Chitina, AK 99566 (tel. 907/823-2202), open May to November only. It's got just two rooms, though.

McCARTHY

The narrow, winding McCarthy Road extends 61 unpaved miles up the abandoned Copper River & Northwest Railroad bed. It takes about four hours to make the trip in normal summer conditions; when it rains, the muddy conditions make a four-wheel-drive vehicle essential. From the parking area at end of the road, two hand-pulled trams cross the Kennicott River to McCarthy. Travelers should ask ahead at the Chitina ranger station for current road conditions.

Only about a dozen people still live in McCarthy, one of the more remote Alaskan communities connected to the rest of the world by road (however bad). From 1910 to 1938 this was "town" to the men who worked at the Kennicott Copper Mine, six miles north. The colorful buildings of the abandoned mine are still basically intact.

Historic artifacts and photographs are on display at the **McCarthy-Kennicott Museum.** There's also a country store in McCarthy.

Accommodation is available mid-May through September. The **McCarthy Lodge,** McCarthy, AK 99588 (tel. 907/333-5402), provides full board and local transportation starting at $75 per person; it also has bunkhouse lodging for $15. More deluxe trappings can be found at the old mine in the **Kennicott Glacier**

Lodge, P.O. Box 103940, Anchorage, AK 99510 (tel. 907/258-2350). Private rooms are $75 single, $95 double; bunkhouse berths are $40 per person; full board packages run $125 a day. **McCarthy Wilderness Bed & Breakfast,** P.O. Box 111241, Anchorage, AK 99511 (tel. 907/277-6867), has lodging in three rustic rooms for $45 single, $55 double; a former territorial commissioner's cabin which sleeps ten rents for $125 a night.

McCarthy Trailrides offers rides up the Erie Mine wagon trail to the old mine and excursions to Root Glacier and Stairway Ice Falls for prices starting at $20 per person. Full-day trips, including lunch, run $120, and custom overnight rides are $140. **St. Elias Alpine Guides,** with headquarters in the Mother Lode Powerhouse, schedules white-water rafting and hiking trips at rates from $25 per person. The McCarthy Lodge has the details. The lodge itself rents mountain bikes for $12 a day.

WRANGELL–ST. ELIAS NATIONAL PARK AND PRESERVE

Chitina and McCarthy are encompassed in this 12.4-million-acre parkland, which stretches from the Gulf of Alaska at Yakutat Bay 200 miles north to the headwaters of the Copper River, and from the Canadian border 150 miles west to Glennallen.

The Wrangell Mountains are the park's centerpiece. Of 20 peaks in the United States over 14,000 feet, 17 of them are in Alaska and 3 of them are here—Mount Blackburn (16,390 feet), Mount Sanford (16,237 feet), and Mount Wrangell (14,163 feet). In terms of sheer mass, Mount Wrangell is the largest—bigger by four times even than Washington state's Mount Rainier, no mole hill itself. Mount Wrangell is also a semi-active volcano. Though it hasn't formally erupted since 1912, when it sent a stream of lava to its base and threw ash beyond Glennallen, it has shown signs of reawakening since the mid-1970s. On cold clear mornings it's easy to see wisps of steam rising from Mount Wrangell's vents.

The main park headquarters is at Mile 105 of the Old Richardson Hwy., ten miles south of Glennallen and four miles north of Copper Center. A **visitors center,** P.O. Box 29, Glennallen, AK 99588 (tel. 907/822-5234), is open daily during the summer months, making maps and other information available to the public. There are National Park Service district ranger stations at Chitina (tel. 823-2205) and Nabesna (tel. 822-5238).

Together with Kluane National Park in Canada's Yukon, Wrangell–St. Elias has been designated a World Heritage Site by the United Nations.

SPORTS

Salmon and trout fishing are popular year round in hundreds of lakes and streams throughout the region. Hunters seek bear, moose, mountain goats, and especially dall sheep, with August and September the popular big-game-hunting seasons. About one-third of the national parkland is designated a "preserve" where hunting is permitted.

Because so much of this region is inaccessible by road or trail, bush planes are essential. Fly-in costs average $190 an hour for plane charter. Many operators offer package trips; typical charges are $245 to $850 for one-day trips, $550 to $1,000 for three-day/two-night forays including cabin or tent camp, boat, and motor, for two to three persons.

Backpacking, mountaineering, and cross-country skiing are also very popular on marked trails or self-created ones. The sport surging in popularity here is river rafting, mainly on the Copper and/or Chitina Rivers.

A six-day excursion down the Chitina River is offered by **Keystone Raft and Kayak Adventures,** P.O. Box 1486, Valdez, AK 99686 (tel. 907/835-2606). The first day is spent traveling by road from Chitina to McCarthy; the second day is free for exploring. Then follow three days on the river, through undisturbed wilderness surrounded by spectacular mountains and ever-present wildlife. The price of $600 includes meals, lodging, equipment, and transportation from Anchorage or Valdez.

At the park's northern extreme, Carey Davis's **Nabesna Whitewater Rafting,** Star Route A, Box 1455, Slana, AK 99586 (tel. 907/822-3426), works out of the Devils Mountain Lodge at the 42-mile end of the Nabesna Road. Davis offers several fly-in, raft-out trips, but the most intriguing is an excursion from the headwaters of the Copper River on Mount Sanford. Trips are run from June through early August. Room and full board at the **Devils Mountain Lodge** (same address and phone number as Nabesna Whitewater Rafting) is $65 a day. Lodging and meals are also available at the **Silvertip Lodge,** Mile 25.5 on Nabesna Road (Star Route A, Box 1260), Slana, AK 99586 (tel. 907/337-2065), for $20 to $35 a night.

4. Matanuska-Susitna Valleys

The twin valleys of the Matanuska and Susitna Rivers, known to most Alaskans simply as "Mat-Su," comprise a rich agricultural region at the head of the Cook Inlet. The dual hubs of the district, Palmer and Wasilla, are about 11 miles apart, each 40 miles north of Anchorage—Palmer on the Glenn Highway heading east to Glennallen and Tok, Wasilla on the George Parks Highway heading north toward Denali National Park and Fairbanks.

It's easy to dismiss the Mat-Su Valley as a slightly distant suburb of Anchorage. A significant percentage of the population in fact commutes to the "big city." But tarry a while: the valley boasts such singular attractions as the headquarters of the Iditarod Trail sled-dog race, the historic Independence Mine at spectacular Hatcher Pass, the state fairgrounds, and the Museum of Alaska Transportation and Industry. You'll also find excellent fishing, hiking, rafting, and other leisure pursuits.

Two factors played key roles in Mat-Su's historical development: the building of the Alaska Railroad and the establishment of the Matanuska agricultural colony. The Anchorage–Fairbanks rail line was completed in 1915, and within two years Wasilla had been established as the trade and commercial center for a growing community of Hatcher Pass gold miners and Mat-Su homesteaders. In 1935 the Matanuska Colony was created as a place to give a new start to Midwest American farmers ruined by the Great Depression. This federally sponsored agricultural experiment helped develop the 15,000 cultivated acres of farmland around Palmer; more than half of Alaska's farms today are in the Matanuska Valley. The growing season is short, but long hours of daylight produce record vegetables—like 80-pound cabbages!

The climate in the Mat-Su Valley is very much like that of Anchorage, with slightly greater extremes of summer heat (record high: 89°F) and winter cold (record low: −40°F). Temperatures typically range between 4°F and 21°F in mid-winter, with eight to ten inches of monthly snowfall, and between 44°F and 68°F in midsummer, with two inches monthly rainfall.

For more information on Mat-Su facilities and activities, write the **Matanuska-Susitna Convention & Visitors Bureau,** 191 E. Swanson Ave., Suite 201, Wasilla, AK 99687 (tel. 907/376-8000).

GETTING THERE

As noted, the two major highways serving the Mat-Su Valley are the George Parks and Glenn Highways, both emanating from Anchorage. Because many of the valley's best attractions are off the main roads, you're best served by driving a private vehicle. Commuter bus service is provided, however, by **Alaskan Star Charters** (tel. 345-2432 in Anchorage).

The **Alaska Railroad** passes through Wasilla twice daily in summer—once each, northbound (at 9:50 a.m.) and southbound (at 6:40 p.m.)—and less frequently in winter. It takes about 1½ hours to reach Anchorage (one-way adult fare: $14), 4¾ hours to Denali Park (fare: $49.50), and 8¼ hours to Fairbanks (fare:

$76). Call for information and reservations (tel. 265-2685 in Anchorage, or toll free 800/544-0552).

As befits Alaska, there are small airports in both Palmer and Wasilla, as well as in several smaller communities in the valley. These serve private pilots and charter services. Regularly scheduled flights go through Anchorage.

Tours of the valley are offered by two large agencies and three smaller ones. **Gray Line of Alaska,** 547 W. Fourth Ave., Anchorage (tel. 277-5581, or toll free 800/544-2206), operates a six-hour trip including visits to an experimental farm and a musk-ox farm. Trips depart Anchorage daily at 10:30 a.m., mid-June to mid-September; fare is $31, half price for children under 12. **Alaska Sightseeing Tours,** 543 W. Fourth Ave., Anchorage (tel. 276-1305), offers a similar trip.

Bed and Meals on Wheels, P.O. Box 190411, Anchorage, AK 99519 (tel. 907/248-3747), runs a more personal nine-hour motorhome excursion to the Mat-Su Valley, including the Museum of Transportation and Industry, for $35 per person including lunch (maximum of four adults). **Alaska Heritage Tours,** P.O. Box 210691, Anchorage, AK 99521 (tel. 907/696-8687), offers custom tours of the valley; among its specialties is handicapped tours. Daily tour service between Anchorage and the valley is provided by **Mat-Su Motor Tours** (tel. 373-5455).

PALMER

Palmer's 3,200 people owe the existence of their community to the Matanuska Colony. These 202 families were resettled here in 1935 under President Franklin Roosevelt's "New Deal" to establish the only farm colony in American history. They drew lots for 40-acre tracts, then lived in tent camps while they cleared the land, planted it, and built their log homes and barns. The surviving structures are testimony to the colony's perseverance and success, as is the fact that the main street through downtown Palmer is called Colony Way, and the biggest local annual event (in June) is called Colony Days.

The **Greater Palmer Chamber of Commerce,** P.O. Box 45, Palmer, AK 99645 (tel. 907/745-2880), maintains its offices in the **Visitor Information Center and Museum** at 723 S. Valley Way, just across the railroad tracks from the intersection of South Colony Way and East Fireweed Avenue. This rustic log cabin, open daily in summer from 9 a.m. to 5 p.m., weekdays only the rest of the year, displays many memories of the Colony era in its downstairs collection. It also has a gift shop.

Valley Hospital, 515 E. Dahlia Ave. (tel. 745-4813), serves residents for many miles around. Palmer has 11 churches and numerous fraternal organizations.

Colony Days is celebrated annually over the third weekend of June. Events include a parade, open-air market, various games, and exhibits. The **Alaska State Fair,** of course, draws folks from all over the state to Palmer during the 11 days ending Labor Day. The fair includes the standard agricultural exhibits (a great place to see oversize Matanuska Valley vegetables), lots of animals, 4-H and homemaker displays, a carnival and parade, horse shows, and a rodeo.

Where to Stay and Eat

The **Fairview Motel,** P.O. Box 745, Palmer, AK 99645 (tel. 907/745-1505), is across from the fairgrounds at Mile 40½ on Glenn Hwy. To an initial 20 rooms, it plans to add another 10 plus a restaurant/lounge. All rooms have queen-size beds and other standard furnishings, local TV, free local phone calls, and thermostat-controlled hot-water heating. Three rooms have kitchenettes; all have access to the guest Laundromat. Rates are $41 to $51 single, $46 to $56 double.

The **Pioneer Motel,** 124 W. Arctic St., Palmer, AK 99645 (tel. 907/745-3425), has 19 rooms from $40 and eight ground-floor apartments with kitchenettes from $65. All rooms have cable TVs. The **Valley Hotel,** 606 S. Alaska St., Palmer, AK 99645 (tel. 907/745-3330), has rooms for $40 and $42 a night and a 24-hour restaurant.

Russell's Bed & Board, HCO 1-6229-R, Palmer, AK 99645 (tel. 907/376-

7662), is actually closer to Wasilla (four miles) than Palmer (seven miles) at De-Camp Road, Mile 38 on the Parks Hwy. One of several bed-and-breakfasts in the area, it has private-entrance guest rooms for $35 single, $45 double, with use of laundry facilities and a cable-TV room. Full board—including a packed lunch and a home-cooked dinner with dessert—runs just $10 more.

Right in Palmer is another B&B, the **Tannenhof Llama Inn,** P.O. Box 3434, Palmer, AK 99645 (tel. 907/745-2309, or 745-1361 days). This German-style house on a small llama ranch off Laurel Street charges $55 single, $65 double, in summer, and $10 less in winter. Llama pack trips can be arranged by reservation.

Palmer has the 45-space municipal **Matanuska River Park** for RVs in a wooded section of town, on East Arctic Avenue. It has picnic tables, toilets, showers, and sewage disposal. Contact the visitor center for information and rates. There are several state campgrounds nearby as well, including the **Moose Creek Wayside,** five miles north on the Glenn Hwy.

Popular Palmer restaurants are **The Bounty,** Mile 0.2 on the Palmer–Wasilla Hwy., just off Glenn Hwy. (tel. 745-4040), open daily from 9 a.m. to 11 p.m.; the **Colony Kitchen,** Mile 40.7 on Glenn Hwy., by the fairgrounds (tel. 745-4330), open daily from 6 a.m. to midnight; and **Pizzaria Delphi,** in the 100 block of West Arctic Avenue (tel. 745-2929), open from 11 a.m. to 11 p.m. daily for pizza and pastas. You can eat well at any of these restaurants for $10 or less.

What to See and Do

Start your exploration at the **Alaska State Fairgrounds,** with its main entrance at Mile 40.2 on Glenn Hwy. Something is always going on here, even when the fair is not.

The grounds of the **Museum of Alaska Transportation and Industry** (tel. 745-4493) are adjacent to the fairgrounds. This largely open-air museum appeals to kids, with its variety of trains, boats, planes (civilian and military), trucks, farm machinery, and parts thereof. Some of the vehicles are of the "climb aboard" variety. Inside three rail cars is a very interesting Alaska Railroad historical exhibit. Open Tuesday through Saturday from 8 a.m. to 4 p.m. Admission is $3 for adults.

Also at the fairgrounds is **Colony Village** (tel. 745-4827), which has preserved five of the early Matanuska Colony buildings. A church, barn, and two private homes today house historical displays. Open from 10 a.m. to 4 p.m. Monday through Saturday June through August. Admission is free. The Valley Performing Arts group (tel. 745-2484) makes its home in the Lutheran church building, now a theater.

The last of the original three Colony churches still in regular use is the so-called **Church of a Thousand Logs,** a United Protestant church (Presbyterian), two blocks east of the visitor center on Elmwood Avenue. Built in 1936 and 1937, it has handmade pews and a pulpit overlaid with birch bark.

The **University of Alaska Agricultural Experiment Station,** on Trunk Road off the Parks Highway (tel. 745-3278), was established in 1917. A center for dairy farm testing, it also has developed numerous crop adaptations for subarctic growing conditions. Guided tours of the facilities are offered daily, June 1 to September 1, by appointment. The station is open for general viewing from 8 a.m. to 4 p.m. Monday through Friday.

The **Musk Ox Development Corp.** has a unique musk-ox farm about two miles north of downtown on Archie Road, just west of the Glenn Highway (tel. 745-4151). More than 100 of these shaggy beasts live at an old Colony farm, where their downy underwool (*qiviut*) is harvested to be knit into clothing by Natives of several western Alaska villages. There are numerous educational displays in the barn, and guided tours are conducted half-hourly from 9 a.m. to 7 p.m. daily, May 15 to September 15, and from 10 a.m. to 3 p.m. on Saturday, October 15 to May 15. Adults pay $3 admission; seniors and students, $2.

A half mile west of the Glenn Highway, on the Palmer-Wasilla Highway, is the **Palmer Tsunami Observatory** (tel. 745-4212). Scientists at this head-quarters of the Alaska Regional Tsunami Warning System, a division of the National Weather Service, record seismic and tidal information. Public tours are offered on Friday from 1 to 3 p.m.; groups can make special arrangements.

Sports

BASEBALL The semi-pro **Mat-Su Miners,** a member of the Alaska Baseball League, play in June and July at Hermon Brothers Field on the state fairgrounds. Home games start at 7:30 p.m. Monday through Saturday, with Sunday doubleheaders at 1 p.m.

FISHING Trout angling is popular in the Palmer area, mainly in the valley's numerous small lakes. Try the Kepler-Bradley Lakes, half a dozen of which are interconnected by foot trails starting at Mile 37.3 on Glenn Hwy. The **Alaska Department of Fish and Game** has an office in Palmer at the corner of South Alaska Street and West Cedar Avenue (tel. 745-4247).

HIKING There are dozens of trails, ranging in difficulty from easy to strenuous, in the Palmer area. Chuck Kausic at the Mat-Su Borough office (tel. 745-4801) has detailed information on conditions and terrain. Cross-country skiers use the same trails in winter.

One short steep trail that offers a fine view over the Mat-Su Valley and the Knik Glacier goes half a mile up Bodenburg Butte south of Palmer. Access is from Mile 11.5 on Old Glenn Hwy.

HORSEBACK RIDING Riding is a very popular activity in the Mat-Su Valley. As evidence, no fewer than ten different **horse shows** are held at the state fairgrounds between May and September.

Two local riding stables offer mounts for trail rides. **Matanuska Guest Ranch,** on the Trunk Road west of Palmer (tel. 745-3693), offers horseback and pony rides daily, June to August; weekends only in spring and fall. It also has a private camper park and camp facilities for kids 8 to 15. **Rafter T Ranch,** Mile 50 on Glenn Hwy. (tel. 745-2894), 2.2 miles north of Palmer, has trail rides, and buggy and hay rides.

RIVER RAFTING An hour's drive northeast of Palmer, **NOVA Riverunners,** P.O. Box 1129, Chickaloon, AK 99645 (tel. 745-5753), offers thrilling white-water day trips on the scenic Matanuska River ($40 in mid-week, $45 on weekends; children under 12, half price) and rugged Lions Head River ($55). Remote 2- to 12-day expeditions are also plotted. The rafting season is May through September.

SWIMMING There's an indoor pool at Palmer High School, West Arctic Avenue (tel. 745-5091) and a "Man-Made Lake" on the Knik River for summer dips.

TENNIS Public tennis courts are four blocks east of the visitor center at South Gulkana Street and East Elmwood Avenue.

GLACIERS

The **Knik Glacier** is one of the closest glaciers to a major population center in Alaska, yet it's one of the least visited. It cannot be reached by road, but is easily accessible traveling by air or by boat up the Knik River. Between 1915 and 1966 this glacier was a natural wonder, damming its own meltwater in the winter to create a 25-square-mile lake, then overflowing the ice dam in late June in a two-week, 150-million-gallons-a-minute flood. By 1967 the glacier had receded to a point where the ice dam was no longer created, but it's still an impressive sight.

Two firms take visitors close to the foot of the glacier. **Knik Glacier Scenic**

Tours, P.O. Box 876805, Wasilla, AK 99687 (tel. 373-2628), offers three-hour airboat tours for $69. They're located at Mile 5.5 on Old Glenn Hwy. **Knik Glacier Raft Tours,** HCO 2-7669, Palmer, AK 99645 (tel. 907/745-1577 or 272-3269), touts its 3½-hour float trip, including a picnic lunch and hike, priced at $30 for adults, $20 for kids. Trips begin at Mile 1.2 on Knik River Road. The outfit also has a bed-and-breakfast cabin available near the river at $50 double.

Numerous air-charter services offer short tours of Knik Glacier and iceberg-laden Lake George, high in the Chugach Mountains. **Knik Air,** at the Wasilla Airport (tel. 376-4888), asks $65 per person (minimum of three people) for a one-hour tour.

An awesome sight about an hour's drive east of Palmer, at Mile 102 on Glenn Hwy., is the **Matanuska Glacier.** Some 27 miles long, 4 miles wide, and 1,000 feet thick, it is stable and accessible enough to allow visitors to walk on it. A side road gives access to a state park and campground at Mile 101 on Glenn Hwy., from which a trail leads a short distance to the foot of the glacier. Watch out for crevasses!

Stop for a snack at the **Long Rifle Lodge,** Mile 102.2 on Glenn Hwy. (Star Route C, Box 8445), Palmer, AK 99645 (tel. 745-5151), with a deck overlooking the glacier; or stay at the **Sheep Mountain Lodge,** Mile 113.5 on Glenn Hwy. (HCO 3-8490), Palmer, AK 99645 (tel. 907/745-5121), a well-kept secret since the 1940s. Dall sheep often clamber across the rocky peak behind the lodge. Six cabins, some with private baths, are priced at $50 double. A sauna and Jacuzzi are available. The restaurant specializes in sourdough pancakes, homemade soups and chili, and rich desserts. Twelve miles of groomed cross-country ski trails surround the lodge. From May to October Sheep Mountain's dorm cabins are an official American Youth Hostel, also open to nonmembers.

A good source of information on the Matanuska River country northeast of Palmer is the **Greater Sutton Chamber of Commerce,** P.O. Box 24, Sutton, AK 99674.

WASILLA

Built between and around the shores of two beautiful long lakes—Wasilla Lake and Lake Lucille—it's no wonder that Wasilla is growing fast. Many of its 3,900 people commute to work in Anchorage. Few are descendants of the miners and homesteaders who gave the town its start in 1917.

You can see many reminders of early Wasilla, however, in the **Wasilla Museum and Visitors Center,** on Main Street at Swanson Avenue (tel. 376-2005), less than two blocks north of the George Parks Hwy. A log house built in 1931 as a community social center, it was restored in 1967 by the Wasilla–Knik–Willow Creek Historical Society to preserve artifacts pertaining to local history. Open Tuesday through Saturday from 10 a.m. to 6 p.m., on Sunday and Monday from noon to 6 p.m.

Additional information can be obtained from the **Greater Wasilla Chamber of Commerce,** P.O. Box 871826, Wasilla, AK 99687 (tel. 907/376-1299), in Cottonwood Creek Mall where the Palmer-Wasilla Road joins the Parks Hwy. It's open weekdays from 9 a.m. to noon and 1 to 5 p.m.

To get around Wasilla and vicinity, you can rent a car from **Avis,** Mile 1.2 on Lucille Street (tel. 373-2847), or from **Ford Rent-a-Car,** Mile 40 on Parks Hwy. (tel. 376-5656).

The train station is right in the middle of town, where Main Street crosses the Parks Hwy., though it's not in active use: you'll have to stand up outside as you wait for the Alaska Railroad and hope it's not late (as it often is). Wasilla also has a small airport used by private planes and air-taxi services.

From their Wasilla offices, the semi-weekly *Frontiersman* newspaper and weekly *Valley Sun* keep the Mat-Su area informed. Valley Hospital in Palmer serves Wasilla as well, though medical assistance can be obtained at **Arctic Insta Care** on Swanson Avenue (tel. 376-2437), an emergency clinic.

Given Wasilla's location between the lakes, it's no surprise that the town's biggest celebration of the year makes use of them. **Wasilla Water Days,** over the July 4 weekend, includes a family picnic, parades (land and water), waterski competition, raft races, and even an underwater tricycle race. The **Iditarod Winter Carnival,** held the first weekend of March to coincide with the start of the Iditarod Trail sled-dog race, includes a costume ball, a Monte Carlo night, and a golf tournament on frozen Wasilla Lake. Shuttlebus service carries musher fans to the Iditarod restart point at Settlers Bay.

Where to Stay and Eat

The valley's finest lodging is the quiet **Mat-Su Resort,** 1850 Bogard Rd., Wasilla, AK 99687 (tel. 907/376-3229). Built of split logs in 1939, it was expanded and renovated in 1980.

Here you can step out on the back porch of your deluxe room and feed the ducks waddling up from Wasilla Lake. Each of the 15 newer units, including three suites and three private cabins, has a kitchenette, queen-size bed, sofa and coffee table, satellite TV, phone (free local calls), electric baseboard heat, and more-than-adequate lighting. They're decorated in brown and rust tones, with slatted red blinds and rich wood furnishings. Summer rates, including tax, are $68 for deluxe rooms, $83.75 for suites or cabins. The resort also has 22 older economy rooms without TV or phone that go for just $36.50 a night. Winter rates run $5 to $10 less.

The main resort lodge houses the extremely popular restaurant (tel. 376-3228) and lounge. A huge brown bear and musk ox in trophy cases greet you at the entry; elsewhere you'll spy record-class moose and caribou racks and a set of enormous walrus tusks. The lakeside dining room offers a wide variety of full dinners such as petite filet mignon and scampi ($21.75) and deep-fried frogs' legs ($14). Open for lunch weekdays from 11 a.m. to 2:30 p.m., on Saturday to 3 p.m.; for dinner, Sunday through Thursday from 5 to 10 p.m., on Friday and Saturday to 11 p.m. Sunday brunch is served from 10:30 a.m. to 2:30 p.m. The lounge has live music and dancing on weekend evenings.

Rowboats and paddleboats are available for rent in the summer, and there are covered picnic facilities for 600 people. During the winter, hayrides are offered on Friday and Saturday nights and on Sunday afternoons, and the lake is ideal for skating and cross-country skiing.

The **El Toro II Motor Lodge,** Mile 40 on Parks Hwy. (P.O. Box 874907), Wasilla, AK 99687 (tel. 907/376-4908), has 12 rooms appointed in blue, with queen-size beds but few other furnishings; they do have cable TVs, phones (free local calls), and electric baseboard heat. Rates are $55 single, $60 double, from May through September; $5 less the rest of the year.

Check in at the El Toro II restaurant, off Herman Road via Sun Mountain Avenue. This coffeeshop, with its Aztec plaques on the walls, prides itself on its Guadalajaran chef and Mexican specialties, like enchiladas rancheras ($7.50) and chiles rellenos ($8). There's a prime-rib special ($10); lunches are priced from $4.25. Open from 11 a.m. to 11 p.m. Sunday through Thursday, to midnight on Friday and Saturday (shorter hours in winter). The lounge, with its round bar and country-western band playing Wednesday through Sunday nights, is known as the favorite watering hole of the Wasilla City Council.

The **Kashim Inn,** 181 W. Parks Hwy. (Mile 42), Wasilla, AK 99687 (tel. 907/376-5800), has made its 11 small rooms feel like grandma's house, with lacy calico bedspreads and drapes and mountain pictures on the green-striped walls. But it's hard to ignore the noise from the nearby highway and railroad tracks. The standard furnishings include cable TV, a dressing table, and hot-water thermostat heating, but no phone. Rates are $49, single or double, in summer; $39 in winter.

The coffeeshop, open 24 hours daily, offers burgers from $4, omelets from $4.50, and an eight-ounce New York steak-and-prawns dinner for $10.50. The lounge has a big dance floor and top-40 bands Thursday through Saturday.

The Windbreak, 2201 E. Parks Hwy., Wasilla, AK 99687 (tel. 907/376-

4484, or 376-4209), has ten small rooms nicely appointed with blue carpeting and bedspreads, and wildlife pictures on the walls. Pick up your key at the bar. The furnishings are basic but sufficient; TVs are available on request, and there's a courtesy phone at the foot of the stairs. You'll pick up a little bar noise, but the price is right: $45, single or double (you pay per room), from mid-May to mid-September; $35 the rest of the year. For reservations, write 1890 Glenn Hwy. South, Palmer, AK 99645.

The Windbreak Café, open daily from 6 a.m. to midnight in summer, to 10 p.m. in winter, has simple wood décor and mounted trout on the walls. Breakfast is served all day (try the four-egg "Windbreak special"; $6.25), quarter-pound burgers with "the works" cost just $3.50; and for dinner you can feast on sirloin steak and all the shrimp you can eat for only $10. There's also a complete children's menu. After eating, you can enjoy the pool table, darts, and big-screen TV in the lounge.

Bed-and-breakfast enthusiasts should contact the Matanuska-Susitna Convention & Visitors Bureau (tel. 907/376-8000) for a full listing of the 22 B&Bs in the valley. One that stands out is **Yukon Don's,** 1½ miles off the Parks Hwy. on Fairview Loop Road (HC31-5086), Wasilla, AK 99687 (tel. 907/376-7472). Don Tanner is a Yukon River outfitter; his wife, Kristan, a former Miss *and* Mrs. Alaska, and their children help run this delightful inn. Five guest rooms and one suite have fishing, hunting, dog-sledding, or logging décor, and the 900-square-foot recreation room has a barrel stove, pool table, and bar. There's even a sauna and exercise room. Rates start at just $25 and go up to $80 for the suite. Don won't take credit cards, but he'll accept gold dust.

For campers, the **Finger Lake Wayside** on Bogard Road has 41 sites with water, toilets, and picnic tables. The **Greenridge Camper Park,** 1130 Vicky Way, Mile 29.4 on Parks Hwy. (tel. 907/376-5899), and **Rainbow Acres RV Park,** Mile 49 on Parks Hwy. (tel. 907/376-8897), have full hookups.

The **Country Kitchen,** in Wasilla Center (tel. 376-6357), serves French and Italian meals, as well as homemade baked goods. Open Sunday through Thursday from 6 a.m. to 11 p.m., on Friday and Saturday until midnight. The **Peking Chinese Restaurant,** Mile 42.5 on Parks Hwy. (tel. 376-4919), has a dedicated following.

One of the valley's unique new eateries is the **Yamakawa Japanese Restaurant,** 290 N. Yenlo St., in Meta Rose Square (tel. 373-6117). It has daily lunch specials in the $5 to $6 range, and full dinners for $13.50 to $17.50, with beer, wine, and sake available. Korean dishes are also served. Open from 10 a.m. to 9 p.m. Monday through Thursday, until 10 p.m. on Friday and Saturday; closed Sunday.

A favorite lunching spot for Wasilla business people is **The Deli,** in the Wasilla Business Park, on Swanson between Main and Yenlo (tel. 376-2914). It's open from 8 a.m. to 6 p.m. Monday through Friday and noon to 4 p.m. on Saturday.

What to See and Do

After dropping into the Wasilla Museum and Visitors Center, you can head out the back door to **Frontier Village,** a restoration of early Wasilla on Boundary Street at Swanson Avenue. Two different styles of log cabins, Wasilla's first school, a smokehouse, smithy, and public bath have been preserved here. Admission is $1 for adults, 50/ for children. Open from 10:30 a.m. to 6 p.m. daily except Sunday.

The Iditarod sled-dog race, called by some "The Last Great Race" on earth, has its headquarters at the **Iditarod Trail Sled Dog Race Gift Shop and Visitors Center,** Mile 2.2 on Knik Road (tel. 376-5155). Slide or video shows of past races are shown on request. You can buy videotapes, photos, posters, and other gifts and souvenirs. Visitors get a free card autographed by the mushers. Open in summer Monday through Friday from 8 a.m. to 5 p.m., and on Saturday and Sunday from noon to 5 p.m.

There are those who claim that the musher who wins the arduous Iditarod race should be considered the world's most durable athlete. An Alaskan woman, Susan Butcher, won the race three years in a row, from 1986 to 1988. (Past winners have come from Alaskan villages with names like Red Devil, Coldfoot, Clam Gulch, and Trapper Creek.) Beginning on or about March 1, normally consuming two to three weeks of time, teams of 12 to 18 dogs and their solo musher follow the Iditarod National Historic Trail over two mountain ranges, down the great Yukon River, and around a corner of the frozen Bering Sea. They retrace the route used during the Nome gold rush to move mail, supplies, and (later) diphtheria serum from the ice-free port of Seward. Millions of dollars in gold were transported by dog teams returning from Nome along the same route. For information on the modern race, write the **Iditarod Trail Committee**, Pouch X, Wasilla, AK 99687.

An important stop along the trail, then as today, was **Knik,** the first white settlement in what is now the Mat-Su Borough. The trade and supply center for the Willow Creek and Iditarod gold-mining districts between 1898 and 1919, it is remembered today only by historians and by two surviving structures. One of them is the **Bjorn Cabin,** restored by members of the Knik–Wasilla–Willow Creek Historical Society.

The other is the former pool hall, now the **Knik Museum and Sled Dog Mushers Hall of Fame,** Mile 14 on Knik–Goose Bay Road (tel. 376-7755). Many artifacts of the old town are preserved here. But most visitors come to see its dog-sled memorabilia and portraits of famous mushers, past and present—such as four-time Iditarod winner Rick Swenson. The curator is Vi Redington, wife of renowned racer Joe Redington, Sr. Open in summer from noon to 6 p.m. Wednesday through Sunday; in winter, arrangements can be made by calling the Wasilla Museum (tel. 376-2005). Admission is $1 for adults, 50¢ for children.

If Joe Redington, Sr., born in 1917, competes in the 1990 Iditarod race, it will be his 16th. He finished fifth in 1988 at the age of 71. Called the "father of the Iditarod," he moved to Knik in 1948, opened much of the trail to mushing, promoted the race to Nome, and launched it in 1973 with a $25,000 purse. Now it's $250,000 and rising. You might have seen Redington mush down Pennsylvania Avenue in President Ronald Reagan's 1981 inaugural parade. Redington's **Knik Kennels,** Mile 12 on Knik–Goose Bay Road (tel. 376-5562), is said to be the largest sled-dog kennel in the world. Visitors are welcome, but call for an appointment.

Sports

BOATING   The **Mat-Su Resort** (tel. 376-3228) has paddleboat and rowboat rental for use on Wasilla Lake.

BOWLING   On the Palmer-Wasilla Highway just east of town, **Valley Lanes** (tel. 376-9737) is open from 10 a.m. to midnight daily. Its Golden Nugget Lounge has live country-and-western music on Friday and Saturday nights.

CANOEING   The Little Susitna River, north and west of downtown Wasilla, is a favorite place. **Chimo Guns** (see "Fishing," above) rents canoes for $18 the first day, $15 a day for two or more days.

FISHING   Wasilla Lake has good trout fishing. Lake Lucille and Finger Lake, east of Wasilla on Bogard Road, are stocked with silver (coho) salmon. **Chimo Guns,** next to Carr's Shopping Center on Yenlo Street (tel. 376-5261), open daily, sells fishing gear and licenses.

GOLF   The **Settlers Bay Country Club,** south of Wasilla on Knik–Goose Bay Road (tel. 376-5466), has a nine-hole public golf course and pro shop.

HORSEBACK RIDING   The **Mountain Creek Guest Ranch** (tel. 373-7433) offers custom trail rides. **Settlers Bay Stables** (tel. 376-9690) has trail rides and boarding. **Scenes of Yesteryear,** Mile 1.7 on Pittman Road (tel. 376-2379), and **Wilosa**

Ranch, Mile 5 on Fishhook Road (tel. 376-5617), offer horse-drawn carriage rides and rentals.

ROLLER SKATING **Let the Good Times Roll-er Rink** is just off the Parks Hwy. on Broadview Avenue (tel. 376-8858).

SWIMMING There's year-round indoor activity at Wasilla High School's **Mat-Su Pool** on Bogard Road (tel. 376-4222), open daily from 6 a.m. to 9:30 p.m. Call for schedules and fees. At **Wasilla Lake,** there's a roped-off municipal swimming area and picnic spot next to the Parks Hwy.

TENNIS The Wasilla city courts are downtown on Swanson Avenue, at Town Site Park. Settlers Bay Village Inn, Mile 8 on Knik Road, has courts.

WINTER SPORTS Cross-country skiing and skating, icesailing, and ice fishing are popular on the surrounding lakes. More serious skaters appreciate the **Mat-Su Ice Arena** at Wasilla Junior High School, Crusey Street at Bogard Road (tel. 376-9260).

HATCHER PASS

High above timberline, yet only a short drive from Palmer or Wasilla, is spectacular Hatcher Pass. Dotted with decaying mine buildings, the narrow, winding, unpaved road follows the Little Susitna River to the summit (3,886 feet), yielding glorious alpine views of the Mat-Su Valley, Cook Inlet, and Chugach Mountains, and providing access to popular hiking, horseback riding, cross-country skiing, and snow-machining terrain.

This southern end of the Talkeetna Mountains was actively mined for gold from the early 20th century until World War II. Today the **Independence Mine State Historic Park** recalls that era. This mining complex, which once produced 48,194 ounces of gold ($1,686,790 in value) in a single year, is slowly being restored for public viewing. The visitor center in the former mine manager's quarters features interpretive displays on the mine, which opened in 1908 but never recovered from World War II closures, and was finally shut down in 1951. A "touch tunnel" at the entrance to the visitors center simulates a gold mine, complete with miners' voices. The park includes an assay building (which is being turned into a hard-rock mining museum), bunkhouses, mess halls, a tipple, and other structures.

The visitors center and other facilities are open from 11 a.m. to 7 p.m. Thursday through Monday in summer. On weekends from July 4 to Labor Day, guided tours (at $3 per person) follow the trails among a dozen abandoned buildings. At any time of year, trails wind throughout and beyond the park for self-guided tours.

The Alaska Division of Parks is also trying to work out an agreement for tours of the adjacent Gold Cord Mine, which reopened in 1979 to process the old Independence claims. For more information, contact the Parks Division's Mat-Su office at Finger Lake on Bogard Road (tel. 745-3975).

Close by the Independence Mine at 3,000 feet elevation is the **Hatcher Pass Lodge,** P.O. Box 2655, Palmer, AK 99645 (tel. 907/745-5897). Co-owner Tom Murphy moved to this large red A-frame in 1974 because the terrain closely approximated his beloved Swiss Alps.

In summer the lodge serves breakfast, lunch, and dinner in its intimate restaurant. Specials include bratwurst on a bun ($5.25), Swiss-style fondue for two with Gruyère and Emmentaler cheeses, kirsch and wine ($7.50), and beef Stroganoff ($14.50). There's also an espresso bar and cocktail service. Four private cabins rent for $75 double, and four small attic rooms with double or bunk beds are available for bed-and-breakfast at $40 single, $55 double. A propane-heated sauna sits outside beside a "dipping hole" in the Little Susitna headwaters. Open daily from June 1 through September 15, then Friday through Sunday only until April 30; closed in May.

Twenty kilometers (12 miles) of set-track cross-country ski trails surround the lodge in winter. A ski school teaches cross-country and Telemark skiing, and a ski patrol is on duty every weekend.

In 1988 a Japanese company, Mitsui, was awarded a 55-year lease and rights to develop an 11,000-acre alpine ski resort at Hatcher Pass. Plans are currently underway.

BIG LAKE

One of south-central Alaska's largest recreational playgrounds, Big Lake is the largest of many dozens of small, low-lying, glacier-dug lakes that dot the lower Mat-Su Valley. Anchorage residents and others build vacation homes along the shore of this lovely island-studded body of water.

Big Lake Road joins the George Parks Highway at Mile 52. Turn southwest here and drive about six miles to a land of marinas, resorts, campgrounds, and picnic areas. Fishing (for salmon, trout, grayling, and burbot), swimming, sailing, boating, and waterskiing are the preferred sports here in summer; in winter, snow-lovers turn to ice fishing, skating, cross-country skiing, and snow-machining on the frozen lake. The year's big events reflect seasonal sports interest—the Big Lake Sailing Regatta is held the third weekend of July and the Big Lake 500 Snowmachine Race takes place in March.

There are several places to rest your head around the lakeshore. With a couple of the lodges having fallen on hard times and awaiting new ownership, my preference is the **Big Lake Motel,** P.O. Box 520728, Big Lake, AK 99652 (tel. 907/892-7976). Built in 1986, this 20-room accommodation at Mile 5 on South Big Lake Road is adjacent to the Big Lake Airport and a mile from the lake by road. Each room has a navy-blue color scheme, queen-size beds, custom-built oak furnishings, sliding windows with screens and blinds, remote-control color TV, a clock-radio, indoor and outdoor entrances, and thermostat-controlled hot-water heat. There's a pay phone in the lobby. Year-round rates are $50 single, $55 double, $60 twin. A licensed restaurant is planned shortly.

The most popular restaurants on Big Lake itself are inaccessible most of the year except by water or ice. But that doesn't slow business down. The **Islander Restaurant,** on Long Island (tel. 892-7144), is open daily for steaks and seafood. The owners operate the *Big Wheel Jessica A.,* a 58-foot paddlewheeler that carries up to 60 people on Big Lake sightseeing tours beginning at noon and 4 p.m. Monday through Friday in summer. The tour, leaving from the Burkeshore Marina, costs $27.50, including lunch at the Islander, $34.50 with dinner. Reservations are required.

On a promontory near the west end of the five-mile-long lake is the **Call of the Wild** restaurant and bar (tel. 892-6274), locally famous for its burgers and rib-eye steaks. It's open daily for lunch and dinner, and features live music for dancing from 9 p.m. to 1 a.m. on Friday and Saturday and 4 to 8 p.m. on Sunday. Get there via 24-hour water taxi from the marina, or drive across the ice in winter.

WILLOW

A Talkeetna Mountain gold-mining camp from 1897 to 1940, Willow was revived from virtual ghost-town status by the completion of the George Parks Hwy. in 1972. Its star flared in 1976 when Alaska voters selected a nearby 100-square-mile site as the location of their new capital city. Six years later when voters refused to release funds to move the capital from Juneau, however, Willow (pop. 500) resigned itself to being just another outpost on the highway.

The community center is the **Willow Trading Post,** half a mile east of Mile 69.5 on Parks Hwy. (P.O. Box 49), Willow, AK 99688 (tel. 907/495-6225). Five nicely appointed rooms and small cabins beside a small lake vary in size and furnishings, but all are spacious and homey, with wall-to-wall carpeting and oil heat. Rates are just $45 double in summer, $40 in winter. Toilets are in a separate bathhouse; showers cost $3. You can use the pay phone in the bar, which prides itself on its beer selection and its live piano music on Saturday nights.

A short snack menu is offered at the Willow Trading Post, but for meals, you're best off heading three miles back toward Wasilla to **White's Crossing Café,** Mile 66.5 on Parks Hwy. Open from 7 a.m. to 9 p.m. daily, it offers some of the best prices on the road: ham and eggs is $4 for breakfast, soup and sandwich runs $3.25 for lunch, New York steak goes for $8 at dinner.

Between Willow and Houston, the **Nancy Lake State Recreation Area** preserves a beautiful forested flatland speckled with 130 lakes, most of them interconnected by streams (to the delight of canoeists and fishermen). During the summer, rangers lead a variety of naturalist programs, including campfire talks and a children's discovery hike. Although swampy ground limits hiking, 40 miles of trails are maintained within the recreation area, including the mile-long Tulik Trail, a self-guided nature walk. The Lynx Lake Loop canoe trail makes a leisurely weekend excursion with few portages.

The **Alaska Division of Parks** maintains an office at the Nancy Lake Wayside, Mile 66.5 on Parks Hwy. (tel. 495-6273). The Nancy Lake Parkway turns off the Parks Hwy. at Mile 67.3 and runs south and west 6½ miles to the South Rolly Lake campground, with 100 units open to campers. Nancy Lake Wayside has another 30 sites, and there are 11 more campsites along the canoe trail system.

The **Nancy Lake Marina and Resort,** Mile 64.5 on Parks Hwy. (P.O. Box 114), Willow, AK 99688 (tel. 907/495-6284), has five rustic cabins in a lakefront birch forest that rent for $25 year round. If you don't mind bringing your own bedding (sleeping bags) and using a separate bathhouse, you'll get a carpeted, wood-paneled cabin with beds, kitchen facilities, a dining table, and wood or electric heat. There are also 50 campsites without hookups. The lodge/general store rents everything from boats, motors, and fishing tackle to aircraft fuel and snow machines.

DENALI NATIONAL PARK

1. WHERE TO STAY AND EAT
2. WHAT TO SEE AND DO
3. SOUTH OF THE PARK
4. NORTH OF THE PARK

Measured from its base to its summit, and taking into account its enormous girth, there is no greater mountain on earth than Mount McKinley.

The Athabaskan Indians called the mountain Denali, "The High One." The white man named it Mount McKinley in 1896, after Republican presidential candidate Sen. William McKinley. First scaled in 1913, it became the centerpiece of Mount McKinley National Park in 1917. The park area was tripled in size (to six million acres) in 1980 and its name (but not the mountain's) was changed to Denali National Park and Preserve.

At 20,320 feet, Mount McKinley is North America's highest point. The towering centerpiece of the 600-mile-long Alaska Range, it dominates a wilderness of tumbling glaciers and of braided, silt-filled rivers, of subarctic taiga and tundra vegetation, and of an exceedingly rich wildlife.

Indeed, it's the animals that attract most of Denali's annual visitors, now exceeding 500,000 during the brief summer season. Brown (grizzly) bears, moose, caribou, dall sheep, wolves, and numerous smaller mammals thrive in the park, along with a varied birdlife.

For all its 9,300 square miles, there are only about 100 miles of road in the park. Of that, only 18 miles is unrestricted. Because of the negative effect that the throngs of summer visitors were having on the wildlife population, park authorities several years ago began limiting private vehicle traffic, and operating a shuttle bus service and wildlife tours. The ploy worked; the bears, sheep, and caribou are now more commonly seen along the road than they were in the late 1970s.

Park headquarters is located about 3½ miles west of the George Parks Highway junction, where Riley Creek meets the Nenana River, 249 road miles north of Anchorage and 126 miles south of Fairbanks. Two miles nearer the highway are the Denali Park Hotel (the only private concession in the national park wilderness area) and the Denali railway station and post office. All other hotels and restaurants servicing park visitors are located outside the park boundary, along the Nenana River. Some are located half a mile north of the park road junction; another handful are scattered between 6 and 13 miles south. There are several campgrounds in the park and three wilderness lodges (of varying degrees of rusticity) at Kantishna, an almost-

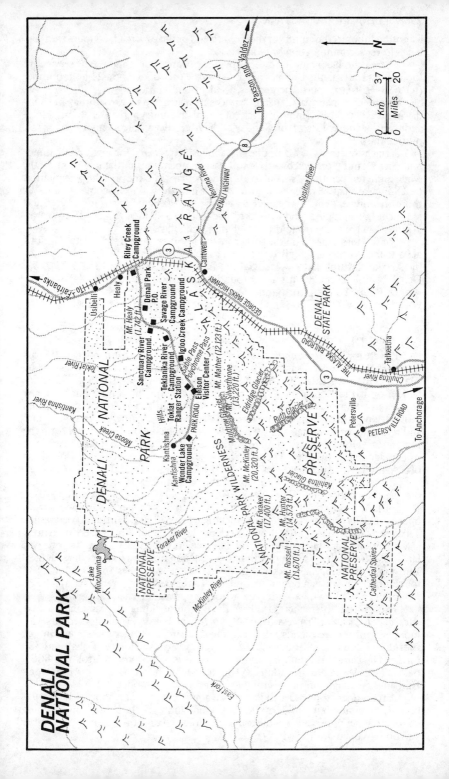

DENALI
NATIONAL PARK

N

Km 37
Miles 20

To Paxson and Valdez

ALASKA RANGE

Nenana River

Susitna River

DENALI HIGHWAY

8

Cantwell

GEORGE PARKS HIGHWAY

3

Riley Creek Campground

To Fairbanks

Healy

Usibelli

Denali Park P.O.

Mt. Healy (1,742 ft.)

Savage River Campground

Sanctuary River Campground

Teklanika River Campground

Igloo Creek Campground

Sable Pass

Polychrome Pass

Toklat Ranger Station

Eielson Visitor Center

Mt. Mather (12,123 ft.)

Mt. Silverthrone (13,220 ft.)

Eldridge Glacier

Muldrow Glacier

Ruth Glacier

DENALI STATE PARK

THE ALASKA RAILROAD

3

Talkeetha

Chulitna River

Petersville

PETERSVILLE ROAD

To Anchorage

Tokat River

DENALI

NATIONAL

Kantishna Hills

Toklat River

PARK ROAD

PARK

Kantishna

Wonder Lake Campground

Moose Creek

Kantishna River

NATIONAL PARK WILDERNESS

PRESERVE

Kahiltna Glacier

Mt. McKinley (20,320 ft.)

Mt. Foraker (17,400 ft.)

Mt. Hunter (14,573 ft.)

Mt. Russell (11,670 ft.)

Cathedral Spires

NATIONAL PRESERVE

NATIONAL PRESERVE

Foraker River

Lake Minchumina

McKinley River

East Fork

forgotten mining community at the western end of the park road, 88 miles from the next closest accommodation or food service.

There is no hospital within the park—the nearest clinic and rescue service are located in Healy, about 12 miles north—but the park does have a 24-hour number (tel. 683-9100) to report emergencies, accidents, or injuries.

Interdenominational Christian services are held at 6 p.m. on Saturday and Sunday in the Riley Creek Campfire Circle, at 9 a.m. on Sunday at the Denali Park Hotel auditorium; and at 11 a.m. on Sunday at the McKinley Chalets activity center just outside the park.

As far as weather goes, only one rule applies: be prepared for anything. Summer tendencies can be predicted—days will have temperatures in the low to mid-60s, while night temperatures will fall to 40°F and perhaps into the 30s; the precipitation (a 2.8-inch annual average in July, the wettest month) will likely come as rain. But those are only tendencies; the mercury climbed to 90°F one day in June 1969, and ten inches of snow fell (and drifted to five feet) in a sudden August 1984 storm. Weather can change very rapidly in high mountain regions.

For full information on the park, contact the **Superintendent, Denali National Park and Preserve,** P.O. Box 9, Denali Park, AK 99755 (tel. 907/683-2294), or the **Alaska Natural History Association,** P.O. Box 230, Denali Park, AK 99755. Denali National Park also has a year-round **information line** (tel. 907/683-2686). **Alaska Public Lands Information Centers** are located in Anchorage at 605 W. Fourth Ave. (tel. 271-2737) and in Fairbanks at 250 Cushman St. (tel. 451-7352).

GETTING THERE

Private car is the first choice; it's a 5- to 6-hour drive from Anchorage, 2½ to 3 hours from Fairbanks. Denali Park is also served by numerous tour buses and by **Alaska-Denali Transit,** P.O. Box 4557, Anchorage, AK 99501 (tel. 907/276-6443), or at the Denali train station (tel. 683-2798). The private bus company charges just $35 one way from Anchorage to Denali, and makes photo stops en route. It operates daily from June through August, leaving Anchorage at 8:30 a.m. and returning from Denali at 2:30 p.m. **Alaska Sightseeing Tours** buses leave the Denali Park Hotel daily at 2 p.m. to Fairbanks (tel. 452-8518) and via Talkeetna to Anchorage (tel. 276-1305). There's also seasonal van service aboard the **Denali Express,** 405 L. St., Anchorage (tel. 907/274-8539, or toll free 800/327-7651).

Two alternative means of arriving at the park can be spectacularly beautiful, if the weather cooperates. The **Alaska Railroad,** 411 W. First Ave. (P.O. Box 107500), Anchorage, AK 99510 (tel. 907/265-2623, or toll free 800/544-0552), operates a daily express run between Anchorage, Denali, and Fairbanks (via Wasilla, Talkeetna, and Nenana) from the last week of May until mid-September. Train no. 1 leaves Fairbanks at 8:30 a.m. and arrives in Denali Park at 12:15 p.m.; the one-way fare is $34 for adults, $17 for children 5 to 12. Train no. 2 leaves Anchorage at 8:30 a.m. and arrives in Denali Park at 3:45 p.m.; the one-way fare is $62 for adults, $31 for children. Or you can buy an Anchorage–Fairbanks ticket (or vice versa) for $88 (children pay $44), with no extra charge for a stopover at Denali Park.

Express-train passengers also have the option of riding in Gray Line's deluxe *McKinley Explorer* or Princess Tours' *Midnight Sun Express,* private domed cars with more elegant service than is offered in the standard passenger cars. **Gray Line of Alaska** (tel. toll free 800/544-2206) charges $95 for Anchorage–Denali and $50 for Denali–Fairbanks; children pay half price. **Princess Tours** (tel. toll free 800/647-7750) asks $295 for adults, $185 for children, for one-way Anchorage–Fairbanks fare, including an overnight stay at the Harper Lodge.

A train does stop at Denali Park twice a month (both northbound and southbound) in winter, but you'd have to pack a tent and warm gear and plan on doing some snow camping were you to stay: all facilities close for the season in September and don't reopen until May.

The other transportation option is by air. **ERA Aviation,** the Alaska Airlines commuter line (tel. 907/248-4422, or toll free 800/426-0333), has daily Anchorage–Denali Park service in summer. But even if you come to the park by another means, you should try to set aside some time for a clear-weather flightseeing excursion around Mount McKinley. It's the one way to get a grasp of the mountain's true magnitude. Contact **Denali Flying Service,** P.O. Box 82, Denali Park, AK 99755 (tel. 907/683-2261), or most Anchorage and Fairbanks air-taxi services for current schedules and rates.

The following companies are among those offering two-day/one-night tour packages between Anchorage and/or Fairbanks and the park: **Alaska Sightseeing Tours,** 808 Fourth Ave. and Battery Building, Seattle, WA 98121 (tel. 206/441-8687, or toll free 800/621-5557); **Atlas Tours,** 609 W. Hastings St., Dept. 104, 5th Floor, Vancouver, BC V6B 4W4 (tel. 604/669-1332); **Gray Line of Alaska (Westours),** 300 Elliott Ave. West, Seattle, WA 98119 (tel. 206/281-3535, or toll free 800/544-2206); **Midnight Sun Tours,** P.O. Box 103355, Anchorage, AK 99510 (tel. 907/276-8687, or toll free 800/544-2235); and **Princess Tours,** 2815 Second Ave., Suite 400, Seattle, WA 98121 (tel. 206/728-4202, or toll free 800/647-7750).

1. Where to Stay and Eat

As noted, hotels serving park visitors are spread across more than a dozen miles of the George Parks Highway and a couple more miles of the park road. Because their number is limited, they are treated here as if they were all in the same community—which, in a way, they are. Remember, hotels at Denali open no earlier than mid-May and shut their doors by late September. Don't expect TVs or room phones: you won't find them anywhere. You also won't find a room tax.

THE PARK HOTEL

The **Denali National Park Hotel,** Denali Park, AK 99755 (tel. 907/683-2215), may be all things to all people. To those who don't stay here (as well as those who do), it's a focus of national park activities, a place to dine or drink, to hear a naturalist's lecture or to join a nature walk. To those who do rest their heads here, it's a quiet, luxury accommodation.

Surrounded by a rail depot theme, you do indeed feel as if you're walking to a ticket window when you step into the lobby to register. Behind you in the khaki-painted wood building, surrounding a pot-bellied wood stove are the hard-backed benches typical of stationary seating. Oldtime ceiling fans whir on the low rafters, and there are luggage lockers on the platform outside. Where you might expect to find arrival and departure timetables, however, lists of the day's events are posted. And when you sidle up to the sideboard where clerks await your arrival 24 hours a day, you'll be greeted with a room key rather than a train ticket.

Giant blow-up photos of Mount McKinley decorate the lobby walls, and usefully point out the major climbing routes to the summit. At the far end, on the right, are the Denali Dining Room and the Whistle Stop snackshop. The dining room—open daily from 7 a.m. to 10 p.m., and from 5 to 6:30 a.m. with a light breakfast for those leaving on a wildlife tour—has a garden atmosphere, with high-backed chairs and wood dividers on green carpeting, surrounded by hanging plants and green-patterned wallpaper. Breakfasts, including blueberry pancakes and bagels with smoked salmon, are priced from $4.75 to $6.75; lunches and dinners, ranging from quiche and pasta to salmon and sirloin steaks, run $4.25 to $11.75. The Whistle Stop, open from 10 a.m. to midnight daily, features burgers, chili, tuna sandwiches, and the like for about $3 to $5.

Just beyond the rear of the main lobby is the Gold Spike Saloon (open from noon to midnight daily), crowded into a pair of railcars. Off to the left, past the gallery of Denali wildlife photographs, is the large gift shop (open from 9 a.m. to 9:30 p.m. daily), which specializes in Native crafts.

If you continue through a covered passageway to the main guest section of the hotel, you'll come to the 300-seat auditorium. Films are shown daily at 12:30 and 7 p.m., and most nights at 9 p.m. there's a naturalist's presentation or slide show.

The 100 standard guest rooms (priced at $93 single, $103 double) are wood paneled and decorated in earth tones with red-orange carpeting and upholstery. Each spacious room is furnished with a pair of double beds, a desk/dresser, working chair, and easy chair. There's hot-water heat and a sink with a large mirror outside the bathroom.

Unfortunately, the hotel's budget rooms have been phased out. They were previously found in the Pullman compartments of four retired Alaska railcars whose colorful yellow-and-blue panels still lend a festive air to the hotel.

Finally, anyplace where the employee housing is called "The Tapeworm" and the mess hall is known as "The Zoo" has got to be a fun place to work. And when the employees enjoy themselves, you know the visitors will too.

The Denali National Park Hotel is open May 19 to September 9 only. It's owned and managed by ARA Outdoor World Ltd., the same group that operates the McKinley Chalet Resort and McKinley Village Lodge. Write or call year round for reservations: 825 W. Eighth Ave., Suite 240, Anchorage, AK 99501 (tel. 907/276-7234). Ask about their "2-for-1" special—two nights for the price of one if you visit before mid-June.

DELUXE ACCOMMODATIONS

The **McKinley Chalet Resort**, Mile 239 on George Parks Hwy., Denali Park, AK 99755 (tel. 907/683-2215), is the modern complement to Park Hotel tradition. It truly is a resort, with 216 elegant rooms in 18 one- and two-story cedar log chalets connected by covered boardwalks and gravel paths, high on a bluff overlooking the raging Nenana River. The resort enfolds the Chalet Club spa, with glassed-in swimming pools, Jacuzzi, sauna, masseur, Universal gym, sun table, and aerobics classes; a meeting hall and convention center that has hosted such celebrities as Chuck Yeager in speaking engagements; a theater featuring nightly VHS movies and other programs; a very tasteful jewelry and gift shop; and a sophisticated dining room and cocktail lounge.

As you enter the hotel from its spacious parking area, you'll get the red-carpet treatment—literally. Reception is straight ahead. The restaurant and bar are to your right, the gift shop and theater to your left. Ask at the desk about shuttlebus service to the railroad station and Denali Park Hotel.

The food at Denali National Park has come a long way from the days when airplane pilots and co-pilots would be sure to eat at separate restaurants to reduce the likelihood that both would become ill! The Chalet Dining Room offers full dinner entrees like poached salmon in dill-hollandaise sauce ($16.50), veal piccata ($19), steamed king crab legs ($24.50), and for non–meat eaters, the vegetable boutiquetière ($12.50). This is also the place to get an authentic baked Alaska dessert—individually baked as a "mini-McKinley" ($4.25). Lunches are priced $4.75 to $9.50; breakfasts, from $4.50 to $7. Wildlife photos, Native antiques, and fine woodwork set the Chalet Dining Room apart from other restaurants in the Denali area. One particular room, the Jewel Box, entered by sliding glass doors and featuring a pyramidal glass ceiling, affords a bird's-eye view of river rafting some 500 feet straight down. Open daily from 5 to 6:30 a.m. for early breakfast, 7 to 10:30 a.m. for full breakfast, 11 a.m. to 2:30 p.m. for lunch, and 5 to 9:30 p.m. for dinner.

For more casual meals, the Denali Deli (open daily from 10:30 a.m. to midnight), has omelets, pastas, sandwiches, and light seafood and steak dinners. It also has outside seating around an array of flower boxes. The Chalet Lounge (open from noon to 2 a.m. daily) offers live solo entertainment five nights a week.

Fannie Quigley's **Alaska Cabin Nite,** in a turn-of-the-century wilderness cabin near the Nenana River, is the Denali area's most popular nighttime attraction. An all-you-can-eat family-style dinner of salmon, ribs, blueberry pie, and trimmings is followed by a 45-minute show of singing, dancing, and tall tales spun by a colorful troupe of prospectors, trappers, and other "sourdoughs." There are seatings at 5:30 and 8:30 p.m. nightly from Memorial Day weekend through Labor Day weekend. Adults pay $19; children 11 and under pay $11.

With a 93½% room occupancy rate throughout its season, it's no wonder that the McKinley Chalet Resort—already the area's largest hotel—is planning to expand again. Of its current 216 rooms, 36 are furnished with queen-size beds, all others with twins: they're more appropriate for package tour groups, which comprise the largest part of the resort's clientele. You enter the typical quiet guest accommodation to a red-carpeted sitting room with a desk and hideaway sofa-bed; the bedroom, with its orange-checked drapes and bedspreads, adjoins. All rooms have fabric walls and are electrically heated. Rooms are priced at $112 single, $122 double, plus $10 for each additional guest up to five in a room. There are also two executive suites priced at $200 to $350 a day. Two-for-one rates are available before June 15. The hotel is open only from May 19 to September 16.

For off-season bookings, contact ARA Outdoor World Ltd., 825 W. Eighth Ave., Suite 240, Anchorage, AK 99501 (tel. 907/276-7234).

With three seasons of operation already under its belt, the splendid **Harper Lodge Princess,** Mile 238.5 on Parks Hwy. (P.O. Box 110), Denali Park, AK 99755 (tel. 907/683-2282), needn't have done more to prove itself a worthy competitor to the Chalets for the title of Denali's finest accommodation. But Princess Tours prepared for the 1990 season by adding a new 32-room wing, bringing the total capacity to 192 rooms.

An Athabaskan prospector named Walter Harper was the first man to climb Mount McKinley (in 1913); the rustic theme and furnishings of this $6.3-million hotel are a tribute to his era. Exterior walls and interior front walls are done up in log siding, giving the appearance of entering the lobby and individual guest rooms through log passageways. The three wings are attached to a central lobby, with a gift shop and tour desk. A covered walkway leads to the Summit Restaurant (open from 5 a.m. to 10 p.m. daily) and Base Camp Bar with a panoramic view of the Nenana River and Horseshoe Lake. Walter's Burger Bar has light meals. There's shuttle service to the train station and to various activities at park headquarters and the Denali Park Hotel.

Rooms are furnished with twin or double beds, dressers, tables, phones, and color TVs. Six VIP suites have Jacuzzis; two rooms are equipped for disabled travelers. High-season rates for standard rooms run $126, single or double, with a $10 charge per additional guest. Suites are $225 a night. The lodge is open late May to mid-September.

Off-season bookings are made with Princess Tours, 2815 Second Ave., Suite 400, Seattle, WA 98121 (tel. 206/728-4202, or toll free 800/647-7750).

A few miles south is the **McKinley Village Lodge,** Mile 224 on Parks Hwy., Denali Park, AK 99755 (tel. 907/683-2265). It was established by the late Gary Krabb, one of the pioneers of tourism in the Mount McKinley area (he lived here from 1959 until his death in 1987), who also built the North Face Lodge (see "Wilderness Lodges," below). Today it's owned and operated by ARA Outdoor World Ltd., 825 W. Eighth Ave., Suite 240, Anchorage, AK 99501 (tel. 907/276-7234).

The hotel lobby is very large and it presents access to a lovely candlelit lounge that is carpeted and upholstered in red, with a big fireplace and a small jukebox. The more contemporary restaurant specializes in steaks, chicken, and seafood in the $8 to $14 range.

There's a meeting and banquet room, the Kantishna Room, which seats 200; national-park films are shown at 8 p.m. nightly. On the wall is a true relic: a dog sled pulled by 16 dogs to the 17,000-foot elevation of Mount McKinley.

The "village" includes a gift shop, coin-operated guest laundry, recreation center with covered and outdoor picnic tables, even a small sandy riverside beach. A rafting outfitter starts his downriver trips next door.

There are 50 spacious rooms, brightly decorated with orange-gold carpeting and gold-colored bedspreads and drapes. All have two double beds, large hexagonal tables with chairs, desk/dressers, and thermostat-controlled hot-water heating. The walls are partially wood paneled. Half the rooms have a view of the Nenana River. Rates are $86 single, $96 double, from mid-June to September 1; before and after those dates, the price is $10 cheaper. The lodge is open from June 2 to September 9.

MODERATELY PRICED ACCOMMODATIONS

In this price range, we've stepped out of hotels and into private cabins.

The **Denali Crow's Nest Log Cabins,** Mile 238.5 on George Parks Hwy. (P.O. Box 70), Denali Park, AK 99755 (tel. 907/683-2723), are the pick of the litter in this category. Owners Carol and Mike Crofoot and their children, Tiko and Koro, have the best of both worlds: they summer here at Denali National Park and winter on an island in tropical Fiji. The winters must be good to them, because they return to Alaska with tremendous energy for their summer business.

The Crofoots began with a river-rafting operation, then added 39 rough-hewn spruce cabins on three levels at the foot of the Sugarloaf Mountain reserve for dall sheep, across the Parks Hwy. from the McKinley Chalets. (Reach the cabins by turning off the highway at the McKinley/Denali Salmon Bake and driving 200 yards uphill.) Each cabin is angled to provide a 180° vista of the mountains and river. They contain two double beds with calico bedspreads, picnic tables, propane heating, and historical photographs on the walls, personally selected by Carol from National Park Service archives. All cabins have private baths, and all windows are screened to keep pesky insects out. There are also two open-air hot tubs. Planter boxes with colorful flowers brighten decks on each cabin level, with benches to look across the river valley at Horseshoe Lake. The charge per cabin is $98 a night for one to four guests. Two family cabins with room for six guests go for $125. Cabin guests get 10% discounts on Crow's Nest raft trips (see the "What to See and Do" section, below).

The Crow's Nest's Overlook Bar & Grill (tel. 683-2641) gives diners the choice of sitting inside or on a large sunny deck looking across the Nenana River at the park. The grill opens at 5 a.m. for continental breakfast, serves a full lunch and dinner menu featuring moderately priced steaks, seafoods, chicken, and burgers, and finally closes around midnight. Box lunches will be packed on request. The lounge is the Crofoots' eclectic delight—done up in the unlikely marriage of Fiji and Alaska motifs. South Pacific artifacts, Alaskan paintings and prints, and even baleen whale speckle walls covered with Fijian tapa cloth!

The **Denali Cabins,** Mile 229 on George Parks Hwy. (P.O. Box 229), Denali Park, AK 99755 (tel. 907/683-2643 in summer, or 907/258-0134 in winter), are another lodging-plus-rafting enterprise. Gary and Denae Kroll have a burgeoning village of 53 varnished wood cabins of various configurations on nicely landscaped riverside grounds. They sleep two, four, or six, and have private baths or (for nine units) share a central facility. (The shower house is central to everyone; there are also two small hot tubs and a third, giant-size tub on the riverbank.) Two-thirds of the carpeted, propane-heated units are set up for four guests, with two double beds and private baths. Rates start at $74 for four-person cabins without private bath, $75 for two-person cabins with private bath, $94 for four-person cabins with private bath, and $130 for six-person cabins with private bath.

The village has its own generator, well, and sewage system. A grocery sells items for cooking on barbecue grills. There's a gift shop in the office. Courtesy pickup is provided to guests who arrive at the park via train or bus. Denali Cabins guests get 10% discounts on trips with Denali Raft Adventures (see the "What to See and Do" section, below).

The **McKinley Wilderness Cabins,** Mile 224 on George Parks Hwy. (P.O. Box

89), Denali Park, AK 99755 (tel. 907/683-2277), has 11 simple duplex cabins of unfinished wood beside gurgling Carlo Creek, 13 miles south of the park junction. Each unit contains single beds with light bedding, a dresser, a table and two chairs, venetian blinds on the windows, and propane heating. Six units sleep two, and five sleep four. Showers and toilets are in the rear of the big red A-frame that marks the facility from the highway. Rates—$75 to $90 per cabin—include a continental breakfast.

BUDGET ACCOMMODATIONS

Pickings are slim in this category.

The **Grizzly Bear Cabins and Campground,** Mile 231.1 on George Parks Hwy. (P.O. Box 7), Denali Park, AK 99755 (tel. 907/683-2696), has a real variety of options. Thirteen cabins, including two renovated prospectors' cabins, sleeping two to six, rent for $49 to $96 a night; most are $60 to $68. Each cabin (though every one is different) has wood heat; all but the smallest have running water and propane cooking stoves. Beds are doubles, singles, and hideaway sofas, in various combinations. These units—whose individual histories are described on plaques on the front walls—have a real pioneer feel, shrouded as they are in spruce and aspen forest overlooking the Nenana River. There are also a handful of unheated but rainproof tent cabins, with cots on wood floors, priced at $18 to $20 a night. A central washhouse contains toilets, hot showers, and laundry facilities. RV, camper, and tent sites are available by the riverside; they cost $13 a night, including the tent if you need one. For bookings during the off-season, contact Grizzly Bear, 5845 Old Valdez Trail, Salcha, AK 99714 (tel. 907/488-3932).

The **Carlo Creek Lodge,** Mile 223.9 on George Parks Hwy. (P.O. Box 103), Denali Park, AK 99755 (tel. 907/683-2573), has five rustic log cabins on a wooded 25-acre plot 13 miles south of the park entrance. All have two beds and standard furnishings, with toilets, showers, and propane heat. They are priced in the $60 range. There are also 25 RV and tent sites, at $10 a night, with a dump station. The lodge includes a general store and gift shop.

Shoestring travelers may be glad to find **The Happy Wanderer Hostel,** Mile 238.6 on Parks Hwy., at a destination with normally high prices. A rustic two-room cabin across the road from Lynx Creek Pizza, it has eight bunks, with a curtain separating men from women. There's a community kitchen, but no indoor plumbing on running water. Write P.O. Box 108, Cantwell, AK 99729, or call 907/683-2690, to learn the day's security-lock combination.

RESTAURANTS IN THE PARK VICINITY

Besides those in the hotels, there are only a couple, but they're definitely worth visiting.

The **McKinley/Denali Salmon Bake,** Mile 238.5 on Parks Hwy. (tel. 683-2733), is open from 6 a.m. to 10 p.m. daily in a freely constructed wood-frame structure with crushed rock for a floor and transparent plastic for windows. A sourdough breakfast is served until 11 a.m., after which you can help yourself to salmon, halibut, or beef ribs broiled over an outdoor grill, plus homemade soup and baked beans, a salad bar and beverage (beer, wine, and soft drinks). Lunch will run you about $7.50; an all-you-can eat dinner, around $18.

Lynx Creek Pizza, Mile 238.6 on Parks Hwy. (tel. 683-2547), offers delectable deep-dish pizza for prices ranging from $8 (8-inch pizza, three cheeses only) to $20 (16-inch pizza, five toppings). The restaurant also has calzones at $6.50, deli sandwiches from $6 to $8, and a selection of beers and wines. The atmosphere is cozy, with a big fireplace and indoor-outdoor seating. Open from 11 a.m. to 11 p.m. daily, it's in the rear of a log cabin that also serves as a gas station, liquor store, and campground office. It operates from mid-May to mid-September.

After these two and the hotel restaurants, the next closest restaurant is the Healy Roadhouse, eight miles north (see the "North of the Park" section, below).

CAMPGROUNDS

Within **Denali National Park** itself are seven campgrounds containing 225 sites. No advance reservations are taken, so everything is on a first-come, first-served basis—and in the peak of the season, is frequently gobbled up by 11 a.m. You must register in person between 8 a.m. and 7 p.m. at the Riley Creek Visitor Access Center, a quarter of a mile west of the George Parks Hwy. junction with the park road. The maximum stay permitted is 14 nights.

The largest campground is at Riley Creek, with 102 sites. Facilities include flush toilets, piped water, and a sewage dump station. Cost per night is $10. Two of the campgrounds in the park's interior—Igloo and Wonder Lake—are off-limits to private vehicles and are reached by shuttle bus only.

Outside the park boundary, the **Lynx Creek Campground,** Mile 238.6 on Parks Hwy. (tel. 907/683-2547), has 46 campsites with a central bath and shower, piped water, Laundromat, and dump station. Rates are $18.75 with electricity, $14.50 without, $1.50 per additional person over four. Open May 12 through September 16. The **Grizzly Bear Campground** and **Carlo Creek Lodge** (see the listings above) charge $13 and $5 a night, respectively, for tent and vehicle campers.

WILDERNESS LODGES

If you are enthralled by the idea of waking up on a crisp, cloudless summer morning and gazing across a meadow of wildflowers at North America's largest mountain, you don't want to stay in the main Denali National Park resort area. You want to make the 90-mile trek west to Kantishna.

Four lodges, each with its own distinct style, operate in or near this historic mining district within the national park, but outside the wilderness boundaries.

Camp Denali, P.O. Box 67, Denali Park, AK 99755 (tel. 907/683-2290 in summer), is the cream of the crop. Comprising 18 cabins, a dining cabin, a log lodge, and outbuildings spread across 60 acres of hills not far from Wonder Lake, it offers an all-inclusive vacation experience in the great outdoors.

Camp Denali places great emphasis on environmental education. Full-time naturalist-guides are among its 22-member staff, and frequent workshops are offered on such subjects as botany, ornithology, glaciology, photography, and local history. Activities include wildlife observation, hiking, canoeing, fishing, goldpanning, and mountain biking. Lowell Thomas, Jr., son of the famous adventurer, offers flightseeing excursions from an airstrip four miles west of Camp Denali.

Each cabin, of spruce construction with pine interior, has a wood stove and propane hotplate; twin, double, or queen-size beds with handmade quilts; and a table with a mirror and washbasin. Each has its own outhouse, though there are also flush toilets in a central shower house. Smaller cabins sleep two; family cabins can accommodate up to five on bunks.

The lodge, where audio-visual programs are shown each evening, also houses a library. A science resource center features exhibits and a microscope, a photo darkroom, a piano, and a sports-equipment cache. The spacious dining room, decorated with an old-fashioned wood-burning cook stove, mountaineering photos, and nature prints, provides a family atmosphere. A self-sufficient operation, the lodge has its own vegetable garden and greenhouse, carpenters' shops, and hydroelectric system.

"We're in the vacation business, not the hotel and restaurant business," stress proprietors Wallace and Jerryne Cole. With that in mind, they provide transportation from Denali station to the camp only three times in two weeks from early June to early September. With few exceptions, all-inclusive vacation packages are for three nights ($675 per person), four nights ($900), or five nights ($1,125). Children under 12 get 25% off.

The **North Face Lodge,** P.O. Box 67, Denali Park, AK 99755 (tel. 907/683-2290 in summer), was built in 1974 on a hilltop facing Mount McKinley. The Coles bought it in 1988. As you sit in plush leather chairs and couches in the lounge, you can gaze out full-size picture windows at the great mountain, or search for bears, caribou, or other animals through a telescope.

The big dining room, with long tables for communal eating, offers a menu ranging from New York charbroiled steaks to grilled salmon. If you're in the mood for Arctic grayling for breakfast some day, show your Alaska fishing license and the lodge will outfit you with fishing gear and send you off to Moose Creek, behind the lodge. Gold pans are also available to would-be prospectors.

The North Face Lodge has 15 carpeted, wood-paneled units, all with twin beds, gas heat, and private bath with shower, plus a family suite for a capacity of 35 guests. Rates are $225 per person (double occupancy) with a minimum two-night stay, including round-trip transportation and three meals.

From September to May, information on Camp Denali or the North Face Lodge can be obtained from the Coles at P.O. Box 216, Cornish, NH 03746 (tel. 603/675-2248).

The **Kantishna Roadhouse,** P.O. Box 130, Denali Park, AK 99755 (tel. 907/733-2535 or 683-2710), was established in 1905 as a way station for miners (more than 3,000 once prospected here) and other travelers. Today, rustic cabins for two to four guests or heated tent cabins beside a stream recall the mining days of yore. Unlike yesteryear, all have private baths. A hot tub and sauna are centrally located, and family-style meals with home-cooked pastries are served in the dining hall. A cocktail lounge called the Topless Cabbage is open at night. Rates are $349 per person for a three-day tour package, or $75 to $140 per night to independent travelers, June 8 to September 10. Winter packages are offered March 1 to April 15.

Denali Mountain Lodge, P.O. Box 229, Denali Park, AK 99755 (tel. 907/683-2643 in summer, 907/258-0134 in winter), was opened in 1989 by the owners of the Denali Cabins on Parks Hwy. Guests in the 24 individual cabins pay $150 a day; the price includes transportation, dinner, and breakfast.

Just outside the park's remote northwestern boundary, the **Denali West Lodge** offers a true bush getaway on the shores of Lake Minchumina, AK 99757 (tel. 907/733-2630 or 276-8687). Rates are $100 a day, plus $199 round-trip air transportation from Denali Park or Fairbanks. The price includes lodging in private log cabins with wood stoves, all meals in the main lodge, a riverboat wildlife tour, guided fishing trips, canoeing, and a sauna.

2. What to See and Do

The first thing every visitor wants to see is, appropriately, **Mount McKinley.** Ironically, the mountain cannot be seen from the central Denali National Park hotel area. **Mount Healy,** a mere baby at 5,716 feet, is the dominant peak in the park headquarters area.

If you arrived from the south on a clear day, you had a splendid view of McKinley and its huge neighbor, 17,400-foot **Mount Foraker,** as you drove up the George Parks Hwy. For your first view of the mountain from within the park, though, you must drive about 10 miles down the park road, en route to the Savage River campground and check station (at 12 miles). You'll start to get good views of the Alaska Range from about 39 miles on. With few cloudless days in the park, especially in summer, you should plan on rising with the sun to maximize your chance of getting a good view. Early mornings are often cloudcap-free, and the rising sun paints a pinkish glow on the peaks' eastern faces.

Admission to the park is $3 for adults, and free for children and students under 17, seniors (62 and older), and disabled individuals. An annual pass is $15; a Golden Eagle Pass, providing annual access to all federal areas, is $25.

Because of the restriction on park traffic, the best way to see wildlife is to either take the park-operated shuttle bus or the private wildlife tour operated through the leading hotels.

Free **shuttlebus** rides—with no guides to provide a narrative—begin from the Visitor Access Center daily, late May to mid-September, at half-hourly intervals from 6 a.m. to 4 p.m. (except hourly from 1:30 to 3:30 p.m.). The last round-trip bus returns to the center at 11:15 p.m. One midmorning bus has a wheelchair lift. Because of the great number of people who sign up for this tour, you'll be given a ticket for boarding the next available bus. During July and August, that may mean the following day.

From mid-June, depending on snow and road conditions, the shuttle bus runs 85 miles (11 hours round trip) to the Wonder Lake Ranger Station. Earlier, it goes 53 miles (7 hours round trip) to the Toklat Ranger Station or 66 miles (8 hours round trip) to the Eielson Visitor Center. It makes scheduled stops, wildlife stops, and extra stops on a "flag" system: the bus will drop you off anywhere you like and pick you up again at no cost. There's just one catch: the bus must have an empty seat because there's no "standing room only" on this road. Bring warm clothes and your own food and drink, as there are no concessions along the road.

The **Tundra Wildlife Tour,** a six- to-seven-hour excursion operated by ARA Outdoor World Ltd., leaves the McKinley Village Lodge, McKinley Chalet Resort, and Denali National Park Hotel twice daily in summer, at 6 a.m. and 2 p.m. Reservations are required. This tour features a driver/naturalist who acts as narrator for the journey. A trail lunch and hot beverage are included in the $40 cost ($20 for children 12 and under). Tours operate from mid-May to mid-September.

The Kantishna Roadhouse operates a deluxe **Wilderness Trails Tour,** leaving the Harper Lodge daily at 5:45 a.m. and returning at 6 p.m. after a 95-mile round-trip odyssey. The price of $79 includes a narrated wildlife tour by van, lunch at the roadhouse, and a horse-drawn wagon ride to El Dorado Creek for an hour of gold panning.

Before Memorial Day weekend and after mid-September, road restrictions are lifted, and you can drive your own vehicle. Should you choose to do this, be aware that the park road is narrow, winding, and mostly gravel. (The first 14 miles were repaved in 1989.) It's kept in tolerable condition, but the 35-mph speed limit often seems like speedway velocity, and you'll more often find yourself traveling 20 to 25 mph. All wild animals are dangerous, so if you see some along the road, stay in your car. Do *not* attempt to approach them closely.

Some of the main sights you'll see along the road include:

Riley Creek Information Center, Mile 0.2, open from 5:45 a.m. to 7 p.m. daily starting the Saturday before Memorial Day, until the third week of September. This is the place to go for general park information, campground registration, and backcountry camping permits. The Alaska Natural History Association sells a variety of books and maps about the park and its wildlife in the information center. "The Denali Road Guide" is an especially worthwhile purchase. Be sure also to pick up a free copy of the *Denali Alpenglow* newspaper. (Many of the center's functions were scheduled to be taken over by the new Visitor Access Center in 1990.)

Denali National Park Headquarters, Mile 3.4. About 15 families make this their year-round home; this is as far as the road is kept open in midwinter. As might be expected at an Alaskan winter outpost, there's a sled-dog kennel behind the headquarters, down a short trail from the parking lot. Half-hour **sled-dog demonstrations** are given daily at 11 a.m., 3 p.m., and 4 p.m., with free transportation provided from the Denali Park Hotel.

Savage River Campground, Mile 12.8. From 1922 until 1938, when the park road was completed to Wonder Lake, this was as far as most tourists went. Horse-drawn stagecoaches carried visitors to the Savage River camp, where they slept overnight on cots in canvas tents. Today the paved road ends two miles farther, at the bridge over the Savage River.

Teklanika Campground, Mile 29.1. The park's second-largest campground with 50 sites, it is two miles from the broad, braided Teklanika River. (The Athabaskan Indian name means "much gravel, little water.") Look for caribou here.

Sable Pass, Mile 39.1. This is prime grizzly bear country, being especially rich in berries, flowers, and other vegetation. The immediate vicinity is closed to any deviation from the park road.

Polychrome Pass, Mile 45.9. You'd almost feel as if you were in Arizona's Painted Desert here, were not the alpine scenery and wildlife so grand. Glacial chaos, and wind and water erosion have created a spectacular and colorful landscape, especially on the east side of the pass. At the foot of the climb, on the east fork of the Toklat River, you'll see a cabin used today by scientific researchers, occupied in the 1930s by biologist Adolph Murie during his renowned study of wolves.

Highway Pass, Mile 58.3. At 3,980 feet elevation, this is the highest point on the park road (park headquarters is at 2,055 feet).

Eielson Visitor Center, Mile 66.0. Named for pioneer bush pilot Carl Ben Eielson, this facility is only 33 miles from the summit of Mount McKinley. Telescopes are set up to search for animals in the valley below and on the slopes of surrounding peaks. There's an information desk, exhibits on mountaineering and wildlife, rest rooms, a water fountain, and a book sales counter. You can accompany a naturalist on a 30- to 60-minute tundra walk at 11:30 a.m. and 1:30 p.m. daily. The visitor center itself is open from 9 a.m. to 8:15 p.m. daily, early June to mid-September.

Wonder Lake, Mile 84.6. This young glacial lake, about four miles long, is a home for lake trout, burbot, arctic char, and ling cod. Because of the fish, numerous diving and migratory birds often visit here, and caribou and moose are frequently seen. The Wonder Lake Ranger Station is two miles north, and the Wonder Lake Campground, with 30 tent sites, is 1½ miles south on a side road. This is the closest point to Mount McKinley—just 27 miles—on the park road, and mountaineering parties making north-side assaults usually start here.

The **Kantishna** mining district with its trio of lodges begins at Mile 87.9, at the Denali National Park Wilderness boundary. The road ends about two miles farther on.

SPORTS

If you have any active blood in your veins at all, don't miss the opportunity to do some adventuresome exploring in this phenomenally beautiful park.

Hiking and Backpacking

You can get your bearings with a one-hour "Morning Walk" beginning at 8 a.m. daily in summer from the porch of the Denali Park Hotel. Free hikes of half a day or longer, accompanied by a park naturalist, begin daily from the Park Hotel or the Eielson Visitor Center; times and locations are posted at all information centers.

Several day hikes, ranging from one-half to nine miles, leisurely to strenuous, are recommended by park officials. Horseshoe Lake, just over a mile from the Park Hotel, and Mount Healy, overlooking the park headquarters area, are especially popular destinations.

Backpackers (those who intend to camp at least one night in the wilderness area) must obtain permits from a naturalist at the Visitor Access Center. The permit is free; it's simply a means of limiting and distributing park use within the 43 backcountry units, each with quotas. You must stay within the boundaries of the unit designated by your permit.

It's wise to attend an evening backpacking program at the Morino Campground, a half-mile walk from the railway station. There you'll learn how to hike the Denali backcountry, where there are no trails, few trees, plenty of subarctic tundra, and many glacial rivers to cross. You should boil all water because of the threat of giardiasis, a nasty parasite-transmitted disease. Campfires are prohibited, though you may use a small stove. No camping is allowed within half a mile of the park road, and your camp must be out of sight of the road.

In all hiking and backpacking, make sure before you start that you know how to handle yourself in the event of a bear encounter, should one occur, or other emergencies.

Mountaineering

Serious climbers from all over the world tackle Mount McKinley each year, mainly in the spring. There may be 40 or more expeditions on the mountain at once. Several thousand have stood on North America's pinnacle since it was first scaled in 1913. Nearly 50 have died trying, however, and more than 150 have been involved in serious accidents. In good years, the climbers' success ratio is about 50%. The whimsical weather, which can bring severe blizzards and gale-force winds at any time of year, is the biggest factor in success or failure.

Talkeetna, on the south side of the mountain, is the most popular start-off point. Most climbing teams prefer to begin their ascent from the 8,000-foot level of the mountain, after being dropped at the Kahiltna Glacier base camp by a ski plane. The **Takleetna Ranger Station,** P.O. Box 588, Talkeetna, AK 99676, is set up as Denali National Park's main contact point for climbers on the mountain. Anyone contemplating a climb in the national park should write for general or specific information (free) and registration forms.

Seven guide services are authorized by the National Park Service to lead trips to Mount McKinley and other Alaska Range peaks. Three are Alaska-based: Alaska Denali Guiding, P.O. Box 326, Talkeetna, AK 99676; Genet Expeditions, Talkeetna, AK 99676; and Mountain Trip, P.O. Box 41161, Anchorage, AK 99509. The others are the American Alpine Institute of Bellingham, Washington; Rainier Mountaineering of Tacoma, Washington; the National Outdoor Leadership School of Lander, Wyoming; and Fantasy Ridge of Telluride, Colorado.

River Rafting

This is one of the most popular sports in the national park area. Several firms are ready to help you test your mettle against the Nenana. All operate from approximately mid-May to mid-September, depending on water conditions. Raingear and lifejackets are provided, but you should dress warmly, with two pairs of wool socks if possible. Food is not provided, so bring your own if you're the munchie sort.

Owl Rafting (tel. 683-2684) will take you for a two-hour trip from the McKinley Chalet Resort to the town of Healy, through ten miles of the Nenana River canyon. Departures are at 9 a.m. and 3 and 7 p.m. daily. Cost is $34 per person; children must be at least 12.

Crow's Nest Rafting (tel. 683-2723 or 683-2321) offers two options, one for the adventurous and one for the slightly more faint-of-heart. The "Canyon Run" is a two-hour trip through the white water of the steep Nenana Canyon, while the "McKinley Float" starts farther upriver and gives more relaxation and wildlife-watching opportunities. Both cost $34 for adults, $24 for children under 12 ("McKinley Float" only). Departures are at 9 a.m. and 3 p.m. for each trip, plus 7 p.m. for the "Canyon Run" only.

Like Owl and Crow's Nest, **McKinley Raft Tours** (tel. 683-2392) begins from near the McKinley Chalet Resort. Tour A ($30) takes in 2½ hours of upriver scenery; Tour C ($30) is the standard two-hour white-water run to Healy; Tour B ($40) combines the two, for a 22-mile voyage. Tours A and B start at noon daily; Tour C starts at 9 a.m., noon, and 6:30 p.m.

Denali Raft Adventures (tel. 683-2234) leaves from the Mt. McKinley Village hotel, Mile 231 on George Parks Hwy. The four-hour "Healy Express" run, covering 22 miles through the canyon for $45 per person, is a favorite. (Children must be at least 12.) Departures are at 9 a.m. and 2:30 p.m. daily. There's also a more gentle 2½-hour "McKinley Run," leaving at 9 a.m. and 2:30 and 7:30 p.m., and a two-hour, ten-mile "Canyon Run," leaving at 11 a.m., and 4:30 and 7:30 p.m. The latter two, suitable for families, cost $30 for adults, $20 for children under 12.

Winter Sports

Skiing and dog sledding are the main options. Cross-country skiers have the entire park road beyond headquarters at their disposal. Ski mountaineers enjoy flying into the Ruth Glacier from Talkeetna. Dog-sled enthusiasts, on the other hand, can take advantage of some organized trips.

Denali Dog Tours and Wilderness Freighters, P.O. Box 670, Denali Park, AK 99755 (tel. 907/683-2722), provides a real-life mushing experience within the national park wilderness area. Participants are actively involved in driving a freight team, riding the brake or guide-pole skis, breaking trail with snowshoes, feeding and caring for the dogs. Six-hour trips, including a trail lunch, cost $125; overnight tours to the Sanctuary River, including meals and lodging in a National Park Service cabin, are $175. Longer trips of three, six, and ten days are also offered, at an approximate cost of $125 per person per day. The firm also provides support for cross-country skiers, snowshoers, and mountaineers, at a rate of $150 per day per group. Write for full information and requirements.

Chugach Express Sled Dog Tours, P.O. Box 261, Girdwood, AK 99587 (tel. 907/783-2266), offers an all-inclusive three-day/two-night "family adventure" to the Ruth Glacier, with meals and overnight lodging at the Tokosha Mountain Lodge on the south side of the park. The charge of $495 per person includes round-trip transportation from Anchorage. Participants can drive the dog team, ride in the sled, or ski beside it.

FLIGHTSEEING

Several times a day, from sunrise to sunset, pilots for **Denali Wilderness Air,** P.O. Box 82, Denali Park, AK 99755 (tel. 907/683-2261), lift their wings for "totally awesome" trips around the park. Several tour packages are offered. Most popular, as it should be, is the 70-minute "Round Denali" trip, weather permitting. The tour costs $110 per person, based on a three-person minimum. Flights leave every two hours starting at 8 a.m.

Fifty-minute helicopter tours leave every hour, beginning at 9 a.m. They cost $135 per person, with a two-person minimum.

Many air taxis fly trips around Mount McKinley from the Anchorage and Fairbanks area. There are others in Talkeetna (see "South of the Park," below).

---

3. South of the Park

Traveling south from Denali National Park, it's 27 miles from the park road junction to **Cantwell,** a tiny community two miles west of the George Parks Highway surrounded by magnificent snow-capped mountains. The main street of town, a 100-yard-long paved oasis in the middle of a gravel strip, has little more than a café, general store, and bar. There are a couple of restaurants and service stations at the junction of the **Denali Highway** (open summers only). Once the only route to the park from Anchorage, it threads its way 133 miles east to Paxson, where it intersects the Richardson Highway between Fairbanks and Valdez.

Six miles south of Cantwell, the George Parks Highway crosses the divide between the Gulf of Alaska and Yukon River drainages at **Broad Pass.** Though it sketches a line between peaks exceeding 12,000 feet elevation to its east and west, Broad Pass itself is only 2,300 feet above sea level.

Another 35 miles south, the highway enters the 421,000-acre **Denali State Park,** through which it runs for 47 miles. Camping, fishing, and hiking are popular in this state-administered reserve. At Mile 135, three miles from the south highway entrance to the park, a turnout with a display board is perhaps the best place to view and identify the peaks of the Alaska Range during fine weather.

State parks division officials are developing plans for a multi-million-dollar tourist center and hotel in the southeast corner of the park, near the Susitna River and the railroad community of Curry. Developers also have elaborate plans for a 150-room resort hotel in the state park, off the George Parks Highway. Until such time as either or both become reality, accommodations between the village of Talkeetna and the park road junction are limited. Those currently in existence include:

The **Reindeer Mountain Lodge,** Mile 209.5 on Parks Hwy. (P.O. Box 7), Cantwell, AK 99729 (tel. 907/768-2420 or 768-2942), with 26 comfortable motel rooms priced at $55 to $65 a night (double), and a café serving New York steak dinners for $17 and breaded prawns for $14.

The **Chulitna River Lodge,** Mile 156.2 on Parks Hwy. (Star Route, Box 8396), Trapper Creek, AK 99683 (tel. 907/733-2521), more notable for its quaint log-cabin gift shop and café and its overnight rafting expeditions than for its guest cabins ($65 with bath, $45 without).

The **Trapper Creek Trading Post,** Mile 115.5 on Parks Hwy. (tel. 733-2315), which has a café and grocery, cabins at $40 a night for two people, gift shop, and information on the **Tokosha Mountain Lodge,** the only Denali National Park wilderness lodge on the south side of Mount McKinley. Located near the foot of the Ruth Glacier between the Tokositna River and Pirate Lake, the lodge is accessible only by air, raft, or in winter, dog sled. The most popular package is a three-day/two-night fishing trip, priced at $565 including round-trip air taxi from Talkeetna. Contact P.O. Box 13-188, Trapper Creek, AK 99683 (tel. 907/733-1034).

TALKEETNA

At the end of a paved 15-mile dead-end road, branching off the Parks Hwy. at Mile 98.7, is this quaint village of 400 people that is proud to remain just what it is, no more and no less: the hub of an old mining district, the jumping-off point for most Mount McKinley climbing expeditions, and a popular center for wilderness recreation.

Located near the confluence of the Talkeetna and Chulitna Rivers with the broad Susitna, some 80 miles upriver from the Cook Inlet, the community began as an Alaska Railroad construction camp in 1920 and as a freight and supply point for gold miners in the Talkeetna Mountains and other areas. Today it is what Joe McGinniss, author of *Going to Extremes,* described as "a quintessential Alaskan settlement: it had more pool tables (three), and more airfields (two) than it had gasoline stations (one)." Venture off the main street and you'll find yourself on dirt roads looking at log cabins built by some of the early miners and still occupied.

One of Talkeetna's attributes is that it's on the main Anchorage–Denali Park–Fairbanks railroad line. The *Denali Express* stops here daily in the summer season, at 11 a.m. northbound and 4 p.m. southbound, and during winter the train stops on its twice-monthly milk runs.

At festival time, Talkeetna is especially busy with outside visitors. The big occasions are Miners Day in May and the Moose Dropping Festival (yes, really) in July.

For information, you can contact the **Talkeetna Chamber of Commerce,** P.O. Box 334, Talkeetna, AK 99676 (tel. 907/733-2330). The new **Talkeetna Visitor Center,** located at the junction of the George Parks Hwy. and Talkeetna Spur Road (tel. 907/733-2223), is open in summer.

Where to Stay and Eat

You have your choice of several accommodations in Talkeetna, ranging from moderate in price and standard to downright pioneer.

The **Latitude 62° Lodge/Motel,** Mile 14 on Talkeetna Road (P.O. Box 1478),

Talkeetna, AK 99676 (tel. 907/733-2262), is the newest and the nicest. Set back off the road in a spruce and birch forest, it has the feel of a modern hunting lodge, with animal heads and hides mounted on the walls, snowshoe chandeliers, and a honky-tonk piano beneath a mural of Mount McKinley. The 12 small but comfortable rooms contain double or twin beds, private bathrooms, and hot-water heating. They are priced from $45 single, $50 double, April to September; winter rates are some-what lower. TV addicts can watch in the impressive bar, adjacent to the restaurant (open from 7 a.m. to 10 p.m. daily) that serves 14-ounce charbroiled steaks for $15.50 and sautéed jumbo prawns for $15. Winter is a big time here: cross-country skiing, skating, ice fishing, and dog sledding are just out the door, and the lodge rents snow machines.

The **Swiss-Alaska Inn,** Boat Landing Road (P.O. Box 565), Talkeetna, AK 99676 (tel. 907/733-2424), as you might have guessed, is run by Swiss immigrants (Renamary and Werner Rauchenstein). Their casual approach to business is indi-cated by a sign on the front door: "Open most of the time. Closed part of the time." Regardless, it's a favorite place for European mountaineering teams to stay. Located on an often-muddy backstreet, the inn has 12 pleasant rooms decorated in blues with twin or double beds, private baths, and electric heat. They are priced at $50 single, $60 double. The spacious restaurant-bar, partially papered with old news clippings about climbing teams, is open daily for three meals—including chicken béarnaise ($11.75) and wienerschnitzel ($10.75) for dinner.

Talkeetna's most famous building is the **Fairview Inn.** P.O. Box 379, Talkeetna, AK 99676 (tel. 907/733-2423). Located right on the main drag, it's fa-mous for its bar, not for its six upstairs rooms. But in their defense, the rooms (with shared toilets and bathing facilities) do have, ah, character. Antique décor, including double beds with quilted comforters, would make them pleasant overnight stops were it not for the roars and laughter of successful mountaineering teams celebrat-ing downstairs in the spring months. Their glee can be almost as deafening as the silence of expeditions turned away short of McKinley's summit. During my stay the voices and jukebox music weren't as sleep-preventive as the wailing baby in Room 1 and the screeching parrot (seriously) in Room 4 which contributed to the cacopho-ny. But the price is right ($25 a night), the people are friendly, and you can say you've stayed in a building listed on the National Register of Historic Sites. The white wood-frame structure, built in 1923, was famed for years as *the* place for min-ers and trappers to congregate. There's no restaurant at the Fairview Inn, but wild-game potluck dinners are commonly sponsored during the winter.

While you're at the Fairview, inquire about the Talkeetna Bachelors Society. Forty-seven strong at this writing, it is dedicated to "the preservation in perpetuity" of bachelorhood. Male members who succumb to nuptial bliss also surrender $100 to the society. Since its inception in 1980, only $400 has been added in this manner to the society's party fund. More profitable is the annual Wilderness Women Con-test and Bachelor Auction at the Fairview the first weekend of December, at which a drink and dance with each of the society members is auctioned off to the highest-bidding woman. Eligible women are expected to demonstrate their prowess in such Alaskan bush skills as target shooting, water toting, and firewood hauling.

Four Talkeetna-area bed-and-breakfasts are administered by **Golden Spike Ac-commodations,** P.O. Box 525, Talkeetna, AK 99676 (tel. 907/733-2741). Among them is Goldilocks' Lodge, a cabin on Papa Bear Lake ten minutes' flight from town. Rates for all homes are $40 single, $60 double.

Outside of the hotels, there are limited choices for meals. The **McKinley Deli** (tel. 733-1234), one block west of the Fairview Inn on the main street, has sand-wiches priced from $6 to $8, pizzas from $10 (including the "Kitchen Sink," for $18.25), and yummy baked goods. It's open from 10 a.m. to 10 p.m. daily.

Across the road from the deli is the homey **Talkeetna Roadhouse** (tel. 733-2341). Breakfast is served from 7:30 to 11:30 a.m. (three-egg omelets start at $3.25), lunches from noon to 4 p.m. (meatloaf sandwiches run $5). Family-style dinners are served to parties of six or more at 7 p.m. (reservations must be made by 3 p.m.). Eat all you want of whatever the chef prepared for just $10; children, $5.

Talkeetna maintains two **campgrounds,** both with shelters, outhouses, picnic tables, and boat launches. Talkeetna River Park is at the west end of the main street through town. Christianson Lake Camper Park is a few miles south and east, via Comsat Road.

What to See and Do

If any two men can be said to have been accorded the status of "immortals" in Talkeetna, those two are mountaineer Ray Genet (1931–1979) and bush pilot Don Sheldon (1921–1975). Genet, sometimes called "The Pirate," was a Swiss-American who climbed Mount McKinley 25 times, including the first winter ascent (in 1967) and the first dog-team ascent (in 1979). He froze to death during an attempted climb of Mount Everest in the Himalayas. Sheldon, who knew McKinley as only a skilled pilot could, and who saved countless climbers from certain death on its flanks, was taken by cancer.

The **Talkeetna Historical Society Museum** (tel. 733-2487) is housed next to the downtown airstrip in a 1936 schoolhouse. The museum contains many pioneer artifacts, local artworks, and a library of old papers and books. Most of all, it contains a series of displays on the history of climbing and flying around Mount McKinley, featuring special sections on Genet and Sheldon. It also boasts a 12- by 12-foot scale replica of the mountain and surrounding peaks, with 15 gigantic photographs by Bradford Washburn. Open daily in summer from 10 a.m. to 6 p.m. The **B&K Trading Post** (tel. 733-2411), catty-corner from the Fairview Inn, also has a small museum devoted to local mountaineering, piloting, and outdoor life.

To keep up on the ongoing history of Mount McKinley climbing, you'll have to drop by the **Talkeetna Ranger Station,** easily found in the same downtown hub area. Denali National Park staffs this outpost—set up to register and monitor mountaineering expeditions in the park—with rangers who are also experienced McKinley climbers. New parties are shown a slide show, given a briefing, and asked to fill out an application to determine how prepared they are and to assist them on questions of equipment and skill. CB radios are monitored 24 hours a day here, at the Kahiltna Glacier airstrip at McKinley's 7,000-foot level, and at a National Park Service camp at the 14,000-foot level, two days' climb from the top of the mountain. Between 800 and 1,000 climbers, from countries as far away as Brazil, Finland, and Vietnam, tackle the peak each year. Despite precautions, in a typical April-to-July climbing season, there will be four to ten airlift evacuations and several deaths on McKinley.

Getting Around by Air

There are four air-taxi services in Talkeetna, and it's difficult to recommend any one over its competition. They are **Doug Geeting Aviation,** P.O. Box 42, Talkeetna, AK 99676 (tel. 733-2366); **Hudson Air Service,** Main Street, Talkeetna, AK 99676 (tel. 733-2321); **K2 Aviation,** P.O. Box 290, Talkeetna, AK 99676 (tel. 733-2291); and **Talkeetna Air Taxi,** P.O. Box 73, Talkeetna, AK 99676 (tel. 733-2218). If you figure $200 an hour for the plane and divide it by the number of people in your party, you'll have a pretty good idea of your cost.

Geeting, a mountaineers' favorite, offers tourists an 80-minute round-trip flight and landing on the Kahiltna Glacier, at the McKinley base camp. K2's Jim Okonek, a retired military pilot, includes a champagne lunch with his two-hour Circle McKinley tour. David Lee of Talkeetna Air Taxi makes direct trips to Kantishna, on the north side of McKinley.

Getting Around by Land

If you're a mountaineer looking for an expedition, you won't go wrong by talking to **Genet Expeditions,** P.O. Box 1525, Palmer, AK 99645 (tel. 733-2272 or 376-5120) or **Alaska-Denali Guiding,** P.O. Box 326, Talkeetna, AK 99676 (tel. 733-2649). Both lead expeditions by different routes to the summit of McKinley and other Alaska Range peaks, as well as Denali National Park treks and cross-country ski expeditions. The prices are rather high, especially for the mountaineering trips . . . but so are the risks.

For winter skiers, a nordic ski trail, with a ten-mile outer loop and five-mile inner loop, begins in a park between the Fairview Inn and Talkeetna Railway Station.

Getting Around by Water

Several boat operators offer sightseeing tours of the Talkeetna Canyon and an adjacent gorge called Devil's Canyon, plus fishing and rafting opportunities on several rivers and jetboat excursions to the Tokosha Mountain Lodge. Check with **Talkeetna Riverboat Service,** P.O. Box 74, Talkeetna, AK 99676 (tel. 733-2281), in the Village Arts and Crafts Shop on Main Street; **Mahay's Riverboat Service,** P.O. Box 133, Talkeetna, AK 99676 (tel. 733-2223), on Boat Landing Road; or **Tri-River Charters,** P.O. Box 312, Talkeetna, AK 99676 (tel. 733-2400).

River waters around Talkeetna boast all species of salmon plus grayling, Dolly Varden, and rainbow trout. Fishing-boat charters may cost $75 to $125 per person for an eight-hour day, including guide service and equipment, depending in part on the number of people sharing the boat. Shore fishing can also be excellent, especially at Christianson Lake, a short drive southeast of Talkeetna.

Denali Floats, P.O. Box 330, Talkeetna, AK 99676 (tel. 733-2384), offers a wide variety of one- to six-day rafting expeditions throughout the region. More experienced white-water rafters can contact **Nova Riverrunners,** P.O. Box 1129, Chickaloon, AK 99645 (tel. 907/745-5753), about their Talkeetna River trips.

---

4. North of the Park

The George Parks Highway north of Denali Park junction follows the Nenana River 67 miles downstream to Nenana, then up the Tanana River valley another 58 miles to Fairbanks. As you leave the mountains and cross a broad basin, you'll know that you're in the Interior.

HEALY

It's 11 winding miles down the Nenana Canyon to the village of Heaiy (pop. 400). Alaska's largest commercial coal operation, the Usibelli Mine, is just across the river from here. It markets 1.7 million tons of the black mineral each year, mainly to South Korea; you'll see it put on trains for freighting to Seward and ultimate shipment to Pusan.

A little south of the Healy junction, at Mile 245 on Parks Hwy., is the **Healy Roadhouse,** P.O. Box 33, Healy, AK 99743 (tel. 907/683-2273). Its rustic but elegant restaurant, dimly lit, with candles on red tablecloths in a dark-wood décor, serves full 14-ounce prime-rib dinners for $14.50, and fresh halibut and salmon entrees for $11, including soup, salad bar, potato, bread, and coffee. Open from 6 a.m. to 9 p.m. daily. Luncheon sandwiches are available at the bar starting at 11:30 a.m. There are also 21 comfortable motel units. Smaller double ($50) and single ($25) rooms have semiprivate baths, shared between two rooms. The family units, priced at $85 year round, are lovely suites, with a double and two twin beds, a full bath and kitchen, and a living room with a sofa. A campground is planned.

Meals and lodging are also available at the **Totem Café & Motel,** Mile 248.7 on George Parks Hwy. (P.O. Box 105), Healy, AK 99743 (tel. 907/683-2420). The café, a friendly log-cabin coffeehouse, is open 24 hours a day with hearty meals like breakfast steak and eggs for $8 and a full fried chicken dinner for $9. Old Atco trailer units, a common sight in the Interior, contain 21 rooms kept full year round by transient workers. A few rooms, priced at $65 double, $60 single in summer ($55 and $45 in winter), have private bath; most use a communal bath and are $10 cheaper. The motel has a Laundromat and TV room with free use of videotapes.

Nearby is the **McKinley KOA Kampground,** at Mile 248.5 on George Parks Hwy. (P.O. Box 34), Healy, AK 99743 (tel. 907/683-2379). Open mid-May to mid-September, it's the only facility in the neighborhood of Denali National Park with full and electric hookups for RVs and campers. Full hookups cost $20.75 a night. There are 77 sites in all, with fireplaces, picnic tables, and showers; reservations are accepted. The campground also has a grocery, Laundromat, and gift shop.

Healy Junction is at Mile 248.8. The town is spread for several miles east along the road to Usibelli; it has a medical clinic (Healy Clinic; tel. 683-2211), volunteer fire department, state trooper station, grocery, community center, schools, churches, and post office.

Almost exactly halfway between Healy and Nenana is the **Tatlanika Trading Co.,** Mile 276 on George Parks Hwy. (tel. 582-2341). A unique gift shop with a museum atmosphere, it offers such items as moose-antler jewelry, trapper hats, and a variety of furs and original paintings. About 7½ miles farther north is a turnoff to **Clear Air Force Site,** an integral part of the ballistic missile early-warning system. Sorry, you can't visit without advance permission.

NENANA

The symbol of this river port of 600 people is a five-legged tripod. Now, everyone knows that a tripod only has three legs . . . everyone, that is, but the residents of Nenana. This quintapod, as it were, set into the winter ice of the slow-moving Tanana River, is connected to a clock that stops the exact moment of breakup. When that occurs, some lucky Alaskan wins $100,000 or more in the annual **Nenana Ice Classic.** Guess-the-time tickets, at $2 each, are sold throughout Alaska in February and March. (It's a fairly safe bet that breakup will occur some afternoon between April 28 and May 12.)

The Ice Classic aside, Nenana is a pleasant town to visit. The **Nenana Valley Visitor Information Center** (tel. 832-9453), in a sod-roofed log cabin where A Street forks off the George Parks Hwy., can get you started exploring. It's open from 8 a.m. to 6 p.m. daily, Memorial Day to Labor Day. Several small gift shops are located near the visitor center.

Nenana is situated at the confluence of the Nenana and Tanana Rivers, 58 miles southwest of Fairbanks. It's the home of the **River Port Authority,** through which 80% of the villages along the Yukon River, from Fort Yukon to St. Michaels, are supplied with food and freight when the river is free of ice. A tug and barge fleet do the honors.

Also big in Nenana is dog mushing; you can drive past a large dog yard on C Street south of 3rd Street, and elsewhere around town you'll see dogs tethered beside small houses. The **Nenana Dog Mushers** headquarters is in a modern log building on 1st Street between A and Market Streets.

Local Athabaskan Natives, members of the Doyon Ltd. corporation, are very active in cultural activities. Inquire at the visitor center about potlatches or dance performances scheduled around the time of your visit.

FAIRBANKS AND THE INTERIOR

Of all Alaska's cities, large and small, Fairbanks feels most like what an Alaskan city *should* feel like.

Spread for more than eight miles along the banks of the meandering Chena River, a tributary of the Tanana, this modern frontier settlement still carries reminders of the mineral wealth on which it was built. Gold dredges and mining camps speckle its outlying areas. Tom Sawyer paddlewheelers still ply the shallow, muddy rivers, sled-dog teams scamper through the long winter nights, and follies-style revues are a nightly occurrence in saloons and at the re-created Alaskaland pioneer village.

The Trans Alaska Pipeline, which crosses the rolling terrain a stone's throw northeast of the city, brought a new era of progress to Fairbanks in the mid-1970s. Today at the University of Alaska's main campus scientists study the aurora borealis and permafrost, the life cycles of arctic wildlife and the effect on agriculture of 21-hour summer days. The university also has a superb museum. North of the city is a satellite-tracking station. And throughout are modern hotels and restaurants, the equal of those in other cities in Alaska and the American West.

Nowhere else in North America, and in few other places on earth, do this many people live in a community this far north. Only Tromsö, Norway, and three or four Soviet cities scattered across the Arctic at this latitude are larger. The Arctic Circle is only about 200 miles north of Fairbanks. So it comes as a surprise to many visitors to learn that Fairbanks experiences the hottest—as well as the coldest—temperatures in the state of Alaska.

Clear summer days, often reaching into the 90s (though the mean is around 60°F), never really get dark; the Fairbanks Goldpanners baseball team plays a game at midnight on June 20 without lights! On the other hand, average winter temperatures drop below −10°F from December through February, and there can be fewer than four hours of dim daylight. Springs are dry and cool; autumns, crisp with occasional light snow. No time of year is really wet, though August is the rainiest month (with frequent afternoon cloudbursts) and April is the driest. The only really unpleasant time to visit Fairbanks is when the temperature drops to −40°F, as it sometimes does in midwinter, and a stinging ice smog forms around pollutants caught in the air.

A SHORT HISTORY

Fairbanks owes its existence to a low river and a lucky strike, and to two men named E.T. and Felix. And we're not talking movies or comic books.

E.T. Barnette, an ex-convict seeking to establish a trading post up the Tanana River in 1901, was marooned with his goods on the banks of the Chena River when the steamer on which he was traveling hit the shallows and was forced to turn back. While Barnette was contemplating how to move his supplies to a more marketable location, an Italian prospector named Felix Pedro happened upon gold near Fox, about 12 miles north. The date of the discovery, July 22, 1902, is still celebrated every year in Fairbanks as Golden Days.

The rush was on, and Barnette's new trading post became the focus. E.T. became mayor, of course. As a favor to Judge James Wickersham, the first peacemaker to set up court in the Interior, he named the settlement after Indiana Sen. Charles Fairbanks, a Wickersham benefactor who later became vice-president under Theodore Roosevelt. Barnette had trouble staying on the right side of the law, however. He soon became "the most hated man in Fairbanks" for his role in a bank failure that cost many their savings.

Fairbanks history since then has been a series of peaks and valleys. Its population stood at around 11,000 in 1910, but dropped drastically during World War I, and slowly crept back up to around 4,000 with the construction of the Alaska Railroad and the establishment in 1922 of Alaska Agricultural College, now the University of Alaska. World War II saw the construction of the Alaska Highway and brought thousands of military personnel to Eielson Air Base and Ladd Field, now Fort Wainwright. A disastrous flood put much of the city under eight feet of water in August 1967, but the damage—though significant—was quickly forgotten when oil was discovered on the North Slope in 1968. The pipeline construction boom that followed in the mid-1970s brought new wealth and ballooned Fairbanks' population up over 70,000.

Today the 7,400-square-mile Fairbanks North Star Borough claims about 75,000 residents, of whom 20% are military or dependents. Fairbanks itself has a population of around 25,000.

---

1. Orientation

The Chena River runs from east to west through Fairbanks, paralleling the course of the Tanana River until it turns south to meet the larger stream just past the Fairbanks Airport, five miles west of downtown. It's not difficult to keep your sense of direction if you remember where the river is.

Downtown Fairbanks is on the south side of the river. Numbered avenues curve around a bend in the Chena. The avenues are crossed by several north-south streets that fan out like spokes on a bicycle. **Cushman Street,** running one-way north, is the main drag. **Barnette Street,** to its west, is the major southbound thoroughfare. To Cushman's east, **Noble Street** (northbound) and **Lacey Street** (southbound) are two other main byways.

Airport Way demarcates the southern limit of downtown, below 12th Avenue; it's a four-lane highway heading west to the airport and the George Parks

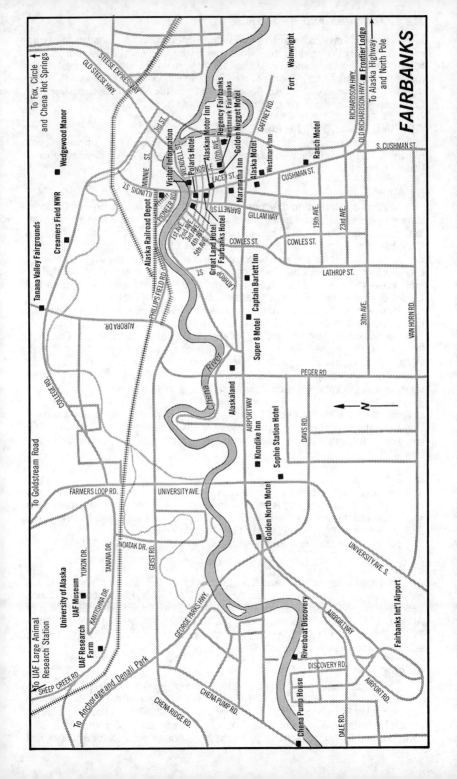

Highway, which proceeds south to Denali National Park and Anchorage. At its eastern end, Airport Way divides the Richardson Highway, which heads south and east toward Delta Junction and the Alaska Highway, from the Steese Expressway, the major northbound artery. North of the Chena River, **College Road** wends its way west to the University of Alaska. **Illinois Street** provides the interface between the Cushman Street bridge and College Road.

GETTING TO AND FROM FAIRBANKS

Name your preferred means. Any form of transportation but ship will get you to Fairbanks, and even then—if you're willing to seek out a Yukon Basin tugboat—you might get lucky.

By Air

Fairbanks International Airport is served by several leading carriers. On arrival, as you descend by escalator from an upper level where you'll find a restaurant, lounges, and gift shops, you'll see before you a black-and-white panoramic photo of the Fairbanks landscape. The main lobby contains a four-panel original oil painting of walruses on float ice and a single-engine antique bush plane suspended above the corridor linking the baggage-claim area with the car-rental counters. A detailed exhibit shares the history of aviation in the Interior. The Fairbanks Convention and Visitor Bureau maintains an **information center** at the airport.

Here are the Fairbanks phone numbers for leading airlines serving domestic traffic: **Alaska Airlines** (tel. 907/452-1661, or toll free 800/426-0330, 800/426-7464 in Alaska); **United Airlines** (tel. toll free 800/241-6522); **Delta Airlines** (tel. 907/474-0238, or toll free 800/221-1212); and intrastate only, **MarkAir** (tel. 907/474-9166, or toll free 800/426-6784). All have offices at the airport. Alaska Airlines offers nonstop flights six times daily from Anchorage and direct daily flights via Anchorage from San Francisco, Seattle, Dallas, and Houston.

GETTING TO AND FROM THE AIRPORT It's a six-mile, 15-minute drive east on Airport Way from the airport to downtown. Many hotels offer courtesy pickup service. If yours does not, you'll have to travel by taxi. Taxis are typically expensive, $8 to $10 for the journey to downtown.

By Car

As North America's northernmost major town, Fairbanks is a goal for many northbound drivers. The city is 206 miles west of Tok, at the junction of the Alaska and Glenn Highways; 364 miles north of Valdez via the Richardson Highway; and 358 miles north of Anchorage via the George Parks Highway.

For a current report on road conditions, dial 452-1911 or 456-ROAD.

By Bus

Fairbanks is served by charter lines, and tour bus lines. Most of these operate in the summer only. They include two American lines—**Alaska Sightseeing Tours,** 250 Cushman St., Fairbanks, AK 99701 (tel. 907/452-8518); and **Gray Line of Alaska,** 1521 S. Cushman St., Suite 123, Fairbanks, AK 99701 (tel. 907/456-7742). **Atlas Tours,** P.O. Box 4340, Whitehorse, Yukon Territory Y1A 3T5 (tel. 403/668-3161), serves Fairbanks from Canada.

By Rail

The **Alaska Railroad,** P.O. Box 7-2111, Anchorage, AK 99510 (tel. 907/265-2494 or 265-2685, or toll free 800/544-0552), operates daily express service in summer (May 24 to September 13) between Fairbanks and Anchorage via Nenana, Denali National Park, Talkeetna, and Wasilla. The express leaves Fairbanks at 8:30 a.m., arriving in Anchorage at 8 p.m.; the northbound train leaves Anchorage at

8:30 a.m., reaching Fairbanks at 8 p.m. From September to May there is weekly service. The one-way fare is $88 for adults, $44 for children 5 to 12.

The Fairbanks passenger depot is across the Chena River bridge from downtown, at 280 N. Cushman St. (tel. 907/456-4155).

GETTING AROUND

The preferred means are bus, taxi, and rental car. Fairbanks is flat enough, however, that bicycling and cross-country skiing are popular in the appropriate seasons.

Buses

Fairbanks's city bus system is called **MACS,** which stands for **Metropolitan Area Commuter Service.** Its two color-coded routes link the downtown **Transit Center** at Fifth Avenue and Cushman Street (tel. 452-6623) with the university, Alaskaland, Fort Wainwright, and residential neighborhoods in all directions. Regular service is available Monday through Friday from 6:45 a.m. to 10:40 p.m., and on Saturday from 7:15 a.m. to 9:40 p.m. Buses don't operate on Sunday.

Fares are $1.50 for adults; 75¢ for students through grade 12, seniors, and handicapped; free for children 5 and under. A day pass costs $3. For more information, write MACS, 3175 Peger Rd., Fairbanks, AK 99701, or call the **public transit hotline** (tel. 907/452-3279).

Taxis

If you've got to get somewhere fast, you can't beat the convenience of a taxi. Fairbanks has a slew of 'em. Four majors, all with 24-hour dispatch, are **Checker Cab** (tel. 452-3535), **Independent Cab** (tel. 452-3375), **King Cab** (tel. 452-5464 or 456-5464), and **Yellow Cab** (tel. 452-2121).

Car Rental

All the large automobile-rental agencies, and many smaller, locally owned firms, are represented at Fairbanks International Airport and/or at downtown offices. I've been pleased with **National,** at the airport (tel. 474-0151, or toll free 800/227-7368). Here's a short list of others: **All Star Rent-a-Car,** 4870 Old Airport Rd. (tel. 479-4229, or toll free 800/426-5243); **Avis,** at the airport (tel. 474-0900, or toll free 800/331-1212); **Budget,** at the airport (tel. 474-0855, or toll free 800/527-0700); **Hertz,** Airport Road and Cushman Street (tel. 452-4444, or toll free 800/654-3131) and at the airport (tel. 456-4004); **Holiday/Payless,** at the airport (tel. 452-2177, or toll free 800/237-2804); and **Rent-a-Wreck,** 2105 S. Cushman St. (tel. 452-1606, or toll free 800/421-7253 outside Alaska).

TOURIST INFORMATION

The **Fairbanks Convention and Visitor Bureau** maintains its headquarters and information center in a log cabin overlooking the Chena River, on First Avenue just east of Cushman Street. Write or visit the FCVB at 550 First Ave. (tel. 907/456-5774, or toll free 800/327-5774) for full information on all area attractions, right down to restaurant menus and language services. Open daily from 8 a.m. to 6:30 p.m. in summer, 8:30 a.m. to 5 p.m. in winter. Free guided walking tours are offered daily at 10 a.m. and 3 p.m., Memorial Day through September. You can also listen to a 24-hour recorded message of attractions and events (tel. 456-INFO).

The **Fairbanks Chamber of Commerce** office is at 250 Cushman St. (tel. 907/452-1105). For information on outdoor pursuits, try the **Alaska Public**

Lands Information Center, 250 Cushman St., Suite 1A (tel. 907/451-7352), or the **U.S. Geological Survey,** 101 12th Ave. (tel. 907/456-0244).

USEFUL INFORMATION

The *Fairbanks Daily News-Miner,* the city newspaper, is a Gannett-affiliated publication. For **emergency** assistance from police, fire department, or ambulance, dial 911. **Fairbanks Memorial Hospital** is located a short distance south of downtown at 1650 Cowles St. (tel. 452-8181). **Banks,** generally open from 10 a.m. to 6 p.m. Monday through Friday, are easily located in the downtown and university areas. Mt. McKinley Mutual Savings Bank, 531 Third Ave. and 530 Fourth Ave. (tel. 452-1751), handles the greatest variety of foreign currencies. For **dry cleaning,** Norge Village Laundry & Dry Cleaning is open from 8 a.m. to 8 p.m. seven days a week at 1255 Airport Way (tel. 456-5211). **Midnight Sun Babysitting Service,** 1120 Kodiak St. (tel. 451-8400), will help you with the kids.

In addition to the dozens of churches and religious organizations, there's also a Dial-A-Devotion phone line (tel. 452-2222). Most major fraternal organizations have lodges here.

SPECIAL EVENTS

The year's biggest celebration is **Golden Days,** annually scheduled the third through fourth full weekends of July (it begins July 21 in 1990, July 20 in 1991). Commemorating Felix Pedro's 1902 gold discovery, it began in 1952 with a 50th anniversary fest; everyone had such fun, it has continued each year since. The whole town dresses up in turn-of-the-century attire; events include a parade, air show, concerts, beard and moustache contests, and even a Felix Pedro look-alike competition. You can get more information from the Golden Days Manager, Greater Fairbanks Chamber of Commerce, P.O. Box 74446, Fairbanks, AK 99707 (tel. 907/452-1105).

Other annual events include the week-long **Fairbanks Ice Festival** in March, including sled-dog races, ice sculptures, a parka parade, Native potlatch, and dances; the **Festival of Native Arts** at the University of Alaska, also in March; the **Flying Lions Air Show** and **Summer Solstice Festival** in June; the **Tanana Valley State Fair** in August; and **Oktoberfest** in October.

---

2. Where to Stay

There are about 2,000 guest rooms available in Fairbanks and its immediate vicinity. Yet accommodation is at a premium in midsummer—and the innkeepers know it. Hotels typically raise their room rates 20% to 95% for the May-to-September tourist season, and the latter rate hike is far from an exception. When you tack onto this an 8% city tax on rooms, you're staring at what could be a very big bill to visit Fairbanks during the summer months.

The following price breakdown for a double room is based on summer rates, though I've also listed the off-season rates with individual hotel descriptions. Luxury hotels are those charging $110 and up a day, the upper bracket is $85 to $110, the middle bracket is $60 to $85, and the bargain basement is under $60. Quite often the winter rates are more indicative of the relative quality of the accommodation.

THE LUXURY BRACKET

There's little question which is the finest full-service hotel in Fairbanks: it's the **Westmark Fairbanks,** 820 Noble St., Fairbanks, AK 99701 (tel. 907/456-7722, or toll free 800/544-0970). Owned and operated by Westours (80% of the summer clientele is comprised of tour groups), this rambling, four-story, 240-room inn sprawls across two city blocks on the south side of the downtown district.

As you drive into the inn, you'll pass through a gateway dividing the lobby from the restaurant/lounge wing. The entry is informal and the staff very friendly. The lobby features potted trees and vinyl-upholstered sofas on a tile floor, with a Westours/Gray Line sales and service desk next to reception, and a gift shop and hair salon nearby. Courtesy-car service is available to most locations in Fairbanks. The *Wall Street Journal* and *USA Today* are available to guests, as well as Anchorage and Fairbanks dailies.

The Bear 'n Seal (tel. 456-7722 for reservations) is recognized by many as Fairbank's elite restaurant. Richly appointed and dimly lit, it specializes in continental cuisine. Plan on an outlay of $80 to $100 for two, not including drinks or wine. Seafood appetizers, such as coquilles St-Jacques and lobster bisque, tempt the palate; entrees are mainly steaks and seafood, including steak Diane flambé and prawns Bombay. Flambé desserts are specialties.

The hotel also has a mid-priced coffeeshop and a cocktail lounge, the Kobuk Room, with solo entertainment nightly except Sunday. A large banquet room can seat up to 500 guests.

Rooms are impressively decorated in pastel shades of mauve, gray, blue, and/or peach, with matching carpets, blackout drapes, and bedspreads. Silk-screened landscapes hang on the walls. Free local phone calls, 24-channel cable television, and thermostat-controlled hot-water heating are standard, as are a variety of complimentary toiletries. Rates are $140 single, $152 double, May 15 to September 15; $92 single, $102 double, the rest of the year. Executive suites, priced $10 higher, have queen-size beds, large desks, elaborate sitting rooms, remote-control TVs and clock-radios, and in winter, complimentary continental breakfasts.

Westours also owns the **Westmark Inn**, 1521 S. Cushman St., Fairbanks, AK 99701 (tel. 907/456-6602, or toll free 800/544-0970). Smaller (171 rooms) than its sister property and half a mile farther south, it has a charming pioneer atmosphere that its counterpart lacks.

A shake roof and railing mark the entrance to Felix's coffeeshop, where old mining photos and rustic wood décor seem to add flavor to the barbecue rib specialties ($9 to $11) and potato bar. The adjoining Husky Lounge features a backyard patio.

Courtesy-car service is readily available. In the lobby are a gift shop and Gray Line sales and service counter. Nearby is a guest laundry.

The clean and spacious guest rooms are air-conditioned for the hot days of summer. The carpeting and bedspreads in the newer wing are in shades of burgundy and gray, with silkscreened landscapes on the walls and wicker furniture; the older wing is done up in rust tones with autumn-print bedspreads. Most rooms have two double beds, blackout drapes, vanities, free local phone calls, TVs with local reception, and thermostat-controlled hot-water heating.

Rooms are priced at $120 single, $133 double. The hotel is open only during the mid-May to mid-September tourist season.

The **Regency Fairbanks,** 95 Tenth Ave., Fairbanks, AK 99701 (tel. 907/452-3200, or toll free 800/478-1320 in Alaska), is a first-class hotel in every respect.

Located just off the Steese Expressway but within easy walking distance of the central downtown area, the Regency has a feeling of opulence to it. Crystal chandeliers hang from the ceiling of the warm, two-level lobby. Plush lavender-and-burgundy carpeting lines the corridors. Bell service is available 24 hours.

The pastel shades are carried over into the décor of the restaurant and piano bar. A breakfast buffet (summer only) is priced at $7, while lunches are in the $6.50 to $11 range. Dinner entrees, including veal Oscar, seafood fettuccine, and prime rib, cost $13 to $18.

A courtesy van provides free transportation to arriving and departing guests. Princess Tours has a sales desk in the lobby. The hotel also contains a coin-op guest laundry.

Half the 128 guest rooms contain kitchenettes with refrigerators, four-burner stoves, and microwave ovens. Dishes and other utensils are available on request from the bell stand at no charge. Forty of the units have Jacuzzis. Each room has two queen-size beds, nouveau antique wood furnishings, satellite television, telephones (free local calls), and thermostat-controlled hot-water heating. Burgundy and peach dominate the color scheme.

Standard room rates are $120 single, $130 double, in summer; $75 single, $85 double, in winter. Two rooms for the handicapped are available.

En Route to the Airport

Very much in the same mold as the Regency is the **Sophie Station Hotel,** 1717 University Ave., Fairbanks, AK 99709 (tel. 907/479-3650). It, too, has kitchenettes—and much else to recommend it.

The centerpiece of an impressive condominium development on the east side of the airport, the Sophie Station presents itself as an elaborate railway depot. Walk in through double doors, with station-style seating in the entryway, to an elegant bilevel lobby featuring potted palms on green carpet and mirrored walls reflecting custom-made wood furnishings.

Zach's restaurant is acclaimed by Fairbanksans as one of the city's finest. Elegant steak and seafood dinners are priced in the $11 to $18 range. It's open daily from 6 a.m. to 10 p.m. in summer, 7 a.m. to 9 p.m. in winter. A gift shop and deli, the Cornerstore (open daily from 6 a.m. to 12:30 a.m.), adjoin the lobby. The plush, relaxing Express Room lounge, on the second floor, serves as a meeting room during the day and is open for cocktail service from 4 p.m. to midnight daily (5 to 10 p.m. on Sunday). Courtesy-van service is provided to guests, 80% of whom are corporate businessmen and government workers.

The Y-shaped hotel has 147 sophisticated rooms (all suites) on its three floors. They are richly appointed with wall-to-wall beige carpeting and burgundy upholstery and trim. Each living room has a couch and easy chair, coffee table, cable television, and desk. There's additional seating at the dining bar. The kitchen comes complete with cookware and utensils, from stove and refrigerator right down to toaster and coffeemaker. The bedrooms are furnished with one or two queen-size beds, custom-made dressers, blackout drapes, and clock-radios; there's a phone beside the bed as well as in the living room (local calls free). The wardrobe closet, with sliding mirror doors, is very large, and the dressing table is a nice addition. All units have hot-water baseboard heating. Guests have use of laundry facilities and access to the tennis courts and jogging track of the adjacent Sophie Plaza Apartments.

Rates are $120 single, $130 double, in summer; $100 single, $110 double, in winter.

THE UPPER BRACKET

Perhaps the most "Alaskan-feeling" hotel in this thoroughly Alaskan city is the **Captain Bartlett Inn,** 1411 Airport Way, Fairbanks, AK 99701 (tel. 907/452-1888, or toll free 800/544-7528, 800/478-7900 in Alaska). Of spruce log construction, with totem poles and a food cache outside the front door, it carries the theme through the whole hotel. The log-cabin interior is like that of a hunting lodge, with a bearskin and rams' heads on the walls, a mounted wolf and dog sled in the rafters. Electric candles brighten the hardwood floor, and an antique grandfather clock tick-tocks against one wall. Down the corridors and throughout the hotel are historical photos of old Fairbanks. (Capt. Robert Bartlett, the hotel's namesake, was an arctic explorer, an associate of Robert Peary on his North Pole expeditions.)

The Captain's Table restaurant, open daily from 6 a.m. to 10 p.m., offers a breakfast buffet, luncheon sandwiches ($4.25 to $8), and such tasty dinner entrees as chicken Bartlett ($13) and sautéed scallops ($17). More game heads and a set of moose antlers hang over the enormous fireplace. A small stage and dance floor are at the rear of the restaurant for after-dinner dancing to a jazz combo. The Dog Sled Saloon, entered through swinging circa-1900 gates, is open until 1 a.m. daily.

The lobby contains the Captain's Treasure Chest gift shop. Courtesy-car service is available to guests.

The hotel's 198 rooms, simply but tastefully decorated in green and mauve tones, contain queen-size or twin beds, desks, and dressers, as well as 27-channel cable TVs, phones (free local calls), and thermostat-controlled hot-water heating. Six units have kitchenettes. Rates are $95, single or double, from May 15 to September 15; $50 single, $55 double, during the off-season.

In the Downtown Hub

At ten stories, the **Polaris Hotel,** 427 First Ave., Fairbanks, AK 99701 (tel. 907/452-5571), is the tallest building in the Interior. Built in the early 1950s, it's one of the older hotels in the city, but through continued renovation it has kept its standards high.

The blue-carpeted lobby contains a gift shop, liquor store, and the Black Angus, a coffeeshop open from 6 a.m. to 10 p.m. daily, and featuring a salad bar, lunch sandwiches in the $5 to $8 range, and filling beef and seafood dinners, such as prime rib ($14) and king crab ($3 per ounce). An adjoining lounge (open from 11 a.m. to 2 a.m.) has a jukebox and large-screen TV.

In the penthouse, the Tiki Cove restaurant (tel. 452-1484; open from 5 p.m. to midnight Monday through Saturday, from 2 p.m. on Sunday) offers Chinese and Polynesian cuisine. No single item on the menu is priced higher than $10.75 (shrimp with lobster sauce); a deluxe combination dinner for two or more runs $18 per person. The décor alone is worth a trip up the elevator. As you disembark, you're greeted by hanging lanterns depicting a Chinese immortal and a Grecian maiden. Potted plastic bamboo stands on red or light-green carpeting. At the tables are wicker chairs with cushions featuring bamboo and bird-of-paradise patterns. The rest rooms are marked with the Hawaiian words for man ("kane") and woman ("wahine").

The 135 spacious guest rooms are much more tastefully appointed in earth tones, with wood paneling on some of the walls, reproductions of classic French paintings on the others. Most contain two double beds, a dresser, desks, chair and mirror, satellite TV, and phone (free local calls), plus lots of closet space. There's hot-water heating (but what's that Holiday Inn bathmat doing beside the toilet?). Rates are $83 single, $93 double, from June 1 to Labor Day; $53 and $63 the rest of the year. Twenty-four suites, a few with kitchenettes, are available at additional cost.

The **Great Land Hotel,** 723 First Ave., Fairbanks, AK 99701 (tel. 907/452-6661), overlooks the Chena River at the intersection of Barnette Street, just two blocks from the visitor information center. Jon Van Zyle sled-dogging prints hang in the small lobby, which also contains an Atlas Tours desk and a comfortable chaise lounge. There's a small lobby cocktail lounge; under separate ownership, but within the hotel, is Ruby's Café II, a coffeeshop open from 6 a.m. to 9 p.m. daily.

The 90 guest rooms aren't the largest in town, but they are clean and well kept. Rust-colored carpeting and peach walls are accented by autumn-patterned bedspreads. Rooms contain a double bed or a double and a single, blackout drapes, easy chairs, and desk/dressers with 12-channel satellite TV. Local phone calls are free. There's hot-water heating for cold nights, and electric fans are available for warm days. Courtesy transport is available. Rates are $85 single, $90 double. Four suites are priced at $125. The hotel is closed in winter.

At the **Golden Nugget Motel,** 900 Noble St., Fairbanks, AK 99701 (tel. 907/452-5141), the wood-shingle and flagstone exterior opens to a small but pleasant lobby with floral décor and a couple of plush couches. A coffeeshop serves breakfast and lunch daily year round (6 a.m. to 2:30 p.m.). A small cocktail lounge adjoins the restaurant.

The 37 guest rooms, which feature handsome wood décor, beige carpeting, and crimson bedspreads and drapes, have reproductions of classic paintings on the walls. Each room has two double beds, 12-channel cable television, free local phone calls, and thermostat-controlled hot-water heating. Standard rates are $94 single, $104 double, in summer; $69 single, $79 double, in winter.

The North Side

One of Fairbanks's best bargains is the **Wedgewood Manor,** 212 Wedgewood Dr. (off College Road), Fairbanks, AK 99701 (tel. 907/452-1442). A segment of an apartment complex on the north side of the city has been set aside as a hotel; guests get all the advantages of full-time residents, and then some. It's bordered on the north and west by the Creamers Field state bird sanctuary, with trails for hiking or cross-country skiing year round.

Reception is in Building R, near the center of the complex. As you enter on grass-green carpeting, the desk is to your left, the lobby area two steps down to your right, with a central fireplace, big-screen TV, and bookshelf and woodcarved art set into the walls. A garden area is bathed in continuous light, and coffee is always available.

All rooms are one- or two-bedroom suites. There are 116 set aside for the hotel—47 in Building P open year round, and the remainder in Buildings M and N open in summer only. Extremely spacious, clean, and well kept, their only drawback is the carpeting: it's like Astroturf. The walls are wood paneled throughout. In the living room are two couches, two tables, and cable television (video and VCR rentals are available). A balcony overlooks the complex's spacious lawn. The bedroom has two double beds and a double dresser, a clock-radio, and an enormous wardrobe closet. Local calls are free. The full kitchen has all utensils and appliances, including toaster and coffeepot, and settings for four. Each building has a token-operated Laundromat, individual mailboxes for guests, and ramps for the handicapped.

There's a restaurant in Building R where continental breakfasts are served, at no charge to hotel guests, from 6 to 11:30 a.m. Within the Wedgewood Manor complex are an indoor swimming pool, racquetball and basketball courts, four saunas, a family-size Jacuzzi, and a game room. Equipment can be checked out at the front desk at no additional charge. A courtesy car is available.

Summer rates are $100 to $110 single, $10 more double. Winter rates are somewhat less. There are significant corporate discounts.

THE MIDDLE BRACKET

For a single-story city motel, the **Klondike Inn,** 1316 Bedrock St., Fairbanks, AK 99701 (tel. 907/479-6241), covers a lot of ground. Located just off Airport Way near University Avenue, these renovated apartment units spread like a ranch on both sides of Bedrock Street and across adjacent Rewak Drive. The friendliness and wide-open spaces associated with a ranch are consistent throughout the motel.

There are 46 one-, two-, and three-bedroom units, all with kitchenettes. Wood paneling, beige upholstery, and lush chocolate-brown carpeting set a tone of warmth. Bedrooms all are furnished with queen-size beds; a couch, chair, six-channel satellite TV/radio, and phone (free local calls) are in the living room. The kitchen area includes a four-burner stove, large refrigerator, microwave oven, and plenty of cabinet space—but you must provide your own utensils. Hot-water heating is thermostat controlled. Pets are accepted with a deposit.

The Klondike Lounge and Dining Hall (tel. 479-2224) has a good-time, rustic appeal. Prime rib is the specialty. You can get a prime-rib sandwich for lunch, with soup or salad, for $7.50; or a 16-ounce dinner cut for $16.75, served au jus with sautéed mushrooms, and including baked beans, potato, hot bread, and soup or salad. The restaurant is open Monday through Saturday from 6 a.m. to midnight and on Sunday from 2 to 11 p.m. The lounge is open daily from 8 a.m. to 5 a.m.

Courtesy-car service is available, and there's a coin-op Laundromat on the premises. Rates are $63 single, $68 double, from May 15 through October 31; $53 single, $58 double, the rest of the year.

The **Super 8 Motel,** 1909 Airport Way (at Wilbur Street), Fairbanks, AK

99701 (tel. 907/451-8888, or toll free 800/843-1991), is everything you expect a Super 8 to be—clean, well kept, reasonably priced . . . and a bit sterile.

Each of the 77 guest rooms (there are two suites) has wall-to-wall brown or rust carpeting, matching patterned bedspreads, and watercolor prints on the walls. Rooms contain queen-size beds, desk, luggage rack (but no dresser), 12-channel cable TV, direct-dial phones (free local calls), and hot-water heating. One room with facilities for the handicapped is available. There's a coin-op laundry, and courtesy-van service to the airport or train station.

There's no restaurant, but Denny's (open 24 hours) is next door, and this stretch of Airport Way is fast-food city: within one long block are McDonald's, Wendy's, Pizza Hut, Shakey's Pizza, Sizzler Steak House, and a 7-Eleven grocery.

Standard room rates at the Super 8 are $68 single, $76 double, $83 twin, between May and September. Rates are slightly less from October through April.

On the South Side

The **Ranch Motel,** 2223 S. Cushman St., Fairbanks, AK 99701 (tel. 907/452-4783), has 31 very nicely appointed rooms with cobalt-blue carpets and floral wallpaper. Each room has double or queen-size beds, two plush chairs, a smoked-glass coffee table, a handsome wood desk/dresser, and a closet with sliding mirror doors. There's also a ten-channel cable TV, a phone (free local calls), gas heat, and an electric fan.

Motel rates are $60 single, $65 double, $50 twin, in summer; $50 single, $60 double or twin, in winter.

THE BARGAIN BASEMENT

The **Alaskan Motor Inn,** 419 Fourth Ave., Fairbanks, AK 99701 (tel. 907/452-4800), has 32 rooms right in the downtown hub, about half of them with kitchenettes. Each room has double or queen-size beds and other standard furnishings, including four-channel TV, free local phone, and hot-water heat. Native-theme prints are mounted on the wood-paneled walls. The kitchenettes have four-burner stoves, but you must bring your own utensils. Summer rates are $40 single, $50 double; $10 more for a kitchenette; $10 less in winter.

The **Alaska Motel,** 1546 Cushman St., Fairbanks, AK 99701 (tel. 907/456-6393), has 35 units (28 with kitchenettes) in two buildings. Each room has two double beds, a desk and dresser, 12-channel cable television, free local phone, thermostat-controlled hot-water heating, light-brown carpeting, and wood-paneled walls. The kitchen has a two-burner stove and refrigerator, and a table with three chairs. A coin-op laundry and a barbershop are on the premises.

Rates are $46 single, $55 double, in summer; $39 single, $45 double, in winter. Weekly rates offer one night free in summer; it's just $150 a week in winter.

The **Golden North Motel,** 4888 Old Airport Way (at Karen Way), Fairbanks, AK 99701 (tel. 907/479-6201), is an excellent value if its slightly inconvenient location doesn't bother you. The 62 units are small but exceedingly clean. Appointed with chocolate-brown carpeting and yellow-and-orange-checked bedspreads, they contain queen-size beds, desk/dressers, 12-channel cable TVs, free local phones, thermostat-controlled hot-water heat, and courtesy coffee. But the management provides courtesy-van transportation wherever you want to go, even to dinner; and a complimentary continental breakfast with doughnuts is provided in the cozy lobby every morning.

Rates are $40 single, $60 double, in summer; $30 single, $45 double, during the off-season.

The **Frontier Lodge,** on the south side of the city at 440 Old Richardson Hwy., Fairbanks, AK 99701 (tel. 907/456-4733), consists of a two-story log cabin facing the highway and a newer building, containing the office, at the rear. The 20 rooms, all with kitchenettes, have double beds, dressers, couches, dining tables with chairs, large closets with shelf space, TVs (local reception), and hot-water baseboard heating. There are two pay phones in the lobby, and a coin-op guest Laundromat on the premises.

Summer room rates are $50 single, $55 double, $60 twin; winter rates are $10 less. Weekly rates are available. Credit cards are not accepted; payment must be made in cash or traveler's checks.

Back downtown, the **Fairbanks Hotel,** 517 Third Ave., Fairbanks, AK 99701 (tel. 907/456-6440), is a survivor from the 1930s. Each of the 36 rooms, small but clean, contains double or twin beds, a dresser, a desk, and chairs. Some have small private baths; others share a central facility. A pay phone and television are in the lobby. Heating is by hot-water radiator.

Summer rates for a room with private bath are $32 single, $39 double; with a shared bath, $27 single, $33 double. They're slightly lower in winter. Here, too, payment must be made in cash or traveler's checks.

BED-AND-BREAKFASTS

The main reservation and referral service in the city is **Fairbanks Bed & Breakfast,** P.O. Box 74573, Fairbanks, AK 99707 (tel. 907/452-4967). An effort is made to place travelers with families of similar interests. Most lodging is priced at $36 single, $48 double, including a continental breakfast.

Among private B&Bs, **Karen's Bed & Breakfast,** 1222 Fourth Ave., Fairbanks, AK 99701 (tel. 907/452-3511), is one of the most centrally located. Hostess Karen Dullin is proud of the homemade sourdough specialties she offers for breakfast. Rates are $36 single, $48 double. Open in summer only.

If you **Bed & Breakfast at Bev & John's,** P.O. Box 75269, Fairbanks, AK 99707 (tel. 907/456-7351), you'll get not only a warm family atmosphere but a color TV with a movie channel in each guest room. A full breakfast or lunch is served, and laundry facilities are available. Free transportation is provided to and from the airport and train stations, and to the downtown area. Rates are $35 single, $45 double.

Other B&Bs in the same price range include **Alaska Seven Gables,** P.O. Box 80488, Fairbanks, AK 99708 (tel. 907/479-0751); **Eleanor's Inn,** 360 State St., Fairbanks, AK 99701 (tel. 907/452-2598); and **Midnight Sun Traveler,** 1009 Tenth Ave., Fairbanks, AK 99701 (tel. 907/451-8106). About 30 more B&Bs are located in Fairbanks. Contact the Fairbanks Convention and Visitor Bureau for a complete listing.

HOSTELS

The **Fairbanks Youth Hostel,** P.O. Box 1738, Fairbanks, AK 99701 (tel. 907/479-4114 days), is located adjacent to the Tanana Valley Fairgrounds at College Road and Aurora Drive, in a quonset hut behind the Farmer's Market on the north side of the city. It's on the Red Line of the city bus system. Open mid-May through mid-September, it offers dorm space (provide your own sleeping gear), common bathrooms, showers, and laundry, but no kitchen. Registration is between 6 and 8 p.m. Cost per night is $10 for American Youth Hostels members, $13 for nonmembers.

CAMPGROUNDS

There are several campgrounds within the city. The **Chena River State Campground,** University Avenue on the south side of the river, has 64 sites with rest rooms, water, a dump station, tables, fireplaces, and a boat ramp. There's a $10 camping fee and a five-day limit. The **Tanana Valley Campground,** at the fairgrounds where Aurora Drive meets College Road (tel. 907/456-7956), has 31 sites with rest rooms, showers, water, a dump station, a laundry, tables, fireplaces, and wood for sale. There's space for recreational vehicles, but no hookups. The overnight charge is $10. The **Norlite Campground,** 1660 Peger Rd., just south of Airport Way (tel. 907/474-0206), has 25 tent sites and 250 trailer sites. Facilities include rest rooms, showers, water, a dump station, a laundry, a grocery and liquor store, and full electric and sewer hookups for RVs. The fee is $13 for tents, $18 for full hookups. **Gold Hill RV Park,** Mile 355 on Parks Hwy. (P.O. Box 60769), Fairbanks, AK 99706 (tel. 907/474-8088), charges $12 for its 31 units with electric hookups. **Pioneer Trailer Park,** 2201 S. Cushman St., Fairbanks, AK 99701 (tel. 907/452-8788), has 40 units at $14 per day for full hookups and showers. Self-contained RVs are also permitted overnight parking (with a five-night limit) at **Alaskaland,** on Airport Way, at $5 for the first two nights and $7 per night thereafter. The city dump station is nearby on Second Avenue.

There are numerous other state campgrounds within an hour's drive of downtown Fairbanks on the Elliot, Steese, and Richardson Hwys. and Chena Hot Springs Road. For information and a complete listing, contact the **Alaska Division of Parks,** 4420 Airport Way (on Sportsman's Way), Fairbanks, AK 99707 (tel. 907/451-2695).

---

3. Where to Eat

As the gateway to the frontier, Fairbanks doesn't have the variety of restaurants you'll find in Anchorage. But neither is the city an ungourmandized outpost.

The restaurants listed below are categorized by location and approximate price range. As a rule of thumb, figure $20 and up per person for a complete dinner at a "Deluxe" restaurant, $12 to $20 at a "Moderate" restaurant, and $5 to $12 at a "Budget" restaurant.

DOWNTOWN

The downtown area, bounded by the Chena River on the north and Airport Way on the south, between the Steese Hwy. and Lathrop Street, has some of Fairbanks's highest-class restaurants—the Bear 'n Seal at the Westmark Fairbanks and the Black Angus and Tiki Cove at the Polaris Hotel. Its other restaurants, however, are very reasonably priced.

Probably Fairbanks's most popular restaurant at the end of the 1980s was **Gambardello's,** an art deco Italian spot next to Nordstrom's department store at 706 Second Ave. (tel. 456-3417). Alice Gambardello, once owner and chef of the San Remo restaurant in New Haven, Connecticut, sought to open a quiet hole-in-the-wall in Fairbanks, but her culinary touch gave her away, and lines now extend into the street at lunchtime.

This is really two different restaurants. From 11 a.m. to 5 p.m. daily it's a frenetic Italian deli with counter service and a blackboard menu. Pasta, gourmet pizzas, and submarine sandwiches run $4.50 to $8. From 5 to 9 p.m. Gambardello's is a more serene sit-down restaurant, with veal, chicken, and other dinners priced from $9 to $15. The house special is seafood Fra Diablo—calamari, shrimp, scallops, crab, and halibut in a tomato sauce with linguine, for $14. Meals include homemade bread and house minestrone or salad. Alice's cheesecake is a great way to finish off.

The **Peking Garden,** 1101 Noble St. (tel. 456-1172), is three short blocks south of the Westmark Fairbanks. The interior is elaborate: after being greeted by a huge painted woodcarving of a pair of sea dragons, you'll walk through a moongate and beneath hanging lanterns into a gaudy Chinese art museum. An all-you-can-eat lunch buffet is $7, but dinner is what everyone looks forward to. For $30 a couple can dine on Mandarin specialties like wonton or sizzling-rice soup, eggrolls, barbecued pork, Mongolian beef, garlic chicken, and steamed rice. Or order à la carte and try white cucumber/bean-curd soup ($5), ants on a tree (shredded pork with green onions and vegetables, at $8), or sautéed happy family (sautéed abalone, shrimp, scallops, and vegetables, for $15). Open Monday through Saturday from 11:30 a.m. to 11 p.m. and on Sunday from 3 to 10 p.m.

Before you climb the stairs to the second-story **Hunan Garden,** 513 Fourth Ave. (tel. 456-8847), pause a moment to drop a penny in the wishing well for Kuan Yin, the Chinese goddess of mercy. Then step up to this pleasant downtown eatery. It's not so much the décor that tells you this restaurant is authentic—the red hanging lanterns or the Japanese fan pattern on the wallpaper—as the incense sticks and oranges in the altar devoted to Tien Kung, a major Chinese folk deity. Five regional cuisines (Hunan, Szechuan, Mandarin, Shanghai, and Cantonese) are prepared here. As a lover of spicy food, I recommend the harvest beef or the Yushan chai tai (a pork dish), each $10. There's an all-you-can-eat luncheon buffet for $6.75 on weekdays. Open Monday through Saturday from 11:30 a.m. to 10 p.m. and on Sunday from 4 to 9 p.m.

THE WEST SIDE

This section of Fairbanks takes in a lot—from busy Airport Way to the university district and beyond. Some of the better moderately priced hotel restaurants, like the Captain's Table in the Captain Bartlett Inn and the Klondike Dining Hall at the Klondike Inn, are located in this area. So, too, is Fairbanks's most famous restaurant, the Pump House.

Deluxe Riverside Restaurants

Back in 1933 the Chena Pump House was built on the Chena River as part of an ingenious hydraulic system that sent river water 400 feet uphill through a three-mile ditch to a gold-dredging operation at Cripple Creek. In 1978 the **Pump House,** Mile 1.3 on Chena Pump Road (tel. 479-8452), was reconstructed as a fine restaurant, preserving many of the relics of that era. So successful was its effort at becoming a "period piece" that the restaurant has been designated a National Historic Site. One pool table, for example, was built in 1898 and used during the Klondike Gold Rush. Other antiques are as much as 150 years old.

The corrugated iron exterior makes it look like a minor warehouse, but within its doors the Pump House exudes class. There's the Senator's Saloon, with a mahogany bar built in Kansas City; the Dining Room, whose hardwood floor and simple décor is reminiscent of a bygone era; and the Cook's Tent, a deck facing on the river, where you can wave at the paddlewheeler as it glides past.

In winter you can opt for a "family-style" dinner (adults are charged $15; children, $6.50) and you'll be served huge platters of whatever the chef saw fit to prepare today, including soup, salad, bread, entree, and dessert. Anytime, you can select prime rib ($17), halibut princesse ($14.75), or chicken à la Oscar ($15) from the menu. Lunch features an all-you-can-eat buffet for $8.75. The Senator's Saloon—which boasts the Farthest North Oyster Bar in the World (mussels and clams too)—has easy-listening guitar vocals Thursday through Sunday nights. For highbrow entertainment, come for Sunday brunch (from 10 a.m. to 2 p.m.) and be serenaded with chamber music by members of the Fairbanks Symphony.

The Pump House is open daily for lunch from 11 a.m. to 2 p.m. and for dinner from 5 to 10 p.m. (to 11 p.m. in summer). The saloon stays open till the wee hours. Call or ask your hotel about the restaurant's free transport service.

Moderately Priced Restaurants

Half the fun of the **Alaska Salmon Bake** (tel. 452-7274) is its location in the Mining Valley exhibit at Alaskaland theme park. When you're not gathered around the outdoor barbecue pit (or in the covered seating), you can wander through an old mining tunnel and see sluice boxes, gold dredge buckets, and other memorabilia of Fairbanks's roots. Dinner—salmon, halibut or ribs for $15 (kids pay $7.50, $6 on weekends)—includes a salad bar, sourdough rolls, blueberry cake, and a non-alcoholic beverage. Beer and wine are extra. Lunch costs $9. Open daily during the summer season only (late May into September) from 11:30 a.m. to 1:30 p.m. and 5 to 9 p.m.

The **Sizzler Steak House,** 1694 Airport Way (tel. 456-3581), is another in the well-known chain of low-cost family steakhouses. Like the others, it's friendly and serves its purpose well. You can pay as little as $7 for a steak dinner, up to just $17 for steak and lobster. Sizzler also features a fresh-fruit salad bar and fresh fish. Open Sunday through Thursday from 11 a.m. to 9:30 p.m., on Friday and Saturday to 10 p.m.

Lighter Fare

Frère Jacques, 4001 Geist Rd., in West Valley Plaza (tel. 479-0875), is a real French pâtisserie and bistro. Cakes and deli items aren't super-cheap—a morning pastry and cup of coffee will cost you $2.25—but a flight to Paris would make a much bigger dent in your wallet. Open Monday through Saturday from 8 a.m. to 5 p.m.

Hot Licks, 3549 College Rd. (tel. 479-7813), is more than just the neighborhood soda fountain. It is best known for its homemade ice cream and espresso bar, but it really gets hopping from 8 p.m. to midnight on Thursday, when a jazz band performs here with its rhythm section! Homemade soups ($2.50 a bowl) and breads satisfy hunger pangs. Open Monday through Saturday from 11 a.m. to midnight, and on Sunday from noon to 10 p.m.

THE SOUTH SIDE

Cushman Street heads south from downtown, eventually branching east as the Old Richardson Hwy. Several restaurants are out this way.

Budget Restaurants

Los Amigos, 636 28th Ave. (tel. 452-3684), was once a popular steakhouse called The Boardwalk. The boardwalk is still there, leading from the parking area to the front door, but the name and cuisine have changed. Mexican specialties are now offered in a $6 all-you-can-eat luncheon buffet on weekdays. Tacos, tamales, enchiladas, and the like are available as combination meals for $7 to $11. In the basement, the "Lower L.A." bar has pool tables and a big-screen TV. Open Monday through Saturday from 11 a.m. to midnight, and on Sunday from 2 to 11 p.m.

If you're in the mood for Mexican food but your partner is not, you might compromise at **El Sombrero/Drop Inn Café,** 1420 S. Cushman St. (tel. 456-5269). Twin restaurants occupy this white-trimmed red building. The Drop Inn is strictly a breakfast-lunch spot (where you can get two poached eggs on toast for $3), while El Sombrero is open for lunch and dinner. If you're very hungry, try the Chihuahua combination, one each of a tostada, taco, taquito, enchilada, and chile relleno, plus rice, beans, chips, and salsa, for $13. I also like the logo: a Mexican taking a siesta against a melting igloo. Live country-western music plays seven nights a week in the adjacent Greyhound Lounge. The Drop Inn is open daily from 6 a.m. to 5 p.m.; El Sombrero, Sunday through Thursday from 11 a.m. to 10 p.m., on Friday and Saturday to 11 p.m.

The **Sunset Inn,** 345 Old Richardson Hwy. (tel. 452-4696), offers reasonable prices in a rustic coffeehouse décor. Examples: a quarter-pound burger with fries for lunch, at $5.25; a ten-ounce king salmon steak for dinner, with salad, potato, vegetables, and bread, for $10. Open Sunday through Thursday from 6 a.m. to 10 p.m., and all night on Friday and Saturday. Sunday brunch is served from 10 a.m. to 2 p.m.

The **Food Factory** has two locations: 17th Avenue and Cushman Street (tel. 452-6348) and 36 College Rd. in the Bentley Mall (tel. 452-3313). You can dine in ("Parents: Ropes and gags available upon request," reads the menu note) or call for delivery ("Food just like Mom used to send out for!"). Cheese steaks ($6.25 to $8.50) are a specialty, and there are also hoagies, hamburgers, deli sandwiches, and pizza. There are 106 domestic and imported beers on the menu. Open Monday through Thursday from 10:30 a.m. to 11 p.m., on Friday and Saturday to midnight, and on Sunday from noon to 9 p.m.

THE NORTH SIDE

This category takes in everything north of the Chena River and east of the university district, except for those restaurants several miles from downtown listed under "Fox/Chatanika."

Moderately Priced Restaurants

Clinkerdagger, Bickerstaff & Petts Public House, better known simply as Clinkerdagger's, is the crown jewel of the Bentley Mall, 24 College Rd. (tel. 452-2756). From the outside it looks like a Chaucerian manor. Within, it's a 17th-century English tavern, with high wood beams, brick fireplaces, stone walls lined with prints and coats-of-arms, pewter mugs, and stained-glass windows. Even the waitresses get into the act, dressed in white as alehouse wenches.

The cuisine is hearty. Dinner favorites include teriyaki steak ($16.25), blackened redfish ($13), and chicken Marlano with artichoke hearts ($14). Daily fresh fish specials from Alaskan and Hawaiian waters start at $11. Don't miss Jan Holtzmeister cheesecake for dessert ($3). For lunch, you can count on fresh quiche ($6 with soup or salad) and homemade steak potage with vegetables and chopped beef ($1.25 a cup). Maui-style kal-bi ribs ($6.75) and Cajun-style chicken fettuccine ($7) are popular. The full bar specializes in draft beer and Irish coffee, and features live blues or light rock music Thursday through Saturday nights. Lunch is served Monday through Friday from 11:30 a.m. to 2 p.m., and dinner is Sunday through Thursday from 5:30 to 9 p.m., to 9:30 p.m. on Friday and Saturday.

Flannigan's Restaurant and Cantina, in Northgate Square at Old Steese Hwy. and Minnie Street (tel. 451-6100), is the Mexican equivalent of Clinkerdagger's, but perhaps just a bit overdone. The feeling of dining amid hanging plants in the courtyard of an adobe hacienda is nice . . . but neon sombreros? I mean, really! In the cantina (lounge), the neon extends to cactuses and beer mugs on stucco walls, and there are stained-glass scenes of Mexican desert life over the bar. The menu is split between Sonoran specialties (pozole soup for $2, avocado con pollo for $8, tostada del rey for $8) and gourmet American foods (steamed clams for $7.50, scallops mornay for $14, prime rib au jus at $16). Lunch is strictly Mexican. A guitarist plays Tuesday through Saturday nights in the cantina. Open Monday through Saturday from 11:30 a.m. to 10 p.m., on Sunday from 4 p.m. The cantina, of course, stays open later.

Don Diego's, 710 Old Steese Hwy. (tel. 456-3667), is a small but colorfully decorated Mexican restaurant near Bentley Mall. A favorite meal is the "build-your-own" fajita: a soft burrito stuffed with charbroiled meat (beef, pork, or chicken, for $8) or shellfish (snow crab or shrimp, at $9). For the more gourmet taste, consider the mojo de ajo (shrimp and crab claws in a fiery garlic butter with jack-cheese sauce) or the pescado con papaya, each around $15. Of course there are Mexican beers, sangría, and wine. Open from 11 a.m. to 10 p.m. daily.

The most unforgettable feature of the décor at **Geraldo's,** 701 College Rd. (tel. 452-2299), is the huge collection of beer cans and bottles around the rafters. But this Italian restaurant is no beer hall. Dining in Geraldo's comfortable wooden booths, you can order dinners like steak, shrimp, or veal Geraldo (each $13), chicken, or clams Geraldo ($12). Geraldo sautés his specials with broccoli, cauliflower, green onions, red peppers, and mushrooms, and serves them in a lemon-garlic sauce. He also has daily specials like spaghetti and meat sauce ($10, including salad bar). Open Monday through Thursday from 11 a.m. to 9 p.m., on Friday and Saturday to 11 p.m.

Budget Restaurants

I am extremely impressed by some of the restaurants on the north side of Fairbanks. Without exceeding $10 for a meal at any of the following, I can succumb to the temptation of Vietnamese, French, Greek, or American deli food and go away feeling absolutely sated.

Foong's, 1753 College Rd. (tel. 452-4399), is a tiny but worthy palate-pleaser for anyone with a taste for Asian cooking. A faint odor of incense wafts from a Buddhist altar through hanging lanterns, and numerous family heirlooms—like an ebony cabinet inlaid with intricate mother-of-pearl designs—decorate the room. There are only eight tables, but that allows Mai Foong to pamper her patrons. The menu shows Westernized Vietnamese dinners like barbecued duck, pork, or fried chicken, including soup and rice, from $7.75, but if you have a special request, she'll try to oblige. Open Monday through Saturday from 11 a.m. to 10 p.m. and on Sunday from 2 to 8 p.m. An Oriental grocery and gift shop adjoins.

The **Café de Paris,** 801 Pioneer Rd. (tel. 456-1669), occupies several rooms of a house half a block from the railroad station. An old organ stands against one wall; local artwork hangs on others; relaxing classical music is piped through the restaurant. A large deck allows diners to enjoy the sunshine. The blackboard menu changes daily, but always features croissant sandwiches for $6 to $6.50, crêpes, quiches, homemade soups, and salads. Open Monday through Saturday from 10 a.m. to 3 p.m.

A Moveable Feast, in Northgate Square at 338 Old Steese Hwy. (tel. 456-4701), is most popular among local business people for lunch. Homemade pastas (around $6) are a favorite. Dinners, of a limited but gourmet selection, change daily; they run to $9. Open Monday through Friday from 7 a.m. to 8 p.m. and on Saturday from 9 a.m. to 5 p.m.

The Bakery coffeeshop, 69 College Rd. (tel. 456-8000), is also proud of its egg dishes. It offers them with soup or salad and a sandwich for $6.25. An even better bargain is the halibut steak dinner, served with mushrooms, potato or rice, soup or salad, bread, dessert, and coffee for $9. Baked goods, especially cinnamon rolls, are a favorite of patrons—as the restaurant's name implies. Open Monday through Friday from 7 a.m. to 8 p.m., on Saturday to 4 p.m., and on Sunday from 8 a.m. to 3 p.m.

Souvlaki, 112 N. Turner St. (tel. 452-5393), has Greek sandwiches (gyros) and salads for minimal prices. Open Monday through Saturday from 10 a.m. to 6 p.m.

FAST FOOD

If you just want to grab a quick sandwich or milkshake or bucket of chicken, you'll know most of these names: Baskin-Robbins, Burger King, Dairy Queen, Denny's, Kentucky Fried Chicken, McDonald's, Royal Fork, Taco Bell, Wendy's, and Woolworth's.

Fairbanks seems to have an unusually large number of pizza parlors per capita. National or regional chains represented here include Domino's, Godfather's, Pizza Hut, and Shakey's.

FOX/CHATANIKA

Some of the best restaurants in Fairbanks aren't in Fairbanks at all. That is, they aren't in the city itself—they're in the Fairbanks North Star Borough several miles north or west, either in unincorporated areas or in the smaller communities of Fox, Chatanika, or Ester.

Unincorporated Fairbanks

A transplanted New Yorker named Sam Galindes serves arguably the best Italian cuisine in the Fairbanks area at the **Vallata,** Mile 2.5 on Goldstream Road, at Ballaine Road (tel. 455-6600 or 455-6664). The octagonal building has windows on all sides, offering views of Mount McKinley and other peaks from between hanging plants and chianti bottles. Specialties include clams oreganata ($7.50), saltimbocca alla romana on a bed of spinach ($16.50), and veal cutlet parmigiana with eggplant ($16). New York–style pizzas are $10 to $14, and a variety of steaks and seafood are also on the menu; there's also a nice Italian wine list. Open daily from 5:30 to 11 p.m.

Feel like something really different, but typically Alaskan? Try the Nome reindeer Baden Baden at **Ivory Jack's**, in a modern log cabin at Mile 1.5 on Goldstream Road (tel. 455-6665). Breaded in almonds and served with game sauce, mushrooms, and a stuffed pear, it's priced at $15. For a complete Alaskan meal, you might start with a king crab cocktail ($7) and finish off with strawberries Romanoff ($2.75). Steak, prime rib, and stuffed prawns are other popular menu items. There's also an all-you-can-eat salad bar. Open daily except Tuesday from 5 to 10 p.m. (on Friday and Saturday to 11 p.m.). Cocktails are served till 1 a.m.

At Fox

This old gold-mining community, which grew up at the turn of the century around Felix Pedro's landmark discovery, is still the place many Fairbanksans head for good steak.

The **Fox Roadhouse,** Mile 11 on Steese Hwy. (tel. 457-7461), opposite the Elliott Hwy. junction, has been sharing its homey atmosphere with travelers since 1908. Red-draped tables with high-backed wooden chairs nestle around a big stone fireplace. Steak, prime rib, and seafood dinners include a baked potato and salad bar. You might start with mushrooms amaretto ($4.50), then try the steak montande ($20), baked halibut ($16), or simple liver and onions ($12). Open Monday through Thursday from 11 a.m. to 3 p.m. and 5 to 10 p.m., until midnight Friday through Sunday. Sunday brunch is served from 10 a.m. to 2 p.m.

The Turtle Club, Mile 10 on Steese Hwy. (tel. 457-3883), limits its menu to three items: prime rib ($11 to $21.75), prawns ($17 and $24), and barbecued ribs ($10.50, but not on Friday and Saturday). It does them well enough to keep folks flocking back to the rustic atmosphere—and to stop into "Theotherbar" for a before-dinner drink. Open Monday through Saturday from 6 to 10 p.m. and on Sunday from 5 to 9 p.m.

The **Dredge Master** restaurant, at Goldstream Dredge No. 8, Mile 9 on Old Steese Hwy. (tel. 457-6058), does everything in a big way—just like in the mining camp that it once was. A blackboard menu offers the likes of rib-eye steak ($19.50), beef kebab ($15), and teriyaki chicken ($13). Open for lunch buffets and dinners Monday through Saturday to 9 p.m., on Sunday to 6 p.m. The Bunkhouse Bar with its turn-of-the-century brass décor is opposite the restaurant entrance.

At Chatanika

It's about a 45-minute drive from downtown Fairbanks to this old mining community. Many folks come to visit the **Old F.E. Company Camp,** Mile 27.5 on Steese Hwy. (tel. 389-2414), where the Fairbanks Exploration Company once made its headquarters. An old Rock-Ola jukebox in the dining hall still plays Guy Lombardo and Jo Stafford records, and there are plenty of other antiques. Owners Pam and Larry McLaughlin raise much of their own meat and cook it in a ten-foot, cast-iron, coal-fired, circa-1923 stove. A full barbecued-ribs dinner is $12.50; fresh fish and prime rib are served Friday through Sunday. Luncheon sandwiches cost $4.75 to $8.75. Open daily from 9 a.m. to 10 p.m. An all-you-can-eat sourdough buffet breakfast (adults pay $10.50; kids, $5) is served on Saturday and Sunday to 2 p.m.

The **Chatanika Lodge,** Mile 28.5 on Steese Hwy. (tel. 389-2164), is like a pioneer roadhouse. Skins, traps and snowshoes, miners' cookware, carved walrus tusks, and various other knickknacks are mounted on the walls. The initials of visitors from all over the world are carved into the long bar. Yet this is only a reincarnation of the original lodge, built from a horse barn, hay barn, and tool shed after its turn-of-the-century predecessor burned to the ground in 1975. The kitchen serves up 16-ounce T-bone steak dinners for $15; cheese-steak sandwiches with onions and hot peppers

($6) are popular for lunch. A country fried chicken dinner ($8.50; with salad bar, $11), served on Sunday only, is a favorite. Open daily from 9 a.m. to 10 p.m.

NORTH POLE

This town of 1,000 people some 14 miles east of Fairbanks on the Richardson Hwy. is more than just the home of Santa Claus. Anyway, the old guy in the white beard has to eat sometime, doesn't he?

When he does, it's more than likely at **The Elf's Den,** Mile 14 on Richardson Hwy. (tel. 488-3268). Chef Tommy Tsakalos is a culinary wizard with such dishes as veal Cordon Bleu ($16 with pasta and salad bar) and stuffed capon ($14). For lunch, try the souvlaki in pocket bread ($5.75). Open Monday through Saturday from 11 a.m. to 10 p.m. and on Sunday from 10 a.m. to 10 p.m.

Many Fairbanksans wouldn't consider having a steak anywhere but at **Club 11,** Mile 11 on Richardson Hwy. (tel. 488-6611). A charcoal-broiled filet mignon or New York cut with mushrooms, including a seafood cocktail, salad bowl, baked potato, and garlic bread, is priced at $17.50. The seafood at this popular roadhouse-style restaurant is also superb. Open Tuesday through Sunday from 5 to 10 p.m. (on Saturday to 11 p.m.). Even if you don't care to linger in the cocktail lounge, duck your head in to admire the collection of Jim Beam bottles.

CHENA HOT SPRINGS ROAD

Fairbanks's favorite escape is the hot springs resort over an hour's drive east of the city. There's one fine restaurant at the resort, and another about a third of the way there.

The menu at **Chena Hot Springs Resort,** Mile 56 on Chena Hot Springs Road (tel. 452-7867), is 20 pages long. But take heart: only four pages are devoted to food. The rest is a wine list and historical treatise. Dinner specials include "What a Crock" ($8.50), a hearty meat stew served with bread and salad. Drinks include the "Bathhouse Ax" ($3). As the menu explains: "A permanent fixture of the log bathhouse that graced the springs in early days was a heavy ax used to hammer open the rough-hewn door when it froze shut. But when even this failed, a cold miner warmed himself with 8-year-old Serbian plum brandy and orange juice . . . and waited for the ice to melt." Open daily from 8 a.m. to 8 p.m.

The **Two Rivers Lodge,** Mile 16 on Chena Hot Springs Road (tel. 488-6815), is locally famous for its seafood, steaks, and cocktails, served in a relaxed and rustic log setting. You might start with sautéed soft-shell crab ($6), and follow it with flame-broiled rib-eye steak Delmonico ($17) or seafood Newburg Marsico in phyllo dough ($19). The desserts are excellent. Open Wednesday through Saturday from 5 to 10 p.m. and on Sunday from 3 to 10 p.m. Reservations are suggested.

4. What to See and Do

You could easily spend a week in Fairbanks and not see everything the city has to offer. Indeed, tourist attractions are the gold nuggets of the "new" Fairbanks.

The Fairbanks Convention and Visitor Bureau has compiled excellent city walking and driving tours which take in most of the outstanding sights in the area. Brochures are available at their offices and at many other locations. Some sights, of course, will entice you to linger or to return for longer periods of time. But a walking tour is a good way to get oriented. The following tour is not as detailed as the one suggested by the convention and visitor bureau.

A DOWNTOWN WALKING TOUR

Start at the Fairbanks Convention and Visitor Bureau's handsome **Visitor Information Center,** at First Avenue and Cushman Street, on the banks of the Chena

River (tel. 907/456-5774, or toll free 800/327-5744). Built of white spruce, birch, and fir, it has a sod roof. Pioneers appreciated the insulation offered by sod during winter, and often used it as a garden in summer.

Directly across the Cushman Street Bridge is the **Immaculate Conception Church,** built in 1904 on the south side of the river at First Avenue and Dunkel Street. It was moved to this site seven years later, pulled across log rollers by horses when the Chena froze over. It still has an active congregation and is listed on the National Register of Historic Sites.

Walking west on First Avenue, at the corner of Wickersham Street is the **Masonic Temple,** from whose false façade President Warren Harding addressed Fairbanks in 1923 after driving the golden spike of the Alaska Railroad. A couple of blocks farther, past Kellum Street, **St. Matthew's Episcopal Church** features a stained-glass nativity scene which depicts Mary and Joseph as Eskimos.

Twenty murals and two parks were created in 1979 as part of a Downtown Beautification Project. You'll see a mural of the midnight sun at Second Avenue and Cowles Street, and pass numerous murals on this walking tour. Farther down Cowles, between Fourth and Fifth Avenues, are several prestigious early Fairbanks homes. In the block east of Cowles on Fourth, you'll spot a unique dwelling with a picket fence made out of army surplus skis and a clothesline created from moose antlers. Just beyond you'll cross the last surviving section of early Fairbanks's ubiquitous boardwalks. Farther east on Fourth Avenue, between Barnette and Cushman Streets, was The Line, a red-light district blocked from public view by a ten-foot-high fence until the mid-1950s.

Courthouse Square, at the corner of Third Avenue and Cushman Street, was the site of Fairbanks's first courthouse and jail early in the city's history. The copper roof and marble floors of the present building were installed in 1934. There are numerous private offices and retail shops inside, but of most interest to the short-term visitor is the **Alaska Public Lands Information Center** in the basement off Third Avenue (tel. 451-7352). Open daily in summer from 8:30 a.m. to 9 p.m., it offers excellent dioramic displays of Alaskan wildlife, landscapes, and Native culture; 30 short videotapes presented continuously on mini-screens; and longer films and slide shows every two hours in a public theater.

When completed in 1952 as the Northward Building, the eight-story **Alaska National Bank Building,** at Third Avenue and Lacey Street, was the first steel-girder skyscraper in the Interior. If you proceed down Lacey to Seventh, then turn east across Noble Street, you'll pass through a restored 1930s neighborhood and wind up in the **Clay Street Cemetery,** the final resting place for many hundreds of early Fairbanks pioneers. Cross through the cemetery and head west again on Fifth Avenue. The residences between Hall and Dunkel Streets are typical of an early Fairbanks neighborhood.

Proceed north on Noble Street. At the corner of First Avenue is the **Wickersham Monument,** on the original site of Judge James Wickersham's frame house. (Today the house is in Alaskaland.) Probably Alaska's greatest statesman, Wickersham moved from a federal judgeship to Congress, from which he introduced the bills that created the Alaska Railroad, Denali National Park, and the University of Alaska, and offered the first Alaska statehood bill in 1916.

ALASKALAND

This 44-acre theme park (tel. 452-4529), built on Airport Way at Peger Road for the Alaska '67 Centennial Exposition, may be a disappointment to visitors who have read its hype and expect something akin to Disneyland. That's not what Alaskaland is trying to be. Temper your expectations and you'll enjoy several hours here.

Owned by the City of Fairbanks, Alaskaland is open Memorial Day to Labor Day, daily from 11 a.m. to 9 p.m., with free admission. Here's what you'll find:

The retired riverboat **S.S. Nenana** was known as "The Queen of the Yukon" during its 1933 to 1954 heyday. The boat, designated a National Historic Landmark, now contains the visitor information center.

After looking at the boat, start your counterclockwise tour of the park. You may want to linger longest in **Goldrush Town,** comprised of 29 early Fairbanks cabins and buildings donated by pioneers' descendants, moved here and renovated. More than half the homes are now occupied by gift shops and art galleries of one sort or another. (That's why there's no admission charge.) Clerks and proprietors are dressed in period costumes. You'll also find a New York deli, a Greek souvlaki café, an ice-cream parlor, and a photo shop. The **Palace Saloon** has G-rated can-can revues every evening. The nearby **Pioneer Hall** houses a small museum of Fairbanks history and the Big Stampede Klondike Gold Rush Show, a narrated presentation at 1, 3, 4, 7, and 8 p.m. daily (admission is $1).

Just past Goldrush Town is the depot for the narrow-gauge **Crooked Creek & Whiskey Island Railroad,** which takes passengers for a $2 (kids pay $1), one-mile ride around the park grounds. It's a good way to orient yourself. You'll see the newly opened **Pioneer Air Museum,** four structures in a re-created Native village called **Alaska Kkaayah,** a public boat launch and fishing pier on the Chena River, the Farthest North Square and Round Dance Center, a children's playground, and numerous picnic shelters. You can return to any or all of them when your ride is complete.

In the park's southwest corner is the **Mining Valley,** complete with a hard-rock mine tunnel and a waterfall with sluices for gold panning. The **Alaska Salmon Bake** also makes its home here (see the "Where to Eat" section, above).

On Barlett Plaza, facing the park's main entrance, is the **Fairbanks Civic Center.** The building contains a 384-seat theater (in use year round), meeting rooms and exhibit halls, an important art gallery, and the offices of the Fairbanks Arts Association.

Visitors can elect to travel to the grounds aboard a "tram train," which does a circuit of city hotels hourly from 11:30 a.m. to 10:15 p.m. for a fare of $1.

RIVERBOAT CRUISE

A cruise down the Chena and Tanana Rivers aboard the sternwheeler *Discovery III* is always a visitor favorite. Capt. Jim Binkley was apprenticed from childhood to be a river pilot, and no one has worked the waters of the Tanana longer than Binkley: he started in 1940. Binkley's knowledge of Alaska's Interior makes this narrated tour something quite out of the ordinary. You'll make stops at an Athabaskan Indian trapping camp and at a sled-dog training outpost, where you'll be given a demonstration of the dogs' prowess. You'll learn how fish wheels operate to assist commercial fishermen; how gold is trapped between layers of quartz, to be washed out by miners; and why ugly but efficient surplus truck tires are used to reduce erosion on riverbanks.

The tour covers 20 miles of river in four hours. An afternoon voyage leaves the boat landing (off Dale Road near the airport) at 2 p.m. daily mid-May to mid-September, and a morning trip departs at 8:45 a.m. daily mid-June to Labor Day. The fare is $25 for adults, $17.50 for children 3 to 12. Advance reservations are suggested. For more information, write or phone **Alaska Riverways,** P.O. Box 80610, Fairbanks, AK 99708 (tel. 907/479-6673).

UNIVERSITY OF ALASKA–FAIRBANKS

There's so much to see and do at UAF that it could easily take up two days of your time all by itself. Your best way to get acquainted with this 2,250-acre campus, located four miles west of downtown, is to join a free walking tour. Weather permitting, the 1½- to 2-hour tour is offered at 10 a.m. Monday through Friday, June through August (except July 3 and 4), and again at 2 p.m. on Monday only. It begins at the UA Museum and takes in several of the university's arctic research institutes, the Rasmuson Library (with its renowned collection of polar literature); Constitution and Signers Halls (sites of the 1956 state constitutional convention);

Davis Concert Hall (home of the Fairbanks Symphony Orchestra and other performing arts groups); and Patty Athletic Center (with its ice hockey arena and other facilities). For more information, contact the University Relations office in Signers Hall (tel. 474-7581, or 474-6397 for a recorded message).

UAF got its start in 1915 when Fairbanks was selected by Judge James Wickersham and approved by Congress as the location of the land-grant Alaska Agricultural College and School of Mines. The college opened its doors in 1922 with one building, six students, and six professors. Today it has 120 buildings, 8,300 students, and 400 faculty. Renamed the University of Alaska in 1935, its system now includes two other university campuses (in Anchorage and Juneau) and 11 community colleges across the state.

The main Lower Campus area, reached by turning west on Taku Drive off Farmers Loop Road, is connected by a free shuttle bus to the West Ridge area, where the museum and most of the research institutes are located. Schedules are available at Wood Center, the student union building.

The campus's single most outstanding visitor attraction is the **University of Alaska Museum,** 907 Yukon Dr. (tel. 474-7505). Exhibits, which focus on the five major geographical regions of Alaska, emphasize Native cultures, natural history, and mineral resources. A display incorporating Alaska's largest gold collection explains the formation of gold and various types of mining. Here also you can see "Blue Babe," the world's only fully restored Pleistocene bison. The museum also has an excellent shop specializing in publications on Alaska subjects. Open from 9 a.m. to 7 p.m. May to September, from noon to 5 p.m. October to April; closed Thanksgiving, Christmas, and New Year's Days. Admission is $3 for adults, $2.50 for senior citizens, free for children under 12.

Nearby in the Elvey Building on Koyukuk Drive is the **Geophysical Institute** (tel. 474-7558), established in 1946 to study the aurora borealis and its effect on communications. Since then it has grown to become a center of expertise in arctic and subarctic geophysics, including permafrost, glaciation, ice dynamics, earthquakes, and volcanoes. Tours—at 2 p.m. every Thursday from mid-June through August; other times, by appointment—include slide shows on the aurora and on quakes, a talk in the Globe Room, and visits to the remote sensing and seismology laboratories.

The **Mineral Industry Research Laboratory** is on Lower Campus in the O'Neill Building (tel. 474-7135). Associated with the School of Mineral Engineering, it's devoted to finding, developing, and utilizing Alaska's mineral wealth. Prospectors and mine operators seek advice here throughout the year. Tours are offered at 2 p.m. every Wednesday from mid-June through August, starting at the Fountain of Flags facing Signers Hall.

Visitors marvel at the size of the vegetables grown at the **Fairbanks Research Farm** of the Agricultural and Forestry Experiment Station on Tanana Drive, at the far west end of campus (tel. 474-7627). The station's purpose is twofold: to find out what crops (and animals) will grow and thrive in a subarctic climate, with short summers but long hours; and to discover how they can be made most economically feasible and competitive with outside markets. Free tours are offered at 2 p.m. on Friday mid-June through August, but you can drop by anytime (August is best) and look at the oversize veggies (especially note the cabbage, carrots, and broccoli) and flowers in the Demonstration Garden. There are displays of comparative farming techniques in the visitors center. A 40-minute round-trip walking trail leads through the experimental arboretum. Remember that this is a working farm with cows, swine, and other animals, so watch where you put your feet!

At the **Large Animal Research Station,** on Yankovich Road, on the north side of the campus a mile west of Ballaine Road (tel. 474-7207), herds of musk oxen, caribou, reindeer, and moose are studied. It was established in 1962 as a division of the Institute of Arctic Biology, and its scientists study animal nutrition, physiology, breeding, and ecology. This may be your only chance to see suckling musk oxen calves. Tours, priced at $2 (children under 12 go free), are offered at 1:30 and 3 p.m. on Tuesday and Saturday, June through September.

Wood Center, the student union building on Yukon Drive opposite Chandalar Avenue North (tel. 474-7211), is the center of student activities. It includes a cafeteria and snackbar, Sir Walter's pub (open Monday through Friday for light lunches and dinners, at $3.50 to $5.75), a bowling alley and games areas, and the headquarters for Wood Center Outdoor Programs to many wilderness areas around the state.

TANANA VALLEY FAIRGROUNDS

In August, the finest horse show and rodeo in the Interior are held during the Tanana Valley Fair at this College Road site, two miles west of the Steese Hwy. A **Farmers Market** is open during the summer months only. On the east side of the fairgrounds is **Creamer's Field National Wildlife Refuge,** where more than 100 species of resident and migratory birds might be seen during the various seasons.

THE STEESE HIGHWAY

The most-traveled highway north from Fairbanks, the Steese runs 162 miles to the village of Circle on the Yukon River. Only the first 44 miles are paved, but that includes the communities of Fox and Chatanika, where most attractions of immediate interest to Fairbanks visitors are located. (There are two roughly parallel roads as far as Fox: the Old Steese Hwy. and the newer Steese Expressway.) Take a drive up this road to see several old or re-created mining camps, a pair of scientific research stations, and the **Trans Alaska Pipeline.**

The best place to see the pipeline near Fairbanks is from a turnout at Mile 7 on Steese Expressway. A small display and information board will tell you that the pipeline is 48 inches in diameter and pumps 1.9 million barrels of oil each day from Prudhoe Bay to Valdez. The pipeline parallels the highway for a short distance. If you're well equipped and feeling adventurous, you can turn left at Fox and follow the Elliott and Dalton Hwys. up the treacherous "Pipeline Haul Road" to Disaster Creek, 295 miles north of Fairbanks. (Traffic is restricted over the final 205 miles to Prudhoe Bay.) To learn more about the pipeline, read this book's sections on Valdez (Chapter V) or Prudhoe Bay (Chapter VIII).

Gold Dredge No. 8, at Mile 9 on Old Steese Hwy. south of Goldstream Road (tel. 457-6058), is a national historic district. It preserves a fascinating floating factory, 250 feet long and five decks high, that dug gravel from the front edge of a pond, separated the gold out, then spewed the washed tailings behind. Built in 1928, it shut down in 1959 when the company that owned it refused to give union workers a 5¢-an-hour wage increase. Today the dredge is open May through September daily from 8 a.m. to dusk. Winter visits are by appointment. An admission fee of $5 includes a tour and gold panning. The bunkhouse has been turned into a small hotel (rooms are $45 a night, year round) and the old mess hall is the Dredge Master restaurant (see the "Where to Eat" section, above).

One mile off the Steese Hwy.—turn left at Fox on the Elliott Hwy. and proceed to the sign—is the **Little El Dorado Gold Camp** (tel. 456-4598 in Fairbanks). A narrow-gauge railroad, the "El Dorado Express," carries visitors from the parking lot to a miners' tent city, where you have an opportunity to try your hand at drift and shaft mining and at using a gold hound, suction dredge, and sluice box. Gold panners can keep the nuggets they're guaranteed to find. A two-hour tour is priced at $18 for adults, $12 for children.

Free tours are offered year round at the **Satellite Tracking Station** (tel. 451-1200), operated by the National Aeronautics and Space Administration (NASA) and the National Oceanic and Atmospheric Administration (NOAA). To reach it, turn off the Steese Hwy. at Mile 13.5 and climb about six miles into a wilderness area near Gilmore Creek.

Pedro's Monument, Mile 16.6 on Steese Hwy., commemorates the discovery of gold near here in 1902 by Italian immigrant Felix Pedro. His find started a gold rush that led to the removal of more than seven million troy ounces of gold from the Tanana Valley. Pedro died in Fairbanks in 1910; his remains were returned to Italy, where he was buried in Trignano.

In 1925 the Fairbanks Exploration Co. opened a gold camp near Chatanika, at Mile 27½ of the Steese Hwy. As many as 400 men lived and worked in the 48-acre camp's 15 buildings until it closed in 1955. Today it has new life as the **Old F.E. Company Camp** (tel. 389-2414). You'll be welcomed to the camp year round to see the vintage mining equipment, old foundry, petting zoo, and gold-panning equipment. The camp, registered as a national historic district, also has a restaurant (see the "Where to Eat" section, above) and hotel (rooms from $22.50), a mercantile store, and a gift shop. Call ahead to arrange an all-day tour from Fairbanks, including brunch and stops at Gold Dredge No. 8 and the pipeline, for $40 (children 6 to 12, $20).

CHENA HOT SPRINGS

Some 57 miles east of Fairbanks, at the end of a lovely wilderness road, is this mineral hot springs resort. Ever since its discovery in 1907 it has been an important out-of-town getaway for Fairbanks residents. Over the years a village of lodges and small cabins has grown up around Monument and Cold Spring Creeks, so that today this year-round resort offers a variety of indoor and outdoor activities in all seasons.

Mineral baths and hot pools are the main attractions. There are also whirlpool baths and a big indoor pool. Says the management: "Different soaks for different folks." Displays of pioneer mining and farming equipment stand beside the vegetable garden and sundeck. You can play volleyball, badminton, miniature golf, croquet, or horseshoes, or opt to go fishing or hiking. In winter, cross-country skiers have their run of the summer hiking trails; nordic rentals are available in the ski lodge. Ice skating, sledding, and snowmobiling are also popular.

The main lodge contains the dining room and bar (see the "Where to Eat" section, above). Prices for overnight lodging in rooms or cabins are $68 and $78 double (children free with adults). For reservations and further information, write Chena Hot Springs Resort, 331 Seventh Ave., Fairbanks, AK 99701 (tel. 907/452-7867).

En route to Chena Hot Springs, you might want to stop at Mile 22 and check out the new **Pleasant Valley Animal Park** (tel. 488-3967), where you can take a horse-drawn buggy ride to see a variety of native animals in their natural habitat.

MILITARY BASES

Tours of the two facilities near Fairbanks can be scheduled by appointment. To visit **Fort Wainwright Army Post,** whose main gate is off Gaffney Road on the east side of the city, contact the Public Affairs Office, Building 3409, Fort Wainwright, AK 99703 (tel. 907/353-7117). To see **Eielson Air Force Base,** 23 miles east of Fairbanks on the Richardson Hwy., contact the Public Affairs Department, Eielson Air Force Base, AK 99702 (tel. 907/377-2116).

NORTH POLE

This Richardson Hwy. community of 1,000 happy souls, 14 miles east of Fairbanks, is indeed the home of Santa Claus. In fact, Con Miller's **Santa Claus House,** built even before the town was incorporated in 1953, is far and away North Pole's biggest attraction.

Miller, then the struggling young proprietor of a Fairbanks trading post, first donned a red Santa Claus outfit on business trips in 1949 to bring the Christmas spirit to hundreds of children in the Interior Alaskan bush. He moved to the current site of North Pole in 1952 and erected his new trading post. Miller served as the mayor of North Pole for 17 years and his two sons became state legislators (and one the lieutenant-governor), but they all stayed involved in the family business. Today it's a huge and unique gift shop, with a wide variety of Alaska souvenirs and a constant stock of tasteful toys and Christmas ornaments.

Every Christmas, Santa Claus sends a special letter to children all over the world from North Pole, along with a deed to one square inch of Santa Claus Subdivision. You can hear all about it here, or you can write Santa Claus House, Santa Land, North Pole, AK 99705 (tel. 907/488-2200).

There's free overnight parking for self-contained RVs in the Santa Land lot.

Also in North Pole is **Jesus Town,** a missionary community of a dozen beautiful hand-hewn spruce-log cabins, all with sod roofs. Radio station KJNP ("King Jesus North Pole") broadcasts on a 50,000-watt AM station and a 25,000-watt FM frequency in the English, Inupiat, Athabaskan, and Russian (for Siberia) languages. TV station KJNP is local Channel 4. Visitors are welcome daily between 8 a.m. and 10 p.m. (tel. 488-2216). To reach Jesus Town, turn north off the Richardson Hwy. at Mission Road, where the **North Pole Chamber of Commerce and Visitors Center** (tel. 488-2242) is located.

SPORTS

Well, you can't surf in the Fairbanks area and jai alai isn't a big crowd pleaser. But virtually every other kind of sports activity is available here.

AUTO RACING During the summer, there's stock car competition every Saturday at 7 p.m. and/or Sunday at 2 p.m. at the **Greater Fairbanks Raceway,** Van Horn Road and Lathrop Street (tel. 452-3500). The season runs from Memorial Day to Labor Day; admission is $5 for adults, $2.50 for students, $10 for families. On Saturday nights there's more action at the **North Pole Speedway,** Mile 9 on Badger Road (tel. 488-6295).

BASEBALL The **Fairbanks Goldpanners,** a nationally famous semi-pro team that has seen the likes of Tom Seaver, Chris Chambliss, and Dave Kingman in uniform, play their home games at 7:30 p.m. in June, July, and August at Growden Field, at the corner of Wilbur Street and Second Avenue. Their archrivals in the Alaska Baseball League, the **North Pole Nicks,** play at their own field on Newby Road in North Pole. The Goldpanners are annual hosts to Alaska's most famous baseball tradition: a midnight-sun baseball game, played without artificial lights at midnight on June 21, the longest day of the year. The *News Miner* newspaper carries game schedules.

BASKETBALL The University of Alaska–Fairbanks has men's and women's teams in NCAA Division II. Their rivals are schools like UA–Anchorage, University of Puget Sound, and Eastern Montana University. Home games are played November to March at Patty Athletic Center (tel. 474-7205) on the UAF campus. Area high schools also have teams.

BICYCLING There is an extensive bike-path system all over Fairbanks. Rentals can be arranged from **Lucky Sourdough's Bicycle Shop** (tel. 456-2522).

BOWLING There are two facilities: **Arctic Bowl,** 940 Cowles St. (tel. 456-7719), and the new **Alaska Lanes** in The Center, Airport Way between Market and Rewak Streets (tel. 479-3800).

CANOEING The extensive system of lakes, creeks, and rivers in the Interior makes this an exceptionally popular sport here. For rentals, contact **Wilderness Canoe Adventures** (tel. 452-8968). For information on trips and tours, check out **General Bull Moose Canoe Tours,** 1437 Ithaca Dr. (tel. 479-4061).

CURLING   This European sport, something like shuffleboard on ice, has undergone a renaissance of popularity in Fairbanks. Their "Super Bowl," with numerous teams from Canada participating, is the International Bonspiel every April. Contact the **Fairbanks Curling Club,** 1962 Second Ave. (tel. 452-3011).

DOG MUSHING   If you're in Fairbanks in the winter, you'll have lots of opportunities to experience Alaska's official state sport. Local mushers practice at the **Jeff Studdert Racing Grounds** at Mile 4 on Farmers Loop Road, north of the university. The year's biggest event is the 1,000-mile **Yukon Quest International Sled Dog Race,** held annually in February and March between Fairbanks and Whitehorse (it starts in each city on alternate years). The $50,000 race is sponsored by the **Alaska-Yukon Trail Association,** which maintains a museum and store with displays and videos at 552 Second Ave. (tel. 452-7954).

   TIVI Kennels, on Kallenberg Road in Ester (tel. 457-2047, radiophone 5683), takes summer visitors on its ArfMobile to visit its sled dogs. It offers live demonstrations and videos of winter racing from mid-June to mid-September. Admission is $6.

FISHING   Your first contact should be the **Alaska Department of Fish and Game,** 1300 College Rd. (tel. 452-1531), for full information on licensing restrictions and local regulations. Fish and Game also has a year-round recorded **hotline** of hunting and fishing locations (tel. 452-1525).

   The waters of the Interior produce grayling, turbot, salmon, northern pike, whitefish, sheefish, and rainbow and lake trout. Drop a line straight into the Chena River, meander to a proven nearby fishing hole like Chena Lake (19 miles east) or the Chatanika River (39 miles north), or take advantage of the packages offered by numerous outfitters in the Fairbanks area. You might consider **Arctic Grayling Outfitters,** P.O. Box 83707, Fairbanks, AK 99708 (tel. 907/452-5201), offering nine-hour trips for as little as $75; or **Bob Elliott Guide Service,** 5920 Airport Way, Fairbanks, AK 99707 (tel. 907/479-6323), with fly-in northern pike and trout fishing from $105. You can rent equipment from **Backcountry Logistical Services,** 469 Goldmine Trail (tel. 457-7606).

GOLF   Play a round at the nine-hole, par-35 **Fairbanks Golf and Country Club,** at Yankovich and Ballaine Roads (tel. 479-6555), and you'll be given a certificate verifying that you've tackled the world's northernmost golf course. The **Chena Bend Golf Course** at Fort Wainwright (tel. 355-6749) is the best in the area. Both are open for summer business, and they welcome visitors.

HEALTH CLUBS   The most complete modern facilities are at the **Fairbanks Athletic Club,** 751 Old Richardson Hwy. (tel. 452-6801), and **The Athletic Club,** 150 Eagle Ave. (tel. 456-1914).

HIKING AND BACKPACKING   After making a stop for information and maps at the Public Lands Information Center, Third Avenue and Cushman Street, day and overnight hikers would do well to drive 40 to 50 miles east on the Chena Hot Springs Road to the **Chena River Recreation Area.** Popular tracks include the 6-mile Granite Tors Trail and the 29-mile Chena Dome Loop Trail. Another fine walk is the 20-mile **White Mountains Trail,** leaving the Elliott Hwy. at Wickersham Dome, 30 miles northwest of Fairbanks.

Wilderness backpacking expeditions of one to two weeks, many of them in the Brooks Range, are operated by a number of Fairbanks-based agencies. **Roger Rom's Alaska Wilderness, Inc.,** P.O. Box 81267, Fairbanks, AK 99708 (tel. 907/455-6060), emphasizes conservation aspects and works closely with the University of Alaska outdoor program. Ten-day trips are priced from $1,375. Others to consider: **Alaska Wilderness Expeditions,** P.O. Box 73297, Fairbanks, AK 99707 (tel. 907/457-7715); **Arctic Treks,** P.O. Box 73452, Fairbanks, AK 99707 (tel. 907/455-6501); and **Tundra Treks,** 1819 Musk Ox Trail, Fairbanks, AK 99701 (tel. 907/479-2754).

HORSEBACK RIDING   Trail rides are offered by **Wynfromere Farms,** Mile 0.2 on Bennett Road, off Chena Hot Springs Road (tel. 457-7902); **Midnight Sun Ranch,** Mile 1 on Grange Hall Road, off Chena Hot Springs Road (tel. 488-3272); or **North Pole Ranch,** Mile 8.5 on Badger Road (tel. 488-9414). Expect to pay about $25 an hour.

HUNTING   Again, contact the **Alaska Department of Fish and Game,** 1300 College Rd. (tel. 452-1531), for full information on licensing restrictions and local regulations, and for their year-round recorded **hotline** of hunting and fishing locations (tel. 452-1525). For guide service to reach the best hunting grounds for bear, moose, caribou, and sheep, you won't go wrong in contacting **Alaskan Back Country Guides Co-operative,** P.O. Box 81533, Fairbanks, AK 99708 (tel. 907/479-2754).

ICE HOCKEY   The **University of Alaska–Fairbanks** varsity hockey team, known as the Nanooks, and the **Gold Kings** semi-pro team play with the best in the country of their caliber. UAF plays its matches in winter at Patty Ice Arena (tel. 474-7602). Such major university teams as Michigan and Princeton are on the schedule. For the Gold Kings' schedule, call 452-2492.

ICE SKATING   If you have your own skates, you won't need to be told what to do. Even the Chena River is frozen over in midwinter, although it's not regarded as safe for skating. If you're at the mercy of rental equipment, try the **Big Dipper Ice Rink,** 19th Avenue and Lathrop Street (tel. 456-6683), or the **UAF Patty Ice Arena** (tel. 474-7602). **Chena Hot Springs Resort** (tel. 452-7867) also has great ice and rentals.

LUGE   This perilous Olympic sport, relatively unknown except in the European Alps, has recently established a foothold in Fairbanks. Alaska's only luge course is at the **Birch Hill Recreation Area,** northeast of downtown off City Lights Boulevard. Lessons and rentals are available from late October to early April, snow permitting. The luge, for the uninitiated, is an open one-man bobsled.

MOUNTAINEERING   Fairbanks itself isn't a mountaineering center, although it does offer some interesting rock climbs at the Granite Tors in the **Chena River Recreation**

Area, 40 miles east of the city. Numerous alpine organizations are based here, however, and outfitters frequently travel to peaks in Denali National Park and the Brooks Range. Check with **Clem's Backpacking Sports,** 315 Wendell St. (tel. 456-6314), for information.

RACQUETBALL AND HANDBALL   The major health clubs have excellent court facilities.

RAFTING   From Fairbanks, you can arrange trips of 2½ hours to a week or longer, on rivers as slow and silty as the Chena to streams with Class IV white water. Some outfitters emphasize the aspect of adventure, others are oriented toward wildlife viewing and photography, and still others are geared mainly for fishermen. Shop around to find the firm that meets your particular needs. **Teklanika Tours,** P.O. Box 10367, Curry's Corner, Fairbanks, AK 99710 (tel. 907/457-7194), offers a variety of wilderness floats and backpack trips in the Interior basin, Denali Park, and Brooks Range. **Rainbow Riverrunners,** P.O. Box 74202, Fairbanks, AK 99708 (tel. 907/479-5859), takes 55-mile fishing floats down the Gulkana River, starting 170 miles south of Fairbanks. There are many others; check with the Visitor Information Center.

RIVERBOATS   A real network of boats operates on the Chena and Tanana Rivers, for commercial and fishing purposes as well as for touring and sightseeing. You can travel downstream to Nenana, for example, with **Alaska River Charters,** P.O. Box 81516, Fairbanks, AK 99708 (tel. 907/455-6827).

A proper riverboat is 22 feet long. Powered by a 60-horsepower engine, it can travel more than 60 miles per hour. On the summer solstice in June, Fairbanks riverboats compete in the **Yukon 800 Marathon,** a 24-hour race down the Chena, Tanana, and Yukon Rivers to Galena and back. The **Mayor's Cup** races are held in July and the **Besco Lord Memorial** race to Nenana in August.

ROLLER SKATING   If you prefer wheels to blades, you can practice your pirouettes at **Roller Tech** in The Center, Airport Way between Market and Rewak Streets (tel. 479-3800), or at **Skate Country Mile,** 6 Dennis Rd. in North Pole (tel. 488-9444).

SHOOTING   Contact the **Tanana Valley Sportsman's Association,** Sportsman's Way and Boat Street off Airport Way (tel. 479-4425), for information on rifle ranges, skeet shooting, and matches.

SKIING   Cross-country skiers have a virtual paradise in Fairbanks, especially after the long December and January nights give way to much longer hours of daylight in February and March. On the University of Alaska campus alone there are 35 miles of cross-country trails, and there are many more at Birch Hill Recreation Area (site of the 1984 World Cup championships), Chena Lakes Recreation Area, and other nearby spots. Overnight cross-country ski tours are organized by **Alaska Fish & Trails Unlimited,** 1177 Shypoke Dr., Fairbanks, AK 99709 (tel. 907/479-7630). You can rent equipment from a number of local sporting goods stores, including the **Alpine Haus,** 719 Second Ave. (tel. 456-5520), and **Beaver Sports,** 3480 College Rd. (tel. 479-2494).

The best downhill facilities close to Fairbanks are at the **Cleary Summit Ski Area,** Mile 21 on Steese Hwy. (tel. 456-5520). The views from here are terrific at any time of year. The smaller **Skiland** area (tel. 456-4518), a better spot for beginners, is on a hilltop accessible from Mile 13 on Steese Hwy.

SLEIGH RIDES The same folks who took you horseback riding in the summer will hook up Old Nell to the proverbial one-horse sleigh for a high-stepping trip through the countryside or downtown Fairbanks when winter comes. Also check with the **Pleasant Valley Animal Park** (tel. 488-3967) or **Helgesino Livestock** (tel. 457-6539).

SWIMMING Summer swimmers usually head for the **Chena Lakes Recreation Area,** 19 miles east of Fairbanks via North Pole, or the Chena Hot Springs Resort. Four heated indoor pools are open year round; call for times and prices: **Hamme Pool,** 901 Airport Way (tel. 456-2969); **Mary Siah Recreation Center,** 1025 14th Ave. (tel. 456-6119); **Patty Gym Pool,** University of Alaska (tel. 474-7205); and **Wescott Pool,** Eighth Avenue in North Pole (tel. 488-9401).

TENNIS The Fairbanks North Star Borough Parks and Recreation Department has six outdoor courts open on a first-come, first-served basis at the **Hez Ray Recreation Center,** 19th Avenue and Lathrop Street (tel. 456-4218), and the **Mary Siah Recreation Center,** 1025 14th Ave. (tel. 456-6119).

VOLLEYBALL The University of Alaska women's volleyball team competes against the likes of the Air Force Academy and the University of California from September to November at Patty Gym (tel. 474-7205).

WORLD ESKIMO INDIAN OLYMPICS If you happen to be in Fairbanks in late July, don't miss this. Alaskan Natives have met here each year since 1961 to celebrate not only their sports, but also their dance, art, and culture.

In recent years, events have been held over four days at the Big Dipper Recreation Arena, 19th Avenue and Lathrop Street. Among the 26 events are the ear pull, in which a loop of string is placed over the same ear of two contestants, who then stage what amounts to a tug-of-war; and the blanket toss, in which contestants try to jump the highest with the best form. There are also competitions in knuckle hopping, muktuk eating, fish cutting, seal skinning, greased pole walking, sewing, team dancing, and high-kicking. A Miss WEIO Queen contest, Native baby contest, and intertribal pow-wow are also part of the festivities.

For more information and tickets, call the WEIO office (tel. 452-6646).

TOURS

There are good local tour operators. **Red Hat Tours,** P.O. Box 10622, Fairbanks, AK 99710 (tel. 907/457-3000) offers a regular schedule from May 15 to September 15, with tours by arrangement the rest of the year. A three-hour morning and afternoon tour, leaving the Captain Bartlett Inn at 9 a.m. daily except Sunday and 2:30 p.m. every day, is priced at $19 for adults, $9 for children 3 to 12.

Gray Line of Alaska (tel. 456-5816 at the Westmark Fairbanks) offers city tours (including the university and Gold Dredge No. 8) at 9 a.m. daily, May through September, and at 2:30 p.m. daily, June 1 through September 15 ($18.50 for adults and half price for children). **Princess Tours** (tel. 456-8131) is the only operator including a stop at the University of Alaska Museum; the three-hour city tour is offered daily, May 20 to September 25 (adults pay $18; children, $9). **Alaska Sightseeing Tours** (tel. 452-8518) includes the UAF experimental farm on a three-hour itinerary, offered twice daily (at 9 a.m. and 2:30 p.m.) from May 15 to September 30 ($16 for adults, $8 for children 5 to 11). **Atlas Tours** (tel. 452-7373 in the Great Land Hotel) also has a city tour at 9 a.m. and 2:30 p.m., June 1 through September 10 ($18 for adults, $9 for children under 12). Check with any of these operators for additional tour options.

Flightseeing

No fewer than ten different flightseeing services offer trips from Fairbanks over the Interior, from Gates of the Arctic National Park to Denali National Park. Among them are **40-Mile Air**, 6262 Old Airport Rd. (tel. 474-0518); **Larry's Flying Service,** 3822 University Ave. (tel. 474-9196, or toll free 800/478-5769); and **Wright Air Service,** 3842 University Ave. (tel. 474-0502). The Fairbanks Convention and Visitor Bureau can provide you with a complete list.

If you prefer a helicopter trip, contact **ERA Helicopters** (tel. 474-0838, or toll free 800/478-1947).

---

5. Shopping

With the sole exception of Anchorage, Fairbanks has the best selection of souvenir items of any settlement in Alaska.

NATIVE ARTS AND CRAFTS

Handcrafts of the Interior and Arctic are what you should look for here. Athabaskan art forms, designed and created by the Native peoples of the Yukon River basin, are worth seeking out. Unlike Eskimo crafts, they're hard to find elsewhere. (Look for a tag with an open hand, indicating an authentic handcrafted Alaskan Native product.) In particular, you might seek these out:

Tanned caribou- and moose-skin products, often decorated with fine beadwork: these include purses, pouches, gloves, slippers, parkas, and key rings.

Furs and products made from furs—caribou, wolf, wolverine, beaver, fox, and ground squirrel: slippers, hats, and collars are good examples.

Jewelry made from moose skin, beads, feathers, porcupine quills, and shells.

Baskets: birch-bark baskets in particular are beautiful. Willow may be used on top or as a reinforcement, and spruce roots are used for stitching. Grass, willow, or spruce root may also be woven into complete baskets. Some baskets are decorated with beads and moose skin.

Walrus ivory carvings, masks, and jewelry: most of these items come from Bering Sea islands—King, St. Lawrence, and Little Diomede—and from Nome and various coastal villages.

The **Alaska Native Arts & Crafts Center of Fairbanks,** in a big log cabin at 1603 College Rd. (tel. 452-8164), is the single best place to find all of these items. A division of the K'oyitl'ots'ina Limited, Native corporation, it features exclusively Native handcrafted goods.

You'll also find good collections of Native Alaskan crafts at the **Arctic Traveler's Gift Shop,** 201 Cushman St. (tel. 456-7080); and at **Xanadu,** 250 Third Ave. (tel. 452-3714) and in North Pole Plaza (tel. 488-0574). Both shops also have outlets at Alaskaland.

GEMS

You won't have to look far in Fairbanks to find the mineral the town was built upon. Any jeweler will be happy to show you a wide selection of gold-nugget jewelry. I like **Alaskan Prospectors,** 504 College Rd. (tel. 452-7398), which doubles as a dealer in recreational mining equipment. Gold, jade, ivory, and other minerals can be purchased. A couple of good bets in the downtown area are **Gold Mine Jewelers & Gift Shop,** 402 Fifth Ave. (tel. 452-4682), and **24-Karat Alaska Inc.,** 525 Fourth Ave. (tel. 456-5337).

FURS AND QIVIUT

At **Gerald Victor Furs,** 212 Lacey St. (tel. 456-6890), you will find high-quality coats of fox, mink, beaver, muskrat, otter, and fur seal, and hats of sable, coyote, lynx, and marten. The **Fur Factory,** 121 Dunkel St. (tel. 452-6240), deals in raw hides as well as finished products.

Weavers might like to purchase some *qiviut,* the soft underwool of the musk ox. The University of Alaska's Large Animal Research Station is offering one-pound lots of *qiviut* at $110 plus $5 postage and handling. (If you think that's a lot, take a look at what *qiviut* scarves and hats sell for!) If interested, write Muskox Research, Institute of Arctic Biology, University of Alaska, Fairbanks, AK 99775.

FINE ARTS

There are some fine artists in the Fairbanks area, both in traditional painting forms and in cottage industries.

A good place to get an overview of Interior artisans' work is **The Craft Market,** 401 Fifth Ave., at Noble Street (tel. 452-5495). More than 100 different artists are represented here.

Several galleries deal in modern adaptations of Native designs. I like the **New Horizons Gallery,** 211 Cushman St. (tel. 456-2063). You'll also find excellent collections at **Eye Appreciation Gallery,** 122 N. Turner St. (tel. 456-7015), and **The Artworks,** 3055 College Rd., at University Avenue (tel. 479-2563).

For other types of art—carvings, weaving, and pottery—check out the **House of Wood,** 411 Sixth Ave. (tel. 456-7958); **Log Cabin Fibers,** 1074 McGrath Rd. (tel. 457-2786); and **Helen's Ceramic Studio,** 97 Timberland Dr. (tel. 456-7134).

CAMERAS AND BOOKS

Fairbanks Fast Foto has an excellent selection of photographic equipment and supplies. There are three locations: in the Gavora Mall at 250 Third Ave. (tel. 456-3397), in the Shopper's Forum at 1255 Airport Way (tel. 456-8896), and in the North Pole Plaza (tel. 488-1970). **Alaskan Photographic Repair Service,** 551½ Second Ave. (tel. 452-8819), carries used equipment and parts.

Among the most interesting bookstores in Fairbanks is **Baker & Baker Booksellers,** open seven days a week at Eagle Plaza, 418 Third St. (tel. 456-2278). In addition, **Waldenbooks,** the nationwide chain store, is represented at 32 College Rd. (tel. 456-8088).

GIFTS

Aside from hotel gift shops, here are a couple of suggested spots where souvenir hunters can browse: **Last Rush Trading Post,** Mile 4 on Old Steese Hwy., at the Chena Hot Springs Road junction (tel. 457-4535), and **TCR's Ivory,** 555 Second Ave. (tel. 452-1817).

GAME

Reindeer Shop of the Arctic, 59 College Rd., Room 208, Regency Court (tel. 456-4800), sells Indian Valley Meats gift packs with reindeer sausage, "squaw candy" (smoked salmon), and many other items.

6. Culture and Nightlife

For a city on the edge of the frontier, Fairbanks has a surprisingly active cultural life.

You can find out what's happening in Fairbanks at any time of year by calling the Fairbanks Convention and Visitor Bureau's 24-hour **information line** (tel. 456-4636). The **Fairbanks Daily News-Miner** carries more detailed information in its Thursday "Arts/Entertainment" section and its Sunday supplement, "The Weekender."

FAIRBANKS SUMMER ARTS FESTIVAL

No time is more active than the two weeks in late July and early August when the annual Fairbanks Summer Arts Festival is held. Workshops and concerts in classical music, jazz, dance, theater, and the visual arts are presented by well-known guest artists from all over the United States.

Most events are staged on the university campus in association with **Jo Scott's Center for Cultural Development** (tel. 479-6778). Tickets are available at J.C. Penney's downtown and the Wood Center on the UAF campus. Many of the guest artists assist with the **UAF Summer Fine Arts Camp** for children (tel. 474-7555 for information).

THEATER

It's not serious theater, but it's lots of fun to catch the *Good as Gold* revue at Alaskaland's **Palace Theater and Saloon** (tel. 456-5960) nightly from late May to mid-September. Billed as a portrayal of "the comic life and musical times of Fairbanks," the sometimes-slapstick show takes its audience from the city's gold-rush era to modern times. There are two shows daily, at 7:30 and 9 p.m. Admission is $6. The bar opens at noon daily (at 2 p.m. on Sunday).

Another rollicking repertoire is offered summer nights at the Cripple Creek Resort's **Malemute Saloon,** made famous by the Robert Service ballad "The Shooting of Dan McGrew." The Malemute looks like a converted barn with classic swinging doors and a sawdust floor. Tables are mere boards on kegs; a sign at the bar urges patrons to "Please Use Spittoon." The show *Service with a Smile*, complete with ragtime music and Service poetry, begins at 9 p.m. Monday through Saturday. The show costs $5 (children pay $3); with drinks, it's $11, and with dinner, $15.

Also at Cripple Creek, in the **Fire House Theater,** the *Crown of Light* multimedia program combines concert music with spectacular slides of the aurora borealis. It is presented at 6 and 8 p.m. nightly in July, 8 p.m. only in June and August, by Photo Symphony Productions (tel. 479-2130). Adult admission is $4.

Cripple Creek Resort (tel. 479-2500), a 1906 gold camp, is in Ester, eight miles west of Fairbanks. It's reached via a short dirt road that turns off the George Parks Hwy. at Mile 351.7.

For more serious theater, several local troupes have seasons that occasionally extend into summer. Contact any of the following for schedules and ticket information: **Fairbanks Drama Association,** 558 Gaffney St. (tel. 456-7529); **Fairbanks Light Opera Theater,** 122 N. Turner St. (tel. 456-5631); and **UAF Drama Department,** Fine Arts Building (tel. 474-7751).

CINEMA

Moviegoers in Fairbanks have several theaters to choose from for first-run films. The newest is **The Picture Show** twin cinema at The Center, Airport Way between Market and Rewak Streets (tel. 479-3800). Others include **Goldstream Cinemas,**

1855 Airport Rd. (tel. 456-5113), and **Alaskaland Cinema,** 1656 Tamarack St. (tel. 456-8906).

Revivals and some first-run films are presented weekly at the **University of Alaska;** call for titles and schedules (tel. 474-7037). Free Alaska documentaries can be seen daily at the **Alaska Public Lands Information Center,** 250 Cushman St. (tel. 451-7352), and at 7 p.m. on Monday at the **Noel Wien Library,** 1215 Cowles St. (tel. 452-5177).

CLASSICAL MUSIC AND DANCE

The **Fairbanks Symphony Orchestra** (tel. 479-3407), with headquarters at the Fine Arts Building on the University of Alaska campus, has an active October-to-April season. Year-round presentations by visiting artists in music, dance, ballet, opera, and other performing arts are hosted by the **Fairbanks Concert Association** (tel. 452-8880) and are presented at the UAF's Davis Concert Hall or at the Alaskaland Civic Center. Native shows are sometimes offered by the **Institute of Alaska Native Arts** (tel. 456-7491 or 456-7406).

NIGHTCLUBS

To begin with, Fairbanks liquor laws are hardly "strict." They go to the limit allowed by the state: every establishment serving alcoholic beverages must close for at least one hour at 5 a.m. That relaxed attitude sets the scene for an effusive nightlife.

The scene changes, of course. At this writing, the hottest spot in town was **The Roof,** the spacious and sophisticated second-floor penthouse of The Center, on Airport Way between Market and Rewak Streets. Top-40 rock acts from the West Coast perform Monday through Thursday from 8 p.m. to 1 a.m., and on Friday and Saturday from 9 p.m. to 2 a.m. For a little variety, there's classical piano on Sunday from 5 to 8 p.m. and local jazz on Sunday from 8 to 11 p.m. On Friday and Saturday nights a $2 cover is charged.

While you're in The Center, spend a little time looking around. Fairbanks's most complete entertainment center, it includes a twin cinema (The Picture Show), a roller-skating disco rink (Roller Tech), a '50s-style diner, an ice-cream parlor, a video shop, and various other spots that appeal mainly to high-school-age youth.

Rock 'n' Roll

The biggest hangout for Fairbanks's large population of single military men is the **Sunset Inn,** 345 Old Richardson Hwy. (tel. 456-4754). Hard-rock or top-40 acts perform nightly except Monday from 9:30 p.m., closing at 4 a.m. on Friday and Saturday, at 2:30 a.m. on other nights. The lounge itself, remarkable only for its large size and almost total lack of atmosphere, is open from 10 a.m. to 5 a.m. seven days a week. Lip-sync contests and tequila night (Tuesday) are big occasions.

Cabaret, 410 Second Ave. (tel. 456-1663), is on the notorious downtown Fairbanks strip known during the Pipeline days simply as "Two Street." Every worker from Prudhoe Bay to Valdez knew that Two Street was where the action was: if you had the money, you could get anything you wanted. Today it's considerably tamer, but the reputation clings. This club features live music for dancing nightly except Sunday from 10 p.m. to 4 a.m.; the bar is open from 9 p.m. to 5 a.m.

Country-and-Western Music

If you're a C&W aficionado, you'll have lots of company in this city, especially on the south side. Behind the frontier façade of the **Silver Spur,** 285 Old Richardson Hwy. (tel. 456-6300), is Fairbanks's newest country club, with music nightly and a big dance floor made for Texas two-stepping. The **Frontier Lodge,** 440 Old Richardson Hwy. (tel. 452-2266), has a band on Friday and Saturday nights from 9:30 p.m. Farther out is the **Circle M,** Mile 6.5 on Old Richardson Hwy. (tel. 488-9956), with "country rock" and a bar open till 5 a.m. nightly.

The Greyhound Lounge, 1351 Cushman St., at Airport Way (tel. 452-7977), attracts a big following in town. Stetson-hatted patrons from their 20s through 60s dance in this dimly lit, low-ceilinged club from 9:30 p.m. to 3 a.m. nightly except Sunday.

Square Dancing
The **Northern Lights Council of Dancers** (tel. 452-5699) lists five different local clubs that keep Alaskaland's Square and Round Dance Hall occupied every Thursday, Friday, and Saturday night.

Burlesque
Reflections, 2406 S. Cushman St. (tel. 456-6433), features go-go tiger cages on either side of the stage in a shocking-pink art-deco atmosphere. It's currently Fairbanks's most popular strip joint, open till 5 a.m. nightly. Some voyeurs prefer **The Lonely Lady,** 4625 Old Airport Way (tel. 479-4162).

Local Bars
Pikes Landing, Mile 4.5 on Airport Way (tel. 479-6305), is best known locally as the launching point for the annual Tanana Raft Race to Nenana in early June. But this riverside tavern is a popular student hangout too, thanks to its all-you-can-eat Tuesday hot-dog night, Thursday taco night, and Sunday spaghetti night. Open daily from before noon to 5 a.m.

For some true local color, make the drive out to Fox and drop in at the **Howling Dog Saloon,** Mile 11.5 on Steese Hwy. (tel. 457-8780). This rustic remnant of better days is packed to the rafters most nights, especially Thursday through Saturday, when a neighborhood band plays its version of rock 'n' roll. In midsummer the volleyball net in the backyard is in use all night.

---

7. Short Trips from Fairbanks

Beyond Fairbanks is the bush. The **Dalton Highway,** better known as the Pipeline Haul Road, struggles 500 miles through the Brooks Range to Prudhoe Bay on the Beaufort Sea. The last 205 miles past Disaster Creek are restricted to drivers who hold commercial or industrial permits. The Dalton is gravel all the way, but it does offer the only opportunity in Alaska to drive north of the Arctic Circle (which you'll cross 200 miles out of Fairbanks). Wildlife is prolific and the scenery is spectacular, especially after **Coldfoot,** a tiny way station 260 miles from Fairbanks. It has a restaurant, motel, grocery, and gas station. The owners are an Iditarod sled-dog musher, Dick Mackey, and his wife, Cathy.

THE STEESE HIGHWAY
Few visitors make the one-way-and-turn-around drive up to Coldfoot, however. There are numerous more worthwhile destinations within shorter driving distance of Fairbanks. The Steese Hwy., for instance, runs 162 miles from Fairbanks to Circle, on the banks of the Yukon River. En route it passes through the town of Central, with a side road to the popular Arctic Circle Hot Springs.

There are several campsites and numerous abandoned mining camps along the Steese Hwy. beyond Chatanika's Old F.E. Company Camp (see the "What to See and Do" section, above). On the divide of the Yukon and Tanana River drainages, between Miles 85 and 108, you're likely to see a carpet of wildflowers in May and June, or herds of migrating caribou in August and September. Eagle Summit (elevation 3,624 feet) at Mile 108 is a popular place for Fairbanksans to view the summer solstice.

It's downhill from there—over 2,600 feet in less than 20 miles—to **Central.**

The permanent population of about 100 grows to around 800 in summer. In town you'll find the interesting Circle District Museum, a couple of restaurants, a motel, and a campground.

Eight miles southeast of Central via a side road, 136 miles from Fairbanks, is **Arctic Circle Hot Springs,** Central, AK 99730 (tel. 907/520-5113). The highly mineralized springs, flowing at a rate of 386 gallons per minute and a temperature of 139°F, are considered very medicinal. They have a high sodium and chloride content, and significant amounts of sulphate and silica. The resort hotel, built in 1930, offers year-round lodging at $35 and $40 single, $50 and $55 double, or $15 per bed in the hostel-style dormitory. Many of the vegetables served in the restaurant, which is open for breakfast, lunch, and dinner, are grown in greenhouses heated by the springs. Meal prices are moderate: for example, the 16-ounce T-bone steak dinner, including salad, potatoes, and vegetables, costs $17.

At **Circle** (pop. about 75), another 34 miles northeast of Central, you'll find a virtual ghost town that from 1894 to 1897 was the biggest boomtown the Far North had (to that time) ever seen. Circle City, as it was known, was a log-cabin metropolis with an opera house, hospital, and library, plus myriad hotels and bars. It was soon surpassed by Dawson City in the Klondike, but the town hung on as supply center for the mining camps of the Circle Mining District until the Steese Hwy. connected it with Fairbanks in 1927. The Yukon Trading Post houses a café and general store, and books flightseeing and charter-boat expeditions.

THE ELLIOTT HIGHWAY

Manley Hot Springs is almost exactly as far west of Fairbanks as Circle is northeast—163 miles. It's located at the end of the Elliott Hwy., which forks off the Steese Hwy. at Fox, 11 miles north of Fairbanks. The road turns to gravel 17 miles farther on.

This route offers spectacular views, access to good river fishing, and side trips to the communities of Livengood and Minto. **Livengood** (pop. 100), 86 miles from Fairbanks, is little more than a ghost town, but it thrived between 1914 and 1920, when miners sluiced $9.5 million in gold out of the nearby hills. The Athabaskan Indian residents of **Minto** (pop. 230), 131 miles from Fairbanks and 11 miles off the Elliott Hwy. on the banks of the Tolovana River, are mainly hunters and fishermen. An arts and crafts center displays their birch-bark basketry and items of fur and skin clothing. Accommodations and meals are available at the lodge and general store.

Manley Hot Springs, situated where Baker Creek empties into the Tanana River, has a permanent population of 65 which swells to 150 in summer. Frank Manley built a resort hotel here in 1907 when the settlement was the principal mining supply center for the Eureka and Tofty gold districts, but today it's the hot springs—located about three-quarters of a mile east of the town itself—that attract the most attention. Bubbling out of the earth at a temperature of around 136°F, they are unusual in that they have no sulfur content, and thus none of the acrid smell that usually characterizes hot springs.

Manley's old hotel is now the **Manley Roadhouse,** 100 Front St., Manley Hot Springs, AK 99756 (tel. 907/672-3161 or 672-3221), a veritable "period piece" furnished with antiques and prehistoric artifacts. Open May 15 to October 1, it has a restaurant and saloon, plus rooms and cabins priced at $30 to $65. Or you can pay $2 at the roadhouse to use the Manley Hot Springs Park Association's nearby campground.

The new **Manley Hot Springs Resort,** Old Manley Hwy. and Spring Drive, Manley Hot Springs, AK 99756 (tel. 907/672-3611), offers year-round swimming in a pool at the springs. The main lodge, housing the restaurant and lounge, is a lovely log building with a jade fireplace and a cozy, rustic feeling. There are 24 rooms with private bath; rates were not available at this writing. The resort also has an RV park, Laundromat, and gift shop. It arranges fishing trips and riverboat charters, and books tours to fishing camps, gold mines, and sled-dog kennels.

FORT YUKON

The largest Athabaskan village in Alaska is Fort Yukon, a settlement of about 650 people eight miles north of the Arctic Circle, some 140 air miles northeast of Fairbanks. It's a fascinating, friendly community with a subsistence lifestyle (note the fish wheels, traps, and garden plots) amid the accouterments of the late 20th century (telephones, satellite television, and off-road vehicles).

The Hudson's Bay Company first established a trading post here in 1847, on a great bend of the Yukon River near its confluence with the Porcupine. The community's subsequent missionary, gold-rush, and riverine commercial history is eloquently told at the **Dinji Zhuu Enjit Museum.** The **old fort** houses the Fort Yukon Native Council. Nearby are the **Old Mission House,** listed on the National Register of Historic Places, and Alaska's first Episcopal church, with its beaded mooseide altar cover. The Gwitchyaa Athabaskans are noted for their fine beadwork. It can be purchased at the museum.

Lodging and food are available year round in riverside log cabins at the **Elderly Lodge,** P.O. Box 10, Fort Yukon, AK 99740 (tel. 907/662-2468 or 662-2634). Room rates are $30 to $45 a night. For a change of scene, you can dine at the old **Sourdough Inn** on First and Sled Street (tel. 662-2402). Fort Yukon has been "dry" since its residents voted in 1984 to ban the sale and importation of alcoholic beverages.

Regular flights and package tours are offered by **Arctic Circle Air,** P.O. Box 60049, Fairbanks, AK 99701 (tel. 907/456-1112); **Audi Air,** P.O. Box 60370, Fairbanks, AK 99701 (tel. 907/451-0225); and **Friendship Air,** 3806 University Ave., Fairbanks, AK 99701 (tel. 907/456-4411).

---

8. The Alaska Highway

Southeast of Fairbanks, the Richardson and Alaska Highways coincide as far as Delta Junction, a distance of 98 miles. From here, the Richardson Highway turns south toward Glennallen and Valdez (266 miles away), while the Alaska Highway continues in a southeasterly direction. The Canadian border is another 200 miles; Dawson Creek, British Columbia, is 1,422 miles on.

DELTA JUNCTION

A farm center of about 1,100 people serving an area population of some 5,600, Delta Junction lies in a stretch of fertile land between the Delta and Tanana Rivers. The town proudly calls itself the end of the Alaska Highway: a sign outside the Visitor Information Center underscores that declaration, and inside, you can pay $1 for a certificate stating that you've driven the highway. The **Visitor Information Center,** in a log cabin at the junction of the two major highways, is open from 9 a.m. to 6 p.m. daily, late May to Labor Day (tel. 907/895-9941).

Where to Stay and Eat

The **Alaska 6 Motel,** Mile 270.3 on Richardson Hwy. (P.O. Box 1115), Delta Junction, AK 99737 (tel. 907/895-4848), is four miles northwest of the junction toward Fairbanks, but offers better quality for price than any other accommodation in the area. All 16 well-kept rooms, decorated in earth tones with wood paneling, have two double beds, a large desk, television, and hot-water heating. Half the rooms have kitchenettes. Year-round rates are $39 single, $45 double; children under 10 stay free with their parents.

C's Motel, Mile 265.5 on Richardson Hwy. (P.O. Box 1121), Delta Junction, AK 99737 (tel. 907/895-4437), is half a mile south of the junction toward Valdez. The 42 rooms and eight suites have double or twin beds, refrigerators, phones, and TVs with in-house movies. Most have private baths; these rooms are priced at $40 single, $47 double, year round. Rooms that share baths are $5 less; the two-room suites are $25 more. Korean chef Lee Dok Sun's Oriental flair keeps the adjoining Arirang Restaurant and Lounge packed with servicepeople from nearby Fort Greely. The restaurant serves a full breakfast beginning at 6 a.m., offers half-pound burgers for $5 at lunch, then slips into high gear at dinnertime with a wide choice of Korean and American foods. They range from English cheese steak with Worcestershire sauce ($6.75) to a spicy octopus-and-vegetable dish called nak-gee bokum ($16.50 for two). You can listen to rock 'n' roll bands in the lounge every weekend.

The **Delta Youth Hostel,** P.O. Box 971, Delta Junction, AK 99737 (tel. 907/895-5074), is nine miles out of town. Follow the highway toward Fairbanks to Mile 271.8, turn right on Tanana Loop Road, and follow the signs another three miles. The hostel is open from June 1 to September 1. Overnight rates are $10 for members, $13 for nonmembers.

A popular local restaurant is **Pizza Bella,** Mile 266 on Richardson Hwy. (tel. 895-4841). You can either sit at a red tablecloth, ignoring the adjacent video room, or place an order to go. Spaghetti and meatballs is $8.75; baked lasagne with Italian sausage, $10; a 12-inch pepperoni-and-mushroom pizza, $11.50. Open daily from 11 a.m. to midnight.

What to See and Do

The **Delta Agricultural Project,** started in 1978, has created 37 farms on 85,000 acres in the Delta Junction area. Farms grow mainly barley and forage crops. You can see many of the farms by driving out Clearwater and Jack Warren Roads. Ask directions locally. The agricultural community celebrates at the **Deltana Fair,** held annually over the first weekend of August.

Fort Greely, five miles south of Delta Junction off the Richardson Hwy., contains the U.S. Army's Northern Warfare Training Center—which emphasizes Arctic survival, military snow skiing, mountaineering, glacier crossing, and inland waterway navigation—and the army's Cold Regions Test Center for food, clothing, and equipment. Visitors can get a pass at the front gate. Call the Fort Greely Public Affairs Office (tel. 873-4161 or 872-4206) for more information.

Big Delta State Historic Park is 9½ miles north of Delta Junction toward Fairbanks. In the park is Rika's Roadhouse, an early-20th-century lodge at an important ferry landing on the Tanana River. The Alaska Division of Parks (tel. 895-4226 or 479-4114) has restored the roadhouse, with 1920s period furnishings, as a bed-and-breakfast that also serves meals. There's also a barn, the ferryman's house, and a blacksmith's shop.

Don't be surprised to see a large **herd of American bison** in this area. A herd of 23 was transplanted in 1928 from the National Bison Range in Moiese, Montana; that group has grown to about 375, and hunting is permitted on a restricted basis from October to March.

In the heart of buffalo country is one of the great lodging bargains in Alaska. Dan Splain's **Pioneer Cabins,** Mile 1404 on Alaska Hwy., Delta Junction, AK 99737 (tel. 907/895-4157), are lovely new pine-construction cabins with charcoal-gray wall-to-wall carpeting, full bathrooms with shower and sauna, full kitchens with four-burner stove and refrigerator, a sleeping loft, and propane heat. Up to six can stay in one unit—and the price is a miniscule $35 a night per cabin. The only catch is that you must bring your own utensils or drive eight miles west to the nearest restaurant. The Silver Fox Roadhouse next door sells groceries, and The Nearest Bar is literally a stone's throw away. Splain is also an outfitter who arranges horse pack trips into the Granite Mountains and McComb Plateau to look for buffalo and caribou.

TOK

Located 206 miles from Fairbanks and 125 miles from the Canadian border near Beaver Creek, Yukon Territory, this unincorporated settlement of about 1,200 summer residents (less than half that in winter) spreads around the junction of the

Alaska Highway and Glenn Highway. Travelers coming from Canada make a decision here: Do they continue straight ahead to Fairbanks or turn south toward Anchorage? As a result, it's a popular overnight stop for independent and package tourists.

Your first stop in town should be the state-operated **Tok Information Center,** Mile 1314.1 on Alaska Hwy. (tel. 883-5667). It has excellent exhibits of regional history and wildlife and a huge number of brochures from sites all over the state of Alaska. It also shares a building with the state troopers and a medical clinic. The information center is open daily, Memorial Day through September, from 7 a.m. to 10 p.m., and in winter Monday through Friday from 8 a.m. to 4:30 p.m.

Where to Stay and Eat

DELUXE ACCOMMODATIONS   Tok's two largest (and most expensive) motels are seasonal operations, owned by outside interests and geared primarily to handling the busloads of tourists who stop here overnight.

The **Westmark Tok,** Alaska and Glenn Hwys. junction (P.O. Box 130), Tok, AK 99780 (tel. 907/883-5174, or toll free 800/544-0970), comprises a series of eight-plexes centered around rock gardens. The 72 long, narrow rooms were once pipeline trailer units; the shape has resulted in awkwardly placed bathroom facilities. Otherwise, the rooms are very nice: wall-to-wall blue-gray carpeting, checkered covers on double or twin beds, dresser and table, clock-radio, and electric baseboard heat. There's no TV or phone, but you can watch a *Never Cry Wolf* video in the lobby at night, and there are pay phones near reception.

The warm lobby has a propane fireplace, lots of sofa and chair seating, and piped-in classical music. A friendly dining room with a garden décor serves breakfast from 6 to 9:30 a.m. daily and dinner from 5 to 10 p.m. (no lunch). Help yourself to a 20-item salad bar for $6, or order a full dinner of halibut Olympia ($13.50) or broiled rib-eye steak ($17). The lounge is open from 4 p.m. to midnight.

The Westmark Tok opens its doors on Memorial Day weekend and keeps them open through the third week of September. The rate for singles is $112; doubles, $126.

The **Westmark Inn,** Mile 1315 on Alaska Hwy. (P.O. Box 336), Tok, AK 99780 (tel. 907/883-2291, or toll free 800/544-2206), is a modern hotel of log-house construction one mile north of the junction. Each of the 67 rooms, decorated in earth tones and varnished wood, has two double beds and other standard furnishings, including electric baseboard heat. There's no TV; a pay phone is in the lobby. Rates are $112 single, $126 double, May 15 to September 30.

The Caribou Dining Room and Lounge extend the homestead atmosphere of the rustic lobby. Breakfast is served from 6 to 10:30 a.m. daily, and dinner is from 5 to 10 p.m.; box lunches can be prepared with advance notice. Prices are moderate: a stack of pancakes is $4.75; an old-fashioned pot roast dinner costs $11; brook trout stuffed with snow crab is $13. The lounge opens at 4 p.m. daily. Also adjoining the lobby is a small sundry shop.

A **KOA Kampground** shares the grounds. It has 54 wooded sites, most serving RVs with four-way power outlets and sewer and water hookups. All sites also have barbecue grills and picnic tables; there's a 24-hour shower house and Laundromat.

MODERATELY PRICED ACCOMMODATIONS   Three motels in Tok fall into this more affordable price range.

The **Golden Bear Motel and Camper Park,** Mile 124.4 on Glenn Hwy. (P.O. Box 276), Tok, AK 99780 (tel. 907/883-2561), half a mile south of the junction, boasts 44 new rooms and eight older log units with kitchenettes. Rooms are decorated in autumn tones with double or queen-size beds, large desk/dressers and tables, electric baseboard heating, and satellite TV with radio. Bathrooms are huge: through the swinging saloon-style doors are a sink, dressing table, and wardrobe closet; the toilet and shower/bath are in a second room. Summer rates are $55 single, $60 double; off-season rates are $5 less. The camper park has 15 full hookups and 12 partial, with tent sites, firepits, canopied tables, a heated bathhouse, and a Laundromat. The Golden Bear also has a large and complete gift shop.

Young's Motel, Mile 1313.3 on the Alaska Hwy. (P.O. Box 482), Tok, AK 99780 (tel. 907/883-4411), has 11 spacious rooms appointed in shades of brown, with double beds, desk/dressers, satellite TVs, fluorescent ceiling lamps, and hot-water baseboard heating. Register in adjoining Fast Eddy's Restaurant which offers everything from omelets to pizzas to steak and lobster at reasonable prices. There's also a guest Laundromat. June through August, singles are $45; doubles, $50. Rates are $5 cheaper the rest of the year.

The **Gateway Motel,** Mile 1314 on the Alaska Hwy. (P.O. Box 559), Tok, AK 99780 (tel. 907/883-4511), has 14 new two-room suites with private bath and television for $50 single, $55 double. (Rates are $5 less in winter.) There are 24 additional units in pipeline trailers sharing a central bath; small and spartan, with twin beds and little else, they cost $25 single, $30 double.

Tok International Youth Hostel, P.O. Box 532, Tok, AK 99780 (tel. 907/883-5113), is located eight miles west of the junction, on Pringle Road a mile south of Mile 1322.5 on the Alaska Hwy. Open June through September, it offers ten beds in a wall tent and additional tent space. It goes without saying that toilet facilities are outhouses.

What to See and Do

Tok calls itself the "Sled Dog Capital of the World." It's estimated that every third resident is in some way involved with raising dogs—breeding, training, or mushing.

The **Tok Dog Mushers Association** headquarters, at Mile 1310 on the Alaska Hwy. (tel. 883-5612), has a small museum with a slide presentation. The Race of Champions, last major race of the Alaskan winter season, is held here over the third weekend of March.

The **Burnt Paw,** a gift shop just west of the Glenn Hwy. junction on the Alaska Hwy. (tel. 883-4121), presents sled-dog demonstrations at 7:30 p.m. daily except Sunday during the months of June, July, and August.

EAGLE

Situated on the banks of the Yukon River 175 miles north of Tok via the narrow, winding Taylor Highway, Eagle (pop. 200) is a worthwhile stop for travelers en route to or from Dawson City, the capital of the Yukon's Klondike district. Founded in 1898 by Klondike gold miners as the nearest American settlement to the rush, it rapidly grew in importance, being established as the first incorporated city in the Alaskan Interior by declaration of President Theodore Roosevelt in 1901.

There's a lot to see in Eagle. The original **Wickersham Courthouse,** built in 1901 to establish the federal court in the Interior, today houses one of the city museums. Another museum occupies the old **Customs House** on the banks of the Yukon River. Reconstructed **Fort Egbert,** a U.S. Army post from 1899 to 1911, offers an interpretive exhibit and photo display, and a 58-stall mule barn (with name plates for each mule). Free **walking tours** are conducted at 10 a.m. daily, Memorial Day to Labor Day, by the Eagle Historical Society.

Eagle is also the headquarters for the 2.2-million-acre **Yukon-Charley Rivers National Preserve,** comprising 115 miles of the Yukon River between Eagle and Circle and the entire 88-mile-long drainage of the Charley River. The preserve encompasses scenic beauty, gold-rush relics and ghost towns, ancient archeological sites, and a plethora of wildlife. Float trips are the most popular means of access. For information, contact the National Park Service, P.O. Box 64, Eagle, AK 99738 (tel. 907/547-2233).

Yukon River Cruises re-create the gold-rush era in summer cruises down the Yukon River between Dawson City and Eagle, aboard the M/V *Yukon Queen*. Fully narrated, one-day bus-cruise round trips are offered most days in summer. The fare includes transportation and lunch. Contact **Gray Line of Alaska,** 1980 Cushman St., Fairbanks, AK 99701 (tel. 907/456-7742).

There is no road access to Eagle in the winter when the Taylor Hwy. is closed, but air taxis, snow machines, and dog teams make the trip easily. Meals and lodging are available in town.

THE ARCTIC

North of the Arctic Circle, the longest day has no night and the longest night has no day. The landscape is mostly frozen desert, a region underlain by permafrost, where little precipitation falls but what does remains on the ground all winter. Myriad lakes, from a few feet to 35 miles long, reveal the unseen action of permafrost's summer thaw. There are no trees, only sparse bushes and colorful wildflowers that seasonally speckle the earth. The sea itself is frozen ten months of the year, and even during the brief July-August period when it is not, there is no noticeable tidal shift, no wave action to speak of, leaving only an eerie flatness. This is a stark land. Man's adaptability to the Arctic is one of the great survival stories to be discovered in Alaska.

Temperatures in the Arctic are not as extreme as in Alaska's Interior, but are definitely cooler on average. Barrow, for instance, has an average July high of 44°F (over 50°F is tropical) and an average January low of −24°F. Nome and Kotzebue, farther south and west-facing, expect highs and lows 10° to 15° higher. Barrow gets 4 inches of precipitation annually (10 inches of snow equal 1 inch of rain), Kotzebue gets 8 inches, and Nome, 15 inches.

Who lives in the Arctic? Traditionally, it's the hardy Inupiat Eskimos. At home in settlements scattered along the coasts and rivers, they originally earned their living from the sea, fishing and sealing and whaling. Today there is nowhere safe from the influence of "progress": in most villages, snowmobiles have taken the place of dog sleds and satellite television has replaced tribal councils. In the two largest Eskimo communities, Kotzebue and Barrow, no visitor can avoid observing the conflict between old and new.

Most Native villages have wisely banned the sale and/or importation of alcoholic beverages, stemming another problem that has assailed Native populations throughout Alaska. Prudhoe Bay, founded in the 1970s as the northern terminus of the Trans Alaska Pipeline, also limits alcohol sales. Nome, though, has no such restrictions. The turn-of-the-century gold-rush town can still be the wildest community in the north, especially in March when the Iditarod dog-sled racers arrive from Anchorage.

Towns, of course, aren't representative of the Arctic as a whole. An enormous chunk of the landscape, mainly in the Brooks Range, has been set aside by the federal government as national park, preserve, or wildlife refuge. The extra effort it takes to reach this wilderness repays backpackers, canoeists, and other outdoor enthusiasts with the experience of a lifetime.

GETTING THERE

The only practical way to travel to Alaska's Arctic is by air. **Alaska Airlines** (tel. toll free 800/426-0333) operates regular daily flights from Anchorage to Nome and Kotzebue, and from Anchorage and Fairbanks to Prudhoe Bay. **MarkAir** (tel. toll free 800/426-6784, 800/478-0800 in Alaska) has the concession on travel to Barrow from Anchorage and Fairbanks, and also visits Prudhoe Bay. Several air taxis, listed under the appropriate gateway city, service the region.

Most visitors travel to the Arctic as part of a summer tour. A number of options are available. Most popular are an overnight Nome–Kotzebue excursion ($429 from Anchorage) and a full-day trip to Barrow ($389 from Anchorage, $309 from Fairbanks). Since you cross the Arctic Circle on both trips, your airline provides a certificate stating such. For information, contact the airlines or your travel agent. **Alaska Airlines Vacations** (tel. toll free 800/468-2248) handles most trips.

---

1. Nome

Nome isn't technically in the Arctic. It's spread along the flat, barren Bering Sea coast 150 miles south of the Arctic Circle. Its climate can be downright balmy compared to that of Barrow. (On the other hand, no visitor would mistake Nome for the tropics.) But the city is isolated from most sizable Alaskan towns, and it has more in common with the Arctic than with any other region. Besides, many tourists combine a visit to Nome with one to Kotzebue, which *is* north of the Arctic Circle. And so Nome winds up in this Arctic chapter.

Whether intentionally or not, Nome is a living relic of a bygone era. Prospectors still search for gold along the shores and in the low, rolling hills of the Seward Peninsula. The dog sled remains a form of winter transportation. There are probably more bars per capita—at least nine in a town of 4,400 people—than anywhere else in Alaska.

Nome owes its establishment to the discovery of gold on Anvil Creek in 1898. News of the strike reached the Klondike goldfields that winter, and by the following spring "Anvil City" (soon to be renamed "Nome") had a population of 10,000 fortune seekers. When the beach sands were found to contain a little gold themselves, steamships from Seattle and San Francisco braved the Bering ice to assault the place where, according to rumor, "the beaches are made of gold."

No trees grew here, so there was no way to build log cabins without importing lumber. Tents soon dotted the landscape and lined a 30-mile stretch of beach. The U.S. Census of 1900 showed that one-third of all whites living in Alaska were in Nome: its official population then was 12,488, though estimates ranged upward to 20,000. So sophisticated was Nome that it even had a French lingerie shop and four piano movers. But several violent storms and major fires, coupled with the increasing difficulty of finding easy wealth from gold, drove the population down near its current level after World War I.

Whence the name Nome? Credit it to a spelling mistake. A British naval officer charting this coast in the 1850s wrote the inscription "? Name" next to a prominent unnamed point. Another draftsman later took that to be "C. Nome," and it appeared on a map as "Cape Nome."

Today about 60% of the population is Native, mainly Yupik Eskimo. But Nome remains much more a "white man's town" than any other in western Alaska. Three major gold-mining companies are still in operation, along with many family-run operations, and Alaska's reindeer industry is based in Nome. Oil and gas leases in Norton Sound could bring additional wealth to the city.

Average July temperatures range from 44°F to 55°F; average January temperatures from −3°F to 12°F. Average annual precipitation is 18 inches, about one-third of which drops as winter snow (56 inches annually).

ORIENTATION

It's hard to get lost in Nome. Almost everything is within walking distance of your accommodation. **Front Street,** where most businesses are located, sprawls along the waterfront in an east-west direction. Numbered avenues (First through Sixth) parallel it to the north. Near the western end of Front Street, **Bering Street** branches north as the main thoroughfare inland.

Nome Airport, about a mile west of downtown via Seppala Drive, is served by **Alaska Airlines** (tel. toll free 800/426-0333), with regular daily flights connecting Nome with Anchorage and Kotzebue. Several smaller airlines provide service within the Norton Sound region, including **Bering Air** (tel. 907/443-5464), **Cape Smythe Air** (tel. 907/443-2414), **Olson Air** (tel. 907/443-2229), and **Ryan Air** (tel. 907/443-2005).

Nome has three 24-hour taxi companies—**Checker Cab** (tel. 443-5211), **Gold Rush Taxi** (tel. 443-5922), and **Nome Cab** (tel. 443-3030)—whose fares run approximately $3 to anywhere in town. You can rent a car ($65 per day) from **Jim West Car Rental** (tel. 443-2611), and a pickup truck ($65 per day) or van ($80 to $100 per day) from **Bonanza Car Rentals** (tel. 443-2221).

The **Nome Convention and Visitors Bureau,** P.O. Box 251, Nome, AK 99762 (tel. 907/443-5535), maintains an efficient office with plenty of brochures and a free slide show on Front Street at Division Street. Its slogan is a natural: "There's no place like Nome!"

Nome's weekly newspaper, the *Nome Nugget,* has been continuously publishing since 1901. The city has a 20-bed hospital, a community college, one bank, and 14 churches.

The year's big event is the **Iditarod Trail Sled Dog Race,** which begins in Anchorage on the first Saturday in March and ends some two weeks and about 1,100 miles later in Nome. Sometimes called "The Last Great Race," more commonly just "The Iditarod," it challenges 60 to 90 men and women—and over 1,000 dogs—with a snow- and ice-covered obstacle course of mountains and rivers, windswept tundra, and ice-locked seacoast. The top 20 finishers (in a good year, 70% of the starters will finish) share a $250,000-plus purse. Nome's **Month of Iditarod** also includes shorter dog-sled races, dog weight pulling, snowmachine races, ice golf on the frozen Bering Sea, basketball and volleyball tournaments, Eskimo sports competitions, crafts exhibits and sales, special receptions, and an awards banquet for the Iditarod mushers.

In the week of June 21, when Nome receives 22½ hours of direct sunlight, the **Midnight Sun Festival** is held. Highlights are the Nome River raft race (the perpetual trophy is a fur-lined honey bucket), a softball tournament, and Eskimo cultural events including the Miss Alaska Native Brotherhood Pageant.

Other important annual events are the **Polar Bear Swim,** a Memorial Day dip in the Bering Sea; the **Fourth of July** parade and street games; and the hilarious **Great Bathtub Race** down Front Street on Labor Day.

WHERE TO STAY

Accommodations in Nome are limited to two hotels, three bed-and-breakfasts, two VIP apartment complexes, and a small inn. City tax on lodging and meals is 4%.

If you're planning to be in Nome during Iditarod Month (March), it's essential that you book well in advance. If you still can't find a room, contact the Convention and Visitors Bureau: local families often make extra space for guests at this time.

Most tour groups lodge their guests at the **Nome Nugget Inn,** Front Street at Bering Street (P.O. Box 430), Nome, AK 99762 (tel. 907/443-2323). In fact, between mid-May and mid-September, 35 of the 47 rooms are reserved strictly for tour groups. Most of the small rooms in this hotel, which is co-owned by the King Island Native Corporation, have twin beds (only one has queen-size). Wood paneled and carpeted, they contain basic furnishings (no TV or phone) and three-quarter baths. Year-round rates are $85 single, $95 double.

The lobby of this hotel is its most impressive feature. An antique organ and Victrola, a beautiful sideboard, and wrought-iron railings around the circular staircase give it a real Gay '90s feel. The theme is carried into the nice Gold Dust Lounge, where a big-screen TV is located. Fat Freddie's restaurant, serving three meals daily, adjoins the hotel. Outside are life-size carvings of a prospector with his shovel and an Eskimo with his dog and harpoon.

The **Polaris Hotel,** First Avenue at Bering Street (P.O. Box 741), Nome, AK 99762 (tel. 907/443-2000), is a lower-standard lodging that caters mainly to village travelers. Its new wing, which contains 16 double or twin rooms off wide, well-lit corridors, offers private baths and showers, nice wood furnishings, and satellite television. The 13 single units in the old section are a last resort, with communal bathroom facilities, metal furnishings, and paper-thin walls. All units are wood paneled and carpeted, with hot-water heating. Year-round rates are $40 single (old wing), $80 double (new wing). The red-carpeted Polaris Bar has a jukebox and dance floor, pool tables, and dartboards.

Nome's first bed-and-breakfast, the **Ocean View Manor,** is on the seacoast at 490 E. Front St., near Moore Street (P.O. Box 65), Nome, AK 99762 (tel. 907/443-2133). Shirley Bronston has a spacious and comfortable home which offers better facilities for the price than either of the hotels. Each of three private rooms has a TV and phone. One has a private bath; the other two share. Guests have kitchen privileges, and the makings of continental breakfasts are provided. The living room, library, and outside deck offer a seemingly endless view of the Bering Sea. Rates are $55 single, $60 double, year round.

The Sitnasuak Native Corporation's **Nanuaq Manor VIP Apartments,** Third Avenue at Linton Way (P.O. Box 905), Nome, AK 99672 (tel. 907/443-5296), are another real bargain, especially for businessmen or couples traveling together. The two- and three-bedroom apartments are homes away from home. Decorated in shades of brown and white and furnished with a couch, chairs, and coffee table, each unit has 1¾ baths, satellite TV, phone, washer-dryer, and a full kitchen with a refrigerator, four-burner stove, double sink, electric dishwasher (the only one I saw in Alaska), a dining table with six chairs, and lots of cabinet space (kitchenware provided). The bedrooms have double or twin beds, large closets, and dressers. Year-round daily rates are $70 single, $100 double, $150 for three or four. If you stay a week or longer, rates drop to $60, $80, and $120 per day. Register in the corporation's office at 223 E. Front St. While you're there, admire their display of Native ivory crafts.

The **Polar Arms Apartments,** on Front Street (P.O. Box 880), Nome, AK 99762 (tel. 907/443-5191), comprise four fully furnished one-bedroom units and one two-bedroom suite with phones, TVs, and kitchen facilities for $80 to $95 single, $90 to $110 double, $10 per additional person. The **Ponderosa Inn,** Third Avenue and Spokane Street (P.O. Box 125), Nome, AK 99762 (tel. 907/443-2368 or 443-5737), has seven deluxe suites and nine smaller rooms, all with full baths, TVs, and phones. Guests can use the kitchen, laundry, and living room (with its stereo and other furnishings). Suites are $110 a night; standard rooms are $65 to $75 single, $75 to $85 double.

Two newer B&Bs are **Aurora House,** P.O. Box 1318, Nome, AK 99762 (tel.

907/443-2700), with rooms at $55 single, $65 double; and **Candlelight Camp,** Second Avenue at West D Street, Nome, AK 99762 (tel. 907/443-5600), with singles at $40 and doubles for $52.

WHERE TO EAT

Nome's longest-established restaurant is the **Fort Davis Roadhouse** (tel. 443-2660), housed in a nondescript barn-like red building two miles east of downtown on the Nome–Council Hwy. The large dining room has a rustic atmosphere, with hanging wagon-wheel lamps and ferns, wood tables and wood-paneled walls, and red drapes and carpets. Dinners, priced from $12, include potato and salad bar. Consider the Friday seafood buffet, at $16; the "Tundra Special" (reindeer steak with prawns or a king crab leg), for $17; or the 34-ounce porterhouse steak, at $35. The adjoining Starlight Lounge (with a dance floor and live entertainment on Friday and Saturday nights) will mix you its famous "Bering Ball" cocktail. Open every day from 5 p.m. to midnight for drinks, 6 to 10 p.m. for dinner. Closed in January and February. Credit cards aren't accepted, but out-of-state checks are.

New on Front Street, next door to the Nugget Inn, is **Fat Freddie's** (tel. 443-5899). Delicious buffet meals featuring steak, seafood and chicken are served daily for lunch ($7 to $9) and dinner ($15).

The Old Federal Building in the 200 block of East Front Street houses both an Italian and a Mexican restaurant. The Korean-owned and operated **Milano Pizzaria** (tel. 443-2924) has low-lit Italian décor, with imitation brick walls and hanging stained-glass lamps, and a menu of pizzas ($9.25 to $18.75), pastas (from $9.50), veal parmigiana ($12), and Japanese lunches (from $7.25). Open weekdays from 11 a.m. to 11 p.m., on weekends from 4 p.m. **Nacho's** (tel. 443-5503) has a south-of-the-border atmosphere with stuccoed walls and private booths. Menu offerings include standard taco-enchilada combinations from $10 and an excellent steak picado (diced and simmered in salsa and vegetable sauce) for $16. Open from 7 a.m. to 10 p.m. weekdays, 8 a.m. to 9 p.m. on Saturday, and 8 a.m. to 7 p.m. on Sunday.

For Chinese food, the **Twin Dragon,** Bering Street at Second Avenue (tel. 443-5552), is surprisingly authentic for its remote location. The tiny main dining room (four tables seat 15) is nicely decorated with ornate mirrored walls, dragon-and-phoenix motifs on the ceiling, and a large central hanging lantern. (There is additional seating upstairs and downstairs.) Lunch specials, such as pork chow mein and various beef, chicken, and shrimp dishes, are priced from $7 including soup, rice, eggroll, tea, and fortune cookie. Family-style dinners—take your pick of Mandarin, Szechuan, Cantonese, or Peking cuisine—start at $11 per person. Open from 11:30 a.m. to 2:30 p.m. and 5 to 10 p.m. every day.

A popular local café is the **Polar Cub Restaurant,** on Front Street opposite Federal Street. Look for the backdoor entrance behind the Polar Gift Shop and Polar Bar and Liquor Store. A clean, comfortable coffeeshop, it offers pancake breakfasts from $4.50 (with coffee), a burger and fries for $5, and daily lunch specials, including soup, salad bar, dessert, and coffee or tea, for $9. Fresh baked goods from the Billikin Bakery are always on the menu. Open daily from 6 a.m. for breakfast and lunch only.

Fast-food fanatics head for the **Glue Pot** (tel. 443-5474), where they can get a double-bacon-burger for $6.25, a small pizza for $4.75, or ham and eggs for $5.75. It's almost always open in summer, closing only from 3 to 6 a.m. weekdays (it stays open 24 hours on weekends); in winter it's open from 10 a.m. to 3 a.m. weekdays, to 6 a.m. weekends, and 24 hours during Iditarod. Ask directions locally.

WHAT TO SEE AND DO

The **Carrie McLain Memorial Museum,** on Front Street opposite Lane's Way, is a good place to start your exploration of downtown Nome. It's located in the Kegoayah Kozga Library building. A wealth of historical photographs show how the city looked during its glitzy heyday. Various artifacts and exhibits provide a glimpse both of the area's Native heritage and gold-rush past. Hours vary with the season. Inquire upon arrival.

The visitors bureau will provide you with a thoughtfully produced pamphlet to guide you on a 30- to 45-minute historical **walking tour.** The tour visits Nome's oldest standing building, a log cabin dating from 1898 or 1899; the only part of the city to escape a devastating 1934 fire (caused by an exploding whisky still during Prohibition); the one-time red-light district, whose working residents paid a $10 monthly "fine" (in lieu of arrest) which funded the Nome fire department; remnants of the Wild Goose Railroad, which ran from the city to tundra goldfields beginning in 1900; and the seawall that kept Nome from being "washed away" by a terrible storm in 1974.

En route, I enjoy poking my head into the local **butcher shop** to see what the Eskimo population eats. The meat of the *oogruk,* the bearded seal, is a favorite—along with its flippers, liver, and kidneys. You'll also find *coak* (walrus meat), *muktuk* (whale blubber), and reindeer steaks.

Many of the **gift shops** in downtown Nome specialize in ivory carvings. This is probably the best place in Alaska to buy ivory articles. Prices may be 50% to 100% lower than in Anchorage. Gold-nugget jewelry, furs, and Eskimo handcrafts are also good buys. There are several shops on Front Street; I like **Maruskiya's Gift Shop,** next door to the visitor center, and the **Arctic Trading Post,** between Bering and Division Streets.

The nearest working reminders of Nome's gold rush are found near town at the **Little Creek Mining Station,** an original mining claim where visitors can keep the gold they pan. Tour buses make a stop here.

The beach for miles east of Nome is cluttered with the rusted litter of nine decades of gold mining. In the summer months you may see miners camped on the beach, sluicing for gold. The mineral is not as plentiful as it once was, but if you're a scavenger you may get lucky: in 1985 a tourist found a 3¼-inch gold nugget (1.29 ounces, valued at about $520) right at the end of the city seawall!

Driving Tours

Although it's impossible to drive to Nome from other parts of Alaska, if you have a car at your disposal here ($1.75-per-gallon gas notwithstanding) there are over 350 miles of roads to travel. Three main (dirt and/or gravel) highways lead east 72 miles to Council, west 71 miles to Teller, and north 85 miles to Taylor.

NOME–COUNCIL HIGHWAY Tour buses often drive the 13 miles east to Cape Nome, from which there's an expansive shoreline view. Several fish camps are near here: dried fish can be seen hanging from driftwood racks during salmon season. Also near here is a **dog camp** where musher Howard Farley, an Iditarod veteran, gives an excellent overland demonstration with his team. He'll welcome you to pet his pups and he'll encourage your photography, but don't get too friendly with his adult dogs. Follow that rule wherever you see sled dogs chained outside small houses in the Nome area. The dogs' temperaments are unpredictable, and they may become territorial and overprotective.

The road follows the coast for 30 miles, then turns inland to **Solomon,** a once-prosperous community with an active railroad, now a virtual ghost town with just four families resident. As you drive northeast across the Seward Peninsula from here, you're in prime wildlife country. Wild musk oxen are occasionally seen near Hastings Creek and elsewhere. You may also spot reindeer, moose, or grizzly bears. If you do, don't get out of your vehicle!

When you pass into an area of trees—the nearest trees to Nome—you'll know you're only seven miles from **Council.** This village has a population of two families in winter, but 30 to 40 in summer. You'll have to park across the Niukluk River from the village and hitch a ride on a local boat.

NOME–TELLER HIGHWAY Teller became famous in 1985 when resident Libby Riddles became the first woman ever to win the Iditarod Trail Sled Dog Race. About 200 people live here on Port Clarence year round. There's no restaurant or lodging, but you will find a small gift shop and general store.

NOME–TAYLOR HIGHWAY Eight miles north of Nome, a small community called **Dexter** has a popular roadhouse and seasonal fishing camps. This route traverses many old mining areas, remembered by abandoned log cabins, water ditches, and railroad bridges. The **Salmon Lake** campground at Mile 38 is a popular weekend excursion site for Nomeites. This highway is locally known as Beam Road or Kougarok Road. **Taylor,** a tiny settlement at the head of the road, gives overland access (by trail) to Serpentine Hot Springs and Bering Land Bridge National Preserve (see "Short Trips from Nome," below).

Sports

FISHING After getting your Alaskan fishing license—$10 for three days for nonresidents—at the country store or the Alaska Department of Fish and Game, both on Front Street, you can go after salmon, northern pike, grayling, or arctic char on the Seward Peninsula's inland waterways. Peak fishing times are June through September. Some of the best fishing is on the Nome River north and east of the city and on the Snake River a few miles west.

GOLD MINING Most productive mining areas near Nome have been staked and are off-limits. Unstaked areas may be panned, but it's up to the individual to research possible ownership of the land, whether it be state, city, federal, private, or Native owned.

No permit is required for mining of a recreational nature—which means that you're limited to panning or using a small rocker box or portable dredge with an intake of less than two inches. Specific mining questions in Nome may be directed to the **Bureau of Land Management** (tel. 443-2177).

WINTER SPORTS The Nome Kennel Club—the oldest **dog-mushing** organization in the world—sponsors local races for the Nome area's 40 teams every Sunday from January through March. Visitors can participate in the sport year round. Richard and Linnea Burmeister's **Flat Dog Kennels,** 914 E. Sixth Ave. (P.O. Box 1103), Nome, AK 99762 (tel. 443-2958), offers sled trips in winter, and simulated sled trips on a wheeled rig in summer. The cost is $25 for a half hour, which may seem like a lot . . . but in that time you can travel six to eight miles.

Cross-country skiing, sledding, and **snowmachining** are all popular on the Seward Peninsula. Skis can be rented from the Nome Recreation Center (see below) for $5 a weekend, with a $20 refundable deposit.

SWIMMING When the Bering Sea warms to 45°F in the middle of the summer, locals deem it warm enough for swimming. Some even allow their nerves to be numbed by waterskiing and windsurfing. Visitors are welcome to join in the fun—but most prefer the warmth of the indoor pool at **Nome-Beltz High School** (tel. 443-5717), three miles north of town. The fee for public pool use is $2.

MISCELLANEOUS In a huge new building at 425 E. Sixth Ave. near Steadman Street, the **Nome Recreation Center** (tel. 443-5431) has a variety of facilities, including a six-lane bowling alley, racquetball courts, gymnasium, weight equipment, and aerobic dance classes. It's open from 9:30 a.m. to 11 p.m. Monday through Saturday and 1 to 11 p.m. on Sunday.

Nomeites go ga-ga over **softball** in the summer. The City League fields are two miles west of town near the airport.

Birdwatchers also love Nome. Merely sitting on the city seawall, you can spot migratory Asiatic species and various Beringian birds—those that breed only in the Bering Sea. The visitor center will provide a free checklist of birds found in this area.

Tours

Nome Tour & Marketing (tel. 443-2651), with an office at the Nome Nugget Inn, is the major summer tour operator. The $35 half-day package includes an introductory slide show at the Nugget Inn, a tour of town, and visits to the Little Creek Mining Station and Howard Farley's dog camp. Meals and accommodation are not included.

Between February and April, **Iditatours** (tel. 443-2636) picks up the slack. Farley, a commercial fisherman most of the year, will provide town tours with airport pickup and delivery, visits to gold dredges and dog camps (including a dog-team ride), and ice fishing for those who don't mind braving the cold. He also offers an overnight dog-sled excursion to the White Mountain Lodge, about 65 miles east of Nome, for $80.

Customized local tours are offered by **J & D Outdoor Adventures** (tel. 443-5124 or 443-5917). In addition to $35 tours of the town and surroundings, guided fishing trips ($150 per day), hunting expeditions, and photography and gold-panning excursions are available. The firm also rents canoes and boats ($10 an hour or $40 per day) and jet boats ($250 per day, maximum of three people).

NIGHTLIFE

Despite the proliferation of saloons, there's a lot of sameness in this category: dingy bars and drunks. Your best bets for a nice evening out are the Nome Nugget Inn and the Fort Davis Roadhouse. If you really want to soak up some atmosphere, try the **Board of Trade (BOT) Saloon** on Front Street. The BOT has a big dance floor and live rock band nightly, but a largely inebriated clientele.

SHORT TRIPS FROM NOME

Nome is the gateway to 100-mile-long St. Lawrence Island, tiny Little Diomede Island, and the Bering Land Bridge National Preserve.

The Yupik Eskimos of **St. Lawrence Island** cling to many of their ancient traditions, especially the reliance on the bounty of the sea. Visitors are welcomed to the main town, Gambell (formerly Sivuqaq), on a one-day tour from Nome. Village guides lead a slow 1½-mile, five-hour hike through the community, sharing stories of their heritage and lifestyle. The tour includes lunch, a dance performance, and demonstrations of ivory carving and skin sewing. To reserve a place, contact the Northwest Tourism Center, 110 Seppala Dr., at West C Street (P.O. Box 1318), Nome, AK 99762 (tel. 907/443-2700). Cost of the tour is $249.

A good time to visit is when the annual **Savoonga Walrus Carnival** is held in May or June in the island's only other community of size, Savoonga. Accommodation is available in Gambell. Inquire at the City of Gambell offices (tel. 907/985-3112) for details.

Little Diomede Island has the distinction of being the nearest U.S. land mass to the Soviet Union. The two-square-mile rock, 125 miles northwest of Nome in the middle of the Bering Strait, is a mere three miles from Big Diomede Island, across the International Date Line in the U.S.S.R. Most of the island's 150 Yupiks live in primitive plywood houses built in the mid-1970s by the Bureau of Indian Affairs.

Bering Land Bridge National Preserve covers much of the northern part of the Seward Peninsula. This 2½-million-acre parkland protects a wealth of features of geographical and archeological importance. The early North Americans who crossed the prehistoric land bridge (now beneath the Bering Strait) left sparse but priceless clues of their having passed this way. Birdlife is prolific in the gently rolling tundra, and nearly 250 varieties of wildflowers have been identified (best seen in late August and early September). Hot springs and lava beds are a reminder of ancient volcanic activity. The only accommodation in the preserve is a primitive shelter with cots, but planes can be chartered to numerous subsistence Eskimo villages like **Shishmaref** (pop. 425) or to **Serpentine Hot Springs,** a lovely oasis on the south-central side of the preserve. For information, contact the park superintendent at P.O. Box 220, Nome, AK 99762 (tel. 907/443-2522).

Flightseeing tours and charters (usually $180 to $200 an hour) can be arranged with the following: **Bering Air** (tel. 443-5464), **Foster's Aviation** (tel. 443-5292), **Olson Air** (tel. 443-2229), and **Evergreen Helicopters** (tel. 443-5334).

Arrangements for marine trips can be made with **Jim West Boat Charters** (tel. 443-2611).

---

2. Kotzebue

Alaska's most appealing Eskimo village, as well as its largest, with a population nearing 4,000, Kotzebue is located a mere 26 miles north of the Arctic Circle. It's situated on a barren gravel-and-tundra spit at the end of the Baldwin Peninsula, a long finger of land extending into the Chukchi Sea opposite the mouths of the Noatak, Kobuk, and Selawik Rivers.

Because of its location near the deltas of several important inland trading routes, the Inupiat Eskimo village called Kikiktagruk ("land that is almost an island") had been a thriving commercial center for a full three centuries when it was visited in 1816 by a Russian navy lieutenant named Otto von Kotzebue. Today, despite the importation of 20th-century culture in the form of TVs and snowmobiles, many Inupiat (80% of the population) still pursue traditional subsistence lifestyles. Indeed, until hunting of the animal was banned in 1972, Kotzebue was known as the "polar bear capital of the world." You can still look out the window of your hotel on Front Street to see fish drying on crude racks and handmade sealskin fishing boats braving the early-summer float ice.

The 21st century, however, may be upon Kotzebue before the townspeople know what hit them. Construction at the world's largest lead-zinc mine, the Red Dog Mine, 90 miles north of Kotzebue, began in 1986. Some 250 workers are involved in the $400-million construction of a port and a 52-mile access road to the mine, located in the DeLong Mountains on the edge of Noatak National Preserve. By 1991, when the first of 85 million tons of ore is scheduled to be extracted, there will be 650 employees. The Northwest Alaska Native Association (NANA) owns the mineral deposit and operates it in partnership with Cominco Alaska. NANA has succeeded in getting voter approval for a new Northwest Arctic Borough, thereby detaching the mine from the oil-rich North Slope Borough and ensuring that the local government will control and benefit from taxation and land-use regulations.

The climate in Kotzebue is similar to Nome, but a little cooler and drier. Annual average temperatures range from a July high of 58°F to a January low of −11°F, with extremes of 85°F and −52°F. The annual precipitation is nine inches, half of which is recorded as snow (47 inches).

ORIENTATION

Front Street, alternatively called Shore Road, is the main street in town, running south to north for about 1½ miles along the waterfront. It's paralleled to the east by numbered avenues. Second Avenue passes the NANA Regional Corporation offices en route to Kotzebue Airport. Named streets, including Lagoon Street and Tundra Way, connect Front Street with the avenues. The airport—whose runway is the only stretch of pavement this side of Nome—divides Kotzebue town from the rest of the Baldwin Peninsula. One road leads a few miles south across the tundra to a World War II air force station.

Alaska Airlines (tel. 907/442-3474, or toll free 800/426-0333) has three flights a day connecting Kotzebue with Anchorage and Nome. Several smaller carriers provide service within the region, include **Cape Smythe Air** (tel. 442-3020), **Ryan Air** (tel. 442-3347), and **Bering Air** (tel. 442-3943).

Somehow, Kotzebue supports three 24-hour taxi companies: **Arctic Cab** (tel. 442-3713), **Midnight Sun Cab** (tel. 442-3394), and **Papa Joe's Cab** (tel. 442-2530). Motor vehicles can be rented from **V&G Ltd.** (tel. 442-3647).

The closest things Kotzebue has to visitor information offices are the museums (see "What to See and Do," below). But you can write the **Arctic Circle Chamber of Commerce,** P.O. 284, Kotzebue, AK 99752, or to the **NANA Regional Corporation,** P.O. Box 49, Kotzebue, AK 99752 (tel. 907/442-3301), for information.

The year's most festive period extends for a week beginning the **Fourth of July.** The nation's birthday observance includes a beluga whale–hunting celebration, beauty pageants, and Eskimo games such as seal-hook throwing and muktuk eating. It's followed by the **Northwest Native Trade Fair,** which draws Native peoples from throughout Arctic and Bering Alaska to participate in more cultural demonstrations, feasting and dancing, handcraft trading, and Eskimo games.

Kotzebue has a modern 50-bed **Public Health Services Hospital** (tel. 442-3321), a bank (Bank of the North), a community college and vocational training school, eight churches, and a library.

WHERE TO STAY AND EAT

The only accommodation in town, at this writing, is the **Nullagvik Hotel,** 308 Front St., at Tundra Way (P.O. Box 336), Kotzebue, AK 99752 (tel. 907/442-3331). Owned and operated by NANA, the Nullagvik—its name means "overnighting place" in the Inupiat dialect—is the nicest hotel in Alaska's Arctic. It has 46 spacious rooms with full baths, direct-dial phones, thermostat-controlled hot-water heating, and even orange shag carpeting. On the oceanfront side of the hotel are second- and third-floor sitting rooms where you can watch the Kobuk ice floes crunching and tinkling their way down the coast of Kotzebue Sound long after the winter icepack has broken up and disappeared. The hotel contains a lobby gift shop with good prices on local crafts, a barbershop and beauty parlor, a coin-op guest laundry, and even an attorney's office. The restaurant—open from 6 a.m. to 10 p.m. in summer, 7 a.m. to 9 p.m. in winter—features such local specialties as grilled arctic sheefish (a full dinner for $13) and reindeer stew ($7.50 for lunch). Year-round room rates are $85 single, $110 double.

Outside of the one in the hotel, my favorite Kotzebue restaurant is the **Arctic Dragon** (tel. 442-3770), on Front Street four storefronts south of the Nullagvik. A Korean-owned Mandarin Chinese restaurant, it features combination dinners from $12.50, lunch specials at $8, and American-style breakfasts. The décor is far from elaborate, but it's quite comfortable, with a large aquarium against one wall and hanging Oriental lanterns. Open daily from 6:30 a.m. to 11 p.m.

There's also the **Dairy Queen Brazier Restaurant,** Second Avenue and Lagoon Street (tel. 442-3269), the "world's farthest north" DQ. In this reddish log-style building two blocks from the airport, you can get a burger for as little as $2.25, a three-piece chicken dinner for $8, a 12-ounce New York steak for $14—and if it strikes your fancy, a banana split for $4.

Other food alternatives in Kotzebue are the **Hamburger Hut,** 513 Front St., with burgers from $2.50; and the **Kotzebue Pizza House** (tel. 442-3432 for delivery).

WHAT TO SEE AND DO

Kotzebue's "must" attraction is the **NANA Museum of the Arctic** (tel. 442-3304), located on Second Avenue next to the regional corporation's headquarters. But don't expect an impersonal collection of artifacts. This is a living museum, a place built—according to the directors—so "generations of Eskimos would know who they were and why. So would the rest of America."

The full presentation takes an hour and a half. Upon arrival, you are ushered into an indoor diorama of Arctic wildlife complete with a soundtrack of the different animal calls. After a visit to the adjoining Jade Mountain factory (see below) you return to the diorama room for a multimedia show, *The Roots of Kotzebue*. Finally, Inupiat natives offer a cultural demonstration of such time-honored crafts as skin sewing and ivory carving. The Kotzebue Native Dancers perform several traditional dances, inviting the audience to join in. The show concludes with an Eskimo blanket toss. Various handcrafts are offered for sale. Admission to the full show is $25 for adults, $12.50 for children, though the cost is included in tour packages.

A viewing window atop a flight of carpeted steps next door to the museum lets visitors peer into the jade factory. NANA owns all mineral rights to Jade Mountain, Alaska's chief source of jade, 130 miles up the Kobuk River. Fire is used to dislodge boulders from permafrost during the summer; the rocks are then barged to Kotzebue. (When the icepack is frozen, summer fishermen become winter jade workers.) The factory sells its jade tiles worldwide.

A more traditional museum is **Ootukahkuktuvik,** "Place Having Old Things," in a small wood-shingle house at 341 First Ave. You won't miss the polar bear sculpture on its roof. The museum has a small collection of items of local ethnographic and historical significance, including fishing and hunting artifacts, seal-oil lamps, and walrus-intestine rain parkas. Open from 2 to 4 p.m. and 7 to 9 p.m. daily June through August for tour groups.

Even more enjoyable is just to stroll around town at leisure, appreciating the different cultural perspective of these hard-working Eskimo people. Some of the earliest homes are at the north end of Front Street.

Sports

Fishing and hunting are popular in summer, mainly in the surrounding wilderness. **Walker Air Service,** 503 Front St. (tel. 442-3263), is a registered guide-outfitter. If you have questions, consult the **U.S. Fish and Wildlife Department** (tel. 442-3799).

In winter, dog-sled races and snowmachine competitions are big local events, and cross-country skiers find endless tundra to trek across.

Tours

The half-day tour offered by **Alaska Airlines Vacations** (tel. 442-3331 at the Nullagvik Hotel) includes a tour of the city, lengthy stops at both museums, an inspection of the tundra and permafrost layer, and a visit to "Kotzebue National Forest." (The tongue-in-cheek designation refers to a single, desperate spruce tree, the only tree for a good 100 miles, planted outside the former U.S. Air Force station south of town.) The tour costs $35, with airport pickup and dropoff but no meals or accommodation.

SHORT TRIPS FROM KOTZEBUE

Kotzebue is the principal gateway to numerous federally protected lands. Chief among them are the 540,000-acre Cape Krusenstern National Monument, the 1.7-million-acre Kobuk Valley National Park, and the 6.5-million-acre Noatak National Preserve. Also nearby are the Selawik and Koyukuk National Wildlife Refuges. Gates of the Arctic National Park and Preserve are only slightly farther away. You can get full information on all these destinations and view an exhibit of their wildlife at the Northwest Alaska Areas headquarters of the **National Park Service,** P.O. Box 287, Kotzebue, AK 99752 (tel. 907/442-3573 or 442-3890). The offices are lodged in the NANA Regional Corporation building on Second Avenue.

Cape Krusenstern National Monument, whose closest point is only about ten miles from Kotzebue across the Hotham Inlet, is important as a living archeological repository of 6,000 years of Eskimo history. Its 114 lateral beach ridges, formed by wind and wave action and by changing sea levels, contain various artifacts that recall marine mammal hunts when Mediterranean cultures were in their infancy. Eskimo men still hunt seals along the cape's outermost beach, only now they use rifles instead of harpoons. The women still trim and render the catch for the hides, meat, and seal oil vital to their diet.

The centerpiece of **Kobuk Valley National Park** is its 25 miles of shifting sand dunes, the largest active dune field in Arctic latitudes in the world. Summer temperatures can exceed 100°F. Most of the park is a vast tundra steppe supporting great herds of caribou, plus moose, bears, fish, waterfowl, and many edible and medicinal plants. Signs of human habitation date back 12,500 years at Onion Portage, the oldest known site in the North American Arctic. The Kobuk River and its tributary, the Salmon, offer easy canoeing and kayaking.

Noatak National Preserve protects the largest virgin river basin in the United States. So important is the 425-mile Noatak River as a corridor between subarctic and arctic environments for plants and animals that it has been designated an International Biosphere Reserve by the United Nations Educational, Scientific and Cultural Organization (UNESCO).

The river runs from glacial melt atop Mount Igikpak in the Brooks Range out to Kotzebue Sound, en route cutting the scenic Grand Canyon of the Noatak. Except for its headwaters, the entire route is slow moving and gentle, making it popular with wilderness canoeists and kayakers. Large mammals are prolific in the preserve, among them grizzly and black bears, caribou, wolves, lynx, and dall sheep. The Noatak abounds in arctic char, whitefish, grayling, and salmon.

Unless one or more of them has folded, all of the following Kotzebue-based air services offer charter flights to federal lands: **Arctic Air Guides** (tel. 442-3030), **Baker Aviation** (tel. 442-3108), **Bering Air** (tel. 442-3943), **Cape Smythe Air** (tel. 442-3020), **Northwestern Aviation** (tel. 442-3525), **Ryan Air** (tel. 442-3347), **Shellabarger Flying Service** (tel. 442-3187), and **Walker Air Service** (tel. 442-3263).

---

3. Barrow

Contrary to what you may read or be told, Barrow is not the northernmost point on the North American continent. That honor belongs to Canada's Boothia Peninsula, which extends to 71°58' North Latitude. (Point Barrow reaches to 71°23'N). But that minor discrepancy doesn't diminish the value of a visit to the self-proclaimed "Top of the World."

There are few more memorable experiences than to stand in utter silence by the edge of the Arctic Ocean on a summer night and stare across a virtually frozen sea. Away from the city, with little contour to the barren earth, it can be hard to tell where land ends and water begins. Only for a few weeks at the peak of the summer does the ice pack drift away from shore enough for barges to navigate their way here.

When the sun rises here on May 10, it doesn't set again until August 2—bringing 84 days of continuous daylight. But when it sets on November 18, another 67 days pass before the sun rises again on January 24.

It takes a special breed of person to adapt to these unusual conditions. Few white settlers are able to last more than a couple of years here before midwinter depression takes a severe toll. Yet Inupiat Eskimos have lived here for 1,500 years, subsisting mainly on the bounty of the sea. Their culture is evident everywhere you turn.

Charted by the Royal Navy in 1825 and named for Sir John Barrow of the British Admiralty, Barrow became an important supply station for Boston whalers working the Arctic Ocean at the turn of the 20th century. It was incorporated as a first-class city in 1974, just in time to benefit from the oil boom at Prudhoe Bay. Barrow's position as seat of the 88,000-square-mile North Slope Borough—the world's largest municipal government—left it with millions of dollars to invest in modern schools, offices, stores, and health services. Despite its alien climate, the city has modern electric, water, and sewer systems.

It's hard to convince folks who see Barrow's winter snowpack, but the city is located in a veritable Arctic desert with average annual precipitation of just 4.9 inches. (Ten inches of snow equal one inch of precipitation.) The average July high is 46°F (though a record high of 78°F was once attained), and the average January low is −24°F.

ORIENTATION

Barrow's 3,000 people actually live in two adjoining settlements on either side of the freshwater Isatkoak Lagoon. Most businesses and visitor services are on the south side of the lagoon in Barrow proper. Many citizens live north of the lagoon in the residential neighborhood known as Browerville.

The **Barrow Airport** faces on Ahkovak Street. Opposite the airport, at the intersection of Momegana Street, is the chamber of commerce office. Momegana leads north five blocks into the main part of town, ending in a "T" junction at Agvik Street. To your right (east) are the boroughs offices, hospital, and Isatkoak Lagoon; to your left (west) are the big Alaska Commercial Co. department store and the Top of the World Hotel. Stevenson Street, which follows the coast north to Browerville, intersects Agvik at the hotel.

Means of traveling to Barrow are, for all practical purposes, limited to one: **MarkAir** (tel. 907/852-7377 in Barrow, or toll free 800/426-6784, 800/478-0800 in Alaska). The statewide carrier offers several flights daily to and from Anchorage (tel. 907/243-6275) and Fairbanks (tel. 907/452-7577). Connecting service to villages and locations near Barrow is provided by **Cape Smythe Air** (tel. 852-8333) and **Barrow Air** (tel. 852-2334).

The efficient city bus service—the **Inuich Commuter Express** (tel. 852-2611, ext. 368)—operates year round, daily except Sunday, every 20 minutes from 6:20 a.m. to 10 p.m. The adult fare is 50¢ (children pay 25¢) within Barrow and Browerville. Taxi service is provided by **Barrow Cab** (tel. 852-3111), **Arcticab** (tel. 852-2227), and **Polar Taxi** (tel. 852-3030). If you don't mind paying upward of $2.50 a gallon for gas, you can rent a vehicle from **Julie's and Chuck's Trucks** (tel. 852-6732).

The **Barrow Chamber of Commerce,** P.O. Box 942, Barrow, AK 99723 (tel. 907/852-5211 to city offices), has a visitor center across from the MarkAir terminal, at the corner of Ahkovak and Momegana Streets. Local crafts are also sold.

The year's biggest festival is **Nalukataq,** held in June following a successful whaling season. If you're in Barrow between mid-April and the end of May when the bowhead whales migrate through this area (depending on the ice pack), you'll likely be greeted by businesses with signs reading: "Closed, Gone Whaling." Alaska's nine whaling communities from Barrow to St. Lawrence Island together are allowed 32 strikes a year with no more than 52 in two years. When village whalers in their walrus-skin umiaks (boats) harpoon a whale, they haul it onto the ice and drag it back to their settlement by dog sled. No part of the creature goes to waste. The meat and muktuk (inner skin and blubber) are eaten and used for oil; the bones were traditionally used in shelter construction. Even baleen—a long black fiber which hangs like a plate from certain whales' mouths to strain out plankton, their dietary mainstay—is used in etching and basket weaving. (New Englanders once used it for corset stays.)

The **Piuraagiaqta** spring festival in mid-April bids farewell to long winter nights with a parade and a variety of Native competitions, from dog-sled and cross-country ski races to speed contests with the participants toting tea and wearing mukluks (moccasins). Special observances are also scheduled on the Fourth of July and New Year's Eve, and there's a big home-lighting contest every Christmas.

Modern **Barrow Hospital** is at the east end of Agvik Street (tel. 852-4611). The city's only bank, the **Bank of the North,** at Agvik and Kiogak Streets (tel. 852-6200), is open from 9 a.m. to 2:30 p.m. Monday through Thursday and 11 a.m. to 6 p.m. on Friday. The weekly newspaper is called *Ukpiagvik's Edgington Unedited*. There are six churches but no bars—Barrow is dry. While you're permitted to import alcoholic beverages for your own consumption, you can't buy or sell them here.

WHERE TO STAY

Utility prices and the cost of importing all construction materials has resulted in extremely high prices on hotel rooms in Barrow. Then again, everything in Barrow costs at least twice what you'd pay in Anchorage. Tag a 6% tax on quoted room rates.

If you arrive on an organized tour, you'll be lodged at the **Top of the World Hotel,** Agvik and Stevenson Streets (P.O. Box 189), Barrow, AK 99723 (tel. 907/852-3900). Operated by Tundra Tours, a wholly owned subsidiary of the Arctic Slope Regional Corporation, the hotel charges independent visitors $110 single, $120 double. Each of the 40 rust-carpeted rooms has queen-size or twin beds, a desk/dresser, reclining chair, 11-channel cable TV, free (local) direct-dial telephone, electric baseboard heat, and full bath. Some also have a small refrigerator. The spacious lobby, with its huge mounted polar bear, has a 24-hour desk, plush seating, a gift counter, and a snack corner. An airport shuttle and guest laundry are also provided. Room service is available from Pepe's North of the Border (see the "Where to Eat" section, below).

Rod Benson's homey **Barrow Airport Inn,** 1815 Okpik St., at Momegana Street (P.O. Box 933), Barrow, AK 99723 (tel. 907/852-2525), is just a block from the airport on the bus line. A typical well-lit room has brown carpeting, double bed with autumn-pattern cover, standard furnishings, 12-channel cable television, free local phone, a three-quarter bath, and hot-water baseboard heat. Nine of the 16 units have kitchenettes with stoves, refrigerators, and cabinet space. The cozy lobby has couches and chairs amid standing plants and a large bookshelf, with complimentary coffee. Year round, singles are $100; doubles, $120; and kids stay free (rollaways are provided).

WHERE TO EAT

Visitors are always surprised to find a highly reputable Mexican restaurant in a location as isolated as Barrow. But the fame of **Pepe's North of the Border,** next to the Top of the World Hotel on Agvik Street at Kiogak Street (tel. 852-8200), has spread far and wide. Its zealous owner, Fran Tate, has appeared on Johnny Carson's "The Tonight Show" and other national telecasts; besides Pepe's, she also runs a fast-food diner, a water-delivery service, and Elephant Pot Sewage Haulers.

Fran's crustiness is typical of Barrow, though the restaurant doesn't reflect it (other than to warn diners who find a rock in their pinto beans that there are "not enough rocks for everyone"). Each of three dining rooms has fine décor, including the spacious El Toro room with bullfighting paintings and matador jackets on the walls around a tiled fireplace. Meal prices reflect the expense of decoration: chiles rellenos are $16; a taco, cheese enchilada, rice, beans, and salad costs $13.75. You can pay $22.50 for a crab Louis or $22.75 for a ten-ounce New York steak. Coffee and soft drinks with meals are $1.35. Open Monday through Saturday from 6 a.m. to 10 p.m. and on Sunday from 9 a.m. to 8 p.m.

Perhaps the major point of interest in Browerville is **Mattie's Eskimo Café,** on Simmonds Street overlooking the ocean (tel. 852-2170). Mattie is a granddaughter of Barrow's first white settler, Charles Brower, who was a prolific gentleman: his Eskimo wives gave him 14 children. The café is decorated with paraphernalia of whaling days past—rusty harpoons and dramatic oil paintings on wood-paneled walls. Omelets cost around $7.50 for breakfast, cheeseburgers run $6 for lunch, and a reindeer or arctic fish steak is $15 at dinnertime. Between meals you can snack on caribou soup or Eskimo doughnuts. Open Monday through Saturday from 8 a.m. to 8 p.m. and on Sunday from 9 a.m. to 7 p.m. Be sure to drop in next door at Charles Brower's store, the Cape Smythe Whaling and Trading Post, established in 1886 and still in the family.

Elsewhere in Barrow, **Ken's Café,** upstairs in the MarkAir building at the airport (tel. 852-8888), offers home-cooking at reasonable prices (a grilled half chicken is $10.50 for dinner) daily except Sunday from 6 a.m. to 6 p.m. Ken also has the cheapest coffee in town (50¢). **Arctic Pizza,** 125 Apayauk St., near Pisokak Street (tel. 852-4222), has pizzas ranging from small cheese-only at $13.50, to large with "the works" at $44.50 (for that price, you might expect caviar). Gyros are $12.50; spaghetti dinners, $16. Open on Sunday from 2 to 11 p.m., on Monday from 5 to 11 p.m., and Tuesday through Saturday from 11 a.m. to 11 p.m. **Sam and Lee's,** Kiogak Street at Aivik Street (tel. 852-5555), is a 24-hour Korean-owned Chinese restaurant locally praised for its Mongolian beef. Dinners run $12 and up. The **Burger Barn,** on Takpuk Street near Okpik Street (tel. 852-2276), is a high-school hangout and fast-food drive-in.

WHAT TO SEE AND DO

The most interesting thing to do in Barrow is to wander with your eyes open, observing how painfully the old Eskimo culture is adjusting to the 9-to-5 society forced on it by Americanization. Here, 330 miles north of the Arctic Circle, you'll see a multi-million-dollar high school with fish and caribou hides hanging to dry outside, and modern racquetball courts and a tanning salon only a few blocks from a centuries-old archeological site.

The old village, **Uqiagvik** ("high place with good view"), was discovered in 1982 on a city bluff overlooking the Arctic Ocean. Subsequently excavated by University of Washington archeologists, its sod igloo sites have been dated back five centuries. These early Eskimos dug holes in the ground and covered them with canopies of skins on frames of whalebone and driftwood. You can walk to the site, which faces Apayauk Street opposite Ogrook Street, but be sure to respect tribal traditions by not treading on homesites and not taking souvenirs. Sixteen dwelling mounds have been uncovered at the earlier (A.D. 500–900) **Birnirk** archeological site about three miles up the coast at Pignaq (see below).

Jump from the ancient to the modern by browsing in a couple of Barrow's stores—like the **Arctic Cash and Carry** supermarket, on Pisokak Street at Apayauk Street (open from 11 a.m. to 1 a.m. daily), or the **A.C. Stuaqpak** department store, on Agvik Street near Kiogak Street (open from 1 p.m. to 9 p.m. Monday through Saturday and on Sunday from noon to 5 p.m.). You'll wonder how anyone can afford to live in Barrow after pricing milk at $7 a gallon and eggs just over $2 a dozen. The steep prices extend to the shortage of decent housing: studio apartments were renting in 1989 for an average of $700 a month, not counting an additional utility bill of about $300 a month. Native handcrafts, on the other hand, can be purchased quite reasonably. Look for articles of carved walrus-tusk ivory and etched baleen, plus leather-and-fur masks, mittens, mukluks, and parkas. You can call **The Eskimo Shop** (tel. 852-5025) for custom orders.

North of Barrow a couple of miles and inland a few more is the site of the **Naval Arctic Research Laboratory,** built by the federal government in 1955 as an operations base for the 23-million-acre Naval Petroleum Reserve No. 4, and to study Arctic survival and adaptation. The lab closed a few years ago and is now owned by an

Inupiat corporation and used for storage and housing. A small weather station remains. The site is adjacent to the DEW (Distant Early Warning) radar system, which serves as a reminder of the close proximity of Soviet Siberia.

Non-Eskimos normally aren't welcome to stop at **Pignaq,** a summer shantytown three miles north of Barrow where many Inupiats maintain second homes on Birnirk sacred ground. It's known as the Duck Camp Shooting Station to Native hunters who base themselves here while pursuing waterfowl. This area is beautiful in July, when the tundra grass turns green and speckled with wildflowers. By August annoying mosquitoes have taken much of the joy out of an excursion.

Point Barrow, the northernmost point in the United States, is four miles beyond Pignaq, out a long gravel-and-tundra spit. The point has a 50-foot tower and little more. All-terrain vehicles negotiate the spit with ease.

Fifteen miles south of Barrow is a **Wiley Post–Will Rogers Memorial,** erected where the famed pilot and the great humorist were killed in a 1935 airplane crash. En route from Fairbanks to Siberia, they stopped to ask directions to Barrow, stalled on takeoff, and plunged 50 feet into a river. A newer monument, dedicated in 1982, is directly opposite the Barrow Airport beside the chamber of commerce office.

Sports

The obvious pursuits are outdoor recreations. Cross-country skiing, snow-machining, and ice skating are winter favorites, while camping and boating are popular in the short summer season.

Fishing and hunting licenses can be purchased in Barrow, but sportsmen should be aware that, first of all, no guide services are available; and second, only Native Alaskans are allowed to take marine mammals.

Swimmers can earn a membership certificate in the **Polar Bear Club** by being "willfully submerged in the Arctic Ocean." The water temperature in mid-August is typically 28°F (salt water has a lower freezing point); the air is around 45°F. Submersion must be total, though you can wear whatever clothes you want. Search and Rescue officials are present. If you're not that hardy, Barrow High School, at Okpik and Takpuk Streets (tel. 852-8950), has an indoor pool.

Facilities at the new **Piuraagvik recreation center,** on Ahkovak Street east of the airport, include racquetball and basketball courts and a sauna. Call the adjacent City Hall (tel. 852-5211) for information and hours.

Tours

Out-of-town visitors inevitably are greeted at the airport by **Tundra Tours,** owners of the Top of the World Hotel (tel. 853-3900). The prebooked package tour includes a whirl around city points of interest, a stop for Eskimo doughnuts at Mattie's Café, and an excellent show of Inupiat dancing and handcrafts. Dancers perform to a chorus of flat drums (from various animal skins and membranes), the only musical instruments, and chanting. Native elders demonstrate how seal, caribou, polar bear, and other hides are worked to make warm clothing. Every body part is used, from sinews (which become threads) to bones (used for needles, especially the polar bear leg bone and walrus tusk).

Tundra Tours is represented outside of Barrow by Midnight Sun Tours in Anchorage (tel. toll free 800/544-2235).

Pausan Arctic Adventures, P.O. Box 68, Barrow, AK 99723 (tel. 907/852-7780), is geared much more to the adventure traveler. In summer owners Mike and Patsy Aamodt offer three-hour guided tours to Point Barrow or the Post-Rogers Memorial on four-wheel-drive Honda all-terrain vehicles. A 20-minute training session on the four-wheelers precedes the tour, which costs $50 per person (maximum of ten). Casual four-wheeler rentals cost $15 an hour. You can also join the Aamodts on a wildlife photo tour by boat mid-July to October, weather permitting. Prices start at $100. Between November and May, snowmachine tours are offered anywhere from

Point Barrow to the village of Atkasuk, 70 miles south. The price is negotiable, from $50 up. If you choose, you can ride on a dog sled behind the snowmachine. Patsy, by the way, is an Inupiat Eskimo and Barrow's first Harvard graduate.

Young **Matt Davis,** P.O. Box 246, Barrow, AK 99723 (tel. 852-6745), also leads tours to Point Barrow and the Post-Rogers Memorial. Those who join Davis are promised more adventure aboard three-wheelers (all-terrain vehicles) for a reduced price of $40 per person.

Flightseeing enthusiasts can contact **Cape Smythe Air,** P.O. Box 549, Barrow, AK 99723 (tel. 907/852-8333), about its 30-minute excursions to Point Barrow and the Post-Rogers Memorial. The charter rate for a Cessna 207 is $300 an hour; for a Cessna 185, $200 an hour. Find four other visitors to split the cost.

SHORT TRIPS FROM BARROW

There's little to see of tourist interest close to Barrow. The nearest village, **Atkasuk** (pop. 200), 70 miles south on the Meade River, has good fishing but no visitor accommodations. **Wainwright** (pop. 450), another Inupiat village 95 miles southwest along the coast, is famed statewide for its superb craftsmen and Native dance troupe. The **Olgoonik Hotel,** Wainwright, AK 99782 (tel. 907/763-2514), has 12 basic rooms; rates were not available. Fly there by commuter aircraft from Barrow.

---

4. Prudhoe Bay

The most famous oil-drilling site in the United States, and perhaps the world, was built in the early 1970s on a permanently frozen desert 280 miles north of the Arctic Circle. The story of the discovery and exploitation of the vast petroleum reserve, and the subsequent pipeline boom, have been recounted elsewhere in this volume (see "A Capsule History" in Chapter I).

Modern history comes alive with a visit to Prudhoe Bay. Enormous controversy over its environmental impact preceded the industrialization of the North Slope, but today pump stations and drill pads share the tundra ecosystem with myriad nesting migratory birds and a herd of 10,000 caribou. It was truly a technological triumph to be able to tap the oil reserve while preserving the delicate Arctic environment.

Prudhoe Bay and its adjoining service village of **Deadhorse** are strict working communities with a combined population, transient but stable, of around 5,000. Most of the workers—90% of them men—live at Prudhoe eight days a fortnight and elsewhere in Alaska the other six. Although the population is down from about 18,000 during the mid-'70s pipeline construction era, the town is remarkable for a remote area which had no settlement whatsoever prior to 1967, when exploratory drilling began.

The Prudhoe Bay oilfield is the largest in North America and the 18th largest on earth. It pumps 1.9 million barrels of oil a day and accounts for 85% of Alaska's revenues (the state takes a 12.5% royalty interest). More than 700 offshore wells have been drilled in the 400-square-mile field. Each cost about $2.9 million, compared to $250,000 per well in Texas. The cost difference is attributable to the difficulty of drilling through a 2,000-foot layer of permafrost.

By 1987 the Prudhoe Bay field's estimated reserves of 9.6 billion barrels of crude oil and 26 trillion cubic feet of natural gas had been about half depleted. Intensive exploration is continuing in offshore areas and in the 23-million-acre National Petroleum Reserve, west of Prudhoe Bay, to locate and exploit new oil reserves. Several smaller fields are now being developed.

Located 400 miles almost due north of Fairbanks near the mouth of the Sagarvanirktok River, Prudhoe Bay has a climate similar to that of Barrow. Very sparse precipitation (a seven-inch annual average) falls mainly as snow in the late fall and early spring months. Winter temperatures average 20° to 30° below zero Fahrenheit, and not infrequently drop to −60°F, with a high wind-chill factor of −115°F. Normal summer temperatures are 40°F to 50°F, but occasionally climb above 70°F. Winters see 56 consecutive days of darkness, but summers enjoy 75 days of continual daylight.

The North Slope tundra is very flat and pockmarked with small lakes created by permafrost thaw. If you arrive in midsummer, don't be surprised to find it extremely beautiful. An astonishing variety of plant and animal life call this vast tundra home.

ORIENTATION

The Prudhoe Bay field is operated by Arco and Sohio on behalf of all 15 oil companies with North Slope oil and gas leases. (Lease owners share costs of developing and maintaining the field to minimize cost, maximize efficiency, and reduce negative environmental effects.) Security clearance is required to pass the checkpoints to the **Arco Prudhoe Bay Operations Center,** a complete village with a population of 560, or the **Sohio Base Operations Center,** which numbers its residents at 476. Each self-contained community, constructed on pilings above the permafrost, has a hospital, theater, library, and full sports facilities, including gymnasiums and running tracks. Sohio even has a heated swimming pool which doubles as a water reservoir and a glass arboretum landscaped with trees and flowers. In addition to the operations centers, Sohio has three construction camps for 500 workers each and Arco has a single construction camp housing another 1,900 workers.

Deadhorse, where the airport and hotel facilities are located, is the headquarters of highly specialized oilfield contractors—folks who haul water and treat sewage, who manufacture mud and cement, who stabilize oil temperatures, cap wells, and recover spills.

Getting There

Alaska Airlines (tel. toll free 800/426-0333) and **MarkAir** (tel. toll free 800/426-6784, 478-0800 in Alaska) both fly daily to Deadhorse from Anchorage and Fairbanks. The 6,500-foot paved airstrip is on the southeastern side of the Prudhoe Bay field, within easy walking distance of several hotels and construction camps.

The **Dalton Highway,** otherwise known as the Haul Road, connects Prudhoe Bay with Fairbanks, a rugged 510 miles south. The northernmost 205 miles of the gravel road above Disaster Creek are restricted to drivers who hold commercial or industrial permits. In an average month, 150 trucks carrying seven million pounds of goods move over the road, which is kept open year round. It is not normally accessible to tourists, although Princess Tours began taking trips down the Haul Road in 1987 (see "Tours," below).

Within the Prudhoe Bay oilfield itself are some 200 miles of interconnecting gravel roads. Most of them are off-bounds to all but oil company–approved drivers. There are no vehicle-rental agencies in Deadhorse, although one contractor has developed a vehicle with low-pressure tires for traveling on the tundra with minimal environmental impact. It's called the Rollagon. Even that, however, is forbidden from traversing the tundra until the waterfowl have completed their spring nesting cycle, about mid-July.

Barges, tugboats, and lighters may visit Prudhoe Bay during the six-week period in August and September when the shore ice has broken up and the polar ice shelf has moved away from the coast. They have no provision for passengers.

Useful Information

There's no chamber of commerce or visitors center. **Sohio Alaska Petroleum Co.,** Pouch 6-612, Anchorage, AK 99502, or **Alyeska Pipeline Service Co.,** 1835 S. Bragaw St., Anchorage, AK 99512, both have excellent brochures on their operations and general information on Prudhoe Bay. The hotels, especially the facility operated by the Northwest Alaska Native Association (NANA), also have information.

The *Prudhoe Bay Journal* is published biweekly in Anchorage and distributed in Prudhoe Bay.

WHERE TO STAY AND EAT

All facilities for overnight visitors, except those invited by Sohio or Arco, are in **Deadhorse.** Each hotel is a self-contained city providing accommodation, dining facilities, and living space for employees of smaller companies—mainly independent contractors—who don't have "camps" of their own. In every case, hotels are of modular construction, trailer units strung together on pilings in the permafrost. None of them is fancy and all are expensive, but they're extremely functional for their alien environment. In their favor, all have public cafeterias with all-you-can-eat meal hours three times daily. Unless otherwise noted, they're within a stone's throw of the airport terminal.

The **NANA Oilfield Services Hotel,** Pouch 340112, Prudhoe Bay, AK 99734 (tel. 907/659-2840), is owned and operated by the Northwest Alaska Native Association, based in Kotzebue. (NANA also operates Prudhoe Bay's local tour service.) The hotel accommodates 190, although 160 beds are more or less permanently occupied by Prudhoe Bay employees. The rooms are basic, with twin beds, dresser, desk, and wardrobe cabinet, plus electric heat (the hotel has its own powerhouse). Toilet and shower facilities are shared. Within the hotel are a TV room with satellite reception and a VCR, a weight room and sauna, and a recreation room with pool, Ping-Pong, darts, and video games. Pay-phone booths are in some corridors. Nightly rates are $100 single, $160 twin, including all meals. The cafeteria is open 24 hours, with breakfast ($10) served from 5 to 8 a.m., lunch ($12.50) from 11:30 a.m. to 1 p.m., and dinner ($15) from 5 to 8 p.m. Substantial snacks are available at all other times. Nonresidents can buy meal chits at reception.

The **Arctic Caribou Inn,** Pouch 340010, Prudhoe Bay, AK 99734 (tel. 907/659-2368), is situated on Colleen Lake, about 300 yards from the airport. Operated in summer only by NANA for the benefit of Princess Tours' package travelers, it has 208 beds in a variety of single- and double-room configurations, some with private or semiprivate baths, a few with room/office combinations. Hotel facilities include TV rooms with satellite reception, a recreation room with pool and Ping-Pong, a weight room with a Universal gym, laundry rooms, and public pay phones. Independent travelers should expect to pay $150 per night, inclusive of three meals. The dining room is warm and cozy, with a menu that changes nightly. Meals are served from 5:30 to 7:30 a.m., noon to 1 p.m., and 6 to 8 p.m. Also offered are a salad bar and homemade dessert carousel. Prices are equivalent to other hotels. Beverages, snacks, and sandwiches are available anytime. Next door to the Arctic Caribou Inn is the Trading Post, Prudhoe Bay's largest retail store, with clothing, office supplies, nonprescription drugs, and a variety of gifts and souvenirs. It's open from 9 a.m. to 10 p.m. daily.

The **Prudhoe Bay Hotel,** Pouch 340004, Prudhoe Bay, AK 99734 (tel. 907/659-2449), is another full-service accommodation located opposite the airport. Its rooms have a double or two twin beds, a wardrobe closet, dresser and desk, and electric heat. The hotel also has a TV room, a weight room, a sauna, a sun room, a 24-hour commissary, and pay phones. Rates (including all meals) are $90 single, $150 double, with shared bath. A limited number of rooms with private baths—priced at $110 single, $170 double—must be reserved far in advance. The dining room serves breakfast from 5:30 to 8 a.m., lunch from 11:30 a.m. to 1 p.m., and dinner from 5:30 to 9 p.m., with snack service between meal hours and until 10 p.m.

WHAT TO SEE AND DO

Most visitors to Prudhoe Bay are anxious to look at the **oil production and pipeline facilities.** Unless you're a working visitor or a guest of the oil companies, you'll have to join a **half-day tour** in order to be cleared to pass the security checkpoints. I enjoyed the tour offered by NANA (tel. 659-2840); MarkAir has a similar four-hour tour in conjunction with the Prudhoe Bay Hotel (tel. 659-2449). Both tours cost about $70 per person. The NANA tour begins with a 30-minute film at the NANA Hotel. Then you'll proceed by van to the massive Arco operations center on the east side of the oilfield and the Sohio complex on the west. Their raised construction minimizes environmental impact on the permafrost. Both companies have three oil-gas separation plants located in strategic locations around the field. Your guide will point these out, as well as drill pads and the vital satellite communications system.

Between the two operating centers, but nearer the Sohio complex, is **Pump Station One,** the beginning of the 800-mile Trans Alaska Pipeline. Two 34-inch-diameter transit lines deliver 1.6 million barrels of oil daily to the pump station, one from each half of the field. Alyeska, the pipeline operator, meters the oil and pumps it south through a 48-inch-diameter pipeline. It takes the oil about six days to reach Valdez on Prince William Sound. An interpretive pavilion at Pump Station One helps explain its facilities and operation.

Aside from the industrial tour, the most popular activity at Prudhoe Bay is enjoying nature. The **tundra** here is thickly carpeted with some 250 species of colorful wildflowers, berries, and fully grown alder and willow trees that stand barely knee high. The Central Arctic caribou herd, 10,000 strong, migrates through the region, and some 200 different birds, mainly shorebirds and waterfowl such as snow geese and tundra swans, have been identified in the Prudhoe Bay summer nesting grounds. Polar bears and musk oxen are rarely seen, but grizzly bears, arctic foxes, arctic hares, ground squirrels, lemmings, wolves, and other wildlife roam the coastal plain, and moose sometimes come in from the Brooks Range foothills.

The oil companies have invested a great deal of money to minimize their environmental impact on the North Slope. Sohio engineers, for example, address air and water quality, solid-waste disposal, hazardous-waste handling and disposal, spill cleanup, recovery and contingency planning for oil and hazardous substances, archeological site assessment, tundra vegetation monitoring, and gravel site restoration.

Sports

Fishing for arctic char, grayling, and Dolly Varden is good on the Sagarvanirktok and Kuparuk Rivers. Licenses can be purchased at the Trading Post. The river ice breaks up around the first of June, and the river doesn't freeze again until about mid-September. No hunting is permitted in the Prudhoe Bay field.

In winter the vast, open tundra is ideal for **cross-country skiing** and **snow-machining.** But white-out blizzard conditions and gale-force winds can arise quickly, so sportsmen should always let others know the direction they are headed in.

Hardy **scuba-divers** with highly efficient wetsuits will be fascinated by **"The Boulder Patch,"** a unique site discovered in 1971 in 20 feet of water off the mouth of the Sagarvanirktok River. Whereas most of the Arctic Ocean seafloor is rather barren, these boulders—which, scientists speculate, may have been ice-rafted here from elsewhere—harbor a rich marine life of colorful coral, anemones, sponges, and algae. It's not far from an Exxon drilling site.

Tours

Princess Tours, 2815 Second Ave., Seattle, WA 98109 (tel. 206/728-4200), in 1987 began offering tours of Prudhoe Bay combined with a two-day, 510-mile bus trip down the Haul Road. Participants fly from Fairbanks to Deadhorse, get a tour of oilfields, then head back south over the two-lane gravel road, stopping overnight at Coldfoot. Or they can do the four-day/three-night trip (including a night in Fairbanks) in reverse. Either way, the price tag is $889.

MarkAir (tel. toll free 800/426-6784, 800/478-0800 in Alaska) offers a two-day Barrow–Prudhoe Bay tour, with an overnight in Barrow, for $434 from Fairbanks or $585 from Anchorage. The trip is available June through August.

5. The Brooks Range

The Brooks Range, spanning Alaska north of the Arctic Circle from the Chukchi Sea to the border of Canada's Yukon, has been called "one of the world's last true wildernesses." The northernmost extension of the Rocky Mountains, it has an austere beauty and grandeur, with magnificent views down pristine river valleys and across treeless, sedge-covered slopes.

Most of the range is contained within federally protected lands. Gates of the Arctic National Park and Preserve, 7.95 million acres straddling the range's crest, is the centerpiece. To its west are Noatak National Preserve and Kobuk Valley National Park (see "Short Trips from Kotzebue" in Section 2, above); to its east is the 18-million-acre Arctic National Wildlife Refuge. The only break in the protected belt is the narrow Trans Alaska Pipeline corridor.

The Brooks Range is not a particularly high mountain range—its highest point, Mount Isto near the Canadian border, is only 9,058 feet—but its sheer isolation makes it forbidding. From its spruce-and-taiga southern flank facing the Interior to its semi-arid and frigid North Slope, this wilderness is inhospitable to humankind. Grizzly bears, wolves, caribou, and dozens of other mammals range the fragile tundra. A few scattered tribes of Native Alaskans—Athabaskan Indians on the south, Inupiat Eskimos on the north—eke a meager subsistence living from hunting and fishing.

Though it's possible to walk into **Gates of the Arctic National Park and Preserve** directly off the Haul Road, most visitors to the park climb aboard scheduled flights on **Frontier Flying Service** (tel. 907/452-1014) from Fairbanks to the villages of Anaktuvuk Pass or Bettles, and hire outfitters and/or charter aircraft there to take them deeper into the wilderness. Get full information on park access and services from the Superintendent, Gates of the Arctic National Park and Preserve, P.O. Box 74680, Fairbanks, AK 99707 (tel. 907/456-0281).

Anaktuvuk Pass (pop. 260), an Eskimo village which lies in a historic 2,200-foot pass connecting the Interior with the Arctic, has some overnight accommodations and a pleasant little museum. Trips to the Endicott Mountains, Chandler Lake, and other North Slope destinations often begin here. The pass is 260 miles from Fairbanks.

Bettles (pop. 92), also known as Evansville, began in 1899 as a trading post on the south bank of Upper Koyukuk River in the Brooks Range foothills, 185 miles northwest of Fairbanks. There's still a trading post here, and year-round accommodation is available at the **Bettles Lodge,** Bettles, AK 99726 (tel. 907/692-5111). Trails lead 85 miles north to Anaktuvuk Pass and 35 miles southwest to the Athabaskan village of **Allakaket.** In addition to air and foot, Bettles is accessible by boat in summer and by snowmachine in winter.

Bettles-based outfitters offer a wide variety of wilderness experiences, from combination backpack-river trips (in kayak or canoe) in summer, to dog-sled and cross-country ski excursions in winter. Contact Dave Schmitz's **Brooks Range Wilderness Trips,** Bettles, AK 99726 (tel. 907/692-5312); **Brooks Range Expeditions,** Bettles, AK 99726 (tel. 907/692-5333); or Dave Ketscher's **Sourdough Outfitters,** Bettles, AK 99726 (tel. 907/692-5252). Prices typically run from $1,000 for a seven-day trip to $2,500 for a three-week expedition. Private air-charter service is available in Bettles from **Brooks Range Aviation** (tel. 907/692-5444).

The only fishing lodge in Gates of the Arctic National Park is about 70 air miles northwest of Bettles. Nick and Susan Jennings's **Walker Lake Wilderness Lodge,** Bettles, AK 99726 (tel. 907/692-5252), is a modern three-story lodge overlooking

17-mile-long Walker Lake. It's open June 10 to September 15; rates begin at $950 per person for four days/three nights, including meals, guide service, and round-trip air transportation from Bettles. The lodge also has several remote log cabins for rental scattered through the Brooks Range.

Some of the best prices for summer backpacking and canoeing/kayaking expeditions in the Brooks Range are offered by **Wilderness: Alaska/Mexico,** 1231 Sundance Loop (Star Rte. 30537), Fairbanks, AK 99701 (tel. 907/479-6226 or 452-1821). (Owner Ron Yarnell escapes to Mexico from December to March.) **Alaska Fish and Trails Unlimited,** 1177 Shypoke Dr., Fairbanks, AK 99701 (tel. 907/479-7630 or 479-4732), has a wide selection of trips, while **Roger Rom's Alaska Wilderness** offers study treks into the Brooks Range in conjunction with the University of Alaska. Contact Conferences and Continuing Education, 117 Eielson Building, University of Alaska, Fairbanks, AK 99775 (tel. 907/474-7800).

If you're a river runner, see what **Alaska Treks n Voyages,** P.O. Box 625, Seward, AK 99664 (tel. 907/224-2960 in summer or 288-3610 in winter), has planned: 10 days kayaking the John River, $1,253; 12 days kayaking the Kobuk River, $1,638.

The Seward-based outdoor agency also offers a 13-day trip (priced at $2,278) down the Hulahula River in the **Arctic National Wildlife Refuge,** a combination of rafting, kayaking, and hiking from the mountains to **Kaktovik,** an Eskimo village on Barter Island in the Arctic Ocean. The refuge, the northernmost and remotest one in the United States, supports the 180,000 caribou of the Porcupine herd. Increasing oil exploration is progressing on its Arctic plain.

SOUTHWEST ALASKA

Southwest Alaska is at once the state's vastest region and its most difficult to categorize. Stretching from Cook Inlet to the Yukon River Delta to the tip of the 1,000-mile-long Aleutian archipelago, it contains bustling fishing communities and wind-ravaged wastelands, lush lowlands and smoldering volcanoes. Its tortured, rocky coastline limits boat landings but has created a paradise for marine mammals and birds.

If any two threads can be said to bind this region, they are the Russian heritage and fishing, both commercial and sport.

Kodiak Island was the site of the first Russian settlement in North America in the late 18th century, and the headquarters for the Russian American Company until its later move to Sitka. The company established numerous fur-trading outposts through the Alaska Peninsula, the Aleutians, and even the Pribilofs, simultaneously absorbing the Native Aleut people into their old-world culture. Today virtually every Aleut settlement—all of them in southwest Alaska—is centered around its own Orthodox church.

Fishing, which grew in importance after the American purchase of Alaska, provides the modern economic base. Bristol Bay, on the north side of the Alaska Peninsula, is considered by many to be the world's richest salmon ground, and the waters around Kodiak Island were once famed for their king crab. The Bristol Bay–Kodiak fishery has been restricted to permit holders since 1922. Additionally, the rivers and lakes of the Alaska Peninsula attract sport fishermen from all over the world to cast their lines for trophy-size salmon, trout, northern pike, arctic char, and grayling. The dozens of lodges that accommodate these anglers frequently charge $3,000 a week and more. The rates normally include not only room and board, but also round-trip transportation from Anchorage, use of boats and small planes from the lodge, guide service, all sports equipment—in short, virtually everything you'll need but your own alcoholic beverages.

1. Kodiak

The largest city in the southwest is hardly a metropolis. Buried in pumice by the 1912 eruption of Katmai's Mount Novarupta, badly shaken by the 1964 Good Friday earthquake and leveled by the subsequent tidal wave, Kodiak has nevertheless emerged like a phoenix from the ashes to become a bustling modern town of 6,700 people (twice that many in the island borough), most of them somehow engaged in commercial fishing as a livelihood.

The town is nestled in a protected harbor at the northeast end of mountainous 3,588-square-mile Kodiak Island. The largest island in Alaskan waters, it is deeply indented with fjords on all sides, forested with spruce in the east, covered with lush tundra on the west, and inhabited everywhere but the city by the great Kodiak brown bear (a subspecies of the grizzly) and a wealth of other animal life.

About 260 miles southwest of Anchorage and a mere 100 from the tip of the Kenai Peninsula and the mouth of the Cook Inlet, Kodiak lies virtually in the middle of the Japan Current. Its maritime climate gives it mild temperatures (summer days in the 50s and 60s, winter days in the 20s and 30s), moderate rainfall (70 inches annually, especially in the fall, with several feet of winter snowfall), and more than its share of fog and wind.

ORIENTATION

The city of Kodiak is laid out in a southwest-to-northeast direction, the main street, **Rezanof Drive,** extending from the airport (five miles southwest of downtown) to Fort Abercrombie State Park (four miles northeast). **Marine Way,** the center of most activity, branches off Rezanof Drive just as it reaches the Small Boat Harbor at the head of St. Paul Harbor and winds along the narrow strait facing Near Island, itself newly connected to the Kodiak Island mainland by a bridge. Many shops, restaurants, government buildings, and private offices are on Marine Way or Center Avenue, a block north. Rezanof Drive is paralleled to the east by Mission Road, which starts at Marine Way, and to the west by Mill Bay Road. The entire island has a very limited road system, only 87 miles in length—all in the northeast.

Getting There

Kodiak State Airport is efficiently served several times daily from Anchorage by **MarkAir** (tel. 907/487-2424, or toll free 800/426-6784, 800/478-0800 in Alaska). **ERA Aviation** (tel. toll free 800/426-0333) also offers passenger service to Kodiak from Anchorage, Kenai, and Homer. Four air-charter services are based on Kodiak Island (see "Short Trips from Kodiak," below).

Kodiak is also served by the ferries of the **Alaska Marine Highway System** (tel. 486-3800, or toll free 800/544-0552). The M/V *Tustumena* plies the waters between Kodiak, Port Lions (a village on the north side of Kodiak Island), the Kenai Peninsula, and Prince William Sound three times weekly throughout the year, except for a week-long trip to Dutch Harbor in the Aleutians once a month between May and September, and a ten-week maintenance period in Seattle beginning January 1. Under its normal schedule, the ferry leaves Kodiak for Homer and Seldovia every Monday at 3 p.m. and Tuesday at 9 p.m., and for Seward, Valdez, and Cordova every Thursday at 8:15 a.m. The passenger fare is $38 to Homer, $80 to Valdez —vehicle, berth, and meals not included. The terminal is on Marine Way at the end of Center Avenue.

Travelers who prefer to have the arrangements made for them will find a variety of Kodiak tour packages offered from Anchorage.

One local Kodiak operator is also in on the package business. MarkAir books its visits with **Island Terrific Tours,** P.O. Box 3001, Kodiak, AK 99615 (tel. 907/486-4777). You're met at the airport by a driver/guide who will introduce you to all the major attractions. The cost is $199 for one day, $239 overnight (double occupancy), plus tax. If you're already in Kodiak, you can book the tour alone for $45.

Getting Around

For $5 the **Airporter Bus Service** (tel. 486-5200) will carry you the five miles from the airport to town, or you can opt for the **Ace Mecca Taxi Cab Service** (tel. 486-3211), with a rather steep fare of $3 at flagfall and $1.50 per mile. That should make the run from the airport $10.50.

There are several car-rental agencies at the airport: **National** (tel. 486-4751); **Rent-a-Heap** (tel. 486-5200); **Avis** (tel. 487-2264); **Hertz** (tel. 487-2261); and **Budget** (tel. 486-5815).

Useful Information

The **Kodiak Visitor Information Center,** 100 Marine Way (near the ferry dock), Kodiak, AK 99615 (tel. 907/486-4070), is open from 8:30 a.m. to 5 p.m. daily in summer, weekdays year round. It's maintained by the **Kodiak Island Convention & Visitor Bureau,** downstairs in the same building: 100 Marine Way, Kodiak, AK 99615 (tel. 907/486-4782).

The *Kodiak Daily Mirror* is published Monday through Friday. **Kodiak Island Hospital** is at 1920 E. Rezanof Dr. (tel. 486-3281, or 911 in an emergency). The town has five banks and numerous churches.

Festivals

The year's biggest celebration is the **Kodiak Crab Festival,** held over Memorial Day weekend to mark the end of the crab season and pay homage to the commercial fishing industry. Parades, the Miss Kodiak contest, sporting events, and even the state "survival suit championships" play second fiddle to the blessing of the fleet.

The Russian Orthodox church, which follows the Gregorian calendar, celebrates Christmas about two weeks after most folks—usually January 7 or 8—with **Starring,** a tradition in which a child twirls a beautifully decorated star while accompanying house-to-house carolers. One week later the new year is rung in with the **Russian Orthodox Masquerade Ball** at the Kodiak Elks Club. An important local holiday is **St. Herman's Day,** on August 9, honoring the first saint of the Russian Orthodox church in North America.

Other important dates on Kodiak's calendar are **Com Fish** (the Alaska Fisheries and Marine Trade Fair) in March and the three-day **Kodiak Rodeo and State Fair** in late August at the Jaycees Fairgrounds in Bell's Flats. Also in August, the theatrical show *Cry of the Wild Ram* is presented over three weekends at the Frank Brink Amphitheater (see "Culture and Nightlife," below).

WHERE TO STAY

Kodiak city has three hotels, a motel, and a bed-and-breakfast association. Borough bed tax is 8%.

The best of the bunch is the **Westmark Kodiak,** 236 S. Rezanof Dr. (P.O. Box 1547), Kodiak, AK 99615 (tel. 907/486-5712, or toll free 800/544-0970 outside Alaska). Located on the town's main street overlooking the Small Boat Harbor, it has 89 rooms decorated in muted masculine tones of navy blue and lavender. Each standard unit has two queen-size beds, a four-drawer dresser and other natural-wood furnishings, a large closet with sliding mirror doors, 17-channel cable TV, a direct-dial phone (local calls are 50¢), and thermostat-controlled electric heat. Room rates are $90 single, $98 double, in the summer season; $70 and $78 in the off-season.

The Chart Room restaurant, open from 6:30 a.m. to 10 p.m. daily, is on the second floor facing the harbor, at the top of a circular staircase leading from the mid-size lobby. Breakfasts and lunches are in the $4 to $7 price range; dinner entrees are priced from $11 to $25. A personal favorite is the scampi flamed in Pernod, at $19.

The **Kodiak Buskin River Inn,** 1395 Airport Way (P.O. Box 89), Kodiak, AK

99615 (tel. 907/487-2700), is removed from the city but a short walk from the airport. Its 51 rooms and six suites have been newly renovated with a bright color scheme. Each room has queen-size or double beds and other standard furnishings, cable television, direct-dial phone (local calls are 25¢), and electric baseboard heat. Rates are $76 single, $84 double, June 1 to September 15; $60, single or double, the rest of the year. Suites start at $115. Children under 12 stay free in their parents' room. If you're without a car, you can make arrangements to be dropped in town.

The inn's Eagle's Nest Restaurant overlooks the salmon-rich Buskin River, so it's appropriate that a catch of the day be its dinnertime specialty, at $13. Breakfast prices start at $4, and lunch sandwiches at $4.50. It's open weekdays from 7 a.m. to 2 p.m. and 6 to 10 p.m., on Saturday and Sunday from 8 a.m.

Back in the city, the **Shelikof Lodge,** 211 Thorsheim Ave. (P.O. Box 774), Kodiak, AK 99615 (tel. 907/486-4141), is a nondescript but adequate accommodation a quiet three blocks from Marine Way. Its 39 dimly lit rooms, with blue carpeting and orange spreads on the double beds, have ample furnishings including cable TV, telephone (free local calls), and electric baseboard heat. Year-round rates are $45 single, $58 double.

In the hotel but under separate ownership is The Fox Inn restaurant. Open Monday through Saturday from 5 a.m. to 2 p.m. and 5 to 9 p.m., and on Sunday from 9 a.m. to 3 p.m.

Kodiak Bed and Breakfast, 308 Cope St., Kodiak, AK 99615 (tel. 907/486-5367), places guests in island homes for $44 single, $55 double. Write or phone coordinator Mary Monroe for details.

All three state parks on Kodiak Island have **camping and RV facilities** (without hookups). There are 18 sites at Buskin River State Recreation Site (four miles southwest of Kodiak), 15 at Fort Abercrombie State Historic Park (four miles north of Kodiak), and 9 at Pasagshak River State Recreation Site (47 miles south of Kodiak). All have fireplaces, latrines, and water.

WHERE TO EAT

The **Chart Room** in the Westmark is the city's best restaurant for a formal atmosphere, and the other two hotel eateries are also good. But Kodiak has many more meal options.

Young immigrants from Hong Kong operate Kodiak's original Asian restaurant, the **China House,** 202 W. Rezanof Dr. (tel. 486-8589). Oriental art hangs on the walls, red lanterns are suspended over the tables, and even the wallpaper has a Chinese calligraphy pattern. The service is Hong Kong efficient, and the food—Cantonese, Mandarin, and Szechuan—is quite good. Full dinners are priced from $11 per person. There's also a children's menu. Open Sunday through Thursday from 11:30 a.m. to 10 p.m., on Friday and Saturday to 11 p.m.

Some of the best Mexican food in Alaska can be found at **El Chicano,** 104 Center Ave. (tel. 486-6116). A campy concrete fountain depicting a little Mexican boy in a sombrero greets diners to this spacious second-floor restaurant in the Center Avenue Plaza Building. Seating is in imitation brick alcoves, with basket shades over hanging lamps. The Mexican chefs are generous with their portions at lunch ($6 to $7) and dinner ($8 to $9.75). Chicken mole ($8.25) is one of my favorite Mexican dishes, and this is one of the few places north of California I've been able to find it. Several imported Mexican beers are on the menu to douse the fire from the chili sauce, homemade with real chilies. Open daily except Sunday from 11 a.m. to 10 p.m.

Across the street in the Bakery Mall is **Out to Lunch,** 103 Center Ave. (tel. 486-4868), a pleasant and friendly deli-style café with fresh flowers on the tables and original watercolors and silkscreens on the walls. Order your choice of soup ($3), salad ($3), and/or sandwich (from $5) from the buffet line. Rolls are made fresh daily, and there's always something for vegetarians. Open daily except Sunday from 8 a.m. to 6 p.m.

Locals recommend the **Kodiak Café,** 203 Marine Way (tel. 486-5470), for its hamburgers and daily specials (open Monday through Saturday from 6 a.m. to 3 p.m. and on Sunday from 7 a.m. to 2 p.m.), and **Kodiak Pizza,** 1819 Mill Bay Rd. (tel. 486-4090), for its Greek food (open daily from 10 a.m. to midnight). And yes, Kodiak has a **McDonald's,** near the Rezanof Drive–Lower Mill Bay Road "Y" junction (open daily from 6 a.m. to midnight). You can't miss the golden arches, even if you want to.

WHAT TO SEE AND DO

An excellent way to get acquainted with the town of Kodiak is to take the **walking tour** detailed in the "Kodiak Island Visitors Guide," available at the Visitor Information Center.

On Foot

The **Baranov Museum,** lodged in the Erskine House at 101 Marine Way, at Center Avenue (tel. 486-5920), is one of the state's outstanding small museums. The oldest standing Russian building in Alaska, it was constructed around 1792 of logs and was used as a warehouse for sea otter pelts and a commissary in Alexander Baranov's capital. It subsequently belonged to the Alaska Commercial Company (1867–1911) and to W. J. and Nellie Erskine, who lived in the house until 1948. In 1962 it was declared a national historic landmark. The museum's collection includes fine samovars and other memorabilia from the Russian era, 18th- and 19th-century period furnishings, and artifacts from Aleut and Koniag Eskimo prehistory. Many authentic Russian and Native crafts are sold in the museum's sophisticated gift shop. May through mid-September the museum is open from 10 a.m. to 3 p.m. Monday through Friday, and noon to 4 p.m. on Saturday and Sunday; in the winter season hours are 11 a.m. to 3 p.m. on Monday, Tuesday, Wednesday, and Friday, and noon to 3 p.m. on Saturday. Admission is $1; children under 12 are free.

Holy Resurrection Orthodox Church, just north of the museum at the corner of Kashewarof Avenue at Mission Road, is the focus of much of the spiritual life in Kodiak. It was, in fact, the first Christian parish in Alaska. Within the sanctuary are numerous precious icons, rare paintings, and handmade brass works. It's open by appointment (tel. 486-3524). Note the remains of eight bells beside a small bell-tower in the churchyard. A plaque on the tower wall tells how the bells were cast at a Kodiak foundry in 1794–1796, but were destroyed, along with the church, by fire in 1943. The church was rebuilt immediately after the war, but it was 1980 before the congregation could afford to have new bells cast and shipped from France.

Any young Alaskan who wants to become a Russian Orthodox priest will spend several years at **St. Herman's Theological Seminary,** Mission Road past Third Avenue. One of only three Orthodox training institutes in the United States, and the only one in Alaska, it also houses the St. Innocent Veniaminov Research Institute museum, containing many important items from church history in Kodiak and elsewhere in Alaska. It's open from 10 a.m. to 5:30 p.m. Monday through Saturday and 1 to 5:30 p.m. on Sunday, June through September.

While the church may be Kodiak's spiritual center, the **Small Boat Harbor** is unquestionably its economic center. Stroll through and chat with the fishermen working on their boats or mending their nets. Most will be pleased to point out the different types of gear and rigs for salmon fishing, bottom fishing, and crab or shrimp fishing. You can watch the boats come and go from the loading dock in front of the Harbormaster Building on Marine Way. Directly in front is the heart-rending **Fishermen's Memorial,** dedicated to the dozens of Kodiak fishermen lost at sea. It's a grim reminder that commercial fishing is one of the world's most dangerous professions. As the largest commercial fishing port in the United States, Kodiak is bound to have its casualties.

If you wander up Rezanof Drive past Center Avenue and the "Y" junction, you'll spot a plaque marking the spot where the 86-foot crab boat M/V *Selief* came to rest following the 1964 earthquake and tidal wave. The boat was repaired and is still operating as a fishing vessel. Another block uphill on Lower Mill Bay Road, a plaque on the outer wall of the police station marks the high-water level of that same '64 tsunami, which wiped out Kodiak's business district.

While most fishing vessels have slips in the Small Boat Harbor, pleasure craft generally are found across the strait in the **St. Herman Boat Harbor** on Near Island. A ferry shuttled to and from Near Island until the bridge was completed in 1986.

A surplus World War II liberty ship, the *Star of Kodiak,* was set beside Marine Way near the ferry dock as an emergency cannery following the disaster of 1964. Intended as a temporary facility, it has long since become a permanent feature of the city.

With Wheels

Just over four miles north of downtown Kodiak is the rain-forest-clad site of an important World War II outpost. **Fort Abercrombie State Historic Park** was built in 1941 as a top-secret radar station, with artillery added in 1943 (after the Japanese attack on Attu) to protect the Fort Greely Garrison at Naval Air Station Kodiak. Between 150 and 200 men were stationed here on 780 acres until the spring of 1944. Wander the trail and road system and see the radar tower, observation posts, strategic spotting and plotting room, war reserve magazine, and other facilities. Plans are under way to develop an interpretive museum in the ready ammunition bunker beneath the gun emplacements, at Miller Point devoted to the World War II Aleutian Campaign.

In addition to being a site of historic value, the fort is a lovely spot to enjoy nature. The rugged coastline is rife with seabird rookeries and tidepools. Virgin Sitka spruce cloak the peninsula, ash from the 1912 eruption of Mount Novarupta still observable on their branches; flowering plants, berries, and lush moss carpet the forest floor. The ranger's office and visitor center near the park entrance has historical displays and interpretive literature. Contact the Alaska State Parks System, Southwest District, Kodiak Area Ranger, Star Route, Box 3800, Kodiak, AK 99615 (tel. 907/486-6339), for more information.

The navy turned its air station over to the U.S. Coast Guard in 1972. Today the **USCG Support Center Kodiak** (tel. 487-5267)—the Coast Guard's North Pacific operations base—occupies the entire Nyman Peninsula near the state airport, six miles west of downtown Kodiak, and additional surrounding land, making it the largest in area of any Coast Guard base. About 3,000 Coast Guardsmen and their families live here. Their duties extend from patroling Alaska's waters for illegal (inside the 200-mile limit) foreign fishing to performing search-and-rescue services.

Visitors are welcome but must make prior arrangements to be met by a Coast Guard bus. Call the Public Affairs Office (tel. 487-5259) for details on this, or on how to schedule a boat tour or hangar inspection.

Also in the Buskin River area, but on the city side of the airport opposite Lake Louise, is the **Kodiak National Wildlife Refuge Visitor Center.** The western two-thirds of Kodiak Island and three smaller islands are part and parcel of this 1,865,000-acre reserve. The variety and quantity of wildlife here is remarkable: the Kodiak brown bear, the world's largest carnivore (males range up to 1,500 pounds), is the central attraction of the refuge; all five species of Pacific salmon spawn in its streams and lakes; and at least 200 pairs of American bald eagles have been counted, among 200 species of other birds. But dense vegetation and a mountainous spine make the land virtually impenetrable by trail, so that boat and float plane are the only practical means of arrival. Nine recreational cabins in different parts of the refuge are available for use on a reservation basis.

The visitor center on Buskin Beach Road offers displays, interpretive programs, and trip-planning information. Free films on the island's wildlife are shown at 1, 2, and 3 p.m. on Saturday and Sunday through the summer. The center is open from 8 a.m. to 4:30 p.m. weekdays, and noon to 4:30 p.m. on weekends.

Driving Tours

Beyond the state airport, Rezanof Drive—now known as **Chiniak Road**—zigs and zags around several bays to Cape Greville, 47½ beautiful miles from downtown Kodiak. En route, it passes the residential district of Bell's Flats at the head of Women's Bay, skirts Holiday Bay on Middle Bay, and traverses the Olds River where it flows into Kalsin Bay. The **Kalsin Inn Ranch,** P.O. Box 1696, Kodiak, AK 99615 (tel. 907/486-2659), and the **Northland Ranch and Resort,** P.O. Box 2367, Kodiak, AK 99615 (tel. 907/486-5578), both offer lodging and meals: cabins are $35 to $62 at the inn, $40 to $75 at the ranch; and steak dinners run $10 to $15 at both. (The beef is local: this is open range country.)

From Kalsin Bay the road weaves down a rugged coastline to **Road's End,** P.O. Box 1305, Kodiak, AK 99615 (tel. 907/486-2885), another friendly and casual lodge with excellent steak and seafood lunches ($6 to $8) and dinners ($10 to $15). Year-round room rates are $35 to $40. It's not far from here to Cape Greville and Cape Chiniak, Kodiak Island's easternmost point. In March and April you may see folks gazing out to sea in the hope of spotting a migrating gray whale.

Pasagshak Bay Road branches south off Chiniak Road at the Northland Ranch and climbs 16½ miles over the Mann Range to Fossil Beach at Pasagshak Bay State Recreation Area. Near the airport, Kodiak Island's only other road, **Anton Larsen Bay Road,** leaves Rezanof Drive/Chiniak Road for a scenic 11½-mile trip to its namesake. Bears are occasionally spotted at Anton Larsen Bay, a quiet cove on the island's north shore.

Sports

FISHING Freshwater fishing is excellent any time of year. Many of the island's lakes have been stocked with rainbow trout, silver (coho) salmon, or grayling. All five species of Pacific salmon, steelhead, and Dolly Varden spawn in major streams between May and November, with the particular run depending on the species. Kodiak also has many enthusiastic ice fishermen.

Deep-sea charter vessels, working out of St. Herman's (formerly Dog Bay) Small Boat Harbor on Near Island, bring in fine catches of salmon, halibut, black bass, and cod year round. **Kodiak Sea Charters,** P.O. Box 2156, Kodiak, AK 99615 (tel. 487-2683), is one of half a dozen charter services that offer fishing, hunting, and sightseeing trips around the island. The Visitor Information Center will recommend charters.

Remember to get your Alaskan fishing license before you drop your first line. A 3-day ($10) or a 14-day ($20) nonresident sport-fishing license can be purchased at **Mack's Sport Shop,** 117 Lower Mill Bay Rd. (tel. 486-4276). Ask at the **Alaska Department of Fish and Game** office, 211 Mission Rd., at Kashewarof Avenue (P.O. Box 686), Kodiak, AK 99615 (tel. 907/486-4791), for their thorough "Kodiak Area Sport Fishing Guide." Fish and Game operates a 24-hour **"fishing hotline"** (tel. 486-4559) to answer up-to-the-minute questions about what's hot and what's not.

You needn't charter a boat or plane to take you fishing. The Buskin River, which empties into the Gulf of Alaska right beside the state airport, is one of the best fishing streams on the island, with spawning runs of Dolly Varden, sockeye, pink, and silver salmon. The island's best fishing stream, however, is the Karluk River (see "Short Trips from Kodiak," below).

HUNTING If it's the Kodiak brown bear you're seeking, and if you're not a resident of Alaska, it'll cost you. Be prepared to part with a $60 license fee, a $350 brown bear permit fee, and—unless you're hunting with a close relative who *is* an Alaska resident—$5,000 or so for an experienced guide. Bears are in season April 1 to May 15 and October 25 to November 30. You can also go after elk, Sitka black-tailed deer, or reindeer, as well as ducks.

You can get licenses and information in the same places as noted under "Fishing," above. In addition to the charter services listed in that category, **Kodiak Island Charters,** P.O. Box 1396, Kodiak, AK 99615 (tel. 486-5380 or 486-5140), handles hunting expeditions with great efficiency.

HIKING The visitors bureau's Kodiak map lists no fewer than 24 recommended hiking trails within easy reach of the town of Kodiak by road or boat. A good start might be to walk up the road to the communication saucer atop 1,270-foot **Pillar Mountain,** overlooking Kodiak town. The road starts just above downtown. The five-mile **Termination Point** trail is quite popular; it starts at the end of the Monashka Bay Road beyond Fort Abercrombie. Or get a boat to drop you off on **Woody Island,** only a couple of miles due east of downtown. The site of a Christian summer camp, it also harbors an old Russian cemetery, sawmill, and ice-packing plant.

WINTER SPORTS Where there's snow, there are skiers and skaters. The island trails are ideal for cross-country skiers, while skaters find ample ice on several ponds—including Lilly Lake and Potato Patch Lake—within the city limits.

OTHER SPORTS **Baranof Park,** off Baranof Street between Powell and 14th Avenues near Kodiak High School, is operated as a recreation ground by the Kodiak Parks and Recreation Department. It contains lighted tennis and basketball courts, a sports field surrounded by a track, and two children's playgrounds. The high school **swimming pool** is open to the public for a small fee after school and on weekends during the school year.

There's **bowling** at Tropic Lanes, 120 Marine Way (tel. 486-6257); **horseback riding** and pack trips at Northland Ranch on Chiniak Road (tel. 486-5578); **stock-car races** at the fairgrounds on summer weekends; and **weight equipment** at Doc's Nautilus Fitness Center, 326 Center Ave. (tel. 486-4971).

CULTURE AND NIGHTLIFE

The event of the year in Kodiak is a historical drama presented every August in Alaska's only outdoor theater. As the sun sets over Monashka Bay and balalaikas play spirited Russian folk music, *Cry of the Wild Ram* begins in the Frank Brink Amphitheater (named for the playwright) near Fort Abercrombie. Since 1967 this acclaimed play has traced the history of the first Russian colony in America through the eyes of its enigmatic and beleaguered governor of 30 years, Alexander Baranov. Most of the cast is local, though some professionals from the Lower 48 are brought in to direct the play and take several major roles.

Ten evening performances are spread over the first three weekends of August. Reserved seats are $15, general admission is $12, student tickets are $10, and those for senior citizens and children run $5. The production plays rain or (moon) shine, so the audience is advised to dress warmly and bring raingear . . . just in case. Russian food is served during intermission. Contact the **Kodiak Arts Council,** P.O. Box 1792, Kodiak, AK 99615 (tel. 486-5291), for more information.

The rest of the year, nightlife is pretty much what you might expect in a fishing town: casual and lively, sometimes crossing the fine line to rowdy. Most of the action is within a couple blocks of the Harbormaster's Building. In the Mall on Marine Way you'll find **Solly's Office,** a large, dimly lit lounge with live rock bands playing Tuesday through Saturday nights. **Tony's Bar,** just across a corridor, has a funky round bar, pool tables, and live music on weekends. **The Mecca,** on the opposite side of the Mall (tel. 486-3364) has live music Tuesday through Saturday and a very spacious dance floor. Nearby are **The Village,** with a country-and-western soloist Thursday through Sunday nights, and the **Ship's Bar,** a traditional fishermen's watering hole. About two miles north on Mission Road, **The Beachcomber** also has live music but not quite as many fishermen. Most bars are open nightly until 5 a.m., with music from 10 p.m. to 4 a.m. For a quieter drink, enjoy it in the comfort of your hotel lounge.

SHORT TRIPS FROM KODIAK

The city of Kodiak is not the only settlement on Kodiak Island. There are, in fact, five other villages on the island and another just offshore.

Ouzinkie (pop. 233), on the west coast of Spruce Island, is the closest to Kodiak city. Spruce Island is only about five miles from Fort Abercrombie, and easily visible from there; Ouzinkie nestles in a grove of spruce trees on its western shore. St. Herman is buried on this island, where he lived in a hermitage; today the New Valaam Monastery and a Russian Orthodox church are the foci of villagers' social lives. Chris and Kathy Opheim's **Pleasant Harbor Lodge,** P.O. Box 8049, Kodiak, AK 99615 (tel. 907/486-6526), is a great place for a getaway at $200 per day per person, for full board. The island is a favorite of hunters, fishermen, beachcombers, and nature lovers.

Port Lions (pop. 291), 19 miles northwest of Kodiak city on Kizhuyak Bay, may be the only community in the world named for a Lions Club. When the 1964 earthquake and tidal wave destroyed 28 of 33 homes in the village of Afognak and caused salt water to contaminate the freshwater supply, villagers relocated here at Settler Cove with the assistance of several service organizations, including the Mennonites, Salvation Army, the U.S. Navy, and, yes, Kodiak's 49th District Lions Club. Today the village—which is served by the state ferry system—has schools and churches, a library and a medical clinic, two grocery stores, and a café. The **Lions Den Lodge,** P.O. Box 266, Port Lions, AK 99550 (tel. 907/454-2301), has bed-and-breakfast accommodation for $50 per person.

The Native fishing village of **Karluk** (pop. 102), 75 miles southwest of Kodiak on Shelikof Strait, actually consists of three village sites near the mouth of the salmon-rich Karluk River. Archeologists have found many prehistoric artifacts at two of them. An Orthodox church, left over from a former Russian trading post, overlooks a massive abandoned cannery. Accommodation is available at Rob and Martha Sikes's **Aleut Fishing Village,** Karluk, AK 99608 (tel. 907/241-2229). Full fishing packages, including food, lodging, boats, and guides, vary according to season, but run $160 to $250 a day.

There's another large cannery at **Larsen Bay** (pop. 180), 15 miles east of Karluk on Uyak Bay, built at the turn of this century by the Alaska Packers Association. It operated until 1984. As at Karluk, prehistoric artifacts such as ulus, spearpoints, and oil lamps have been found in this area. Visitors who want to shoot bears with rifle or camera will find **Mike Munsey's Bear Camp** not far from Larsen Bay. Contact Munsey at Amook Pass, Kodiak, AK 99615 (tel. 907/847-2203). His rates are $1,400 to $1,700 for five days.

On the south shore of Kodiak Island are **Akhiok** (pop. 102), 90 miles southwest of Kodiak city, and **Old Harbor** (pop. 355), 50 miles southwest. Akhiok was established as a sea-otter hunting settlement on the barren, grassy shores of deep Alitak Bay. Old Harbor, which faces Sitkalidak Island, is the closest settlement to Three Saints Bay, site of Gregori Shelekhov's first Russian America colony in 1784. Old Harbor villagers erected a cross on the site in 1984 to celebrate its bicentennial.

Afognak Island, just north of Kodiak Island and part of the borough, is a wilderness island with no permanent settlements. But you can stay in the rustic **Afognak Cabins** by contacting the office at 203 Marine Way (P.O. Box 1277), Kodiak, AK 99615 (tel. 907/486-6014). Rates start at $65 depending on the season. Also available is a 14-foot skiff with an outboard motor. The cabins sleep six. They're available on Kazakof Bay from April to December.

Shuyak Island, immediately north of Afognak Island, is a state park. A popular stop for sea kayakers en route from Homer to Kodiak (or vice versa), it can also be reached by boat or plane from either city. Four rustic cabins on the island can be reserved for $15 a night by contacting Alaska State Parks (tel. 486-6339 in Kodiak). There's a puffin rookery on the island, and many sea otters and sea lions.

All of Kodiak's small air companies perform a variety of services, from air-taxi shuttles to flightseeing, fishing, and hunting expeditions to freight hauling. **Peninsula Airways,** P.O. Box 890, Kodiak, AK 99615 (tel. 487-4014), regularly flies a Grumman Goose to King Salmon and Cold Bay. **Island Air Service,** P.O. Box 125, Kodiak, AK 99615 (tel. 486-6196), serves Chignik from June to September. **Uyak Air Service,** P.O. Box 4188, Kodiak, AK 99615 (tel. 487-4443), flies Cessnas back and forth to Larsen Bay, where it has cabins for rent. A newer service is **Sea Hawk Charters,** P.O. Box 500, Kodiak, AK 99619 (tel. 487-2477).

2. The Alaska Peninsula

The 450-mile-long Alaska Peninsula, from huge Iliamna Lake to False Pass, contains some of Alaska's most rugged wilderness and most prolific fishing grounds. Its terrain is everywhere mountainous, although the spruce forests of the northeast are replaced by barren tundra in the southwest. By stretching the peninsula's boundaries just slightly to the north of Iliamna, it can be said to contain two national parks (Lake Clark and Katmai) and a national monument (Aniakchak). Population is sparse: no town on the peninsula has as many as 1,000 residents.

LAKE CLARK

A maze of jagged peaks, smoldering volcanoes, and high alpine lakes, four-million-acre Lake Clark National Park and Preserve encompasses the territory where the Alaska Range meets the Aleutian Range. The awesome, granite-spired Chigmit Mountains, formed by violent earth movement and sculpted by glaciers, provide the link; they have been called the Alaskan Alps. Looming over the western shore of Cook Inlet, with a broad view across the Kenai Peninsula, are the great twin volcanoes Mount Redoubt (10,197 feet) and Mount Iliamna (10,016 feet). Behind the range, fed by hundreds of waterfalls, is turquoise, 50-mile-long Lake Clark, a key spawning ground for red salmon in the Bristol Bay fishery.

The park's features vary from fossil-rich cliffs and marshy lowlands on the Cook Inlet coast to tundra-covered foothills and boreal spruce forest on the mountains' western flanks. Brown and black bears, moose, caribou, dall sheep, wolves, and smaller mammals inhabit the environs. Most visits are made between June and August, after the spring thaw and before the first snow. Float trips on three designated wild rivers (the Chilikadrotna, the Mulchatna, and the Tlikakila), backpacking and fly-in fishing and hunting (the latter in the preserve only) are popular wilderness activities.

Port Alsworth, within the preserve on the eastern shore of Lake Clark, is the headquarters of the park and preserve. Air charters from Anchorage, Kenai, and Iliamna land here, and a variety of lodging, from primitive to modern, is available. You can get a list of lodges, air charters, and outfitters licensed to operate in the park and preserve by contacting the Superintendent, Lake Clark National Park and Preserve, 701 C St. (P.O. Box 61), Anchorage, AK 99513 (tel. 907/271-4224).

Among the wilderness lodges on Lake Clark are Chuck and Sara Hornsberger's unique **Koksetna Wilderness Lodge,** Port Alsworth, AK 99653 (tel. 907/781-2227), open year round at an all-inclusive rate of $250 per person per day; **Alaska's Wilderness Lodge,** 1 Lang Rd., Port Alsworth, AK 99653 (tel. 907/781-2223), with packages starting at $1,000 for three nights; and **Haeg's Wilderness Home,**

Chitina Bay (contact P.O. Box 338, Soldotna, AK 99669; no phone), for $200 per day per person.

ILIAMNA LAKE

By far Alaska's largest natural freshwater lake, with a surface area of an even 1,000 square miles, Iliamna Lake bridges the gap between the Chigmit Mountains and the Bristol Bay lowlands.

There are two villages on the lake's north shore, **Iliamna** (pop. 100) and **Newhalen** (pop. 150). Inhabitants of Newhalen are mainly Tanaina Indians, a branch of Athabaskan. Iliamna village, on the other hand, is a bustling resort community in the summer months with large numbers of fishermen and hunters staying at its lodges.

Among the wilderness lodges on Lake Iliamna are the **Igiugig Lodge,** P.O. Box 4022, Igiugig, AK 99613 (tel. 907/533-3216) in summer, or P.O. Box 871395, Wasilla, AK 99687 (tel. 907/376-2859) in winter, charging $250 daily per person from June through September for modern accommodation at the lake outlet; **Iliaska Lodge,** P.O. Box 228, Iliamna, AK 99606 (tel. 907/571-1221) in summer, or P.O. Box 30, Homer, AK 99603 (tel. 907/235-6188) in winter, at $3,600 weekly per person, with three float planes and ten jet boats available for guest use; **Lake View Lodge,** P.O. Box 109, Iliamna, AK 99606 (tel. 907/571-1248), with year-round rates of $90 per person; and the **Newhalen Lodge,** P.O. Box 102521, Anchorage, AK 99510 (tel. 907/279-4236), at $3,150 weekly June to October.

KING SALMON

This small town (pop. 550) is the gateway to Iliamna Lake and numerous other lakes, to Katmai National Park and Preserve, and to Aniakchak National Monument. King Salmon is served twice daily by commercial flights from Anchorage via **MarkAir** (tel. toll free 800/426-6784) and from Kodiak and Cold Bay via **Peninsula Airways** (tel. 907/246-3372). Many state and federal agencies are located here, including a small U.S. Air Force base (with a complement of 375 men and women), the National Park Service (tel. 246-3305) and the Alaska Department of Fish and Game (tel. 246-3340).

King Salmon is the main town, but not the governmental seat, of the Bristol Bay Borough. That honor falls to the fish-processing center of **Naknek** (pop. 320), 15 miles down the Naknek River on Bristol Bay. The village has hotels, restaurants, schools, a medical clinic, and a civic center.

A 25-mile, all-weather road connects Naknek with King Salmon and the western boundary of Katmai National Park, near the point where the Naknek River empties out of Naknek Lake. The river, ice free from May to October, has some minor rapids and is a popular spot for float and fishing trips.

More specific information can be obtained by writing the **Bristol Bay Borough,** P.O. Box 189, Naknek, AK 99633.

Where to Stay and Eat

The **King Ko Inn,** P.O. Box 346, King Salmon, AK 99613 (tel. 907/246-3378), open year round, is a reasonably priced, full-service hotel-restaurant. Manager Jacques Marshall or staff will pick you up at the airport, arrange car or boat rentals, send you on guided hunting, fishing, or rafting trips, provide jet-boat service to Brooks Lodge in Katmai National Park, then urge you to relax at night in front of their lounge's big-screen satellite TV. The rooms are simple but comfortable, with standard rates of $65 single, $90 double with shared bath, or $75 single, $100 double with semiprivate bath. Deluxe trailer units with a separate bedroom, kitchen, and private bath are $85 single, $125 double.

The King Ko Inn charters fishing trips with local guides. Normal charges are $150 per person per day. Rainbow trout from 8 to 15 pounds run in the Naknek River in the spring and fall; Dolly Varden, arctic grayling, and northern pike are also common in Naknek Lake, as well as the five species of Pacific salmon. Full fishing packages, including round-trip transportation from Anchorage, lodging, lunches, and guided fishing, are available.

The only other hotel in King Salmon is the **Ponderosa Inn,** P.O. Box 234, King Salmon, AK 99613 (tel. 907/246-3444), whose 25 rooms all have private baths. Package rates—$495 per person for three nights, $990 for a week—include three family-style meals a day, a boat, motor, gas, and transfers.

Wilderness lodges on the Naknek River include the **Eskimo Creek Lodge,** P.O. Box 196, King Salmon, AK 99613 in summer, or 3605 Arctic Blvd., Suite 372, Anchorage, AK 99503 (tel. 907/258-6529) in winter, and **Prestage's Sportfishing Lodge,** P.O. Box 213, King Salmon, AK 99613 (tel. 907/246-3320), at both of which rates were unavailable at press time. Slightly farther out are the **Alaska Rainbow Lodge,** P.O. Box 101711, Anchorage, AK 99510 (tel. 907/287-3059), charging $3,500 weekly per person; the **Becharof Lodge,** P.O. Box 104, Egegik, AK 99579 (no phone), at $300 daily per person; and the **Mother Goose Lake Lodge,** 4203 Minnesota Dr., Anchorage, AK 99503 (tel. 907/562-4541), whose rates were undeclared at this writing. All are open from June to October.

Year-round local air-taxi service is offered by **Bay Air** (tel. 246-4268) and **King Flying Service** (tel. 246-4414).

KATMAI NATIONAL PARK AND PRESERVE

The 1980 eruption of Mount St. Helens was nothing compared to the blast that shook the Alaska Peninsula on June 6 and 7, 1912. In one of the most violent cataclysms ever recorded, Mount Katmai collapsed into itself, while a side vent called Novarupta spewed seven cubic miles of flaming ash and sand, burying a 50-square-mile valley up to 700 feet deep. The sparse Native population in the area weathered about 60 hours of total ash-induced darkness. Some 1,500 miles away, in Vancouver, British Columbia, rain laden with sulfuric acid ate away linens hung outside to dry, and all that summer, Northern Hemisphere temperatures were unusually cool due to the high concentration of dust particles in the atmosphere.

Today the **Valley of Ten Thousand Smokes** that Novarupta created is the best-known attraction of the 4.2-million-acre Katmai National Park and Preserve—created as a national monument in 1918 at the behest of the National Geographic Society, which sent four separate expeditions to explore the eruption site during the interim years. At that time the valley contained millions of fumaroles which issued steam hot enough to melt zinc. Only a few fumaroles remain active today, and Mount Katmai's crater holds a lake.

Elsewhere in the park and preserve, however, there is pristine wilderness relatively unaffected by the great eruption. A coastline of plunging cliffs and islets is home to seals and sea lions, sea otters, and a rich birdlife, including puffins, auklets, and kittiwakes. West of the Aleutian Range, where creeks and rivers tumble as waterfalls from the mountain glaciers, are numerous large lakes—Naknek, Brooks, Grosvenor, Coville, Nonvianuk, Kulik, and Kukaklek.

This is prime territory for the Alaska brown bear, the grizzly, which feasts all summer on migrating salmon in park streams. Katmai National Park and Preserve has the world's largest population of unhunted brown bear; in fact the park's boundaries have been expanded four times, most recently in 1978, primarily to protect the habitat of these bears through their annual cycle. Other land mammals found in the park are the moose, caribou, wolf, fox, wolverine, porcupine, lynx, beaver, otter, marten, weasel, hare, squirrel, and vole.

The park's most popular destination is the **Brooks Lodge,** operated by Katmailand, Inc., 4700 Aircraft Dr., Suite 2, Anchorage, AK 99502 (tel. 907/243-

5448, or toll free 800/544-0551). Located on the short stream connecting Lake Brooks with Naknek Lake, the lodge was established by pioneer aviator Ray Petersen in 1950. Today it has 16 modern guest cabins with hot and cold running water, private baths and showers, and electric heat. Most cabins have twin bunk beds. Family-style meals are served three times a day in the dining hall, and the lodge bar allows guests to relax around a large circular fireplace. Standard rates in 1989 were $99 per adult ($110 in July) or $50 per child, double occupancy, plus another $42 a day for meals. (They were expected to rise in 1990.) A better deal is to buy an all-inclusive package from Anchorage, providing round-trip air transportation to King Salmon, a floatplane ride to Brooks Lodge, two nights' lodging, and a guided bus tour to the Valley of Ten Thousand Smokes for $589 per person ($619 in July).

If you're staying in King Salmon and drop into Brooks for the day, you're still welcome to join the 22-mile bus tour to see the valley from a National Park Service cabin on Overlook Mountain. The tour runs $50 with lunch, $43 without. Flightseeing tours are also offered for $70 a head.

At the Katmai National Park and Preserve **visitor center,** on the lakeshore near Brooks Lodge, you can watch nightly slide presentations. There's also a campground with tables, fireplaces, wood, water, shelters, and a food cache (to deter bears). Space is limited, so if you plan to stay—or if you need more information—contact the Superintendent, Katmai National Park and Preserve, P.O. Box 7, King Salmon, AK 99613 (tel. 907/246-3305).

Katmailand, Inc., the folks who operate Brooks Lodge, also have the only other two concessions in the park—all of which operate from late May into September only. Both the deluxe **Kulik Lodge,** between Kulik and Nonvianuk Lakes, on the edge of the preserve, and the more rustic **Grosvenor Camp,** on the narrows between Lakes Coville and Grosvenor, are fly-in wilderness fishing lodges. All-inclusive rates, which cover round-trip air transportation from Anchorage are $1,950 for three nights or $3,550 per week per person at the Kulik Lodge; and $1,150 for three nights, $2,030 per week, at the Grosvenor Camp. Contact Katmailand, Inc., 4700 Aircraft Dr., Suite 2, Anchorage, AK 99502 (tel. 907/243-5448). There are a few other lodges in the preserve on Nonvianuk and Kukaklek Lakes; contact the park service for a list.

Don't expect to see the sights of Katmai National Park under sunny skies, by the way. Wind and rain are the norm here, where weather systems from the Bering Sea and Gulf of Alaska collide. Summer temperatures average in the 50s and 60s in the daytime, but tempests can arise very quickly. Don't go on an outing, no matter how brief, without being prepared for the worst.

McNEIL RIVER

If it's bears you want to see, it's bears you'll get at the **McNeil River State Game Sanctuary.** Surrounded on the south and west by Katmai National Park and Preserve, on the east by Cook Inlet, and on the north by the rugged Chigmit Mountains, this sanctuary offers a unique opportunity for wildlife photographers, amateur as well as professional. The large concentration of brown bears here don't seem to mind that humans watch them: they go about their business as usual, tolerant of humans as long as their actions fall within an established pattern of noninterference.

That established pattern requires that no more than ten people a day accompany armed rangers to McNeil River Falls (the prime viewing spot) in July and August. A lottery held May 15 determines who will be included in these daily visits. Apply to the Alaska Department of Fish and Game, Game Division, 333 Raspberry Rd., Anchorage, AK 99502, by May 1, enclosing a completed questionnaire (which you must request in advance) and a $5 fee.

It's a short hike or boat ride from the river mouth to the falls. You can arrive by plane or boat from Homer at high tide, and you can camp at the river mouth for up to a week.

The **Chenik Wilderness Camp,** an outpost of the Kachemak Bay Wilderness Lodge, P.O. Box 956, Homer, AK 99603 (tel. 907/235-8910), is the only permanent facility near the sanctuary. The minimum stay here is five days, with arrival on Saturday and departure on Thursday; the price of $2,000 per person includes the $300 round-trip floatplane trip to and from Homer. A maximum of six guests stay in tent cabins with sun porches and outside "privies"; the lodge, where all meals are served, also has a library, big fireplace, and—nearby—a wood-heat sauna. Hosts Michael and Diane McBride will gladly put your name in the McNeil River lottery pool; they point out that the permit system is not in effect in June, and even if you miss out in July or August, there's a good chance that a no-show will leave a space open for you. When you're not watching the bears, there's excellent hiking, fishing, and beachcombing. Only a few miles off-shore, in the Cook Inlet, is the recently active Augustine Island volcano.

ANIAKCHAK NATIONAL MONUMENT AND PRESERVE

If Mount Katmai's 1912 eruption was colossal, there are few words to describe what might have happened at Aniakchak at some point in the distant past. Sometime since the last Ice Age, the caldera exploded and collapsed, creating a crater six miles wide and 30 square miles in area. That's half again as big as Oregon's Crater Lake. But here the only water is in small (and aptly named) Surprise Lake. Hot springs heat the lake, which feeds the Aniakchak River, which cascades through a 1,500-foot rift in the crater wall to empty into Bristol Bay. Sockeye salmon spawning up the river have a distinctive flavor of soda and iron. Aniakchak last erupted in 1931 from its caldera cone, Vent Mountain. The 586,000-acre national park and preserve was established in 1980.

For information, contact the Superintendent, Aniakchak National Monument and Preserve, P.O. Box 7, King Salmon, AK 99613 (tel. 907/246-3305). It's a singular experience to cruise over Aniakchak's moonscape in a floatplane from King Salmon, 150 miles north, or **Port Heiden** (pop. 100), the nearest village, and land on Surprise Lake.

THE WESTERN EXTREMITY

West of Aniakchak, the Alaska Peninsula is mainly cold, rainy, windswept tundra, dotted with scattered Aleut villages and fish-processing plants. **Chignik** (pop. 180), **Sand Point** on Popof Island (pop. 800), **King Cove** (pop. 530), and **Cold Bay** (pop. 250), all served by the Alaska state ferry system five times between May and September, are the major settlements.

From Katmai National Park and Preserve south, all the land on the Gulf of Alaska side of the peninsula is owned by the federal government. The 1.2-million-acre **Becharof National Wildlife Refuge,** P.O. Box 277, King Salmon, AK 99613 (tel. 907/246-3339), abuts Katmai on the south and contains 458-square-mile Becharof Lake, Alaska's second largest. The 3.5-million-acre **Alaska Peninsula National Wildlife Refuge** (same address as Becharof) flanks Aniakchak National Monument and Preserve on either side. The tip of the long, snake-like peninsula comprises 320,000-acre **Izembek National Wildlife Refuge,** P.O. Box 2, Cold Bay, AK 99571 (tel. 907/532-2445).

---

3. Bristol Bay

The most productive red (sockeye) salmon fishery on earth is this 170-mile-wide bay where the Togiak, Wood, Nushagak, Kvichak, and King Salmon Rivers, among others, enter the Bering Sea after tumbling from alpine lakes and mountain glaciers. This is an angler's paradise, land not only for the commercial fishermen who ply their trade in the often-foggy waters of the bay. Sportspeople flock here from around the world to test the freshwater lakes and rivers for rainbow and lake trout, arctic char, Dolly Varden, grayling, steelhead, northern pike, and sheefish.

DILLINGHAM

Spread across lush tundra on the shore of Bristol Bay, near the confluence of the Wood and Nushagak Rivers, this growing town of 2,000 people, 320 miles west of Anchorage, is the home of a 500-boat salmon fleet and a center for sport fishing and hunting.

Few towns in Alaska have a longer history. A Russian fort, known as Aleksandrovski Redoubt but later renamed Nushagak, was built at the mouth of the Nushagak River in 1818 and an Orthodox mission established in 1837. American entrepreneurs built the first salmon cannery in the Bristol Bay region at Nushagak in 1884 and another in 1886 on the site of modern Dillingham. U.S. Sen. W. P. Dillingham of Vermont visited the cannery in 1903. His name was bestowed on the town the following year when a post office was established.

Dillingham has a climate called "marine transitional"—Bristol Bay's warmer air collides with cool weather fronts from the Interior, bringing mild temperatures but almost perpetually cloudy skies, strong winds, and moderate precipitation. Average temperatures are in the 50s and 60s in summer, between 0°F and 20°F in winter, with annual extremes of 92°F to −36°F. Average annual precipitation is 25 inches, including 71 inches of snow.

Dillingham is best regarded as a base for visiting the outdoors rather than a destination in itself. The town does have a **Heritage Museum** (tel. 842-5610) with a varied collection of Native Yupik Eskimo arts and crafts. The **Bristol Bay Native Corporation** has its headquarters here. And in March there's a three-day festival called the **Beaver Roundup,** which celebrates the end of the winter trapping season with dog-sled and snowmobile races, a Miss Dillingham pageant, and other activities.

Local air-taxi services include **Armstrong Air Service** (tel. 842-5940) and **Yute Air Alaska** (tel. 842-5333). Cars can be rented for the 20-mile drive to **Aleknagik** (pop. 250), a Native village on Lake Aleknagik in Wood-Tikchik State Park.

The **Alaska Department of Fish and Game** (tel. 842-5925) maintains an office in Dillingham. For further information about the area, contact the **Dillingham Chamber of Commerce,** City of Dillingham, P.O. Box 191, Dillingham, AK 99576.

Where to Stay

The town has two hotels. The **Bristol Inn,** P.O. Box 196, Dillingham, AK 99576 (tel. 907/842-2240), has 30 rooms with private bath, cable television, and in-room phone. The Cannery restaurant and lounge is open daily for all meals. Courtesy-van service is offered to and from the airport year round. Rates are $79 to $125.

The **Dillingham Hotel,** P.O. Box 194, Dillingham, AK 99576 (tel. 907/842-5316), has 32 rooms, several with kitchenettes, all with TVs and phones. It also has a courtesy car. Year-round rates are $62 to $76.

WOOD-TIKCHIK STATE PARK

Alaska's largest state park is a wilderness wonderland of two separate water systems, each with half a dozen long, fjord-like lakes interconnected by cascading rivers and streams, all emptying into Nushagak Bay (an arm of Bristol Bay) at Dillingham. Its 1.4 million acres are one of the state's lesser-known secrets. The tundra-cloaked slopes of the Kilbuck Mountains enclose the western shores of the Tikchik lakes and some of the Wood River lakes, while spruce forests tickle the eastern shores. Contact the **Alaska Division of Parks,** 619 Warehouse Ave., Suite 210, Anchorage, AK 99501 (tel. 907/274-4676), to learn more.

As might be expected in a rich natural area, there are numerous fishing lodges in the park. They include **Bristol Bay Lodge,** Rte. 1, Box 580, Ellensburg, WA 98926 (tel. 509/964-2094), charging $3,495 weekly per person, June through September; the **Golden Horn Lodge** on Mikchalk Lake, P.O. Box 190748, Anchorage, AK 99519 (tel. 907/243-1455), at $3,495 weekly per person, June to October; the **Royal Coachman Lodge,** P.O. Box 1887, Anchorage, AK 99510 (tel. 907/842-2725 in summer, or 907/346-2595 in winter), at $3,575 weekly per person at the lodge or $2,700 for its wilderness camp, June to October; the **Tikchik Narrows Lodge,** P.O. Box 220248, Anchorage, AK 99522 (tel. 907/243-8450), charging $3,500 weekly per person; and the **Wood River Lodge,** 4437 Sanford Dr., Fairbanks, AK 99701 (tel. 907/479-0308), at $3,495 weekly per person, June 9 through September.

Outside the park boundary, the **Ekwok Lodge,** on the Nushagak River, P.O. Box 1769, Dillingham, AK 99576 (tel. 907/464-3364 in summer, or 907/694-1589 in winter), takes 14 guests from May 15 to September 15 for $300 daily per person.

NATIONAL WILDLIFE REFUGES

Togiak National Wildlife Refuge, 4.1 million acres with nearly every major wildlife species in Alaska represented, covers the Ahklun Mountains and most of the western shore of Bristol Bay adjoining Wood-Tikchik State Park. Its headquarters are at P.O. Box 10201, Dillingham, AK 99576 (tel. 907/842-1063). Offshore, the Walrus Islands and Round Island are part of the expansive **Alaska Maritime National Wildlife Refuge.** Round Island in particular is a rare and highly restricted sanctuary for walrus, of which as many as 10,000 bulls may congregate on its rocky shores at once. Contact the Alaska Maritime NWR, 202 Pioneer Ave., Homer, AK 99603 (tel. 907/235-6546).

No visitors are allowed without permits, but you can expect to see a lot of marine life if you go out with **Trapper Don's Round Island Boat Charters,** General Delivery, Togiak, AK 99678 (tel. 907/493-5927).

4. Yukon-Kuskokwim Delta

Alaska's two greatest river systems, the Yukon and the Kuskokwim, empty into the Bering Sea. Though their mouths are about 200 miles apart, they come as close as 30 miles to one another as they flow from the vast Interior onto the barren, flat tundra of the western plains. The final 150 to 200 miles of their courses are marshy and meandering, and an ideal environment for birdlife. Indeed, the nation's largest wildlife refuge—the Yukon Delta National Wildlife Refuge—covers most of this boggy tundra.

BETHEL

The largest town in western Alaska lies along the northern bank of the Kuskokwin River, 90 miles from the Bering Sea at the head of narrow Kuskokwim Bay. The trade and transportation center for the 57 villages of the Delta region, this town of 3,700 people also has a substantial commercial fishing business and a sizable service sector. Yet it is at the mercy of the river, which annually tears large chunks of land from the city waterfront, and nearly as often floods its banks.

Once known as Mumtrekhlagamute, Yupik for "smokehouse village," Bethel got its name from Scripture in 1885 when a Moravian mission was established near a trading post. The climate, similar to but drier than Bristol Bay, has mean temperatures in summer of 53°F (record high 86°F) and in winter of 11°F (record low −46°F). Annual precipitation is 17 inches, including 50 inches of snow.

Bethel's long, dreary winter is made survivable by the **Yukon-Kuskokwim State Fair,** which runs from mid-January to mid-February annually. The high-light is the Kuskokwim 300 Sled Dog Race; other events include a one-dog sled race for children, a fishing derby for village elders, a Native olympics, Yupik dance contests, and the exhibit and sale of traditional handcrafts from throughout the Delta region. Write P.O. Box 388, Bethel, AK 99559, for more information. Spring is ushered in with the **Kuskokwim Ice Classic,** modeled on the more famous Nenana Ice Classic: lottery entrants must try to guess the precise day and minute that the ice will move on the Kuskokwim River at Bethel. Contact P.O. Box 271, Bethel, AK 99559 (tel. 907/543-4239).

Alaska Airlines (tel. 543-3905, or toll free 800/426-0333) serves Bethel twice daily on weekdays, and once daily on weekends, with flights from Anchorage. District and superior courts are here, as well as a regional hospital (tel. 543-3711) and offices of the Alaska Department of Fish and Game, the U.S. Fish and Wildlife Service, and the federal Bureau of Indian Affairs. Bethel has a weekly newspaper, the *Tundra Drums,* 13 churches, Kuskokwim Community College, and head offices of the Native Calista Corporation. For information, contact the **Bethel Chamber of Commerce,** P.O. Box 329, Bethel, AK 99559, or call the city offices (tel. 907/543-2097).

Recent travelers have found the town's only hotel, the long-established **Kuskokwim Inn,** P.O. Box 218, Bethel, AK 99559 (tel. 907/543-2207 or 543-2218), in need of a major renovation. Rooms have private baths, cable TVs, and phones, and rent for $40 to $95 a night. There's a restaurant on the premises.

Bed-and-breakfast may be the way to go here. **Porterhouse Bed and Breakfast,** P.O. Box 868, Bethel, AK 99559 (tel. 907/543-3551 or 543-3552), charges $50 single, $75 double. There are cable TVs in every room, and full breakfasts served on fine china with a river view. **Wilson's Hostel Bed and Breakfast,** P.O. Box 969, Bethel, AK 99559 (tel. 907/543-3841 or 543-2783), has rates from $59. No smoking or drinking here.

Bethel's pride and joy is the **Yugtarvik Regional Museum,** located in a log building on Third Avenue (tel. 543-2098). Dedicated to the preservation of Yupik Eskimo culture, its purpose is twofold: to display artifacts from the past (such as kayaks, hunting implements, household items, and clothing) and to encourage modern works. To the latter end, this is a living museum where master artisans and apprentices shape works of ivory and wood, weave grass baskets, and design skin clothing, while bantering in their native Yupik tongue and talking freely (in English) to visitors who ply them with questions about the "old way" of life. Works are sold in the excellent museum shop. Admission to the collection is free.

YUKON DELTA NATIONAL WILDLIFE REFUGE

The 19.6-million-acre refuge, larger than several states in the Lower 48, is home to more than 100 million migratory waterfowl. It also harbors a large colony of reindeer and musk oxen on huge Nunivak Island, just across the Etolin Strait. Between May and September **Nunivak Island Guide Service,** P.O. Box 31, Mekoryuk, AK 99630 (tel. 907/827-8213), offers a rare opportunity to visit the offshore island for wilderness trips, photography, fishing, or hunting. (Limited hunting for musk oxen is permitted in season.) Refuge offices are at P.O. Box 346, Bethel, AK 99559 (tel. 543-3151).

5. Pribilof Islands

The Pribilofs are one of Alaska's most isolated enclaves and one of its most fascinating, both for their Russian heritage and for their thriving colonies of northern fur seals and sea birds.

Here on these barren rocks, 880 miles west of Anchorage and 350 miles from the North American mainland in the middle of the Bering Sea, fortunate visitors can peer over the edges of cliffs directly into the rookeries of puffins, auklets, and 209 other species of avian life. And two blinds have been set up—accessible by permit or with a tour guide—for a closeup view of up to a million seals in their rookeries. It's a wildlife photographer's dream.

Slaughtered nearly to extinction by the 18th- and 19th-century Russians, the fur seals have come back from the brink, protected by an international treaty barring their harvest on the high seas. Today they are harvested in limited numbers (typically about 5,000 or 6,000) by the Aleut population of the Pribilofs as part of their subsistence lifestyle, under the management of the federal Department of Commerce.

Neither of the main islands of **Saint Paul** (pop. 600) and **Saint George** (pop. 220)—there are also three smaller islets—was inhabited until 1786, when Russian fur traders founded the communities with Aleuts from the Aleutians. The Aleut inhabitants of these tiny villages, which cling like limpets to the tundra, still bear Russian names and other signs of the European lifestyle. None is so evident as their churches, both on the National Register of Historic Places—Saints Peter and Paul Russian Orthodox Church on Saint Paul, Saint George the Great Martyr Russian Orthodox Church on Saint George.

The climate in the Pribilofs is cool and wet, with heavy fog expected between May and August. Temperatures are typically in the 40s in summer (record high is 63°F), in the teens in winter (record low is −7°F on Saint George, −19°F on Saint Paul). Annual precipitation is 23 to 30 inches (heavier on Saint Paul), with around 50 inches of snow.

As the larger of the two villages, Saint Paul has the more complete visitor facilities. The **King Eider Hotel,** P.O. Box 88, Saint Paul Island, AK 99660 (tel. 907/546-2312), owned by the Native Tanadgusix Corp., has a handful of clean, spartan rooms with shared bath (rates were not available). There are several restaurants, a clinic, a general store, and four gift shops, but no banks. Off-road vehicles can be rented. For more information, write City of St. Paul, P.O. Box 1, Saint Paul Island, AK 99660 (tel. 907/546-2331).

The historic **St. George Hotel,** Saint George Island, AK 99660 (tel. 907/859-2255), is operated by the Saint George Tanaq Corp., with most rooms going to participants in the corporation's naturalist tours from mid-June to Labor Day. Contact the corporation at 4000 Old Seward Hwy., Suite 302, Anchorage, AK 99503 (tel. 907/562-3100), for details.

Both islands have telephone, radio, and television, as well as electricity and water and sewage systems.

Reeve Aleutian Airways (tel. 907/243-4700 in Anchorage) serves St. Paul with Boeing 727s flying three times weekly from Anchorage via Cold Bay. Most Pribilof visitors, however, go to the islands as part of a package tour.

Midnight Sun Tours, P.O. Box 103355, Anchorage, AK 99510 (tel. 907/276-8687, or toll free 800/544-2235), operates the primary Pribilof tour in conjunction with Reeve Airways. The three-day/two-night trips depart from Anchorage on Tuesday and Thursday, June through August. Packages include round-trip transportation, shared hotel accommodations, and full guide services, but no meals. The tour costs $799 plus 3% tax.

6. Aleutian Islands

Perpetually buffeted by violent winds, fog, and rain, the bleak and barren 1,000-mile-long Aleutian archipelago sweeps in a broad arc from the tip of the Alaska Peninsula nearly to the Kamchatka Peninsula of the Soviet Union. As the submarine extension of the Aleutian Range, the islands are mountainous and volcanic, with a high degree of seismic activity.

Extending beyond 173° East Longitude—the International Date Line must make an abrupt dogleg to keep the Aleutians in the same day as the rest of Alaska—they represent both the westernmost (179°10' West, Amatignak Island) and easternmost (179°46' East, Semisopochnoi Island) points in the United States.

There are 80 named islands in the Aleutian chain, 72 of them uninhabited except for the sea birds and marine mammals protected by the **Alaska Maritime National Wildlife Refuge.** They are covered with a tundra vegetation of tussock grasses and heath, with some dwarf trees and occasional taller shrubs along streambeds. Nearly 20,000 sea otters, bouncing back from near extinction, make their principal home in Aleutian waters. For general information, contact the Alaska Maritime NWR, Aleutian Islands Unit, P.O. Box 5251, FPO Seattle, WA 98791 (tel. 907/592-2406).

Dutch Harbor and **Unalaska** on Unalaska Island, near the eastern end of the archipelago, are the largest settlements, with a combined population of about 2,000 people. A U.S. Navy base on **Adak,** an air force base on **Shemya,** and a Coast Guard station on **Attu,** the farthest west island, together employ about 2,250 military personnel.

Aleut villages at **Atka** (pop. 100) and **False Pass** on Unimak Island (pop. 70) are the only surviving Native villages from an island chain that once supported thousands of Aleuts. There are other small fishing communities at **Akutan** (pop. 200) and **Nikolski** on Umnak Island (pop. 50).

Even on the uninhabited islands—**Kiska,** in particular—there are traces of the battles fought with the Japanese for control of this archipelago during World War II (see "A Capsule History" in Chapter I). Miles of abandoned military installations, including landing strips and roads, warehouses, and quonset huts, are reminders of a time not so long past.

That time is well recalled in the "1000 Mile War Tours" offered by **Alaskabound,** 1621 Tongass Ave., Ketchikan, AK 99901 (tel. 907/225-8800, or toll free 800/544-0808). As the agent fits the itinerary to the particular desire of the traveler, this tour is suited for veterans of the Aleutian campaign who want to sneak a latter-day look at the grim battlefield of the 1940s. Prices vary from $795 to $1,195; tours are offered only from April 14 to October 20.

Reeve Aleutian Airways (tel. 907/243-4700 in Anchorage), which has been flying to this island chain since 1932, provides regular service on Boeing 727s from Anchorage to Adak, False Pass, and Shemya. Unalaska (Dutch Harbor) is served from Anchorage by **MarkAir** (tel. toll free 800/426-6784) and from Kodiak and Dillingham by **Peninsula Airways** (tel. toll free 800/544-2248). The **Alaska Marine Highway System** (tel. toll free 800/544-0552) takes the ferry M/V *Tustumena* as far as Dutch Harbor from Kodiak monthly, May to September.

DUTCH HARBOR/UNALASKA

Hardly thriving, these twin fishing villages on the eastern side of Unalaska Island, 920 miles southwest of Anchorage, nevertheless are seeing an increasing trade in tourism.

There are two accommodations. The **Unisea Inn,** P.O. Box 503, Dutch Harbor, AK 99692 (tel. 907/581-1325), has 46 rooms with phones and TVs. The hotel has a restaurant and lounge, a gift shop, game room, and beauty salon. Year-round rates range from $71 to $92. **Carl's Motel,** 100 Bayview Ave. (P.O. Box 109), Unalaska, AK 99685 (tel. 907/581-1230), has 12 rooms with phones, cable TVs, kitchens, and full baths. Rates start at $55.

The best way to see Unalaska Island is with **Aleutian Islands Transport,** P.O. Box 248, Unalaska, AK 99685 (tel. 907/581-1644), which offers five-hour sightseeing tours in a six-wheel-drive World War II troop carrier for $59. The guide takes you to Bunker Hill and Mount Ballyhoo, the site of Fort Mears and a Japanese prisoner-of-war camp, and to the hulk of the S.S. *Northwestern.* You'll also visit Alaska's oldest Russian Orthodox church, sample Russian tea, and learn about the Aleut culture. Tours operate May 15 to October 15.

Flightseeing and inter-island transport can be arranged through **Aleutian Air Ltd.,** P.O. Box 330, Dutch Harbor, AK 99692 (tel. 581-1686), or **Maritime Helicopters,** P.O. Box 597, Dutch Harbor, AK 99692 (tel. 581-1771).

INDEX

Accommodations, 42–4
see also specific places
Admiral Cruises, 34
Admiralty Island, 110–11
Afognal Island, 343
Air travel:
  Alaska, 29–31, 36–7
  Anchorage, 142
  Denali National Park, 270
  Fairbanks, 276
  Southeast Alaska, 48
Akhiok, 343
Alaska:
  climate, 14–15
  getting around, 36–9
  history of, 4–10
  language, 41–2
  map of state, 2–3; airline routes, 31
  natural environment of, 14–20
  nightlife and entertainment, 45–6
  people of, 10–14
  preparing for your trip, 21–4
  sights and attractions, 45
  state symbols, 40–1
  time zones, 40
  tourist information, 23
  transportation to, 29–36; air, 29–31; bus, 32; by car, 32; sea, 30, 32–6
  wildlife, 16–18
  see also South-Central Alaska; Southeast Alaska; Southwest Alaska
Alaska, University of:
  Anchorage, 174–5
  Experimental Agricultural Station, (Palmer), 245
  Fairbanks, 293–5
Alaska Aviation Heritage Museum (Anchorage), 173
Alaska Center for the Performing Arts (Anchorage), 172
Alaska Chilkat Bald Eagle Preserve (Haines), 125
Alaska Highway, 32, 308–12
Alaska Indian Arts Skill Center (Haines), 124
Alaska Kkaayah (Fairbanks), 293
Alaskaland (Fairbanks), 292–3
Alaska Marine Highway, 48
Alaska Maritime National Wildlife Refuges:
  Aleutian Islands, 353
  Bristol Bay, 350
  Homer, 217
Alaska National Bank Building (Fairbanks), 292
Alaskan Coastal Studies, Center for (Homer), 219
Alaska Pacific University (Anchorage), 174
Alaska Peninsula, 344–8

Alaska Railroad Depot (Anchorage), 171
Alaska Southeast, University of (Auke Bay), 105
Alaska State Museum (Juneau), 102–3
Alaska Transportation and Industry, Museum of (Palmer), 245
Alaska Wildlife and Natural History Museum (Anchorage), 173
Aleutian Islands, 13, 352–4
Alsworth, Port (Alaska Peninsula), 344
Alyeska, Mount (near Anchorage), 187–8
Alyeska Pipeline Terminal (Valdez), 230–1
Anaktuvuk Pass, 333
Anan Creek (near Wrangell), 69–70
Anchorage, 140–93
  accommodations, 147–61; bed-and-breakfast, 159–60; budget, 154, 157–9; camping, 160–1; downtown, 148–54; East Anchorage, 158–9; luxury, 154–5; middle bracket, 152–4, 156–8; midtown/Spenard, 154–7; South Anchorage, 157–8; top, 148–51; upper bracket, 151–2, 155–8
  getting around, 145–6
  history of, 140–1
  map of, 143
  nightlife and entertainment, 182–6
  orientation, 141
  restaurants, 161–70; Alaskan, 163, 165–8; American, 164, 167–9; budget, 163–8; delis, 164, 167; deluxe, 161–2; downtown, 161–5; Eastern European, 168; East of Anchorage, 169–70; fast-food, 169–70; Greek, 165; Italian, 165–6, 168–9; literary, 164; Mexican, 163–5, 168, 169; midtown/Spenard, 166–8; moderately priced, 162–3, 165–6; natural foods, 168; Oriental, 163, 165, 166, 169; seafood, 162–3, 167–8; South Anchorage, 168–9; steaks, 165
  shopping, 180–2
  short trips from: Eagle River, 192–3; Girdwood, 197–90; Hope, 191–2; Portage Glacier, 190–1; Turnagain Arm, 187
  sights and attractions, 170–5;
    downtown walking tour, 170–2; flightseeing, 180; museums, 172–3; parks, 174; special events, 147; tours, 179–80; universities, 174–5; zoo, 173–4
  sports and recreation, 175–9
  tourist information, 146–7
  transportation to, 141–2, 144–5
Anchorage, Port of, 171
Anchorage cemetery, 172

NOW, SAVE MONEY ON ALL YOUR TRAVELS!
Join Frommer's™ Dollarwise® Travel Club

Saving money while traveling is never a simple matter, which is why the **Dollarwise Travel Club** was formed 31 years ago. Developed in response to requests from Frommer Travel Guide readers, the Club provides cost-cutting travel strategies, up-to-date travel information, and a sense of community for value-conscious travelers from all over the world.

In keeping with the money-saving concept, the annual membership fee is low — $18 (U.S. residents) or $20 (residents of Canada, Mexico, and other countries)— and is immediately exceeded by the value of your benefits, which include:

1. Any TWO books listed on the following pages.
2. Plus any ONE Frommer City Guide.
3. A subscription to our quarterly newspaper, *The Dollarwise Traveler*.
4. A membership card that entitles you to purchase through the Club all Frommer publications for 33% to 50% off their retail price.

The eight-page *Dollarwise Traveler* tells you about the latest developments in good-value travel worldwide and includes the following columns: **Hospitality Exchange** (for those offering and seeking hospitality in cities all over the world); **Share-a-Trip** (for those looking for travel companions to share costs); and **Readers Ask . . . Readers Reply** (for those with travel questions that other members can answer).

Aside from the Frommer Guides, the Serious Shopper Guides, and the Gault Millau Guides, you can also choose from our Special Editions. These include such titles as **California with Kids** (a compendium of the best of California's accommodations, restaurants, and sightseeing attractions appropriate for those traveling with toddlers through teens); **Candy Apple: New York with Kids** (a spirited guide to the Big Apple by a savvy New York grandmother that's perfect for both visitors and residents); **Caribbean Hideaways** (the 100 most romantic places to stay in the Islands, all rated on ambience, food, sport opportunities, and price); **Honeymoon Destinations** (a guide to planning and choosing just the right destination from hundreds of possibilities in the U.S., Mexico, and the Caribbean); **Marilyn Wood's Wonderful Weekends** (a selection of the best mini-vacations within a 200-mile radius of New York City, including descriptions of country inns and other accommodations, restaurants, picnic spots, sights, and activities); and **Paris Rendez-Vous** (a delightful guide to the best places to meet in Paris whether for power breakfasts or dancing till dawn).

To join this Club, simply send the appropriate membership fee with your name and address to: Frommer's Dollarwise Travel Club, 15 Columbus Circle, New York, NY 10023. Remember to specify which single city guide and which two other guides you wish to receive in your initial package of member's benefits. Or tear out the next page, check off your choices, and send the page to us with your membership fee.

FROMMER BOOKS
PRENTICE HALL TRAVEL
15 COLUMBUS CIRCLE
NEW YORK, NY 10023
212-373-8125

Date_____

Friends:
Please send me the books checked below:

FROMMER™ GUIDES

(Guides to sightseeing and tourist accommodations and facilities from budget to deluxe, with emphasis on the medium-priced.)

☐ Alaska	$14.95	☐ Germany	$14.95
☐ Australia	$14.95	☐ Italy	$14.95
☐ Austria & Hungary	$14.95	☐ Japan & Hong Kong	$14.95
☐ Belgium, Holland & Luxembourg	$14.95	☐ Mid-Atlantic States	$14.95
☐ Bermuda & The Bahamas	$14.95	☐ New England	$14.95
☐ Brazil	$14.95	☐ New York State	$14.95
☐ Canada	$14.95	☐ Northwest	$14.95
☐ Caribbean	$14.95	☐ Portugal, Madeira & the Azores	$14.95
☐ Cruises (incl. Alaska, Carib, Mex, Hawaii, Panama, Canada & US)	$14.95	☐ Skiing Europe	$14.95
☐ California & Las Vegas	$14.95	☐ South Pacific	$14.95
☐ Egypt	$14.95	☐ Southeast Asia	$14.95
☐ England & Scotland	$14.95	☐ Southern Atlantic States	$14.95
☐ Florida	$14.95	☐ Southwest	$14.95
☐ France	$14.95	☐ Switzerland & Liechtenstein	$14.95
		☐ USA	$15.95

FROMMER $-A-DAY® GUIDES

(In-depth guides to sightseeing and low-cost tourist accommodations and facilities.)

☐ Europe on $40 a Day	$15.95	☐ New York on $60 a Day	$13.95
☐ Australia on $30 a Day	$12.95	☐ New Zealand on $45 a Day	$13.95
☐ Eastern Europe on $25 a Day	$13.95	☐ Scandinavia on $60 a Day	$13.95
☐ England on $50 a Day	$13.95	☐ Scotland & Wales on $40 a Day	$13.95
☐ Greece on $35 a Day	$13.95	☐ South America on $35 a Day	$13.95
☐ Hawaii on $60 a Day	$13.95	☐ Spain & Morocco on $40 a Day	$13.95
☐ India on $25 a Day	$12.95	☐ Turkey on $30 a Day	$13.95
☐ Ireland on $35 a Day	$13.95	☐ Washington, D.C. & Historic Va. on $40 a Day	$13.95
☐ Israel on $40 a Day	$13.95		
☐ Mexico on $35 a Day	$13.95		

FROMMER TOURING GUIDES

(Color illustrated guides that include walking tours, cultural and historic sites, and other vital travel information.)

☐ Australia	$9.95	☐ Paris	$8.95
☐ Egypt	$8.95	☐ Scotland	$9.95
☐ Florence	$8.95	☐ Thailand	$9.95
☐ London	$8.95	☐ Venice	$8.95

TURN PAGE FOR ADDITONAL BOOKS AND ORDER FORM.

0190

FROMMER CITY GUIDES

(Pocket-size guides to sightseeing and tourist accommodations and facilities in all price ranges.)

☐ Amsterdam/Holland	$7.95	☐ Minneapolis/St. Paul	$7.95
☐ Athens	$7.95	☐ Montréal/Québec City	$7.95
☐ Atlantic City/Cape May	$7.95	☐ New Orleans	$7.95
☐ Barcelona*	$7.95	☐ New York	$7.95
☐ Belgium	$7.95	☐ Orlando/Disney World/EPCOT	$7.95
☐ Boston	$7.95	☐ Paris	$7.95
☐ Cancún/Cozumel/Yucatán	$7.95	☐ Philadelphia	$7.95
☐ Chicago	$7.95	☐ Rio	$7.95
☐ Denver/Boulder*	$7.95	☐ Rome	$7.95
☐ Dublin/Ireland	$7.95	☐ San Francisco	$7.95
☐ Hawaii	$7.95	☐ Santa Fe/Taos/Albuquerque	$7.95
☐ Hong Kong*	$7.95	☐ Seattle/Portland*	$7.95
☐ Las Vegas	$7.95	☐ Sydney	$7.95
☐ Lisbon/Madrid/Costa del Sol	$7.95	☐ Tokyo*	$7.95
☐ London	$7.95	☐ Vancouver/Victoria*	$7.95
☐ Los Angeles	$7.95	☐ Washington, D.C.	$7.95
☐ Mexico City/Acapulco	$7.95	*Available June, 1990	

SPECIAL EDITIONS

☐ A Shopper's Guide to the Caribbean	$12.95	☐ Manhattan's Outdoor Sculpture	$15.95
☐ Beat the High Cost of Travel	$6.95	☐ Motorist's Phrase Book (Fr/Ger/Sp)	$4.95
☐ Bed & Breakfast—N. America	$11.95	☐ Paris Rendez-Vous	$10.95
☐ California with Kids	$14.95	☐ Swap and Go (Home Exchanging)	$10.95
☐ Caribbean Hideaways	$14.95	☐ The Candy Apple (NY with Kids)	$12.95
☐ Honeymoon Destinations (US, Mex & Carib)	$12.95	☐ Travel Diary and Record Book	$5.95

☐ Where to Stay USA (Lodging from $3 to $30 a night) $10.95
☐ Marilyn Wood's Wonderful Weekends (Conn, Del, Mass, NH, NJ, NY, Pa, RI, VT) $11.95
☐ The New World of Travel (Annual sourcebook by Arthur Frommer for savvy travelers) $16.95

SERIOUS SHOPPER'S GUIDES

(Illustrated guides listing hundreds of stores, conveniently organized alphabetically by category.)

☐ Italy	$15.95	☐ Los Angeles	$14.95
☐ London	$15.95	☐ Paris	$15.95

GAULT MILLAU

(The only guides that distinguish the truly superlative from the merely overrated.)

☐ The Best of Chicago	$15.95	☐ The Best of Los Angeles	$14.95
☐ The Best of France	$16.95	☐ The Best of New England	$15.95
☐ The Best of Hong Kong	$16.95	☐ The Best of New York	$14.95
☐ The Best of Italy	$16.95	☐ The Best of Paris	$16.95
☐ The Best of London	$16.95	☐ The Best of San Francisco	$14.95

☐ The Best of Washington, D.C. $14.95

ORDER NOW!

In U.S. include $2 shipping UPS for 1st book; $1 ea. add'l book. Outside U.S. $3 and $1, respectively.
Allow four to six weeks for delivery in U.S., longer outside U.S.

Enclosed is my check or money order for $_____

NAME_____

ADDRESS_____

CITY_____ STATE_____ ZIP_____

0190